THOMAS HARDY

AND PARADOXES

OF LOVE

H. M. DALESKI

University of Missouri Press • COLUMBIA AND LONDON

D0082074

Copyright © 1997 by
The Curators of the University of Missouri
University of Missouri Press, Columbia, Missouri 65201
Printed and bound in the United States of America
All rights reserved
5 4 3 2 1   01 00 99 98 97

Library of Congress Cataloging-in-Publication Data

Daleski, H. M. (Hillel Matthew), 1926–
   Thomas Hardy and paradoxes of love / H. M. Daleski.
      p.   cm.
   Includes bibliographical references and index.
   ISBN 0-8262-1125-9 (alk. paper)
   1. Hardy, Thomas, 1840–1928—Fictional works.   2. Love stories,
English—History and criticism.   3. Paradox in literature.   4. Love
in literature.   I. Title.
   PR4757.L65D35   1997
   823'.8—dc21   97-15472
                                                                        CIP

∞ ™ This paper meets the requirements of the
American National Standard for Permanence of Paper
for Printed Library Materials, Z39.48, 1984.

Designer: Mindy Shouse
Typesetter: BOOKCOMP
Printer and Binder: Thomson-Shore, Inc.
Typefaces: Garamond

To Shirley

OTHER BOOKS BY H. M. DALESKI

The Forked Flame: A Study of D. H. Lawrence
Dickens and the Art of Analogy
Joseph Conrad: The Way of Dispossession
The Divided Heroine: A Recurrent Pattern in Six English Novels
Unities: Studies in the English Novel

But criticism is so easy, and art so hard: criticism so flimsy, and the life-seer's voice so lasting.

—Thomas Hardy, preface to
Select Poems of William Barnes

Contents

ACKNOWLEDGMENTS

Although my view of Hardy has changed considerably over the years, particularly with regard to my reading of *Tess of the d'Urbervilles,* I have drawn where this seemed appropriate on some parts of previously published material as follows: *"Tess of the d'Urbervilles:* Mastery and Abandon," in *Essays in Criticism* 30 (October 1980); an expanded version of this essay appeared as Chapter 4 of *The Divided Heroine: A Recurrent Pattern in Six English Novels* (New York and London: Holmes and Meier, 1984); and "Hardy's Reluctant Heroines," in *Unities: Studies in the English Novel* (Athens: University of Georgia Press, 1985).

A somewhat different version of Chapter 1 appeared in *Victorian Literature and Culture* (New York: AMS Press, 1991), in the journal's new section of chapters from works in progress.

An expanded version of section 3 of the Introduction was delivered as part of a lecture at a seminar on periodization, organized by Lawrence Besserman for the Hebrew University's Center for Literary Studies. I am grateful to him for the invitation to lecture. The essay has now appeared in Lawrence Besserman, ed., *The Challenge of Periodization: Old Paradigms and New Perspectives* (New York and London: Garland, 1996).

I wish to thank a number of institutions for assistance extended while I was at work on the book: the Rockefeller Foundation for a period of residence at the magnificent Bellagio Study and Conference Center and for provision of work space even though I was present on this second visit as a spouse and not as a fellow; the University of California at Berkeley for appointments as a Visiting Scholar and the granting of library privileges in its fine library; and the Hebrew University for sabbatical leaves during which most of the book was written.

On a more personal note, I would like to express my gratitude to a number of friends and colleagues: to Sanford Budick, who read a first version of the opening chapter and made some helpful suggestions; to those who were kind enough to read the whole book in typescript—Leona Toker, who offered a whole series of acute comments; to Shlomith Rimmon-Kenan, who most perceptively drew my attention to a significant blind spot in the analysis and who also brought her narratological expertise to bear on the typescript; and to Ruth Nevo, who has been my guide and mentor for more than thirty years and who once again has left me inestimably in her debt both by fixing unerringly on stylistic infelicities and, in one major instance, by drawing out the unguessed implications of my argument and so helping to tighten it considerably.

Finally, I wish to thank my wife, Shirley Kaufman Daleski, to whom the book is dedicated. She read the typescript as it was being composed, chapter by chapter, and so gave me an invaluable immediate response to what I was doing. With her fine sense for language, she helped improve the quality of the writing; and, with a major suggestion, she transformed the presentation of the material in the crucial opening chapter.

NOTE ON THE TEXTS

Wherever possible I have used the Penguin English Library editions of the novels (Harmondsworth, 1978) as follows:

Under the Greenwood Tree, ed. David Wright
Far from the Madding Crowd, ed. Ronald Blythe
The Return of the Native, ed. George Woodcock
The Mayor of Casterbridge, ed. Martin Seymour-Smith
The Woodlanders, ed. James Gibson (1981)
Tess of the d'Urbervilles, ed. David Skilton
Jude the Obscure, ed. C. H. Sisson.

I have checked all my quotations from *Tess of the d'Urbervilles* and *The Woodlanders* against the following definitive editions of these novels and in a few instances have made substantive changes:

Tess of the d'Urbervilles, ed. Juliet Grindle and
Simon Gatrell (Oxford: Clarendon Press, 1983)
The Woodlanders, ed. Dale Kramer (Oxford: Clarendon Press, 1981)

The Penguin English Library texts have been supplemented by the Penguin Classics edition of *A Pair of Blue Eyes,* ed. Roger Ebbatson (Harmondsworth, 1986), and by the New Wessex editions (London: Macmillan, 1975) of *Desperate Remedies, A Laodicean,* and *The Well-Beloved.*

Thomas Hardy and Paradoxes of Love

INTRODUCTION

I

Virginia Woolf roundly declared that "on or about December 1910 human character changed." We might now add that in or about 1970, with the publication of Roland Barthes's *S/Z*, the character of literary studies changed. The change in criticism of Thomas Hardy is summed up by Lance St. John Butler in his introduction to a collection of essays on Hardy published in 1989: "[T]he new languages of criticism—semiotic, structuralist, poststructuralist—the feminist revision of literary meaning, political and religious interpretations, a more adventurous style of biographical enquiry, all these have been applied to Hardy in the last ten years"; and the change is epitomized in the title that he chose for his collection: *Alternative Hardy*.[1] It seems to me that, with the inevitable swing of the critical pendulum, the time is now ripe for the reinstatement of a different Hardy and for a new look at what is central in his work. This book, at all events, is dedicated to that proposition. Commenting on Barthes's analysis of Balzac's "Sarrasine" in *S/Z*, Philip M. Weinstein has said: "Barthes' interest in the tale, and his capacity to find the tale interesting, are remarkable. What is generally missing, however, is Balzac."[2] It is the missing Hardy, an absence amid the brilliance and sophistication of "the new languages of criticism," that I try to recuperate, to give substance to.

1. Lance St. John Butler, ed., *Alternative Hardy*, xi.
2. Philip M. Weinstein, *The Semantics of Desire: Changing Models of Identity from Dickens to Joyce*, 12.

1

The basic principles of the new critical theories are forcefully presented in Catherine Belsey's influential *Critical Practice*. The mode of nineteenth-century fiction is termed "expressive realism," but she states that "the logical possibility" of such a mode is "put in question by post-Saussurean linguistics" to a degree that "the theory of literature as expressive realism is no longer tenable." Similarly, subjectivity, like the literary text, is only "a discursive construct." Winds of change, however, are blowing in this direction too. Shlomith Rimmon-Kenan has impressively demonstrated, both theoretically and practically, that it is possible "to re-instate representation and re-humanize subjectivity" by "integrating the contemporary destabilization of these concepts and going beyond that destabilization by viewing narration as access." And even Belsey herself seems at times to succumb to the existence of an extratextual dimension: "Ignoring the process of production of the text, dazzled by its brand name, and preoccupied by the assessment of its value, the reader is effectively diverted from the work of producing the play of contradictions which *in reality* constitutes the literary text."[3]

"Classic realism," Belsey maintains, "cannot foreground contradiction," which, where it exists, does so only "in the margins" of such texts. In "the case [of] Hardy," for instance, he " 'recognizes' " only "contradictions in the world," and this ensures he views them as "tragic (inevitable)." It is one of the persistent thrusts of what follows in this book that contradiction is writ large in all Hardy's major novels; and that this has nothing to do with a "transcendent" worldview of the author but with his narrators overtly saying one thing and showing another in relation to pivotal issues. Nor does my attempt to dig out these contradictions have anything in common with the doctrines of deconstruction, with viewing the classic realist text "as a *construct,*" as Belsey says, and so treating it "as available for *deconstruction.*" It is not at all my aim to show that Hardy's deconstructed novels are in effect "unreadable"; rather that it is possible to offer a reading (presupposing this to be only one of endless possible readings) that takes full account of such discrepancies without being overcome by them. The

3. Catherine Belsey, *Critical Practice,* 37, 46, 54, 128 (my emphasis); Shlomith Rimmon-Kenan, *A Glance beyond Doubt: Narration, Representation, Subjectivity,* 1.

"readable text," says Belsey scornfully, is "merchandize to be consumed"; accordingly, "deconstruction in order to reconstruct the text as a newly intelligible, plural object is the work of criticism."[4] What such a doctrine dogmatically advocates is the kind of mechanical application that ensures that the (modern) critic will set out—with malice aforethought, as it were—to deconstruct whatever he touches. This book is a plea for a return not only to the texts but also to critical openness, to the kind of criticism that, as far as this is humanly possible, allows the texts discussed to determine both the nature and the substance of the response to them. Moreover, the great nineteenth-century novels, with those of Hardy not least among them, the novels that Belsey calls classic realist texts, are far from now being the dead "consumerist" artifacts she takes them to be; in their unregenerate and undeconstructed state, as the following analyses of Hardy's major novels, I trust, will demonstrate, they offer a range of complexities that may well tease any critic out of thought.

II

What follows is a study of Hardy's treatment of gender in his major fiction. I set out to analyze the codes of both masculinity and femininity that are inscribed in his texts and offer a revisionary account of his view of both male and female sexuality. It is revisionary in two respects. First, I try to move beyond much feminist criticism of Hardy's essentialism and of his "sexism," as of the supposed domination of his female characters in a male-dominated world. His female characters are repeatedly and sympathetically portrayed as at the center of his fictional worlds, and they are always granted the freedom of choice, refuting the view of them as victims and of the novelist as a crass determinist weighting the scales against them. Second, Hardy is preoccupied with two opposed conceptions of male sexuality, fascinated and repelled by his rake figures and wary and skeptical of his sexually diffident heroes. To the best of my knowledge, this aspect has not previously been the subject of detailed study.

I wish to place Hardy's treatment of sexual relations at the center of his work, currently the missing center. In this he goes far beyond any of

4. Belsey, *Critical Practice,* 82, 104 (her emphasis), 105.

his Victorian predecessors, not only in what he dares to say as opposed to their inhibitions but also in the originality and profundity of his intuitions. One of his major insights, transcending all essentialism, is that the sexual responses of both men and women may be inhibited by what, in terms of the mythology he employs, I call "the Diana complex": a sense of self-sufficiency so strong that it inhibits a need or the ability to open the self to a sexual partner. As opposed to much commentary on Hardy and sexuality, I furthermore maintain that his portrayal of passion is strongly ontological, fundamentally an issue of being, not a matter to be viewed either socially or culturally in terms of class or wealth, though he forcefully presents such aspects too. In his depiction of both male and female sexuality, it seems to me, Hardy is not outdone by D. H. Lawrence—and indeed leaps right out of his time. This does not mean, of course, that we should cease to read him within the context of his own Victorian culture; on the contrary, my book throughout insists on the need to read him in his own terms, not those of contemporary critical theories. It also does not mean that we should take him at his extratextual word: in contradistinction to his (generally accepted) account of his abandonment of fiction in consequence of the public abuse heaped on him after the publication of *Tess of the d'Urbervilles* and *Jude the Obscure,* I also seek to show how a study of the major novels, taken in chronological order, reveals that he in fact drove himself to a dead end. His unremitting pursuit of his central subject finally exhausted it.

III

In many of his critical pronouncements and novelistic practices, Hardy appears as quintessentially Victorian, a writer in the tradition of Dickens and Thackeray and George Eliot, accepting both the realistic ethic of the Victorian novel and its mimetic techniques. He accepted, that is, the need for realistic settings for his fictions; for the telling of a story and its organization in a plot with a tight mechanism of cause and effect; for the development of character and the adherence (for the most part) to a principle of consistency in the characterization; and for a straightforward method of narration, regularly and unadventurously employing an omniscient narrator who copiously avails himself of the opportunity for commentary that the omniscient stance naturally affords.

At the same time, however, Hardy's work is also characterized by its strikingly modernist techniques, techniques that align him with the great modernists such as Joseph Conrad, James Joyce, and D. H. Lawrence and reveal him to be their inventive forerunner.

One aspect of the modernist approach to fiction is vividly expressed by Conrad in a passage that is virtually a manifesto: "My task which I am trying to achieve is, by the power of the written word to make you hear, to make you feel—it is, before all, to make you *see*. That—and no more, and it is everything. If I succeed, you shall find there according to your desserts . . . —all you demand—and, perhaps, also that glimpse of truth for which you have forgotten to ask."[5] What this implies is a kind of literary impressionism, and indeed Conrad was concerned not only with problems of focalization (who sees?) but also with how things are seen. Somewhat surprisingly, given his often didactic omniscient commentary, Hardy's view of fiction is also impressionist. He repeatedly insisted that his art was personal and impressionistic, stating categorically that "a novel is an impression, not an argument" and likewise declaring that all he had attempted to do in *Jude the Obscure* was "to give shape and coherence to a series of seemings, or personal impressions."[6] There is indeed a suggestive parallel between Hardy's descriptive technique and that employed in impressionist art, as J. B. Bullen has noted,[7] and it is generally agreed that modernism in the arts was initiated or launched by the impressionists in the eight exhibitions held in Paris between the years 1874 and 1886. Certainly Hardy was quick to grasp the way impressionism could be seen as confirming his own intuitions:

> At the Society of British Artists there is good technique in abundance; but ideas for subjects are lacking. The impressionist school is

5. Joseph Conrad, preface to his *The Nigger of the "Narcissus,"* x.

6. Hardy, preface to *Tess of the d'Urbervilles;* Hardy, preface to *Jude the Obscure;* Hardy, *Thomas Hardy's Personal Writings,* ed. Harold Orel, 38, 39 (Orel has conveniently gathered together all the "Prefaces to Hardy's Writings").

7. J. B. Bullen, *The Expressive Eye: Fiction and Perception in the Work of Thomas Hardy,* 181–82. Cf. Norman Page, who remarks that "if Dickens's greatest natural gift was his ear, as Angus Wilson has said, Hardy's was surely his eye," and adds that Hardy "goes well beyond most other novelists in presenting his scenes with minute attention to their visual qualities . . ." (*Thomas Hardy,* 66, 71).

strong. It is even more suggestive in the direction of literature than in that of art. As usual it is pushed to absurdity by some. But their principle is, as I understand it, that what you carry away with you from a scene is the true feature to grasp; or in other words, *what appeals to your own individual eye and heart in particular* amid much that does not so appeal, and which you therefore omit to record.[8]

Hardy included what he called "an impression-picture," delineated in terms accordant with the notebook entry of the year before in *The Woodlanders* (1887), when he describes Barber Percomb looking through a window at Marty South: "In her present beholder's mind the scene formed by the girlish spar-maker composed itself into an impression-picture of extremest type, wherein the girl's hair alone, as the focus of observation, was depicted with intensity and distinctness, while her face, shoulders, hands, and figure in general were a blurred mass of unimportant detail lost in haze and obscurity."[9]

Hardy's own literary impressionism—that is, when he himself composed rather than described impression-pictures—is exemplified in two very different passages in *Tess of the d'Urbervilles*. In the first passage Angel Clare observes Tess:

> She was yawning, and he saw the red interior of her mouth as if it had been a snake's. She had stretched one arm so high above her coiled-up cable of hair that he could see its satin delicacy above the sunburn; her face was flushed with sleep, and her eyelids hung heavy over their pupils. The brimfulness of her nature breathed from her. It was a moment when a woman's soul is more incarnate than

8. Hardy, notebook entry, December 7, 1886 (Hardy's emphasis), in *The Life and Work of Thomas Hardy*, ed. Michael Millgate, 191. J. B. Bullen also refers to this note and says: "Impressionist technique focused on some elements in the visual matrix to the exclusion of others, but it reflected, above all else, the characteristics, the prejudices, and the disposition of the perceiving mind" (*Expressive Eye*, 182).

9. Hardy, *The Woodlanders*, 48. The passage is also quoted by Sheila Berger, who adduces it as an instance of the way Hardy uses windows as a framing device, achieving in this case "an effect like that in Impressionist painting" (*Thomas Hardy and Visual Structures: Framing, Disruption, Process*, 69–70).

Ian Gregor, in his introduction to the Penguin English Library edition of *The Woodlanders*, refers both to this passage and to the notebook entry about the British "impressionist school" (13, 14).

at any other time; when the most spiritual beauty bespeaks itself flesh. . . . [10]

This, clearly, is not meant to be a "realistic" or photograph-like description of Tess; it is overtly presented as Angel's impression of her. Consequently, though the snake comparison may do little to objectify the redness of Tess's mouth, it does convey Angel's sense of her earthiness, of the sensuality that is evident too in her thick hair and heavy eyelids, a satiny sensuality, it is also intimated, that he finds somewhat menacing. At the same time he receives an impression—and this subtly modulates into the narrator's view of things, merging with it—of what he cannot even see, her soul, and of how spirit meets flesh in her and is one with it in a "brimfulness" of being, in the kind of wholeness he himself aspires to.

In the second passage it is the narrator who is suddenly impressionistic in a comparison he makes. The simile he uses is representative of the startling and original images that abound in the novels. The occasion is a breakfast at the dairy farm Talbothays, at which Tess says, "I don't know about ghosts, but I do know that our souls can be made to go outside our bodies when we are alive." The dairyman's response is to turn to her "with his mouth full, his eyes charged with serious inquiry, and his great knife and fork . . . planted erect on the table, like the beginning of a gallows."[11] If the dairyman is vividly seen here in all the fullness of his breakfast, this is rendered fairly conventionally; it is the gallows simile that is impressionistic (in Hardy's sense of the term)—and may even strike us at first as outrageous. But the comparison does in fact make us give full weight to the size of the dairyman's knife and fork and register just how he is surprised into holding them on the table in a massive interruption of his breakfast; moreover, that "beginning" of the gallows not only gives the simile a possible pictorial justification but also, in its unfinished tentativeness, exactly provides a tone for the dairyman's questions in response to Tess's statement: "What—really now? And is it so, maidy?" Nor is Hardy merely fixing an impressionist eye

10. Hardy, *Tess of the d'Urbervilles*, 231.
11. Ibid., 175.

on the scene at the breakfast table. The simile expands to an imaginative vision that suddenly takes in the whole sweep of the narrative. Though the scene occurs less than halfway through the novel, he will make us see by its conclusion that it is Tess's propensity to make her soul go outside her body that has led her to the gallows, for it has allowed her to give herself as mere flesh to Alec d'Urberville—and then to kill him when her husband returns to her. "In all failures," it is said of the engagement of Rosamond and Lydgate in *Middlemarch,* "the beginning is certainly the half of the whole," a statement that incidentally provides us with yet further perspectives from which to view those remarkable gallows.

The direct use of an impressionist detail by the narrator, as in this passage, should be distinguished from that in which the impressionism reflects the view of a character, as with Angel and Tess. In the former instance it may possibly be objected that the gallows simile is not genuinely impressionistic at all and that it has been deliberately planted by the narrator for proleptic purposes. Though there is no way to establish—as in the case of the chicken and the egg—which came first, the impressionistic detail or the proleptic design, a writer as skillful as Hardy, if he had started with the intention of establishing a proleptic significance, would surely have found a more realistic means of doing so than that blatant knife and fork.

Hardy's capacity for an impressionistic responsiveness to things is implicitly related to what he called "the scientific basis" of his art: "To see in half and quarter views the whole picture, to catch from a few bars the whole tune, is the intuitive power that supplies the would-be storywriter with the scientific bases for his pursuit." The writer's ability to supply what is not actually seen is extended, in Hardy's art, to making visible that which by its very nature is invisible: "My art is to intensify the expression of things, as is done by Crivelli, Bellini, etc., so that the heart and inner meaning is made vividly visible." Hardy's art of intensification is suggestively close to James Joyce's modernist art of epiphany, for "the heart and inner meaning" it seeks to elicit are like the *"quidditas"* or "whatness" that a Joycean object is made to body forth when, in the moment of epiphany (and in Stephen Dedalus's formulation), "its soul, its whatness, leaps to us from the vestment of its appearance."[12] The epiphanic mode, as developed by Joyce and exemplified by his well-known description of Stephen's response to the wading girl in *A Portrait of the Artist as a Young Man,* is another distinctive feature of modernist fiction.

In *Jude the Obscure,* to cite one instance, Hardy provides us with as fine an example of the epiphanic mode as any in Joyce. It is when Jude, from afar, first sees Christminster:

> Some way within the limits of the stretch of landscape, points of light like the topaz gleamed. The air increased in transparency with the lapse of minutes, till the topaz points showed themselves to be the vanes, windows, wet roof slates, and other shining spots upon the spires, domes, freestone-work, and varied outlines that were faintly revealed. It was Christminster, unquestionably; either directly seen, or miraged in the peculiar atmosphere.
>
> The spectator gazed on and on till the windows and vanes lost their shine, going out almost suddenly like extinguished candles. The vague city became veiled in mist. Turning to the west, he saw that the sun had disappeared. The foreground of the scene had grown funereally dark, and near objects put on the hues and shapes of chimaeras.[13]

All the elements of an epiphany are present here. There is the intense gaze of the observer, making the object yield its whatness. There is the sudden revelation of its inner, spiritual essence, as Jude sees the university city manifesting itself as a city of light, gleaming and shining, the light that will thereafter long beckon him. But the novelist also makes us see more than Jude sees—or more than he is able to grasp. It is intimated that what Jude sees is perhaps no more than a mirage or chimaera; and when the city loses its shine and suddenly goes out, the image points proleptically to the way in which all the hopes Jude will attach to the university city will in turn be extinguished, leaving him in the funereal dark.

12. Hardy, "The Science of Fiction," in *Personal Writings,* 137, and notebook entry, January 3, 1886, in *Life and Work,* 183; James Joyce, *Stephen Hero,* 213. It is perhaps also worth noting that the title of one of Hardy's volumes of verse is *Moments of Vision.*
13. Hardy, *Jude the Obscure,* 61.

Hardy's capacity to reveal "the heart and inner meaning" of what he describes has an obvious application to his method of characterization. If his approach to character would seem to be thoroughly traditional and based on the Victorian notion of consistency, it also incorporates elements that are opposed to this. When Virginia Woolf talked about human character suddenly changing, she presumably meant it was ways of regarding people (and character) that changed; and Hardy was there before her. In *A Laodicean,* published in 1881, the narrator admittedly views Captain de Stancy as an exception, but his characterization effectively breaks the prevailing rule:

> The peculiarly bifold nature of Captain de Stancy, as shown in his conduct at different times, was something rare in life, and perhaps happily so. That mechanical admixture of black and white qualities without coalescence, on which the theory of men's characters was based by moral analysis before the rise of modern ethical schools, fictitious as it was in general application, would have almost hit off the truth as regards Captain de Stancy.[14]

Toward the end of his career as a novelist, moreover, Hardy was taking a decidedly modernist view of character: "I am more than ever convinced," he wrote, "that persons are successively various persons, according as each special strand in their characters is brought uppermost by circumstances." Such a view is dependent on the kind of artistic vision that discerns and reveals aspects of being that have remained quite hidden, unsuspected even by the character himself or herself. Like objects in an epiphany, characters too are made to body forth their inner essence.[15] It is a view that accepts so-called inconsistency as a fact of life, a view, indeed, that notably anticipates D. H. Lawrence's idea of character as a series of allotropic states, an idea that is exemplified in *The Rainbow,* his revolutionary modernist novel. Hardy's concern is not Lawrence's "carbon," though he too reveals

14. Hardy, *A Laodicean,* 230.
15. Hardy, notebook entry, December 4, 1890, in *Life and Work,* 241. Cf. Robert Langbaum, who says "Hardy's much criticized use of coincidences and other 'clumsy' narrative devices" may be viewed as sacrificing verisimilitude in order "to set up highly concentrated scenes that permit the explosive revelation of internal states of being" (*Thomas Hardy in Our Time,* 25).

the inner, unconscious being of his characters, but from early on he certainly intuits that a character may be "successively various persons"— both diamond and coal, in Lawrencean terms. Hardy shows this in his depiction of the mystery of sexual relations and sexual attraction from the time of his first major novel, *Far from the Madding Crowd,* and even while adhering to an overall notion of the need for consistency in character portrayal. In his love triangles, when the woman repeatedly swings in deep involvement from one man to the radically opposed other, she is, as it were, various persons.

This view of character, however, though anticipating modernist conceptions, cannot of itself be said to be modernist since the depiction of such self-division is a steady feature of Victorian fiction. One has only to think of Catherine Earnshaw in *Wuthering Heights,* whom Nelly Dean succinctly epitomizes as both a "lady" and a "savage," or of Maggie Tulliver in *The Mill on the Floss,* who, like Hardy's heroines, is torn between two very different men. But Hardy decisively broke with a traditional mode of characterization and fully anticipated Lawrence in his creation of Sue Bridehead in *Jude the Obscure.* Jude, having in mind Sue's ideas, says to her, "how modern you are"; but nowhere is she more modern than in her inconsistency, in what Jude comes to rue as "her colossal inconsistency." Inconsistency is Sue's principle of being, the very breath of her life, and consequently her actions are said to be "always unpredictable." To the end she remains bewildering and mysterious, prompting one critic to dub her, not inappropriately, "Sue the Obscure."[16]

Hardy also anticipates another of Lawrence's well-known modernist techniques. In *Women in Love,* Lawrence perfected a special kind of symbolic action whereby a dramatic scene, rendered in vivid immediacy, is made to project a significance far beyond its apparent meaning. It is true that instances of a traditional form of symbolic action may be found in Victorian novels, as in *Great Expectations,* for example, when Magwitch turns Pip upside down on first meeting him—as he will in due course turn his life upside down. But Lawrence imparted a distinctively modernist twist to the technique when he yoked it to animals and sex,

16. Hardy, *Jude the Obscure,* 187, 231, 233; see Mary Jacobus, "Sue the Obscure."

showing how the attitudes of men and women to animals may reveal their own sexual proclivities. In one such famous scene in *Women in Love,* Gerald Crich forces the frightened red Arab mare he is riding to stand at a railway crossing while a colliery train slowly passes. As he digs his spurs into the mare's sides, making them bleed, he is watched by Gudrun Brangwen, who is horrified but spellbound. Lawrence contrives to suggest that Gerald's treatment of the mare and Gudrun's reaction are indicative of their sexual attitudes and postulate the nature of their later sexual relationship. The scene at the crossing is magnificently done, but one cannot help wondering whether Lawrence was perhaps building on something he had come across in Hardy. Certainly the episode in *Tess of the d'Urbervilles* when Tess rides with Alec in his smart gig on the way to Trantridge (which is analyzed in Chapter 7) is a startling prefigurement of Lawrencean method. It is not only in his depiction of sexuality that Hardy is in advance of his time and fully of the company of a writer such as Lawrence; he needs too to be recognized and valued for his remarkable technical innovations.

1

Figures in the Carpet

I

When he was roughly at the midpoint of his career as a novelist, Hardy recorded the following observation:

> As, in looking at a carpet, by following one colour a certain pattern is suggested, by following another colour, another; so in life the seer should watch that pattern among general things which his idiosyncrasy moves him to observe, and describe that alone. This is, quite accurately, a going to Nature; yet the result is no mere photograph, but purely the product of the writer's own mind.[1]

The statement is couched in general terms, but it is clearly a product of Hardy's personal experience as a writer. It is one of the most intriguing of the notebook entries, suggestively posing a number of questions as to both the nature and the substance of his art.

Looking at life as at a carpet, the seer is exhorted to "watch that pattern among general things which his idiosyncrasy moves him to observe, and describe that alone." It is interesting that, in contradistinction to Henry James's single master figure, Hardy's multicolored carpet allows for unlimited possible patterns, according to the idiosyncrasy of the observer. His own idiosyncrasy—the contours of his disposition—soon made him regard himself as different from other novelists. Committing himself to a career as a novelist following the success of *Far from the Madding Crowd*

---

1. Hardy, notebook entry, June 3, 1882, in *Life and Work*, 158.

in 1874, he noted the following year that, though he realized he would be expected "to look for material in manners—in ordinary social and fashionable life as other novelists did," he "took no interest in manners, but in the substance of life only."[2] What he saw when he looked at substantive or general things was sex—and sorrow; and toward the end of his career, he was ready to say so emphatically: "Life being a physiological fact, its honest portrayal must be largely concerned with, for one thing, the relations of the sexes, and the substitution for such catastrophes as favour the false colouring best expressed by the regulation finish that 'they married and were happy ever after,' of catastrophes based upon sexual relations as [they are]."[3] Given the physiological fact, relations between the sexes were not to be depicted as, say, a Jane Austen saw them. His subject was, rather, "the elementary passions," or, as he said of the concern of his last novel (though this applies to most of his work), "the fret and fever, derision and disaster, that may press in the wake of the strongest passion known to humanity."[4] This is the distinctive note of Hardy's fiction—and a new note in the history of the English novel. Not only was sexual passion to be foregrounded in a manner not previously attempted; it was to be seen as catastrophic.

Hardy's refusal to regard the relations of the sexes as first and foremost a social matter means that his portrayal of passion has a pronounced ontological dimension. For his protagonists passion is bound up with the nature of being, and love is less a matter of class and wealth than self-realization—or self-destruction. It is more often the latter, given Hardy's sense of the disastrous nature of sexual relations. Rejecting the happy-ever-after formula for marriage, he shows it is marriage itself that is the issue and that becomes the locus of catastrophe.

2. Ibid., "at this date" (1875), 107. Hardy's lack of real interest in manners, even when he attempted a conventionally social setting for a novel, is sadly apparent in a work such as *The Hand of Ethelberta* (1876).

3. Hardy, "Candour in English Fiction," in *Personal Writings*, 127–28.

Referring to the same "pattern among general things," Deborah L. Collins maintains the "pattern in the carpet" that Hardy "traces" is "that God is no more than the machine which powers Nature"; and she repeats that "the pattern in the carpet . . . reveals God to exist only as 'rapt Determiner,' 'Prime Mover,' 'Immanent Will' " (*Thomas Hardy and His God: A Liturgy of Unbelief*, 32, 54).

4. Hardy, general preface to works (1912), in *Personal Writings*, 45; preface to *Jude the Obscure*, in *Personal Writings*, 32.

Love, in Hardy, means pain, as the narrator in *The Mayor of Casterbridge* roundly asserts: the "period in the history of a love when alone it can be said to be unalloyed with pain," he states, is that when there is "a delicate poise between love and friendship." The rule of marriage consequently is disillusionment. This usually applies to both partners, as in the case of Bathsheba and Troy in *Far from the Madding Crowd;* the form such disillusionment may take for a woman is graphically evoked by Bathsheba when she experiences the first major failed marriage in the novels:

> "It is only women with no pride in them, [Bathsheba says] who run away from their husbands. There is one position worse than that of being found dead in your husband's house from his ill-usage, and that is, to be found alive through having gone away to the house of somebody else. . . . A runaway wife is an encumbrance to everybody, a burden to herself and a byword—all of which make up a heap of misery greater than any that comes by staying at home—though this may include the trifling items of insult, beating, and starvation. Liddy, if ever you marry—God forbid that you ever should!—you'll find yourself in a fearful situation; but mind this, don't you flinch. Stand your ground, and be cut to pieces. That's what I'm going to do."[5]

Bathsheba has had a lot to try her, and by the end of the narrative she will be ready to essay marriage again, but her outburst provides us with a map of marriage in Hardy—a woman's guide to the terrain, as it were. Marriage precipitates the woman into "a fearful situation," a condition characterized by "ill-usage." The only adequate response to such usage is endurance, a readiness to stand one's ground and be hacked to bits by the lacerating ministrations of one's partner. Marriage, then, is the ultimate paradox of love. If it holds out the promise of self-realization, it results only in a stifling of being, the self's encompassment by "a heap of misery." It is clearly Troy's sword exercise during his courtship of Bathsheba that provides the imagery behind her determination to stand her ground again even if that means being cut to pieces; the exercise may also be taken to

5. Hardy, *The Mayor of Casterbridge,* 246; Hardy, *Far from the Madding Crowd,* 366.

supply us with an implicit image of love and marriage: "Love," Hardy said, "lives on propinquity, but dies of contact."[6]

Though Hardy wrote *Far from the Madding Crowd* before he himself married, it would seem likely that the dire view of marriage he continued to take throughout his career was not unrelated to his own troubled relationship with his first wife, Emma. His love for her is expressed in the astonishing and moving poems that he wrote about her after her death, but poems written before this evoke a stark sense of the marriage:

> When I bade me not absolve you on that evening or the morrow,
> Why did you not make war on me with those who weep like rain?
> You felt too much, so gained no balm for all your torrid sorrow,
> And hence our deep division, and our dark undying pain.[7]

More prosaically, Robert Gittings says that by 1895 Hardy and his wife had reached "the lowest depths of married estrangement"; and both Gittings and Michael Millgate, Hardy's major biographers, have discussed at length the various causes of the marital dissension that led to the "undying pain."[8]

Hardy's personal experience of such pain, however, may be taken to have fed into a generally tragic sense of life: "The tragical conditions of life," he wrote to a correspondent, "imperfectly denoted in The Return of the Native [*sic*] & some other stories of mine I am less & less able to keep out of my work. . . . All comedy is tragedy, if you only look deep enough into it."[9] Hardy is quoting Ruskin here—"Comedy is Tragedy

---

6. Hardy, notebook entry, July 14, 1889, in *Life and Work,* 230.

7. Hardy, "Had You Wept" (originally published in the volume *Satires of Circumstance,* which also included the love poems written after Emma's death, grouped as "Poems of 1912–13"), in *The Complete Poetical Works of Thomas Hardy,* 2:97. On the face of it, it seems reasonable to read this poem as bearing on Hardy's marriage.

8. Robert Gittings, *Young Thomas Hardy,* 134. See Robert Gittings, *The Older Hardy,* 20, 37, 38, 63–64, 67, 80–82, 93, 96, 117, 139; and Michael Millgate, *Thomas Hardy: A Biography,* 164, 166, 204, 269–70, 298, 312–13, 355–56, 394–96, 398–99, 454, 477, 480–83. In *Hardy,* his recent biography, Martin Seymour-Smith presents a "revisionary" view of Emma (and Hardy's second wife) and persistently challenges the accounts of Gittings and Millgate (particularly the latter), but his counterassertions seem to be more a matter of opinion than fact.

9. Hardy, letter to John Addington Symonds, April 14, 1889, in *The Collected Letters of Thomas Hardy,* 1:190.

if you only look deep enough" *(Fors Clavigera)*—but tragedy was what his own seeing penetrated to, a disposition to the tragic being deeply ingrained in him. In his poems he is preeminently a poet of loss—lost love and lost life—a poet repeatedly asking, "And why unblooms the best hope ever sown?" and holding that "if way to the Better there be, it exacts a full look at the Worst."[10] This insistent view of things expressed itself in his personal life in the most unlikely circumstances; even in a letter of condolence to parents who had lost their ten-year-old son, he could not help saying: "Though to be candid, I think the death of a child is never really to be regretted, when one reflects on what he has escaped." Hardy was a long-lived man, but his eighty-seven years must have been achieved in the face of some persistent wishes of his own to escape from life: "As to despondency," he wrote to another correspondent, "I have known the very depths of it—you would be quite shocked if I were to tell you how many weeks & months in byegone years I have gone to bed wishing never to see daylight again. . . ."[11] It is not surprising, then, that many of the novels are dark, but Hardy was confident that at least by fellow souls the gloom would not be regarded as arbitrary: "[S]ome of these novels of Wessex life," he wrote, "address themselves more especially to readers into whose souls the iron has entered, and whose years have less pleasure in them now than heretofore. . . ."[12]

II

It is fascinating to watch the way Hardy slowly embodied his tragic view of life in the pattern that repeatedly characterizes his mature work, the pattern that bears his idiosyncratic stamp. In his first novel, in line with what he took to be the prevailing fashion, Hardy would seem to have

10. "Hap," originally published in the volume *Wessex Poems,* in *Complete Poetical Works,* 1:10; "In Tenebris, II," originally published in the volume *Poems of the Past and the Present,* in ibid., 208.

11. Hardy, letter to H. Rider Haggard, Monday [May 1891?], in *Collected Letters,* 1:235; and letter to Edmund Gosse, August 30, 1887, in ibid., 167. Michael Millgate also states that "in February 1896 [Hardy] insisted in conversation with [Edward] Clodd that he wished he had never been born and, 'but for the effort of dying, would rather be dead than alive' . . ." (*Thomas Hardy,* 411).

12. Hardy, preface to *A Laodicean,* in *Personal Writings,* 15.

tried to contain his somber sense of "the relations of the sexes" within a social context. We can only guess that this was the case since *The Poor Man and the Lady* was never published and the manuscript has not survived; but the title of the work is one indication, and another is provided by the story "An Indiscretion in the Life of an Heiress," which the editor of *The Stories* describes as "adapted" from the novel, adding that "in his old age [Hardy] rather disparagingly described the story he had salvaged as 'a sort of patchwork of the remains.' "[13] In the story Hardy explores the nature and the effect of the social gulf that separates the lovers, but it is an anemic tale, a pale remnant of Hardy's false start as a novelist.

Desperate Remedies, Hardy's first published novel, is also of little value, and he later differentiated it from his major writings, classifying it as one of three lesser "Novels of Ingenuity"; but in it he nonetheless seems to have stumbled on the pattern that came to dominate his work. The pattern is based on the simple and traditional figure of the love triangle, but as Hardy eventually came to employ it, it provides the contours of his distinctive rendering of experience. Whereas the triangle in most love stories is a means of showing how the protagonists work through to a meaningful choice of sexual partner, a choice that is itself often the climax of the narrative and the validation of the happy-ever-after formula, in Hardy the triangle figures the problematics of choice. In most of the mature novels the love triangle poses a woman in relation to two men, though in *Jude the Obscure* the pattern is reversed and a man is placed in relation to two women. In contradistinction to traditional handling of the triangle, in Hardy the figure dramatizes both the making of a wrong choice and the sexual mystery that may draw a woman equally strongly to two men (or a man to two women) who are depicted as polar opposites. In *Desperate Remedies,* however, Hardy seems to have conceived of the triangular patterning—there are three overlapping triangles—only in terms of complicating his plot. That he has not yet grasped the possibilities of such patterning is indicated by the way in which the dilemmas posed by the triangles are initially resolved—not by choice but by compulsion.

13. Hardy, *The New Wessex Edition of the Stories of Thomas Hardy,* 3:9.

The choice at issue is specifically matrimonial in nature, but its repetition in the novels that followed points to the general significance of choice in Hardy. Indeed, Roy Morrell says "it is difficult to recall one of Hardy's novels or stories which does not at some point or other focus our attention upon the meaning of choice"; and he also states that Hardy's plots imply "a basic Existentialist concern with choice. His treatment of choosing and evading is . . . so exhaustive that to call it an exploration of the psychology of choice would be no exaggeration."[14] This, in the face of the widespread determinist view that there is little or no freedom of choice in Hardy, seems to me to be a salutary emphasis; but it should be weighed against Hardy's own sense of the context of such freedom. In *The Dynasts,* he wrote to a correspondent, "I went on using [the philosophy of life] which I had shaped out in my previous volumes of verse (& to some extent prose) . . .":

> [My] theory . . . seems to me to settle the question of Free-will v. necessity. The will of man is, according to it, neither wholly free nor wholly unfree. When swayed by the Universal Will (as he mostly must be as a subservient part of it) he is not individually free; but whenever it happens that all the rest of the Great Will is in equilibrium the minute portion called one person's will is free, just as a performer's fingers will go on playing the pianoforte of themselves when he talks or thinks of something else & the head does not rule them.[15]

As Hardy indicates, however, this view applies only "to some extent" to the novels; and in fact in the novels characters are offered and exercise a far greater freedom of choice than the image of the performer's fingers implies. His characters are subject, of course, to massive pressures of various kinds; and the Universal Will makes itself felt (among other things) in the play of

14. Roy Morrell, *Thomas Hardy: The Will and the Way,* 146, 144.

Hardy's use of the love triangle as a recurring narrative figure has also occasioned a less sympathetic response. Patricia Ingham, seemingly ignoring the fact that matrimonial choices are open to—and made by—both sexes, says that "the implications of this narrative pattern . . . are . . . clear: that a husband is a woman's only goal and reward," and she adds that such a "narrative structure is, to a feminist, deeply tainted" (*Thomas Hardy,* 30).

15. Hardy, letter to Edward Wright, June 2, 1907, in *Collected Letters,* 3:255.

chance in their lives, as in the notorious instance in *Tess of the d'Urbervilles* when Tess's confession to Angel slips under the carpet—but it should not be forgotten that Hardy arranges for Tess to discover this and then choose to let the matter rest.

The pattern of choice is initiated in the novel that followed *Desperate Remedies, Under the Greenwood Tree.* Fancy Day, the heroine of this novel, has three suitors. It is interesting that, as Hardy begins to come to grips with the problematics of choice in the early novels—in *A Pair of Blue Eyes* and *Far from the Madding Crowd* as well as in *Under the Greenwood Tree*—the distinctive triangular pattern of the later works is only implicit, for though a real dilemma for the heroine is posed in each case by two men, she is involved with at least three, and in *A Pair of Blue Eyes* with four. Fancy is in love with Dick Dewy and manages to dispose of another suitor, Frederic Shiner, but Mr. Maybold, the vicar, proves to be a more serious rival to Dick. Not knowing that Fancy has agreed to marry Dick, Maybold proposes to her. It is a striking and unexpected development in the narrative when she accepts him, saying (though this mystifies him), "[T]he temptation is, O, too strong, and I can't resist it." This moment of temptation is a turning point in Hardy, for it opens up possibilities that will be thoroughly and repeatedly explored in the later works. When Fancy succumbs to it, she enacts what will become a typical Hardyan displacement of love, and she grasps not only at the prospect of a better kind of life but also at the chance of being someone else—a different self. Fancy, in short, is a first rough sketch of Grace Melbury in *The Woodlanders*.[16]

In this serene novel, however, the possible consequences of such a choice on Fancy's part are not pursued, and she is given the chance to recant. She duly marries Dick, and, in line with novelistic tradition, we are to understand they are all set for smooth weather as they take their departure sitting "side by side" in the tranter's new cart. Fancy, however, contrary

---

16. Hardy, *Under the Greenwood Tree*, 200.

It is interesting that Horace Moule, in his 1872 review of the novel in the *Saturday Review*, refers twice to the "episode with the vicar," calling it "curious," but declaring that, "whether wisely introduced or not," it is "too brief to signify much in the working out of the story" (R. P. Draper, ed., *Thomas Hardy: Three Pastoral Novels*, 43, 45).

to Maybold's advice to her, does not tell Dick about what has passed between her and the vicar even though her husband says, as they drive along, "We'll have no secrets from each other, darling, will we ever?—no secret at all." Instead, in the closing words of the narrative, she thinks of "a secret she [will] never tell." They may be sitting happily side by side, but—in a scene that points to developments in subsequent novels—there is already something that separates them.

III

From as early as *Desperate Remedies* and then repeatedly in the mature work, another distinctive feature of the triangular pattern is that the opposed men are presented not only as opposites but also as distinct types, conforming to a recurrent sexual typology. The opposition is figured most clearly because most simply in one of Hardy's best short stories, "The Fiddler of the Reels," in which a mysterious musical prowess is used transparently as an index of sexual potency. Wat Ollamoor, nicknamed Mop, is said to be "a woman's man . . . —supremely so—externally little else"; he is "not attractive" to men, even "perhaps a little repulsive at times," but his great gift is for playing the fiddle, on which he produces "heart-stealing melodies."[17] He has a general "power over unsophisticated maidenhood," a power that seems on occasion to have "a touch of the weird and wizardly in it" (124), but this has a most pronounced effect on Car'line Aspent. When she hears him play—his eyes then are "closed in abandonment to instrumentation"—she is "seized" with "a wild desire to glide airily in the mazes of an infinite dance," and she gives herself to "compelled capers" (125–26). Opposed to Mop is Ned Hipcroft, to whom Car'line is engaged to be married before she meets Mop. A "manly and simple wooer," a "respectable mechanic," he "devotedly" woos Car'line "in ignorance of her infatuation," but, though he has the support of her father and sister, he cannot "play the fiddle so as to draw your soul out of your body like a spider's thread" as Mop does; indeed, Ned has "not the slightest ear for music" and cannot "sing two notes in tune, much less play

17. Hardy, "The Fiddler of the Reels," in *The Stories*, 2:123, 125. Further page references to this story are incorporated parenthetically in the text.

them." He is "measured and methodical in his ways," is given to plodding along in "outward placidity," and his is "a nature not greatly dependent upon the ministrations of the other sex for its comforts" (126–28).

The lines, then, are clearly drawn, and the issue is never in doubt. Ned backs down the moment he is put off by Car'line and goes away, resolving both to accept and to respect her "sad entreaty" (127). Four years later she suddenly appeals to Ned to marry her, and when he agrees, she arrives— together with "a little girl of three or so," the product of Mop's fiddling, as it were, before he took his music elsewhere. After a while Car'line and Ned decide to return to their home village, and on the last leg of their journey she goes on ahead with the child, stopping to rest at an inn. A dance is in progress, and "a tremor [quickens] itself to life" in her as she "thrills" to "the notes of that old violin" and "the witchery" she has "so well known of yore." Mop's "cunning instrument" has lost none of its power, and "seized" by the desire to dance she joins in, "convulsively" dancing on and on. The "seductive strains" of the music overwhelm her, "projecting through her nerves excruciating spasms, a sort of blissful torture," and she dances on and on until she drops and lies prone (134–36). She is brought around, but the fiddler has disappeared—together with the child, Mop having claimed his own.

"The Fiddler of the Reels" is a late story, first published in 1893, but the opposition between the two men that it dramatizes is one that concerned Hardy from early on. We may say that the opposition is one between a man who can call the tune sexually and a man who has no music in him. The first man is a libertine, a reckless womanizer, and if he is drawn to women compulsively, he is also able to compel them sexually. The second is a good fellow, honorable, temperate, and restrained by nature, decent to women, but sexually either diffident or inhibited or ineffective.[18] Why

18. Lascelles Abercrombie, one of Hardy's earliest critics, registers a typological division among Hardy's men, but he refers to only three novels and does not see the opposition in primarily sexual terms (*Thomas Hardy: A Critical Study*, 108–9). Albert J. Guerard also defines a male typology in Hardy but differentiates between his two categories primarily in terms of "masculine aggressiveness" (*Thomas Hardy*, 117, 114–15). Leon Waldoff has suggested a Freudian typology: "[T]he attitude toward woman [in *Tess of the d'Urbervilles*] . . . is split into two characters, Alec and Angel, one taking an attitude that woman is primarily a sexual object, the other an attitude that denies her sexual nature through idealisation"

such an opposition should have so preoccupied Hardy is difficult to say, but a difference between his father and himself is certainly suggestive. Michael Millgate says that "many women . . . are said to have found the elder Hardy's manners charming and his person attractive. As a young man he had a reputation as a womanizer and an occupation which provided ample opportunities for sexual adventure."[19] Hardy described his father as "handsome" and noted that he was an "open-air liver and a great walker"— and good at dancing. Most revealingly, Hardy (writing in the third person of the ostensible "biography") said of himself: "His immaturity . . . was greater than is common for his years [he was then about twenty] and . . . a clue to much of his character and action throughout his life is afforded by his lateness of development in virility, while mentally precocious." He also noted that "he tried . . . to avoid being touched by his playmates. One lad, with more insight than the rest, discovered the fact: 'Hardy, how is it that you do not like us to touch you?' This peculiarity never left him, and to the end of his life he disliked even the most friendly hand being laid on his arm or his shoulder. Probably no one else ever observed this."[20]

Another way of viewing the personal significance of Hardy's sexual typology is suggested by the idea of "decomposition," which Robert Rogers says is "a minor concept in psychoanalytic theory" but—as he shows—is a phenomenon widely prevalent in literature. Rogers takes over Ernest Jones's definition of decomposition (in his study of *Hamlet*): decomposition is the process whereby "various attributes of a given person are disunited and several individuals are invented, each endowed with one group of the original attributes." Rogers states categorically that "decomposition in literature . . . always reflect[s] psycho-sexual conflict, however obliquely."[21] In the light of Hardy's own admission of his "lateness of development in virility," it is possible that his diffident men and his

("Psychological Determinism in *Tess of the d'Urbervilles*," 147). It seems to me, however, that the problem of "the heroes" is not that they deny the woman's sexual nature but their own and that what is at issue with the rakes is, more fundamentally, the nature—and the limitation—of the power they are able to exert over women.

19. Millgate, *Thomas Hardy,* 20.

20. Hardy, *Life and Work,* 17–18, 37, 502 (Millgate lists this note as one of those added to *Life and Work* by Florence Hardy after Hardy's death).

21. Robert Rogers, *A Psychoanalytic Study of the Double in Literature,* 13, 12, 15, and passim.

rakes—his sharply paired lovers—reflect a conflict between his sense of himself and what he perhaps wished (and feared) to be. They certainly seem to point to a split between passive and active male roles.

Without doubt Hardy was fascinated by pronounced virility. In *Desperate Remedies* the libertine, Aeneas Manston, is by far the most striking character. The first of a line of unscrupulous sexual adventurers in the novels, he is a representative figure. When Cytherea Graye first sees him, he seems "to be of towering height" and is "dark in outline"; he is "an extremely handsome man, well-formed, and well-dressed," with an "almost preternatural clearness of . . . complexion," and his lips are "full and luscious to a surprising degree, possessing a womanlike softness of curve, and a ruby redness so intense as to testify strongly to much susceptibility of heart where feminine beauty [is] concerned"; but his mouth is also "reckless" and "voluptuous."[22] The pattern is completed by the look of his eyes, which more than anything else express his capacity for penetration: when she first meets him, Cytherea feels that "his eyes are going through" her (162), and afterward his "black eyes seemed piercing her again" (169). This capacity typically goes together with a compelling power. To Cytherea it seems that it is the lightning and thunder that "[compel] her, willingly or no, to accept his invitation" to enter his house (163), but it soon becomes apparent that she is "compelled to do as she [is] bidden" by him (166). Manston's power is directly manifested when even the touch of his clothes "[sends] a thrill through Cytherea" (164); but it is also metonymically embodied in the storm: the "thunder, lightning, and rain" increase "to a terrific force," and Cytherea, "in spite of herself," is "frightened, not only at the weather, but at the general unearthly weirdness" that seems to "surround" her (166). The weirdness would seem to be linked in Hardy's imagination with the effect of music, for Manston's power—like that of Mop in "The Fiddler of the Reels"—is associated with a performative musical ability. Manston plays an organ for Cytherea, an organ that he himself has made. He plays "powerfully," and she, who has "never heard such music in the completeness of full orchestral power," is greatly "moved"; indeed, the "varying strains" are

22. Hardy, *Desperate Remedies*, 162, 163–64, 169. Further page references to *Desperate Remedies* in this section will be incorporated parenthetically in the text.

said to "[shake] and [bend] her to themselves, as a gushing brook shakes and bends a shadow cast across its surface" (167). As she continues to listen, "new impulses of thought [come] with new harmonies, and [enter] into her with a gnawing thrill" (168). The writing may be overwrought, but sexual capitulation is so insistently suggested in the imagery deployed in this encounter that it is a pity Hardy thereafter turned to different kinds of compulsion in portraying her submission to him, using the contrivances of plot to undo her.

Edward Springrove, the honorable man who is opposed to Manston in the contest for Cytherea, is shown in an early scene that typifies his sexual diffidence. His advances are characterized by their measured cautiousness, and his commitment to another woman effectively serves to inhibit him, enhancing his natural timidity:

> She breathed more quickly and warmly: he took her right hand in his own right: it was not withdrawn. He put his left hand behind her neck till it came round upon her left cheek: it was not thrust away. Lightly pressing her, he brought her face and mouth towards his own; when, at this the very brink, some unaccountable thought or spell within him suddenly made him halt—even now, and as it seemed as much to himself as to her, he timidly whispered "May I?" (80–81)

It is true that he does finally kiss her, but with his moves orchestrated in punctuated pauses, he is not exactly a compelling figure. Indeed, after Cytherea's first encounter with Manston, Edward's image is said to rise before her "like a shadowy ghost" (169)—and he is never much more substantial than that.

The sort of opposition figured by Manston and Edward and the manner in which it patterns the recurrent love triangles are among the topics that I propose to trace in the more significant novels that followed *Desperate Remedies*. Edward's insubstantiality in relation to Manston is redressed in *A Pair of Blue Eyes*, in which the two main opposed men are both in the honorable mold—and there is no libertine. Stephen Smith and Henry Knight represent different possibilities of the type as Hardy comes to develop it, Stephen being a good, straightforward, simple man, and Knight a complicated intellectual. Thereafter the major novels regularly pose a libertine against an honorable man: Frank Troy against Gabriel Oak (and also Farmer Boldwood) in *Far from the Madding Crowd;* Damon Wildeve against Clym Yeobright in *The Return of the Native;* Edred Fitzpiers against Giles Winterborne in *The Woodlanders;* and Alec d'Urberville against Angel Clare in *Tess of the d'Urbervilles.* C. H. Salter, with reference to a similar list of what he calls repeated "structural contrasts," cites it as indicative of Hardy's lack of inventiveness, of "an element of monotony" in his work that "survives differences of character and situation."[23] It seems to me, however, that the repeated pattern is embodied in a rich diversity of "character and situation"—and presented with steadily increasing psychological depth. And anyway, as Proust's narrator says to Albertine (in C. K. Scott Moncrieff's translation of *Remembrance of Things Past*), "[T]he great men of letters have never created more than a single work, or rather have never done more than refract through various mediums an identical beauty which they bring into the world."

One exception to Hardy's insistent patterning of the men in his love triangles is seemingly *Jude the Obscure,* but in effect the pattern is maintained since the same kind of opposition is depicted, though in this case it is figured by two women (in relation to a man)—that between Arabella Donn and Sue Bridehead. Another apparent exception is *The Mayor of Casterbridge.* Though this novel turns on the opposition between two men, Michael Henchard and Donald Farfrae, and though they are involved in a love triangle, Hardy's main concern in this work is not with setting a woman between two men but with the relationship of the men themselves. Neither man, moreover, appears to conform to the dominant male typology. But, as I shall seek to show, *The Mayor of Casterbridge* fits into the prevailing pattern in several unexpected ways.

IV

These, then, are the main figures in the carpet of Hardy's fiction. Their depiction is complicated, however, by the role of "the writer"—or narrator— in presenting them, for as stated in the notebook entry quoted at the

23. C. H. Salter, *Good Little Thomas Hardy,* 112.

beginning of this chapter, he regards himself as a "seer." The term is ambiguous, and ambiguities in the fiction may well be traced back to it.

In the given context the word "seer" would seem to refer to the one who sees, a see-er who "watches" the pattern he is moved to "observe." But the Oxford English Dictionary lists such a meaning for "seer" as "rare," and I imagine most readers, on first encountering the word in the quoted passage, would assume it has one syllable and refers to a prophet or sage. Hardy goes on to insist that what the see-er sees bears the imprint, when it is recorded, of "the writer's own mind," an imprint that may thus also incorporate the sage's view of things. The passage suggests that the artist, for Hardy, compounds the functions of watcher and sage—that he is, in another of his terms, a "life-seer."

That the use of the word "seer" in the quoted passage is indeed ambiguous is exemplified by the divergence between the readings of two critics, the first taking it to mean only the one who sees, the second only the sage. Thus, George Wotton says: "In so far as Hardy believed that the function of the artist was to draw aside the veil of the apparent, he defined himself as a seer whose art was not concerned with the mirroring of reality or the expression of ideas but with seeing into the structure of the real." But J. T. Laird contends that "as a 'seer' . . . Hardy conceived of the novelist's purpose as giving direct expression to the 'pattern' observed among 'general things', the pattern in his case being a philosophic interpretation of the nature of existence. . . ."[24] Certainly the narrators in the novels amply project a compound presence, though not all readers have been enamored of it. Praise is freely elicited by the direct description of the see-er, the fine observer of nature and pastoral activity and young love; but antagonism is generated as often as not by the authorial commentary of the seer, the ponderous moralizer and the gloomy prophet of doom.

24. George Wotton, *Thomas Hardy: Towards a Materialist Criticism*, 7; J. T. Laird, "Approaches to Fiction: Hardy and Henry James," 51.
My sense of the term—in contradistinction to both Wotton and Laird—is supported by J. B. Bullen's view of its meaning: "For [Hardy] the artist is a 'seer,' not only in the conventional sense that he is gifted with spiritual and moral insight, but also in the sense that a seer is one who watches and observes the life around him" (*Expressive Eye*, 13).

Support for viewing Hardy's "seer" as both watcher and sage is provided by his use of the term in his fiction. So far as I know, the term is used with narratorial authority only once in the novels—when it is applied to Elizabeth-Jane in *The Mayor of Casterbridge*. (It is also used, though ironically, in *Tess of the d'Urbervilles* when Tess thinks Angel Clare's soul "the soul of a saint, his intellect that of a seer" and in *Jude the Obscure* when Jude Fawley, as his relationship with Sue Bridehead collapses, despairingly laments his sense of her as having formerly been "a woman-poet, a woman-seer.")[25] Elizabeth-Jane, having often been perceived as mouselike and elicited considerable unsympathetic criticism, is an unlikely stand-in for Hardy, but the fact remains that she alone of all his characters is depicted as relating to the world around her in a way that is analogous to that of the novelist as presented in the carpet passage.

Elizabeth-Jane is repeatedly shown silently observing others—she is the quintessential watcher in the novels—but her watching is the concomitant of other attributes. When she becomes suspicious of the relations between Lucetta and Farfrae, for instance, "the reflective Elizabeth" is made "more observant" of Farfrae and begins to "read" Lucetta: "A seer's spirit took possession of Elizabeth, impelling her to sit down by the fire and divine events so surely from data already her own that they could be held as witnessed."[26] Elizabeth-Jane is possessed by "a seer's spirit," as a writer by his daemon, but the spirit emanates from close and direct "observation"; the observation, in turn, issues in "reflection" and in a "reading" or interpretation of what is seen. The act of seeing thus becomes a penetration, a seeing through; sight becomes insight. The seeing, in other words, is a function—as in the carpet passage—of the perceiving mind: "Elizabeth-Jane, surveying the position of Lucetta between her two lovers from the crystalline sphere of a straightforward mind, did not fail to perceive that her father, as she called him, and Donald Farfrae became more desperately enamoured of her friend every day" (250).

Elizabeth-Jane, however, also "divines events," intuiting and predicting what will occur with absolute surety. Her seeing, that is, is not only a

---

25. Hardy, *Tess of the d'Urbervilles*, 257; Hardy, *Jude the Obscure*, 426.
26. Hardy, *The Mayor of Casterbridge*, 242–43. Further page references to the novel in this section will be incorporated parenthetically in the text.

seeing through but also a foreseeing, and her divining fuses the functions of watcher and sage, joining them in the seer and serving as a bridge to the view of her as prophet. Hardy clearly intends her to be seen as such, filling her with a moral passion for the truth, like a figure from the Old Testament. When Lucetta refuses to admit that she ought, as Elizabeth maintains, "to marry Mr Henchard or nobody—certainly not another man!" the girl makes her steely pronouncement: "Admit it or not, it is true!" And when Lucetta confesses she is already married, she is indeed put into a biblical dock: " 'You—have—married Mr Farfrae!' cried Elizabeth-Jane, in Nathan tones" (289). Elizabeth's role in this respect is not only hortatory or denunciatory; she is also presented as wise. Though much younger than Lucetta, she plays "the part of experienced sage" in discussions with her (245) and makes "wise little remarks" to Farfrae (246). But she is preeminently the Hardy seer as prophet in her darkly disillusioned view of life: "Her experience had been of a kind to teach her, rightly or wrongly, that the doubtful honour of a brief transit through a sorry world hardly called for effusiveness, even when the path was suddenly irradiated at some half-way point by daybeams rich as hers" (410–11). The idea is hammered home in the reluctantly qualified assertion that concludes her story (and the novel): though she is finally "forced to class herself among the fortunate," she does not forget that her "youth had seemed to teach that happiness was but the occasional episode in a general drama of pain."

In the carpet passage quoted from the notebooks, the task of seeing, though suggestively modified, is presented as primary. Hardy's view is in line with an emphasis on the importance of seeing that goes back to Wordsworth and on through Browning and Ruskin; it also points ahead to the famous statement made by Joseph Conrad some fifteen years later.[27] The importance of seeing was in the air, as it were, and Hardy may be regarded as continuing to endorse its primacy in a (presumably appreciative) copying in his *Literary Notebooks* of statements by other writers that support such a view. He made the following note, for instance, from an article on J. M. Barrie that appeared in the *Academy* in November 1900:

27. See the Introduction, 5 above.

The great artist may force you to laugh or to wipe away a tear, but he accomplishes these minor feats by the way. What he mainly does is to *see* for you. If, in presenting a scene, he does not disclose aspects of it which you would not have observed for yourself, then he falls short of success. In a physical and psychical sense his power is visual, the power of an eye seeing things always fresh, virginally, as though on the very morn of creation itself.

He also copied the following passage from Ruskin's *Modern Painters:* "*The greatest thing* a human soul ever does in the world is to *see* something, & tell what it *saw* in a plain way. . . . To see clearly is poetry, prophecy & religion all in one."[28] And in his life in the world outside his art, Hardy "preferred" to observe rather than to act, to be "the man with the watching eye."[29]

He did not always incline, however, to a subordination of philosophizing to seeing. In an essay he granted that "excursions into various philosophies, which vary or delay narrative proper, may have more attraction [for some readers] than the regular course of the enactment," and he said that the "judicious inquirer may be on the look-out for didactic reflection." He also declared that the "true object" of novels is "a lesson in life, mental enlargement from elements essential to the narratives themselves and from the reflections they engender. . . ." And if he copied out the extract from Ruskin, he had many years before made a note of a very different kind of pronouncement by Matthew Arnold (in an essay on Wordsworth that appeared in an 1879 issue of *Macmillan's Magazine*): "The noble & profound application of ideas to life is the most essential part of poetic greatness."[30]

The question of the subordination—or the insubordination—of the sage is crucial to an understanding of Hardy's art. He himself, despite

28. *The Literary Notebooks of Thomas Hardy,* ed. Lennart A. Björk, entry 2072, 2:102 (the editor describes the entry as an "annotation and quotation with slight variations" from the original [518]); entry 2152, in ibid., 117 (Hardy's underlining; the editor describes the entry as an "abridged quotation with slight variations" [522]).

29. In his (disguised) autobiography, Hardy wrote: "Early in January 1926, feeling that his age compelled him to such a step, Hardy resigned the Governorship of the Dorchester Grammar School. He had always been reluctant to hold any public offices, knowing that he was by temperament unfitted to sit on committees that controlled or ordained the activities of others. He preferred to be 'the man with the watching eye'" (*Life and Work,* 465).

30. Hardy, "The Profitable Reading of Fiction," in *Personal Writings,* 112–13, 114; Hardy, *Literary Notebooks,* entry 1102, 1:118.

the quoted statements above, seemed in practice to believe in a necessary subordination and to believe too that he had succeeded in controlling the seer throughout most of his career as a novelist: "[This is] almost the first book of mine," he wrote to a correspondent of *Jude the Obscure,* "of which I feared that the Job-cum-Ezekiel moralist loomed too largely behind the would-be artist." That *Jude* was in fact the first such book is doubtful, as that "almost" appears to concede; and Robert Gittings has indicated what the "would-be artist" had to contend with: "Hardy, more than most creative artists, was deeply self-centred. He regarded himself as one of the chosen few who had a mission to his age; his obsessive markings in his Bible show a belief not in the message of that book—like so many Victorian thinkers, he lost his faith in the 1860s—but in himself as a kind of latter-day seer and prophet, an Isaiah or an Ezekiel."[31] Nor is the extent to which the prophet looms large behind the artist merely an aesthetic question: the issue of subordination is crucial because the seer in Hardy is often at odds with the see-er. It is one of the objects of this study to explore the relation between the two and to assess the significance of divergences between them and of consequent discrepancies in the fiction. In this respect I should say at once that I am not proposing to unearth a poststructuralist Hardy who deconstructs himself and so leaves us with a body of work whose meaning cannot be determined. My concern is with the writer whose seeing proved in effect (and in a strange variant of Bloomian misreading) to be liberating, for it enabled him to continue to pursue his career as a novelist despite the seer's black pronouncements on what had been seen in a given work—so black they should have sufficed to silence him. The silence—in the novel, at any rate—came when he could take things no further, when in this respect *Jude the Obscure* finally brought the see-er and the sage together in the seer.

V

In their relations with the woman of the love triangle, the libertine and the good fellow are seen to function—as she with them—in terms of certain rules of love. In *Desperate Remedies,* it is true, the narrator queries whether

31. Hardy, letter to William Archer, November 14, 1895, in *Collected Letters,* 2:96; Gittings, *The Older Hardy,* 12.

"any rule at all can be laid down in a matter which, for men collectively, is notoriously beyond regulation";[32] but Hardy nonetheless provides a number of rules both in this novel and in *Far from the Madding Crowd,* his first fully achieved work. An account of these rules, which, though formulated early, have their bearing on Hardy's whole oeuvre, may serve to complete the pattern descried by the seer "among general things."

The rules of love fall into two sets, one relating to the self of the lover, the other to the object of his love. With regard to the first, the rule that has perhaps the most far-reaching implications is stated when Gabriel Oak (in *Far from the Madding Crowd*) looks down at Bathsheba Everdene (whom he does not yet know by name) through a hole in the roof of a shed:

> In making even horizontal and clear inspections we colour and mould according to the wants within us whatever our eyes bring in. Had Gabriel been able from the first to get a distinct view of her countenance, his estimate of it as very handsome or slightly so would have been as his soul required a divinity at the moment or was ready supplied with one. Having for some time known the want of a satisfactory form to fill an increasing void within him, his position moreover affording the widest scope for his fancy, he painted her a beauty.

In a notebook entry Hardy had earlier declared that "the poetry of a scene varies with the minds of the perceivers."[33] The view is sharpened here: what we see, it is held, is not merely necessarily subjective but "coloured and moulded" by our "wants." Accordingly, even the beauty of a woman is conferred on—or withheld from—her by a man who cannot but look at her through his own needs. Such a man is transformed into a lover and she into a beauty when he is aware of a "void within him" that he seeks to fill. One's falling in love, that is, is an index of a lack in the self, and whether one falls in love or not is dependent on the degree of one's self-sufficiency—or self-awareness. It follows, therefore, that "the rarest offerings of the purest loves are but a self-indulgence, and no generosity at

32. Hardy, *Desperate Remedies,* 244.
33. Hardy, *Far from the Madding Crowd,* 64; notebook entry for August 23, 1865, in *Life and Work,* 52.

all." Far from being generous, indeed, love is acquisitive, seeking as large a return as possible on invested feeling: "Love," we are told, is "an extremely exacting usurer (a sense of exorbitant profit, spiritually, by an exchange of hearts, being at the bottom of pure passions . . .)."[34] When there is no bottom to passion or need, when there is only "an increasing void" within the self that is not filled, then the self is swallowed up in its own emptiness. Alternatively, the void may effectively be denied—for a time—and there is thus a line of characters in the major work who appear (or try) to be self-sufficient: Knight in *A Pair of Blue Eyes,* Bathsheba and Boldwood in *Far from the Madding Crowd,* Grace Melbury in *The Woodlanders,* and Sue Bridehead in *Jude the Obscure,* though she in her insistence on self-containment despite her need of men represents a variation of the desire. The phenomenon is exemplified preeminently by Henchard in *The Mayor of Casterbridge,* which is a full-scale study of attempted self-sufficiency as an alternative to unhappy marriage.[35]

A number of the rules that relate to the object of love are initially formulated in *Desperate Remedies.* The first is the attraction of indifference, a rule that the young novelist buttresses with a quotation from Terence: "It was plain then, Cytherea said, that Edward did not care deeply for her, and she thereupon could not quite leave off caring deeply for him:

Ingenium mulierum
Nolunt ubi velis, ubi nolis cupiunt ultro."

And in turn Cytherea's "supreme indifference" is said to add "fuel to Manston's ardour."[36]

34. Hardy, *Far from the Madding Crowd,* 181, 73.

35. J. Hillis Miller also comments on the importance of this rule of the void in Hardy: "Each of Hardy's protagonists has . . . the sense of a void within. This inner emptiness is the absence of any absolute ground for the self. These characters seek escape from their ontological insufficiency by way of relations to other people, in a yearning movement of one subjectivity toward another which generates the dramatic action of Hardy's fiction . . ." (*Thomas Hardy: Distance and Desire,* 184).

36. Hardy, *Desperate Remedies,* 173, 244.
The editor of this text provides the following note on the quotation: " 'I know the disposition of women: when you will, they won't; when you won't, they set their hearts upon you of their own inclination.' From Terence's comedy *Eunuchus (The Eunuch),* Act IV, sc. vii, 1.42" (427).

The obverse of this rule, though it is implied rather than formulated, is dramatized by a puzzling development in *Far from the Madding Crowd:* Troy's abandonment of Fanny Robin in view of the love for her that he later demonstrates. It is true that he feels publicly humiliated when he is made to wait in vain for her in the church on what was to have been his wedding day, but it is difficult to ascribe his rejection of her to such passing resentment. It is implied, rather, that—in contradistinction to the pull of indifference—it is her loving dependence on him, her submissive and clinging availability, that repels him. Bathsheba initially behaves in an analogous manner to Gabriel. And in *The Mayor of Casterbridge,* once Lucetta has "quickened" Henchard's "feelings with regard to her," she becomes "indifferent to the achievement."[37]

Desperate Remedies also provides some rules pertaining to the logic of love. For the man, the condition of conquest is persistence: Manston is said to see "for the hundredth time in his life" that "perseverance, if only systematic, [is] irresistible by woman kind." For the woman, it is a rival who counts even more than a lover, a rival who may mediate not only desire but rejection, as is made evident in Adelaide Hinton's sudden marriage to Farmer Bollens: "I think I can see my lady Hinton's reason for choosing yesterday to sickness-or-health-it," says Mr. Crickett. "Your young miss [Cytherea Graye], and that one, had crossed one another's path in regard to young Master Springrove; and I expect that when Addy Hinton found Miss Graye wasn't caren to have en, she thought she'd be beforehand with her old enemy in marrying somebody else too. That's maids' logic all over, and maids' malice likewise."[38] J. Hillis Miller, indeed, following René Girard's general formulation, goes so far as to assert that "the law of mediated desire" is the impelling force in Hardy's work: "The most important and pervasive barrier between Hardy's lovers . . . is . . . the presence of a third person. His fiction might be defined as an exploration of the varieties of mediated love. The third person standing between most inflames love and most successfully prevents the lover from reaching his goal." He cites Eustacia (in *The Return of the Native*) as "the clearest

37. Hardy, *The Mayor of Casterbridge,* 236.
38. Hardy, *Desperate Remedies,* 250; 268.

example in Hardy's fiction" of the operation of this law;[39] but the law applies not at all to her relations with the two men in the love triangle— and is relevant only in regard to her less important rivalry to Thomasin in relation to Wildeve. The law, though certainly evident, is of only minor importance in Hardy and plays little or no part in the configurations of the love triangle that I have outlined. It is these configurations, it seems to me, that form the most significant pattern in the novels—and it is these that I aim to trace in what follows.

39. Miller, *Thomas Hardy*, 158–59.

2

A Pair of Blue Eyes
The Displacement of Love

I

A Pair of Blue Eyes was the first of Hardy's novels to appear under his own name, neither *Desperate Remedies* nor *Under the Greenwood Tree* having previously been so distinguished. In retrospect the announcement of his name appears portentous, for the novel marks his coming into self, the finding of a durable literary identity. It is true that in the artificialities and improbabilities of its plot it looks back to *Desperate Remedies*—Hardy himself commented on the "immaturity" of its "views of life" and its "workmanship"[1]—but in the freedom of his immaturities, he seems almost inadvertently to have come upon what was to be an abiding concern of his work as a novelist. This is evident in a subtext that runs counter to a textually professed intention and is an early instance of the seer's seeing better than he knew when he began to look closely at the multicolored carpet spread before him.

The overt intention of the novel is proclaimed in its epigraph:

"A violet in the youth of primy nature,
Forward, not permanent, sweet, not lasting,
The perfume and suppliance of a minute;
      No more."

The lines are not attributed, and as they stand seem to point innocuously

---

1. Hardy, 1912 postscript to *A Pair of Blue Eyes,* 48. Further page references to this novel will be incorporated parenthetically in the text.

only to the transitoriness of the violet and of the titular blue eyes of the heroine, Elfride Swancourt, whose life is prematurely extinguished. The violet soon leads, indeed, to a bier, for we are told that "every woman who makes a permanent impression on a man is usually recalled to his mind's eye as she [appears] in one particular scene," and Stephen Smith always remembers Elfride's singing of "the closing words of the sad apostrophe" to Shelley's "When the Lamp Is Shattered":

> "O Love, who bewailest
>   The frailty of all things here,
> Why choose you the frailest
>   For your cradle, your home, and your bier."
>   (67–68)

The violet, however, has a specific context (*Hamlet* 1.3.5–10), and the epigraph is taken from what Laertes says about Hamlet to Ophelia:

> "For Hamlet, and the trifling of his favor,
> Hold it a fashion and a toy in blood,
> A violet . . . no more."

The lines thus refer more pointedly to the transitoriness of love rather than of life, and the violet that warns Ophelia against Hamlet's passing fancy seems intended to epitomize the inconstancy of Elfride's blue eyes. Elfride, we gather, is to be apprehended as the very model of a fickle female, a woman who gaily flits from man to man—she is involved with four in all—and whose physical propensities as she "[hovers] about . . . like a butterfly" (74) imply her emotional constitution. Her supposed fickleness is steadily insisted on: her "capacity for being wounded" is said to be "surpassed" only by that "for healing, which rightly or wrongly is by some considered as an index of transientness of feeling in general" (170); in her the pain of love is naturally transformed into more salutary feeling, for she can "slough off a sadness [at parting from a lover] and replace it by a hope as easily as a lizard renews a diseased limb" (190); the need to dissemble dictates in her "a fickle behaviour almost as imperatively as fickleness itself" (222); when she realizes she loves Henry Knight more than Stephen, we are told not only that there is perhaps "a proneness to inconstancy in her nature" but also that it is a "fickle resolve" that makes her determine to have "no more to do with Stephen Smith" (314–15); and she herself is made to acknowledge "her fickleness" when she is glad to shift "responsibility" for it, if only in part, from "her own shoulders to her father's" (318). Indeed, her blue eyes would appear, from the opening description of her, to be an emblem of this capacity. She "lives" in her eyes, we are told, and they are "blue as autumn distance—blue as the blue we see between the retreating mouldings of hills and woody slopes on a sunny September morning. A misty and shady blue, that had no beginning or surface, and was looked *into* rather than *at*" (51). Elfride's eyes, in their misty indistinctness, figure an absence of firmness, even, in their unpredictable depths, an unplumbed duplicity.

The authorial insistence on Elfride's fickleness has been faithfully reflected in critical responses to her. Peter J. Casagrande talks of her "essential fickleness" and of "something indefinably treacherous in her"; James R. Kincaid calls her a "devious female"; and (most extreme of all) J. Hillis Miller says: "[Elfride] moves through life from betrayal to betrayal. One man has already died for love of her before the novel begins. Later she leaves Stephen Smith to turn to Henry Knight. . . . Then she betrays Knight to marry Lord Luxellian."[2] But this is not at all what we are shown in the novel. Felix Jethway may have died for love of Elfride, and his mother may consequently believe Elfride killed him, but she was never in love with him and certainly does not betray him. As she tells Mrs. Jethway, she could not help his loving her, but broke with him when he tried to kiss her (332–33). Nor does she betray Knight when she marries Lord Luxellian; she does so only after Knight has ruthlessly abandoned her and the marriage is as much a nonrelationship (for all we ever learn about it) as her involvement with Jethway. What she does do is leave Stephen for Knight and so in a measure betray him—and him alone; but even in this instance we miss the point if we characterize her as fickle. She may

2. Peter J. Casagrande, *Unity in Hardy's Novels: "Repetitive Symmetries,"* 92; James R. Kincaid, "Hardy's Absences," 209; Miller, *Thomas Hardy,* 167–68. In a continuing—and what has proved to be a long-held—view, Raymond Chapman says that "Elfride proves to be what the Victorians called a flirt . . ." (*The Language of Thomas Hardy,* 8).

play at love with Stephen, and so is certainly irresponsible, but there are numerous indications that she is never deeply in love with him and in relation to him gives undue weight to extraneous considerations. When he calls her his "queen" and says he "would die" for her, she responds to "a proud moment": "She was ruling a heart with absolute despotism for the first time in her life" (107). We are told furthermore that without "the mystery" that attends Stephen's initial appearances at the rectory she would perhaps "never have seriously loved him at all" (119); when he reveals his humble origins and suggests she give him up, she declares the "hopelessness in [their] affairs" makes her "care more" for him (126); and, it is asserted, "it is certain that the young girl's love for Stephen received a fanning from her father's opposition which made it blaze with a dozen times the intensity it would have exhibited if left alone" (149).

It is not Stephen himself, therefore, who can bind Elfride to him, and when he bungles their planned elopement, she is quick to leave him, responding to an instinctive compulsion: " 'O Stephen,' she exclaimed, 'I am so miserable! I must go home again—I must—I must! Forgive my wretched vacillation. I don't like it here—nor myself—nor you!' " (166). Her vacillation, that is, is between waves of her own feeling and is not occasioned by a third party. When Knight appears on the scene after Stephen's departure for India and she falls in love with him despite her own sense of being "irretrievably committed" by the earlier relationship (170), this is illustrative not of the inconstancy of her nature but of the nature of love. "Love," says the narrator, "frequently dies of time alone—much more frequently of displacement" (314). The statement marks a seminal moment in Hardy, for with it he moves from a conventional view of female frailty and fickleness to a more profound grappling with the mystery of sexual impulses and compulsions. Elfride's feeling for Knight absorbs "her whole soul and existence": "A greater than Stephen had arisen, and she had left all to follow him" (359). The veering that was aborted in Fancy Day in *Under the Greenwood Tree* (as we have seen) is here played out in all its consequences. Henceforth the displacements of love (in this non-Freudian sense) as they center in one heroine after another become Hardy's repeated concern. He had found a major subject.

II

Elfride is involved with four men, but she is emotionally torn between only two of them; and in his handling of her relationships with Stephen and Knight, Hardy now begins what was to become his prolonged exploration of the love triangle as the basic figure of his fiction. In this early novel he also establishes what was to emerge as the characteristic feature of the triangle: the men in it are not only opposed to each other as lovers of the heroine but are themselves presented as decided opposites.

In *A Pair of Blue Eyes* the opposition is presented in simple, if not crude, terms and is worn outwardly, like a badge: "[Stephen's] complexion was as fine as Elfride's own; the pink of his cheeks almost as delicate. His mouth as perfect as Cupid's bow in form, and as cherry-red in colour as hers. Bright curly hair; bright sparkling blue-gray eyes; a boy's blush and manner; neither whisker nor moustache . . ." (60). Stephen's absence of facial hair is worked hard. It is not merely that he is young and immature, a mere "boy," who is so untouched by life that his "open countenance"— though he comes from London—"could never even have seen anything of 'the weariness, the fever, and the fret' of Babylon the Second" (60); with a complexion "as fine as Elfride's" and a face as "pretty" (60), he is also clearly marked as effeminate. His effeminacy is as much a matter of temperament as physique: he is said to have "a plastic adaptability more common in woman than in man" (144), and "the emotional side of his constitution" is "built rather after a feminine than a male model" (420). Stephen is caught for us in one of those memorable little scenes at which Hardy excels, scenes in which the everyday slides effortlessly into the symbolic. Setting out on an excursion with Elfride, he moves to help her mount her horse, taking her "slight foot upon his hand." "One, two, three, and up!" she says, but "unfortunately not so: He staggered and lifted, and the horse edged round; and Elfride was ultimately deposited upon the ground rather more forcibly than was pleasant. Smith looked all contrition" (105). The boyish Stephen, clearly, is not man enough for Elfride, a fact that is further emphasized when the rector's man, blatantly named Worm, steps forward to help her mount and she is "in the saddle in a trice" (105). The scene, moreover, has a strong proleptic force. In the contest that (unknown to them) is to develop between Stephen and

Knight, it is neatly intimated that Stephen will not be the man to hold Elfride; rather, it is also suggested, he will let her down, as he does with the marriage license, leaving her to take a fall.

The opening description of Knight pits him point for point against Stephen:

> A man of thirty in a speckled coat, with dark brown hair, curly beard, and crisp moustache. . . .
>
> Knight's mouth and eyes came to view now. Both features were good, and had the peculiarity of appearing younger and fresher than the brow and face they belonged to, which was getting sicklied o'er by the unmistakable pale cast. . . . [T]he eyes, though keen, permeated rather than penetrated: what they had lost of their boy-time brightness by a dozen years of hard reading lending a quietness to their gaze which suited them well. (181–82)

Not only does Knight have the requisite amount of hair to make him firmly masculine and the necessary number of years to establish him as overtly mature; in further contrast to Stephen, who feels wretchedly inferior to Elfride since she is the kind of woman who writes her father's sermons for him and has herself written a novel ("Ah, you are cleverer than I," he tells her. "You can do everything—I can do nothing!" [102]), Knight is an intellectual, who, if not ravaged by hard thought and reading, bears their mark upon him. He is a barrister and reviewer, and to come into his presence makes Elfride feel she has "[entered] a cathedral" (228). Knight is the bearer and wearer of another telltale Hardy sign, though it is only later that its meaning becomes apparent: his eyes are not penetrating. We remember that in *Desperate Remedies* it was Manston's piercing eyes that proclaimed his sexual power.

The contrast between Knight and Stephen is further developed through a pleasing symbolic parallelism. Elfride and Knight are together on the leads of the tower of West Endelstow Church when she remembers "a giddy feat" she has previously performed: "It was to walk round upon the parapet of the tower—which was quite without battlement or pinnacle, and presented a smooth flat surface about two feet wide, forming a pathway on all the four sides. Without reflecting in the least upon what she was doing she now stepped upon the parapet in the old way, and began walking along" (218). It is, first, Elfride who is epitomized by this scene. Bound to Stephen (who is in India) but drawn to Knight and allowing her relationship with him to develop, she seems to believe she can safely balance between the two men in much the same way she initially does on the parapet. And she engages in both giddy feats "without reflecting in the least" about possible consequences, and with complete confidence she is in control of what she is doing—"I am safe enough," she says in response to Knight's objection (218). What the scene dramatizes, however, is that she is unable to maintain her balance; and when she loses it, what she risks is death and disaster. Fortunately for her (and in contradistinction to her ultimate fate), she totters "to the inner edge of the parapet instead of to the outer" and falls only a few feet to the roof below. She is badly shaken nonetheless and swoons away. When she comes to, Knight, despite her protests, insists on carrying her down: "He took her into his arms, entered the turret, and with slow and cautious steps descended round and round" (218–20). In contrast to Stephen, who, it has been suggested, will not be able to hold her, Knight shows that he can carry her off. The earlier scene with Stephen is further recalled when Knight and Elfride emerge from the tower and he makes her take his arm: she feels "like a colt in a halter for the first time at thus being led along" (221). It is not only that Knight here displays a mastery clearly lacking in the hapless Stephen; it is the masterful Elfride who is mastered. The scene with Stephen is once again brought to mind at a crucial moment in the episode that takes place on the Cliff without a Name. When both Elfride and Knight are in danger of plunging over the precipice, he tries to save her by helping her climb to level ground: "She placed her feet upon the stirrup he made of his hand, and was high enough to get a view of the natural surface of the hill over the bank. . . . She made a spring from the top of his shoulder, and was up" (267). The image of the stirrup recalls Stephen's misfortune in the horse-mounting scene and points by contrast to Knight's ability to give Elfride the support she needs—or so it seems. Knight's resourcefulness is matched by that of Elfride in saving him when she makes a rope of her underclothes and enables him to climb to safety. It is the besetting irony of their relationship that he is then unable to match the passion that their adventure releases in her.

Knight's Laodiceanism in the sphere of passion is matched, however, by that of Stephen; and in this respect the opposition between them dissolves in likeness. If Hardy discovered a major subject in *A Pair of Blue Eyes,* he did not take up the kind of opposition portrayed between Manston and Springrove in *Desperate Remedies* and further develop what was to become the characteristic sexual typology of his presentation of the men in the love triangle. Both Stephen and Knight are in their own way sexually diffident, and there is no dashing rake-figure in the narrative. It is perhaps of some incidental interest that in this novel, which draws on clear autobiographical elements, Hardy, who (as has been remarked earlier) commented on his own "lateness of development in virility" should have concentrated on two sexually immature men.

Stephen's temperamental inability to assert himself is nicely caught on his first appearance. Moved to enthusiasm about Elfride and what he takes to be her way of life, he says, "I could live here always"; but when she remarks that he cannot, he agrees, and then "[draws] himself in with the sensitiveness of a snail" (69). The readiness to withdraw into his shell is perhaps Stephen's main characteristic; and if it points in one direction to his willingness both to withdraw altogether from Elfride when he goes to India and then, on his return, when it appears she has not kept faith with him, to take himself off to Birmingham rather than to "[provoke] a catastrophe of some sort" (297), such retraction is also not without sexual implications. Though his "shyness" will "not allow him to look her in the face" (95), he nevertheless does declare his love for her on his return to the rectory some months later. "I must tell you how I love you," he says. "All these months of my absence I have worshipped you":

> "Let me kiss you—only a little one," he said with his usual delicacy, and without reading the factitiousness of her manner.
> "No; not one."
> "Only on your cheek?"
> "No."
> "Forehead?"
> "Certainly not."
> "You care for somebody else, then? Ah, I thought so!"
> "I am sure I do not."

"Nor for me either?"

"How can I tell?" she said simply, the simplicity lying merely in the broad outlines of her manner and her speech. There were the semitone of voice and half-hidden expression of eyes which tell the initiated how very fragile is the ice of reserve at these times. (102–3)

We see how the "delicacy" that is born of diffidence is in effect obtuse, for it prevents Stephen from "reading the factitiousness of her manner"; it also makes him notably submissive, begging for what he might take, and defeatist, ready at once to believe in his own supplanting. In a word, he is not sexually "initiated," and his worship of her and slack inexperience combine to prostrate him before her, making it impossible for him to crack "the ice of [her] reserve."

Their tortuous relationship inches along nonetheless, only to reach an impasse when Elfride's father banishes Stephen on learning of his working-class origins. It is overtly a social constraint, therefore, that prevents the lovers from coming together, but Hardy makes it clear that it is another kind of bar that is really operative. Stephen reflects that "had Mr Swancourt consented to an engagement of no less length than ten years," he would have been "comparatively cheerful in waiting," and then gives himself to further fancies:

"I wish we could marry now," murmured Stephen, as an impossible fancy.

"So do I," said she also, as if regarding an idle dream. " 'Tis the only thing that ever does sweethearts good!"

"Secretly would do, would it not, Elfie?"

"Yes, secretly would do; secretly would indeed be best," she said, and went on reflectively: "All we want is to render it absolutely impossible for any future circumstance to upset our future intention of being happy together; not to begin being happy now."

"Exactly," he murmured in a voice and manner the counterpart of hers. "To marry and part secretly, and live on as we are living now; merely to put it out of anybody's power to force you away from me, darling." (148)

When Elfride says that marriage is "the only thing that ever does sweethearts good," she is presumably thinking—along the lines of the Pauline injunction—that it is better to marry than to burn; but the scene in fact suggests that these sweethearts would far prefer to procrastinate than to bring about the happy consummation. Stephen can face a prospect of ten years' waiting with (comparative) equanimity. "All" that these lovers "want" is to ensure their exclusive possession of each other, but the last thing either seems to want is to enter on that possession; consequently a secret marriage that will insure the future but ensure that they go on "as [they] are living now" is what will "do" nicely for both of them. They are indeed counterparts. It is with a vivid if simple depiction of the mutual fear of these immature lovers that Hardy begins his protracted exploration of the causes and effects of sexual inhibition. For the same reason, it would appear, Stephen proves to be incapable of going through even with the secret marriage he has proposed. His mishandling of arrangements for the marriage license—a piece of everyday psychopathology that is to recur in the fiction that follows—betrays once more an underlying unreadiness for the marriage, as does his acquiescence in Elfride's change of mind. His "offence," it is asserted, is "his very kindness in letting her return," for she has "her sex's love of sheer force in a man" and he should have dragged her to the altar and "peremptorily [married] her" (179). But that, of course, is the whole point; he is quite incapable of such force. Hardy's diffident men always pause to dither, where his rakes act to compel.

A somewhat more complex layer in the presentation of Stephen is suggested by his relationship with Knight. It is notable that Stephen is given both to hyperbole in his talk of his friend Knight and to seemingly compulsive mention of him in the presence of Elfride. When he returns to Endelstow Rectory to court her, he tells her that it was "[his] friend Mr Knight" who taught him to play chess and at once adds that he is "the noblest man in the world" (99). On the same occasion and apropos of Knight's having instructed him in the classics, he declares that his friend is "the best and cleverest man in England" and, moreover, that he is "one in a thousand" (101). Later, at the very moment when he is discussing with her the most opportune time for talking to her father about their engagement, she notices that he seems distracted and to be thinking deeply of something else:

"I was thinking how my dear friend Knight would enjoy this scene. I wish he could come here."

"You seem very much engrossed with him," she answered, with a jealous little toss. "He must be an interesting man to take up so much of your attention."

"Interesting!" said Stephen, his face glowing with his fervour; "noble, you ought to say." (112–13)

It is with a sure if jealous instinct that Elfride registers there is something peculiar in the way Stephen is "engrossed" with Knight; we see too, though she apparently does not, that his face never "glows" in response to her and that she does not seem capable of arousing such "fervour" in him. She does, however, accuse him of liking Knight "better" than he does her when, on the same occasion, he confesses to an overt ambition to "try to be his intimate friend" and to "hob and nob with him" when he is "richer and better known"—at which point his eyes "sparkle" (113). Stephen denies the preference for Knight, but it is clear he is more deeply involved emotionally with the man than the woman. His diffidence in relation to Elfride, it now appears, is at least in part a measure of his latent homosexuality. The narrator, seemingly with the ancient Greeks in mind, is at pains to hint at this condition when Stephen discovers it is Knight who is his rival: "That his rival should be Knight, whom once upon a time he had adored as a man is very rarely adored by another in modern times, and whom he loved now, added deprecation to sorrow, and cynicism to both" (303). Hardy seems to have had some interest in the subject of homosexuality: there is a strange, lesbian-like encounter between Cytherea Graye and Miss Aldclyffe in *Desperate Remedies;* and the issue arises again (as we shall see) in *The Mayor of Casterbridge.* But the matter is not pursued further in *A Pair of Blue Eyes;* and the homosexual theme is subsumed by Hardy's interest in the displacement of love: in his persistent adulation of Knight in the presence of Elfride, Stephen—even before she meets his friend—prepares the ground for his own replacement.

Not that Knight is without his brand of sexual diffidence. This is masked, first, by an overt preoccupation with the spirit rather than the flesh. He is said to be "a bachelor by nature," a man who seemingly asserts a natural self-sufficiency, but he nonetheless falls in love with Elfride. The way in which he begins to love her, however, serves as a "disproof of the assumption" that love, "like flame," is made "palpable at the moment of generation," for it is only when he is parted from her and she is "sublimated in his memory" that he falls "in love with her soul" (245). Rather than the embrace of spirituality, this suggests a flight from flesh; and then it emerges that he is a conditional—not a natural—bachelor: "Inbred in him was an invincible objection to be any but the first comer in a woman's heart. He had discovered within himself the condition that if ever he did make up his mind to marry, it must be on the certainty that no cropping out of inconvenient old letters, no bows or blushes to a mysterious stranger casually met, should be a possible source of discomposure" (246). In this passage periphrasis does double duty, serving to indicate what the narrator only dares to hint to his readers and, at the same time, what the character does not dare acknowledge to himself. That the issue is ostensibly a man's being "the first comer in a woman's heart"—a notable phrase—is one way of intimating that the woman must be a virgin; and in this early novel Hardy deals gingerly with the subject he was to treat so magisterially in *Tess of the d'Urbervilles,* both Elfride and Knight (as remains to be seen) being anticipatory in this regard of Tess and Angel Clare respectively. Or, as Hardy himself put it in the 1912 postscript to the novel, *A Pair of Blue Eyes* may be said to exhibit "the romantic stage of an idea which was further developed in a later book" (48). But Knight's objection to being any but the first comer is said to be "inbred in him," to be innate rather than inculcated, a condition he has "discovered within himself" rather than one that is culturally determined. Nor does the requirement appear to be even the disguised issue of the woman's virginity, for if it is concretized as the avoidance of letters and bows and blushes, these are imagined as "discomposing" him rather than the lady. What is at question, it seems, is a fear rather than a principle, the fear of his own discomfiture, though the true nature of that which may crop out as "a possible source of discomposure" is not revealed at this point.

Elfride and Knight move to a mutual disclosure of their feeling for each other after each saves the life of the other on the Cliff without a Name:

> He was saved, and by Elfride.
> He extended his cramped limbs like an awakened sleeper, and sprang over the bank.

At sight of him she leapt to her feet with almost a shriek of joy. Knight's eyes met hers, and with supreme eloquence the glance of each told a long-concealed tale of emotion in that short half-moment. Moved by an impulse neither could resist they ran together and into each other's arms.

At the moment of embracing, Elfride's eyes involuntarily flashed towards the *Puffin* steamboat. It had doubled the point, and was no longer to be seen. . . .

Regarding their attitude, it was impossible for two persons to go nearer to a kiss than went Knight and Elfride during those minutes of impulsive embrace in the pelting rain. Yet they did not kiss. Knight's peculiarity of nature was such that it would not allow him to take advantage of the unguarded and passionate avowal she had tacitly made. (278–79)

The sound that is wrung from Elfride when Knight appears is indeterminate in nature—it is "almost a shriek of joy"—but it effectively expresses the dual significance of this moment in her life. It is, first, a moment of revelation, the point at which the depth of her feeling for Knight becomes clear to her, for her joy is not merely at the saving of a life but of a loved one, and then it is revealed to him by her eloquent eyes. It is also a moment of release as the "long-concealed" feeling bursts out and throws her into his arms. Elfride, that is, is impelled by an irresistible impulse, not a fickle vagary, by a feeling that possesses her entirely and so drives out the more superficial emotion that Stephen has aroused in her. Stephen is aboard the *Puffin,* which is bringing him home to her, but at this moment it is "no longer to be seen." What is enacted is the displacement of love—and his displacement.

For Knight the moment seems to have a corresponding significance. He too has discovered the full extent of his love for her, his eyes too declare his feeling to her, and he too is irresistibly impelled into her arms. It is not merely from the nightmare of his experience on the cliff that he seems to waken, as he extends "his cramped limbs," but from a condition of partial and restricted existence as a compulsive bachelor, for the sleeper's resumption of waking life seems to be accompanied by a movement toward expansive physical being as he impulsively embraces her. Yet what the scene actually enacts is the strength of his inhibition. It is "impossible," we are told, for two people to go "nearer to a kiss" than do Knight and Elfride; but they do not kiss, and it is he who holds back. The narrator asserts that he holds back in a refusal "to take advantage" of her, and this is perhaps what Knight tells himself, but what is dramatized in a scene in which impulse has hitherto been irresistible is the still greater power of that which inhibits him. It is to a "peculiarity of nature" that is other than a fineness of moral scruple that we are adverted here.

It is some time before Knight can bring himself to kiss Elfride, but when he does, he also proposes to her:

> Now, though it may seem unlikely, considering how far the two had gone in converse, Knight had never yet ventured to kiss Elfride. Far slower was he than Stephen Smith in matters like that. . . . So Elfride's cheek being still forbidden fruit to him he said impulsively:
> "Elfie, I should like to touch that seductive ear of yours. Those [earrings] are my gifts; so let me dress you in them." . . .
> "And you shall," she whispered, without reserve, and no longer mistress of the ceremonies. . . .
> At the touch, the sensation of both seemed to be concentrated at the point of contact. All the time he was performing the delicate manoeuvre Knight trembled like a young surgeon in his first operation.
> "Now the other," said Knight in a whisper. . . .
> She was powerless to disobey, and turned forthwith; and then, without any defined intention in either's mind, his face and hers drew closer together; and he supported her there, and kissed her. . . .
> "Elfride, when shall we be married?" . . .
> And Knight laughed, and drew her close and kissed her the second time, which operation he performed with the carefulness of a fruiterer touching a bunch of grapes so as not to disturb their bloom. (337–38, 340)

Edward Springrove in *Desperate Remedies* was Hardy's first exemplar of the diffident man, and his sexual advances were characterized by their supreme cautiousness. Knight, however, emerges here as a still more extreme version of the type. The man whose face has "the unmistakable pale cast" is not only given to thought but also verbalizes everything, carefully expressing a wish to touch rather than touching. And to be described as "far slower" than Stephen Smith is to be established as a very tortoise among lovers.

But it is in the images used to evoke the quality of the lovemaking that he is given his distinctive stamp. Impelled by the self-imposed prohibition of "forbidden fruit" to abjure her cheek, as if to keep off the grass, he ventures on a path that will lead him to her ear. The mature man is then transformed into the "young surgeon in his first operation," subject to trembling inexperience, but professionally engaged—and suitably antiseptic. The images are made to converge neatly. When Knight claims his second kiss, this too is an "operation," and his abstinence from forbidden fruit gives way to the "carefulness of a fruiterer touching a bunch of grapes so as not to disturb their bloom." The metaphor subversively suggests that the lover's care is occasioned by a desire to preserve things in their full intactness. Knight, it seems, has as strong a fear of being the first comer as he has a wish to be so privileged.

What lies behind the wish is a particular fear, as Knight himself unwittingly reveals in a confessional exchange with Elfride. He admits rather shamefacedly, since he sees that his "avoidance of women" has been "rather absurd," that the only women he has kissed have been Elfride and his mother (353). His taste, he explains, making use of a phrase that is even more suggestive than that of the first comer though doubling for it and so conjuring up what he would perhaps prefer to ignore, has always been for "untried lips" (355). When pressed as to why he has "[held] aloof," he says he could only like a woman as "unpractised" as he and despaired of finding one until he met Elfride. Her lack of practice, he states, ensures that she "can't draw invidious comparisons" if he should do his "engaging improperly" (354). The invidious comparisons are safely restricted to her "opinion of [his] addresses" (354); but as the untried lips graphically declare, it is another kind of performance that is at issue and fear of another sort of "discomposure" that has proved so thoroughly inhibiting.[3]

3. Knight's preference for "untried lips" has been variously explained. My view is similar to that of Ronald Blythe and of Rosemarie Morgan. Blythe says: "[I]t is . . . plain that Knight rejects [Elfride] more out of terror at having to cope, as he thinks, with an experienced woman than because she might be scandalous" (introduction to *A Pair of Blue Eyes,* 19). Morgan says that Knight is a "pathetic victim of his own sexual anxiety and, we infer, atrophied sexual potency, which have bred in him a predilection for what

The fear is at once activated when Knight discovers that Elfride has had a lover before him, but it is deflected when she admits, under the pressure of his questioning, not only that she was "away alone with him" but also that she did not return home on "the same day" she left it:

> It is a melancholy thought that men who at first will not allow the verdict of perfection they pronounce upon their sweethearts or wives to be disturbed by God's own testimony to the contrary, will, once suspecting their purity, morally hang them upon evidence they would be ashamed to admit in judging a dog. . . .
>
> The scene was engraved for years on the retina of Knight's eye: the dead and brown stubble, the weeds among it, the distant belt of beeches shutting out the view of the house, the leaves of which were now red and sick·to death.
>
> "You must forget me," he said. "We shall not marry, Elfride."
> (399–400)

Knight's inhibiting fear may be strengthened by Elfride's revelations, but it is also transformed into revulsion from her supposed impurity. Discovering that his "idol" is "secondhand" (384), he disdains to have her, recoiling from the very idea of used goods. Knight, as previously suggested, is an Angel Clare in the making, and the submerged issue of the woman's virginity now rises to the surface of the narrative.[4] But since his suspicion is in fact unfounded, he will be haunted for years by the scene of his rejection of her, the scene—as so often in Hardy's poetry, as notably in "Neutral Tones"—being the landscape of an emotion. Just as the beeches shut out the view of the house, so his suspicion shuts out his view of her; and the stubble that is "dead and brown" and the leaves that

---

he calls 'untried' lips (metonymically, virgins)" (*Women and Sexuality in the Novels of Thomas Hardy*, 12). Rosemary Sumner tends more charitably to take Knight at his word: "[H]e wants the woman to be 'bungling' in her first kiss so that his own inexperience and incompetence will not be shown up" (*Thomas Hardy: Psychological Novelist*, 123). Michael Steig gives Knight's "sexual inadequacy" an oedipal slant: "He must be the first, and the oedipal implications of this are clear" ("The Problem of Literary Value in Two Early Hardy Novels," 60).

4. Cf. F. R. Southerington, who says "Knight . . . is obviously a first draft for Angel Clare, and in his idealisation of his own dreams, and his refusal to accept Elfride when she falls below his ideal, he bears more responsibility than any other figure" (*Hardy's Vision of Man*, 53). See also Richard H. Taylor, *The Neglected Hardy: Thomas Hardy's Lesser Novels*, 54.

are "sick to death" are engraved in his memory, encapsulating his sense of an ending. But the stubble and the leaves also point to what Knight himself never sees (though he cannot forget that day): the scene of death also figures the death of Elfride, which must ultimately be traced back to his rejection of her. Elfride of the vital blue eyes leaves Stephen Smith with a memory of the lines from Shelley that she sings—and Knight with that of the sickening countryside.

III

To regard Elfride as the betrayer of the men in her life, as J. Hillis Miller does, is in effect to see her as victimizing them, though such a view might well elicit the retort that it is she, if anyone, who is the victim, first of Stephen's bungling and then of Knight's rejection of her. It seems to me, however, that neither view is tenable, the former for reasons already indicated and the latter since she is responsible for her entanglements with both men. If Elfride is the first heroine in Hardy to enact the displacement of love, she is also the first really to confront the problem of choice. At crucial points in the narrative she is the one who makes decisive choices.

It is of interest that Hardy inaugurates what are to become protracted dramas of choice in his fiction with a tableau in which Elfride on a momentous occasion elects not to choose. She is on her way on horseback to St. Launce's, where she is to entrain for Plymouth and the secret marriage to Stephen, when she suddenly looks back:

> They were now on an open table-land, whose altitude still gave her a view of the sea by Endelstow. She looked longingly at that spot.
>
> During this slight revulsion of feeling Pansy had been still advancing, and Elfride felt it would be absurd to turn her little mare's head the other way. "Still," she thought, "if I had a mamma at home I *would* go back!"
>
> And making one of those stealthy movements by which women let their hearts juggle with their brains, she did put the horse's head about, as if unconsciously, and went at a hand-gallop towards home for more than a mile. By this time, from the inveterate habit of valuing what we have renounced directly the alternative is chosen, the thought of her forsaken Stephen recalled her, and she turned about, and cantered on to St. Launce's again.

> This miserable strife of thought now began to rage in all its wildness. Overwrought and trembling, she dropped the rein upon Pansy's shoulders, and vowed she would be led whither the horse should take her. (162)

If the allusion to the way in which "women let their hearts juggle with their brains" bares Hardy's essentialist view of gender—and such a view is apparent throughout his work—we do well to read him in his own terms, from within, as it were, rather than deplore his "sexism" in our terms, from without. Such a reading should not be regarded as an endorsement of his judgments or an evasion of charged feminist issues. We need to read him, in such matters, with a willing suspension of current beliefs, reserving our energy for the deciphering of what steadily become more and more complex texts and constantly bearing in mind the frame of reference of his own Victorian culture.

With her female brain juggled by her heart, then, it is clear that, when it comes to the test of action, Elfride shrinks not only from the escapade of the elopement but also from the proposed marriage to Stephen. It is home she "looks longingly" at, and if her "revulsion of feeling" is so "slight" as to make it seem "absurd" that she should turn back, it is strong enough to make her go toward home "for more than a mile." Her imagined "mamma" may be invoked to sanction her distaste for the elopement, but she is her own mamma when it comes to turning her back on Stephen and the marriage—as she in fact does later in London. The turnabout for St. Launce's, when it comes, is an enactment in miniature of what will be a repeated tendency among Hardy's heroines, for the "habit of valuing what we have renounced directly the alternative is chosen" is, as the narrator insists, "inveterate," though this habit, presumably, is a weakness of men as well as of women since it is one "we" are all given to. But the ostensible abrogation of choice when Elfride then decides to "be led" wherever the horse takes her is uniquely hers. And her decision not to choose is itself, of course, a choice, perhaps the most momentous of her life, for it leads her to Stephen when the horse, contrary to her expressed wish, turns toward St. Launce's (163). It leads her, that is, to a man she does not deeply love, and if she is strong enough not to go through with the marriage, this does not prevent her entanglement with Stephen from being the cause of her loss of the man she does profoundly love. Elfride's behavior in this crucial scene is strikingly irresponsible, but—even though she tells herself her "rash action" is "not her own" (163)—she bears full responsibility for it.[5]

The second crucial choice Elfride makes is not to tell Knight about his predecessor. The narrator remarks that "when women are secret they are secret indeed; and more often than not they only begin to be secret with the advent of a second lover." Elfride, at all events, "never [alludes] to even a knowledge of Knight's friend," even though "her natural honesty [invites] her to confide in Knight" and though she knows that "as mere policy it would be better to tell him early if he [is] to be told at all" (316). Elfride, that is, is a Tess Durbeyfield in the making; and, facing a similar dilemma, she procrastinates in much the same way—and in the end suffers the same kind of rejection. Like Tess, she even decides to confess everything, but when it comes to the point, she suddenly backs away: "I told you one day," she says to Knight, " . . . what was not true. I fancy you thought me to mean I was twenty my next birthday, but it was my last I was twenty" (330). When Knight finds out and forces her to admit she spent the night away from home, she is in "utter despair of being able to explain matters" satisfactorily (400), though the only apparent difficulty is that she does not even seem to grasp what the issue is: "I would not leave you for such a little fault as mine," she says. "Do not think it was so vile a thing in me to run away with him" (404).

The consequences of Knight's abandonment of her are clearly intimated. In the confession scene she tells Knight that he has been "everything in the world" to her (399), and when he leaves her she has nothing to fall back on. She becomes ill and tells Unity, the parlor maid, that she does not care what happens to her and wishes "she could die" (447). In the event she marries Lord Luxellian but remains in love with Knight: when the maid assumes it is Knight she is going to marry and says so, Elfride

---

5. As opposed to this view of the episode, Roger Ebbatson sees it as showing Elfride's loss of volition: "Elfride's decision to elope is made to depend upon the decision taken by her pony, and it is a sign of the incautious passivity which will rob her of her 'volition' at the later crisis with Knight [the reference is to the scene on the Cliff without a Name], a trait which links her with the more fully imagined Tess" (introduction to *A Pair of Blue Eyes*, 21).

sinks down "like a heap of clothes" and faints (448). Despite her marriage, she never regains the will to live and dies after a miscarriage (449). Her death thus spares her the experience of a failed marriage, which will be the fate of most of Hardy's heroines in the novels that follow.

3

Far from the Madding Crowd
The Only Love

I

Far from the Madding Crowd, says Howard Babb, is "not in the same class with Hardy's later achievements"; and Irving Howe echoes him in stating it is a novel that "by no stretch of affection could be called major."[1] It seems to me, however, that if *Tess of the d'Urbervilles* and *Jude the Obscure* clearly stand alone as Hardy's two great novels, *Far from the Madding Crowd* is nonetheless a major achievement and as good as anything else he wrote. Admittedly, it has one poorly contrived and ineffective sequence— the Greenhill Fair episode, which brings Troy back into the narrative after his disappearance—but its mature mastery, following some of the persistent crudities of *A Pair of Blue Eyes,* is remarkable. The gain in assurance is immediately evident in the tone and the style, which now effortlessly accommodate the vivid and the humorous, as in the following early description of the ways in which Gabriel Oak prepares his person for the proposal of marriage he intends to make to Bathsheba Everdene: "[He] used all the hair-oil he possessed upon his usually dry, sandy, and inextricably curly hair, till he had deepened it to a splendidly novel colour, between that of guano and Roman cement, making it stick to his head like mace round a nutmeg, or wet seaweed round a boulder after the ebb."[2]

1. Howard Babb, "Setting and Theme in *Far from the Madding Crowd,*" 147; Irving Howe, *Thomas Hardy,* 52.
2. Hardy, *Far from the Madding Crowd,* 75. Further page references to this novel will be incorporated parenthetically in the text.

The warm humor plays throughout on the rustics, whose simple, steady lives are set against the passionate upheavals of the protagonists; but it even sports with serious thematic matter: "It may have been observed that there is no regular path for getting out of love as there is for getting in. Some people look upon marriage as a short cut that way, but it has been known to fail" (83). It is this high-spirited narrative that contains Hardy's first major portrayal of a failed marriage. It also presents an exploration of the possibilities of love that is characterized by its originality and profundity; and if some of the action tends to be melodramatic, melodrama is the seedbed of Hardy's genius.

The title of the novel, the strong presence of the rustics, the detailed rendering of the agricultural year—particularly of what might be called "the sheep year," with its lambing, washing, shearing, and marketing scenes—the assertion that, on the day of the shearing, "God was palpably present in the country, and the devil had gone with the world to town" (194), the venerable barn in which the shearing takes place that is said to be "natural to the shearers" as they are "in harmony" with it (196): this kind of emphasis appears to place the narrative in a straightforward pastoral tradition. When the quotation from Gray is restored to its context, however, the title, while still continuing to evoke "pastoral affairs" (74), has a decidedly ironic dimension:

Far from the madding crowd's ignoble strife
  Their sober wishes never learn'd to stray;
Along the cool sequester'd vale of life
  They kept the noiseless tenor of their way.

The narrative may be located in a sequestered vale of life, but the wishes of its characters are hardly "sober" and exhibit a pronounced tendency "to stray."[3] The tendency is exemplified in miniature and in the comic mode by the story told about Bathsheba's father. Mr. Coggan calls him "one of the ficklest husbands alive," a man whose "heart would rove" and who

3. John Goode also remarks that the narrative, "far from ignoring ignoble strife, is the story of wishes and their consequences which are neither sober nor noiseless" (*Thomas Hardy: The Offensive Truth,* 31).

could not help his "wicked heart wandering." But he manages to "cure" his straying when he makes his wife take off her wedding ring: "[A]s soon as he could thoroughly fancy he was doing wrong and committing the seventh," says Coggan, " 'a got to like her as well as ever, and they lived on a perfect picture of mutel love" (111).

That more ominous forces may lurk in the pastoral scene, however, is intimated in the early episode that changes Gabriel's life. His dog drives his ewes over a precipice, and in a typical Hardy landscape—"the attenuated skeleton of a chrome-yellow moon" hangs over "an oval pond" that glitters "like a dead man's eye"—Gabriel looks down on "a heap of two hundred mangled carcases, representing in their condition just now at least two hundred more." It appears that the dog, "under the impression that since he was kept for running after sheep, the more he ran after them the better," had "collected all the ewes into a corner, driven the timid creatures through the hedge," across a field, and finally "hurled them over the edge" (86–87). The scene vividly dramatizes how even in a quiet pastoral setting creatures may be driven to destruction. This episode also has a proleptic symbolic force that establishes it as a frame for the ensuing action. The dog destroys unwittingly, a wayward animal force; in the tale that subsequently unfolds we are invited to watch the operation of a similarly wayward and destructive force in human beings, a force that drives them (though from within) as ineluctably as the dog drives the sheep. Hardy quietly insists on the parallel. Shortly after this scene when Gabriel encounters Fanny Robin and gives her some money, his fingers touch her wrist: "It was beating with a throb of tragic intensity. He had frequently felt the same quick, hard beat in the femoral artery of his lambs when overdriven" (101). And at the end of the narrative, in the climactic scene in which Farmer Boldwood kills Sergeant Troy, we are told that "all the female guests" in the room remain "huddled aghast against the walls like sheep in a storm" (440).

In *A Pair of Blue Eyes* it was sexual inhibition that was shown to have tragic consequences; in *Far from the Madding Crowd* it is sexual passion. In this novel Hardy begins his prolonged engagement with what he conceived as the destructive effects of passion. But he also uses the portrayal of such passion as a foil to what he takes to be a more stable and enduring kind of love, making this the motivating force of the narrative. The contrast is established through the opposition between Gabriel and Troy, who serve as prototypical figures in Hardy's developing male typology, and through Bathsheba's marriages first with Troy and then with Gabriel. Nor is this novel unique in the canon only because it resolves its triangular opposition in *two* marriages; it further complicates it through the heroine's deep involvement with a third man, Boldwood. Keeping Bathsheba (and her choices) firmly at the center of the narrative and more and more tightly enmeshing the lives of the four protagonists, the novelist is effectively able to depict varying possibilities of love.

II

Gabriel Oak, it will be recalled, is the character in Hardy in relation to whom the rule of the void is first prescribed.[4] Once he becomes aware of "an increasing void within him" (64), he is ready for love—and fixes on Bathsheba Everdene as well suited to supply his need. The opening description of him, however, suggests that he is unlikely to appeal to the spirited girl whose "ropes of black hair" tumble over the crimson jacket she wears (64), and who on occasion rides her pony while lying flat on its back, "her head over its tail, her feet against its shoulders, and her eyes to the sky," having glided into this position with "the rapidity . . . of a kingfisher" and the "noiselessness . . . of a hawk" (65):

> In his face one might notice that many of the hues and curves of youth had tarried on to manhood: there even remained in his remoter crannies some relics of the boy. His height and breadth would have been sufficient to make his presence imposing, had they been exhibited with due consideration. But there is a way some men have . . . for which the mind is more responsible than flesh and sinew: it is a way of curtailing their dimensions by their manner of showing them. And from a quiet modesty that would have become a vestal, which seemed continually to impress upon him that he had no great claim on the world's room, Oak walked unassumingly. . . . This may be said to be a defect in an individual if he depends for his valuation more upon his appearance than upon his capacity to wear well, which Oak did not. (52–53)

4. See Chapter 1, 32–33 above.

That the manly Oak still bears the marks of youth and even boyhood in
his face suggests that he is a reworking of the immature Stephen Smith
of *A Pair of Blue Eyes*. There is nothing effeminate, however, about Oak,
whose physique is "imposing" and who has an unbreakable manliness of
temperament that "wears well." The immaturity that clings to him, it is
indicated, is of a sexual nature, for it shows itself too in a "modesty" of
disposition that is not only quiet but virginal. Oak, indeed, is a diffident
man, psychologically so diffident that he appears to be smaller than he is, to
make little of himself in a general "curtailing" of his physical "dimensions"
and reducing of his "claim on the world's room." His diffidence expands,
ramifying into all aspects of his relations with Bathsheba. It makes him
inexpressive, for, though he wants to communicate "his impressions" to
her, he would as soon think of "carrying an odour in a net as of attempting
to convey the intangibilities of his feeling in the coarse meshes of language"
(70–71); and this in turn makes him feel inferior to her (again recalling
Stephen Smith in relation to Elfride): "I can't match you, I know," he
says to her, "in mapping out my mind upon my tongue. I never was very
clever in my inside" (72). It makes him slow—too slow for the kingfisher
and the hawk—and physically timid with her: when he takes her hand, he
holds it "but an instant" for "fear of being too demonstrative," and so only
touches her fingers "with the lightness of a small-hearted person" (72). The
small-heartedness is also projected in a dimness of being that makes him
look, when he is juxtaposed with Troy, "like a candle beside gas" (299).
And it manifests itself too in an acceptance of his subordination to her
"superiority" that implies a readiness for a reversal of traditional sexual
roles: her recognition of her superiority pleases "by suggesting possibilities
of capture to the subordinated man" (73).[5]

When Oak proposes to Bathsheba, she says she "shouldn't mind being
a bride at a wedding, if [she] could be one without having a husband"
(80), making it apparent he has not occupied the blank spot in her

---

5. In contradistinction to this view of Oak, Annette Federico talks of his "sexual
equilibrium": "He is Hardy's version of the male ideal, perfectly balanced between the
flesh and the spirit" (*Masculine Identity in Hardy and Gissing,* 71). Robert Langbaum
remarks on "Gabriel's strong sexuality throughout" and says his name suggests "phallic
strength" (*Thomas Hardy,* 80, 84).

consciousness. She tells him she wants somebody "to tame" her since she is "too independent," and she knows he is not the man for the job. So little is he capable of taming her that he is in retreat before the battle is joined, characteristically reducing his claim to her as he does on the world's room: "But I love you," he says to her, "—and, as for myself, I am content to be liked" (80). All he arouses in Bathsheba is "a yawn" and the conviction, presumably in a number of related respects, that he is not "good enough" for her (126).

Hardy complicates his presentation of Oak—and so quite transforms the male line he had started with in Stephen Smith—by making him masterful in everything other than his relations with women. As is shown time and again in the narrative, he is a natural leader of men, an expert shepherd, and resourceful, conscientious, and reliable in all that pertains to life on a large farm. As a shepherd (if not as a lover), with four lambs hanging over his shoulders, he looks "an epitome of the world's health and vigour" (156); and as a man among men, though he is "one of the quietest and most gentle men on earth," he is capable—when he thinks the rustics are not showing sufficient respect in their talk of Bathsheba—of "[rising] to the occasion with martial promptness" and a ready fist (157). Paradoxically, his tendency to make little of himself is the basis of a self-mastery that even Bathsheba eventually comes to recognize and to envy: it is his selflessness that underlies his general reliability and resourcefulness, for "among the multitude of interests" by which he is surrounded, he shows that those which affect "his personal well-being [are] not the most absorbing and important in his eyes"; and it ensures too that he is always capable of seeing things as they are, for he looks "upon the horizon of circumstances without any special regard to his own standpoint in the midst" (355).

Oak, that is, is an impressive exemplar of the type of decent, honorable, though sexually ineffective man that is to recur in the novels that follow. In posing him against Sergeant Troy as a contender for Bathsheba's affections, the novelist appears to be wryly contemplating the irony that gives Oak all the virtues that his rival so manifestly lacks—and none of the potency that he so manifestly possesses. Nevertheless, it will be the burden of the tale, as we shall see, that Oak's is the only kind of love that endures;

and so from the start his "affection," though limited in force by being
so "placid and regular," is also said to flow "deep and long" (83). When
he loves, however diffidently, it is once and for all: "You know, mistress,"
he says to Bathsheba shortly before she marries Troy, "that I love you,
and shall love you always." And he adds that she is more to him than
his "own affairs, and even life!" (248) He is sincere in what he says, of
course, but in terms of the plan of love propounded by the novelist, the
question that insistently poses itself is how, in the face of Bathsheba's
apparent indifference to him, he keeps his love alive. Love, as we have
seen, is defined as "an extremely exacting usurer" (73), and it demands its
pound of flesh. What saves Oak, it would seem, is that he is prepared to
settle for less than that, as emerges on the day of the sheepshearing: "Poor
Gabriel's soul was fed with a luxury of content by having her over him,
her eyes critically regarding his skilful shears. . . . Like Guildenstern, Oak
was happy in that he was not over happy. He had no wish to converse
with her: that his bright lady and himself formed one group, exclusively
their own, and containing no others in the world, was enough" (197–98).
Oak, moderate and restrained, is satisfied by a metaphorical possession of
the woman he loves: it is "enough" for him that they form "one group"
and so together have possession of something that is "exclusively their
own." Consequently, he does get a return on his usurious love, for his
soul is "fed with a luxury of content"; and though it is the exposure of
"the void" within him that has made him love her, he does not fall into an
unrequited emptiness, for merely to be with her, as in this scene, makes
him "full of [a] dim and temperate bliss" (198). It is a contentment that is
sustained by such contact throughout the period preceding her marriage
to him and by her growing dependence and reliance on him in all that
concerns her farm.

III

Where Gabriel may be seen as a more complex development of Stephen
Smith, Farmer Boldwood takes off, as it were, from Henry Knight. He is
a man of forty-one and, until he receives Bathsheba's valentine, has been
"a confirmed bachelor" (177), as Knight was "a bachelor by nature." But
he too is a more complex conception than his predecessor:

> The phases of Boldwood's life were ordinary enough, but his was not an ordinary nature. That stillness, which struck casual observers more than anything else in his character and habit, and seemed so precisely like the rest of inanition, may have been the perfect balance of enormous antagonistic forces—positives and negatives in fine adjustment. His equilibrium disturbed, he was in extremity at once. If an emotion possessed him at all, it ruled him; a feeling not mastering him was entirely latent. Stagnant or rapid, it was never slow. He was always hit mortally, or he was missed. (171)

The narrator is surely undecided by design here, for in offering two alternative explanations of Boldwood's outstanding feature, his stillness, he contrives to insinuate both possibilities, and, though they may appear to be contradictory, they are in fact complementary. Boldwood's stillness is an outward sign of an assumed self-sufficiency, a self-containment that makes it unnecessary for him to move toward anything. But this seems more like frozen motion than a genuine inner stillness, since what may be taken to be an enormously powerful outward drive is held in "perfect balance" with a neutralizing, "antagonistic" force of withdrawal. And this is indeed "the rest of inanition," though in a more profound sense than may strike casual observers, who presumably see it as exhaustion. But it is a hidden emptiness, the heavy immobility of the void, that the confirmed bachelor bears within in much the same way as the young shepherd. The difference between Oak and Boldwood is that the latter has not yet been made aware of it; it takes Bathsheba's valentine to do the trick. And unlike the temperate Oak, who is throughout an epitome of self-mastery, Boldwood is "mastered" by the feeling that now wells up in him. From the moment he receives the valentine he is a man "possessed."

The change in Boldwood, once he fixes on Bathsheba as a love object, is even apparent physically. When her figure "shines" on his eyes, it "[lights] him up as the moon lights up a great tower," though it is suggested that the light actually comes from within:

> A man's body is as the shell, or the tablet, of his soul, as he is reserved or ingenuous, overflowing or self-contained. There was a change in Boldwood's exterior from its former impassibleness; and his face

showed that he was now living outside his defences for the first time, and with a fearful sense of exposure. It is the usual experience of strong natures when they love. (172)

Boldwood may have a "strong nature," and so be at the opposite pole from a character such as Stephen Smith, but he nonetheless resembles him in one respect. Stephen had a tendency to "draw himself in with the sensitiveness of a snail"; Boldwood too, prior to the valentine, has lived within his "shell," not so much in sensitive withdrawal as in the natural "reserve" of a habitual sense of "self-containment." His reserve has made him physically impassive, for no feeling moves into or out of his hard, shell-like "impassibleness," keeping him closed up like a dark tower or shut book. When Bathsheba comes into his life, the new feeling "overflows," and he then writes himself in his body, "the tablet of his soul"; powerfully lit from within, he now can be read at a glance. Having sallied forth from the tower, he lives "outside his defences for the first time"; or, alternatively, having shed his shell, he has "a fearful sense of exposure." But it is not only that he is now exposed to the outside world; he is also exposed to a consciousness of the void within, and so it is imperative for him to fill it. What he feels for Bathsheba is said to be "genuine lover's love" (173) because it springs directly and urgently from his own need. The need is so strong that the first words he addresses to her are an "offer of marriage" (177).

Just as Oak (as we have seen) tells Bathsheba that he will love her "always" and that she is more to him even than life, so Boldwood, when she informs him "her final decision" is that she "[cannot] marry him" (251), declares that his feeling for her is "a thing strong as death" and that no "dismissal by a hasty letter" can affect it (257). In the end he will show his feeling is so strong that he can deal out death; but it is a paradox of his condition that this man who is mastered by his passion, obsessed and possessed by it, is sexually diffident, as he himself admits in an important exchange with Bathsheba:

> The most tragic woman is cowed by a tragic man, and although Boldwood was, in vehemence and glow, nearly her own self rendered into another sex, Bathsheba's cheek quivered. She gasped, "Leave me, sir—leave me! I am nothing to you. Let me go on!"

"Deny that he [Troy] has kissed you."

"I shall not."

"Ha—then he has!" came hoarsely from the farmer.

"He has," she said slowly, and, in spite of her fear, defiantly. "I am not ashamed to speak the truth."

"Then curse him; and curse him!" said Boldwood, breaking into a whispered fury. "Whilst I would have given worlds to touch your hand, you have let a rake come in without right or ceremony and— kiss you! Heaven's mercy—kiss you! . . ." (262)

Boldwood here takes his stand on the need for "right" and "ceremony" in a man's relations with a woman, speaking out of the knowledge that his own relations with Bathsheba have been marked by an exemplary propriety and decorum. But when this passionate man, who breaks into "a whispered fury" at the idea of Troy's having kissed her, and who ultimately will kill as well as curse him, reveals that he has not dared "to touch [her] hand," we may assume that in the case of the "confirmed bachelor," as in that of the "bachelor by nature" in *A Pair of Blue Eyes,* an underlying inhibition has been at work.

The nature of Boldwood's inhibition—unlike Knight's—is not explored, but in this respect the assertion that the farmer is nearly Bathsheba's "own self rendered into another sex" proves most suggestive. He is said to be overtly like her "in vehemence and glow," but (as remains to be seen in her case) there is perhaps a deeper resemblance in the paralyzing effect sexually of a long-sustained sense of self-sufficiency.[6]

In the face of Bathsheba's denial of him, Oak maintains himself on the crumbs offered him; Boldwood appears to revert to his earlier condition. When she marries Troy, the farmer seems to freeze. Oak looks sympathetically at "the square figure sitting erect" on his horse, his head "turned to neither side," his elbows "steady by the hips," and the brim of his hat "level

6. Marjorie Garson, however, calls "the rigid monklike celibacy" of Boldwood a "parody" of Bathsheba's "wilful self-sufficiency" (*Hardy's Fables of Integrity: Woman, Body, Text,* 25).

A number of critics have also commented (though in different terms) on the resemblance between Boldwood and Henry Knight: John Lucas states that "Boldwood is very like Henry Knight in his romantic vision of women" ("Hardy's Women," 132). And Ronald Blythe says "the farmer, like the man of letters in *A Pair of Blue Eyes,* is sexually timid and uncertain" (introduction to *Far from the Madding Crowd,* 26).

and undisturbed in its onward glide" and finds "something more striking in this immobility than in a collapse" (296). Boldwood might indeed have been expected to collapse, to fall into the void opened up within him and disintegrate, when his aroused feeling meets with no return. He contrives with iron will, however, to repress his feeling, and so, it would seem, to remain immobile on the edge of the void, precariously poised to move away from it if chance should offer or topple over into it. In the event, he enacts both possibilities. He remains locked in the "fond madness" of his "unreasoning devotion to Bathsheba," and "a great hope" germinates in him when it seems possible, a year after Troy's disappearance, that Bathsheba might remarry (392). He renews his suit, but since Troy's body has not been found, Bathsheba will not contemplate marriage until seven years have elapsed from the time of his supposed drowning. Expecting to receive her consent at the Christmas party he is giving some fifteen months after that event, Boldwood asks Oak whether there is "anything so wonderful in an engagement of little more than five years" (421). Like Stephen Smith, it appears, Boldwood is intent on ensuring possession of his beloved but is more than ready to delay it. "It seems long in a forward view," Oak answers laconically. Boldwood's mind, we are to understand, is already "crazed with care and love," as the "extraordinary collection of articles" he has purchased for Bathsheba later reveals (446); when Troy appears at the party and claims Bathsheba, nothing can prevent Boldwood's collapse. His initial "gnashing despair" changes to "a frenzied look" when she screams on Troy's "seizure" of her—and he shoots the sergeant (439).

IV

Bathsheba initially makes all the wrong choices in regard to the men in her life. First, she rejects Oak, whom she ultimately marries and with whom she is set to live happily ever after at the end of the narrative. Then, having registered Boldwood's indifference to her at the Casterbridge cornmarket, she brings him into her life by inciting him with her valentine, which she seals with the words "Marry Me" (147). And she not only sends the valentine to him on a whim but also, in a manner reminiscent of Elfride on her pony in *A Pair of Blue Eyes,* leaves it to the fall of a book as to whether she should send it to him or not. "So very idly and unreflectingly was this deed done," comments the narrator (148), but she so chooses to do. When Boldwood proposes to her, she tells him she is not in love with him and cannot marry him, but she is conscious that love is "encircling her like a perfume" (177), and she is also left with "a strong feeling that, having been the one who began the game, she ought in honesty to accept the consequences" (181–82). Boldwood persists, and she is on the verge of giving way—"I will try to love you," she says, and adds that she has "every reason to hope" that within about six weeks she will "be able to promise" to be his wife (210–11)—when she meets Troy. Then she marries Troy.

She meets Troy for the first time when she is making her nightly tour of inspection of the farm. She is going back to the house "by a path through a young plantation of tapering firs" when, at "the darkest point of her route," she hears footsteps:

> The noise approached, came close, and a figure was apparently on the point of gliding past her when something tugged at her skirt and pinned it forcibly to the ground. The instantaneous check nearly threw Bathsheba off her balance. In recovering she struck against warm clothes and buttons.
> "A rum start, upon my soul!" said a masculine voice, a foot or so above her head. "Have I hurt you, mate?"
> "No," said Bathsheba, attempting to shrink away.
> "We have got hitched together somehow, I think."
> "Yes."
> "Are you a woman?"
> "Yes."
> "A lady, I should have said."
> "It doesn't matter."
> "I am a man."
> "Oh!"
> Bathsheba softly tugged again, but to no purpose. (213–14)

This is one of the scenes in the novels that first bears the unmistakable Hardy stamp. It also strikingly exhibits his new maturity as a novelist as he makes the scene resonate with symbolic and proleptic force. From the moment Bathsheba encounters Troy, we see, she becomes entangled with him, caught up so firmly she cannot get free. In a word, she is "hooked."

When she does try to free herself, she tugs so "softly" that it is "to no purpose." The effect of the sudden contact is nearly to throw her "off her balance," but in trying to recover it she moves only closer to him, becoming conscious of his "warm clothes," of the warmth of his body, that is. It is in more than one sense "a rum start," as Troy says, and a portentous one. It is made even more so by the strange way in which Troy chooses to announce his entry into her life: "I am a man," he says; and Bathsheba, who has already been conversing with the "masculine voice" that has addressed her out of the darkness, can only gasp. It is with masculine strength of a kind she has not previously encountered that she now has to contend: when he later "looks hard" into her eyes, she at once looks down, "for his gaze [is] too strong to be received point-blank with her own" (215), and penetrating looks, we know, have their special significance in the novels. But this is a strength, it has previously been intimated, that she needs to measure herself against: at the Casterbridge cornmarket, "something" in the appearance of the "lithe slip of humanity" she is there said to be suggests her "potentiality" for "alarming exploits of sex, and daring enough to carry them out" (140). Troy, who is utterly unlike both Oak and Boldwood, is the kind of man, it rapidly becomes clear, to test that daring; he is indeed a New Man among Hardy's diffident men (though Manston of *Desperate Remedies* is a villainous forebear).

It is a mark of the novelist's imaginative control that Bathsheba's first instinctive response to bodily contact with Troy is "to shrink away" as much as she can. It is a crucial response as we shall see, and we do well to bear it in mind, for we tend to lose sight of it amid the brilliance of what follows:

> "Is that a dark lantern you have? I fancy so," said the man.
> "Yes."
> "If you'll allow me I'll open it, and set you free."
> A hand seized the lantern, the door was opened, the rays burst out from their prison, and Bathsheba beheld her position with astonishment.
> The man to whom she was hooked was brilliant in brass and scarlet. He was a soldier. His sudden appearance was to darkness what the sound of a trumpet is to silence. Gloom, the *genius loci* at

all times hitherto, was now totally overthrown, less by the lantern-light than by what the lantern lighted. The contrast of this revelation with her anticipations of some sinister figure in sombre garb was so great that it had upon her the effect of a fairy transformation.

It was immediately apparent that the military man's spur had become entangled in the gimp which decorated the skirt of her dress. . . . (214)

When Troy opens the dark lantern, we have one of the first epiphanies in the novels, the use of epiphany being one of Hardy's major techniques for implying significance as opposed to his tendency to provide regular narratorial directives in that regard.7 Troy is the focus of attention, and Bathsheba is the one who looks; what is suddenly illuminated comes to her with the force of a "revelation." In the epiphanic mode, it is Troy's inner essence that is revealed here, and we do well to bear this in mind too, especially in view of what soon becomes the narrator's increasing hostility to him. Troy's "brilliance" is directly attributable to the "brass and scarlet" of his uniform (and we remember the crimson jacket in which Bathsheba makes her first appearance). But it also streams out of him, shattering the darkness as a trumpet would the silence. It is an inner radiance that confounds the spirit of place, the darkness being "totally overthrown, less by the lantern-light than by what the lantern light[s]." It is the darkness, moreover, of a site that, even "gloomy" at "cloudless noontide," is "dark as midnight at dusk, and black as the ninth plague of Egypt at midnight" (213). What emanates from him is a sexual vividness and brightness, as is underscored when the phallic spur finally becomes apparent. To be open to such brightness, it is implied, is liberating: when Troy takes in what has happened, he says to her, "You are a prisoner, miss" (215); the rays of the lantern that reveal this to be the case are said (in an image that otherwise would be incongruous) to "burst out from their prison" when the lamp is opened.8

7. See the Introduction for a discussion of the connection between Hardy and James Joyce in this respect, 8–9 above.

8. There is a lot more to this scene, as I have tried to bring out, than that phallic spur, which is often made a limiting focus of attention. Cf. Richard C. Carpenter, who says "there is patent phallic symbolism . . . in this scene in the cruel potency of the spur and

After this encounter Troy pursues Bathsheba, wooing her with a combination of genuine admiration and designing flattery until one day her
response signifies that she has capitulated, that "the seed" that will "lift
the foundation" has "taken root in the chink," at which point "the careless
sergeant [smiles] within himself, and probably too the devil [smiles] from
a loop-hole in Tophet," for this is "the turning-point of a career" (226).

A more tangible turning point in the relationship is the occasion of
the sword exercise (239–41), which John Bayley calls "one of the greatest
scenes in English fiction." It is also, one may add, an early instance of
Hardy's use of symbolic action to convey sexual significance, a technique
that enabled him to bypass Victorian restrictions in this respect.9 Troy uses
the demonstration, in the first place, to test Bathsheba, and her ability
to stand up to his onslaught bears sharply on his later disillusionment
with her. He starts with "a preliminary test" to learn whether she has
"pluck enough" to let him do what he wants, and he insists that he cannot
"perform" if she is afraid. He lies to her about the sword, denying that it is
"very sharp" when in fact it "will shave like a razor," but she is nevertheless
unflinching when "his cuts" come so close that "had it been possible for
the edge of the sword to leave in the air a permanent substance wherever
it flew past, the space left untouched would have been almost a mould
of Bathsheba's figure." But the performance is also designed, of course, to
demonstrate his skill: "Never since the broadsword became the national
weapon had there been more dexterity shown in its management than
by the hands of Sergeant Troy." He crowns the performance by using the
razor-sharp sword to cut a lock of her hair—"Bravely borne!" he says to
her. "You didn't flinch a shade's thickness. Wonderful in a woman!"—and

---

the soft, enveloping tissues of the gown" ("The Mirror and the Sword: Imagery in *Far
from the Madding Crowd,*" 342). Rosemarie Morgan, in her "revisionary" (that is, feminist)
analysis of the scene, gives even more weight to the momentous spur, "[T]he soft, feminine
folds of the woman's dress pierced through by the man's projecting blade [*sic*] suggests
(and prefigures) not only the act of love-making, but as a material representation of inner,
intangible desires, the erotic seizure now taking hold of the two young lovers" (*Women
and Sexuality,* 33).

9. John Bayley, *An Essay on Hardy,* 121. Another striking instance of Hardy's provision
of a sexual subtext by means of symbolic action is his description of Tess's ride with Alec
in his gig in *Tess of the d'Urbervilles:* see Chapter 7, 156–58 below.

then to spit "upon its point" a caterpillar that has settled on her bosom. When he finally tells her how sharp the sword is, she shudders: "I have been within an inch of my life," she says, "and didn't know it"; but he assures her she has been "perfectly safe": "My sword never errs." In this scene, in which the sexual overtones gather fast and thick, Troy has indeed shown a mastery of his weapon. He also shows he is the kind of man who will not hesitate to put a woman at risk.

For Bathsheba the exercise reenacts and intensifies the visionary experience of her first encounter with Troy. As his "reflecting blade" flashes, catching "beams of light" from the sun, the atmosphere is "transformed to [her] eyes," and she is "enclosed in a firmament of light, and of sharp hisses, resembling a sky-full of meteors close at hand." Troy, that is, is once again all brilliance and sparkle, a fiery, vital force, manifesting himself in strong contrast to the dullness of Oak's restraint and the gloom of Boldwood's obsession. The woman who told Oak she wanted someone to tame her is mastered here, feeling "powerless to withstand or deny" Troy:

> He was altogether too much for her, and Bathsheba seemed as one who, facing a reviving wind, finds it blow so strongly that it stops the breath.
>
> He drew near and said, "I must be leaving you." He drew nearer still. A minute later and she saw his scarlet form disappear amid the ferny thicket, almost in a flash, like a brand swiftly waved.
>
> That minute's interval had brought the blood beating into her face, set her stinging as if aflame to the very hollows of her feet, and enlarged emotion to a compass which quite swamped thought. It had brought upon her a stroke resulting, as did that of Moses in Horeb, in a liquid stream—here a stream of tears. She felt like one who has sinned a great sin.
>
> The circumstance had been the gentle dip of Troy's mouth downwards upon her own. He had kissed her. (241–42)

One has to give full and careful weight to this scene in order to be able later to engage with the narrator's ambivalences. If Bathsheba is overwhelmed by Troy here so that afterward she loves him, loving "in the way that only self-reliant women love when they abandon their self-reliance" (243), her capitulation is presented in positive terms. Troy may for her have become his sword as he disappears "almost in a flash, like a brand swiftly waved," and so the encounter with him may "stop the breath" in its perilousness, but it is also vitalizing, "a reviving wind," waking her to sexual life. And when he kisses her and fires her into passion, making her blood beat and setting her aflame, it is by way of an expansion of being that "enlarges" emotion even if it "swamps" thought. If we may be inclined to regard this as an equivocal gain, the man who works the enlargement and produces the emotion that issues in her tears is seen, like "Moses in Horeb," to possess miraculous powers. Prudent thought would anyway be of no avail.[10]

Subsequently, however, Bathsheba's "culpability" is said to lie in her "making no attempt to control feeling by subtle and careful inquiry into consequences" (244). The view of her relationship with Troy that the narrator now appears to endorse is that she is foolishly infatuated with him and so is led to marry the thoroughly irresponsible and dissolute man that he reveals himself to be, a man who eventually deserts her as he has earlier abandoned Fanny Robin. Justice may be done to Troy's sexual glamour and vitality, but he is otherwise consistently condemned.

He is condemned, first, out of his own mouth: "He had been known to observe casually that in dealing with womankind the only alternative to flattery was cursing and swearing. There was no third method. 'Treat them fairly, and you are a lost man,' he would say" (221). He is condemned too by his own actions, as on the night of the great storm when, instead of taking steps to protect the ricks on Bathsheba's farm (which has now become his responsibility), he leads the farmworkers in a "debauch" that makes for a "painful and demoralizing termination to the evening's entertainment" he has arranged (303). And he is condemned furthermore by the hostile

10. This is to view the scene in radically different terms from a critic such as Susan Beegel, who (with reference to the sword exercise) refers to "Troy's brand of death-dealing passion" and says that "Bathsheba's love for Troy is a love which embraces helplessness; his feeling for her one which exults in the powerlessness of its victims" ("Bathsheba's Lovers: Male Sexuality in *Far from the Madding Crowd,*" 210, 212).

Robert M. Polhemus refreshingly says that "it simply will not do to moralize smoothly on this chapter . . . and deplore Bathsheba's reaction to Troy as 'self-destructive' [the reference is to Beegel], misguided, or tragic. To do so misses the point, slighting and cheapening the soul-shaking power of the erotic." But Polhemus himself diminishes this power by going on to call Troy "the seducer, the huckster of desire and instant gratification" (*Erotic Faith: Being in Love from Jane Austen to D. H. Lawrence,* 240, 246).

commentary of the narrator, who seems bent on maintaining a negative consistency of characterization. A few examples of this must suffice. He is said to be "moderately truthful towards men" but to lie "like a Cretan" to women; since his "vicious phases" are "the offspring of impulse" and "his virtuous phases of cool meditation," the latter have "a modest tendency to be oftener heard of than seen" (220). We are told that his "deformities" lie "deep down from a woman's vision," while his "embellishments" are "upon the very surface" (244). When he plants the flowers on Fanny's grave with what I take to be genuine emotion—I shall discuss his attitude toward Fanny later—the narrator remarks that "in his prostration at this time" he has "no perception that in the futility of these romantic doings, dictated by a remorseful reaction from previous indifference, there [is] any element of absurdity" (372–73). And what Troy has "in the way of emotion" is described as "an occasional fitful sentiment which sometimes [causes] him as much inconvenience as emotion of a strong and healthy kind" (400).

Troy, clearly, is not an admirable character, but the failure of his marriage to Bathsheba is not solely to be attributed to him. Although he is again viewed critically when he and Bathsheba are seen alone for the first time after the marriage, it is also suggested that something more is at issue between the couple than emerges (rather like the scene in Henry James's *The Portrait of a Lady*—published a few years later—in which we first see Mr. and Mrs. Osmond after their marriage and register the change in their relationship):

> "And you mean, Frank," said Bathsheba sadly—her voice was painfully lowered from the fulness and vivacity of the previous summer—"that you have lost more than a hundred pounds in a month by this dreadful horse-racing? O, Frank, it is cruel; it is foolish of you to take away my money so. We shall have to leave the farm; that will be the end of it!"
>
> "Humbug about cruel. Now, there 'tis again—turn on the water-works; that's just like you."
>
> "But you'll promise me not to go to Budmouth second meeting, won't you?" she implored. Bathsheba was at the full depth for tears, but she maintained a dry eye.
>
> "I don't see why I should; in fact, if it turns out to be a fine day, I was thinking of taking you." . . .

"But you don't mean to say that you have risked anything on [the race next Monday] too!" she exclaimed, with an agonized look.

"There now, don't you be a little fool. Wait till you are told. Why, Bathsheba, you have lost all the pluck and sauciness you formerly had, and upon my life if I had known what a chicken-hearted creature you were under all your boldness, I'd never have—I know what." (318–19)

The injured tones of the couple as they engage in mutual recrimination indicate how soon the marriage has lost its gleam, the point being made additionally and emblematically by some "early-withered leaves" that spin across the path of their gig (319). But if Bathsheba is justifiably angered by his prodigal behavior, it is not clear why she—as distinct from her money—should be so diminished, for her voice is "painfully lowered" from its habitual "fulness and vivacity." We recall too that on her first appearance after the marriage she has spoken "listlessly" and "seemed weary" (282). And if Troy, in turn, is led to assert his mastery in the marriage, there is nothing in the scene itself to account for the kind of disenchantment he expresses, neither her nagging nor her chickenheartedness—he, if anyone, should have the full measure of her "boldness"—being presented as so obnoxious as to warrant his implied regret that he has married her.

Shortly thereafter, when Troy is reduced to asking Bathsheba for money (which he wants to give Fanny), we are told that he deems it "necessary to be civil," though he does "not now love her enough to allow himself to be carried too far by her ways" (330). It seems that the decline of his love for Bathsheba may be linked to his chance encounter with Fanny, with whom he has lost touch but not deliberately abandoned, and this impression is strengthened when Bathsheba discovers he keeps another woman's "coil of hair" in the case at the back of his watch (331). The discovery greatly upsets Bathsheba and forces her to review her situation. The account we are then given of her attitude to marriage suggests the cause of Troy's disenchantment with her, though the narrator carefully stops short of stating this himself:

Directly he had gone, Bathsheba burst into great sobs—dry-eyed sobs, which cut as they came, without any softening by tears. But she determined to repress all evidences of feeling. She was conquered; but she would never own it as long as she lived. Her pride was indeed brought low by despairing discoveries of her spoliation by marriage with a less pure nature than her own. She chafed to and fro in rebelliousness, like a caged leopard; her whole soul was in arms, and the blood fired her face. Until she had met Troy, Bathsheba had been proud of her position as a woman; it had been a glory to her to know that her lips had been touched by no man's on earth— that her waist had never been encircled by a lover's arm. She hated herself now. In those earlier days she had always nourished a secret contempt for girls who were slaves of the first good-looking young fellow who should choose to salute them. She had never taken kindly to the idea of marriage in the abstract as did the majority of women she saw about her. In the turmoil of her anxiety for her lover she had agreed to marry him; but the perception that had accompanied her happiest hours on this account was rather that of self-sacrifice than of promotion and honour. Although she scarcely knew the divinity's name, Diana was the goddess whom Bathsheba instinctively adored. That she had never, by look, word, or sign, encouraged a man to approach her—that she had felt herself sufficient to herself, and had in the independence of her girlish heart fancied there was a certain degradation in renouncing the simplicity of a maiden existence to become the humbler half of an indifferent matrimonial whole— were facts now bitterly remembered. (333–34)

The narrator states that the sense of "spoliation" Bathsheba so bitterly registers here is due to her "marriage with a less pure nature than her own," but the rest of the passage suggests it stems from the brute fact of marriage itself. It is not merely that she has "never taken kindly to the idea of marriage." If it was a positive "glory" to her, prior to her own marriage, to know she had remained sexually untouched by any man, this feeling would seem to extend beyond a girlish pride in virginity since she is said to "hate herself now"—to be disgusted, apparently, by sexual experience per se. Such experience, the image of the caged leopard implies, has not been liberating, has failed to realize the hope symbolized in the scene with the dark lantern. Certainly the feeling of self-hatred is evoked in direct response to the recall of those untouched lips and waist. This suggests that her resentment at being "conquered" may also be related to the fact of her sexual submission and that it is not merely disillusionment in Troy that has brought "her pride" low. Similarly, her renunciation of "the simplicity of a maiden existence" for life as "the humbler half of an indifferent matrimonial whole" is felt as a "degradation," and the strength of the revulsion suggests a more profound kind of humbling. Indeed, she was only led into marriage in the first place "in the turmoil of anxiety for her lover," by her jealousy and fear of losing him, that is, as she has previously admitted to Oak: "I went to Bath that night," she tells him, "in the full intention of breaking off my engagement to Troy," but when she learns he has been eyeing a beautiful woman, she is caught "between jealousy and distraction" and marries him (311).

The specific fear of losing Troy would seem to have allayed Bathsheba's more general fear of sexual contact and impelled her to go against her own nature, for it is Diana she "instinctively adore[s]": Bathsheba, that is, is temperamentally a virgin, "sufficient to herself." It is in this more profound sense that Boldwood, as we have seen, may be said to be "nearly her own self rendered into another sex": Boldwood the bachelor, apparently confirmed in his self-sufficiency, and Boldwood the lover, who even when roused out of himself does not dare to touch her hand. Paradoxically, a sufficiency of self, a firm sense of self-establishment, is a precondition for a successful sexual relationship, provided it does not function, as in these instances, to inhibit sexual response. Marriage, even in its "happiest hours," is a "self-sacrifice" to Bathsheba, for her martyrdom to sex entails the violation of her vaunted self-sufficiency. Bathsheba and Boldwood may thus be regarded as victims of what might be called a Diana complex. In this respect Hardy is astonishing in his handling of gender, moving far beyond an essentialist position to a profound understanding of what may be common to both man and woman. And Bathsheba and Boldwood are merely the first of major Hardy characters who are caught in sexual incapacity. Hardy will again explore the working of the complex in his portrayal of Michael Henchard in *The Mayor of Casterbridge,* of Grace Melbury in *The Woodlanders,* and of Sue Bridehead in *Jude the Obscure.* It is interesting that, some two years after the publication of *Far from the Madding Crowd,* there should be an indication of a similar condition in the work of a woman novelist. In Chapter 7 of *Daniel Deronda,* it is said of Gwendolen Harleth that "she objected, with a sort of physical repulsion, to being directly made love to. With all her imaginative delight in being adored, there was a certain fierceness of maidenhood in her." Gwendolen is unmarried at this point, but we may infer that she—like Bathsheba—carries such fierceness with her into marriage.[11]

In the quoted passage from *Far from the Madding Crowd*, however, the narrator both implies that Bathsheba is temperamentally unsuited to marriage and contrives to camouflage this by suggesting at the same time that it is her marriage *to Troy* that is the trouble. What he leaves quite unsaid—though this is of the essence—is what the effect of her attitude is on Troy. Troy is no doubt a wastrel and a philanderer and so the wrong man for Bathsheba, but in the failed marriage there is more to his side of things than the novelist appears willing to admit. Troy's accusation of chickenheartedness on Bathsheba's part now takes on another meaning. In the sword exercise, we recall, Troy said he could only "perform" if she were not afraid; if she did not flinch then, we may suspect she has been inclined to "shrink away" from him now, much as she instinctively did on the occasion of their first encounter in the dark. It is not her nagging about money that is the main cause of his rapid disenchantment with her; it seems reasonable to assume, rather, that she has proved incapable of really opening herself to him. D. H. Lawrence (as I have analyzed in detail in *The Forked Flame*) may instruct us as to what, in all likelihood, lies behind such incapacity (this applying as well to Grace and Sue, to Boldwood and Henchard): in his depiction of a similar inhibition in Constance Chatterley, he shows it is a fear of losing the self that is at issue. Bathsheba, at all events, with her sense of violation, is a prisoner not of Troy, as in the scene with the spur, but of self.[12]

11. I am indebted to my colleague, Joshua Adler, for drawing my attention to this passage in George Eliot's *Daniel Deronda*.

12. See *The Forked Flame: A Study of D. H. Lawrence*, 293–99.

Peter J. Casagrande views the problem as one of lost innocence:

Bathsheba is filled with repugnance toward physical contact and near-hysteria at the thought of having lost her innocence. Sexual union with Troy has left her with a sense of "spoliation," "degradation," and pollution, the unalterability of which she would never "own . . . as long as she lived." Therefore she hates herself, regards herself a bloody victim, a fallen woman. . . . Her instinctive affinity for Diana . . . reinforces this. Her idea of

If this reading is valid, then it is Bathsheba's sexual irresponsiveness that makes Troy feel they are not truly married. Support for this view is provided by one of the most striking scenes in the novel (and in Hardy)—the confrontation of Troy and Bathsheba over the open coffin that contains the bodies of Fanny and her child, whom he has fathered:

> He had originally stood perfectly erect. And now, in the well-nigh congealed immobility of his frame could be discerned an incipient movement, as in the darkest night may be discerned light after a while. He was gradually sinking forwards. The lines of his features softened, and dismay modulated to illimitable sadness. Bathsheba was regarding him from the other side, still with parted lips and distracted eyes. Capacity for intense feeling is proportionate to the general intensity of the nature, and perhaps in all Fanny's sufferings, much greater relatively to her strength, there never was a time when she suffered in an absolute sense what Bathsheba suffered now.
>
> What Troy did was to sink upon his knees with an indefinable union of remorse and reverence upon his face, and, bending over Fanny Robin, gently kissed her, as one would kiss an infant asleep to avoid awakening it.
>
> At the sight and sound of that, to her, unendurable act, Bathsheba sprang towards him. All the strong feelings which had been scattered over her existence since she knew what feeling was, seemed gathered together into one pulsation now. The revulsion from her indignant mood a little earlier, when she had meditated upon compromised honour, forestalment, eclipse in maternity by another, was violent and entire. All that was forgotten in the simple and still strong attachment of wife to husband. She had sighed for her self-completeness then, and now she cried aloud against the severance of the union she had deplored. She flung her arms round Troy's neck, exclaiming wildly from the deepest deep of her heart—
>
> "Don't—don't kiss them! O, Frank, I can't bear it—I can't! I love you better than she did: kiss me too, Frank—kiss me! *You will, Frank, kiss me too!*" . . .
>
> "I will not kiss you!" he said, pushing her away. (359–60)

---

growing up is, in short, a nervous panicky one requiring fulfillment of the impossible dream of regaining the lost "simplicity of a maiden existence." ("A New View of Bathsheba Everdene," 64)

Hardy's characterization here is superb. Troy acts with complete sincerity and spontaneity, and so is unassailable. The commentary, otherwise so hostile, grants him this: as he begins to melt into motion, the unfreezing of his "congealed immobility" is given an affirmative connotation by the parallel established between it and the discerning of "light" in "the darkest night," just as the softening of his features bespeaks the tenderness with which he approaches the dead Fanny.[13] (His feeling now, we may remark in passing, is not different in kind from that which he later exhibits at Fanny's grave, though the narrator is not as charitable to him then.) But the suffering that Troy inflicts on Bathsheba is also sharply rendered. His gentle kissing of Fanny is an "unendurable act" for Bathsheba not alone for the quality of the feeling it reveals toward the dead woman but also in its utter negation of her, his wife, as if he were unaware of her very presence there. The fear of losing him that has led her into the marriage now operates to make her try to save it, though paradoxically it has all along been a threat to "her self-completeness," and this propels her into her grotesque competition with Fanny. But Troy is remorseless. Putting an effective end to their marriage, he proceeds to spell out what has undermined it: "This woman," he says to Bathsheba, "is more to me, dead as she is, than ever you were, or are, or can be," and he then calls Fanny his "very, very wife." He also adds, "heartlessly": "You are nothing to me—nothing. A ceremony before a priest doesn't make a marriage. I am not morally yours" (361). If Troy here brutally insists on Bathsheba's lack of responsiveness to him sexually, we cannot but reflect that the professed depth of his commitment to Fanny and of his love for her must be supposed in turn to have affected his own sexual response to Bathsheba,

13. George Wing is one of the few critics to accept that Troy is sincere here: "There [is] a curious warmth in the shallowness of the dandy's heart, and an unexpected fidelity in his fickleness. As he stands before Fanny's rough coffin . . . he is unequivocal and, I think, sincere" (*Thomas Hardy,* 50).

Cf. Ian Ousby, who takes the more usual view: "With the discovery of Fanny Robin's death and the belated awakening of his guilt, Troy turns on Bathsheba in a misogynistic fury that is anything but feigned. [His] arguments . . . are now advanced over Fanny's coffin with an intensity that loses nothing for being rooted in hypocrisy and self-deception" ("Love-Hate Relations: Bathsheba, Hardy and the Men in *Far from the Madding Crowd,*" 38).

even though he may have believed Fanny to be "miles away, or dead" (320) throughout the marriage.[14]

Troy acts on his sense of Fanny as his "very wife" in the tombstone he puts up for her and in its inscription ("Erected by Francis Troy / In Beloved Memory of / Fanny Robin . . ."); and in due course Bathsheba seems to accept the fact too: her inscription on the same tombstone reads—"In the same Grave lie / The Remains of the aforesaid / Francis Troy . . ." (451).

V

When Troy disappears, Bathsheba, "perceiving clearly that her mistake had been a fatal one," accepts her position and waits "coldly for the end" (386). Eventually, however, Boldwood renews his suit, and she is on the verge of agreeing to marry him within about six years when Troy stages his return at the Christmas party. She is initially prostrated by the killing, but she "[revives] with the spring" (450), and a year after her "legal widowhood" (454) she and Oak decide to marry. Their coming together is celebrated in a passage that is pivotal in Hardy's future development as a novelist:

> They spoke very little of their mutual feelings; pretty phrases and warm expressions being probably unnecessary between such tried friends. Theirs was that substantial affection which arises (if any arises at all) when the two who are thrown together begin first by knowing the rougher sides of each other's character, and not the best till further on, the romance growing up in the interstices of a mass of hard prosaic reality. This good fellowship—*camaraderie*—usually occurring through similarity of pursuits, is unfortunately seldom superadded to love between the sexes, because men and women associate, not in their labours, but in their pleasures merely. Where, however, happy circumstance permits its development, the compounded feeling proves itself to be the only love which is strong as death—that love which many waters cannot quench, nor the floods drown, beside which the passion usually called by the name is evanescent as steam. (458–59)

14. I am indebted to a graduate student, Dorit Ashur, for this view of the presumed consequence of Troy's love for Fanny.

Linda M. Shires maintains that, "though the point is not made directly by Troy, Fanny is the truer wife because she has produced his child, because she is a mother, while Bathsheba is not" ("Narrative, Gender, and Power in *Far from the Madding Crowd*," 172).

The love that Bathsheba and Oak achieve, we are told, is "the only love" worth having, being the only kind of love that is "strong as death" and so will endure. Its various attributes are clearly distinguished. First, it is a love that is akin to friendship, being fundamentally a matter of "good fellowship" or *"camaraderie."* Sometime previously Bathsheba has begun "to entertain" for Oak "the genuine friendship of a sister" (334); by the time this feeling ripens into love, they are "tried friends" and share the mutuality of a friendship that can take their feeling for each other for granted. Second, their love is founded on "substantial affection," a phrase that is carefully chosen. It is based on affection, not "passion," that is, and hence is substantial, for (in Solomonic cadence) it can neither be extinguished nor dissipated, whereas passion is "evanescent as steam." Third, it is a love that is solidly rooted in "hard prosaic reality," flowering out of it; it is thus rooted too in a mutual fullness of knowledge that broadly encompasses "each other's character." Fourth, it is a love that is marked by the compatibility of the lovers, a general affinity of interest that embraces a "similarity of pursuits" and an association not only in their "pleasures" but in their "labours" too. It is, therefore, a multifaceted love, and it is the fact that it is a "compounded feeling" that gives it its strength.

The sentiments expressed in the quoted passage at first seem unexceptionable in view of the tale that has preceded it. Passion indeed seems to have vanished like steam, for there is nothing left of the passion of Troy and Fanny, of Troy and Bathsheba, and of Boldwood for Bathsheba. Where the compounded feeling of camaraderie will foster true love, passion has destroyed the lovers, only Bathsheba of those named above surviving to carry on with ordinary life. It is another matter, however, when this passage is viewed in relation to the novels that follow it. The pronouncement of the seer is so emphatic that it would seem to foreclose any future exploration on his part of the nature of passion, the more especially since its destructiveness was shown to be sordid rather than tragic. And who would want to try to take hold of steam? Yet Hardy proceeded hereafter to devote all his major work (with the exception of *The Mayor of Casterbridge*) to this subject. An explanation of the seeming contradiction perhaps lies in the fact that his see-er had seen and shown aspects of passion that his seer ignores in his final sweeping generalization. He had shown, for instance, that the passion of Bathsheba and Troy (the main focus of interest in the novel) was not destructive per se, that it was, if anything, her lack of passion that was the trouble. This problem of the reluctant or unresponsive woman certainly preoccupied Hardy and led him to persevere in tackling it in varied passionate contexts.[15] Furthermore, the see-er had seen and vividly conveyed that passion could be not only destructive but vitalizing; and if the seer invoked Solomon at its demise, the see-er had called on Moses with no less force at its birth. More needed to be said before the seer could be left to hold such sway. And though Bathsheba is set in the end to flourish in her marriage of camaraderie, we cannot but feel that the see-er has insinuated she will be missing something.[16] It is a fact, at any rate, that the ideal camaraderie does not seem to interest the novelist very much, for analogous relationships founded on it tend to be tacked on to the end of the novels that follow—that is, until he essays a full-scale treatment of it in *Jude the Obscure,* with the sort of consequences that remain to be determined.

15. It is perhaps not irrelevant to note that Hardy's biographer has stated that his wife, Emma, failed "to respond physically" to him (Millgate, *Thomas Hardy,* 166).

16. Only Lionel Adey, so far as I know, points to what Bathsheba stands to lose in the marriage to Oak: "Certainly Bathsheba does right to choose companionate love wherein is no ecstasy, but she also jettisons a part of herself that, had Troy proved a fitting husband [and she a fitting wife, we might add] would have given her life an *élan* it will never know again" ("Styles of Love in *Far from the Madding Crowd,*" 60–61).

4

The Return of the Native
Erratic Histories

I

The descriptions of Egdon Heath in *The Return of the Native* have long impressed both critics and common readers alike. Richard C. Carpenter has rightly called Egdon "one of the great *places* of fiction—like Twain's Mississippi or Conrad's Golfo Placido or Dickens' London."[1] Critics differ, however, in their views of its significance. D. H. Lawrence, in a memorable formulation, holds it is "the primitive, primal earth, where the instinctive life heaves up." John Paterson says it "suggests Tartarus, the gloomy foster-home of rebel-gods . . . the grim underworld of the Greek and Christian imaginations." And Lascelles Abercrombie maintains it typifies "the ceaseless drifting power of material fate," which is "neither malignant nor benevolent, but simply indifferent, unconscious of its freightage of . . . humanity. . . ."[2] Textual support may certainly be adduced for each of these views, these being among the most suggestive of the many accounts of Egdon, but it seems to me they do not sufficiently place it *in* the narrative and that its function is both simpler and more direct.

The most immediately striking feature of the heath is its darkness. Darkness is said to be "the great and particular glory of the Egdon waste," which is "a near relation of night," and only in darkness does "it tell its true

1. Carpenter, *Thomas Hardy,* 91.
2. D. H. Lawrence, "Study of Thomas Hardy," 25; John Paterson, "The 'Poetics' of *The Return of the Native,*" 216; Abercrombie, *Thomas Hardy,* 119.

tale."[3] At twilight the heath is seen to "[exhale] darkness as rapidly as the heavens [precipitate] it," and the two close together—in a vivid phrase—"in a black fraternization" (54). Even when the moon waxes "bright and silvery," the heath is "proof against such illumination" (325). What the darkness points to is the presiding gloom of this tale, which perhaps more than most of Hardy's work directly images the gloom of his universe. And what it projects is the depression of the protagonists who live out their lives on the heath. Hardy himself, as we have seen, would seem to have been subject to periodic bouts of depression,[4] but in no other of his novels are major characters so persistently prone to depression as Eustacia Vye and Clym Yeobright.

Eustacia is said to have an "abiding sense of the murkiness of human life" (179). To Wildeve she declares that "no words can express how gloomy I have been because of that dreadful belief I held . . . that you had quite deserted me," though she archly adds that it is "in [her] nature" to feel "gloomy" (115). To Clym she explains that she took part in the mummers' play "to get excitement and shake off depression," and her answer, when he asks what depressed her, is short and to the point: "Life," she says (202). She hopes that Clym may have the power "to deliver her soul from a most deadly oppression" (187). On the evening of the gipsying, an evening that in effect decides her fate, we are told (in the title of this chapter) that "She Goes Out to Battle against Depression" (317), and on the night of her death her soul sinks into "an abyss of desolation seldom plumbed by one so young" (424). It should not be found puzzling, therefore, that Eustacia, who detests the heath, is pictured in the opening scene as if she were "an organic part" of it (63): what they share is a prevailing aura of darkness.

Clym is temperamentally less gloomy than Eustacia, but his view of the world outside him is so grim that he is—at least in this respect—a match for her. "As for his look," the narrator says, "it was a natural cheerfulness striving against depression from without, and not quite succeeding" (195). He also tells us that Clym "had reached the stage in a young man's life when

3. Hardy, *The Return of the Native*, 53. Further page references to this novel will be incorporated parenthetically in the text.
4. See Chapter 1, 17 above.

the grimness of the general human situation first becomes clear" (247), and Clym himself tells his mother that "any man deserving the name" can see that "half the world [is] going to ruin for want of somebody to buckle to and teach [men] how to breast the misery they are born to" (233). Temperamentally, indeed, as these statements suggest, Clym is perhaps not unlike his creator; and it is worth noting that in rereading his work for the Wessex edition of the novels, Hardy said: "I got to like the character of Clym before I had done with him. I think he is the nicest of all my heroes," and, he added disingenuously, *"not a bit* like me."[5] When Clym turns from the general human condition to his personal situation, the view is not dissimilar. He tells Fairway that he found life in Paris "very depressing" but says it was "not so depressing as something I next perceived—that my business was the idlest, vainest, most effeminate business that ever a man could be put to" (229). He leaves Paris to return to the more congenial gloom of the heath. He is so "permeated with its scenes"—and with its emanations—that "he might be said to be its product" (231).

The darkness of the heath is countered, in the opening section of the novel, by the bonfires that spring up all over it. It is November 5, and these are Guy Fawkes bonfires, but the narrator insists that the lighting of the fires has a further significance: "It indicates a spontaneous, Promethean rebelliousness against the fiat that this recurrent season shall bring foul times, cold darkness, misery and death. Black chaos comes and the fettered gods of the earth say, Let there be light" (67). It is the explicit Promethean motif here that underlies John Paterson's view of the heath (which was quoted above) as "Tartarus, the gloomy foster-home of rebel-gods." And Hardy certainly works hard to give his tale a Promethean dimension. Egdon is said to be Eustacia's "Hades," to which she is "eternally unreconciled"; and her appearance "[accords] well with this smouldering rebelliousness," for "a true Tartarean dignity [sits] upon her brow" (119–20). As for Clym, "the deity that lies ignominiously chained within an ephemeral human carcase [shines] out of him like a ray"

5. Hardy, letter to Florence Dugdale, conjectured date April 22, 1912, in *Collected Letters*, 4:212.

(195); and he is capable of saying to Eustacia, "Now, don't you suppose, my inexperienced girl, that I cannot rebel, in high Promethean fashion, against the gods and fate as well as you" (315). The unreal, forced quality of this announcement is indicative of the way the Promethean theme is imposed on the narrative, for the bonfires have a more down-to-earth significance.

One of the bonfires, the one that lasts the longest on the heath, is the fire that Eustacia is using as a lover's signal to Wildeve. Fire, that is to say, is more effectively connected in the narrative with passion than Prometheanism. Eustacia's tale of love is framed by her bonfires at both its beginning and its end. Her fires are set not against the darkness of the coming winter but the depression that threatens to engulf her. She has her being in fire, and so it is natural to her to turn to passion as an antidote to dejection: "O deliver my heart from this fearful gloom and loneliness," she prays; "send me great love from somewhere, else I shall die" (122). She is equipped, as it were, for such love, since the narrator says, "you could fancy the colour of [her] soul to be flame-like" (119), and Clym remarks on her "inflammable nature" (308). In this respect she is a fit mate for Wildeve, who confesses to her that "the curse of inflammability" is upon him (114) and in whom "the revived embers of an old passion [glow] clearly" when he answers her bonfire signal (116).

As fires burn all over the heath on the opening Guy Fawkes night, the focus is first on the bonfire lit on Rainbarrow; but it soon begins to fail: "The bonfire was by this time beginning to sink low, for the fuel had not been of that substantial sort which can support a blaze long" (78); and in the end "the site of the fire [is] . . . merely a circle of ashes flecked with red embers and sparks, the furze having burnt completely away" (80). The burned-out fire provides a perfect image for Hardy's sense of the self-consuming nature of passion, and the reference to the fuel's not being sufficiently "substantial" to last long points to a continuity of view as between *Far from the Madding Crowd* and this novel. The earlier work ends, as we have seen, in the marriage of Bathsheba and Oak, a marriage that is said to be firmly based on the "substantial affection" between them. Their marriage will last, it is intimated, because it depends on affection, not passion, which (in a change of image, though the end result is the same) is declared to be as "evanescent as steam." Eustacia is committed to a diametrically opposed ethos: "A blaze of love, and extinction," she feels, is "better than a lantern glimmer of the same which should last long years" (122). The inflammable Wildeve is of the same party, and *his* lover's signal supplies an image of the end of passion that is an alternative to that of Eustacia's bonfire. His signal consists in releasing a moth through a chink in the window of Eustacia's lighted room: "The moth made towards the candle upon Eustacia's table, hovered round it two or three times, and flew into the flame" (330). Eustacia later refers to the "skeleton" of the moth that is "getting burnt up in the wick of the candle" (335).

Burned-out fire and burned-up moth: the see-er and the seer would seem smoothly to coalesce in these images, for the visual effect strongly but simply supports a view of passion as either naturally self-consuming or blindly self-destructive. It is a view that the novelist time and again commits himself to. The problem—to keep for the moment to this instance alone—is that a close reading of the actual narrative does not allow us to take so bald a view of the fate of the protagonists. After their tale is done and Eustacia and Wildeve are dead and Clym bereft, the narrator, referring to the dead pair, says: "Misfortune had struck them gracefully, cutting off their erratic histories with a catastrophic dash, instead of . . . attenuating each life to an uninteresting meagreness . . ." (447). The trouble with *The Return of the Native,* given the emphasis of its dominant imagery, is that the histories provided by the narrator are erratic in another sense too.

II

The Return of the Native follows *Far from the Madding Crowd* in having a failed marriage at its center. But where it is primarily the woman, in the earlier novel, who fails the man sexually, in this it would seem to be the man who fails the woman. I say this only seems to be the case because, while the see-er does not actually deconstruct the view of the seer, he so qualifies and modifies it as considerably to blur the crucial issue of the couple's sexual relationship. This may make for an obscure narrative, but it certainly results in an interesting complexity.

It is perhaps apposite though inadvert, therefore, that the relationship of Clym and Eustacia should center in the figure of blurred vision. The figure is concretized in the actual near blindness of Clym, who strains his eyes reading, and it is the consequence of this disability that is the overt cause of tension in the marriage. The figure is reinforced by the metaphorical blindness on both sides that marks the coming together of this mutual pair.

Clym and Eustacia each see the other through the lens of immediate personal need. When he returns to the heath full of plans to establish a school there, he is in need of a wife to help him and is at once ready to believe that she fits the bill. He holds to this belief in the face of all the counterindications that are bountifully provided for him. After the mumming but before he has met her in propria persona, he at once takes up Sam's suggestion that he should see the "handsome girl" by asking whether he thinks she "would like to teach children," and he is in no way deterred by the response he gets: "Quite a different sort of body from that, I reckon" (237). But then he is not discouraged even when Eustacia herself directly disabuses him. Clym asks her whether she would like to help him "clean away [the] cobwebs [of Egdon] . . . by high class teaching" and elicits the reply: "I don't quite feel anxious to. I have not much love for my fellow-creatures. Sometimes I quite hate them" (244). Far from being discouraged, he walks home feeling that "his scheme [has] somehow become glorified. A beautiful woman had been intertwined with it," and this despite the fact that on the same occasion she has in addition forcefully told him she "cannot endure the heath" (245).

Eustacia, for her part, longs to escape from life on the heath and dreams of finding a husband who will both remove her from her Hades and take her abroad, preferably to Paris. Coming home from Paris, Clym seems clearly destined to meet her need. She is as blindly disregarding of his wishes and intentions, however, as he of hers. When he talks of marriage, she says she will promise to marry him if he agrees to go back to Paris. He solemnly says, "I have vowed not to go back, Eustacia," but she persists in her belief that he does not mean this: "You will never adhere to your education plan, I am quite sure," she says, "and then it will be all right for me; and so I promise to be yours for ever and ever" (257). She relies on her being able, "once married to Clym," to "induce" him to return to Paris but is met by his being "as firm in the contrary intention" (300). In the end, when her hopes fade in this respect and she goes out to fight depression at the gipsying and meets Wildeve, she has to admit how much she stumbled when she thought she saw: "[D]o I desire unreasonably much in wanting what is called life?" she asks him, "music, poetry, passion, war, and all the beating and pulsing that is going on in the great arteries of the world? That was the shape of my youthful dream; but I did not get it. Yet I thought I saw the way to it in my Clym" (345).[6]

The motif of blindness is further accentuated in the description of Clym's feeling for Eustacia. Clym is a notable development in Hardy's male typology. In the decent, honorable mold, he is neither diffident sexually, like Stephen Smith or Boldwood or Gabriel Oak, nor is he inhibited, like Henry Knight, a fellow intellectual. He may not have the sexual sparkle of a rake such as Troy, but he initially responds to Eustacia with direct sexual ardor. When they begin to meet on the heath, they embrace and kiss passionately, the narrator commenting somewhat primly, "Such a situation had less than three months brought forth," though he grants their intensity: "They remained long [in their embrace] without a single utterance, for no language could reach the level of their condition . . ." (254). On the same occasion, Clym passionately says to her: "[O]ne thing is certain—I do love you—past all compass and description. I love you to oppressiveness . . ." (255). When he has to contend with the opposition of his mother, however—Mrs. Yeobright is as implacably and unreasonably opposed to Eustacia as Mrs. Morel to Miriam Leivers in *Sons and Lovers*—and realizes how insistent Eustacia is about their going to Paris, he registers that his position has become "indescribably complicated": "Thus as his sight grew accustomed to the first blinding halo kindled about him by love and beauty, Yeobright began to perceive what a strait he was in" (260). Clym may begin to perceive the difficulties he has to confront, but it is the fire of a blind passion that has been kindled in him and that he gives way to in marrying Eustacia. He later feels he must have been "bewitched" in doing so (393).

Eustacia's passion for Clym is the blindness of her need: "To be loved to madness—such was her great desire. Love was to her the one cordial which

---

6. Robert B. Heilman also makes the same point, remarking that "Hardy wonderfully records the way in which each one listens to himself and not to the other" (*"The Return: Centennial Observations,"* 73).

could drive away the eating loneliness of her days. And she seemed to long for the abstraction called passionate love more than for any particular lover" (121). Subject to an "eating" loneliness, Eustacia is also subject to the primary rule of love in Hardy, the rule of the void, for we are to understand that she is consumed by her loneliness, hollowed out by it. Consequently, just as the void in Gabriel Oak makes him fix on Bathsheba in *Far from the Madding Crowd*, Eustacia turns, once she has broken with Wildeve, to Clym. In love with love more than with him, she is "predetermined to nourish a passion" for him (199) and so fill up what has been eaten out. But the likely result of giving way to the importunities of so blind a mouth is prefigured in a dream she has after she has decided to break with Wildeve and before she has met Clym:

> She was dancing to wondrous music, and her partner was the man in silver armour who had accompanied her through the previous fantastic changes, the visor of his helmet being closed. The mazes of the dance were ecstatic. . . . Suddenly these two wheeled out from the mass of dancers, dived into one of the pools of the heath, and came out somewhere beneath into an iridescent hollow, arched with rainbows. "It must be here," said the voice by her side, and blushingly looking up she saw him removing his casque to kiss her. At that moment there was a cracking noise, and his figure fell into fragments like a pack of cards. (174)

The dream figure she dances with conflates both Wildeve and Clym. He embodies, first, her wish to have Clym play the knight in shining armor and rescue her from her desolate life on the heath. But with the visor of the helmet closed, she cannot see the man within the armor; when, "looking up," she is about to see the man as he really is, what she has been holding to collapses. The proleptic significance extends as well to Wildeve, who is evoked by the ecstatic "mazes" of the dance, for they will dance together in a "maze of motion" at the gipsying (323).[7] They will also both dive into "one of the pools of the heath," though then they do not come out of it alive.

7. Elliot B. Gose also notes the significant repetition of the maze image (*Imagination Indulged: The Irrational in the Nineteenth-Century Novel*, 122).

As opposed to the fantastic nature of the dream, developments in Eustacia's relationships with both men are also suggested proleptically in a symbolic scene. It has been read as a "phallic episode,"[8] but this seems to me to strain at a scene that, in its quiet ordinariness, is typical of one dimension of Hardy's symbolism. Wanting to draw some water for Eustacia from her well, Clym ties a pail to a long rope and begins to let it down into the well:

> "I must make fast the end first, or we may lose the whole," he said to Eustacia. . . . "Could you hold this a moment, while I do it—or shall I call your servant?"
> "I can hold it," said Eustacia. . . .
> "I suppose I may let it slip down?" she inquired.
> "I would advise you not to let it go far," said Clym. "It will get much heavier, you will find."
> However, Eustacia had begun to pay out. While he was tying she cried, "I cannot stop it!"

Clym manages to stop the rope, but her hand is bleeding where the rope has "dragged off the skin." "You should have let go," he says (243–44). Eustacia is full of confidence in her own powers, just as she is sure she will get what she wants from Clym; but what the scene dramatizes is how she heedlessly—blindly, in the face of his admonitions—takes on more than she can handle. Having done so, her problem, it is intimated, is that she cannot let go, just as she cannot let go of Wildeve even after her marriage—and gets really hurt in the process.

Even before the marriage of Clym and Eustacia is consummated, on the day they fix the date of the wedding, the narrator sounds an ominous note: "Whether Eustacia was to add one other to the list of those who love too hotly to love long and well, the forthcoming event was certainly a ready way of proving" (267). Nor is the proof long in coming; indeed, given its nature, it is notably fast. Eustacia's hot love returns us to the quickly burning bonfire; and it is the ostensible burden of the tale that the marriage collapses, like a fire that falls in on itself, because the passion

8. Carpenter, *Thomas Hardy*, 102.

that engenders it soon burns itself out. This is repeatedly emphasized: "They were like those double stars which revolve round and round each other, and from a distance appear to be one. The absolute solitude in which they lived intensified their reciprocal thoughts; yet some might have said that it had the disadvantage of consuming their mutual affections at a fearfully prodigal rate" (299). Their married passion is no match for their mutual tendency to depression: "One week and another week wore on, and nothing seemed to lighten the gloom of the young couple" (309). Within a few months they themselves recognize what is happening to them:

> "How cold you seem this afternoon! [said Clym,] and yet I used to think there never was a warmer heart than yours."
> "Yes, I fear we are cooling—I see it as well as you," she sighed mournfully. "And how madly we loved two months ago! You were never tired of contemplating me, nor I of contemplating you. Who could have thought then that by this time my eyes would not seem so very bright to yours, nor your lips so very sweet to mine? Two months—is it possible? Yes, 'tis too true!" (315)

And after Eustacia's death, Clym reflects that "every pulse of loverlike feeling" has been stilled in him: "His passion for her had occurred too far on in his manhood to leave fuel enough on hand for another fire of that sort . . ." (453).

The novelist's conclusion is all too clear: passion is not enough, is not a sufficiently substantial basis for a lasting marriage. The only basis for that, we are meant to see, "the only love which is strong as death," is that based presumably on the sort of camaraderie that binds Bathsheba and Oak together. Eustacia and Clym are not mutually compatible as they are, are not friends as well as lovers, do not have the fullness of knowledge of each other that Bathsheba and Oak have. The seer's verdict is uncompromising, but what we are also made to see in this erratic history is that the marriage fails not because passion is not enough but because there is not enough of it.

The contradictory reading is due to the ambiguous presentation of Clym. On the one hand, as I have remarked, he is distinguished by the

freedom of his passion. On the other, he is "a modern man," and the
"beauty" of his features, we are accordingly informed, will "in no long
time be ruthlessly overrun by its parasite thought," for in him "an inner
strenuousness" is "preying upon an outer symmetry":

> He already showed that thought is a disease of flesh, and indirectly
> bore evidence that ideal physical beauty is incompatible with emo-
> tional development and a full recognition of the coil of things.
> Mental luminousness must be fed with the oil of life, even though
> there is already a physical need for it; and the pitiful sight of two
> demands on one supply was just showing itself here.
> When standing before certain men the philosopher regrets that
> thinkers are but perishable tissue, the artist that perishable tissue has
> to think. Thus to deplore, each from his point of view, the mutually
> destructive interdependence of spirit and flesh would have been
> instinctive with these in critically observing Yeobright. (194–95)

Clym is presented in this way on his initial appearance, and though, in
his passionate courting of Eustacia that follows, we tend to forget it, it
considerably complicates, if it does not altogether undermine, the account
we are given of the cooling of passion in the marriage. The narrative, that
is, confronts us not only with the fire of passion that naturally consumes
itself but also with a "mental luminousness" that is fed by and presumably
burns on the "oil of life."

The fiery nature of Clym's mind is insisted on. When his mother
maintains that, in giving up his position in the "large diamond estab-
lishment," he shows that he is "getting weary of doing well," he replies:
"Mother, what is doing well?"—and this is characterized as a "burning
question" (234). This kind of fire, however, just like that of passion,
is seen to be self-consuming: after his mother's death he believes he
has "sinned against her" and "[consumes] himself by the gnawing of
his thought" (373–74). He also nearly blinds himself when he pursues
a program of strenuous reading. The doctor pronounces "the disease"
to be "acute inflammation" of the eyes (309), this being set against the
inflammability of the souls of Eustacia and Wildeve. The inflammation is
also a tangible manifestation of the "disease of flesh" that thought is said
to be, though there is no indication of flesh preying on spirit, despite the

narrator's assertion of "the mutually destructive interdependence of spirit and flesh."

Clym's near blindness is a crucial factor in the collapse of the marriage. When as a result of it he begins to work as a furze cutter, it is this that seemingly vitiates the marriage. To Eustacia, anyway denied the hope of moving to Paris, Clym's descent to such work is "a positive horror" (311) and is "degrading to her" (313). "I would starve rather than do it!" she exclaims. "And you can sing! I will go and live with my grandfather again!" (314) This is so excessive that we are led to suspect an undisclosed source of dissatisfaction is compelling her. A hint of what this might be is given us when she tells Wildeve at the gipsying that Clym is "not ill—only incapacitated" (324), a disability that is still more sharply focused when she dances with Wildeve on the same occasion and the "change of atmosphere" she then experiences is said to be from the "arctic frigidity" in which she has been "steeped" to "the tropical sensations" of the dance (323). We may assume that sexual energy as well as thought is fueled by the oil of life and that "one supply" is inadequate to sustain both in the economy of depletion outlined by the narrator. Clym's near blindness, that is, is richly evocative of his condition in a further respect and points also to sexual incapacity, if not to "a kind of castration," as has been somewhat wildly asserted.9 This no doubt illuminates the nature of the depression Eustacia goes out to battle against on the day of the gipsying, but it considerably blurs the view we are to take of the failure of the marriage. This now appears to be the result not of the self-consuming nature of passion per se, of a mutual exhaustion of sexual ardor, but of a deficiency of passion on the part of Clym. This unexpectedly establishes a parallel between the marriage of Clym and Eustacia and that of Bathsheba and Troy. In both cases passion as a possible alternative to camaraderie is not given the chance of a substantial blaze. More, not less of it, seems called for. The absence of a "zest for existence" that is evident from the outset in Clym's face (and that will be a feature of "the typical countenance of the future") (225) points not merely to the cost of thought but to the loss of vital sexual being.

9. Marjorie Garson says: "Certainly Clym's emblematic eye-trouble unmans him. . . . [Clym's] blinding is, practically as well as symbolically, a kind of castration" (*Hardy's Fables*, 72–73).

Despite the novelist's apparent skepticism as to the value of passion in a marriage, the fine parting scene between Clym and Eustacia dramatizes how it could possibly have saved it. Clym demands to know whether it was Wildeve who was with her when the door was closed against his mother:

> "Why did you not kick him out, and let her in, and say, I'll be an honest wife and a noble woman from this hour? Had I told you to go and quench eternally our last flickering chance of happiness here you could have done no worse. Well, she's asleep now; and have you a hundred gallants, neither they nor you can insult her any more."
> "You exaggerate fearfully," she said in a faint, weary voice; "but I cannot enter into my defence—it is not worth doing. You are nothing to me in future, and the past side of the story may as well remain untold. I have lost all through you, but I have not complained. Your blunders and misfortunes may have been a sorrow to you, but they have been a wrong to me. All persons of refinement have been scared away from me since I sank into the mire of marriage. . . ." (394)

Bathsheba came to regard her marriage to Troy, we recall, as her encompassment in "a heap of misery"; Eustacia's sense of failure in her relationship with Clym is not dissimilar, for it has meant her sinking into "the mire of marriage." But her ostensible abasement cannot be compared with Bathsheba's actual humiliation. Indeed, the fact that Eustacia says she has lost "all" through Clym and that his misfortunes have been "a wrong" to her would seem to point once again to the personal deprivation that underlies her feeling of social shame. When Clym refers to her having quenched their last "flickering chance of happiness," it is the embers of their passion that he inadvertently evokes. The only hope for the marriage, it is now contradictorily intimated, would seem to lie in their tending this flame.

This is emphasized again in the wonderful moment that marks their final parting:

> She hastily dressed herself, Yeobright moodily walking up and down the room the whole of the time. At last all her things were on. Her little hands quivered so violently as she held them to her chin to fasten her bonnet that she could not tie the strings, and after a few moments she relinquished the attempt. Seeing this he moved forward and said, "Let me tie them."

She assented in silence, and lifted her chin. For once at least in her life she was totally oblivious of the charm of her attitude. But he was not, and he turned his eyes aside, that he might not be tempted to softness. (395)

When Clym spontaneously moves forward to tie the strings of her bonnet, it is the habit of true intimacy that manifests itself in spite of everything. At this moment Clym has it in his power to save his marriage by giving way to her charm—and to the tenderness of his hands. But in a culminating instance of the motif, he "turn[s] his eyes aside," making himself blind to her, lest he "be tempted to softness," strikingly prefiguring the response of Angel Clare to his wife on a similarly climactic occasion.[10]

The marriage of Clym and Eustacia, then, is subject to contrary strains. The narrator's account of it is further complicated, if not muddied, by the fact that their separation is due in no small measure to the play of chance. The immediate cause of the separation is Eustacia's failure to admit Mrs. Yeobright to their house and the latter's subsequent death. Although she believes that Clym will open the door for his mother, Eustacia is responsible for her own choice in not doing so herself and thus for what follows; but it must be said that her choice is also the end product of an overwhelming series of chance events. Before her crucial refusal to open the door, the "ghastly breach" (334) between Clym and his mother that is occasioned by the marriage is duplicated by that between Eustacia and Mrs. Yeobright—and their division is the result of a number of chance occurrences. Christian gambles away the money that Mrs. Yeobright has asked him to deliver to Clym and Thomasin; Venn retrieves the money but mistakenly gives it all to Thomasin; Christian confesses to Mrs. Yeobright that he lost the money to Wildeve, and she, assuming he has returned it by giving it to Eustacia rather than Clym, tactlessly asks her whether she has "received a gift from Thomasin's husband" (302). The inflammable Eustacia "[fires] up all too quickly" (302), and the mutual recrimination

10. Ian Gregor says that the showdown between Clym and Eustacia "disintegrates largely into rant. It comes to that because there has never been any intensity of feeling between them in the first place," though he does grant that "genuine feeling breaks through" in the bonnet scene (*The Great Web: The Form of Hardy's Major Fiction*, 97–98).

that follows ends with Eustacia telling Mrs. Yeobright that she has "caused a division which can never be healed" (304). For good measure Eustacia then says to Clym, "I have seen your mother; and I will never see her again!" (306). Eustacia's refusal to open the door to Mrs. Yeobright is thus hemmed in by the chance events that precede it: "[H]ow can I open the door to her," she says to Wildeve, "when she dislikes me—wishes to see not me, but her son? I won't open the door!" (346). And her refusal is also subject to the greatest chance of all: that Wildeve is visiting her at the time and that both he and Mrs. Yeobright should pay their first unannounced and unexpected visits to the home of the couple on the same day and at the same hour.

In all of Hardy's novels there are certain scenes that bear his distinctive, if idiosyncratic, imaginative stamp. One thinks, for instance, of the scene on the Cliff without a Name in *A Pair of Blue Eyes* or of the destruction of the sheep by the wayward dog in *Far from the Madding Crowd*. An equivalent scene in *The Return of the Native* is that of the gambling of Venn and Wildeve on the heath. As they throw the dice in the deep darkness of the heath at night, they are "surrounded by dusky forms between four and five feet high, standing a few paces beyond the rays of the lantern." These are forty or fifty heath-croppers, which "[gaze] intently" at the players. Wildeve chases them away, but then a large moth extinguishes their candle. Desperate to recoup his losses, Wildeve proceeds to gather thirteen glowworms, and the gambling continues by the light of "the thirteen tiny lamps" that throw "a pale phosphoric shine" (292–93). This weird scene is in the sense indicated at the center of the plot; but the glowworms throw their light not only on the game of chance but also on the play of chance that collapses the marriage of Clym and Eustacia.

III

When Eustacia sends her signal to Wildeve at the beginning of the narrative, he is irresistibly drawn by her fire, even though he was supposed to have been married to Thomasin on that very day. The symbolism is simple but effective. Having inflammability of being in common, they would seem to be natural partners; and they have in the past been full sexual partners, as Hardy made clear in the 1895 Uniform edition: whereas the current edition has Eustacia chide Wildeve for having deserted her as if she had never been his "life and soul so irretrievably" (113), the 1895 version substituted "body" for "life." And anyway at the same meeting she says to him, "[You] may tempt me, but I won't give myself to you any more" (115). What is not clear is why they have previously broken off the relationship.

On the one hand it is intimated that it was only to be expected that he should have deserted her since he is no more than a philanderer. In introducing him, the narrator remarks on the singular "grace of his movement," but in what becomes a continuing vein of hostile commentary, he adds: "it was the pantomimic expression of a lady-killing career" (93). Wildeve, that is, is to be seen as the male equivalent of the supposedly fickle Elfride in *A Pair of Blue Eyes,* who "hovers about like a butterfly." Even D. H. Lawrence refers to him as "the unstable Wildeve."[11] But, in fact, he is not a simple rake, being as much of a modification of the type as Clym is of the honorable but sexually diffident man. Though he suffers "the curse of inflammability," he is also "cursed with sensitiveness" (95) and so is not heartlessly free for adventures. It becomes evident, moreover, that he has always and only been in love with Eustacia, though the definitive statement of his feeling comes late in the narrative (on the fateful day of "the closed door"). In response to her blaming him for having "turned aside" to Thomasin, he replies:

> "I meant nothing by it. . . . It was a mere interlude. Men are given to the trick of having a passing fancy for somebody else in the midst of a permanent love, which reasserts itself afterwards just as before. On account of your rebellious manner to me I was tempted to go further than I should have done; and when you still would keep playing the same tantalizing part I went further still, and married her. . . . [Clym] may know what it is to come down in the world . . . but he probably doesn't know what it is to lose the woman he loved." (344–45)

11. Lawrence, "Study of Thomas Hardy," 23.

Wildeve admits here to the waywardness of his "passing fancy" and to the irresponsibility of his marrying out of pique, but he is quite unambiguous—and sincere—in his declaration of the "permanence" of his love for Eustacia. His behavior throughout would seem to confirm the truth of what he says.

In the on-again, off-again nature of Wildeve's initial relationships with Eustacia and Thomasin, even though he is the apex of the triangle, it is Eustacia who exemplifies René Girard's "law of mediated desire" and who, as we have seen, fluctuates dramatically in her feelings.[12] Her passion, the narrator remarks, stems from a "super-subtle, epicurean heart" (155–56). He also insists that Wildeve's desire is mediated in the same way, as is supposedly apparent in his reaction to the news of Eustacia's marriage to Clym: "The old longing for Eustacia had reappeared in his soul: and it was mainly because he had discovered that it was another man's intention to possess her." For good measure the narrator adds: "To be yearning for the difficult, to be weary of that offered; to care for the remote, to dislike the near; it was Wildeve's nature always. This is the true mark of the man of sentiment" (274). The hostile sarcasm is pronounced, but on the same occasion we are told that when Wildeve hears the news of Eustacia's marriage, "a sudden expression of pain [overspreads] his face" (274), a reaction that bespeaks a "longing in his soul" that has never left him rather than suddenly stimulated desire. And when Eustacia's opening bonfire calls him up, he goes to her in direct and unmediated response. At their second meeting, Eustacia says to him, "You will love me all your life long. You would jump to marry me!" "So I would!" he answers, and

---

12. See Chapter 1, 34–35 above.
    J. Hillis Miller gives the following account of the process in *The Return of the Native:*

> Eustacia Vye is the clearest example in Hardy's fiction of . . . submission to the law of mediated desire. . . . When Eustacia has Wildeve to herself she soon tires of him, but as soon as he turns from her to Thomasin he becomes desirable again. . . . As soon as she learns that Thomasin no longer wants Wildeve and that she can have him wholly to herself again, he is magically drained of his attractions for her. She becomes once more indifferent. . . . (*Thomas Hardy,* 159–60)

indeed he proposes that she come away with him to America (139). He repeats the offer to marry her and take her away, but by then she has lost interest in him. He responds as unhesitatingly to her second bonfire a year later and, though they are both married then, once again offers to leave everything and go off with her. For a man of sentiment he is remarkably steady in his feeling for her. For an unscrupulous philanderer he proves on that occasion to be unexpectedly responsible and notably concerned with her well-being, as his response to the "great misery" he detects in her—she has by then left Clym—indicates:

> "O, Eustacia, forgive me for the harm I have done you in these two past years! I see more and more that I have been your ruin. . . . I ought never to have hunted you out; or, having done it, I ought to have persisted in retaining you. But of course I have no right to talk of that now. I will only ask this: can I do anything for you? Is there anything on the face of the earth that a man can do to make you happier than you are at present?" (406–7)

Following their marriages, Eustacia and Wildeve renew contact when they meet by chance and dance at the gipsying. (In passing, it should be noted that chance plays as large a part in their tragic end as it does in the breakup of her marriage. It is Charley, wishing to please the depressed Eustacia, who lights the bonfire when the fifth of November comes around again and so unwittingly calls up Wildeve for their fateful meeting. It is by chance that Wildeve comes into an inheritance just at this time—"I am rich now," he tells her (407)—and so is in a position both to provide for his wife and child and to flee with Eustacia.) It is the general thrust of the narrative that their dancing at the gipsying constitutes their self-destructive plunge into the flames. The dancing takes place on the village green under a large yellow moon, which exerts its influence on them, the scene having a striking parallel in the dancing of Ursula and Skrebensky under the moon in *The Rainbow.* Eustacia experiences a "sudden rush of blood" when she first sees Wildeve (321), and her "pulses [begin] to move too quickly for . . . rumination" when they are "launched" into the dance. As they "[thread] their giddy way," the moon, added to the movement, "drives [their] emotions to rankness" (322), and the dancing becomes for

them "a riding upon the whirlwind": "The dance had come like an irresistible attack upon whatever sense of social order there was in their minds,
to drive them back into old paths which were now doubly irregular" (324).

The irregularity referred to would seem to point to their being driven
to an illicit liaison, and one critic has not hesitated to say Eustacia engages
in "adultery" and Wildeve in an "adulterous affair."[13] But the fact of the
matter is that they meet only once (on the day of the closed door) while
Eustacia is still with Clym, and that meeting is innocent. Even the narrator
grants that "Wildeve's intrigue" is "rather ideal than real" (329); and on
the night of the second bonfire Eustacia says to him: "I did not send for
you! As a wife, at least, I've been straight" (406). Nor does the dancing
point only to their self-destructiveness in what has been called "a ritual
embracing of oblivion and death."[14] For Eustacia, at any rate, it seems
rather to be regenerative. As she dances, "a new vitality [enters] her form"
(322); and if she set out that day to battle depression, she is lit up by the
dance: "She had entered the dance from the troubled hours of her late life
as one might enter a brilliant chamber after a night walk in a wood" (323).

It is not that it is passion that self-destructively drives them to their
doom; it is that passion is not given its due. Though Eustacia has arranged
to let Wildeve help her in her flight, she is at the last moment subject to
undermining doubt:

> To ask Wildeve for pecuniary aid without allowing him to accom-
> pany her was impossible to a woman with a shadow of pride left in
> her: to fly as his mistress—and she knew that he loved her—was of
> the nature of humiliation. . . .
> "Can I go, can I go?" she moaned. "He's not *great* enough for me
> to give myself to—he does not suffice for my desire! . . . If he had
> been a Saul or a Búonaparte—ah! But to break my marriage vow
> for him—it is too poor a luxury! . . . And I have no money to go
> alone!" (420–21)

When Eustacia invokes her Saul and her Búonaparte, she not only
ridiculously gives way to a schoolgirlish, romantic pomposity but also

13. See Marjorie Garson, *Hardy's Fables*, 57, 58. Cf. too Carpenter, *Thomas Hardy*, 94.
14. Leonard W. Deen, "Heroism and Pathos in Hardy's *The Return of the Native*," 212.

blinds herself to what was illuminated for her at the gipsying. Just as Clym at the crucial moment averts his eyes from her in the scene with the bonnet strings, so she now turns her back on the revitalizing force of passion. Rejecting passion, and rejecting Wildeve as well as Clym, she leaves herself no way out. Though it is left open as to whether her drowning, which follows, should be viewed as an accident or a suicide, everything points to her taking her own life. Clym, for one, has no doubt about this: "It is I," he says, "who ought to have drowned myself" (443). Eustacia of the flaming soul is apparently meant to be seen as literally enacting her self-destructiveness. In trying to rescue her, Wildeve also drowns; the imagery used by the narrator to describe the pool in which the erstwhile lovers die would seem to imply that they, like the moth in the candle flame, are, in the end, burned up: " 'O, my darling!' exclaimed Wildeve in an agonized voice; and, without showing sufficient presence of mind even to throw off his great-coat, he leaped into the boiling caldron" (437). Wildeve's failure to show presence of mind is no doubt intended to illustrate *his* self-destructiveness, but the hostile narrator might have granted him his selfless devotion to Eustacia.

Some eighteen months after the deaths of Eustacia and Wildeve, a ghost appears on the heath, but this is not *Wuthering Heights*—it is no more than Diggory Venn as "the ghost of [himself]." Red no longer, he now exhibits "the strangely altered hues of an ordinary Christian countenance" (450). Venn's normal color symbolizes the return of the ordinary in this tale of inflamed passions, and the ordinary is further reestablished in the marriage of Venn and Thomasin that follows. He tells her that his "soft sentiments are gone off in vapour like" (458), a declaration that brings to mind the narrator's announcement in *Far from the Madding Crowd* that passion, in comparison with camaraderie as the basis of marriage, is "evanescent as steam." Indeed, as has often been noted, the relationship of Venn and Thomasin is a replaying of that of Oak and Bathsheba.[15] Initially rejected by Thomasin, Venn remains undeviatingly loyal to her, generous

---

15. Cf. Richard Benvenuto, *"The Return of the Native* as a Tragedy in Six Books," 84; Carpenter, *Thomas Hardy,* 100; Gregor, *Great Web,* 106; and Merryn Williams, *Thomas Hardy and Rural England,* 138.

and selfless in his continued love and protective of her and her interests throughout the time of her marriage to Wildeve. Though the depiction of their relationship does not have the solidity of that of the couple in the earlier novel, their coming together in marriage is convincing enough. It is also structurally appropriate: it nicely brings the narrative full circle, ending with the couple that open the novel. In addition, if the triangle of Eustacia, Clym, and Wildeve is resolved in death, it is contraposed with that of Thomasin, Wildeve, and Venn, and this is resolved in the kind of marriage—and continued life—that are to be seen as a needed antidote to passion. What is somewhat startling is that the novelist should have disowned his own conclusion. In a note added to the Wessex edition of 1912, Hardy wrote:

> The writer may state here that the original conception of the story did not design a marriage between Thomasin and Venn. He was to have retained his isolated and weird character to the last, and to have disappeared mysteriously from the heath, nobody knowing whither—Thomasin remaining a widow. But certain circumstances of serial publication led to a change of intent.
>
> Readers can therefore choose between the endings, and those with an austere artistic code can assume the more consistent conclusion to be the true one. (464)[16]

This is disingenuous, to say the least. Throughout his career as a novelist, Hardy altered in book publication what he felt he had been constrained to provide for the magazines. Furthermore, as has been suggested, the

---

16. Hardy added a similar note to "The Distracted Preacher," a tale published the year after *The Return of the Native:*

Note: The ending of this story with the marriage of Lizzy and the minister was almost *de rigueur* in an English magazine at the time of writing. But at this late date, thirty years after, it may not be amiss to give the ending that would have been preferred by the writer to the convention used above. Moreover it corresponds more closely with the true incidents of which the tale is a vague and flickering shadow. Lizzy did not, in fact, marry the minister, but—much to her credit in the author's opinion—stuck to Jim the smuggler, and emigrated with him after their marriage, an expatrial step rather forced upon him by his adventurous antecedents. They both died in Wisconsin between 1850 and 1860. (May 1912). (*The Stories*, 1:205)

existing conclusion is if anything "the more consistent" of the two. Hardy's
leaving a choice of conclusion to the reader is itself a violation of even
a minimally "austere artistic code." The note, indeed, is symptomatic of
the kind of divided perspective that characterizes the erratic course of the
whole narrative.

5

The Mayor of Casterbridge
The Same Stuff

I

Henchard's sale of his wife in *The Mayor of Casterbridge* makes for the most powerful—and astonishing—opening in Hardy's fiction. The episode is so shocking it arouses expectations that it will be the crux of the narrative; and accordingly the novel has been read as a modern tragedy with analogies to *Oedipus Rex* and *King Lear,* in which Henchard's act of shame invites tragic retribution.[1] But when Farfrae arrives in Casterbridge and offers Henchard his cure for grown wheat, the narrator comments that "had not his advent coincided with the discussion on corn and bread . . . this history had never been enacted."[2] This suggests that the opening is deceptive in its implications, for the statement invites a different view of the focus of Henchard's history. But this too proves to be deceptive since Henchard's relationship with Farfrae is only one of a number of parallel relationships.

Deception, indeed, is a recurrent motif in the plot as characters deceive one another with abandon. Susan Henchard does not tell Elizabeth-Jane that her relations with Newson are not what they seem to be and, when they set out for Casterbridge, does not reveal her own "former relations" with Henchard. Similarly, she does not tell Henchard that Elizabeth-Jane

1. See D. A. Dike, "A Modern Oedipus: *The Mayor of Casterbridge*"; and John Paterson, " 'The Mayor of Casterbridge' as Tragedy."

2. Hardy, *The Mayor of Casterbridge,* 106. Further page references to this novel will be incorporated parenthetically in the text.

is Newson's daughter. Henchard in turn deceives the people of Casterbridge as to the nature of his relations with Susan and her daughter, as he
does too in respect of Lucetta; then he deliberately deceives Elizabeth-Jane
when he discovers the truth about her parentage. Finally, when Newson
suddenly appears in Casterbridge, Henchard lies to him about Elizabeth-
Jane's death and does not tell her about Newson's search for her. Newson
himself admits "it was not in [his] heart to undeceive" Susan of her belief
that the sale was "binding" (366–67) and subsequently deceives her as to
his supposed death. Likewise, Lucetta deceives everyone in Casterbridge,
particularly Elizabeth-Jane and Farfrae, about her previous relations with
Henchard. And Henchard experiences his most piercing agony when
Elizabeth-Jane denounces him for having deceived her: "I could have
loved you always—I would have gladly," she says to him. "But how can I
when I know you have deceived me so—so bitterly deceived me!" (402)

Nor is this all. In order to hide the truth about Elizabeth-Jane's pater-
nity, the narrator too deceives the reader. This is not merely a matter of his
withholding information, as is common enough in plots with surprises up
their sleeve, for on two occasions he deliberately falsifies. Susan is made
to say to the furmity-woman, "Can you call to mind . . . the sale of a wife
by her husband in your tent eighteen years ago today?" (89), when she
must well know, since the second Elizabeth-Jane is eighteen, that it was
nineteen years before, as emerges explicitly some fifty pages later (though
in less obvious circumstances) when Henchard tells Farfrae he lost his wife
"nineteen years ago or so" (147). Second, the narrator himself presents a
false summary of Susan's life following the sale, crudely suppressing the
minor facts of the death of one Elizabeth-Jane and the birth of another:

> The history of Susan Henchard's adventures in the interim can be
> told in two or three sentences. Absolutely helpless she had been taken
> off to Canada, where they had lived several years without any great
> worldly success, though she worked as hard as any woman could to
> keep their cottage cheerful and well-provided. When Elizabeth-Jane
> was about twelve years old the three returned to England, and settled
> at Falmouth. . . . (91–92)

A striking motif in a plot is usually a reliable indicator of thematic
concerns. Since Hardy himself says in the "Author's Preface" to the novel

that "the story is more particularly a study of one man's deeds and character than, perhaps, any other of those included in [his] Exhibition of Wessex life" (67), we do well to regard Henchard's character as the consistent focus of the narrative and to relate the motif to him. It is not only that he resorts often to deception, as indicated above, and that he is the cause of deception by others; primarily, and essentially, he is given to self-deception. This, I shall argue, is at the complicated heart of his portrayal.[3]

The tendency manifests itself early on in two simple instances. When Elizabeth-Jane presents herself to Henchard as "Elizabeth-Jane Newson," introducing herself as what she truly is, he at once deceives himself into thinking this is the deception Susan has practiced on her, for "this at once [suggests] to Henchard that the transaction of his early married life at Weydon Fair [is] unrecorded in the family history" (136). And when he secretly meets Susan and proposes to court and marry her as Newson's widow, being ready then to have Elizabeth-Jane live in his home as his stepdaughter, he triumphantly exclaims, "The thing is so natural and easy that it is half done in thinking o't. This would leave my shady, headstrong, disgraceful life as a young man absolutely unopened . . ." (143–44). Henchard is a very Bulstrode in his conviction that he can successfully put his past behind him, but the meeting with Susan takes place at the Ring, the Roman Amphitheatre, and Casterbridge is everywhere a testimony to how easily the past opens up:

> Casterbridge announced old Rome in every street, alley, and precinct. It looked Roman, bespoke the art of Rome, concealed dead men of Rome. It was impossible to dig more than a foot or two deep about the town fields and gardens without coming upon some tall soldier or other of the Empire, who had lain there in his silent unobtrusive rest for a space of fifteen hundred years. He was mostly found lying on his side, in an oval scoop in the chalk, like a chicken in its shell. . . . (140)

---

3. Juliet M. Grindle draws attention to "the truly remarkable amount of lying which is done" in the novel, citing many of the instances noted above, but sees this as partly accounting for and greatly augmenting "the complexity of the web of relationships between the six major characters" ("Compulsion and Choice in *The Mayor of Casterbridge,*" 96–97).

For an expert treatment of the general problem of the withholding of information by narrators, see Leona Toker, *Eloquent Reticence: Withholding Information in Fictional Narrative.*

The very locale in which Henchard lives thus declares that, despite appearances, the past is far from dead and buried, that it easily rises to the surface, merely waiting, like the soldier in his shell, to be hatched. Just as the skeletons from Henchard's past push up into his life.

Fundamentally, however, Henchard deceives himself about his own nature, about who and what he truly is—the man beneath the mayor. His self-deception manifests itself in all his major relations, those with Susan, with Lucetta, with Farfrae, and with Elizabeth-Jane. These relations, like the directions in his will, are "a piece of the same stuff that his whole life [is] made of" (410). But the stuff is so rich and the relations so varied that Henchard emerges not only as "a man of character" but, as has frequently been asserted, as Hardy's greatest male character, perhaps even his "most brilliant characterization."[4] Indeed J. I. M. Stewart says that Henchard represents Hardy's "nearest approach . . . to creating one of the really great male characters in English literature"; and Albert J. Guerard even calls him "one of the greatest tragic heroes in all fiction."[5] The achievement is perhaps not unrelated to the fact that in this novel there is no divergence between see-er and seer, the kind of divergence that seemingly occurs, as we have observed, when it is passion that is at issue.

II

The opening of the novel is striking not only in itself but also in respect of Hardy's previous work, for it starts with a failed marriage, not working up to this through a woman's wrong choice as between two opposed men, but confronting us at once with the brute fact of the bad marriage through the man's wish to escape from it. From the outset the wish is implicit in the "dogged and cynical indifference" the man shows to his wife and child, the group preserving a "perfect silence" as they move along the road together (69). On his part the silence is an "ignoring silence," negating his wife, and reading, "or pretending to read," as he walks, he appears to want "to escape an intercourse that would have been irksome to him" (69–70). What he wants to escape, in the light of what follows, is suggestive,

4. Collins, *Hardy and His God*, 116. See too, for instance, Abercrombie, *Thomas Hardy*, 125; and Carpenter, *Thomas Hardy*, 104.
5. J. I. M. Stewart, *Thomas Hardy: A Critical Biography*, 114; Guerard, *Thomas Hardy*, 146.

the word "intercourse" reverberating in respect of his relations with the woman. But we are not told what has gone wrong with the marriage, the narrator merely implying sourly that this is the nature of the beast: "That the man and woman were husband and wife, and the parents of the girl in arms, there could be little doubt. No other such relationship would have accounted for the atmosphere of stale familiarity which the trio carried along with them like a nimbus as they moved down the road" (70).

In the tent of the furmity-woman, however, there is talk about marriage, and then it appears the man, married for three years, is convinced the woman has ruined him: "The conversation took a high turn, as it often does on such occasions. The ruin of good men by bad wives, and, more particularly, the frustration of many a promising youth's high aims and hopes and the extinction of his energies by an early imprudent marriage, was the theme"; and the trusser's contribution is to say, "I did for myself that way thoroughly" (74). The trusser is out of work, but it is not evident in what way the woman is responsible for this, as he seems to believe. What does come through is his conviction that close contact with a woman is inimical to a man, not only "doing" for him in a worldly sense but undoing him, destroying his male self at its core, extinguishing his vital force. His conclusion is that "men who have got wives and don't want 'em [should] get rid of 'em as these gipsy fellows do their old horses" (75). The man's not "wanting" a wife, we see, is not merely a matter of his preferring not to have one; more profoundly, it expresses his feeling that he does not need a wife, as the gipsies do not need their old horses. He is a man who does not need a wife because he is sure he is sufficient to himself—and would be far better off without one: "I haven't more than fifteen shillings in the world . . ." he says, but "if I were a free man again I'd be worth a thousand pound before I'd done o't" (74). It is in this context that Michael Henchard's story begins with the sale of his wife.

In his readiness to dispense with women, Henchard is the culminating instance of a line of men in Hardy. He follows Henry Knight of *A Pair of Blue Eyes*, who is "a bachelor by nature," and Farmer Boldwood of *Far from the Madding Crowd*, who is "a confirmed bachelor."[6] Whereas both Knight

6. See Chapter 2, 46 above and Chapter 3, 62 above.

and Boldwood in the end fall in love with women and their prolonged
bachelordom is exposed as a function of sexual inhibition, Henchard,
more dramatically, is, as he himself puts it, "by nature something of a
woman-hater" who finds it "no hardship to keep mostly at a distance from
the sex" (148). Since he has been, in Solomon Longways's words, a "widow
man" (102) for nineteen years following the sale of his wife, and since (as
remains to be discussed) he has lapsed into a relationship with a woman
only once during this time, and that for a short period and only after
sixteen years, Henchard takes the stage at the beginning of the narrative
proper as a man who would seem "by nature" to be sexually self-sufficient.
Without a woman, seemingly enabled to husband his energies rather than
have them extinguished, he appears to have found a viable alternative to
a failed marriage and has become "the masterful, coercive Mayor of the
town" (153). His mastery, of himself and of all around him, is compensation
for the long years of abstinence. In this respect, his abstinence from drink
in accordance with his vow may be regarded as concretizing a more radical
abstention. All his passion goes into his dominating mastery, for when he
"[carries] his point" it is a "blaze of satisfaction that he always [emits]"
(194). Keeping himself to himself, it is thus that in a number of respects
he holds his own.7

When Susan seeks out Henchard after the lapse of nineteen years, his
response is interesting. Arranging to meet her in a note he sends with
Elizabeth-Jane, he encloses five guineas, the amount Newson paid for
her, as if "tacitly [saying] to her that he [buys] her back again" (138).
Henchard, that is, takes her back as a chattel, recovering what belongs
to him. Neither in the note nor at the meeting with her does he express
any love for her or is there any movement of feeling toward her. His "first
words," the narrator stresses, are "I don't drink. . . . You hear, Susan?—I

---

7. Henchard seems to be taken at his word in the criticism. Cf. Ian Gregor, who says
"[Hardy's] eye is not so much on money, as on the notion of 'freedom' [the sale] appears
to offer, and which Henchard is so intent on grasping" (*Great Web*, 119); D. H. Fussell,
who notes that "the family is seen by Henchard as a constraint to self-advancement" ("The
Maladroit Delay: The Changing Times in Hardy's *The Mayor of Casterbridge*," 24); and
Bruce Johnson, who maintains that "the [wife] auction signals the triumph of social and
commercial signification over the more primitive, even atavistic sources of Henchard's
being" (*True Correspondence: A Phenomenology of Thomas Hardy's Novels*, 78).

don't drink now—I haven't since that night" (142), a way of begging her forgiveness that rather leaves her out of account. What he proposes to her is a pro forma marriage in more than one sense, and he sets about courting her "with business-like determination," seeming to school himself "into a course of strict mechanical rightness" toward her to conceal his lack of "amatory fire" (152–53). When Susan moves into his house, however, he does try to "[show] some semblance" of feeling for her by being "kind" to her, "lest she should pine for deeper affection than he [can] give" (157).

What is unclear at this stage is whether his inability to give affection is due to Susan's failure to arouse such feeling in him or whether it is an incapacity on his part that extends to all women. Certainly, the protracted period of his celibacy would seem to indicate a more general incapacity—or lack of desire. We can perhaps profitably relate to this problem by recurring to his kinship with Boldwood and considering Boldwood's own kinship with Bathsheba. Boldwood, we saw, was said to be "nearly [Bathsheba's] own self rendered into another sex"; and Bathsheba is a woman who "[feels] herself sufficient to herself," Diana being "the goddess whom [she] instinctively adore[s]."[8] I suggested that for Bathsheba sex entails the violation of her self-sufficiency and that she is unable to open herself sexually. It seems to me that we can best understand Henchard's varied relations in this novel by viewing him as a male exemplar of the Diana complex. He deceives himself into believing his actions are dictated by his pride in his self-sufficiency and his need for self-enclosure, but in fact he longs to break out of his isolation. The difficulty is that it is only rarely he can bring himself to admit this and that in his fierce manliness he cannot, until it is too late, open himself—to anyone.

When he does succumb sexually to a woman, this takes place in Jersey, where he has gone on business, and in special circumstances, as he tells Farfrae:

> "I fell quite ill, and in my illness I sank into one of those gloomy fits I sometimes suffer from, on account o' the loneliness of my domestic life, when the world seems to have the blackness of hell, and like

8. See Chapter 3, 65 and 75–76 above.

Job, I could curse the day that gave me birth. . . . While in this state I was taken pity on by a woman . . . [who] was as lonely as I. This young creature was staying at the boarding-house where I happened to have my lodging; and when I was pulled down she took upon herself to nurse me. Heaven knows why, for I wasn't worth it. But being together in the same house, and her feelings warm, we got naturally intimate. I won't go into particulars of what our relations were. It is enough to say that we honestly meant to marry. There arose a scandal, which did me no harm, but was of course ruin to her. . . . At last I was well and came away." (148–49)

It is only when Henchard is really ill and so deprived of his habitual sense of independence that his isolation, the "loneliness of [his] domestic life," hits home and undermines him. It undermines him to such an extent that we are to understand it plunges him into a suicidal depression, for in the blackness of the "gloomy fit" he "sinks" into he wants, like Job, to end it all. He later acknowledges this even more directly when he rescues Lucetta from the bull and she cries out, "You—have saved me!"—"saved my life," as she adds; and he replies: "I have returned your kindness. . . . You once saved me" (280, 282). It is thus with an instinctive grasping at life that he responds to Lucetta when she takes pity on him. And it is in the helplessness of his dependence that he allows her to nurse him, for when he is depressed, we are told, "all his practical largeness of view [oozes] out of him" (264): drained and depleted then, his self-supporting sense of mastery falls in on itself. That they eventually become "intimate" would seem to be due more to her than to him, for it is her feelings that are "warm." What is notable is the manner in which he backs away from her when he is restored to himself: he implies that it is the scandal which breaks up the relationship, but this does him "no harm" and would rather be a reason for his standing by her, especially since they mean to marry. But he neither stays with her nor marries her, seeming incapable of moving toward her or of accepting moral responsibility for her "ruin." He tells Farfrae the story three years after his break with Lucetta and begins by indicating he now views his submission to her as a "blunder" (148).

   Henchard's sexual entanglements, it emerges, are characterized by a repetition compulsion on his part. This is pointed, when he meets Lucetta in the Ring as he has previously met Susan, by her "appearing . . . as the double of the first" (324). Initially, he seems driven to reject the woman with whom he has been intimate. This is more startling in the case of Susan, but Lucetta feels no less abandoned, "forsaken," as she says in one of her letters to him (319). The rejection is followed by his attempt eventually to make up to the woman, formally to do right by her. Thus, when Susan appears in Casterbridge, he remarries her; and after three years of Lucetta's badgering, he offers to marry her, though his readiness to make her this "return" (149) is nullified by the advent of Susan.

When Susan dies, his sense of obligation to Lucetta is strong, and he reflects that he "must put her in her proper position": "It was by no means with the oppression that would once have accompanied the thought that he regarded the moral necessity now; it was, indeed, with interest, if not warmth. His bitter disappointment at finding Elizabeth-Jane to be none of his, and himself a childless man, had left an emotional void in Henchard that he unconsciously craved to fill" (219). The passage throws light, first, on his previous abandonment of Lucetta. For him the mere thought of marriage has been an "oppression," so oppressive as to make him flee her and then resist her pleas. Now, however, he is doubly driven. He is driven morally by a need to make a required—and acknowledged—restitution to her; and he is driven emotionally by the need to fill an inner void. The propulsive force of such a void is Hardy's central metaphor for sexual impulsion, for a psychology of sex in which men and women are driven to one another. The idea of the void is definitively formulated in *Far from the Madding Crowd* when Gabriel Oak, "having for some time known the want of a satisfactory form to fill an increasing void within him," fills it with Bathsheba, whom he does not know at that stage but whom he loves steadily thereafter.[9] The crucial difference between Oak and Henchard is that the former is aware of the void within him and consciously seeks to fill it, whereas the latter "unconsciously craves" to do so and is impelled by a need that, in his vaunted self-sufficiency, he would even deny exists.

Henchard's lack of awareness of the void within has several consequences. In his aversion to sexual relationship, he is driven to intense

9. See Chapter 1, 32 above.

emotional involvements of an apparently nonsexual nature, as remains to be discussed in respect to his relationships with Farfrae and Elizabeth-Jane. It is when these relationships fail him that Lucetta comes to Casterbridge, and then "by an almost mechanical transfer the sentiments which [have] run to waste since his estrangement from Elizabeth-Jane and Donald Farfrae [gather] around Lucetta before they [have] grown dry" (220). But if the idea of marriage to her now seems less oppressive, he cannot muster any passion for her: there is no "warmth" or "strong feeling" (219) in his mechanical approach to her.

A further difference between Oak and Henchard is highlighted by the fact that Oak's need makes him not only fall in love with Bathsheba but also "paint her a beauty," whereas the only "charm" Lucetta has for Henchard is that she is "a lady of means," and that "[lends] a charm to her image which it might not otherwise have acquired" (220). Indeed, it is because he has been "dreaming of [her] as almost his property," significantly to be added on to him, as it were, that he lets "his strong, warm gaze [rest] upon her" (247) when he visits her. But by then she no longer feels "that warm allegiance" which she previously bore toward him, and her "pure love" has been "considerably chilled" (226). By then, moreover, she has been drawn to Farfrae. Elizabeth-Jane registers the rivalry of the two men, seeing how they become "more desperately enamoured of her friend every day," but the outcome is not in doubt: "On Farfrae's side it was the unforced passion of youth. On Henchard's the artificially stimulated coveting of maturer age" (250).

III

The repeated pattern in Hardy of triangular relationship is manifested in *The Mayor of Casterbridge* in the rivalry of Henchard and Farfrae for Lucetta. The two men are strongly opposed physically and temperamentally, may indeed be seen as opposites, but they do not conform to Hardy's habitual male sexual typology. Nor is the narrative focus on Lucetta's choice of one of them, or on her marriage to Farfrae when she chooses him. Exceptionally in this novel, Hardy is more concerned with the relationship of the men themselves since the fact that Henchard, the central focus, is conceived as a "woman-hater" serves to subordinate sexual relationships.

The male relationship is inaugurated when Farfrae restores Henchard's grown wheat and the latter offers him a position as manager of the corn branch of his business. Henchard says to him:

> "Your forehead, Farfrae, is something like my poor brother's—now dead and gone; and the nose, too, isn't unlike his. You must be, what—five foot nine, I reckon? I am six foot one and a half out of my shoes. But what of that? In my business, 'tis true that strength and bustle build up a firm. But judgement and knowledge are what keep it established. Unluckily, I am bad at science, Farfrae; bad at figures—a rule o' thumb sort of man. You are just the reverse—I can see that. . . ." (117)

Henchard is drawn to Farfrae as a displacement of his dead brother, seemingly stirred emotionally by his appearance. But in his isolation he is also impelled to Farfrae as a substitution for the kind of close relation with a woman that he has forsworn: "[H]ow that fellow does draw me," he says to himself. "I suppose 'tis because I'm so lonely" (125). In this respect it is significant that he should move so abruptly and apparently inconsequently from the supposed resemblance of Farfrae to his brother to a reckoning of the differences between himself and Farfrae, clearly being drawn to him as his complement, for all the world as if he were relating to a woman. It is repeatedly insisted that "Farfrae's character [is] just the reverse of Henchard's" (185); and on Farfrae's part too "the great difference in their characters" adds to his liking for Henchard (146). From the outset Henchard, who never expresses feeling for or to a woman (other than his stepdaughter), readily declares himself to Farfrae: "[H]ang it, Farfrae," he says, "I like thee well"; and when Farfrae agrees to work for him and be "[his] man," he at once claims him, moving to a different plane of relationship: "'Now you are my friend!' he exclaimed" (133). And his "interest" in his "new friend" is said to be "keenly excited" (138).

On the very day that Henchard takes Farfrae into his business, he is informed by Elizabeth-Jane of Susan's return and arranges, when he meets her that evening, to remarry her. But far from alleviating, this serves only to intensify his sense of loneliness. Returning from the Ring, he insists on Farfrae's having supper with him and, though they are still strangers, unburdens himself of the story of his relations with both Susan and Lucetta: "It is odd," says Henchard, "that two men should meet as we have done on a purely business ground, and that at the end of the first day I should wish to speak to 'ee on a family matter. But, damn it all, I am a lonely man, Farfrae: I have nobody else to speak to; and why shouldn't I tell it to 'ee?" (147). If Henchard, as we have seen, in the gloom of his loneliness and illness, becomes "naturally intimate" with Lucetta, he now forces intimacy on Farfrae. In a parody of sexual intimacy, he bares himself, pouring out what he has for long years kept to himself and finding "great relief" (151) in doing so. The narrator comments that he is "plainly under that strange influence which sometimes prompts men to confide to the new-found friend what they will not tell to the old" (147), but what seems to be decisive is not so much the newness of the friend as his sex. From the start, though the narrator remarks on this explicitly only at the end of the narrative, Henchard's liking for Farfrae is "passionate" (405). That he is driven by the void within him, the sense of which is intensified, if anything, by his alienation on Susan's return, and that he unconsciously wishes to possess Farfrae, to take him into himself, so to speak, is suggested when Elizabeth-Jane's discerning eye detects his devouring feeling for him: though he puts his arm on the manager's shoulder "as if Farfrae were a younger brother," she recognizes "Henchard's tigerish affection for the younger man" (161). Outwardly, however, they are merely friends, as the narrator pointedly remarks when Elizabeth-Jane observes them together on another occasion: "Friendship between man and man; what a rugged strength there was in it, as evinced by these two. And yet the seed that was to lift the foundation of this friendship was at that moment taking root in a chink of its structure" (167).

What makes the chink in this apparently rugged and strong friendship is Henchard's need for mastery. Farfrae has to be *his* man, rendered unto him, as Susan was his woman, even though discarded by him. Their relationship begins to crack when Farfrae countermands Henchard's humiliating punishment of Abel Whittle, ordering him to go home and get his breeches:

"Hullo, hullo!" said Henchard, coming up behind. "Who's sending him back?"

> All the men looked towards Farfrae.
> "I am," said Donald. "I say this joke has been carried far enough."
> "And I say it hasn't! Get up in the waggon, Whittle."
> "Not if I am manager," said Farfrae. "He either goes home, or I march out of this yard for good." (170)

Instead of caving in, as Henchard anticipates, Farfrae stands his ground and directly challenges his employer. He insists that he is master in his own sphere, and it is Henchard who unexpectedly gives way. He knows he is in the wrong, and once he speaks to Farfrae "like a sullen boy" (170), the game is over. What rankles with Henchard as much as the challenge to his authority is his public humiliation: "Why did you speak to me before [the workmen] like that, Farfrae?" he says. "You might have stopped till we were alone" (170). And when one of the men subsequently turns to him for directions, he says, "Ask Mr Farfrae. He's master here!" (171). Henchard thus directly reveals what is at issue for him; at the same time he himself turns Farfrae into a rival, foisting the role on him.

Where he previously expressed his affection for Farfrae, Henchard now draws back: "The corn-factor seldom or never again put his arm upon the young man's shoulder so as to nearly weigh him down with the pressure of mechanized friendship" (173). The narrator's reference to the "mechanized friendship" that Henchard has previously extended to Farfrae retrospectively complicates our view of the tigerish gesture noted above. It would seem that no intense relationship, whether with man or woman, is natural to Henchard, that he cannot give himself to such closeness and has mechanically to force himself to maintain it. In reaction, he retreats, as always, into an entrenched self and moves to reject the one he has favored. But first his passion goes into the rivalry he has created: "fired with emulation," he sets out to better Farfrae in the entertainment he is getting up "in celebration of a national event" (173). What follows is once again his public humiliation; and as a result he dismisses Farfrae, now in effect asserting he does not need him and openly rejecting him, as he has previously rejected Susan and Lucetta.

Far from putting an end to the rivalry, the practical consequence of Henchard's dismissal of Farfrae is to intensify it, for once the younger man sets up on his own in the same line of business, he is "compelled, in sheer self-defence, to close with Henchard in mortal commercial combat" (186). The language in which this commercial struggle is described points proleptically (and precisely) to the climactic physical combat that Henchard finally forces on Farfrae. But first there also develops their rivalry over Lucetta, and "the sense of occult rivalry in suitorship" is "superadded to the palpable rivalry of their business lives" (255). Farfrae is victorious on all fronts and ends by moving with Lucetta into Henchard's old house, while Henchard goes to work for him "as a day-labourer in the barns and granaries he formerly had owned" (302). If it is the reappearance of the furmity-woman and her public denunciation of Henchard that forms "the edge or turn in the incline of [his] fortunes" (291), and if it is he himself who seems to put all his weight into his downward movement, it is surely Farfrae who ensures that the revolution of the wheel of fortune should be felt as so complete: "Here be I, his former master," Henchard says to himself, "working for him as man, and he the man standing as master, with my house and my furniture and my what-you-may-call wife all his own" (302).

There remains one final public humiliation for Henchard, an event that he thinks of as a "crowning degradation" (344). With Farfrae installed as mayor and a royal visit to Casterbridge pending, Henchard asks to be included in the reception of the visitor but is turned down by the mayor. On the day of the visit he drunkenly staggers to the side of the royal vehicle, holding out a hand to "the Illustrious Personage":

> Farfrae, with Mayoral authority, immediately rose to the occasion. He seized Henchard by the shoulder, dragged him back, and told him roughly to be off. Henchard's eyes met his, and Farfrae observed the fierce light in them despite his excitement and irritation. For a moment Henchard stood his ground rigidly; then by an unaccountable impulse gave way and retired. (340)

Since Henchard afterward says "brokenly to himself," "He drove me back as if I were a bull breaking fence" (343), there is a suggestive parallel between this scene, in which Farfrae saves the day, and an earlier episode in which Henchard saves Lucetta and Elizabeth-Jane from a bull that is attacking them. On that occasion Henchard seizes the bull's leading-staff and wrenches its head "as if he would snap it off." The bull's "thick neck" seems to become "half-paralysed," and its nose drops blood. The "creature [flinches]," and Henchard leads it to the door and fastens it outside the barn (279–80). The interesting point in the parallel is not Henchard's bullishness but the manner in which the bull flinches before him, just as he gives in to Farfrae. The parallel seems to lie in the way superior force carries the day, Henchard's courage and physical force in the first instance being matched by Farfrae's courage and force of will in the second. But the narrator says it is "by an unaccountable impulse" that Henchard gives way, suggesting he is unable or unwilling to explain this and at the same time implying that Henchard himself is unwilling or unable to acknowledge what it is that makes him back off. The crucial moment seems to come when Henchard's eyes meet Farfrae's, and this detail links the scene to one that follows it as well as to the one that precedes it, for a meeting of eyes is once again decisive in the physical fight to the death between the two men that ensues, as we shall see. I suggest that Henchard is overcome here not by Farfrae's willpower but by the force, despite the fierceness of his gaze, of his own deepest feeling for the younger man, the kind of feeling that makes him abjure his own superior physical strength, that leads him for once to master himself rather than the other.[10]

Afterward, however, Henchard's public humiliation rankles more and more deeply as he bitterly recalls how he was "shaken at the collar by him as a vagabond in the face of the whole town" (344); and he forces Farfrae to "finish out [the] little wrestle" begun that morning (346) in a fight that

10. Some critics relate Henchard directly to the bull. Cf. Howard O. Brogan, who says the bull is "the very image of Henchard's unruly passions" (" 'Visible Essences' in *The Mayor of Casterbridge*," 308); and Richard C. Carpenter, who calls the bull Henchard's "symbolic alter ego" and says he treats it "as cruelly as life treats him" (*Thomas Hardy*, 108). Other critics have commented on the parallel between the scene with the bull and that of the royal visit. See, for instance, Frederick R. Karl, who says "Henchard is recognizably the bull, or at least suggestive of the bull in its brazen fierceness and then in its flinching half-paralysis once a stronger force masters it" (*"The Mayor of Casterbridge:* A New Fiction Defined," 202); and Grindle, who comments that "images of bulls have, of course, a particular bearing on Henchard who is bull-like in respect of his largeness, slowness, clumsiness, strength, unpredictability, and—in the end, the manner in which he is susceptible to being tamed" ("Compulsion and Choice," 103).

gives body to their earlier "mortal commercial combat." Henchard, as "the strongest man," ties one arm to his side but soon has the advantage:

> "Now," said Henchard between his gasps, "this is the end of what you began this morning. Your life is in my hands."
> "Then take it, take it!" said Farfrae. "Ye've wished to long enough!"
> Henchard looked down upon him in silence, and their eyes met. "O Farfrae!—that's not true!" he said bitterly. "God is my witness that no man ever loved another as I did thee at one time. . . . And now—though I came here to kill 'ee, I cannot hurt thee! Go and give me in charge—do what you will—I care nothing for what comes of me!"
> He withdrew to the back part of the loft, loosened his arm, and flung himself into a corner upon some sacks, in the abandonment of remorse. Farfrae regarded him in silence; then went to the hatch and descended through it. . . .
> Henchard took his full measure of shame and self-reproach. . . . So thoroughly subdued was he that he remained on the sacks in a crouching attitude, unusual for a man, and for such a man. Its womanliness sat tragically on the figure of so stern a piece of virility. (347–48)

If the fight ends unexpectedly in Henchard's unmanning as he crouches like a woman, Elaine Showalter, in a feminist account of the novel—arguably the best piece of criticism on it—maintains that at this point he "finally [crosses] over psychically and strategically to the long-repressed 'feminine' side of himself." She says that Hardy "understood the feminine self as the estranged and essential complement of the male self," that, in selling Susan, Henchard "sells out or divorces his own 'feminine' self" and that his efforts, "first to deny and divorce his passional self, and ultimately to accept and educate it, involve him in a pilgrimage of 'unmanning.' "[11] This is illuminating, but it seems to me that Showalter settles too lightly for the "finality" of the change in Henchard; he is made up a little too much

11. Showalter, "The Unmanning of the Mayor of Casterbridge," 112, 101, 103, 101–2.
  Simon Gatrell cites Showalter, saying that she reaches "a similar conclusion [to him] by a different route," and he also remarks that "in erotic terms [Henchard is] a character subversive of the norms of the dominant culture" (*Thomas Hardy and the Proper Study of Mankind*, 188, 73).

of the same stuff for that. And there are perhaps additional dimensions to the crucial episode of the fight.

The scene, it seems to me, hinges on the issue of giving and taking. All his life Henchard has been habituated, especially in his personal relations, to taking, to taking to himself in acts of possession that have been the only mode of his masterfulness. Farfrae has been his man and has then been rejected by him in the only countermanding mode available to him. Now, on the verge of an ultimate kind of taking, he gives Farfrae's life back to him. This is not the same as giving himself to Farfrae, but it comes close to it. The turning point is their meeting of eyes when all Henchard's deep feeling for Farfrae wells up in him, as earlier that day, and he gives himself to the emotion in the astonishing declaration, given the circumstances, that he has "loved" him. The love is defensively located in the past, but he asserts that it was supreme of its kind, no man ever having loved another as he did Farfrae.[12] It is at this point that his proud self-possession crumbles, and giving way altogether, he lets himself go "in the abandonment of remorse." This is followed by an "overpowering wish," though this is frustrated by Farfrae's departure from Casterbridge, to make it up with him; and this too breaks a habitual pattern, for he does not wish now to make restitution but "to attempt the well-nigh impossible task of winning pardon for his late mad attack" (348).

The first time Henchard says he loves anyone is when he admits to Farfrae that he has loved him. The fact that it is a man and not a woman who elicits this declaration and that he is a self-professed misogynist suggest that he is perhaps confessing to more than he consciously realizes. There is no overt homosexual tendency in his feeling for Farfrae, and the younger man is certainly quite unaware of such a possibility, but to view Henchard as a latent homosexual not only adds further depth to the

12. Robert Kiely, seemingly ignoring the earlier episode, also stresses the importance of the meeting of eyes in this scene, though he attributes a different significance to it: "This is the first scene," he says, "in which Henchard looks into Farfrae's eyes and sees, if only for a moment, that he might not be what he [has] made him out to be. . . . For Henchard, this glimpse of Farfrae as another helpless mortal rather than a cunning viper signals the beginning of an internal disintegration analogous to the one he has already suffered socially and financially" ("Vision and Viewpoint in *The Mayor of Casterbridge,*" 193–94).

powerful scene of their fight but also helps explain his relations with Susan and Lucetta. It throws a different light too on his supposed self-sufficiency and can perhaps be seen as his crowning self-deception. It is suggestive that a later writer and close reader of Hardy, D. H. Lawrence, would seem to have picked up such vibrations in the scene of the fight and then elaborated them in *Women in Love,* in which Birkin's latent homosexuality is more apparent. It is a moot point whether Lawrence was consciously following Hardy, but the parallels are notable.

In *Women in Love,* Birkin's desire for an "eternal union with a man too: another kind of love"[13] is depicted in his relationship with Gerald Crich. He proposes that they "swear a Blutbrüderschaft," that is, that they "swear to love each other" and to be "given to each other, organically" (206–7). The word takes on flesh, as it were, in the well-known wrestling encounter between the two men, in which they strip naked and seem "to drive their white flesh deeper and deeper against each other, as if they would break into a oneness" (270). Henchard may not propose a blood brotherhood to Farfrae, but he is clearly drawn to him, as I have noted, as a displacement of his dead brother; and he is also drawn to him as if to a woman who might be his complement. His "tigerish affection for the younger man" may also be seen as an unconscious wish to take him into himself in a different sense from that previously suggested. When the two men wrestle, at any rate, the struggle knits them together, as it does Birkin and Gerald: they rock and writhe "like trees in a gale"; and Farfrae "[locks] himself to his adversary" (347). And the wrestling, of course, is the occasion of Henchard's declaration of love for Farfrae.

Farfrae also correlates with Gerald Crich in a different connection, thus strengthening the overall parallel. Just as Gerald, the mining magnate, is responsible for the mechanization of his mines, so Farfrae recommends the introduction of a "new-fashioned agricultural implement called a horse-drill" not previously known in that part of the country (238). Where Elizabeth-Jane laments that "the romance of the sower is gone for good," Farfrae declares that it "will revolutionize sowing heerabout":

13. D. H. Lawrence, *Women in Love,* 481. Further page references to *Women in Love* are incorporated parenthetically in the text.

"Each grain," he proudly says, "will go straight to its intended place, and nowhere else whatever!" (240). Comparably, Gerald undertakes "the great reform" of his mines, bringing in new machinery from America, "great iron men" as they are called, and everything is run "on the most accurate and delicate scientific method" (230).

Hardy's critics, however, have tended to raise the question of a possible homosexual dimension to the relationship only to dismiss it. Elaine Showalter emphatically says "there is nothing homosexual in their intimacy; but there is certainly on Henchard's side an open, and, he later feels, incautious embrace of homosocial friendship, an insistent male bonding." She is echoed by Marjorie Garson, who insists that the nature of Henchard's feeling for Farfrae remains "undefined and unexaminable"; by contrast she maintains that it is Lawrence in *Women in Love* who has rewritten the wrestling match "to release its erotic potential." She does, however, grant that "it is possible to feel that there is an erotic dimension to Henchard's attraction for the younger man" but says that "Farfrae's failure to recognize the intensity of Henchard's emotion facilitates the repression of this dimension." Dale Kramer, on the other hand, in terms not altogether dissimilar to those I have proposed, grants the case for seeing a homosexual dimension in the relationship but then brusquely undercuts it when he says that "to turn Henchard into a latent homosexual whose downfall stems from an inability to maintain the latency may stimulate fresh readings of the novel, but it does not help us to understand either the formal or the emotional qualities of the novel." A recent account of this aspect of the novel continues to take back with one hand what it gives with the other: Robert Langbaum says that "Henchard's sudden passion for Farfrae, which is striking after his coolness toward women, suggests homosexuality on his side. . . . But their relationship does not develop in a way that bears out this hypothesis; for it quickly turns into male power rivalry once Farfrae breaks out of Henchard's proprietorship."[14]

It seems to me, however, that the parallels between *The Mayor of Casterbridge* and *Women in Love* are so striking that they cannot be

14. Showalter, "The Unmanning," 107; Garson, *Hardy's Fables*, 110; Dale Kramer, *Thomas Hardy: The Forms of Tragedy*, 86–87; Langbaum, *Thomas Hardy*, 129.

ignored. It is true that the homoerotic dimension of the male relationship in the earlier novel is much more muted, but when we read back from Lawrence to Hardy, the relationship of Henchard and Farfrae is placed in a context that brings out its undertones. The fight between them, at all events, puts an end to the relationship, and Henchard is driven back on himself into customary self-enclosure.

IV

Henchard's isolation at this stage is broken by the renewal of his relationship with Elizabeth-Jane, but that too goes through many vicissitudes. He first initiates a change in their relations three weeks after Susan's funeral by way of claiming her as his own, telling her *he* is her father, not Newson, and asking her to take his surname. He is swept by strong feeling when he speaks to her—he moves "like a great tree in a wind" (193)—but the feeling is proprietary, for his great satisfaction is that she is "his at last": "He was the kind of man whom some human object for pouring out his heat upon— were it emotive or were it choleric—was almost a necessity. The craving of his heart for the re-establishment of this tenderest human tie had been great during his wife's lifetime, and now he had submitted to its mastery without reluctance and without fear" (195). The use of the word "craving" relates this passage to one previously discussed that soon follows it, the passage that describes Henchard's turning to Lucetta in an unconscious craving to fill "an emotional void" within him. In the aftermath of Susan's death and his estrangement from Farfrae, we may assume it is likewise his inner void that impels him to claim Elizabeth-Jane. It is significant, however, that the bond he wishes to establish is described as the "tenderest human tie," more tender, that is, than the tie between husband and wife, for instance, which might seem to have a prior claim to the superlative. It is more tender to Henchard, no doubt, because he backs away from such tenderness in relation to a woman who is his sexual partner; but in relation to a daughter the masterful man allows himself to "[submit] to [the] mastery" of the craving. This would account too for his need to "pour out his heat" since he is a man more accustomed to taking in rather than giving out: whereas we must assume that in the nineteen years following the sale of Susan the expression of this need has been primarily "choleric," in relation to Elizabeth-Jane "his heat" may be safely "emotive."

On the very day Henchard tells Elizabeth-Jane he is her father, he discovers he is not. The proprietary foundation of his "tenderness" is so strong that it turns to revulsion when he has to contend with the fact she is not his: now seeing Newson's face in hers, he "[cannot] endure the sight of her," the terms of his disappointment suggesting that his feeling all along has been ingestive more than anything else: "Like Prester John's, his table had been spread, and infernal harpies had snatched up the food" (197). The heat that was to have been poured out on her is now suddenly dammed up (to continue the narrator's mixed metaphor), his manner becomes "constrained," and she is exposed instead to "coldness," though this soon "[breaks] out into open chiding" (200). And in a reversal of the food image, he now shows "a positive distaste for the presence of this girl not his own" (203). Elizabeth-Jane consequently grasps the opportunity provided by Lucetta to leave him, "his coldness [being] such that it [encourages] her to departure" (213). Having rejected her, Henchard falls into the compulsive pattern of all his relationships with women, being impelled then to make it up to her, and he arranges for her to have "a small annuity," so that he may be "independent" of her (not vice versa, we note) (213).

As suggested in respect to his relations with Lucetta, it is when Henchard is ill and depressed that his sense of self-sufficiency is weakened; and this proves to be the case too in his response to Elizabeth-Jane. Hearing that he is ill, she visits him; and though he resents the intrusion and tries to send her away, "the ice [is] broken," and he becomes "reconciled" to her visits. It is his iciness toward her as much as the constraint between them that is broken; symbolically, he has "caught cold," and "the effect, either of her ministrations or of her mere presence, [is] a rapid recovery." The effect, more significantly, is to take him out of himself, and his recovery marks the first stage of a movement toward her: "He no longer thought of emigration, and thought more of Elizabeth" (301).

After his fight with Farfrae and the fruitless attempt to overcome his adversary's distrust of him, Henchard is plunged in gloom:

[I]n the midst of his gloom [Elizabeth-Jane] seemed to him as a pin-point of light. He had liked the look of her face as she answered him from the stairs [about Lucetta's condition]. There had been affection in it, and above all things what he desired now was affection from anything that was good and pure. She was not his own; yet, for the first time, he had a faint dream that he might get to like her as his own,—if she would only continue to love him. (361)

Once again, as some years before with Lucetta, his gloom is potentially suicidal; feeling he has lost everything, he again invokes Job: "He cursed himself like a less scrupulous Job, as a vehement man will do when he loses self-respect, the last mental prop under poverty" (360). It is Elizabeth-Jane, the "pin-point of light," who seems to offer him the hope, however small, of life. It is to her that he now clings; and this, *pace* Showalter, is the turning point in his history, for what he now wants "above all things," quite beyond his habitual self-enclosure and his need for mastery, is love and affection. Moreover, his feeling for her, apparently shorn of his proprietary instinct, is not corrupted by the fact she is "not his own." That she really now means life to him is suggested when Newson suddenly appears in Casterbridge in search of her and confronts Henchard: the latter's "face and eyes [seem] to die" (366). Henchard's need of her is now so great that he lies to Newson, a rash, stupid lie, the old proprietary feeling once again mastering him, turning him to "a greedy exclusiveness in relation to her" as he seeks to preserve "his last treasure" (368). When he next sees her, he takes her hand "with anxious proprietorship" (370), an act that pleasantly surprises her, but it is regressive on his part, the same stuff proving to be obstinately tenacious.

Convinced that Newson will soon return to claim Elizabeth-Jane, and that life without her will be "unendurable" (371), Henchard becomes actively suicidal and sets out to drown himself at Ten Hatches. He is saved by the sight of his own image (the skimmington effigy) in the water beneath him, being convinced that "Somebody's hand" has intervened to stop him from taking his life (374). But his wish to die—like his actual death later—is testimony to the fact that what undoes a man is not close relationship but the lack of it, being thrown back on oneself alone in an unendurable darkness. When Elizabeth-Jane, sensing his state of mind, offers to live with him, he is "resuscitated" (374). The change in Henchard is perhaps best registered in the narrator's comment when, perceiving the growing closeness of Farfrae and Elizabeth-Jane, he begins to watch her "more narrowly": "Henchard was, by original make, the last

man to act stealthily, for good or evil. But the *solicitus timor* of his love—
the dependence upon Elizabeth's regard into which he had declined (or, in
another sense, to which he had advanced)—denaturalized him" (379–80).
Explicitly it is Henchard's stealth that is unnatural to him, but we may
say that it is love for Elizabeth-Jane, his opening of himself to her in love
and his dependence on her, that has "denaturalized" him. And when he
wrenches himself away from her in the knowledge that Newson's return
is imminent, he is able for only the second time in his life to express his
love: previously, and more ambiguously, it was to Farfrae; now for the first
time it is to a woman, it being the nonsexual nature of the relationship
that seemingly is liberating. "[D]on't let my sins, *when you know them all,*"
he says to her, "cause 'ee to quite forget that though I loved 'ee late I loved
'ee well" (387). He is driven to return to her wedding, hoping to obtain
her forgiveness for his deception of her and wanting now not just to hold
his own but "to hold his own *in her love*" (my emphasis): "[I]t was worth
the risk of repulse, ay, of life itself" (397).

When he is repulsed by her and denied her love, all that is left to him, as
he loses the will to eat, is the death he has risked. His despair brings out the
old stuff in him, and though his first thought is to spare Elizabeth-Jane,
he reverts in his will to a stance of needing no one—for anything:

MICHAEL HENCHARD'S WILL

That Elizabeth-Jane Farfrae be not told of my death, or made to
grieve on account of me.
    & that I be not bury'd in consecrated ground.
    & that no sexton be asked to toll the bell.
    & that nobody is wished to see my dead body.
    & that no murners walk behind me at my funeral.
    & that no flours be planted on my grave.
    & that no man remember me.
To this I put my name.   (409)

The completed testament of Henchard's life makes us revise our initial
placing of him. At first it seems that he is odd man out in Hardy's gallery
of male characters, conforming neither to one nor the other of the two
recurring male types in the novels. But the man who draws away from both

Susan and Lucetta and who can express love to a woman only in a filial context may well be regarded as a variant of Hardy's diffident man. And *The Mayor of Casterbridge* itself, indeed, is more in line with the novelist's continuing preoccupations than at first appears. It may not deal centrally with triangular sexual relationships, but Henchard as a male exemplar of the Diana complex looks both back to *Far from the Madding Crowd* and ahead to *The Woodlanders* and *Jude the Obscure* in their representations of a similar disability in their female protagonists. Furthermore, Henchard's desire for a close relationship with Farfrae, for all its latent homosexuality, may be considered a variant of heterosexual camaraderie. Hardy's fiction too, no less than Henchard, it emerges, would seem to be compounded of the same stuff.

6

The Woodlanders
Sorrow and Sickness of Heart at Last

I

Two episodes in *The Woodlanders*—those relating to the death of Mr. South and to his daughter, Marty, when she cuts her hair—draw attention to themselves by virtue of what retrospectively appears to be their unnecessary elaboration. Mr. South's death is no doubt of crucial importance in the plot since as a result of it Giles Winterborne forfeits his houses and so loses all hope of marrying Grace Melbury; furthermore, it also prepares the way for Giles's death in his lonely hut in the woods. But given that Mr. South is from the outset presented as seriously ill, his death could acceptably have been reported by means of a simple and direct statement of the fact by the narrator instead of its melodramatic linkage to the fate of a tree. The cutting of Marty's hair, which is the focus of the opening sequence of the novel, is handled effectively, but the prominence accorded it—unlike that of the death of her father—can hardly be attributed to its importance in the plot. It is only nominally the eventual means of bringing about Dr. Fitzpiers's separation from Mrs. Charmond, and their parting could easily have been made a matter of straightforward statement since the whole of their escapade in Europe is dealt with summarily and takes place offstage, as it were. The two episodes, however, prove to have an imaginative reverberation quite separate from their role in the plot. They point indeed to basic underlying conceptions in the narrative.

129

Mr. South has become obsessed with the idea that the tall tree outside his house, which is "exactly his own age," will blow down and kill him.[1] When the doctor orders the tree to be felled in order to rid him of his fear, and Mr. South registers its absence, he "[springs] up, speechless": "his eyes rose from their hollows till the whites showed all round, he fell back, and a bluish whiteness overspread him" (150). He dies that day, being so possessed by his kinship with the tree that he psychologically brings about his own death. But the novelist would seem to be intent on concretizing a wider parallel between the life of man and the life in nature. This is further implied in various ways. The "mutual interest" that Grace and Fitzpiers begin to take in each other, for instance, is said to grow "as imperceptibly as the twigs budded on the trees." When the narrator then goes on to describe the coming of spring, he has no need to specify the kind of interest they have aroused in each other: "Spring weather came on rather suddenly, the unsealing of buds that had long been swollen accomplishing itself in the space of one warm night. The rush of sap in the veins of the trees could almost be heard" (183). If a description such as this looks ahead to the opening of *The Rainbow* (as *The Mayor of Casterbridge* is linked in a different way to *Women in Love*), it also looks back to *Far from the Madding Crowd*, in which the flow of human passions similarly moves to the beat of the seasons. It seems at first as if this work, like the earlier one, will also have a pronounced pastoral ambience, for Little Hintock is said to be "one of those sequestered spots outside the gates of the world" (44), another "cool, sequester'd vale of life," that is, but this impression soon proves to be false. Where nature in *Far from the Madding Crowd*, despite eruptions of destructive force, is shown on the whole to be beneficent, in *The Woodlanders* it is for the most part virulent.

The tone is set early on in the narrative when "a lingering wind" brings to Marty's ear "the creaking sound of two overcrowded branches in the neighbouring wood, which were rubbing each other into wounds, and other vocalized sorrows of the trees" (54). Sorrow seems to seep into the very air: "There was now a distinct manifestation of morning in the air,

1. Hardy, *The Woodlanders*, 149. Further page references to this novel will be incorporated parenthetically in the text.

and presently the bleared white visage of a sunless winter day emerged like a dead-born child" (62). When Grace is in Giles's hut in the woods, a bough from a tree sometimes "[sways] so low as to smite the roof in a manner of a gigantic hand smiting the mouth of an adversary, to be followed by a trickle of rain, as blood from the wound" (374). And in the woods there is a continuous Darwinian battle for *Lebensraum:*

> Next were more trees close together, wrestling for existence, their branches disfigured with wounds resulting from their mutual rub-bings and blows. It was the struggle between these neighbours that [Grace] had heard in the night. Beneath them were the rotting stumps of those of the group that had been vanquished long ago, ris-ing from their mossy setting like black teeth from green gums. (378)

Nor is it only the narrator's vivid imagery that underlines the parallels between man's life and that of nature; the sense of this is also felt and directly expressed by one of the novel's characters. When Marty is planting trees with Giles, she says, "How they sigh directly we put 'em upright, though while they are lying down they don't sigh at all"; and then she adds: "It seems to me as if they sigh because they are very sorry to begin life in earnest—just as we be." She is rebuked by Giles, who looks "critically" at her and says, "You ought not to feel like that, Marty" (106), but the point is made, for all the whimsicality of the observation.

The specific thrust of the parallels surfaces in a passage that is at the ideological center of the narrative:

> They . . . skirted trunks with spreading roots whose mossed rinds made them like hands wearing green gloves. . . . On older trees still than these huge lobes of fungi grew like lungs. Here, as everywhere, the Unfulfilled Intention, which makes life what it is, was as obvious as it could be among the depraved crowds of a city slum. The leaf was deformed, the curve was crippled, the taper was interrupted; the lichen ate the vigour of the stalk, and the ivy slowly strangled to death the promising sapling. (93)

If the passage portrays the same kind of struggle for existence that is evident throughout, it focuses the parallels between man and nature in the "Unfulfilled Intention," which "makes life what it is," whether in the wood or in a city slum. That the Unfulfilled Intention is capitalized suggests that it does duty here for the Immanent Will, the ruling force in Hardy's universe. Since this force is unconscious, it should not be thought that life is made what it is because of malicious intent on its part. Things are as they are because of its inability to realize itself, and so the blight that descends on wood and slum alike is a failure of potentiality. Everywhere things fail to be what they might be, what they give promise of being.

The Unfulfilled Intention has a particular manifestation in human affairs in the institution of marriage that purportedly regulates sexual relations—and in the potentiality of love that ostensibly animates it. In Hardy, as we have seen, marriage means failed marriage; and this proves to be the case in *The Woodlanders* as well, as he ruefully remarked in his retrospective preface of 1895: "In the present novel, as in one or two others of this series which involve the question of matrimonial divergence, the immortal puzzle—given the man and woman, how to find a basis for their sexual relation—is left where it stood . . ." (39). The question of such "divergence" is wickedly emblematized before Grace and Fitzpiers marry. They are standing together in the wood near the remains of a fire that some workers have used to make their tea when "two large birds," which have "either been roosting above their heads or nesting there," tumble "one over the other into the hot ashes at their feet, apparently engrossed in a desperate quarrel that prevented the use of their wings." They quickly part and fly up "with a singed smell" to be seen no more, but Marty South is there to comment on such nesting: "That's the end of what is called love," she says (192). The birds thus preside over an idea of marriage as a getting burned prior to a separation. And after their marriage, both Grace and Fitzpiers emphasize the point for us: "Sorrow and sickness of heart at last," he says, are "the end of all love, according to Nature's law" (248), and she wonders if there is "one world in the universe where the fruit [has] no worm, and marriage no sorrow" (260).[2]

2. The ramifications of Mr. South's death and of "the Unfulfilled Intention" have not always been recognized. Cf. Mary Jacobus, who says "the unexplained prominence of the episode [the felling of the tree] makes one return to it as something more. On it Hardy

The particular cause of matrimonial divergence in *The Woodlanders* is pointed by the epigraph to the novel, which is given more than usual weight since Hardy specially wrote it himself:[3]

> "Not boskiest bow'r,
> When hearts are ill affin'd,
> Hath tree of pow'r
> To shelter from the wind!"

There is no refuge, we are to understand, from a marriage that goes wrong, no remedy for a couple who are badly matched. And the mismatching, as in the preceding novels, is a consequence of the woman's choice of partner, the more especially since she is called on to choose between two men who are strongly opposed.

The note of mismatching is struck in the opening pages of the narrative in the description of the first human figure to appear on the deserted country highway: "It could be seen by a glance at his rather finical style of dress that he did not belong to the country proper" (41–42). The man is Barber Percomb, and he is on his way to Little Hintock from the nearby town in order to persuade Marty to cut off her hair for a wig that he is to make for Mrs. Charmond, Marty's hair being "the exact shade" of the lady's (50). This episode, which occupies the first three chapters of the novel, is the second, as noted above, that seems to be given an undue prominence in the narrative.

Marty initially rejects the barber's offer of two sovereigns for her hair, saying to him, "I value my looks too much to spoil 'em" (51). But then she overhears Mrs. Melbury say that Giles "adores" Grace and Mr. Melbury declare that he intends Grace to marry Giles. She herself is in love with

---

pegs the obsessive quality—the adherence to an *idée fixe*—which characterises life in Little Hintock . . ." ("Tree and Machine: *The Woodlanders,*" 125); and Noorul Hasan, who states that "the passage [describing the Unfulfilled Intention] certainly expresses Hardy's keen awareness of the cruelty in nature, but to regard it as a focal point of what the novel is trying to say as a whole is to grant it a structural significance it does not possess" (*Thomas Hardy: The Sociological Imagination,* 83).

3. In a letter to Florence Henniker of August 12, 1895, Hardy said: "I have been looking for a motto for the title page of the 'Woodlanders' & not being able to find one, composed it" (*Collected Letters,* 2:85).

Giles, but she not unreasonably concludes now that "Giles Winterborne is not for [her]!":

> She returned to her cottage. The sovereigns were staring at her from the looking-glass as she had left them. With a preoccupied countenance, and with tears in her eyes, she got a pair of scissors and began mercilessly cutting off the long locks of her hair, arranging and tying them with their points all one way as the barber had directed. Upon the pale scrubbed deal of the coffin-stool table they stretched like waving and ropy weeds over the washed white bed of a stream.
> She would not turn again to the little looking-glass out of humanity to herself, knowing what a deflowered visage would look back at her and almost break her heart; she dreaded it as much as did her own ancestral goddess the reflection in the pool after the rape of her locks by Loke the Malicious. (58)

The reference to Loke the Malicious imparts a sense of wanton destructiveness to Marty's act, for Loke, the Penguin editor informs us, is "the god of destruction in old Norse mythology" (452). The act, furthermore, is given a strong sexual connotation by aligning it with the rape of the goddess's locks and having it issue in "a deflowered visage." What Marty is deliberately and "mercilessly" doing is destroying her sexual attractiveness, and this is presented as a violation of self. "I've made myself ugly—and hateful—that's what I've done," she says in response to Giles's remark that her denuded head "looks like an apple upon a gate-post" (60). Her act, indeed, has suicidal overtones, as the startling image of those "waving and ropy weeds," expressive of a luxuriant sexuality and seeming to have a life of their own, suggests, for it is as if they lie stretched in a drowning body of water, with the "coffin-stool" made ready. Marty, in short, dies to sex at the outset of the narrative, and at its end she is left mourning the dead Giles in virginal forlornness. But the sense of self-violation is so strong that it also reaches out beyond this scene to encompass the flight from sex in Grace's marriage to Fitzpiers. In a number of respects Marty may be viewed as a double of Grace—she too is "a daughter of the woods," she too is in love with Giles—and this opening episode serves to frame Grace's story.[4]

4. A number of critics take a similar view of Marty's act though they do not attribute a further significance to it. Cf. J. I. M. Stewart, who says Marty "seems practically as well as

II

Having completed *Far from the Madding Crowd* in 1874, Hardy said (in the disguised autobiography) that he then "thought of" a "woodland story," which "later took shape in *The Woodlanders.*" He put this aside, however, because he declared he "had not the slightest intention of writing for ever about sheepfarming" and instead made "a plunge in a new and untried direction," producing a social comedy, *The Hand of Ethelberta,* which appeared in 1876. But in November 1885 he noted that he had nonetheless "gone back to [his] original plot for 'The Woodlanders' after all," and the novel was published in 1887. Referring to this chronology, Peter J. Casagrande says that "if *The Woodlanders* seems somewhat out of place among *The Mayor, Tess,* and *Jude,* it can be seen to be very much at home in the company of the *Return* and the *Greenwood Tree,* which it strikingly resembles in structure and in theme."[5] This is suggestive, and it certainly would seem that Grace, the central character in *The Woodlanders,* is imaginatively connected both to Fancy Day of *Under the Greenwood Tree* and to Clym Yeobright of *The Return of the Native.* Grace follows the path that Fancy decides not to take in preferring her superior, educated suitor to her simple, country lover; like Clym, she is a returned native, though, unlike him, she gives way to parental pressure in the choice of a mate.[6]

What Casagrande leaves out, no doubt because it does not conform to the return of a native pattern, is *Far from the Madding Crowd.* But *The Woodlanders* was conceived in the same creative burst as *Far from the Madding Crowd,* and it seems to me that its deepest, most fundamental affinities are with this work. This results in a curious two-level narrative. The upper, more superficial level is devoted to the return of the native,

---

symbolically to be accepting sexlessness" (*Thomas Hardy,* 143); Mary Jacobus, who sees her as "[desexing] herself in mourning as well as self-abnegation (Giles is not for her)" ("Tree and Machine," 120); and Ian Gregor, who regards her act as a "ruthless self-mutilation, her plundering of her selfhood" (*Great Web,* 147).

5. Hardy, *Life and Work,* 105, 182; Casagrande, "The Shifted 'Centre of Altruism' in *The Woodlanders:* Thomas Hardy's Third 'Return of a Native,'" 105.

6. William H. Matchett also comments on the connection between Grace and Clym, though he does so in a different respect: "Grace is related to Clym . . . , being also a native who has returned to discover that she has unfitted herself for the life she must lead" ("*The Woodlanders,* or Realism in Sheep's Clothing," 252).

who is faced with a choice between what Casagrande calls "an 'alien' . . . and a 'native' lover." But the choice for Grace, more profoundly and more decisively, is between two men who represent opposed sexual attitudes and options.[7] In this respect Giles and Fitzpiers take off directly from Oak and Troy, and Hardy once again plays variations on his basic male sexual typology. Nor is it only the men who come out of *Far from the Madding Crowd*. In his portrayal of Grace, as we shall see, Hardy makes yet another attempt to come to grips with a kind of female sexual response that can subvert a marriage as surely as the proclivities of a male philanderer; in this respect Grace is a blood sister to Bathsheba. But because the emphasis in the narrative is on the superficial and more obvious level, *The Woodlanders* is weaker than both *Far from the Madding Crowd* and *The Return of the Native,* and its fabricated quality is sadly apparent in such scenes as the meeting in the woods of Grace and Mrs. Charmond or the horse-sharing ride of Mr. Melbury and Fitzpiers.

Giles, like Oak, is a decent, honorable, faithful man, and like him, when he falls in love, he does so irrevocably.[8] The trouble is that Grace, when she returns to Little Hintock from the superior schooling her father has provided for her, has been educated beyond Giles and simple country ways. Her father feels she is too good for such a lover, and she begins to think so too. The first part of the novel is devoted to showing how socially inept Giles is in comparison with her and how far above him she is intellectually. But the tameness of these scenes would seem to suggest that Hardy was not deeply engaged by this aspect of his theme.

Giles is more interesting as a man than as a native of Little Hintock. In the opening description of him, his marked physical characteristics prove

7. Casagrande, "Shifted 'Centre,' " 106. David Lodge, like Casagrande, maintains the central conflict is that between alien and native: "From out of [the] civilised world, into the woods . . . come strangers, bringing with them habits, attitudes and values that disturb and unsettle the traditional life of the woodland. Hardy's original title for the novel, 'Fitzpiers at Hintock,' indicates that this was, for him, the central source of conflict and interest in the story" (*"The Woodlanders:* A Darwinian Pastoral Elegy," 80).

8. A number of critics have noted the resemblance between Giles and Oak. Cf. Eugene Goodheart, "Thomas Hardy and the Lyrical Novel," 220; George S. Fayen, "Hardy's *The Woodlanders:* Inwardness and Memory," 94; Frank R. Giordano, "The Martyrdom of Giles Winterborne," 65; and David Ball, "Tragic Contradiction in Hardy's *The Woodlanders,"* 18.

to be a trusty sign of what he is: "The door was flung back, and there stepped in upon the mat a man not particularly young for a lover, nor particularly mature for a person of affairs—each of which functions he in some degree discharged. There was reserve in his glance, and restraint upon his mouth" (59). What marks Giles is his tightness, the extent to which he is held in, as the reserve and restraint apparent in his face tellingly reveal, a tightness that makes him a lover only "in some degree." Though he is also said to be notably "self-contained" (59), he should be distinguished in this respect from Henchard in *The Mayor of Casterbridge,* for, constantly yearning for Grace, it is not a personal self-sufficiency that he asserts; rather, it is a habitual self-restraint that makes him sexually unadventurous and ineffective. When they were children, "[Grace's] mouth was somewhat more ready to receive a kiss from his than was his to bestow one," and this childhood reluctance develops into an adult timidity, for when he goes to meet Grace on her return, he is "diffident" in his approach to her, merely trusting to "a promise rather implied than given" (229). His "self-control," in a word, is "shy" (92). What it is exactly that holds him back is not pursued in the narrative, his inhibition functioning as a given, but there is perhaps a hint that he may be fearful of the strength of his own feelings: when he shows the Melburys the horse intended for Grace and reveals that he has "bought her . . . because she has been used to carry a lady," he tells them this "with warmth so severely repressed as to seem indifference" (128). His physicality runs to trees rather than to a woman, as is suggested when he is engaged in planting: "Winterborne's fingers were endowed with a gentle conjuror's touch in spreading the roots of each little tree, resulting in a sort of caress under which the delicate fibres all laid themselves out in their proper directions for growth" (106). Whereas a quarter of the trees planted by the journeymen soon die, all Giles's trees flourish, he being better able to foster their growth than that of his relationship with Grace: "He had a marvellous power of making trees grow. . . . [T]here was a sort of sympathy between himself and the fir, oak, or beech that he was operating on; so that the roots took hold of the soil in a few days" (105).

The kind of relation that exists between Giles and Grace is epitomized in the view Marty has of them as they travel home together on the day of

Grace's return: "Then . . . she dimly saw their vehicle drawing near the lowest part of the incline, their heads slightly bent towards each other; drawn together, no doubt, by their souls; as the heads of a pair of horses well in hand are drawn in by the rein" (79). The imagery is brilliant. Whatever closeness "draws them together" is nonphysical, a matter of long association and of the spirit, though the gap left by their inclination to each other will grow steadily wider; what is clear is that it will not be bridged by sexual contact, for the animal in both of them is strongly restrained, quite reined in. Apart from his inhibitions, Giles, it would seem, is simply incapable of firing her into passion: when Grace's father increases the pressure on her to break with Giles and extorts a promise from her not to meet Giles without Mr. Melbury's knowledge, we are told that "the years-long regard that she had had for [Giles] was not kindled by her return into a flame of sufficient brilliancy to make her rebellious" (140). This is the bottom line of their separation.

The narrator's comment about the lack of fire is made on the occasion of their parting when Giles is lopping the branches of the tree that so disturbs Mr. South. Grace refuses to answer his greeting, and so he stolidly works on, "climbing higher into the sky, and cutting himself off more and more from all intercourse with the sublunary world" (140). He certainly cuts himself off from all intercourse with her. When she informs him that her father wants her to break off their "engagement or understanding," he accepts this in "an enfeebled voice." Strong man though he is, Giles's problem is that he is too feeble. Like Oak, he has all the virtues and no sexual charge or drive, as is underlined by the narrator:

> Had Giles, instead of remaining still, immediately come down from the tree to her, would she have continued in that filial, acquiescent frame of mind which she had announced to him as final? If it be true, as women themselves have declared, that one of their sex is never so much inclined to throw in her lot with a man for good and all as five minutes after she has told him such a thing cannot be, the probabilities are that something might have been done by the appearance of Winterborne on the ground beside Grace. But he continued motionless and silent in that gloomy Niflheim or fogland which involved him, and she proceeded on her way. (141)

The editor's note tells us that "in old Norse mythology, Niflheim was a cold underworld of mist and darkness. Here dwelt those who had died unfulfilled, from illness or old age, as Giles is to do" (455). If this is the decisive moment in his relationship with Grace, Giles dies unfulfilled from sheer incapacity rather—an incapacity that is magnified by the sexual magnetism of his rival, Fitzpiers.

Fitzpiers is an intellectual. As Mr. Melbury says, he is "a gentleman fond of science, and philosophy, and poetry, and, in fact, every kind of knowledge" (69). Mr. Melbury may be overawed by him, but Fitzpiers is certainly fond of quoting poetry, particularly Shelley; and even the narrator says that "though his aims were desultory Fitzpiers's mental constitution was not without its creditable side; a real inquirer he honestly was at times" (172). His interests align him with intellectuals in earlier novels, such as Knight in *A Pair of Blue Eyes* and Clym Yeobright in *The Return of the Native,* and this makes for an interesting crossing of lines in Hardy's male sexual typology, for the earlier characters are in the honorable mold and Fitzpiers is a libertine. He is also well born, being descended from "a line . . . once among the greatest, a family which had conferred its name upon a neighbouring village [to Little Hintock]" (211). In this respect he looks ahead to Hardy's next novel and to his most famous libertine, Alec d'Urberville, though his "line" is spurious.

He also looks back to Oak, for though the sheep farmer is as constant in his affections as Fitzpiers is errant, they are both propelled into love in the same way. Fitzpiers tells Giles:

> "[P]eople living insulated, as I do by the solitude of this place, get charged with emotive fluid like a Leyden jar with electric, for want of some conductor at hand to disperse it. Human love is a subjective thing—the essence itself of man, as that great thinker Spinoza says— *ipsa hominis essentia*—it is a joy accompanied by an idea which we project against any suitable object in the line of our vision, just as the rainbow iris is projected against an oak, ash, or elm tree indifferently. So that if any other young lady had appeared instead of [Grace], I should have felt just the same interest in her, and have quoted precisely the same lines from Shelley about her, as about this one I saw. Such miserable creatures of circumstance are we all!" (165)

Fitzpiers's reference to Spinoza no doubt buttresses his intellectual cre-
dentials, but his description of love harks back more directly to Hardy's
conception of the void, first delineated in respect to Oak and pursued in
subsequent novels, as we have seen. It is an inner void that determines
that feeling should be "projected" against the first suitable object, and so
directs Fitzpiers's attention to Grace. It is notable, however, that whereas
the process is usually depicted as a taking in to the self, a filling in of
an inner emptiness, in Fitzpiers's case this is additionally viewed as a
compulsive discharge of feeling. It also has the effect of "[enkindling] his
soul with a flame that blinds his eyes" (173): Fitzpiers's passionate nature,
that is, is fired by Grace in a way that is foreign to Giles; in turn the flame
kindles Grace in contradistinction to Giles's inability to do this. But, as in
The Return of the Native, the flame of passion "blinds his eyes"; he is quite
unaware of what he is letting himself in for by pursuing Grace, and not
only in respect to what he comes to regard as a social lowering consequent
on the connection.

The relationship between Grace and Fitzpiers is initiated when she
visits his home on a mission for Grammer Oliver. She finds him asleep
but then is surprised by what she sees in a mirror: "An indescribable thrill
passed through her as she perceived that the eyes of the reflected image
were open, gazing wonderingly at her. Under the curious unexpectedness
of the sight she became as if spell-bound, almost powerless to turn her
head and regard the original. However, by an effort she did turn, when
there he lay asleep the same as before" (176). Fitzpiers is between sleep
and waking, and after momentarily opening his eyes he "[relapses] into
unconsciousness, if indeed he [has] ever been positively awake" (176). It
is of some significance that the two should stare first at a reflection of the
partner they are to marry—not the reality that marriage will disclose. "I
did not see you directly," he says to Grace, "but reflected in the glass. I
thought, what a lovely creature! The design is for once carried out. Nature
has at last recovered her lost union with the Idea!" (179). A further irony
of the situation is that the "design" Nature will in fact recover is that of
"the Unfulfilled Intention." But perhaps the main point of the scene is the
effect his condition has on her. She is as if "spell-bound," a response that
is glossed by her later reaction to a similar stillness in the scene outside her

room at dawn: "The tree-trunks, the road, the out-buildings, the garden, every object, wore that aspect of mesmeric passivity which the quietude of daybreak lends to such scenes" (219). From then on (until she breaks free) Grace is compelled by Fitzpiers, mesmerized by a different kind of magnetism, his sexual power.

His power over her is dramatized at the end of the Midsummer-eve ceremony or "enchantment." Lying in wait for her, he puts out his arms as she "[bursts] upon him" and "[captures] her in a moment, as if she had been a bird," as if, indeed, she were one of the birds they had just previously watched fall into the fire. Captured, "she [rests] on him like one utterly mastered," as Bathsheba was mastered by Troy, though in this case the flashing sword is not actually brandished. "You are in my arms, dearest," he says, "and I am going to claim you, and keep you there all our two lives" (198). The Midsummer "enchantment," which is designed to give the village girls "a glimpse of their future partners for life" (194), is thus borne out in at least one instance and in more than one respect. Since Grace's father is constantly at her to favor Fitzpiers, it is inevitable that "so much pressure" should "produce some displacement" of Giles (213); but the actual displacement, as on the originating occasion in the novels in *A Pair of Blue Eyes,* is brought about by the superior force of one suitor in comparison with the other: Fitzpiers, we are told, exercises over her "an almost psychic influence, as it is called" (210). He is "the handsome, coercive, irresistible Fitzpiers" (216). He is also no mean rake. No sooner does Grace leave him on the night of the Midsummer-eve ceremony than he runs off after Suke Damson, "the hoydenish maiden of the hamlet," and it is "daybreak" before the couple reenter Little Hintock (198–200). We are to understand that the affair with her continues throughout the period of his courtship of Grace. He is the kind of man, the narrator says, who is ready to play with a woman "as a toy" (173), though he qualifies this by more charitably adding that he is capable of "spreading the same conjoint emotion" over a number of women at the same time and that the "love of men like [him] is unquestionably of such quality as to bear division and transference": "He had indeed once declared . . . that on one occasion he had noticed himself to be possessed by five distinct infatuations at the same time" (265–66). His capacity for such division is demonstrated in the passion he conceives for Mrs. Charmond within a few months of his marriage to Grace.

What is puzzling, for the narrator is reticent about this, is why Fitzpiers becomes so quickly disenchanted with Grace, seemingly being unable to spare her even some crumbs of a conjoint emotion. An initial clue is provided by Grace's sense that her husband is "disposed to avoid her" and that "the scrupulous civility of mere acquaintanceship [has] crept into his manner" (256). This points to a feeling on his part that they have failed to establish a real intimacy, and the fact that he "often [sits] up late" seems to bear this out. But Grace is inclined to attribute her sense of distance from him to a different cause, and her view appears to be endorsed by the narrator, who pronounces on the issue in the distinctive tones of the seer:

> Grace was amazed at the mildness of the anger which the suspi-
> cion [of her husband's involvement with Mrs. Charmond] engen-
> dered in her. She was but little excited, and her jealousy was languid
> even to death. It told tales of the nature of her affection for him. In
> truth, her ante-nuptial regard for Fitzpiers had been rather of the
> quality of awe towards a superior being than of tender solicitude for a
> lover. It had been based upon mystery and strangeness—the mystery
> of his past, of his knowledge, of his professional skill, of his beliefs.
> When this structure of ideals was demolished by the intimacy of
> common life, and she found him as merely human as the Hintock
> people themselves, a new foundation was in demand for an enduring
> and staunch affection—a sympathetic interdependence, wherein
> mutual weaknesses are made the grounds of a defensive alliance.
> Fitzpiers had furnished nothing of that single-minded confidence
> and truth out of which alone such a second union could spring. . . .
> (258)

What Grace discovers here—to her amazement—is that, though it was his passion for her that mastered her, her sexual feeling for him is not very strong, as the mildness of her anger and the languidness of her jealousy now indicate to her. But if the absence of strong feeling on her part tells a (surprising) tale of "the nature of her affection for him," it also bears witness to what she has brought to him in the marriage, though neither she nor the narrator seems to take account of this. The reflections that follow are characterized by the same kind of half-truth: they may have their own validity, but more needs to be said. If it was "awe towards a superior being" that drew her to Fitzpiers, it is not only "tender solicitude for a lover" that this seems to have displaced, nor is solicitude the only alternative to such awe. If "a new foundation" is needed for "an enduring and staunch affection" in their relationship, this is not merely because the awe has disappeared in "the intimacy of common life" but because the relationship has never had a firm sexual basis. The desired "second union" that should be founded on "a sympathetic interdependence" seems to be a new version of camaraderie, the kind of enduring relationship that is distinguished from one based on passion. But the passion that is "evanescent as steam," we are now led to register, never seems to have been brought to the boil in the marriage of Grace and Fitzpiers. It is the absence of such a second union, it is now asserted, that makes for the failed marriage, but we are made to see that there are other factors at issue.

On the lamentable occasion when Grace and Mrs. Charmond meet and Grace has her unexpected revelation—" 'O, my great God!' she exclaimed, thunderstruck at a revelation transcending her utmost suspicion. 'He's had you! Can it be—can it be!' " (302) (while we wonder what she imagined had been going on), she also tells her rival Fitzpiers will tire of her: "He'll get tired of you soon, as tired as can be—you don't know him so well as I!—and then you may wish you had never seen him!" (297). This says much about Grace's own resentment at the way Fitzpiers would seem to have tired of her, and she appears to imply that this has happened because he is that kind of man. But what follows suggests it is not unconnected with the sort of woman she is.

After Fitzpiers leaves home and informs Grace that he is going on a journey, his hat is found in the woods; that night a cuckoo's cry wakes her: " 'O—he is coming!' she cried, and in her terror sprang clean out of bed upon the floor" (336). "Terror" is a strong word, notably in excess of the distaste she may be presumed to feel at the prospect of having to renew conjugal relations with a renegade husband; what it expresses is her uncontrollable need to flee the marriage bed. This impression is strengthened when sometime later he announces he is returning home, indicating that he has separated from Mrs. Charmond, for her response once again implies more than moral revulsion on her part. Her father urges her to take him back, but the idea of his "reinstatement" strikes her as "intolerable," and she becomes "almost hysterical" (362). When her husband actually appears on the scene, she runs away from him:

> A spasm passed through Grace. The Daphnean instinct, exceptionally strong in her as a girl, had been revived by her widowed seclusion; and it was not lessened by her affronted sentiments towards the comer, and her regard for another man. She opened some little ivory tablets that lay on the dressing-table, scribbled in pencil on one of them, "I am gone to visit one of my school-friends" . . . and, not three minutes after [her husband's] voice had been heard, her slim form . . . might have been seen passing out of the back door of Melbury's house. (362–63)

It is interesting that—as in analogous circumstances in *Far from the Madding Crowd*—the narrator should again have recourse to mythology in order to account for the behavior of the heroine, the mythological reference, in the comparative openness of its connotation, serving perhaps to conceal as well as reveal and so ensure that the question of female sexuality should remain decently veiled. Grace's "Daphnean instinct," at all events, suggests that she is the kind of woman for whom the preservation of her virginity, her maiden self-sufficiency, means more than life itself (in ordinary terms), for it is at her own entreaty that Daphne is changed into a tree when pursued by Apollo. The instinct, which is said to have been "exceptionally strong" in Grace "as a girl," would not seem to have diminished in force in her maturity, for it now impels her to precipitate flight from her husband. We may assume, indeed, since instincts do not easily die, that it not only "revived" in her "widowed seclusion" but also, prior to that, survived in her marriage and that she, like Bathsheba in *Far from the Madding Crowd,* was unable psychologically, if not physically, to open herself to her husband. There is no doubt that, in Hardy's imagination, Grace is another Bathsheba, for she is later said to have "more of Artemis than of Aphrodite in her constitution" (381), more, that is, of Diana, who was widely identified with Artemis. Daphne thus merges with Diana, and we may accordingly suppose that Fitzpiers, like Troy, has had to suffer an unresponsive wife and that it is not in sheer promiscuity that he turns from Grace to pastures new. We may also suppose that for Grace, as for Bathsheba, marriage entails a "perception of self-sacrifice" and that it is a violation of self—one more profound than Marty's cutting of her hair.[9]

III

As Grace is watching Fitzpiers ride off on one of his visits to Mrs. Charmond, Giles comes up:

> He looked and smelt like Autumn's very brother, his face being sunburnt to wheat-colour, his eyes blue as corn-flowers, his sleeves and leggings dyed with fruit-stains, his hands clammy with the sweet juice of apples. . . . Her heart rose from its late sadness like a released bough; her senses revelled in the sudden lapse back to Nature unadorned. The consciousness of having to be genteel because of her husband's profession, the veneer of artificiality which she had acquired at the fashionable schools, were thrown off, and she became the crude country girl of her latent early instincts. (261)

The passage seemingly implies the mismatch of Grace's marriage to Fitzpiers and emphasizes her natural affinity to Giles. He is "Nature unadorned," suffused and permeated with it, "Autumn's very brother." If he later rises "upon her memory as the fruit-god and the wood-god in alternation," she herself is then said to be "the elastic-nerved daughter of the woods" (340–41). Artificiality and sophistication, we are to understand, have repressed her natural bent, forced it out of line, and so the meeting with Giles is liberating, restoring her elasticity and freeing her from depression "like a released bough." Grace and Giles may thus seem to be a natural pair, "two whom nature [has] striven to join together in earlier days" (340), but we know that nature is productive ultimately of the Unfulfilled Intention and that a union between them would be no better than that between Grace and Fitzpiers. Poised between Giles and Fitzpiers, Grace is faced with unrewarding choices, but like all Hardy's

9. In contradistinction, Rosemary Sumner says that "Grace's sexual instincts, though uncertain in the choice of object because of her lack of secure identity, seem to be quite strong and fairly uninhibited . . ." (*Thomas Hardy,* 94).

heroines, she is the one who exercises choice, and she should not be seen, as Giles inclines to see her, merely as "the victim of her father's well-meant but blundering policy" (356). Moreover, though she identifies with Giles in his naturalness in the quoted passage, her sense of being at one with nature is for her also a "lapsing back," a falling off from what she has become and therefore something she cannot sustain, as is vividly brought home to both Giles and herself when he takes her to the simple tavern at Sherton. Living with Fitzpiers, she has "imbibed" his tastes to such an extent that she feels "humiliated" in the tavern and "shrinks" from it (348). Where she may be supposed to shrink from Fitzpiers sexually, she shrinks from Giles and his ambience socially, the "latent early instincts" of the "country girl" asserting themselves in the first instance and not being sufficiently strong in the second.

On the occasion that Giles figures as "Autumn's very brother," it becomes clear to Grace that he knows of Fitzpiers's relationship with Mrs. Charmond, and old feeling stirs in both of them:

> Her abandonment to the seductive hour and scene after her sense of ill-usage, her revolt for the nonce against social law, her passionate desire for primitive life, may have showed in her face. Winterborne was looking at her, his eyes lingering on a flower that she wore in her bosom. Almost with the abstraction of a somnambulist he stretched out his hand and gently caressed the flower.
>
> She drew back. "What are you doing, Giles Winterborne?" she exclaimed with severe surprise. (262)

This is one of those quiet little scenes at which Hardy excels, and it epitomizes the second phase of the relationship of the reluctant lovers. Grace is not the kind of woman who is given to "abandonment" or to "passionate desire," and so when the urge arises in her to let go, she is seduced by the "hour and scene," not the man, and her desire is for "primitive life" rather than for Giles. Consequently, her "revolt . . . against social law" remains strictly—and safely—"for the nonce." Giles, on the other hand, can bring himself only to caress the flower she wears, not her, touching it gently as he does the roots of trees and stretching out his hand in "abstraction" both from her and from himself, for he moves unconsciously, like "a somnambulist." But even this is too much for Grace, who quickly "draws back."

Grace and Giles remain as timid with each other even when Fitzpiers goes abroad with Mrs. Charmond. It is only when Grace believes she is about to obtain a divorce from her husband and is "on the verge of freedom" that she invites Giles to kiss her (354). Though he knows that the hope of a divorce has come to nothing, he cannot resist and gives her a "long embrace and passionate kiss" (355). This is the one and only time that Giles overcomes his inhibiting self-restraint, and the moral is clear—the importance of the difference between aliens and natives notwithstanding—for Grace then says to him: "Giles, if you had only shown half the boldness before I married that you show now, you would have carried me off for your own, first instead of second" (356). When she learns the truth about the divorce, she recoils into the "existence of [a] self-constituted nun," and her feeling for Giles is "rarefied" into "an ethereal emotion" that has "little to do with living and doing" (359). It is from such an existence that she goes to Giles's hut when she runs away from Fitzpiers on his return, but in effect she then adheres to the same constitution. Rather than intrude on her privacy and her sanctity as a married woman, Giles generously gives up his hut to her, even though he is ill and so condemns himself to death by staying outside in the rain. It is a touching scene if one can accept its premises, but it is undercut by the symbolic force of the locked door that stands between them, the door behind which, with her Daphnean instinct, she has taken refuge and keeps closed until it is too late, the door that he, in "the purity of his nature, his freedom from the grosser passions, his scrupulous delicacy" (381), has himself locked.[10]

After Giles's death his noble self-sacrifice is further undercut when on one occasion Grace is said to think of "poor Giles's 'frustrate ghost'"

---

10. Cf. J. I. M. Stewart, who says "Grace is right [not to take Giles into the hut]—if only because Giles is not a Mellors. To take him would have been a kind of rape—a violation of his personality" (*Thomas Hardy,* 139); and Ian Gregor, whose view of Grace is closer to mine: "[Grace draws] on [Giles's] companionship without committing [herself] as a lover, a relationship which instinctually she withdraws from, as his sharing of the hut would have disconcertingly revealed" (*Great Web,* 147).

(415). It is clearly the narrator, not Grace, who quotes from Browning's "The Statue and the Bust" here, and in doing so, he offers perhaps his sharpest (if most indirect) comment on Giles's attitude to Grace.[11] But Giles's relationship with Grace is after all a two-way affair; and, just as the narrator, in summing up the nature of the failure of Grace's marriage to Fitzpiers, confines himself to only half the truth, so here he again tells only half the story. That he is indeed omitting something is indicated by the fact that the very phrase he quotes is only half the phrase in the poem:

> And the sin I impute to each frustrate ghost
> Is—the unlit lamp and the ungirt loin,
> Though the end in sight was a vice, I say.
> You of the virtue (we issue join)
> How strive you? *De te, fabula!*

The sin of the frustrate ghosts in the poem is equally that of the lady and the Duke. There is even a parallel between the life of Grace and that of the lady: if Grace is like a "self-constituted nun," the lady watches the world outside her window "like a convent's chronicler." And the virtue of the lovers in both cases, of the woman as well as the man, ultimately counts for little beside their lack of daring and their failure to consummate their love. The seer may restrict his (camouflaged) criticism to Giles, but we see that Grace too should be included in it. Their mutual story likewise constitutes a sad fable of "the unlit lamp and the ungirt loin"—in short, of the Unfulfilled Intention.[12]

Since Grace has so decisively been shown to be a devotee of Diana, the final problem posed by the narrative is why Fitzpiers should wish to return to her—and since he has so basely abandoned her, why she should

---

11. John Bayley, however, maintains that "Winterborne is the only rustic in his work who is idealized by Hardy" ("A Social Comedy? On Re-reading *The Woodlanders,*" 9).

12. Merryn Williams believes it is a fear of commitment that accounts for Grace's behavior: "Naturally frigid, [Grace] has rejected [Giles] before her marriage, kept him at a distance afterwards . . . and finally driven him into the storm. . . . Her 'selfish correctness' is, in its own way, as negative and cruel as Fitzpiers's promiscuity. They are, in fact related, as both of them spring from a fear of deep commitments" (*Thomas Hardy,* 166).

be ready to take him back. When they meet, he is surprised to find that "though she had been married to him" she could "yet be so coy," but this holds "a certain fascination" for him (411). In like manner it is her apparent reluctance to renew the relationship, her very inaccessibility, that draws a man such as Fitzpiers, serving as a test of his own powers. This can be taken to apply as well to her more fundamental inaccessibility. And he proceeds subtly; he carefully exercises "restraint" in order "not to kill the delicate bud of returning confidence," the very need for such restraint "[feeding] his flame" (425). He tells her, moreover, that though he loves her more than ever before, his feeling for her has changed: "It is a different kind of love altogether," he says. "Less passionate; more profound. It has nothing to do with the material conditions of the object at all; much to do with her character and goodness, as revealed by closer observation" (409). What he seems to be proposing is the substitution of something very much like camaraderie for passion, passion once again in Hardy having supposedly been destructive since it has ostensibly led to their separation and has indeed caused the death of Mrs. Charmond. Fitzpiers, however, may be taken to be speaking too glibly, for a little later we are told that he "passionately [desires]" to take her "to his arms anew" (417).

As far as Grace is concerned, since Giles is dead and she is married to Fitzpiers without hope of a divorce, she seems to take the view that his return to her is the best option available to her. But first she insists on what amounts to a second courtship, needing to be convinced that he cares for her. Proof of this is afforded when she sets off the man-trap that the jealous Tim Tangs has laid for Fitzpiers. When Fitzpiers sees that the trap has been thrown and that part of a woman's clothing is caught in it, he cries out "like one in corporal agony, and in his misery [bows] himself down to the ground" (426). These are the narrator's words and should be given full weight. And Grace later says to him, "I heard what you said when you thought I was injured . . . , and I know that a man who could suffer as you were suffering must have a tender regard for me" (428).

Grace and Fitzpiers are thus reconciled, but there is little assurance that their life in the future will be very different from what it has been in the past. Mr. Melbury, for one, is not hopeful that a chastened Fitzpiers will be ready to give up joint-stock enterprises:

"Well—he's her husband," Melbury said to himself, "and let her take him back to her bed if she will! . . . But let her bear in mind that the woman walks and laughs somewhere at this very moment whose neck he'll be coling next year as he does hers to-night; and as he did Felice Charmond's last year; and Suke Damson's the year afore! . . . It's a forlorn hope for her; and God knows how it will end!" (435)

For good measure, the hollow-turner remarks: "She's got him quite tame. But how long 'twill last I can't say" (437). One would imagine that the indication of the likely course of events is sufficiently strong, but Hardy himself did not seem to think so. In response to a request for permission to adapt *The Woodlanders* for the stage, he also related to the ending:

> You have probably observed that the *ending* of the story, as hinted rather than stated, is that the heroine is doomed to an unhappy life with an inconstant husband.
> I could not accent this strongly in the book; by reason of the conventions of the libraries etc. Since the story was written however truth to life is not considered quite such a crime in literature as it was formerly: & it is therefore a question for you whether you will accent this ending; or prefer to obscure it.[13]

No mention is made, however, either in the novel or outside it, of what we may assume Fitzpiers will continue to encounter in his renewed marriage to Grace. She presumably is Daphne still, and there will be a mutual sorrow and sickness of heart at last.

---

13. Hardy, letter to J. T. Grein and C. W. Jarvis, July 19, 1889, in *Collected Letters*, 1:195. Hardy also told another correspondent that "in the story the reunited husband & wife are supposed to live ever after *un*happily!—or at any rate not quite happily" (letter to W. Moy Thomas, August 7, 1889, in ibid., 196).

7

Tess of the d'Urbervilles
Green Malt in Floor

I

Tess Durbeyfield, in a continuing view of her story, has been regarded by a number of influential critics as a hapless victim of forces beyond her control. It was D. H. Lawrence who set this ball rolling: "It is inevitable for Angel Clare and for Alec d'Urberville mutually to destroy the woman they both loved. Each does her the extreme of wrong, so she is destroyed." Echoing Lawrence, Tony Tanner says that "it is both men who drive Tess to her death." J. Hillis Miller sees Tess as a victim of her genes, rather than of Alec and Angel, but still very much a victim: "The nature [Tess] inherits forces her to enact involuntarily a new version of a life which has been lived over and over again by her ancestors, as if she were no more than a puppet of history. . . ."[1] The text, in various ways, certainly supports a sense of the victimization of Tess. When she first meets Alec at the beginning of her story, the narrator comments: "Thus the thing began. Had she perceived this meeting's import she might have asked why she was doomed to be seen and coveted that day by the wrong man . . ."; and he proceeds to reflect on the imperfect "social machinery" that "jolts us round and along."[2] About midway through the narrative, he remarks that though Tess was "but a girl of simple life, not yet one-and-twenty,

---

1. Lawrence, "Study of Thomas Hardy," 100; Tony Tanner, "Colour and Movement in Hardy's *Tess of the d'Urbervilles*," 230; Miller, *Thomas Hardy*, 103.
2. Hardy, *Tess of the d'Urbervilles*, 82–83. Further page references to this novel will be incorporated parenthetically in the text.

[she] had been caught during her days of immaturity like a bird in a springe" (261). And at the end of the narrative the novelist himself would seem to give his imprimatur to the image of Tess as victim when he sets the scene for her arrest at the sacrificial slab at Stonehenge. Moreover, that is how Tess sees her story, as emerges when she strikes Alec with the gauntlet: " 'Now, punish me!' she said, turning up her eyes to [Alec] with the hopeless defiance of the sparrow's gaze before its captor twists its neck. . . . 'Once victim, always victim—that's the law!' " (411).

The comparison of Tess to the hopeless sparrow recalls an earlier scene in which she herself does some twisting of necks. The episode begins when she is accosted by the "well-to-do boor whom Angel had knocked down at the inn for addressing her coarsely." When he tries to get her to admit that what he said about her was true, she runs away from him, feeling this is the only "escape for her hunted soul." Plunging into a plantation, she makes "a sort of nest" for herself among some "dead leaves" that she heaps together (350–51). Depicted thus as a hunted creature, the context makes it clear that it is by her past she is hunted, this being one of the main forces by which she is victimized. The image of Tess ramifies when in the light of day she discovers what it was that had disturbed her during the night. Nearby there are some pheasants that have literally been hunted, "their rich plumage dabbled with blood," and those that are not dead are still "writhing in agony," their "tortures" not yet ended (352). The birds are the victims of "some shooting-party" and have thus been killed and wounded in the name of what is socially accepted as a sport. Tess's troubles too stem from another kind of sport, for she, the simple country girl, has been fair game for a man such as Alec; and subsequently she has been hunted by the socially accepted idea of what constitutes "a pure woman." The image of Tess as a hunted soul is proleptic as well as analeptic, looking ahead to the time when she too is literally hunted—by the police after the murder of Alec, the prey not merely of social pressures but of the law. The final twist given this sequence is representative of the singular force of Hardy's imagination: "With the impulse of a soul who could feel for kindred sufferers as much as for herself, Tess's first thought was to put the still living birds out of their torture, and to this end with her own hands she broke the necks of as many as she could find . . ." (352–53).

The scene prefigures the way in which she herself, finally hunted down, will be put out of her agony by having her own neck broken. When the hanging is over, the narrator bitterly remarks that " 'justice' was done, and the President of the Immortals . . . had ended his sport with Tess" (489).

The notion of Tess's victimization is seemingly also supported by the fact that at crucial moments in her story she is apparently the victim of chance. This is forcefully dramatized at the outset by the episode in which the horse, Prince, is killed. It is because of her feeling of guilt for the accident that Tess agrees to her mother's proposal that she seek out the d'Urbervilles, and her life may be seen as being determined by her meeting with Alec. The death of Prince is merely one link in a chain of chance: it is chance that Tess's father should have met the parson on the afternoon before the accident; it is chance that the parson, having called Durbeyfield "Sir John" on a number of previous occasions, should choose to tell him of his d'Urberville ancestry on that day, with the result that Durbeyfield gets so drunk that Tess is called on to take the family's beehives to the market. Furthermore, as if to emphasize that Tess has no control over what happens, she is asleep at the time of the accident. It would seem, therefore, that her life is subject to the working of blind chance and, since the episode is so crucial, that her fate is thus determined by accident. But, in fact, Tess is not simply a pawn of chance. When her brother, Abraham, who is keeping her company, becomes drowsy, she lets him go to sleep, thinking that she can "take upon herself the entire conduct of the load" (70). We must register that, taking this upon herself, tired and overburdened and not really up to the demanding task though she may be, Tess is then not simply overcome by sleep: when one knows that one has to stay awake and succumbs to sleep, it is after all because one reaches a point at which, losing control, one *allows* oneself to fall asleep. Tess, that is, must be seen as bearing her share of responsibility for what happens; she herself is unequivocal in this regard: " 'Tis all my doing—all mine!" she cries. "No excuse for me—none" (72).

The most notorious instance of the play of chance in the novel, the one most frequently hurled at the supposedly deterministic head of the novelist (and briefly referred to in that regard in Chapter I above), is the miscarriage of Tess's epistolary confession to Angel before the wedding. Tess has

wanted to tell Angel about her relationship with Alec but has repeatedly
been unable to do so. At last she summons up courage to write to him, but
when she slips the letter under his door, it slides under a carpet and he never
receives it. What, it seems, could be a more glaring instance of a novelist's
"putting his thumb in the scale" (in Lawrence's phrase)? In fact, however,
though Tess is subject to the arbitrary deflection of chance, once again,
as in the episode of the death of Prince, she is granted the freedom of her
own choice. When Angel does not respond to the letter, she investigates
and finds it under the carpet. At that point she gives way to what, in a fine
phrase, is subsequently described as the "reckless acquiescence in chance"
that is "apparent in the whole d'Urberville family" (324–25). She "jumps
at" the misplacing of the letter "as if it [prevents] a confession," though
she knows "in her conscience that it need not." There is "still time" before
the wedding for her to act, but she does not (277). For all the mitigating
circumstances, Tess must be seen as responsible for this failure to do what
she knows she should do, and the failure is at the very heart of her story. It
is the kingpin of the plot, for it results in Angel's abandonment of her; it
is the essential cause of her tragedy, for it is an irreparable error and leads,
in the end, to her murder of Alec and her execution; and it is the crux of
her attitude to Angel, for it signifies her wish to repress the past—and the
carnality it represents for her—in relation to him.

Finally, the third momentous combination of chance and choice occurs
when, a year after her separation from Angel and in the face of the harsh
rigors of her work as a farmhand at Flintcomb-Ash, Tess decides to appeal
for help to Angel's parents. By chance she arrives when they are out,
and then she chances to run into Angel's brothers, overhears them make
disparaging remarks about her, and watches helplessly as her walking
boots, which she has left in a hedge, are appropriated, it being assumed
that they have been "thrown away . . . by some tramp or other" (376–77).
Tess is utterly subdued by "all these untoward omens" and decides it is
"impossible to think of returning to the vicarage" (377). The narrator
leaves no room for doubt as to the consequences of her choice: "[S]he
went her way without knowing that the greatest misfortune of her life
was this feminine loss of courage at the last and critical moment through
her estimating her father-in-law by his sons. Her present condition was

precisely one which would have enlisted the sympathies of old Mr. and Mrs. Clare" (378). The aid they would have been likely to proffer could have prevented the disastrous turn her story takes at this stage. It is on her way home after her aborted mission that she encounters Alec and that he comes back into her life.

If *Tess of the d'Urbervilles* is not only Hardy's finest novel but also a major work of the Victorian period, this is at least in part because, as I trust has been suggested, the narrative has an impressive density of texture and immerses us in a complex action, in which Tess is at the center of carefully contextualized contingencies and choices. Her life is subject to many intolerable pressures, and these are rendered in disturbing particularity: the pressures exerted on her by Alec and Angel; the pressures of her ancestry and of a doom that seems to dog her; the pressures of a "social machinery" that hunts her down and demands that she be sacrificed to her past; the pressures of her own youth and inexperience that make her the sport of time; the pressures of grinding economic necessity, both when she lives with her family and when she is on her own at Flintcomb-Ash; and the pressures of chance, which, unlike the play of coincidence that portends the working of a benign providence in a novelist such as Dickens, function in Hardy's mechanical and godless universe to help undo her. But over and above these various pressures, perhaps so strong they can hardly be borne, Tess is presented not as a helpless victim but as a tragic agent, choosing her own way and creating her own tragic stature. The fact that she is ultimately responsible for what happens to her is one of the sources of the novel's power.[3]

Tess herself is preeminent among Hardy's heroines. In more than one sense, she is the most full-bodied of his female characters. Angel may call her Artemis, but Tess is at the opposite pole from the Diana figures who precede her in the novels. She has a "bouncing handsome womanliness" (52), a "luxuriance of aspect, a fulness of growth" (82), and it is this that

3. Robert B. Heilman is one of the few critics who takes a similar view of Tess's role. He says that Hardy's imagination, working over and above "indignation at people and events that contribute to [Tess's] suffering," makes her "more of a person and less of a helpless victim, more of an agent and less a passive recipient of the actions of others" (*"Gulliver and Hardy's Tess:* Houyhnhnms, Yahoos, and Ambiguities," 288).

makes the grimness of her suffering and the extinguishing of her vibrant young life so poignant—and so moving. But her blooming sexuality is also her problem. At the outset, one of "the elderly boozers" at Rolliver's inn remarks on it in a way that frames her story: "Tess is a fine figure o' fun," he says. "But Joan Durbeyfield must mind that she don't get green malt in floor" (66)—must mind, that is, that she does not get herself pregnant. That the green malt does get in is the pity, if not the terror, of it.

II

Alec d'Urberville is the last of the rakes in the novels, and Hardy takes the figure to extremes. Whereas the rakes who precede him, such as Troy or Fitzpiers, possess a compelling sexual magnetism, this is magnified in Alec to blatant sexual power, to a drive for mastery and conquest. He is a "handsome, horsey young buck" (92), and when Tess first meets him, his sensuality is manifest in his "full lips . . . red and smooth" and in his eyes. But what is most distinctive about him is the force he exudes: "Despite the touches of barbarism in his contours, there was a singular force in the gentleman's face, and in his bold rolling eye" (79). "Despite" seems to be the wrong word here; it is precisely Alec's capacity for unrestraint, a readiness to let go, come what may, that is one of the conditions of his singular force. He has a "reputation as a reckless gallant and heart-breaker" (132), and both his recklessness and his force are concretized in the manner in which he drives Tess in his smart gig on the way to Trantridge.

The ride also figures the sort of relationship Alec wishes to impose on Tess. When they reach a long, steep descent and he begins to drive recklessly down it, it seems at first as if this is merely an expression of his natural flamboyance and high spirits: "Why, Tess," he says in response to her request that he slow down, "it isn't a brave bouncing girl like you who asks that? Why, I always go down at full gallop. There's nothing like it for raising your spirits" (94). The ride, we see, is a replay of Troy's sword exercise, in which Alec both tests Tess and shows his own skill. It soon becomes apparent, moreover, that there is more to his driving than a raising of spirits. For one thing, the horse is a mare; and as the dashing young male urges it into a full gallop, the description of the pell-mell drive downhill, with "the figure of the horse rising and falling in undulations before them"

(95), takes on insistent sexual overtones. These are still further emphasized when, before the end of the drive, Tess is reduced to desperation and "her large eyes [stare] at him like those of a wild animal" (96). For another, the mare is no ordinary horse but "has killed one chap" and has also "nearly killed" Alec himself on another occasion (95). Consequently, the drive downhill also becomes a question of Alec's pitting himself against the horse, of his testing his power over it and demonstrating his mastery: "If any living man," he tells Tess, "can manage this horse I can:—I won't say any living man can do it—but if such has the power, I am he" (94). The scene becomes more and more uncannily evocative of the episode in *Women in Love* in which Gerald Crich subdues the mare at the railway crossing in the presence of Gudrun Brangwen.

Once Alec has loosened the rein and given the mare its head, what he demonstrates in the ride is the degree to which he can impel it to a wild abandon while he himself coolly—if high-spiritedly—retains control of it (95). The motif of abandon, so sharply concretized in the mare's plunge downhill, is of central importance in Tess's story, as becomes clear subsequently. But as the gig speeds along, alternative possibilities in the development of her relationship with Alec are nicely juxtaposed.

With the horse knowing well "the reckless performance expected of her," they go shooting wildly down the first hill they come to. In her alarm Tess clings to Alec, and it is only when they safely reach the bottom of the hill that she disengages herself and realizes how completely she has given way to impulse: "She had not considered what she had been doing; whether he were man or woman, stick or stone, in her involuntary hold on him." She expresses her anger, with "her face on fire" (95), but it is not only anger that her fiery face suggests. Alec then "[loosens] rein" again, they go rocking down a second hill, and the only way she can persuade him to stop is by agreeing to let him kiss her. She implores him not to claim his due, but he is "inexorable" and gives her "the kiss of mastery" (96), a phrase that draws together related significances of the drive. When they come to "yet another descent" and Alec tries to extort another kiss, Tess defeats him by allowing her hat to blow off and refusing to get back into the gig after she has retrieved it. Her eyes light up "in defiant triumph" at this point. In the power struggle that is joined between them on this ride, Tess shows her capacity for resistance, and, demonstrating that she can take a stand, she walks the rest of the way (97–98).

Tess, however, is not always prepared to walk, and her behavior on another occasion is premonitory of what is to come. One night she is drawn into a fierce quarrel with the Queen of Diamonds when suddenly Alec appears on horseback. He urges her to jump onto the horse, and, seeing a chance of "triumphing" over "the contentious revellers," Tess (in a vivid phrase) "[abandons] herself to her impulse" and "[scrambles] into the saddle behind him" (113). This episode immediately precedes the crucial scene in The Chase and, being a striking instance of Tess's capacity for abandon in relation to Alec, would strongly seem to suggest that what follows is a seduction. But, as is well known, critical opinion is sharply divided on this issue. Among others, Tony Tanner, in perhaps the best study of the novel, repeatedly refers to what happens as a rape. Leon Waldoff, among others, thinks the evidence points to a seduction. Ian Gregor, straddling these views, says that the "encounter" in The Chase is "both a seduction *and* a rape."[4] In the murk in which Hardy encompasses the episode, only one thing seems clear: the opposed critical views are the result of a thoroughgoing ambiguity in the presentation of this crucial event in Tess's life, as a number of critics have noted.[5] The real issue is what lies behind the ambiguity and how it is constituted.

It seems to me that the ambiguity is the culminating instance in the novels of divergent views between the seer and the see-er. From the

---

4. Tanner, "Colour and Movement"; see, for instance, 221, 222, 223; Waldoff, "Psychological Determinism," 138, though Waldoff notes that "the text does not permit certainty" (140); Gregor, *Great Web*, 182.

Kaja Silverman reaches a similar conclusion to Gregor, though by a novel route. Her "narratological" approach, however, has the unfortunate effect of implicating the poor narrator as deeply as Alec:

To the degree that the narrator's desire for figural disintegration predominates [that is, with Tess lost in the darkness], Alec's "mastery" of Tess will be perceived as a rape. However, insofar as priority is given to the narrator's erotic gratification at the re-emergence of Tess as image, Alec's action will assume the status of a seduction. In the first instance narratological revulsion is projected onto Tess as non-compliance, whereas in the second narratological desire is projected onto her as acquiescence. ("History, Figuration, and Female Subjectivity in *Tess of the d'Urbervilles*," 11)

5. See, for instance, Kristin Brady, "Tess and Alec: Rape or Seduction?" 133, 144–45.

moment Alec returns to the sleeping Tess, the tones of the seer are very much in evidence. It is not for nothing that the prophet Elijah is at once invoked: lamenting the absence of Tess's "guardian angel," the narrator says, "Perhaps, like that other god of whom the ironical Tishbite spoke, he was talking, or he was pursuing, or he was in a journey, or he was sleeping and not to be awaked" (119). And in the page or so before the novelist drops the curtain on what eventuates in The Chase, the seer unremittingly evokes a rape. Suggestions of violation are strong: Tess is a "white muslin figure" that seems to be swallowed up in the "darkness" and the "blackness" that "[rule] everywhere around" (118–19); the epitome of innocence, hers is a "beautiful feminine tissue" that is "practically blank as snow as yet," but it is "doomed" to have "traced" on it "a coarse pattern." Indeed, it is asked why the coarse should (in a key term) *appropriate* the "finer thus." And though the seer declares that "to visit the sins of the fathers upon the children" is a "morality" that should be "scorned," he nonetheless adds this dimension to what he is clearly presenting as a rape: "One may, indeed, admit the possibility of a retribution lurking in the present catastrophe. Doubtless some of Tess d'Urberville's mailed ancestors rollicking home from a fray had dealt the same measure even more ruthlessly towards peasant girls of their time" (119). Furthermore, the description of Alec's return to Tess ended, in the first edition of the novel, with the following passage (subsequently omitted from later editions):

> Already at that hour some sons of the forest were stirring, and striking lights in not very distant cottages; good and sincere hearts among them, patterns of honesty and devotion and chivalry. And powerful horses were stamping in their stalls, ready to be let out into the morning air. But no dart or thread of intelligence inspired these men to harness and mount, or gave them by any means the least inkling that their sister was in the hands of the spoiler; and they did not come that way.[6]

This pronouncement is echoed in the edition we now have in the comments of a villager on Tess's baby: "A little more than persuading had to do wi' the coming o't, I reckon. There were they that heard a sobbing one

6. See the New Wessex (paperback) edition of *Tess of the d'Urbervilles*, 470.

night last year in The Chase; and it mid ha' gone hard wi' a certain party if folks had come along" (140).

There are a number of reasons for the seer's insistence on rape. In the preceding novels he has time and again presented passion as being destructive; in making the act of passion a rape, a brutal and violent destruction of Tess's innocence, he gives a final turn of the screw to this motif. Second, the seer has shown consistent animosity to the rake figures in the novels, subjecting them to a continuing vein of hostile commentary; in presenting Alec as a rapist, he pushes animus against the type as far as it can go, exposing what might be regarded as a compelling sexual attractiveness as consisting in blatant force, a ruthless exercise in power: it is this that Alec's mastery of a horse is represented as becoming when transposed to a woman. Third, and most important, that Tess should be raped and not seduced is essential to the seer's presentation of her as a victim. Taking on the mantle of prophet to a stiff-necked people, he thus casts his "pure woman" in their teeth.

Given the quoted pronouncements of the seer in the scene in The Chase, it is astonishing that, outside the novel, Hardy should so nonchalantly have lent himself to a very different view of the matter. Writing to a correspondent at about the time the novel appeared in book form, he said: "Clare's character [in the serial version] suffers owing to a mock marriage having been substituted for a seduction pure & simple of the original MS—which I did for the sake of the Young Girl. The true reading will be restored in the volumes."[7] Perhaps this statement is not so astonishing after all, for it is to "a seduction pure & simple" that the novel, of course, also points.

Prior to the scene in The Chase, Alec is certainly not presented as a rapist. For "near three mortal months" he has pursued Tess and, though riled by her "trifling" with him, has accepted her rebuffs (115). On the night in question he tells her that he loves her and asks whether he may not treat her "as a lover" (115). He also reveals that on that day he has presented her father with "a new cob" to replace Prince and given toys to the children of the family (117). Most revealing of all, when he leaves Tess

7. Hardy, letter to Thomas MacQuoid, October 29, 1891, in *Collected Letters*, 1:245–46.

to try to find out where they are, he is compassionate to her: " 'Nights grow chilly in September. Let me see.' He pulled off a light overcoat that he had worn, and put it round her tenderly. 'That's it—now you'll feel warmer,' he continued. 'Now, my pretty, rest there; I shall soon be back again' " (118). It is the see-er, the meticulous recorder of concretized action, who quietly presents this little vignette and who makes us see that neither Alec's concern nor his tenderness casts him as a rapist. He makes us see too that Tess is not quite the innocent victim she is purported to be by the seer. We are told that she has "never quite got over her original mistrust" of Alec (109), but she nonetheless falls asleep when he leaves her, just as she let herself sleep when Prince is killed. She is also remarkably compliant as the episode unfolds. When Alec asks her whether he has often offended her "by love-making," she replies "sometimes"; and when he presses her as to whether it has been "every time," she is "silent" (114). She does not "perceive" that Alec has "not taken the Trantridge track" (115). When he asks whether he may treat her as a lover, she does not say no, and musters no more than a "murmured 'I don't know—I wish—how can I say yes or no when—,' " allowing him to "[settle] the matter by clasping his arm round her as he [desires]" while she expresses "no further negative" (116).

Nor is Tess's behavior after the night in The Chase easily reconcilable with her having been raped. One can conceive how a novelist such as Hardy could lead us to imagine that a woman might fall in love with her rapist; but Tess, both before and after the crucial episode, states that she does not love Alec. However, though the episode takes place on "a Saturday in September" (106), it is not until "a Sunday morning in late October" (123) that she leaves him, having freely lived as his mistress, that is, for about a month after it. This period is crucial: it is once again Tess who freely chooses to do what she does. It is as a responsible tragic agent, not helpless victim, that in this most important of matters we must once again view her.

What is most striking about Tess's feeling when she leaves Alec is her self-loathing, her self-disgust. When he catches up with her, she says to him: "if I had ever sincerely loved you, if I loved you still, I should not so loathe and hate myself for my weakness as I do now! . . . My eyes were dazed by you for a little, and that was all" (125). And when her mother tells her she should have gotten Alec to marry her, she reflects bitterly how little her mother knows the feeling toward him that has made her "detest herself":

> She had never wholly cared for him, she did not at all care for him now. She had dreaded him, winced before him, succumbed to adroit advantages he took of her helplessness; then, temporarily blinded by his ardent manners, had been stirred to confused surrender awhile: had suddenly despised and disliked him, and had run away. That was all. Hate him she did not quite; but he was dust and ashes to her, and even for her name's sake she scarcely wished to marry him. (130)

Tess loathes and hates herself so strongly, it appears, because she now despises and dislikes Alec. Her feeling for him fills her with revulsion from her own body as well as his. She herself, as well as Alec, is reduced to "dust and ashes" because she now feels that what she gave Alec was a body devoid of the love that could truly animate it—and that could alone redeem it in her eyes. Though her eyes were "dazed" and "blinded" by him, they see clearly enough now.[8] Her surrender, moreover, was "confused," we are to understand, because it was not wholehearted, because (as she later maintains) there was not at least a strong physical passion to move her to it: when Alec begins to pursue her for a second time and says, "Here I am, my love, as in the old times!" she answers: "Not as then—never as then—'tis different! . . . And there was never warmth with me!" (410).

The see-er indicates what cold bodies are like in the superb scene of the parting of Alec and Tess, which encapsulates all the elements in their relationship:

> Alec d'Urberville removed his cigar, bent towards her, and said—
> "You are not going to turn away like that, dear? Come!"

---

8. Both Bernard J. Paris and Jane Adamson take a similar view. Paris says "Tess loathes herself because she has never loved Alec" (" 'A Confusion of Many Standards': Conflicting Value Systems in *Tess of the d'Urbervilles*," 69); Adamson says that "the deeper issue for Tess . . . what makes her so 'loathe and hate' herself is the violation of her essential integrity, the inner law of her being, in surrendering herself to Alec when she 'had never wholly cared for him' " (*"Tess,* Time and Its Shapings," 32).

"If you wish," she answered indifferently. "See how you've mastered me!"

She thereupon turned round and lifted her face to his, and remained like a marble term while he imprinted a kiss upon her cheek—half perfunctorily, half as if zest had not yet quite died out. Her eyes vaguely rested upon the remotest trees in the lane while the kiss was given, as though she were nearly unconscious of what he did. (126)

Tess's coldness here may seem to support John Bayley's contention that "Hardy conveys with a total delicacy and accuracy the repulsion this unawakened girl feels for the sexuality of Alec." Bayley further maintains that to suggest that Tess's "real appetite and affiliation are with Alec" is to "vulgarise" a "sex dogma . . . from D. H. Lawrence, and [impose it] upon a situation to which it has not the smallest relevance."[9] It seems to me, however, that we have been made to see that Tess has not only been awakened sexually by Alec but that she has been touched more deeply by him than she is willing to admit: she may have been "blinded" by his "ardent manners," but she has also been "stirred" into surrender, and that implies a passionate response on her part. Moreover, when she says she would not so loathe herself if she had "ever sincerely loved" him or if she loved him "still," that ambiguously suggests that she has had some genuine feeling for him. Since Bayley refers to Lawrence, it is well to note what Lawrence himself has to say about the relationship: "Alec d'Urberville could reach some of the real sources of the female in a woman, and draw from them. . . . And, as a woman instinctively knows, such men are rare. Therefore they have a power over a woman. They draw from the depth of her being."[10]

However we may choose to explain the nature of the power Alec exerts over Tess, it seems indisputable that she is overcome by it. She may speak ironically in the farewell scene, but we must assume that she in fact "succumbed" to Alec because he "mastered" her. If such mastery implies a subduing of her spirit, that in turn implies (in the end) the marble flesh

9. Bayley, *An Essay on Hardy*, 176.
10. Lawrence, "Study of Thomas Hardy," 96.

that she now indifferently yields to him, as if she is "nearly unconscious" of him—and the taste of dust and ashes. Not that she alone is cold. Her marble is matched by the coldness that underlies his will to dominance, for coolness, as we have seen in the episode with the mare, is a condition of such mastery. But like Tess in regard to herself, Alec too is not fully aware of what impels him. His drive for mastery is more complex than he realizes, and he is a more complex character than is generally recognized, for the drive coexists with the authentic tenderness toward Tess that he exhibits on occasion and with the sincere concern for her that is evident even after she has run away from him: "And if certain circumstances should arise—you understand—" he says to her, "in which you are in the least need, the least difficulty, send me one line, and you shall have by return whatever you require" (125). There is in Alec an unacknowledged force of feeling that will later draw him back to Tess, scattering his evangelical pretensions like so much chaff in the wind, even if at this stage of the relationship, he is, for the most part, more concerned with his own needs.

The needs of the body alone are soon sated, though Alec is slower in reaching satiety than Tess, and the narrator beautifully captures the last flicker of his half-extinguished desire as he kisses Tess "half perfunctorily, half as if zest [has] not yet quite died out." Since his desire is fueled not by love but by a will to mastery, it is fired by opposition, not submission; and it is Tess's very yielding that dooms it to extinction, as is suggested by a passage in the manuscript (italicized in the following quotation) that the novelist inserted into his description of Alec's kiss and then deleted (possibly because it was too specific about the length of Tess's stay with him as his mistress): "he imprinted a kiss upon her cheek—half perfunctorily, half as if zest had not yet quite died out *for only a month had elapsed since she had ceased to defend herself against him.*"[11]

III

In its triangular patterning of love, *Tess of the d'Urbervilles* is notably different from the novels that precede it. In them, as we have seen, the pattern repeatedly figures a displacement of love; in *Tess* displacement is

11. See J. T. Laird, *The Shaping of Tess of the d'Urbervilles*, 72.

replaced by succession. Tess becomes involved with Angel when she thinks she has put Alec behind her, and she takes up again with Alec only when she feels sure Angel has completely abandoned her. But the men in the triangle are as strongly contrasted as ever, and they not only conform to Hardy's male typology but are the most striking and complicated of the two recurring types.

Angel is presented (initially, at any rate) as playing the part of the decent honorable man to Alec's libertine, but, unlike his predecessors, he is, interestingly, not a sexual innocent. He, like Tess, has a sexual history (which makes, of course, for the great irony of the confession scene): when he lived in London, we are told, "he was carried off his head and nearly entrapped by a woman much older than himself, though luckily he escaped not greatly the worse for the experience" (172). He confesses to Tess that, "tossed about by doubts and difficulties in London, like a cork on the waves, he plunged into eight-and-forty hours' dissipation with a stranger" (292). He is also an intellectual who wants to become a farmer, thus combining features of a man such as Henry Knight with those of down-to-earth countrymen such as Gabriel Oak and Giles Winterborne. When he returns to Talbothays after a visit to his parents, he is aware that "to come [there] . . . after an experience of home-life [affects] him like throwing off splints and bandages" (230), thus registering a sense of his having regained a vital freedom and fullness of physical function after the restrictive dislocations of his clerical upbringing. But his newly gained physicality does not offset an ingrained tendency to abstraction, and so on one memorable occasion Tess to him is "no longer the milkmaid, but a visionary essence of woman" (187), and on another he says to himself: "What a fresh and virginal daughter of Nature that milkmaid is!" (176).

Most strikingly, Angel, unlike most of his predecessors, is naturally passionate: "[A]s Clare was oppressed by the outward heats," the narrator says, "so was he burdened inwardly by a waxing fervour of passion for the soft and silent Tess" (207). Not that the narrator is more consistent in his presentation of Angel than in that of Alec, for he also roundly declares that Angel is "in truth, more spiritual than animal," that "though not cold-natured, he [is] rather bright than hot—less Byronic than Shelleyan," and that the quality of his love is "more especially inclined to the imaginative and ethereal" (257). Nonetheless, it is indicated that the force of passion is stronger than his supposed disposition: Angel and Tess are said to "[balance] on the edge of a passion, . . . apparently keeping out of it," but "all the while . . . converging, under an irresistible law, as surely as two streams in one vale" (185). Indeed, "the ardour of [Angel's] affection" is described (his asserted Shelleyan temperament notwithstanding) as being "so palpable" that Tess seems "to flinch under it like a plant in too burning a sun" (232), and he is "driven towards her by every heave of his pulse" (215).

Angel shows that he is capable of decisive physical action and spontaneity when, "before he [has] considered anything at all," he strikes the man who has insulted Tess "with the full force of his fist" (274). But he is repeatedly shown to be incapable of a similar spontaneity when it comes to sex. A few examples must suffice. In the famous scene in which he wades through a flooded lane successively carrying each of the milkmaids across the pool for some fifty yards—in the magazine version Hardy was forced to have him wheel them across in turn in a wheelbarrow—Tess's cheeks, when he carries her, "[burn] to the breeze" and she cannot "look into his eyes for her emotion." Angel is about to kiss her, but then he thinks that this would be "somewhat unfairly taking advantage of an accidental position," and so he goes "no further with it" (203). On another occasion when they are milking together, he suddenly "[clasps] her in his arms." Tess is taken by surprise but yields to "his embrace with unreflecting inevitableness," sinking upon him "with something very like an ecstatic cry." He is "on the point of kissing that too tempting mouth, but he [checks] himself, for tender conscience' sake" (209). When, somewhat later, Tess tells him she cannot marry him, he "[withholds] the kiss" he has been intending to give her, her "determined negative [deterring] his scrupulous heart" (245). When on another occasion *he* abandons himself to his impulse, what he allows himself to do is to "[bring] his lips to her cheek for one moment" (247). It is only when she agrees to marry him that he first kisses her; and it is only when she kisses him to "prove" her love that "for the first time" he learns what "an impassioned woman's kisses" are like (255).

Angel's inclination for passion, then, distinguishes him from his typological predecessors in the novels with the exception of Clym Yeobright: but, unlike Clym, Angel resembles them in his inhibited sexuality. What lies behind the inhibition is at this stage more elusive in his case than in theirs, as neither Knight's fear of invidious sexual comparison, nor Oak's small-hearted sexual timidity and diffidence, nor Boldwood's fear of yielding himself sexually, nor Winterborne's fear of giving rein to overstrong feeling seem to apply to Angel. Angel's blocked sexuality appears, in the instances cited, to be a matter of superfine moral scruple, but since his scrupulousness is excessive and uncalled for in the circumstances, it comes across as mere rationalization. Nor does his supposed ethereality explain his behavior since it is contradicted by his passionate tendencies. His inhibition is perhaps best understood by way of his resemblance to Clym Yeobright. Fairly late in the novel Angel is described as being "a sample product of the last five-and-twenty years" (338), just as Clym was said to be an example of "a modern man." And what distinguished Clym as modern man, it will be recalled, was the way his "mental luminousness" was "fed with the oil of life," the way "parasite thought" threatened to "overrun" his body. Angel's sexual vitality is also usurped by thought or consciousness. That this is what inhibits him in the days of his courtship of Tess is borne out by his treatment of her after she confesses to her relationship with Alec, as remains to be seen.

Angel, moreover, rejects the idea of passion as a basis for marriage: "He loved her; ought he to marry her? Dared he to marry her? What would his mother and his brothers say? What would he himself say a couple of years after the event? That would depend upon whether the germs of staunch comradeship underlay the temporary emotion, or whether it were a sensuous joy in her form only, with no substratum of everlastingness" (216). Angel's hesitation before the prospect of marriage to Tess is not dissimilar to his holding back in respect of her body, or "form," as he thinks of it, the periphrasis itself being expressive of his inability to go straight to the heart of the matter. Nor in both instances is it a question of a lack of nerve or "daring": the "temporary emotion," of course, is sexual passion, which, as we know, is evanescent; and the "staunch comradeship" is yet another version of the desiderated ideal of camaraderie, which alone may provide a "substratum of everlastingness." Since he goes ahead with the marriage, Angel is presumably confident that the substratum has been established, but it does not last very long in the face of Tess's confession.

Prior to the marriage, Tess's own passionate nature is held in check at Talbothays, being in notable contrast to the narrator's lavish celebration of the lushness of her surroundings there. Though she is always instinctively responsive to Angel's physical advances, his inhibition is matched by her attempt to repress her sexual being. It is as if after her experience with Alec she would like to dispossess herself of her body. One day at breakfast she tells the assembled company that it is possible to make souls go outside the body: " 'A very easy way to feel 'em go,' continued Tess, 'is to lie on the grass at night and look straight up at some big bright star; and, by fixing your mind upon it, you will soon find that you are hundreds and hundreds o' miles away from your body, which you don't seem to want at all' " (175). Suggestively, it is this little speech that first draws Angel's attention to her.

One evening shortly after this, Tess hears Angel playing his harp in the garden and begins to move toward him, keeping "behind the hedge" so that he may not "guess her presence":

> The outskirt of the garden in which Tess found herself had been left uncultivated for some years, and was now damp and rank with juicy grass which sent up mists of pollen at a touch; and with tall blooming weeds emitting offensive smells—weeds whose red and yellow and purple hues formed a polychrome as dazzling as that of cultivated flowers. She went stealthily as a cat through this profusion of growth, gathering cuckoo-spittle on her skirts, cracking snails that were underfoot, staining her hands with thistle-milk and slug-slime, and rubbing off upon her naked arms sticky blights which, though snow-white on the apple-tree trunks, made madder stains on her skin; thus she drew quite near to Clare, still unobserved of him.
> Tess was conscious of neither time nor space. The exaltation which she had described as being producible at will by gazing at a star, came now without any determination of hers; she undulated upon the thin notes of the second-hand harp, and their harmonies passed like breezes through her, bringing tears into her eyes. (178–79)

This passage has been the focus of considerable critical scrutiny with regard to Tess's place "in nature." I think David Lodge is right when he insists that "even if the reader recoils from the overgrown garden, there is no suggestion that Tess does" and that she seems to be "at home in it." But I doubt whether the point of the passage is to show the "connection between Tess and the natural world" and so to imply "the 'mad,' passionate, non-ethical quality of her sensibility."[12] Surprisingly, what we are shown, it seems to me, is how unnatural Tess is here. She may be at home in the garden as she moves through it like a cat, but whereas the rank grass and mists of pollen and blooming weeds variously epitomize a natural fecundity, and the juices that rub off on to her skin stain her in the flesh, she has abstracted herself from this teeming abundance. "Conscious of neither time nor space," she has abandoned herself to "exaltation," to a condition, that is, as the reference to her stargazing indicates (and the narrator's close juxtaposition of the two passages stresses), in which "you are hundreds and hundreds o' miles away from your body, which you don't seem to want at all." And that is how she approaches Angel.

Bruce Johnson argues, on the contrary, that she moves toward Angel sensually, that it is "clearly a sensual preoccupation on Tess's part [that] turns the notes of Angel's distant harp into his body itself: 'They [the sounds] had never appealed to her as now, when they wandered in the still air with a stark quality like that of nudity.'" But he grants that "her mind transforms the scene," since she is not conscious of either space or time, and says: "The garden is incredibly fecund and sensuous, in keeping with her apprehension of [Angel's] harp notes as nudity itself, but it is also deceptive, as is her transcendent state of mind. . . ."[13] It seems to me, however, that Tess's "state of mind" functions to dissipate that nudity, to deprive it of substance: by the end of the scene she is said to undulate

---

12. David Lodge, *Language of Fiction*, 182, 185.

13. Johnson, *True Correspondence*, 104, 105.

If Tess does not seem to want her body, Elliot B. Gose interestingly suggests that in this scene the novelist subverts her wish:

Although [Hardy] tends to make a dichotomy between mind and body, he always ties them together, always makes us aware that Tess cannot separate her spiritual rapture from her position in the environment. Perhaps the scene where this is brought home most strikingly is the one in which she moves through the garden listening to Angel's flute [*sic*]. Despite the exaltation she feels from the music, her body is being stained by "sticky blights. . . ." ("Psychic Evolution: Darwinism and Initiation in *Tess of the d'Urbervilles*," 266–67) "upon the thin notes of the second-hand harp, and their harmonies [pass] like breezes through her."

As Tess falls in love with Angel, she does not deny to herself that she loves him, "perhaps all the more passionately from knowing that the [other milkmaids have] also lost their hearts to him" (203). When Angel one day suddenly kisses "the inside vein of her soft arm," she is "such a sheaf of susceptibilities" that her pulse is "accelerated by the touch, her blood driven to her finger-ends, and the cool arms [flush] hot" (239). But these are involuntary responses. Consciously, she tries to maintain her condition of spiritual ecstasy, especially after she agrees to marry Angel:

> The days of declining autumn which followed her assent [to Angel], beginning with the month of October, formed a season through which she lived in spiritual altitudes more nearly approaching ecstasy than any other period of her life.
>
> There was hardly a touch of earth in her love for Clare. To her sublime trustfulness he was all that goodness could be—knew all that a guide, philosopher, and friend should know. . . . He would sometimes catch her large, worshipful eyes . . . looking at him from their depths, as if she saw something immortal before her.
>
> She dismissed the past—trod upon it and put it out, as one treads on a coal that is smouldering and dangerous. (257)

Tess is the epitome of repression at this time. Full-bodied and passionate though she is, there is "hardly a touch of earth" in her feeling for Angel; indeed, when she is with him, the "buoyancy of her tread" is "like the skim of a bird which has not quite alighted" (260). When she does tread firmly, it is to dismiss the past, treading on it as on "a coal that is smouldering and dangerous." It is clearly the fire of passion she wants to stamp out; and at Talbothays she tries "to lead a repressed life," though she "little [divines] the strength of her own vitality" (181). Consequently, the coal is liable to flare up suddenly, as on the occasion previously referred to when she passionately kisses Angel. In her repression—as in her movement through the unweeded garden—Tess is not in harmony with nature, this being suggested by the implied gap between the "spiritual altitudes" in which she has her being and the lush days of "declining autumn" through which she is actually living. Having lost touch with earth, she also loses touch with reality, transforming Angel into the godlike figure of her idealizations. How far he is from actually possessing the qualities she attributes to him, she speedily and brutally discovers.

When Tess finally confesses to Angel on their wedding night, she is appalled to find that he will not "forgive" her, as she begs him to. "O Tess," he says, "forgiveness does not apply to the case. You were one person; now you are another. My God—how can forgiveness meet such a grotesque—prestidigitation as that!"—and he insists that the woman he has been loving is "another woman in [her] shape" (298–99). Angel's response suggests that his is a case of love in the head, as Lawrence might have called it; and his recourse to the word "prestidigitation" in such circumstances reveals how he takes refuge in words from the woman in front of him. Angel, that is to say, when shocked back into an old mode of being, is as much given to intellectual altitudes as Tess to spiritual. Tess, for her part, is quite overwhelmed by his reaction: "Terror was upon her white face . . . ; her cheek was flaccid, and her mouth had almost the aspect of a round little hole. The horrible sense of his view of her so deadened her that she staggered . . ." (299). The "round little hole" of Tess's mouth recalls "the hole" through which Prince's "life's blood [spouts] in a stream," until he suddenly "[sinks] down in a heap"(71). If her story essentially starts with that death, it is all of a piece (like that of Michael Henchard), for this deadening is what it leads to. The little hole also suggests the episode in The Chase, evoking the undoubted violence of Angel's response to her even though that of Alec remains in doubt.

In an intensification of the tendency he has manifested throughout the courtship, Angel thereafter deliberately "[smothers] his affection for her" (300). Like Clym Yeobright at an analogous moment of crisis, he suppresses the feeling that might save his marriage and announces it is "advisable" for them to part:

> Tess stole a glance at her husband. He was pale, even tremulous; but, as before, she was appalled by the determination revealed in the depths of this gentle being she had married—the will to subdue the grosser to the subtler emotion, the substance to the conception, the flesh to the spirit. Propensities, tendencies, habits, were as dead leaves upon the tyrannous wind of his imaginative ascendency. (316)

Angel's harshness to Tess is in part occasioned by his sense of having been deceived by her, is in part "the cruelty of fooled honesty . . . after enlightenment" (301); but, more fundamentally than that, it springs from an involuntary revulsion from what he takes to be her defilement, a recoil from tainted flesh. He realizes this long afterward in Brazil and then is "struck" by remorse, perceiving that what he has "inherited with the creed of mysticism" is an "abhorrence of the un-intact state" (422). Angel, that is, is like Henry Knight with his demand for "untried lips" in *A Pair of Blue Eyes;* but though this might seem to imply that a similar sexual fear underlies his abhorrence—Richard C. Carpenter, indeed, says of Angel that "the emphasis on feminine 'purity' usually indicates an obsession with sexuality as something to be feared"[14]—there is no textual support for such an explanation in his case as there is in that of Knight. It is his mind that exerts a tyrannous ascendency over all passionate feeling for Tess, scattering any "propensities" or inclinations of that kind like so many "dead leaves," determinedly subduing "the substance to the conception." The dead leaves point ahead to the nest Tess will make for herself when she flees the man who accosts her; now she is hunted by Angel's implacable morality. It was also in "a deep mass of dead leaves" that Alec made "a sort of couch or nest" for her in The Chase (117), and it was to "the white muslin figure he had left upon the dead leaves" that he returned (118–19). The two men in Tess's life meet in dead leaves.

They meet too in the motif of mastery, for Alec's struggle to master Tess is juxtaposed to Angel's to master himself. As Angel steels himself against Tess, his air is "calm and cold, his small compressed mouth indexing his powers of self-control; his face wearing still that terribly sterile expression which had spread thereon since her disclosure." His is "the face of a man who [is] no longer passion's slave, yet who [finds] no advantage in his enfranchisement" (305). Shakespeare may have come readily to the narrator's pen, but Angel can hardly be said ever to have been passion's slave; he is simply heir to his "enfranchisement," along with other ills. The coldness of his "calm and cold" air is the condition of his kind of mastery as of Alec's, but Angel's coldness is more inhuman, for it is the

---

14. Carpenter, *Thomas Hardy,* 131.

coldness of metal: though he is generally "gentle and affectionate," deep within him there lies hidden "a hard logical deposit, like a vein of metal in a soft loam, which [turns] the edge of everything that [attempts] to traverse it." It is this that "[blocks] his acceptance of Tess," no less than previously of the Church (311).

Angel's is one of those "natures," we are told, for whom "corporeal presence is sometimes less appealing than corporeal absence" (315). This preference is concretized—in effect—in one of the strangest episodes in the narrative, Angel's sleepwalking, yet another scene in the novels that bears Hardy's hallmark. In his "somnambulistic state," Angel lifts Tess from her bed, rolling her in a sheet "as in a shroud," carries her across a narrow foot-bridge, heads for a ruined Abbey-church, and lays her in "the empty stone coffin of an abbot" (317–20). The sleepwalking is a species of dream and clearly expresses Angel's wish to have done with Tess, to have her dead and buried; but this is not all it reveals. As he carries her, he says, "My poor, poor Tess—my dearest, darling Tess! So sweet, so good, so true!" thereby articulating "the words of endearment" that are "withheld so severely in his waking hours," and he also "[imprints] a kiss upon her lips—lips in the daytime scorned" (318). The episode thus also points to what has been evident throughout: it is only when his mind is asleep, when habitual consciousness is suspended, that he is able to materialize his love and express a sexual tenderness toward her.[15] When he is awake thought subdues substance, battening on it like a cancer and consuming it, for he becomes "ill with thinking; eaten out with thinking, withered by thinking" (313), a modern man who leads straight to Lawrence in the next century. It is in "pure reason" that Angel aims to ground his decision as to what he should do. The deadliness of what the "pure woman" is up against is indicated when reason triumphs and his "resolve to separate

15. My view is similar to that of Philip M. Weinstein, who says (with reference to this episode) that "it is as true that Clare's principles must be put to sleep before his deeper tenderness for [Tess] can emerge, as it is true that at the outraged core of his being he wants her to die" (*Semantics of Desire*, 116).

Tony Tanner, on the other hand, says that in the sleepwalking scene, Angel "encoffins the sexual instinct" ("Colour and Movement," 229).

from her" is "denuded of the passionateness which [has] made it scorch and burn; standing in its bones; nothing but a skeleton . . ." (321).

The separation of Angel and Tess marks yet another failed marriage, the quickest in the novels and the most emphatic since it has not even been consummated. It fails, once again, because there has not been enough passion to it, though the fire of passion is recalled on the morning following the confession: "The pair were, in truth, but the ashes of their former fires. To the hot sorrow of the previous night had succeeded heaviness; it seemed as if nothing could kindle either of them to fervour of sensation any more" (307). It is not passion, however, that has burned itself out in a self-consuming fervor; it is consciousness that has done the job. All Angel's passion, at any rate, goes into "the fury of fastidiousness" by which he is "possessed" (324) as he leaves the woman he loves—though he "hardly [knows] that he [loves] her still" (325)—for an abstraction.

IV

Phases the Sixth and the Seventh of Tess's story are notable not only for her propulsion to her tragic end but also for the characterization of both Alec and Angel. Conceived, no doubt, as exemplars of a typological opposition that runs through Hardy's work, they develop in complex ways that move them beyond their originating types.

Alec makes his reappearance in the narrative as a ranter, having altogether unexpectedly undergone a religious conversion. The narrator is as ambiguous about the conversion as he is about the episode in The Chase, and, after Alec abandons preaching, he tries to jerk him back to type by asserting that the conversion was merely "whimsical," no more perhaps than "the mere freak of a careless man in search of a new sensation, and temporarily impressed by his mother's death" (403). He also says that the "black angularities which his face had used to put on when his wishes were thwarted now did duty in picturing the incorrigible backslider who would insist upon turning again to his wallowing in the mire" (383–84). But this hardly accords with Alec's earlier readiness to act on his newfound beliefs, or with the steady strenuousness of his life as a preacher, or with the reputation of being "an excellent, fiery, Christian man" (379) that he has acquired by the time Tess meets him. What is suggested, rather, is his genuine aspiration to a new mode of being, an intense attempt to change his nature:

> It was less a reform than a transfiguration. The former curves of sensuousness were now modulated to lines of devotional passion. The lip-shapes that had meant seductiveness were now made to express supplication; the glow on the cheek that yesterday could be translated as riotousness was evangelized to-day into the splendour of pious rhetoric; animalism had become fanaticism; Paganism Paulinism; the bold rolling eye that had flashed upon [Tess's] form in the old time with such mastery now beamed with the rude energy of a theolatry that was almost ferocious. (383)

What this bespeaks is not whimsicality but re-formation, a determined effort to yoke opposed qualities together: hence, the "transfiguration," though this description is rounded off with the wallowing in the mire referred to above. But Alec is so strongly cast in an original mold that nothing can change its outlines. Even his "lineaments" seem "to complain" at the attempt, and they are eloquent of his inability to break away from their "hereditary connotation" (384), fully to integrate his new "Paulinism" with his old "Paganism."

Alec suddenly sees Tess while he is preaching, and the effect on him is "electric, far stronger than the effect of his presence upon her" (384). What happens to him, that is, is analogous to what happens to Angel when Tess confesses to him: he is shocked back into an earlier mode of being. Within a few days "something of his old passion for her" revives (394), but this should not be viewed as a mere renewal of his lust for her. What is enacted is the process of displacement that has repeatedly occurred in the novels, the displacement not, as heretofore, of a lover, but of one life drive by another in response to a deeper current of feeling. "I own," he says to Tess, "that the sight of you has waked up my love for you, which I believed was extinguished with all such feelings" (396). His feeling for her seems to be genuine enough: having only now discovered she has borne his child and not knowing she is married, he notably offers "to make the only amends" he can and asks her to be his wife (394); he also repeatedly declares his love for her.

It is only after Alec learns she cannot marry him that, in a grotesque parody of his spiritual rebirth, "the corpses of those old fitful passions which had lain inanimate amid the lines of his face ever since his reformation [seem] to wake and come together as in a resurrection" (403). One of the passions that now revives would seem to be his old passion for mastery, for he unguardedly reveals that an important component of his feeling for Tess is that she was not totally subdued by him: "Why I did not think small of you was on account of your being unsmirched in spite of all," he tells her; "you took yourself off from me so quickly and resolutely when you saw the situation; you did not remain at my pleasure; so that there was one petticoat in the world for whom I had no contempt, and you are she" (402). The old compulsion clearly emerges later when, having given up his preaching "entirely" because of his feeling for her, he reappears in "the old jaunty, slapdash guise" under which Tess first knew him (408–9); and after she strikes him in the face with her heavy leather glove and draws blood, he takes hold of her "by the shoulders, so that she [shakes] under his grasp," and says, "Remember, my lady, I was your master once! I will be your master again. If you are any man's wife you are mine!" (412).

After Angel deserts her, Tess is brought back to earth with a vengeance, and, reduced to hard physical labor in the swede-fields of Flintcomb-Ash, she now lives in a place that is "bosomed with semi-globular tumuli—as if Cybele the Many-breasted were supinely extended there" and where are to be seen "myriads of loose white flints in bulbous, cusped, and phallic shapes" (355, 360). It is a meet background for Alec's renewed pursuit of her, and she is not altogether impervious to him: the narrator remarks that "any one who had been in a position to read between the lines [of a letter she writes to Angel at this time] would have seen that at the back of her great love was some monstrous fear—almost a desperation—as to some secret contingencies which were not disclosed" (398). She continues to resist Alec, yet she is conscious that "in a physical sense [he] alone [is] her husband" (442); and in the end she is unable to withstand him after her father dies and she and her family are forced to leave their village home and seek refuge in a nearby town. When even the rooms they hope to rent in Kingsbere are not available to them and the family is literally in the street, she succumbs to Alec's offer to provide for them. This is a new lease on life for her mother and the children, but, though she herself moves with Alec to "a stylish lodging-house" at Sandbourne (464) and has all the material comfort she can want, we are to understand that the spirit goes out of her at this point. "These clothes are what he's put upon me: I didn't care what he did wi' me!" she tells Angel when he returns to England and seeks her out at Sandbourne. Angel receives the impression then that Tess has "spiritually ceased to recognize the body before him as hers—allowing it to drift, like a corpse upon the current, in a direction dissociated from its living will" (466–67). Tess, of course, is laboring here under the shock of Angel's unexpected return and of the realization that "it is too late" (466), but it is into her whole renewed relationship with Alec that she has, in effect, drifted as mere flesh, like a corpse.

Tess's murder of Alec that follows on Angel's return is complexly motivated. Angel wonders "what obscure strain in the d'Urberville blood [has] led to this aberration" (475); and Hardy himself, in a letter concerning a stage production of *Tess,* said that "the smouldering ancestral fire in Tess's nature . . . broke out in the murder."[16] We recall too that, after her confession to Angel, he says to her, "How can we live together while that man lives?—he being your husband in Nature, and not I. If he were dead it might be different . . ." (313); though there is no mention of this at the time of the murder, we may assume it lingers in Tess's consciousness. Tess herself says to Alec before she stabs him, with "her lips . . . bleeding from the clench of her teeth upon them": "O, you have torn my life all in pieces . . . made me be what I prayed you in pity not to make me again! . . . My own true husband will never, never—O God—I can't bear this!—I cannot!" (469–70). It is a poignant moment, and Tess's plight is tragic: pulled between Alec and Angel, her life is torn to pieces—and breakdown is her only recourse. It is in a "moment of mad grief," Angel later supposes, that "her mind [loses] its balance" and she kills Alec in final desperate abandon (475).

Tess then runs out after Angel in order to tell him what she has done:

> By degrees he was inclined to believe that she had faintly at-
> tempted, at least, what she said she had done; and his horror at her
> impulse was mixed with amazement at the strength of her affection

16. Hardy, letter to Harley Granville Barker, October 20, 1925, in *Collected Letters,* 6:362.

for himself, and at the strangeness of its quality, which had apparently extinguished her moral sense altogether. Unable to realize the gravity of her conduct she seemed at last content. . . .

It was very terrible if true; if a temporary hallucination, sad. But, anyhow, here was this deserted wife of his, this passionately-fond woman, clinging to him without a suspicion that he would be anything to her but a protector. He saw that for him to be otherwise was not, in her mind, within the region of the possible. Tenderness was absolutely dominant in Clare at last. He kissed her endlessly with his white lips, and held her hand, and said—

"I will not desert you! I will protect you by every means in my power, dearest love, whatever you may have done or not have done!" (475)

It is a moving scene, as Tess, after all her suffering, finds acceptance at last. But for her there is now nothing left except the week's happiness she snatches with Angel before her arrest at Stonehenge. For Angel, as he comes to believe that she has, at the least, attempted murder, the wheel comes full circle in the rhythm of change, and he is now called on to respond to a Tess whose "taint" is far worse than when he first rejected her, a being whose "moral sense" seems to be altogether "extinguished." What is remarkable is that he is equal to the occasion, his self-mastery being attained now not through a cold self-control but a willingness and readiness to let go. His instinctive reaction of horror at her deed is at once mediated by a deeper understanding of what has led her to it. Faced by a supreme test, Angel does not this time subdue substance to conception: taking "the gravity of her conduct" into account, he nevertheless fully sets beside it the woman who is clinging to him, accepting the "passionately-fond woman" as his "deserted wife," and it is now that woman in all the anguish of her frailty and strength who is his first concern. The change in Angel is epitomized in the "tenderness" that is "absolutely dominant" in him at last, in his tender kisses and protectiveness, for it is in such tenderness that mind meets body, that flesh is made one with spirit. Inhibited no longer, Angel may be regarded as having finally found himself. In the end Alec and Angel meet not only in dead leaves but in their tenderness toward Tess.[17]

Only now, when it is tragically too late, are Tess and Angel ready for a full sexual relationship. Within the house in which they take refuge and at long last consummate their marriage, there may be "affection, union, error forgiven," but outside is "the inexorable" (481). The closing pages of the novel imply that for Angel there may still be left the possibility of a new union with Tess's younger sister. But when he joins hands with 'Liza-Lu after Tess's execution and "[goes] on," he leaves ruin behind him.

17. C. H. Salter takes a determinedly negative view of Angel's tenderness: "[Angel's] 'tenderness' is a euphemism for his lust, his only expression of it endless kisses with his repulsive white lips in a context of triumphant male sexuality" (*Good Little Thomas Hardy,* 81).

8

Jude the Obscure
The Defective Real

I

More than any other novel of Hardy's, *Jude the Obscure* elicited from its author comments on various features of its structure. "Of course the book is all contrasts," he wrote, " . . . e.g., Sue & her heathen gods set against Jude's reading the Greek Testt; Christminster academical, Chr in the slums; Jude the saint, Jude the sinner; Sue the Pagan, Sue the saint; marriage, no marriage; &c., &c."[1] Since many of these contrasts involve reversals, especially in respect to the intellectual positions of Sue and Jude, the narrative, like that of *The Ambassadors,* has a pleasing hourglass shape.[2] But such a thoroughgoing structural principle naturally subserves a thematic purpose; and, though this will require modification, Hardy stated that the central contrast of the novel is that between the ideal and the real: "The 'grimy' features of the story," he wrote to the same correspondent on another occasion, adding this as an afterthought by way of a postscript, "go to show the contrast between the ideal life a man wished to lead & the squalid real life he was fated to lead. The throwing of the pizzle, at the supreme moment of his young dream, is to sharply initiate this contrast. . . . The idea was meant to run all through the novel."[3] The idea is epitomized in miniature in Jude's encounter with the composer.

---

1. Hardy, letter to Edmund Gosse, November 20, 1895, in *Collected Letters,* 2:99.
2. J. I. M. Stewart has also commented on its hourglass form, but he maintains that, compared with *The Ambassadors,* Hardy has only "indifferent success" with this structure (*Thomas Hardy,* 193).
3. Hardy, letter to Edmund Gosse, November 10, 1895, in *Collected Letters,* 2:93.

Much moved by a new hymn, Jude decides on an impulse to seek out the composer, certain that "he of all men [will] understand [his] difficulties," for "he must have suffered, and throbbed, and yearned." Setting out as "a hungry soul in pursuit of a full soul," he finds that the composer is not interested in beauty but money and for that reason is giving up music and going into the wine business.4 As the narrator comments in another context, what may be "perfect and ideal" at night proves by day to be "the more or less defective real" (130).

Hardy furthermore stated that "the plot is almost geometrically constructed" and then elaborated on this sometime later to the same correspondent: "The 'rectangular' lines of the story were not premeditated, but came by chance: except, of course, that the involutions of four lives must necessarily be a sort of quadrille."5 In some ways the movement of the narrative is indeed like that of a quadrille as the protagonists come together as partners, move away to others, and then finally return to their original positions. But the involutions of four lives need not at all necessarily be a sort of quadrille, as the interlinking lives and loves of the four protagonists in a novel such as *Our Mutual Friend,* for instance, indicate since they involve neither exchange nor return. The necessity that drives the dance of the characters in *Jude* seems rather to be a compulsion to repeat. Jude and Arabella and Sue and Phillotson are driven to repeat what they know will be disastrous marriages with their former spouses, and the repetition does not have the airiness and grace of a dance but the deadliness and deathliness of buried matter.6

Repetition is not only the motivating impulsion of the protagonists but also the fundamental structural principle of the narrative. The narrative

4. Hardy, *Jude the Obscure,* 252–54. Further page references to this novel will be incorporated parenthetically in the text.

5. Hardy, letters to Edmund Gosse, November 10, 1895, and January 4, 1896, in *Collected Letters,* 2:93, 105.

6. Cf. William R. Goetz, who says repetition is "the necessary mode of the tragedy"; and who comments as follows on the remarriages: "[B]oth protagonists [reenter] marriages with their original partners in a sort of grotesque parody of the conventionally happy ending of the earlier English novel," the remarriages being a "seemingly necessary return to a condition of marriage whose spiritual bankruptcy and cruelty have already been conclusively exposed" ("The Felicity and Infelicity of Marriage in *Jude the Obscure,*" 211, 191).

is divided into six parts, and these are linked together rhythmically—that is, the design of the narrative is repeated in each part with variation. The design at once becomes evident when we compare the dramatic movement of the first two parts. The main event in "Part First: At Marygreen" is Jude's marriage to Arabella. By the end of this part the marriage ends in failure when she abandons him and goes off to Australia. Significantly, however, the part does not end with Jude's unrelieved gloom. He decides to go to Christminster as soon as his apprenticeship expires, and so he is filled with new hope. The last sentence of the part is: "He returned to his lodgings in a better mood, and said his prayers" (120). The main events in "Part Second: At Christminster" are Jude's failure to gain admission to any of the Christminster colleges and the subsequent loss of his job. His despair now is even greater than before: "He thought of that previous abyss into which he had fallen . . . ; the deepest deep he had supposed it then; but it was not so deep as this. That had been the breaking in of the outer bulwarks of his hope: this was of his second line" (176). The above passage occurs only a page or so before the end of the part, but by its conclusion the curate has opened to Jude the possibility of his entering the church without a university degree as a licentiate, providing he avoids strong drink: "I could avoid that easily enough," says Jude in the final sentence of the part, "if I had any kind of hope to support me!" (177). The design, then, is clear: each part moves to a kind of climax in which Jude suffers a major blow or defeat, but it actually ends on a note of renewed hope as he determines on a new direction.7 It would be tedious to recapitulate the details of the design in the parts that follow, but they conform to this schema (with the exception of the final part, which chronicles the death of the children, the separation of Jude and Sue, and the death of Jude). The structure of the narrative, therefore, generates an overwhelming sense of frustration: if each failure or loss is offset by new hope, each hope in turn is dashed—until there is nothing left.8 And the movement from

7. Gary Adelman has a similar sense of this design, but he gets the detail wrong: "Each of the novel's six parts begins with hope and ends in despair, like an hourglass constantly being turned around, filling and being drained" (*Jude the Obscure: A Paradise of Despair,* 64).

8. Cf. A. Alvarez, who says "the tragedy of *Jude* is . . . one . . . of missed fulfilment, of frustration" and that "frustration is the permanent condition of Jude's life." However, he

place to place in each part further accentuates the repeated frustrations: each new place represents a new start, and so renewed hope, but these all come to nothing; in the end the ultimate effect of Jude's wanderings is to bring him back to where he started: to Christminster, the city to which he first moves, and to Marygreen, the site of his last despairing and suicidal journey to see Sue and the place from which he originally set out. The contrast between the ideal and the real is thus concretized throughout in the systematic frustration of all aspiration.

An unusual feature of the structure of the novel is the initial portrayal of Jude's childhood. In no other of Hardy's works are we given an account of the protagonist as a child. The childhood section is short, only about thirty pages, detailing Jude's life from the age of eleven to the age of nineteen. It does not have the vivid particularity that characterizes the childhood sections of a novel such as *Great Expectations,* for instance, but the opening does place *Jude the Obscure* in the tradition of the English *Bildungsroman,* whose narrative trajectory typically extends from the childhood to the early maturity of the protagonist. Where the *Bildungsroman,* however, characteristically traces the development of the protagonist to fulfillment and self-realization, Jude's story leads only to nullification and self-destruction. Accordingly, it has been called an "inverted *Bildungsroman,*"[9] the inversion aligning itself with the prevailing mode of frustration in a thwarting of our generic expectations.

The childhood section also serves to establish a number of frames for Jude's story. The central fact of Jude's childhood is that he grows up an orphan. (In passing it may be remarked that orphanhood is a recurrent motif in the English *Bildungsroman* and is also the fate of protagonists such as Pip, Jane Eyre, and Henry Esmond, for example.) Jude's status as

---

then backs away from this view when he states that "the essential subject of the novel is not Oxford, or marriage, or even frustration. It is loneliness" (*"Jude the Obscure,"* 113, 114, 120).

David Lodge relates to "the intricate pattern of shifting relationships between the two couples, which leaves them all, in the end, as they began, trapped with uncongenial and incompatible partners" rather than to the structure of the parts, but he too sees frustration as central. He says the design "embodies the idea which I find central to *Jude*—that life is a closed system of disappointment from which only death offers an escape" ("Pessimism and Fictional Form: *Jude the Obscure,*" 108).

9. Collins, *Hardy and His God,* 139.

orphan has two profound effects on his future development. First, he is made to feel that his existence is "an undemanded one" (57). Drusilla, the great-aunt who accepts responsibility for him, does not hesitate to impress on him that "it would ha' been a blessing if Goddy-mighty had took thee too, wi' thy mother and father, poor useless boy!" (51). The result is to make Jude potentially suicidal from the outset. In a mysterious scene, he lies on his back, pulls "his straw hat over his face, and [peers] through the interstices of the plaiting at the white brightness [of the sun], vaguely reflecting." The reflection issues in a wish to "prevent himself growing up! He did not want to be a man" (57). Focused on a desire to avoid adult responsibilities, the suicidal wish is camouflaged but unmistakable, as is soon made evident: a short time later he again watches the sun "through the interstices" of his straw hat and "[continues] to wish himself out of the world" (72). Jude's life is thus punctuated by repeated wishes—and an actual attempt—to end it, until in the end he does in effect kill himself. It is worth noting that the episode of the hat parallels an experience of Hardy himself, who, in the disguised autobiography, says it stands out "more distinctly than any" at the time: "He was lying on his back in the sun, thinking how useless he was, and covered his face with his straw hat. The sun's rays streamed through the interstices of the straw, the lining having disappeared. Reflecting on his experiences of the world so far as he had got he came to the conclusion that he did not wish to grow up."[10]

Second, and of course related to his sense of his undemanded existence, being an orphan makes Jude emotionally insecure. Because he feels so unattached and consequently adrift, it becomes "the yearning of his heart to find something to anchor on, to cling to" (65). The yearning is expressive of the void within him and accounts for the intensity of his attempts to find an anchorage first in Arabella and then in Sue. It also explains his obsession with Christminster. The anchor image occurs in relation to his thoughts about the city (65–66), and, for all the genuineness of his aspirations to study and to be admitted to one of its colleges, Christminster effectively figures in his emotional life as an alternative anchorage, a receptive female substitute. His new Jerusalem speedily begins to take on a female allure:

10. Hardy, *Life and Work*, 20.

"He was getting so romantically attached to Christminster," the narrator says, "that, like a young lover alluding to his mistress, he felt bashful at mentioning its name . . ." (64). When one night Jude finally gets to his beloved city, his encounter with "the first ancient mediaeval pile" he comes across is portrayed in terms of entry and penetration and sensual satisfaction:

> It was a college, as he could see by the gateway. He entered it, walked round, and penetrated to dark corners which no lamplight reached. Close to this college was another; and a little further on another; and then he began to be encircled as it were with the breath and sentiment of the venerable city. . . .
> When the gates were shut, and he could no longer get into the quadrangles, he rambled under the walls and doorways, feeling with his fingers the contours of their mouldings and carving. (125)

The shutting of the gates is ominous, indicative of the response Jude will experience in Christminster. But the way in which he approaches the city and its colleges explains the speed with which he transfers his interest from them to Sue, though the closing of the gates will prove to be an omen in respect to her as well.

Jude's childhood is productive of a third frame to his story. In the opening pages of the narrative, which describe the departure from Marygreen of the village schoolmaster, Mr. Phillotson, an image is stamped on Jude's consciousness that for long serves him as a lodestar. When Jude asks the teacher why he is leaving, he answers:

> "You know what a university is, and a university degree? It is the necessary hallmark of a man who wants to do anything in teaching. My scheme, or dream, is to be a university graduate, and then to be ordained. By going to live at Christminster, or near it, I shall be at headquarters, so to speak, and if my scheme is practicable at all, I consider that being on the spot will afford me a better chance of carrying it out than I should have elsewhere." (48)

If Phillotson thus provides Jude with an idea of a future—and an itinerary —he serves for us as a sad double of the protagonist. Like Jude's, Phillotson's aspirations also come to nothing, and, after moving from place to place, he too ends where he began: he tells Arabella that his coming back to the village school at Marygreen is "a last resource—a small thing to return to after my move upwards, and my long indulged hopes—a returning to zero, with all its humiliations" (388). The return to zero is an apt summary of Jude's peregrinations and applies as well to his movements between Sue and Arabella.

The structure of the novel, then, is intricate and multilayered. But underlying the various structural aspects referred to are two even more fundamental features. There is, first, the recurrent triangular patterning of the love relationships, though in the main instance in this case it is a man who is placed between two women rather than a woman between two men. But the women may be regarded as equivalents of the types of previously opposed men, Arabella being a female libertine and Sue a nonpareil of sexual inhibition. Jude's movement between the two women follows the course traced in the previous novel, being, like that of Tess between Alec and Angel, a matter not of displacement but of succession. Though the triangular patterning is basic to Hardy, seemingly his instinctive means of grappling with the complexities of sexual relationships, it seems to me that in his last novel he is more immediately concerned with an even starker kind of contrast, a fact that possibly accounts for the reversal of the sexes in the main triangle in this novel.

There is some dispute as to whether *Jude* should be regarded as the last novel. The popular view is that it is, but Patricia Ingham (among others) has argued that Hardy's revisions of *The Well-Beloved* (first published in serial form between *Tess* and *Jude*) were so extensive as to make its publication in book form after *Jude* a separate work and that it is thus the last novel. She further maintains that the two versions of *The Well-Beloved* and *Jude* should be "regarded as interlocking treatments of Hardy's obsessive concern with the relationship between the sexes."[11] But the fact remains that *The Well-Beloved*, though much revised, follows the lines of the serial version and does not represent a radical departure from it. In short, it is not a new work but merely the "final form" of the earlier narrative, as Hardy himself stated in his 1912 preface: "The first

11. Patricia Ingham, "Provisional Narratives: Hardy's Final Trilogy," 53.

publication of this tale in an independent form was in 1897; but it had appeared in the periodical press in 1892, under the title of 'The Pursuit of the Well-Beloved'. A few chapters of that experimental issue were rewritten for the present and final form of the narrative."[12] More important, *The Well-Beloved* is precisely not of a piece with the rest of Hardy's work, and particularly with the treatment of sexual relationships in the major novels. It is a light—and slight—fantasy, which Hardy grouped separately from his important work in the category of "Romances and Fantasies." It has none of the novelist's customary brilliance and depth and certainly does not engage his obsessions. I think *Jude the Obscure* should continue to be seen as Hardy's final statement in the novel.

In *Jude*, then, Hardy rounds off his work in the novel by reverting to a contrast that is central to his first major achievement, *Far from the Madding Crowd*, and making that his focus. But he redefines the terms of the contrast. In *Far from the Madding Crowd*, Bathsheba's marriage to Oak, based on camaraderie, is firmly and positively set against her marriage to Troy, based on passion. Though camaraderie is there presented as an ideal basis for relationship between the sexes, it is not tested in a depiction of the marriage itself, and Hardy in a long career as a novelist did not thereafter present a full portrayal of it: the novels tend to end with a mere assertion of the possibility, as in the marriage of Thomasin and Venn in *The Return of the Native* or the renewed marriage of Grace and Fitzpiers in *The Woodlanders*. In *Jude* for the first time Hardy essays a full-scale presentation of camaraderie, and he sets it in opposition not so much to a marriage based on passion (though this is part of the pattern) as to marriage itself, marriage per se. There are two bad, failed marriages in the novel—those of Jude and Arabella and of Sue and Phillotson—and these are contrasted both with each other and, in yet another variation on the difference between the real and a presumed ideal, with the camaraderie of Sue and Jude.

Hardy said that, apart from "the labours of a poor student to get a University degree," the novel is concerned with "the tragic issue of two bad marriages, owing in the main to a doom or curse of hereditary

---

12. Hardy, preface to *The Well-Beloved*, in *Personal Writings*, 37.

temperament peculiar to the family of the parties."[13] It is true that both Sue's and Jude's parents bequeath to them a dowry of marital failure, to a degree that Drusilla believes neither should ever risk marriage, but it does not seem to be the case that it is their hereditary temperaments that doom their marriages. They are doomed, as we shall see, for other manifest reasons. In addition they seem to be doomed by the fact of marriage itself, for the view taken of marriage in the novel is dire. Two examples of the narrator's commentary in this regard must suffice: Mr. and Mrs. Cartlett (Arabella and her Australian husband) are said to be a "pot-bellied man and florid woman, in the antipathetic, recriminatory mood of the average husband and wife of Christendom" (365). When Jude and Arabella remarry, they go into lodgings, but their landlord doubts whether they are married, "especially as he had seen Arabella kiss Jude one evening when she had taken a little cordial; and he was about to give them notice to quit, till by chance overhearing her one night haranguing Jude in rattling terms, and ultimately flinging a shoe at his head, he recognized the note of genuine wedlock; and concluding that they must be respectable, said no more" (464). For good measure, Little Father Time adds his contribution to the prevailing view. When he asks Sue whether she is his real mother and she asks in turn whether she looks like his father's wife, the boy says, "Well, yes; 'cept he seems fond of you, and you of him" (345). The picture given of marriage would seem to spring straight from the failure of Hardy's own first marriage, which was going through one of its worst periods at the time of the writing of the novel. Indeed, Hardy said at this point, "I feel that a bad marriage is one of the direst things on earth, & one of the cruellest things."[14]

In the statement quoted earlier, Hardy insisted that the lines of his story were "not premeditated, but came by chance." We may assume, however, that chance does not play much part in such matters and that the lines took their shape in response to the pressures of the material dealt with. And this material, as we have seen, was in a number of important respects closely related to Hardy's own life. The fact that the narrative is

13. Hardy, letter to Edmund Gosse, November 10, 1895, in *Collected Letters,* 2:93.
14. Hardy, letter to Sir George Douglas, November 20, 1895, in ibid., 98.

productive of compulsive repetition and frustration—the main features of the structure—is perhaps not without its bearing on the novelist's abandonment of fiction after the writing of *Jude the Obscure*. For him too, it may well have seemed, there was nowhere new to go, not to mention that the ideal of camaraderie to which he dedicated himself in *Jude* was almost preordained to prove to be the defective real.

II

Arabella is an embodiment of female sexuality: "She . . . was a fine dark-eyed girl, not exactly handsome, but capable of passing as such at a little distance, despite some coarseness of skin and fibre. She had a round and prominent bosom, full lips, perfect teeth, and the rich complexion of a Cochin hen's egg. She was a complete and substantial female animal— no more, no less . . ." (81). The question is how we should regard her. There is something to be said, I think, for Lawrence's view of her: "The female in her, reckless and unconstrained, was strong enough to draw [Jude] after her, as her male, right to the end. Which other woman could have done this? At least let acknowledgement be made to her great female force of character."[15] Arabella, as the description implies and her behavior shows, has a great sexual verve and vitality. Like Hardy's male rakes, she exudes sexual force, and Jude's first sense of her is of "her magnetism" (83). Such sexual power is not to be despised, but the narrator precisely does despise her, as his contemptuous reduction of her to mere animality first indicates, as his continued association of her with pigs clearly reveals, and as his hostile commentary throughout emphasizes. Perhaps the best way of approaching her, therefore, is through her portrayal in action, and in this respect she is epitomized in the scene in which she initiates contact with Jude.

Jude, quite unaware of Arabella, is walking along when suddenly "something [smacks] him sharply in the ear." At a glance he sees what it is, "a piece of flesh, the characteristic part of a barrow-pig" (80), and it is this that Arabella has hurled at him. That throwing of the pig's pizzle is quintessential Arabella. John Sutherland insists, since a barrow-pig is a

15. Lawrence, "Study of Thomas Hardy," 106.

castrated pig, that "the fact that [the pizzle] is not . . . a symbol of animal potency but of animal impotency (i.e., not an invitation but a taunt), is the key to the scene and to the whole of Arabella's subsequent relationship with the hero."[16] But the only thing to be said for the relationship of Jude and Arabella is that it does possess a sexual vitality or potency, as is dramatized in the natural and spontaneous renewal of their sexual relations when they meet on her return from Australia. And if the hurling of the pizzle is a taunt and a challenge, a sexual equivalent of the throwing down of a gauntlet, it *is* also an invitation, a daring opening of herself to an incited response on Jude's part. All Arabella's boldness and sexual provocativeness are captured in this act; but at the same time it is expressive of her utter vulgarity and coarseness and blatancy, and it is these qualities that ultimately doom the marriage. The status of the barrow-pig intimates her likely effect on Jude: he will come to feel that she emasculates him, that she diminishes his manhood by wanting to reduce him to mere animality. It is not by chance that on their first outing they look together at a "picture of Samson and Delilah which [hangs] on the wall" of the inn they enter (89). Many years later, as Arabella sets about trapping Jude for a second time and into a second marriage, she is said to regard "her shorn Samson" (457).

The pizzle episode, even before there is any sexual contact between Jude and Arabella, invigorates him and gives him a new sense of ordinary life, as if he has suddenly passed through a barrier that has hitherto cut him off from himself: "He had just inhaled a single breath from a new atmosphere, which had evidently been hanging round him everywhere he went, for he knew not how long, but had somehow been divided from his actual breathing as by a sheet of glass" (84). Jude, in a word, is roused to sexual life, fired into it by the "enkindling one of the other sex" whom he is to meet on the following Sunday (84). He feels "as a snake must feel who has sloughed off its winter skin and cannot understand the brightness and sensitiveness of its new one" (86). And after the first outing with her, he reflects that he is "just living for the first time: not wasting life. It was better to love a woman than to be a graduate, or a parson; ay, or a pope!" (92). Arabella, for her part, is also roused by him. In "a curiously low,

16. John Sutherland, "A Note on the Teasing Narrator in *Jude the Obscure*," 160.

hungry tone of latent sensuousness," she tells Anny she must have him:
"I can't do without him. He's the sort of man I long for. I shall go mad if
I can't give myself to him altogether! I felt I should when I first saw him!"
(93). The sexual attraction between them, that is, is spontaneous, mutual,
and genuine, and the narrator meticulously records the facts of its onset
and its existence. But from the start he is adamant that such passion is no
basis for anything else, certainly not for marriage. He remarks that it is as
if "a compelling arm of extraordinary muscular power" has seized hold of
Jude and moved him "in a direction which tended towards the embrace
of a woman for whom he had no respect and whose life had nothing in
common with his own except locality" (87).

Arabella gets her man, but Jude's passion is speedily undermined. He
responds to the revelations of her female deceits and wiles with a sense
of "chill" and "distaste" (103) and "a feeling of sickness" (104). When he
learns that she has tricked him into the marriage, he bitterly laments that
"a new and transitory instinct" should have led to his being "caught in a
gin which would cripple him, if not her also, for the rest of a lifetime"
(107). Arabella too is soon disillusioned. He may feel trapped, but she now
feels he is not "much of a catch" (114); and in the letter she sends him when
she leaves him, she states she has "grown tired of him," that she does not
care for "the sort of life" he leads and sees "no prospect of his ever bettering
himself or her" (117). It is meant to be indicative of the wrongness of this
marriage, of just how bad a marriage it is, that within a very short time—
after only "some months" (115)—even their passion ceases to count at all
and the marriage breaks up. Matters come to a head over the killing of
their pig, which sharply exposes their antithetical attitudes and feelings.
The next morning is the actual occasion of the rupture when she starts
throwing his books to the floor. Her hands are smeared with lard, and she
leaves "very perceptible imprints on the book-covers" (114). This is finally
too much for Jude: it is as if she has laid greasy hands on his very soul,
soiling and violating it, and he realizes it is "all over between them" (115).

The narrator's comment on the breakup of the marriage is nominally
presented as Jude's thought but is prototypical Hardy—and it goes to the
heart of the whole novel: "Their lives were ruined, [Jude] thought; ruined
by the fundamental error of their matrimonial union: that of having based

a permanent contract on a temporary feeling which had no necessary connection with affinities that alone render a life-long comradeship tolerable" (115). The marriage of Jude and Arabella is the worst failed marriage in the novels, the marriage that has the least to be said for it. The very passion that has brought it into being evaporates into thin air and leaves nothing but ruin. The disaster is recorded as a marker of one extreme form of married failure. Not that others are lacking in a text in which such failure stamps its imprint, like that of Arabella's dirty hands, on everything. On the day that Arabella leaves Jude, his great-aunt says to him:

> "Your father and mother couldn't get on together, and they parted. . . . Your mother soon afterwards died—she drowned herself, in short, and your father went away with you to South Wessex. . . .
>
> "It was the same with your father's sister [Sue's mother]. Her husband offended her, and she so disliked living with him afterwards that she went away to London with her little maid. The Fawleys were not made for wedlock. . . ." (116)

The trial and tribulation of marriage is "temporary feeling," the more devastating when it originates in sexual passion, which the narrator insists is by definition temporary. The only thing that can save marriage is mutual affinity. That and "that alone" may provide a basis for a life-long relationship between the sexes. Within some sixty pages of the opening of the novel, and with three bad marriages disposed of, *Jude the Obscure* throws down *its* gauntlet: the essential condition of a lasting marriage is camaraderie. As for Jude, he tries to kill himself, jumping repeatedly on the ice in the middle of a large pond. The ice cracks, but he does not sink. He concludes he is "not a sufficiently dignified person for suicide" (117) and goes home.

As opposed to the marriage of Jude and Arabella, in which sex is the only connection between them, in the contrasted marriage of Sue and Phillotson it is sex that divides them. Initially it seems that the problem is Phillotson, that he is not only old enough to be Sue's father but is also sexually repellent. Drusilla is quite forthright in telling Sue she cannot understand how she could have married Phillotson: "I can mind the man very well," she says. "A very civil, honourable liver; but Lord!—I don't want to wownd your feelings, but—there be certain men here and there that no woman of any niceness can stomach. I should have said he was one . . ." (249). Sue runs out of the room at this, but she then tells Jude that what Drusilla has said is "true" (249). It seems, therefore, that whatever feeling Sue does have for Phillotson—it amounts to a sense of pale affinity, for she says she "respects" him and is "grateful" to him (171), that she finds him "considerate" and "very interesting" (273)—is quite offset by a sexual aversion to him: "[T]hough I like Mr Phillotson as a friend," she tells Jude, "I don't like him—it is a torture to me to—live with him as a husband!" (273). The nature of her torture is further complicated by her own attitudes and by the fact that she has married Phillotson though she is in love with Jude. On the very day of her wedding the narrator pointedly refers to Jude as "her lover" and to her husband-to-be as "the schoolmaster" (230). It is symptomatic of the view taken of marriage in the novel that in neither of the two main contrasted marriages is mutual love a binding factor: it is never mentioned in relation to Jude and Arabella, as if it were simply not a possible dimension of passion, and, though Phillotson loves Sue in his own way, love only figures as a powerful absence where she is concerned, for she merely has a "love of being loved" (305).

Sue's own sexual constitution becomes clearer in the depiction of her relations with Jude, but her marriage to Phillotson provides a number of pointers as to what is to come. She appears to relate her intimated aversion to Phillotson not only to the kind of man he is but also to her own "fastidiousness, or whatever it may be called" (271), and then goes on to call it her "own wickedness," a "repugnance" on her part (273). But at the same time she suggests that what she is experiencing is common to all women and to the nature of marriage:

> "I have only been married a month or two!" she went on, still remaining bent upon the table, and sobbing into her hands. "And it is said that what a woman shrinks from—in the early days of her marriage—she shakes down to with comfortable indifference in half-a-dozen years. But that is much like saying that the amputation of a limb is no affliction, since a person gets comfortably accustomed to the use of a wooden leg or arm in the course of time!" (273)

Sue's comparison is instructive. If getting used to sexual relations is like getting used to an amputation, this reveals how unnatural such relations seem to her rather than what all women may be supposed to shrink from. And indeed the narrator, in offering an authoritative summing up of her condition, clearly indicates it is a personal disability Sue suffers from: "the ethereal, fine-nerved, sensitive girl" is said to be "quite unfitted by temperament and instinct to fulfil the conditions of the matrimonial relation with Phillotson, possibly with scarce any man" (281).

Just where Sue's temperament and instinct take her to in relation to Phillotson is speedily concretized. They take her out of his bed, for a start, as she retreats to "a large clothes-closet" under the staircase (282). The next morning he sees that the closet is full of spiders' webs, and he bitterly reflects, "What must a woman's aversion be when it is stronger than her fear of spiders!" (284). She begs that he agree to her living not only away from him but with Jude; when he refuses to allow this, she wrests from him his consent to her living with him "in a separate way" (287). When the poor man walks absentmindedly into her room one night—it is the room they originally occupied together—Sue goes one better than Grace Melbury in *The Woodlanders*, who, it will be recalled, springs clean out of bed onto the floor when she thinks her husband is coming back to her, for Sue jumps out of the window. She falls to the earth below but does not "[break] her neck" (289). There is not much left of the marriage after that, and Phillotson, with great generosity of spirit, agrees that she should leave him and go to live with Jude. Like the marriage of Jude and Arabella, this marriage too has taken only some months to fall apart.

III

Sue would seem to attract Jude, at least in part, by virtue of her utter difference from Arabella: "He regarded the delicate lines of her profile, and the small, tight, apple-like convexities of her bodice, so different from Arabella's amplitudes" (245). If this is one of the narrator's nicer discriminations, Jude is not alert to the implication of tight closure in Sue, being held rather by the image of her as "the bright-eyed vivacious girl with the broad forehead and the pile of dark hair above it; the girl with the kindling glance, daringly soft at times" (184). Her broad forehead points, of course, to her intellectual capacity, Sue being the first intellectual heroine in Hardy and quite the New Woman—"quite a product of civilization," as Jude tells her (191). She does not "talk quite like a girl," Jude says, as she proceeds to rattle off for him an impressive list of her reading and then states, "I have no fear of men, as such, nor of their books" (201). That "as such" will require considerable limitation before the end of the narrative, but she is superb in her contempt of Christminster: "And intellect at Christminster," she says, "is new wine in old bottles. The mediaevalism of Christminster must go, be sloughed off, or Christminster itself will have to go" (204). Even after her disastrous desertion of him, Phillotson cannot help saying to Gillingham, "Her intellect sparkles like diamonds, while mine smoulders like brown paper. . . . She's one too many for me!" (293).

Even more than her difference from Arabella, it is Sue's availability as an ideal image that holds Jude. Before he has had any contact with her (though he has secretly been observing her), she is for him "an ideal character, about whose form he [begins] to weave curious and fantastic daydreams" (136). She is his main transaction with the ideal, and she becomes the focus too of an old childhood need: "To an impressionable and lonely young man the consciousness of having at last found anchorage for his thoughts, which promised to supply both social and spiritual possibilities, was like the dew of Hermon . . ." (139). When he finally establishes contact with her, it is perhaps above all his sense of unique affinity with her that draws him: she is to him "the one affined soul he [has] ever met" (170). The phrase recalls the epigraph to *The Woodlanders,* which Hardy himself wrote:

> Not boskiest bow'r,
> When hearts are ill affin'd,
> Hath tree of pow'r
> To shelter from the wind!

It is their supreme and mutual affinity, it would seem to be indicated, that can give these two battered warriors of the previous matrimonial engagements—as hopeless mismatchings as any in *The Woodlanders*—lasting shelter.

When Sue leaves Phillotson and goes to Jude, they take up life together, then, on the sole desiderated basis for a successful relationship between a man and a woman. After numerous glancing evocations of affinities among lovers in the work that followed *Far from the Madding Crowd,* as we have seen, Hardy now in his last novel returns fully to the ethos of the earlier narrative. It is the burden of *Jude the Obscure* that the camaraderie of Sue and Jude is even stronger and more intense than that of Bathsheba and Oak, which is so magisterially announced at the end of their narrative, since it is based on the kind of affinity of temperament and character that in effect makes them twin souls.[17] This is insisted on time and again and, because the insistence itself is of the essence, needs to be rehearsed.

When Sue wades through the river in her flight from the Training-School at Melchester, she goes to Jude; he thinks "what counterparts" they are, and when she takes off her wet clothes and dresses in his Sunday best, he sees his double, "a slim and fragile being masquerading as himself on a Sunday" (197–98). On another occasion he tells her she is "just like him at heart," and, though she quickly says "not at head," she admits that in going to the composer (in the episode previously referred to) he did "just what [she] should have done" (262). The narrator remarks that when "they talked on an indifferent subject, as now, there was ever a second silent conversation passing between their emotions, so perfect was the reciprocity between them" (263). Phillotson tells Gillingham that he has been struck with "the extraordinary sympathy, or similarity, between the pair. He is her cousin, which perhaps accounts for some of it. They seem to be one person split in two" (293). He adds a little later that "an extraordinary affinity, or sympathy, [enters] into their attachment" (295). When they go to the Agricultural Exhibition, the narrator says, "That complete mutual understanding, in which every glance was as effectual as speech for conveying intelligence between them, made them almost

17. Cf. Harold Bloom, who calls *Jude* "the most Shelleyan of Hardy's novels" and says that Sue is "Jude's Shelleyan epipsyche, his twin sister (actually his cousin) and counterpart" (introduction to *Thomas Hardy's "Jude the Obscure,"* 4).

In support of Bloom, it may be noted that when Sue is said to be "so ethereal a creature that her spirit [can] be seen trembling through her limbs," there is a direct reference to "Epipsychidion": "the brightness / Of her divinest presence trembles through / Her limbs."

the two parts of a single whole" (360–61). Finally, Sue's response to the death of their children is to say: "O my comrade, our perfect union—our two-in-oneness—is now stained with blood!" (412).

Such likeness, one cannot help feeling, will tend, if anything, to be a recipe for sexual trouble insofar as a sense of the otherness of one's partner is a desideratum for successful sexual relationship; indeed, before they come together, Jude thinks that "a union between them, had such been possible, would have meant a terrible intensification—two bitters in one dish" (224). When they do live together, however, it is the absence of sex that is the problem, for she refuses to consummate the relationship. Since Jude is clearly not sexually repellent to her, the question of aversion on her part as the source of the difficulty does not arise, as may seem to be the case in her relationship with Phillotson. In her relations with Jude the focus, therefore, for all the tortured complexity of their interaction, is firmly on the nature of her sexual being. Hardy's brilliant depiction of this makes Sue the most fascinating of his unresponsive, reluctant heroines.

As Jude contemplates Sue on one notable occasion, it appears that, where sex is concerned, her problems are likely to be not so much psychological as physical:

> Looking at his loved one as she appeared to him now, in his tender thought the sweetest and most disinterested comrade that he had ever had, living largely in vivid imaginings, so ethereal a creature that her spirit could be seen trembling through her limbs, he felt heartily ashamed of his earthliness in spending the hours he had spent in Arabella's company. There was something rude and immoral in thrusting these recent facts of his life upon the mind of one who, to him, was so uncarnate as to seem at times impossible as a human wife to an average man. (245)

If Sue seems to be "so ethereal a creature" that her spirit can "be seen trembling through her limbs," this is less because her spirituality is palpable—though she is indeed intended to be the opposite of Arabella—than because her physicality gives the impression of being so attenuated she hardly appears to be there in the flesh at all. Jude remarks on this repeatedly: "[Y]ou spirit, you disembodied creature," he calls her, "you

dear, sweet, tantalizing phantom—hardly flesh at all; so that when I
put my arms round you I almost expect them to pass through you as
through air" (309). "But you, Sue," he says on another occasion, "are
such a phantasmal, bodiless creature, one who . . . has . . . little animal
passion in you" (324). All this is beautifully caught in one word, in the
vivid coinage "uncarnate," which places Sue at the opposite pole from Tess,
who, in a memorable description of her,[18] is seen at a moment "when a
woman's soul is more incarnate than at any other time; when the most
spiritual beauty bespeaks itself flesh." Yet, paradoxically, Sue is sexually
attractive, rousing Jude to an enduring passion for her, and she herself
declares, seeking to justify her marriage to Phillotson, that she feels she
would not have been "provided with attractiveness unless it were meant
to be exercised" (265). The exercising, however, reveals to her that she is
a woman "with aberrant passions, and unaccountable antipathies" (266).

Despite her antipathies, Sue, as we have seen, has a "love of being
loved" and seems to be driven by a need for relationships with men, not
only with Phillotson and Jude but also with a Christminster student. Her
"friendly intimacy" with the undergraduate, formed when she is eighteen,
epitomizes her desire for a sealed-off closeness of relationship, for, as later
with both Phillotson and Jude, she lives with him but separately. "We
shared a sitting-room for fifteen months," she tells Jude, and adds: "He
said I was breaking his heart by holding out against him so long at such
close quarters; he could never have believed it of woman. . . . His death
caused a terrible remorse in me for my cruelty—though I hope he died
of consumption and not of me entirely" (202).

The kind of closeness Sue permits herself is caught in an early exchange
between her and Jude:

> " . . . we are going to be *very* nice with each other, aren't we, and
> never, never, vex each other any more?" She looked up trustfully,
> and her voice seemed trying to nestle in his breast.
> "I shall always care for you!" said Jude.
> "And I for you. Because you are single-hearted, and forgiving to
> your faulty and tiresome little Sue!"

18. See the Introduction for the full description and an analysis of it.

He looked away, for that epicene tenderness of hers was too
harrowing. (208)

Sue is her nestling voice. With her voice she gives herself to Jude completely
—but incorporeally, as it were. And that precisely, as the repeated image
emphasizes, is what she would like in return from him: " 'Jude, I want you
to kiss me, as a lover, incorporeally,' she said, tremulously nestling up to
him, with damp lashes" (350). Indeed, the narrator finds the exact word
to describe Sue's tenderness: it is "epicene" in the sense that it takes no
account of any difference of sex between him and herself, remains asexual,
that is, in the very assertion of intimacy, and that is why for him it is so
"harrowing." The "epicene" also effectively deconstructs the "tenderness,"
which the nestling context necessarily makes sexual.

Jude finds Sue's intimacies harrowing, but he generously accepts their
limitations. In this regard, though a spontaneously passionate man, he
is aligned with the diffident heroes who precede him in the novels, as is
brought out on the occasion Sue comes to his lodgings in her flight from
the Training-School. She reports it is being said they "ought to marry as
soon as possible, for the sake of [her] reputation":

> By every law of nature and sex a kiss was the only rejoinder
> that fitted the mood and the moment, under the suasion of which
> Sue's undemonstrative regard of him might not inconceivably have
> changed its temperature. Some men would have cast scruples to
> the winds, and ventured it, oblivious both of Sue's declaration of
> her neutral feelings, and of the pair of autographs in the vestry of
> Arabella's parish church. Jude did not. (213)

Jude's restraint here becomes habitual in his response to Sue, and though
Sue's sexual problem is too deep-seated for it to be easily amenable to
change, it is intimated in a fine symbolic scene how Jude might possibly
have helped save her from herself. The occasion is their visit to the flower
pavilion at the Agricultural Exhibition:

> Sue's usually pale cheeks [reflected] the pink of the tinted roses at
> which she gazed; for the gay sights, the air, the music, and the
> excitement of a day's outing with Jude, had quickened her blood

and made her eyes sparkle with vivacity. She adored roses . . . and put her face within an inch of their blooms to smell them.

"I should like to push my face quite into them—the dears!" she . . . said. "But I suppose it is against the rules to touch them—isn't it, Jude?"

"Yes, you baby," said he: and then playfully gave her a little push, so that her nose went among the petals.

"The policeman will be down on us, and I shall say it was my husband's fault!"

Then she looked up at him, and smiled in a way that told so much to Arabella.

"Happy?" he murmured.

She nodded. (365–66)

Sue's response to the roses is suggestive of more general attitudes she clings to. Even when she is aroused, when her "blood" is "quickened," she hangs back from doing what she wants, from pushing her face "quite into" the roses. It is when Jude, however, does not leave her to hang back but gently pushes her past her reluctance, that she—this being the only time in the novel that she does so in direct relation to him—spontaneously acknowledges him as her "husband."

Instead, Jude remains steadfast in suffering acceptance of her inhibition. It is only after long years and the death of the children that he grasps what she herself intimated to him about herself early in their relationship, on the night of her flight from the Training-School. Having listened then to her story of her relations with the Christminster student, he tells her he believes she is "as innocent as [she is] unconventional":

> "I am not particularly innocent, as you see, now that I have
> twitched the robe
> From that blank lay-figure your fancy draped,"

said she, with an ostensible sneer, though he could hear that she was brimming with tears. "But I have never yielded myself to any lover, if that's what you mean! I have remained as I began."

"I quite believe you. But some women would not have remained as they began."

"Perhaps not. Better women would not. People say I must be cold-natured—sexless—on account of it. But I won't have it! Some of the most passionately erotic poets have been the most self-contained in their daily lives." (203)

When Sue says, with an undercurrent of pride, that she has "never yielded" herself to any lover, we recall Bathsheba's boast in *Far from the Madding Crowd*—sounding over the more than twenty years that separate the two novels—that (prior to her marriage) "her lips had been touched by no man's on earth" as "her waist had never been encircled by a lover's arm." And this is not because Sue or Bathsheba is "sexless," as Sue rightly insists about herself, but because virginity is for each the prime value in its signification of their autonomy. What matters to Bathsheba, Diana being the goddess whom she "instinctively adore[s]," is that she be "sufficient to herself"; what matters to Sue is that she be "self-contained," that she remain as she began. These are first and foremost instinctive physical feelings, and we also remember in this respect Grace's "Daphnean instinct" that dispatches her in precipitate flight from her husband in *The Woodlanders,* a precursor of Sue's flight—via the window—from Phillotson. When the desire for self-containment is held so intensely, it undermines the need in personal—and particularly sexual—relations for a positive and desirable self-establishment since the wish for such sufficiency may even survive sexual surrender and leave its stamp on it, as we have previously seen in the case of both Bathsheba and Grace. This finally becomes apparent to Jude, as he ruefully registers: "Yes, Sue," he says, " . . . I seduced you. . . . You were a distinct type—a refined creature, intended by Nature to be left intact. But I couldn't leave you alone!" (418).

Sue insists on preserving her intactness even when their divorce comes through and they are both free to marry. The fact that they never actually marry, despite repeated resolutions on their part to do so, provides a symbolic underlining of her failure ever really to open herself to him. When she does eventually submit sexually, it is in a manner that once more recalls the story of Bathsheba. One night Arabella suddenly erupts again into their lives, begging Jude to meet her at the inn where she is staying overnight, but Sue opposes his going:

> "Well—Arabella has appealed to me for help. I must go out and speak to her, Sue, at least!"
> "I can't say any more!—O, if you must, you must!" she said, bursting out into sobs that seemed to tear her heart. "I have nobody but you, Jude, and you are deserting me! I didn't know you were like this—I can't bear it, I can't! If she were yours it would be different!"

"Or if you were."

"Very well then—if I must I must. Since you will have it so, I agree! I will be. Only I didn't mean to! And I didn't want to marry again, either! . . . But yes—I agree, I agree! I do love you. I ought to have known that you would conquer in the long run, living like this!"

She ran across and flung her arms round his neck. "I am not a cold-natured, sexless creature, am I, for keeping you at such a distance? I am sure you don't think so! Wait and see! I do belong to you, don't I? I give in!" (332)

What finally brings Bathsheba to give in to Troy is her fear of losing him to another woman, as Sue here fears Arabella will infallibly claim Jude if given a chance. And Sue, like Bathsheba, regards her giving in to her lover as a "conquest" on his part not because she is won sexually but because she is defeated in her desire to remain intact. Beaten by life, she is forced to surrender—and can only lament that she "didn't mean to."

We are to understand that their relationship is consummated sexually that night, but the narrator maintains a conspicuous silence about this momentous event. It is true that Sue says to Jude, "I am not a bit frightened about losing you, now I really am yours and you really are mine" (337), but the fact that years later he should blame himself for having seduced her and not left her intact hardly suggests that she does truly open herself to him, that she is ever really his. She proceeds to bear two children and is pregnant with a third when the tragedy strikes, but the palpable textual insubstantiality of the children serves as a mute comment on the continued ethereality of her supposedly achieved sexuality. There is no indication that their lives are much changed by her surrender, though Hardy is more explicit about this outside the novel than in it:

> [T]here is nothing perverted or depraved in Sue's nature. The abnormalism consists in disproportion: not in inversion, her sexual instinct being healthy so far as it goes, but unusually weak & fastidious; her sensibilities remain painfully alert notwithstanding, (as they do in nature with such women). One point illustrating this I cd not dwell upon: that, though she has children, her intimacies with Jude have never been more than occasional, even while they were living together (I mention that they occupy separate rooms, except

towards the end), & one of her reasons for fearing the marriage ceremony is that she fears it wd be breaking faith with Jude to withhold herself at pleasure, or altogether, after it; though while uncontracted she feels at liberty to yield herself as seldom as she chooses. This has tended to keep his passion as hot at the end as at the beginning, & helps to break his heart. He has never really possessed her as freely as he desired.[19]

To be possessed is to be given, and Sue—like both Bathsheba and Grace—has never been able freely to give herself. What lies behind the inhibition, behind the intractable desire for self-containment, is not explored in the narrative, but I think we may assume that the involuntary clinging to self—in the case of all three heroines—is not unrelated to a deep and instinctive fear of losing it in the giving.[20]

Since Jude and Sue never marry, though they live together and have children together, their union, based as it is on their surpassing affinity of being, is in effect presented as a viable alternative to marriage. Sue, as we have seen, calls it their "perfect union" and laments that the deaths of their children should have stained it with blood. But, of course, it is far from being a perfect union and is exposed as such long before the tragedy of the children. What the union is above all productive of, at least for the long-suffering Jude, is frustration, his sexual frustration being perhaps as chilling an instance of this motif as any in a narrative that is predicated on frustration of one kind or another. This is what the ideal

19. Hardy, letter to Edmund Gosse, November 20, 1895, in *Collected Letters*, 2:99.

20. Terry Eagleton's view of Sue is close to mine. He says that her "freedom . . . is in part negative and destructive—a self-possessive individualism, which sees all permanent commitment as imprisoning, a fear of being possessed which involves a fear of giving" ("The Limits of Art," 66). And Martin Seymour-Smith says it "may be" that Sue is "afraid of the loss of identity that [orgasm] entails: of 'letting go' or of feeling 'possessed' . . ." (*Hardy*, 526).

Cf. D. H. Lawrence, who says "[Sue] was born with the vital female atrophied in her. . . . It was wrong for Jude to take her physically, it was a violation of her" ("Study of Thomas Hardy," 108).

Cf. too Anne B. Simpson, who in a feminist account of Sue insists on her "unknowability": "Sue Bridehead . . . occupies the site of unknowability in a text that challenges assumptions about the transparency and coherence of the feminine" ("Sue Bridehead Revisited," 55).

relationship, nominally "the only love which is strong as death," comes down to. Moreover, death proves to be altogether too strong for it.

The deaths of the children are in more than one sense hard to take, but one can see the need for a catastrophe in the narrative. That Little Father Time should be made the agent of the catastrophe is somewhat unfortunate, for he is an alien figure in an otherwise powerfully realistic mode, but given the mood of the author, he must have forced his way into the novel. When he arrives on the scene, Jude expresses some doubt as to whether he is his child, but going by his *Weltanschauung*, there is no question as to his authorial lineage: he seems "mutely to say" that "all laughing comes from misapprehension. Rightly looked at there is no laughable thing under the sun" (342) and then actually does say, "I should like the flowers very much, if I didn't keep on thinking they'd be all withered in a few days!" (366). His deeds lead to another kind of withering—of the ideal relationship. The most devastating criticism of camaraderie as a basis for relationship between the sexes is that it proves wholly inadequate as a support in the face of the tragedy. Instead of being drawn closer together in their time of need, Sue and Jude are driven apart. Ultimately, the perfect union proves to be as little durable as a relationship based on steamlike passion. By the end of *Jude the Obscure,* camaraderie disappears into the two compulsively repeated and detestable remarriages that the disintegrated couple lend themselves to.

Given this conclusion, it should not be found surprising that Hardy gave up fiction after *Jude.* He himself said that it was the abuse accorded both *Tess* and *Jude* that led him to leave off, but no writer worth his salt has been deterred by mere criticism, however abusive. Rather, it was that he had reached a dead end, a blank wall. His engagement for more than twenty years with the problem of relations between the sexes had culminated in a prospect of repetition and frustration alone. His long chronicle of bad marriages and disastrous sexual relations had hitherto been at least partly qualified by the possibility of an alternative kind of relationship: the failures had regularly given way, if only at the end of the narratives, to intimations of viable, nonpassionate relationship, as in the marriages of Bathsheba and Oak in *Far from the Madding Crowd,* Thomasin and Venn in *The Return of the Native,* and Elizabeth-Jane and

Farfrae in *The Mayor of Casterbridge;* in the renewed marriage of Grace and Fitzpiers in *The Woodlanders* (even though this is offset by negative prognostications); and in the implied union of 'Liza-Lu and Angel in *Tess of the d'Urbervilles. Jude* offers no such possibility. The chronicle of failure had also paradoxically been sustained by significant divergences of view between the see-er and the seer, which had had the effect of palliating the direness of the seer and leaving openings for further developments. In *Jude the Obscure* there are no such discrepancies: throughout see-er meets seer—as the heavens meet Egdon Heath—in a black fraternization.

WORKS CITED

Primary Works

NOVELS

Hardy, Thomas. 1871. *Desperate Remedies*. New Wessex Edition. General editor, P. N. Furbank. London: Macmillan, 1975.

———. 1872. *Under the Greenwood Tree*, ed. David Wright, Penguin English Library. Harmondsworth: Penguin, 1978.

———. 1873. *A Pair of Blue Eyes*, ed. Roger Ebbatson, Penguin Classics. Harmondsworth: Penguin, 1986.

———. 1874. *Far from the Madding Crowd*, ed. Ronald Blythe, Penguin English Library. Harmondsworth: Penguin, 1978.

———. 1876. *The Hand of Ethelberta*. New Wessex Edition. General editor, P. N. Furbank. London: Macmillan, 1975.

———. 1878. *The Return of the Native*, ed. George Woodcock, Penguin English Library. Harmondsworth: Penguin, 1978.

———. 1881. *A Laodicean*. New Wessex Edition. General editor, P. N. Furbank. London: Macmillan, 1975.

———. 1886. *The Mayor of Casterbridge*, ed. Martin Seymour-Smith, Penguin English Library. Harmondsworth: Penguin, 1978.

———. 1887. *The Woodlanders*, ed. James Gibson, Penguin English Library. Harmondsworth: Penguin, 1981.

———. 1891. *Tess of the d'Urbervilles*, ed. David Skilton, Penguin English Library. Harmondsworth: Penguin, 1978.

———. *Tess of the d'Urbervilles*. New Wessex (paperback) Edition. General editor, P. N. Furbank. London: Macmillan, 1975.

———. 1896. *Jude the Obscure*, ed. C. H. Sisson, Penguin English Library. Harmondsworth: Penguin, 1978.

———. 1897. *The Well-Beloved*. New Wessex Edition. General editor, P. N. Furbank. London: Macmillan, 1975.

OTHER WORKS

Hardy, Thomas. *The Collected Letters of Thomas Hardy*. Ed. Richard Little Purdy and Michael Millgate. 7 vols. Oxford: Clarendon Press, 1978–1988.

———. *The Complete Poetical Works of Thomas Hardy*. Ed. Samuel Hynes. 3 vols. Oxford: Clarendon Press, 1985.

———. *The Life and Work of Thomas Hardy*. Ed. Michael Millgate. Athens: University of Georgia Press, 1985.

———. *The Literary Notebooks of Thomas Hardy*. Ed. Lennart A. Bjork. 2 vols. New York: New York University Press, 1985.

———. *The New Wessex Edition of the Stories of Thomas Hardy*. Ed. F. B. Pinion. 3 vols. London: Macmillan, 1977.

———. *Thomas Hardy's Personal Writings*. Ed. Harold Orel. Lawrence: University Press of Kansas, 1966.

Secondary Works

Abercrombie, Lascelles. *Thomas Hardy: A Critical Study*. 1912. Reprint, New York: Russell and Russell, 1964.

Adamson, Jane. "*Tess,* Time and Its Shapings." *Critical Review* 26 (1984): 18–36.

Adelman, Gary. *Jude the Obscure: A Paradise of Despair*. New York: Twayne, 1992.

Adey, Lionel. "Styles of Love in *Far from the Madding Crowd*." In vol. 5 of *Thomas Hardy Annual,* ed. Norman Page, 48–63. London: Macmillan, 1987.

Alvarez, A. "*Jude the Obscure*." In *Hardy: A Collection of Critical Essays,* ed. Albert J. Guerard, 113–22. Englewood Cliffs, N.J.: Prentice Hall, 1963.

Babb, Howard. "Setting and Theme in *Far from the Madding Crowd.*"
    ELH 30 (1963): 147–61.

Ball, David. "Tragic Contradiction in Hardy's *The Woodlanders.*" *Ariel* 18
    (1987): 17–25.

Bayley, John. *An Essay on Hardy.* Cambridge: Cambridge University Press,
    1981.

———. "A Social Comedy? On Re-reading *The Woodlanders.*" In vol. 5 of
    Thomas Hardy Annual, ed. Norman Page, 3–21. London: Macmillan,
    1987.

Beegel, Susan. "Bathsheba's Lovers: Male Sexuality in *Far from the Mad-
    ding Crowd.*" In *Modern Critical Views: Thomas Hardy,* ed. Harold
    Bloom, 207–26. New Haven: Chelsea House, 1987.

Belsey, Catherine. *Critical Practice.* London and New York: Routledge,
    1980.

Benvenuto, Richard. *"The Return of the Native* as a Tragedy in Six Books."
    Nineteenth-Century Fiction 26 (1971): 83–93.

Berger, Sheila. *Thomas Hardy and Visual Structures: Framing, Disruption,
    Process.* New York and London: New York University Press, 1990.

Bloom, Harold. Introduction to *Thomas Hardy's "Jude the Obscure,"* ed.
    Harold Bloom. New Haven: Chelsea House, 1987.

Blythe, Ronald. Introduction to *Far from the Madding Crowd,* ed. Ronald
    Blythe, 11–35. Harmondsworth: Penguin, Penguin English Library,
    1978.

———. Introduction to *A Pair of Blue Eyes,* New Wessex edition, 13–31.
    London: Macmillan, 1975.

Brady, Kristin. "Tess and Alec: Rape or Seduction?" In vol. 4 of *Thomas
    Hardy Annual,* ed. Norman Page, 129–45. London: Macmillan, 1986.

Brogan, Howard O. " 'Visible Essences' in *The Mayor of Casterbridge.*"
    ELH 17 (1950): 307–23.

Bullen, J. B. *The Expressive Eye: Fiction and Perception in the Work of
    Thomas Hardy.* Oxford: Clarendon Press, 1986.

Butler, Lance St. John, ed. *Alternative Hardy.* London: Macmillan, 1989.

Carpenter, Richard C. "The Mirror and the Sword: Imagery in *Far from
    the Madding Crowd.*" *Nineteenth-Century Fiction* 18 (1964): 331–45.

———. *Thomas Hardy.* New York: Twayne, 1964.

Casagrande, Peter J. "A New View of Bathsheba Everdene." In *Critical Approaches to the Fiction of Thomas Hardy*, ed. Dale Kramer, 50–73. London: Macmillan, 1979.

———. "The Shifted 'Centre of Altruism' in *The Woodlanders:* Thomas Hardy's Third 'Return of a Native.'" *ELH* 38 (1971): 104–25.

———. *Unity in Hardy's Novels: "Repetitive Symmetries."* Lawrence: Regents Press of Kansas, 1982.

Chapman, Raymond. *The Language of Thomas Hardy.* London: Macmillan, 1990.

Collins, Deborah L. *Thomas Hardy and His God: A Liturgy of Unbelief.* London: Macmillan, 1990.

Conrad, Joseph. Preface to his *The Nigger of the "Narcissus,"* vii–xii. 1898. Reprint, London: Dent Collected Edition, 1950.

Daleski, H. M. *The Forked Flame: A Study of D. H. Lawrence.* London: Faber and Faber, 1965.

Deen, Leonard W. "Heroism and Pathos in Hardy's *The Return of the Native.*" *Nineteenth-Century Fiction* 15 (1960): 207–19.

Dike, D. A. "A Modern Oedipus: *The Mayor of Casterbridge.*" *Essays in Criticism* 2 (1952): 169–79.

Eagleton, Terry. "The Limits of Art." In *Thomas Hardy's "Jude the Obscure,"* ed. Harold Bloom, 61–71. New Haven: Chelsea House, 1987.

Ebbatson, Roger. Introduction to *A Pair of Blue Eyes,* ed. Roger Ebbatson, 13–38. Harmondsworth: Penguin, Penguin Classics, 1986.

Fayen, George S. "Hardy's *The Woodlanders:* Inwardness and Memory." *Studies in English Literature* 1 (1961): 81–100.

Federico, Annette. *Masculine Identity in Hardy and Gissing.* Rutherford, Madison, Teaneck, N.J.: Fairleigh Dickinson University Press, 1991.

Fussell, D. H. "The Maladroit Delay: The Changing Times in Hardy's *The Mayor of Casterbridge.*" *Critical Quarterly* 21 (1979): 17–30.

Garson, Marjorie. *Hardy's Fables of Integrity: Woman, Body, Text.* Oxford: Clarendon Press, 1991.

Gatrell, Simon. *Thomas Hardy and the Proper Study of Mankind.* Charlottesville: University Press of Virginia, 1993.

Giordano, Frank R. "The Martyrdom of Giles Winterborne." In vol. 2 of *Thomas Hardy Annual,* ed. Norman Page, 61–78. London: Macmillan, 1984.

Gittings, Robert. *The Older Hardy.* London: Heinemann, 1978.

———. *Young Thomas Hardy.* London: Heinemann, 1975.

Goetz, William R. "The Felicity and Infelicity of Marriage in *Jude the Obscure.*" *Nineteenth-Century Fiction* 38 (1983): 189–213.

Goode, John. *Thomas Hardy: The Offensive Truth.* Oxford: Basil Blackwell, 1988.

Goodheart, Eugene. "Thomas Hardy and the Lyrical Novel." *Nineteenth-Century Fiction* 12 (1957): 215–25.

Gose, Elliot B. *Imagination Indulged: The Irrational in the Nineteenth-Century Novel.* Montreal and London: McGill-Queen's University Press, 1972.

———. "Psychic Evolution: Darwinism and Initiation in *Tess of the d'Urbervilles.*" *Nineteenth-Century Fiction* 18 (1963): 261–72.

Gregor, Ian. *The Great Web: The Form of Hardy's Major Fiction.* London: Faber and Faber, 1974.

———. Introduction to *The Woodlanders,* ed. James Gibson, 11–29. Harmondsworth: Penguin, Penguin English Library, 1981.

Grindle, Juliet M. "Compulsion and Choice in *The Mayor of Casterbridge.*" In *The Novels of Thomas Hardy,* ed. Anne Smith, 91–106. New York: Barnes and Noble, 1979.

Guerard, Albert J. *Thomas Hardy.* New Directions paperbook. Norfolk, Conn.: James Laughlin, 1964.

Hasan, Noorul. *Thomas Hardy: The Sociological Imagination.* London: Macmillan, 1982.

Heilman, Robert B. "*Gulliver* and Hardy's *Tess:* Houyhnhnms, Yahoos, and Ambiguities." *The Southern Review,* n.s., 6 (1970): 277–301.

———. "*The Return:* Centennial Observations." In *The Novels of Thomas Hardy,* ed. Anne Smith, 58–90. New York: Barnes and Noble, 1979.

Howe, Irving. *Thomas Hardy.* London: Weidenfeld and Nicolson, 1968.

Ingham, Patricia. "Provisional Narratives: Hardy's Final Trilogy." In *Alternative Hardy,* ed. Lance St. John Butler, 49–73. London: Macmillan, 1989.

———. *Thomas Hardy.* New York and London: Harvester Wheatsheaf, 1989.

Jacobus, Mary. "Sue the Obscure." *Essays in Criticism* 25 (1975): 304–28.

————. "Tree and Machine: *The Woodlanders.*" In *Critical Approaches to the Fiction of Thomas Hardy,* ed. Dale Kramer, 116–34. London: Macmillan, 1979.

Johnson, Bruce. *True Correspondence: A Phenomenology of Thomas Hardy's Novels.* Tallahassee: University Presses of Florida, 1983.

Joyce, James. *Stephen Hero.* Ed. Theodore Spencer. New York: New Directions, 1944.

Karl, Frederick R. *"The Mayor of Casterbridge:* A New Fiction Defined." *Modern Fiction Studies* 6 (1960): 195–213.

Kiely, Robert. "Vision and Viewpoint in *The Mayor of Casterbridge.*" *Nineteenth-Century Fiction* 23 (1968): 189–200.

Kincaid, James R. "Hardy's Absences." In *Critical Approaches to the Fiction of Thomas Hardy,* ed. Dale Kramer, 202–14. London: Macmillan, 1979.

Kramer, Dale. *Thomas Hardy: The Forms of Tragedy.* Detroit: Wayne State University Press, 1975.

Laird, J. T. "Approaches to Fiction: Hardy and Henry James." In vol. 2 of *Thomas Hardy Annual,* ed. Norman Page, 51–60. London: Macmillan, 1984.

————. *The Shaping of Tess of the d'Urbervilles.* Oxford: Clarendon Press, 1975.

Langbaum, Robert. *Thomas Hardy in Our Time.* New York: St. Martin's Press, 1995.

Lawrence, D. H. "Study of Thomas Hardy." In *Study of Thomas Hardy and Other Essays,* ed. Bruce Steele, 7–128. Cambridge: Cambridge University Press, 1985.

————. *Women in Love.* Ed. David Farmer, Lindeth Vasey, and John Worthen. Cambridge: Cambridge University Press, 1987.

Lodge, David. *Language of Fiction.* London: Routledge and Kegan Paul, 1966.

————. "Pessimism and Fictional Form: *Jude the Obscure.*" In his *Working with Structuralism: Essays and Reviews on Nineteenth- and Twentieth-Century Literature,* 106–13. London: Routledge and Kegan Paul, 1981.

————. *"The Woodlanders:* A Darwinian Pastoral Elegy." In his *Working with Structuralism: Essays and Reviews on Nineteenth- and Twentieth-Century Literature,* 79–94. London: Routledge and Kegan Paul, 1981.

Lucas, John. "Hardy's Women." In *Thomas Hardy: Three Pastoral Novels,* ed. R. P. Draper, 128–37. London: Macmillan, 1987.

Matchett, William H. *"The Woodlanders,* or Realism in Sheep's Clothing." *Nineteenth-Century Fiction* 9 (1955): 241–61.

Miller, J. Hillis. *Thomas Hardy: Distance and Desire.* Cambridge: Harvard University Press, 1970.

Millgate, Michael. *Thomas Hardy: A Biography.* Oxford and New York: Oxford University Press, 1982.

Morgan, Rosemarie. *Women and Sexuality in the Novels of Thomas Hardy.* London and New York: Routledge, 1988.

Morrell, Roy. *Thomas Hardy: The Will and the Way.* Kuala Lumpur: University of Malaya Press, 1965.

Moule, Horace. Review of *Under the Greenwood Tree* (*Saturday Review* [1872]). Extracts reprinted in *Thomas Hardy: Three Pastoral Novels,* ed. R. P. Draper, 43–45. London: Macmillan, 1987.

Ousby, Ian. "Love-Hate Relations: Bathsheba, Hardy and the Men in *Far from the Madding Crowd." Cambridge Quarterly* 10 (1981): 24–39.

Page, Norman. *Thomas Hardy.* London: Routledge and Kegan Paul, 1977.

Paris, Bernard J. " 'A Confusion of Many Standards': Conflicting Value Systems in *Tess of the d'Urbervilles." Nineteenth-Century Fiction* 24 (1969): 57–79.

Paterson, John. " 'The Mayor of Casterbridge' as Tragedy." *Victorian Studies* 3 (1959): 151–72.

———. "The 'Poetics' of *The Return of the Native." Modern Fiction Studies* 6 (1960): 214–22.

Polhemus, Robert M. *Erotic Faith: Being in Love from Jane Austen to D. H. Lawrence.* Chicago and London: University of Chicago Press, 1990.

Proust, Marcel. *Remembrance of Things Past.* Trans. C. K. Scott Moncrieff. Vol. 10. London: Chatto and Windus, 1951.

Rimmon-Kenan, Shlomith. *A Glance beyond Doubt: Narration, Representation, Subjectivity.* Columbus: Ohio State University Press, 1996.

Rogers, Robert. *A Psychoanalytic Study of the Double in Literature.* Detroit: Wayne State University Press, 1970.

Salter, C. H. *Good Little Thomas Hardy.* Totowa, N.J.: Barnes and Noble, 1981.

Seymour-Smith, Martin. *Hardy.* London: Bloomsbury, 1994.

Shires, Linda M. "Narrative, Gender, and Power in *Far from the Madding Crowd.*" *Novel* 24 (1991): 162–77.

Showalter, Elaine. "The Unmanning of the Mayor of Casterbridge." In *Critical Approaches to the Fiction of Thomas Hardy,* ed. Dale Kramer, 99–115. London: Macmillan, 1979.

Silverman, Kaja. "History, Figuration, and Female Subjectivity in *Tess of the d'Urbervilles.*" *Novel* 18 (1984): 5–28.

Simpson, Anne B. "Sue Bridehead Revisited." In *Victorian Literature and Culture,* ed. John Maynard and Adrienne Auslander Munich, 55–66. New York: AMS Press, 1991.

Southerington, F. R. *Hardy's Vision of Man.* London: Chatto and Windus, 1971.

Steig, Michael. "The Problem of Literary Value in Two Early Hardy Novels." *Texas Studies in Literature and Language* 12 (1970): 55–62.

Stewart, J. I. M. *Thomas Hardy: A Critical Biography.* New York: Dodd, Mead, 1971.

Sumner, Rosemary. *Thomas Hardy: Psychological Novelist.* London: Macmillan, 1981.

Sutherland, John. "A Note on the Teasing Narrator in *Jude the Obscure.*" *English Literature in Transition* 17 (1974): 159–62.

Tanner, Tony. "Colour and Movement in Hardy's *Tess of the d'Urbervilles.*" *Critical Quarterly* 10 (1968): 219–39.

Taylor, Richard H. *The Neglected Hardy: Thomas Hardy's Lesser Novels.* London: Macmillan, 1982.

Toker, Leona. *Eloquent Reticence: Withholding Information in Fictional Narrative.* Lexington: University Press of Kentucky, 1993.

Waldoff, Leon. "Psychological Determinism in *Tess of the d'Urbervilles.*" In *Critical Approaches to the Fiction of Thomas Hardy,* ed. Dale Kramer, 135–54. London: Macmillan, 1979.

Weinstein, Philip M. *The Semantics of Desire: Changing Models of Identity from Dickens to Joyce.* Princeton: Princeton University Press, 1984.

Williams, Merryn. *Thomas Hardy and Rural England.* London: Macmillan, 1972.

Wing, George. *Thomas Hardy.* Edinburgh and London: Oliver and Boyd, 1963.

Wotton, George. *Thomas Hardy: Towards a Materialist Criticism.* Totowa, N.J.: Gill and Macmillan, Barnes and Noble, 1985.

INDEX

The following abbreviations are used for
novels by Hardy:

DR = *Desperate Remedies*
FFMC = *Far from the Madding Crowd*
JO = *Jude the Obscure*
MC = *The Mayor of Casterbridge*
PBE = *A Pair of Blue Eyes*
RN = *The Return of the Native*
Td = *Tess of the d'Urbervilles*
UGT = *Under the Greenwood Tree*
W = *The Woodlanders*

Topics in Applied Physics   Volume 4

Topics in Applied Physics   Founded by Helmut K. V. Lotsch

Interactions
on Metal Surfaces

Edited by R. Gomer

With Contributions by
E. Bauer   M. Boudart   R. Gomer   S. K. Lyo
D. Menzel   E. W. Plummer   L. D. Schmidt
J. R. Smith

With 112 Figures

Springer-Verlag New York Heidelberg Berlin 1975

Professor ROBERT GOMER

The James Franck Institute, The University of Chicago, 5640 Ellis Avenue,
Chicago, IL 60637, USA

ISBN 0-387-07094-X Springer-Verlag New York Heidelberg Berlin
ISBN 3-540-07094-X Springer-Verlag Berlin Heidelberg New York

Library of Congress Cataloging in Publication Data. Gomer, Robert. Interactions on metal surfaces. (Topics in applied physics; v. 4). Includes bibliographies and index. 1. Surface chemistry. 2. Metallic surfaces. I. Bauer, Ernst. II. Title. QD506.G63. 541'.3453. 75-1281.

© by Springer-Verlag Berlin Heidelberg 1975
Printed in Germany

Monophoto typesetting, offset printing and bookbinding: Brühlsche Universitätsdruckerei, Gießen

Preface

Surface phenomena encompass an important but enormously vast field. Any attempt to treat all or even a major portion of them in a book of this size is clearly impossible. I have selected metal surfaces and interactions on them, principally chemisorption, as the main topics of this book because they are of fundamental importance to almost all aspects of surface science and because progress, both theoretical and experimental is now very rapid in this field. Although catalysis goes considerably beyond the confines of the rest of the book a discussion of it has been included (Chapter 7) because of its intrinsic importance, its close relation to other subjects discussed here, and finally to indicate that there is more to interactions on surfaces than the adsorption of hydrogen on the (100) plane of tungsten.

To keep within the limits of this monograph-like series choices had to be made even within these restrictions. The intent of the book is to acquaint the reader with the theoretical underpinnings, the most important techniques currently being used to investigate metal surfaces and chemisorption, and finally to present some of the results of modern research in this area. It was necessary to omit a number of important topics, for instance field emission and field ion microscopy. In part, these omissions were based on the availability of reference books and review articles, and in part on the editor's sense of priorities for this particular book.

Chapter 1 discusses the electronic properties of surfaces, with emphasis on clean surfaces, largely from the point of view of W. KOHN and his school, and indicates how the linear response approach can be extended to treat chemisorption. Chapter 2 devotes itself specifically to the theory of chemisorption with emphasis on LCAO-MO methods, but includes some discussion of other approaches. Chapter 3 gives a very brief summary of the principal techniques used in chemisorption research but is mainly devoted to discussing what is known about a number of actual systems. Chapter 4 deals with various desorption techniques and the theory of such processes. Chapter 5 discusses the theory of electron spectroscopies, specifically field and photoemission, which provide insight into the electronic structure of surfaces and adsorption complexes, and presents a number of quite recent results obtained by these techniques. Chapter 6 is devoted to a discussion of low energy electron diffraction and Auger phenomena, two of the most important techniques for characterizing the geometry of clean and adsorbate covered metal and semiconductor surfaces, and for determining chemical composition on the atomic scale. Chapter 7, as already pointed out, is devoted to a discussion of catalysis.

Discussions of specific adsorption systems occur not only in Chapter 3 but figure importantly also in Chapters 4 and 5. In some cases there is redundancy in subject matter, but generally not in point of view. This comes about because there is as yet a great deal we do not understand about chemisorption. It is rather recent in fact that there is essentially universal agreement on the experimental *facts* for a given system. It is hoped that the occasional disagreements in interpretation, honestly presented, will not confuse the reader and will serve to give him the true flavor of the current status of this field.

Chicago, January 1975   ROBERT GOMER

Contents

6. Low Energy Electron Diffraction (LEED) and Auger Methods.
By E. BAUER (With 28 Figures)

Contributors

BAUER, ERNST

Physikalisches Institut, Technische Universität Clausthal,
D-3392 Clausthal-Zellerfeld, Fed. Rep. of Germany

BOUDART, MICHEL

Department of Chemical Engineering, Stanford University,
Stanford, CA 94305, USA

GOMER, ROBERT

The James Franck Institute, The University of Chicago,
Chicago, IL 60637, USA

LYO, SUNG K.

The James Franck Institute, The University of Chicago,
Chicago, IL 60637, USA

MENZEL, DIETRICH

Physik-Department, Technische Universität München,
D-8046 Garching bei München, Fed. Rep. of Germany

PLUMMER, E. WARD

Department of Physics, University of Pennsylvania,
Philadelphia, PA 19104, USA

SCHMIDT, LANNY D.

Department of Chemical Engineering and Materials Science,
University of Minnesota, Minneapolis, MN 55455, USA

SMITH, JOHN R.

Research Laboratories, General Motors Technical Center,
Warren, MI 48090, USA

1. Theory of Electronic Properties of Surfaces

J. R. SMITH

With 21 Figures

Surface or interface electronic structure has been generally recognized as being of pivotal importance in many technologies: solid state and gaseous electronics, catalysis, adhesion, and corrosion—to name a few. Despite its practical importance, our fundamental understanding of surface electronic properties has been greatly overshadowed by progress in understanding the bulk.

There is good reason for this situation. Experimentally, microscopically clean surfaces have been difficult to obtain. Theoretically, the loss of symmetry in the direction perpendicular to the surface greatly complicates calculations.

Recently, there has been rapid progress in our understanding of surfaces, however. The commercial availability of vacuum systems capable of 10^{-10} Torr as well as a number of analytical tools (see Chapters 3–6), have allowed experimentalists to obtain well characterized, clean surfaces. The well developed methods of bulk theory are being applied with encouraging success to the computation of many surface electronic properties.

In this chapter, it is hoped that the reader will obtain some feeling for the basic physical principles involved in the electronic properties of surfaces. It is not meant to be a review, however. Because of space limitations, we were not able to discuss surface energy determinations, but fortunately there is a recent review by LANG [1.1] (see also [1.2]). The reader interested in the companion field of adhesion is referred to the review of KRUPP [1.3] and the more recent theoretical efforts of FERRANTE and SMITH [1.4]. Small particle properties are related to those of solid surfaces, and for an introduction to the former we suggest the recently successful work of JOHNSON et al. [1.5]. Surface phonons are indirectly related to surface electronic properties, and we refer the interested reader to the review of WALLIS [1.6].

In Section 1.1, the subjects of surface states, continuum states, and local orbitals in the surface region are introduced via a simple example. Section 1.2 is devoted to the electron work function with results for a wide range of metals, including the effects of crystallinity and of fractional monolayers of adsorbed gases. Dielectric response, including impurity screening, is discussed in Section 1.3 with application to chemisorbed hydrogen. Resonance levels, electron scattering cross sections, binding energies, vibrational modes, and electronic charge distributions are considered. In Subsection 1.4.1 the subject of surface states is treated, including recent theoretical results for the (111) plane of Si. In Subsection 1.4.2, surface plasmons are discussed. Experimental and theoretical results are given for Al, as examples. The nature of the charge fluctuation associated with the surface plasmon is investigated. The subject of the local density of states in the surface region is discussed in Section 1.5. Results for a Ni d-band are presented. Finally, Section 1.6 is devoted to a short description of the current status of surface calculations.

1.1. A Simple Example: Surface States, Continuum States, and Local Orbitals

As an introduction to surface electronic structure, consider the simple model surface [1.7] specified by the one-dimensional potential of Fig. 1.1. The potential repeats periodically throughout the bulk and then rises to the vacuum level, forming a surface barrier. This surface barrier may be considered the wall of the box containing the electrons within the solid. Within this surface barrier there is a well whose depth is less than that of the bulk wells. This is reminiscent of a

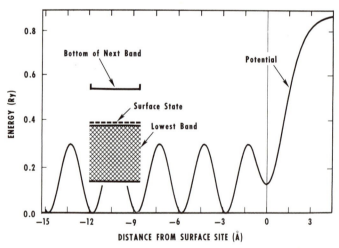

Fig. 1.1. Surface potential plot. The inset shows the relevant part of the energy spectrum of the potential [1.7]

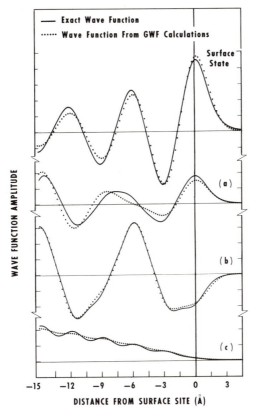

Fig. 1.2a-c. Top curves pertain to the surface state wave function, followed by examples of continuum states near to the top (a), middle (b), and bottom (c) of the lowest band [1.7]

chemisorbed layer, or an atomic layer of foreign particles which is chemically bonded to the surface.

There are two observations that can be made by inspection. The imposition of the surface barrier eliminates the periodicity in the direction perpendicular to the surface. Further, it is a quite strong and yet local perturbation.

The bulk bandwidth of the lowest band and the first band gap are also shown in Fig. 1.1. There is a surface state in the band gap. A surface state is an electronic state bound to the surface region. The local defect produced by the surface barrier can, under certain conditions, bind electrons.

Some of the wave functions of interest are plotted in Fig. 1.2. Let us consider some of the qualitative features of the wave functions.

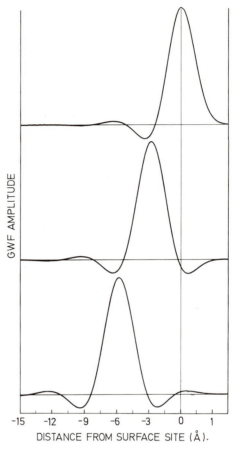

GWF AMPLITUDE

DISTANCE FROM SURFACE SITE (Å).

Fig. 1.3. Generalized Wannier functions belonging to the first three lattice sites [1.7]. The maxima of the GWF's lie very close to the minima of the successive potential wells shown in Fig. 1.1. By the third site in from the vacuum, the local function is essentially the bulk Wannier function

The surface state wave function is unique in that it decays in both the bulk and vacuum directions. Surface states will be discussed further in Subsection 1.4.1. The states within the band, or continuum states, decay only in the vacuum direction. They are, as it were, the tails of the bulk wave functions. This decay of the wave functions leads to a charge asymmetry or, in turn, an electrostatic barrier at the surface which contributes to the electron work function (Sect. 1.2).

This tailing effect and the appearance of surface states means that the local density of states [1.7], the density of states weighted by the square of the local-wave-function-magnitude, will vary in an important way as one proceeds from the bulk through the surface region. The breaking of bonds in forming the surface will generally lead to a narrowing of the local bands, but the appearance of bound or surface states in the band gap will tend to broaden the local density of states. These effects are seen experimentally in, e.g., ion-neutralization, field emission, and photoemission spectroscopies. A discussion of this can be found in Chapter 5 and in [1.8]. The effect of chemisorption on the local density of states will be discussed in Section 1.3, and the results of a calculation of the local density of states for a Ni d-band can be found in Section 1.5.

In Fig. 1.3 are plotted some of the generalized Wannier functions (GWF) for the lowest band [1.7]. The concept of a generalized Wannier function for nonperiodic systems has been quite recently introduced by KOHN and ONFFROY [1.9]. They are local, orthonormal functions, generally one for each lattice site. Total band energies, charge densities and local densities of states can be written in terms of these functions [1.7, 9]. The GWF were all determined via a single four parameter variational calculation. The dotted curves in Fig. 1.2 were obtained using the local functions of Fig. 1.3, showing a rather high accuracy.

Note that in the surface well (top graph of Fig. 1.3) there is considerable asymmetry in the local function. In the first plane in from the surface, the function is somewhat more symmetric. By the second plane in from the surface, the local function is essentially the bulk Wannier function. Thus these "local orbitals" differ from their bulk counterparts only in the first two or three planes in from the vacuum. This is characteristic of the width of the surface region that we deal with for many properties, i.e., 3–12 Å (see also Fig. 1.21).

1.2. Electron Work Function

The electron work function, as usually defined for metals [1.10–12] and for semiconductors [1.13, 14], is depicted schematically for 0 K as the quantity ϕ_e in Fig. 1.4. It is the energy difference between the Fermi level and the vacuum level just outside the surface in the case of both semiconductors and metals. Thus, if the work function of a reference solid surface is known, the work function of another solid surface can be determined from the contact potential difference. For metals, the photoelectric threshold is equal to the work function. This is not true in general for semiconductors [1.14]. For semiconductors

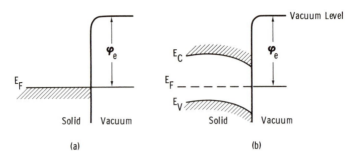

Fig. 1.4a and b. Schematic depicting the electron work function ϕ_e for a) a metal surface and b) a semiconductor surface. E_F is the Fermi energy, while E_c and E_v denote the bottom of the conduction band and the top of the valence band, respectively

the photoelectric threshold is equal to the energy difference between the vacuum level and the top of the valence band (sometimes called the ionization potential) when the bands are flat to the surface over the escape depth of emitted electrons and when surface state emission is negligible. There are many other ways of measuring the work function, and the interested reader is referred to RIVIÈRE's review [1.15] of experimental methods and results.

In the remainder of this section we will concentrate on theoretical calculations of the work function. Further, we will consider only metals, but will return to the semiconductor ionization potential for the case of Si in Subsection 1.4.1.

For a metal at 0 K,

$$\phi_e = - V(\infty) + E_{N-1} - E_N = - V(\infty) - \mu, \tag{1.1}$$

where $V(\infty)$ is the total electrostatic potential just outside the surface, E_N is the ground state energy of the metal with N electrons and μ is the chemical potential. In order to calculate μ, we must introduce a formalism which will be used extensively in later sections of this chapter.

HOHENBERG and KOHN (HK) [1.16] have shown that the ground-state energy E_v of a confined interacting electron gas can be written as a functional of the electron number density $n(r)$. Further, they have shown that $E_v[n]$ assumes a minimum value for the correct $n(r)$, if admissible density functions conserve the total number of electrons. Thus, $n(r)$ can be determined from [1.12]

$$(\delta/\delta n) \{E_v[n] - \mu N\} = 0, \tag{1.2}$$

where $N = \int n(r)\, dr$. HK write

$$E_v[n] = -\int V^{ex}(r)n(r)\, dr + 1/2\iint \frac{n(r)\, n(r')}{|r - r'|}\, dr\, dr' + G[n] \qquad (1.3)$$

(atomic units are used throughout unless stated otherwise), where $V^{ex}(r)$ in the first term is a static external potential (that of the metal ion cores in our clean surface work function calculation); the second term is the ordinary electron-electron interaction energy; and $G[n]$ is the sum of the kinetic, exchange, and correlation energies of the electronic system.

Combining (1.3) and (1.2), we have

$$-V(r) + \delta G[n]/\delta n(r) = \mu, \qquad (1.4)$$

where the electrostatic potential is given by

$$V(r) = V^{ex}(r) - \int \frac{n(r')}{|r - r'|}\, dr'. \qquad (1.5)$$

The point at which the left-hand side of (1.4) is evaluated is arbitrary. It is instructive [1.10] to take the volume average of (1.4) and combine it with (1.1)

$$\phi_e = -[V(\infty) - \langle V \rangle] - \langle \delta G[n]/\delta n(r) \rangle. \qquad (1.6)$$

Equation (1.6) is the desired result because it exhibits the fact that the work function divides into two parts: $-[V(\infty) - \langle V \rangle]$ is the electrostatic barrier at the surface referred to in Section 1.1; $\langle \delta G[n]/\delta n(r) \rangle$ is a bulk term, the bulk chemical potential relative to the mean interior electrostatic potential. Because of the surface term, ϕ_e depends on crystalline plane exposed and impurity effects at the surface. Both of these effects will be discussed later in this section.

Because one can write ϕ_e in terms of volume averages (1.6), one might expect that reasonably accurate polycrystalline work functions of some metal surfaces could be obtained using a uniform-positive-background or jellium model depicted in Fig. 1.5. This is in fact the case, as was first shown for a wide range of metals by SMITH [1.12] (see also JONES and MARCH [1.11]).

The sum of the kinetic, exchange, and correlation energies was approximated by the local and first order terms of a gradient ex-

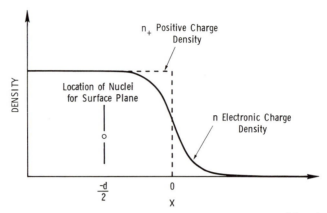

Fig. 1.5. Jellium model. (d is the distance between planes parallel to the surface)

pression [1.16]

$$G[n] = \frac{3}{10} (3\pi^2)^{2/3} \int n^{5/3} dr - \frac{3}{4} (3/\pi)^{1/3} \int n^{4/3} dr$$

$$- 0.056 \int \frac{n^{4/3}}{0.079 + n^{1/3}} dr + \frac{1}{72} \int \frac{(\nabla n)^2}{n} dr .$$

(1.7)

The integrands of the first three terms on the right-hand side of (1.7) represent, respectively, the kinetic, exchange, and correlation energy densities of a uniform electron gas of density n. The Wigner interpolation formula was used to represent the correlation energy of a homogeneous electron gas at metallic densities. The fourth term is the first of the inhomogeneity terms, i.e., those terms containing one or higher orders of the gradient operator acting on n.

The electrostatic barrier is given, in this model, by

$$-(V(\infty) - \langle V \rangle) = 4\pi \int_{-\infty}^{\infty} dx \, x [n(x) - n_+(x)] ,$$

(1.8)

where (Fig. 1.5)

$$n_+(x) = \begin{cases} n_+, & x \leqq 0 \\ 0, & x > 0 . \end{cases}$$

Correspondingly, the bulk contribution to ϕ_e is

$$\langle \delta G[n]/\delta n(r)\rangle = (1/2)\,(3\pi^2)^{2/3}n_+^{2/3} - (3/\pi)^{1/3}n_+^{1/3}$$

$$-\frac{0.056\,n_+^{2/3} + 0.0059\,n_+^{1/3}}{(0.079 + n_+^{1/3})^2}. \tag{1.9}$$

It remains to calculate $n(x)$ variationally, combining (1.2), (1.5), and (1.7). The inclusion of Poisson's equation (1.5) ensures *self-consistency* between the electronic charge density and the potential used to calculate it. Self-consistency is absolutely necessary in metal surface calculations, due to the spread of the electronic density into the vacuum, as shown in Fig. 1.5. To simplify the variational calculation, it was assumed [1.12] that the electron number density belongs to the following family of functions

$$n = n_+ - \frac{1}{2}n_+ e^{\beta x}, \; x < 0$$

$$n = \frac{1}{2}n_+ e^{-\beta x}, \; x \geq 0, \tag{1.10}$$

where β is a family parameter and n_+ is the bulk electron density (Fig. 1.5). The variational results then follow from quite simple analytical manipulations.

For the metals shown in Fig. 1.6, $0.40 \leq 1/\beta \leq 0.43$ Å. Since β is an inverse screening length, one can see that the decay of the electron gas into the vacuum is quite rapid. A comparison with experimental work function data is shown in Fig. 1.6. Rough agreement is obtained over a rather wide range of r_s ($r_s \equiv (1/4\pi\,n_+)^{1/3}$). For large r_s (e.g., C_s), the electrostatic barrier, $-[V(\infty) - \langle V\rangle]$ is only of the order of tenths of eV. Thus for large r_s the surface barrier is primarily due to the exchange and correlation potential part of $\langle \delta G[n]/\delta n(r)\rangle$. There is a gradual increase of the electrostatic contribution as r_s decreases, however. For example for Al, $-[V(\infty) - \langle V\rangle] = 6.0$ eV.

LANG [1.18] and LANG and KOHN (LK) [1.10] refined the jellium calculation of [1.12] by using a more accurate expression for the kinetic energy part of $G[n]$, following KOHN and SHAM [1.19]. In the second calculation, crystallinity was included. LK approximate $G[n]$ as

$$G[n] = T_s[n] - \frac{3}{4}(3/\pi)^{1/3}\int n^{4/3}\,dr - 0.056\int\frac{n^{4/3}}{0.079 + n^{1/3}}\,dr, \tag{1.11}$$

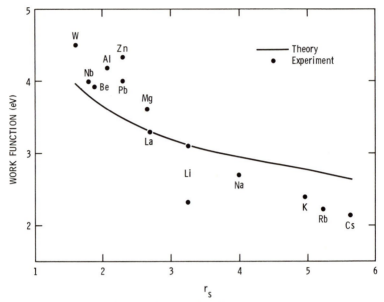

Fig. 1.6. Comparison of theoretical values [1.12] with the results of experiments on polycrystalline samples. For those metals listed in common with Fig. 1.7, the experimental values are those chosen in [1.10]. Otherwise, the data was taken from [1.17]

where $T_s[n]$ is the kinetic energy of a system of noninteracting electrons of density $n(r)$. Then the $n(r)$ which satisfies (1.2), (1.3), and (1.11) is found [1.13] by solving the equations

$$\left[-1/2 \nabla^2 - V(r) - (3/\pi)^{1/3} n^{1/3}(r) \right.$$
$$\left. - \frac{0.056 n^{2/3}(r) + 0.0059 n^{1/3}(r)}{(0.079 + n^{1/3}(r))^2} \right] \psi_i(r) = \varepsilon_i \psi_i(r) \qquad (1.12)$$

and setting

$$n(r) = \sum_{i=1}^{N} |\psi_i(r)|^2 . \qquad (1.13)$$

$V(r)$ is given, as before, in (1.5), thus providing self-consistency. LK take $V^{ex}(r)$ to be the electrostatic potential of the jellium charge density n_+ (Fig. 1.5). Thus their solution for the electron number density n depends only on x. The dipole barrier and bulk contribution to ϕ_e are again given by (1.8) and (1.9) respectively.

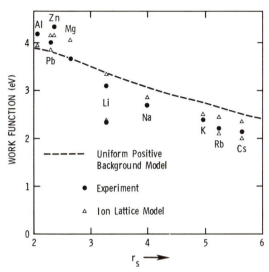

Fig. 1.7. Comparison of theoretical values [1.10] with the results of experiments on polycrystalline sample. The experimental values are those chosen in [1.10]. The ϕ_e values in the ion-lattice model were computed for the (110), (100), and (111) faces of the cubic metals and the (0001) face of the *hcp* metals (Zn and Mg). For qualitative purposes, the simple arithmetic average of these values for each metal is indicated by a triangle (two triangles are shown for those cases in which there are two possible pseudopotential radii r_c). The experimental and theoretical points for Zn should be at $r_s = 2.30$; they have been shifted slightly on the graph to avoid confusion with the data for Pb

Their results for the jellium model are shown as a dashed line in Fig. 1.7. They are quite close to those obtained in [1.12]. (See [1.18] for a direct comparison.)

Their most important contribution was to consider the effect of crystallinity on the work function, which will now be described [1.20]. LK introduce the discrete ion cores via first order perturbation theory, using pseudopotentials of the form employed by ASHCROFT and LANGRETH [1.21]

$$V_{PS}^{ex}(r) = \begin{cases} 0, & r \leqq r_c, \\ z/r, & r > r_c. \end{cases} \qquad (1.14)$$

The difference between an array of pseudopotentials of the form given in (1.14) and the potential of the positive charge density of the jellium provides a perturbing potential $\delta V^{ex}(r)$. Using the definition of the work function given in (1.1), the first order change in ϕ_e due to $\delta V^{ex}(r)$

is then, by standard perturbation theory,

$$\delta\phi_e = \int \delta V^{ex}(\mathbf{r})\, n_\sigma(x)\, d\mathbf{r}\,, \qquad (1.15)$$

where $n_\sigma(x)$ is the difference in the (ground state) electron number density distributions occurring when one electron is removed from the unperturbed system, the jellium metal. Since

$$\int n_\sigma(x)\, d\mathbf{r} = -1\,, \qquad (1.16)$$

$$\delta\phi_e = -\int \delta V^{ex}(x)\, n_\sigma(x)\, dx / \int n_\sigma(x)\, dx\,, \qquad (1.17)$$

where

$$\delta V^{ex}(x) \equiv \int \delta V^{ex}(\mathbf{r})\, dy\, dz\,. \qquad (1.18)$$

The $(N-1)$-electron ground state has, by Gauss's law, a weak electric field perpendicular to the surface at a point outside the surface. For a sufficiently weak electric field, $n_\sigma(x)$ will depend linearly on the field strength (see Section 1.3). Because, by (1.17), $\delta\phi_e$ is homogeneous in $n_\sigma(x)$, $n_\sigma(x)$ can now be taken to be the surface-charge density linearly induced by an *arbitrary* weak electric field perpendicular to the surface. The screening charge density for a weak applied field and $r_s = 2$ (corresponding approximately to Al), is given [1.22] in Fig. 1.8, using the coordinate system defined in Fig. 1.5. LK denote by x_0 in Fig. 1.8 the center of mass of the screening charge,

$$x_0 = \int_{-\infty}^{\infty} x n_\sigma(x)\, dx / \int_{-\infty}^{\infty} n_\sigma(x)\, dx\,. \qquad (1.19)$$

They showed quite generally [1.22] that in fact x_0 is the location of the image plane. This important result was verified in a particular application by YING et al. [1.23]. A knowledge of the image plane location is useful in e.g., chemisorption, field emission, and small-gap condenser analyses [1.22].

Once $n_\sigma(x)$ is known, $\delta\phi_e$ can be calculated via (1.15). A simple arithmetic average of the values for the closest packed planes are listed as triangles in Fig. 1.7. Two results are listed for those elements for which ASHCROFT and LANGRETH gave two choices for the ion core radius, r_c. There is an improvement over the jellium results (dashed line) on comparison with the polycrystalline experimental results indicated by the dots.

More recently, APPELBAUM and HAMANN (AH) [1.24] have treated the (100) surface of Na self-consistently and beyond the perturbative

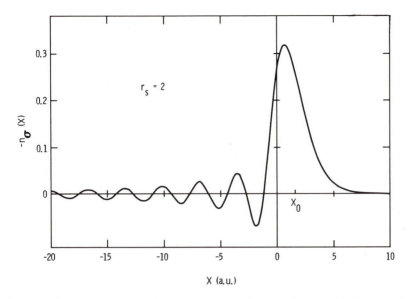

Fig. 1.8. Plot of the screening charge density $n_\sigma(x)$ for a weak applied field at $r_s = 2$, taken from [1.22]. x_0 locates the center of mass of the screening charge and the image plane as well. The edge of the uniform positive background (Fig. 1.5) is at $x = 0$

approximation. They solved (1.5), (1.12), and (1.13) to a good approximation, taking $V^{ex}(r)$ to be of the form given in (1.14). This means that the electron density solution n is three dimensional. They obtained a ϕ_e value for Na(100) of 2.71 eV, which is to be compared with 2.75 eV obtained by LK and 2.93 eV by SMITH. ALLDREDGE and KLEINMAN (AK) [1.25] have computed the three-dimensional charge density and the self-consistent energy band structure of a (001) film of Li. They also solved (1.5), (1.12), and (1.13) to a good approximation, using a non-local ion core pseudopotential $V^{ex}(r, r')$. They obtained $\phi_e = 3.70$ eV. This is 0.4 eV larger than the larger of LK's two results for Li(100) and 0.6 eV larger than SMITH's value. AK point out that the difference with LK may be due mainly to the repulsive (and non-local) part of their pseudopotential not being optimal. The methods of AH and AK will be described in more detail in Subsection 1.4.1.

It was mentioned earlier in this section that adsorbed particles on the solid surface can affect ϕ_e through the surface electrostatic barrier term $-[V(\infty) - \langle V \rangle]$. For example, a monolayer of hydrogen on W(100) increases the work function by ~ 0.9 eV [1.26]. On the other hand, it has been known for many years [1.27, 28] that a fractional

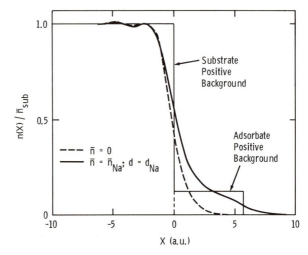

Fig. 1.9. Self-consistent electron density distributions $n(x)$ from [1.31] for a bare-substrate model ($r_s^{(\mathrm{sub})} = 2$, $\bar{n} = 0$), and for a model of substrate with full layer of adsorbed Na atoms ($\bar{n} = \bar{n}_{\mathrm{Na}}$)

monolayer of an alkali metal like Cs can lower the work function of a refractory transition metal by up to 4 eV [1.29]. For a theoretical discussion relating to this comparison see [1.23].

This makes the alkalies quite an interesting theoretical problem. The remainder of this section will be devoted to Lang's [1.31] theory of work function changes induced by alkali adsorption.

Following the lead of the successful jellium ϕ_e calculations, Lang represented the alkali adsorbate layer by a jellium slab (see Fig. 1.9). The metal substrates for which most of the change in work function ($\Delta\phi_e$) vs alkali coverage data are taken are refractory transition metals. Lang argued, however, that many of the data were insensitive to the substrate element. He therefore took $r_s = 2.0$ for the substrate, which is roughly characteristic of the bulk density of Al. The thickness d of the adsorbate slab was taken to be equal to the bulk alkali spacing between closest packed lattice planes. The density $\bar{n}$ of the adsorbate slab was determined so that

$$\bar{n}d = N , \tag{1.20}$$

where N is the number of alkali atoms per unit area.

Since the surface is only a tiny fraction of the total volume of the crystal, $\langle \delta G[n]/\delta n(\mathbf{r}) \rangle$ is changed only infinitesimally by a monolayer

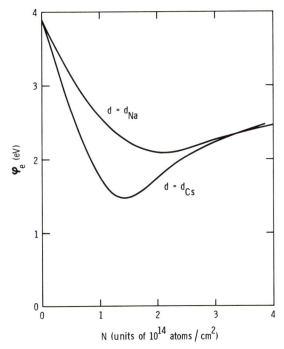

Fig. 1.10. Electron work function ϕ_e as a function of coverage of Na and Cs, taken from [1.31]. Values of the density at the work function minimum indicated here are substantially smaller than those determined for adsorption on a substrate such as W (110), whose zero-coverage ϕ_e is much larger than that of the model

of adsorbed alkali atoms. Thus, from (1.6),

$$\Delta\phi_e = -\Delta[V(\infty)-\langle V\rangle],\tag{1.21}$$

or, the alkali influences the work function by altering the electrostatic barrier at the surface. To find the electrostatic barrier, one need only calculate $n(x)$ via (1.12), (1.13), and (1.5). $V^{ex}(r)$ is the sum of the electrostatic potentials of the substrate jellium ($r_s = 2.0$) and the adsorbate slab of density $\bar{n}$. In Fig. 1.9, $n(x)$ for zero coverage and monolayer coverage are plotted for Na adsorption. The results for ϕ_e for both Na and Cs as a function of adsorbate coverage are shown in Fig. 1.10. These curves exhibit a minimum at fractional monolayer coverage as does the experimental data.

The results of Fig. 1.10 also have a qualitative explanation in terms of an atomic orbital picture first proposed by GURNEY [1.32]. The adsorbed alkali atoms are partially ionized because their broadened valence level lies largely above E_F. The resulting electrical double layer lowers the electrostatic barrier at the surface, and hence the work function. As the coverage of the alkali atoms increases and hence the work function decreases, the broadened valence level is presumably lowered relative to E_F. This means the net positive charge of each alkali adatom is lowered, and hence the contribution per particle to the double layer is decreased. This can lead to the saturation or minimum shown in Fig. 1.10. For more recent employment of this picture see the references listed by LANG [1.31].

1.3. Impurity Screening — Static Dielectric Response

The static (zero frequency) screening of particles and defects, which plays an important role in the physics of bulk metals, is also of considerable interest in the physics of metal surfaces. Some typical applications are: the effect of the metal ions (i.e., crystallinity), on the electron density distribution near the surface; interactions of adatoms with metal surfaces; and mutual interactions of adatoms.

Several workers have dealt with static screening at a solid surface [1.33]. While considerable understanding of surface screening fundamentals has resulted from these treatments, they all deal with an electron gas bounded by an infinite potential step. Self-consistency is now known to be important in surface impurity screening [1.34], as it is also in "bare" or clean surface calculations [1.12, 10, 24, 25]. In the following we consider only a self-consistent response function formalism which will first be presented in quite general form. It will then be applied in approximate form to hydrogen chemisorption as an example [1.35, 23, 30]. Frequency dependent response will be discussed in Subsection 1.4.2.

The formalism of dielectric response follows succinctly from the density functional approach introduced in Section 1.2 [1.30, 34]. Consider first an unperturbed inhomogeneous electron gas in an external potential $V_0^{ex}(r)$ and with electron number density $n_0(r)$. For example, $V_0^{ex}(r)$ might correspond to a crystalline array of metal ion core potentials and $n_0(r)$ the electron number density distribution at a "clean" metal surface. Now introduce an additional small charge density $\varrho_1^{ex}(r)$ (such as an ion core of a chemisorbed particle), giving rise to a perturbing potential

$$V_1^{ex}(r) = \int \left[\varrho_1^{ex}(r')/|r - r'| \right] dr' . \qquad (1.22)$$

What is the resulting change $n_1(r)$ of the electronic density?

Linearizing (1.4 and (1.5), i.e., writing $V^{ex} = V_0^{ex} + V_1^{ex}$, $n = n_0 + n_1$, etc., gives first the equations for the zeroth-order density

$$- V_0(r) + \left[\frac{\delta G[n]}{\delta n(r)} \right]_{n_0} = \mu_0 , \tag{1.23}$$

$$V_0(r) = V_0^{ex}(r) - \int \frac{n_0(r')}{|r - r'|} \, dr' . \tag{1.24}$$

The first order screening density is given by

$$- V_1(r) + \int n_1(r') \left[\frac{\delta^2 G[n]}{\delta n(r) \, \delta n(r')} \right]_{n_0} dr' = \mu_1 , \tag{1.25}$$

$$V_1(r) = V_1^{ex}(r) - \int \frac{n_1(r')}{|r - r'|} \, dr' . \tag{1.26}$$

A calculation of $n_1(r)$ then begins with a (self-consistent) solution of (1.23) and (1.24) for $n_0(r)$ and $V_0(r)$. These results can then be used in (1.25) and (1.26) to find $n_1(r)$ and $V_1(r)$.

One can define the density-potential response function $L(r, r')$ as

$$V_1(r) = \int L(r, r') \varrho_1^{ex}(r') \, dr' . \tag{1.27}$$

It follows from (1.27) that L is the induced potential V_1 due to a point perturbing charge $\varrho_1^{ex} = \delta(r - r')$. Once L is calculated for that system, one can use it through (1.27) to find the induced potential due to a general perturbing charge distribution. It can be shown that [1.23] reciprocity is obeyed:

$$L(r, r') = L(r', r) . \tag{1.28}$$

However, $L(r, r') = L(|r - r'|)$ only for homogeneous systems, and therefore unfortunately not in surface calculations.

Up to now, we have made no approximations other than linearization in our formalism. We would now like to apply it to chemisorption on a metal surface, and make the following approximations:

1) The unperturbed system (substrate) is represented by a jellium model (Fig. 1.5) with appropriate positive charge density.

2) The density functional $G[n]$ is given by (1.7). All of these approximations are discussed at length in [1.23] and [1.30], where it is concluded that they can provide a good zeroth order model for chemisorption on the low index planes of a refractory transition metal

like tungsten. This is a system for which there is considerable experimental data due to the possibility of obtaining clean refractory metal surfaces.

Because of the translational invariance parallel to the surface of the unperturbed (jellium) system, it is convenient to introduce the two-dimensional Fourier transform of the various quantities in the form

$$L(Q, x, x') = \int du e^{-iQ \cdot u} L(u, x; x') \qquad (1.29)$$

etc., when $Q \equiv (0, Q_y, Q_z)$, $u \equiv (0, y - y', z - z')$, $u \equiv |u|$, and $Q \equiv |Q|$. Then (1.25) and (1.26) become [1.30, 1.23]:

$$-\frac{1}{36 n_0(x)} \frac{d^2 n_1(Q, x)}{dx^2} + \frac{1}{36 n_0^2(x)} \frac{dn_0(x)}{dx} \frac{dn_1(Q, x)}{dx}$$

$$+ \left(X + \frac{Q^2}{36 n_0(x)}\right) n_1(Q, x) - V_1(Q, x) = \mu_1 \, \delta(Q) \qquad (1.30a)$$

and

$$\frac{d^2 V_1(Q, x)}{dx^2} - Q^2 V_1(Q, x) = 4\pi [n_1(Q, x) - \delta(x - x')], \qquad (1.30b)$$

where

$$X = \frac{1}{3} (3\pi^2)^{2/3} n_0^{-1/3}(x) - \frac{1}{3} (3/\pi)^{1/3} n_0^{-2/3}(x)$$

$$- \frac{(\nabla n_0(x))^2}{36 n_0^3(x)} + \frac{\nabla^2 n_0(x)}{36 n_0^2(x)}. \qquad (1.31)$$

As discussed immediately following (1.27), we have taken $\varrho_1^{ex} = \delta(r - r')$ in Poisson's equation (1.30). Equations (1.30a) and (1.30b) can now be solved simultaneously (self-consistently) to yield the screening potential V_1 and density n_1 for a point perturbing charge. An immediate application of the results would be to hydrogen chemisorption (see Chapter 2 for a review of theoretical and experimental chemisorption). The proton immersed in the inhomogeneous electron gas of the metallic surface region is the point perturbing charge. We chose $r_s = 1.5$ for n_+ in an effort to approximate [1.12, 30] a close packed surface plane for a refractory transition metal like tungsten.

In the remainder of this section, results are given for a number of observables in the hydrogen-tungsten system.

First we determine the hydrogen ion-metal substrate interaction as a function of the coordinates of the proton $(u = 0, x')$. This is given,

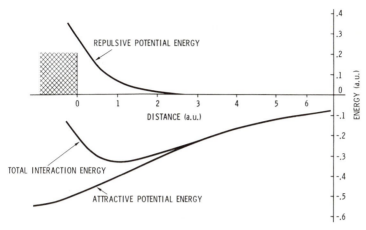

Fig. 1.11. Hydrogen ion-metal interaction energy versus separation distance [1.23, 30]

according to the Hellmann-Feynman theorem, by

$$W(x') = V_0(x') + 1/2\, \bar{V}_1(x=x', u=0), \tag{1.32}$$

where $V_0(x')$ is the electrostatic potential of the "bare" surface and $\bar{V}_1(x=x', u=0)$ is the potential of the screening charge, evaluated at the proton location. The results are shown in Fig. 1.11. There is competition between the repulsive term $V_0(x')$ and the attractive term $1/2\,\bar{V}_1(x=x', u=0)$. This results in a minimum in $W(x')$ at $x' = 1.08$ a.u. The depth of the minimum is the ionic desorption energy, $E_I = 9$ eV. The experimental value [1.35, 36] for hydrogen on tungsten is $E_I = 11.3$ eV. This allows a measure of the accuracy of the calculation. For a first-principles calculation with no adjustable parameters, this sort of agreement is encouraging in light of the state-of-the-art in surface physics today. It should be noted that hydrogen is singular in that its ionic desorption energy E_I is much larger than that of other chemisorbed species.

The adsorbed hydrogen will exhibit vibrational modes in the potential well of Fig. 1.11. The excitation energy is given by the usual relation

$$\hbar\omega = \hbar \left(\frac{1}{m} \frac{d^2 W(x)}{dx^2} \right)^{1/2}_{x_m}, \tag{1.33}$$

where $x_m = 1.08$ a.u. is the position of the proton at its energy minimum, and m is the proton mass. The theoretical value is 200 meV, while the

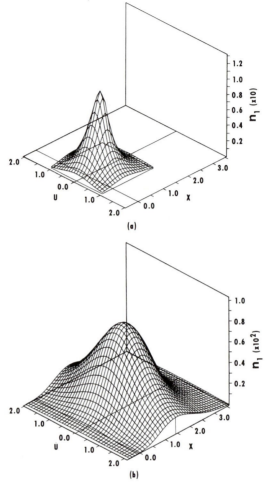

Fig. 1.12a and b. Screening charge density n_1 for two proton positions: a) at $u = 0$, $x = 0.571$ Å, the interaction energy minimum, i.e., the location for chemisorbed H; b) at $u = 0$, $x = 2.29$ Å, a small displacement in the vacuum direction from the adsorption site [1.23, 35]. u is the cylindrical coordinate in the plane parallel to the surface measured from an axis through the proton. Scaled units [1.33] are used for n_1. x and u are given in Å. The vertical line denotes the n_1 peak location. The peak density in a) is 13 times the peak density in b) (note change in scale for n_1)

experimental result is 140 meV [1.38, 39]. This fair agreement between the single-adsorbate theoretical result and experiment is evidence of dissociative adsorption [1.40]. This is consistent with computations [1.23, 30] of the short range (≤ 2 a.u.) interaction energy between hydrogen adatoms. This short range energy is repulsive, indicating dissociation. This supports the numerous experimental contentions (see, e.g., [1.41]), that hydrogen dissociates upon adsorption in the first adlayer on tungsten and certain other metals.

One might well ask, "what does the chemisorbed hydrogen look like?" The screening charge $n_1(r)$ is shown for two positions of the proton in Fig. 1.12, $x' = 0.571$ Å and $x' = 2.29$ Å. When $x' = 0.571$ Å, the hydrogen is located at the energy minimum (Fig. 1.11), and the screening charge is rather symmetric about the proton. However, when the proton moves to $x' = 2.29$ Å, the screening charge is quite asymmetric. Further, the screening charge spreads in the direction parallel to the surface, i.e., in the u direction (note the change in scale on the n_1 axis between Fig. 1.12a and b). As $x' \to \infty$, the spreading becomes complete, and n_1 becomes a function of x only.

With this rapid change in shape of the chemisorbed hydrogen as the proton moves about in the surface, one might expect that low energy electron scattering properties would depend on the location of the hydrogen. We will see later that this is in fact the case. When hydrogen is introduced onto a clean W(100) surface, a $c(2 \times 2)$ low energy electron diffraction (LEED—see Chapter 4) pattern is observed [1.42] which exhibits additional (half-order) beams. The intensity of these extra beams is comparable to the other (integral-order) beams of the pattern. The result is made more interesting by the fact that the isolated atom back-scattering cross sections for hydrogen are an order of magnitude smaller than those of the W atom [1.43] in the 50–100 eV energy range. Analogous data have been obtained for other light adsorbates on heavy substrates. Some authors (see, e.g., GERMER [1.44]) feel these data indicate reconstruction of the substrate. Others (see, e.g., BAUER [1.45a] and TRACY and BLAKELY [1.45b]) believe that reconstruction is not a necessary condition. More recently, JENNINGS and McRAE [1.46] have shown for H on W(100) that inter-layer multiple scattering can lead to fractional-order beams of comparable intensity to neighboring integral-order beams. They used isolated H atom phase shifts, however. In an attempt to obtain further information on the subject, we calculated [1.23, 35] differential scattering cross sections (DCS) for chemisorbed (Fig. 1.12a) and isolated hydrogen atoms. Figure 1.13 exhibits, for the first time, the effect of chemisorption on DCS. Note that the forward scattering DCS are considerably enhanced by chemisorption. Our results appear to support the picture of JENNINGS and McRAE, but one would have to do a multiple scattering calculation using the DCS (or, equivalently, our phase shifts) to be certain.

In Fig. 1.14, the total electronic potential in the vicinity of the chemisorbed hydrogen is plotted. This is the electrostatic potential of the proton (hence the "spike"), plus the electrostatic and (Kohn-Sham)

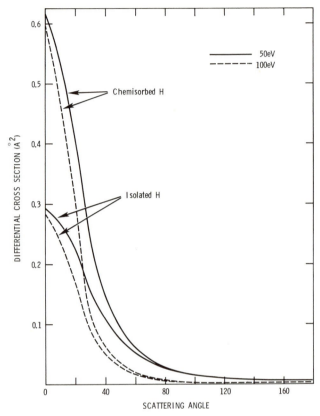

Fig. 1.13. Differential scattering cross sections for chemisorbed and isolated hydrogen atoms. The chemisorbed atom is located at the energy minimum of Fig. 1.11 [1.23, 35]

exchange potential of the screening charge. Notice that the potential dips below zero on the bulk side of the proton. This was much more striking in the earlier example, Fig. 1.1, where the peak at ≈ -1.5 Å is considerably lower than the vacuum level. One might well ask about the virtual energy levels associated with this potential well in Fig. 1.14. That is, it would be of considerable interest to determine the local density of states associated with the chemisorbed hydrogen. This interest is enhanced by the recent ability of experimentalists to detect local densities of states associated with adsorbed layers [1.47, 48]. We have found [1.23, 35] a resonance level associated with the potential well of Fig. 1.14 which lies 5.6 eV below the Fermi level. PLUMMER and WACLAWSKI [1.48] find peaks in their photoemission energy spectra for hydrogen adsorption at 5.7 eV and 6.3 eV below the Fermi level for

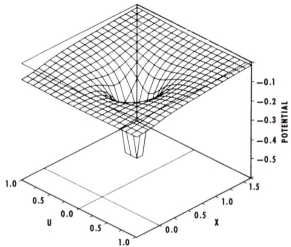

Fig. 1.14. Total electronic potential in the vicinity of the chemisorbed hydrogen. The potential is in a.u., while u and x are in Å [1.35]

W(100) and W(110) respectively. The agreement between theory and experiment indicates that these low-lying states are localized primarily on the adsorbate (compare with [1.49]). Our calculated level width is considerably larger than the observed value, however. We refer the interested reader to [1.23] and [1.35] for a discussion of this. This is the first *a priori* self-consistent calculation of a resonance level associated with an adsorbate potential well.

In Chapter 2, a LCAO-MO (linear combination of atomic orbitals-molecular orbital) treatment of H on W(100) is presented by LYO and GOMER. A resonance at 5–6 eV below the Fermi level is also predicted.

Qualitative considerations [1.23] suggest that none of the approximations listed in the paragraph after (1.28) is unreasonable for the problem at hand. It is noteworthy that agreement between our theory and experiment is quite good. At the same time we consider it very important that improvements on all our approximations be carried out so that the theory can be put on a firmer and more quantitative basis.

1.4. Surface States and Surface Plasmons

1.4.1. Surface States

In Section 1.1 we saw an example of an electronic state which is bound to the surface region, i.e., it decays in both the vacuum and bulk directions. TAMM [1.50] first predicted that surface states could exist at

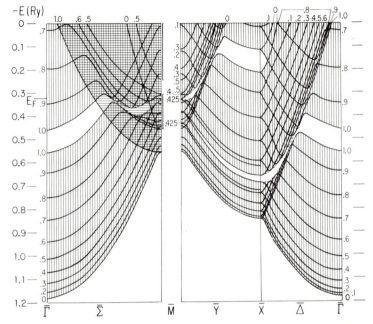

Fig. 1.15. Two-dimensional projection of the three-dimensional energy bands of aluminum [1.55]. The horizontal and vertical crosshatching represent continua of states with different symmetries. The numbers labeling the various bands represent values of k_x in units of $2\pi/a$, where a is the edge length of the fundamental cube

crystal interfaces. Many years later, the then budding semiconductor device industry learned that these states can strongly influence many properties of devices made from these materials. Surface states have also been reported experimentally at metal surfaces using field emission, photoemission, and Auger [1.51]. An extensive review (through 1970) of theory and experiment of surface states has been given by DAVISON and LEVINE [1.52] (see also [1.53]).

Let us consider a crystalline solid-vacuum interface. If there is to be a surface state at energy E with reduced wave vector parallel to the surface $k_{\parallel}$, then: a) the state must be a valid eigenfunction of Schrödinger's equation, b) the energy E must be less than the vacuum level (so that the electron is bound to the solid), c) there must be no continuum (band) states with the same E and $k_{\parallel}$ (so that electron cannot escape into the bulk). A thorough study of these requirements has been made by HEINE [1.54]. In Fig. 1.15 is a two-dimensional (001) projection of the three-dimensional energy bands of aluminum [1.54]. b) and c) require that surface states exist only within energy

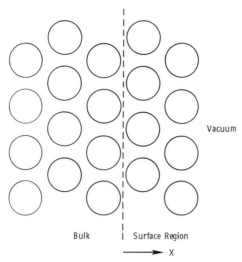

Vacuum

Bulk   Surface Region

→ X

Fig. 1.16. Schematic representation of a solid surface, indicating the mathematical separation into "surface" and "bulk" regions used in [1.58]

gaps of this two-dimensional projection. a) must then be satisfied in order for a surface state to exist in the gap. It is perhaps not surprising that the simultaneous satisfaction of these requirements depends rather sensitively on the potential used [1.56, 57] and hence on self-consistency [1.58, 25].

We will concentrate in the rest of this subsection on the two (very recent) self-consistent calculations of surface states [1.58, 25]. APPELBAUM and HAMANN (AH) have determined the ionization potential (c.f. Section 1.2), charge density, and surface state configuration for Si(111). In the following, their method is briefly summarized. For a review of earlier work on Si, see JONES [1.59]. The ion core potentials that make up $V^{ex}(r)$ [Eq. (1.3)] are represented by pseudopotentials [1.60]. Equations (1.12) and (1.13) are solved for two representative $k_\parallel$ points in the surface Brillouin zone, Γ at the zone center and J at the center of the zone edge (a two point variant of the Baldereschi summation scheme used for bulk semiconductors [1.61]). At both $k_\parallel$'s the equations were solved for all surface states below the Fermi energy and for ten continuum states per bulk valence band. The charge density was computed via these wave functions, which yielded a new potential [(1.5) and (1.12)]. This process was then iterated to self-consistency.

More particularly, AH divide the Si crystal into a "surface" and a "bulk" region by a mathematical plane (Fig. 1.16). These two

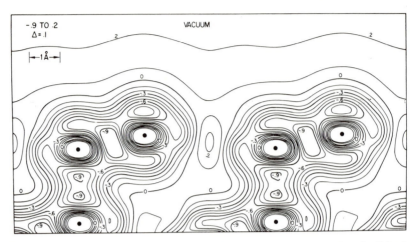

Fig. 1.17. Contours of constant surface potential plotted on a plane normal to the Si(111) surface and passing through a line connecting a surface atom with one of its nearest neighbors in the second plane of atoms [1.58]. The heavy black dots locate the centers of the Si atoms. The energy units are hartrees, the contours are spaced 0.1 hartree apart, and the scale is placed so the valence-band maximum falls at $+0.06$ hartree

regions are solved separately, and the wave functions joined at the plane. Since pseudopotentials are used, a plane wave basis set is manageable. In the bulk region, the potential is assumed to be fully periodic. Thus the solution for the evanescent and Block waves involves a matrix eigenvalue calculation. In the surface region, the wave function is expanded as

$$\psi(r) = \sum_{Q} \psi_{Q}(x)\, e^{i(k_{\parallel} - Q) \cdot r}, \tag{1.34}$$

where the Q are reciprocal lattice vectors parallel to the surface [see (1.29)]. In the basis of (1.34), (1.12) becomes a set of N coupled one dimensional equations, where N is the number of surface reciprocal lattice vectors used (~ 30). These equations can be numerically integrated to the matching plane. The Fermi energy lies in the gap surface-state band for Si, and is determined by filling the surface states until the surface region is neutral.

The resultant surface potential is plotted in Fig. 1.17. It is shown on a plane normal to the Si(111) surface and passing through a line connecting a surface atom with one of its nearest neighbors in the second plane of atoms. Notice the attractive wells between atoms indicative of covalent bonding. More importantly, above the surface atoms there are residual attractive potentials. AH attribute the

Table 1.1. For three different surface geometries, identified by giving the location of the second and first atomic layers relative to the third, the ionization potential (IP), electronic occupancy of the gap surface-state band in electrons per surface atom (n_{ss}) and the number of surface bands present are listed [1.58]. The geometric parameters corresponding to the ideal bulk lattice are 4.44 and 5.92 a.u.

Geometry [a.u.]	IP [eV]	n_{ss}	No. of surface-state bands
4.44, 5.26	5.44 ± 0.05	0.7016	3
4.44, 5.56	5.46 ± 0.004	0.5834	1
4.24, 5.06	5.51 ± 0.07	0.6350	3

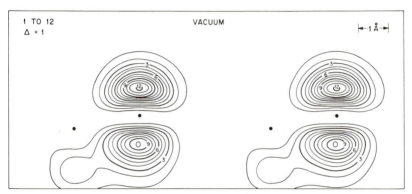

SILICON TOP SURFACE STATE CHARGE DENSITY

Fig. 1.18. "Dangling bond" surface state charge density [1.62] plotted on a plane normal to the Si(111) surface whose orientation is given in the caption of Fig. 1.17

localized "dangling-bond" surface states to these dangling potential wells. These surface states are only partially occupied, as indicated in Table 1.1, containing less than one electron per surface atom. The location of the top of the valence band with respect to the vacuum level (IP) is also given in Table 1.1. It is to be compared with an experimental value of 5.15 eV [1.14].

The charge density of one of the "dangling bond" surface states is shown in Fig. 1.18, again on a plane intersecting atoms in the first and second layers [1.62]. It is calculated for the geometry described by the first entry in Table 1.1. The band of surface states lies completely within the absolute valence band-contribution band gap. About 80% of the charge in the surface state lies in the area covered by the plot; only 20% tails off deeper into the bulk.

PANDEY and PHILLIPS (PP) [1.63] have formulated a simple semi-empirical tight-binding method which reproduces many of the AH results. They [1.64] disagree however, on the number of electrons per surface atom in the gap surface state band (n_{ss} in Table 1.1). PP find that $n_{ss} = 1$ for a relaxed surface (spacings 4.44, 5.26 a.u.—Table 1.1). Kleinman [1.65] has recently provided a rather general argument for the value of unity. PP note that it is possible that the discrepancy arises from the matching plane (Fig. 1.16) being too close to the vacuum. They [1.64] find a substantial density of gap surface states in the fourth layer.

We close this section with a brief discussion of a complementary method which has recently been developed to determine self-consistent surface states for a thirteen layer (001) film of lithium, due to Alldredge and Kleinman (AK) [1.25] (see also [1.55]). AK also solve (1.5), (1.12) and (1.13), using a pseudopotential for the ion cores and a two-dimensional plane wave basis. AK do not divide the crystal artifically into "surface" and "bulk" regions, however. They solve a matrix eigenvalue problem for the entire film. Thus they, unlike AH, can easily accommodate non-local potentials throughout the solid. Further, AK obtain the *complete* band spectrum of the film, without having to search for (and possibly overlook) surface states. However, these advantages are obtained at the price of being limited to thin films (which are of interest in themselves, but only approximate semi-infinite crystals), and apparently taking more computer time than required by AH.

It will be interesting to follow these two approaches as they continue to develop.

1.4.2. Surface Plasmons

Throughout the chapter, we have considered only ground state properties of the solid surface. Our description of electronic properties would not be complete without a consideration of electronic excitation.

As an introductory example, Fig. 1.19 is an energy-loss profile in the (11) diffraction direction for a beam of electrons scattered from Al (100) in the LEED experiment (see Chapter 4) of Burkstrand [1.66]. The dominant peaks near 10 and 15 eV are attributed to surface and bulk plasmon excitations, respectively.

Surface and bulk plasmons have also been detected in transmission experiments [1.67] and by optical studies [1.68].

There have been several reviews recently of the subject of surface plasmons [1.69]. In the following, we will merely indicate the "nature of the beast".

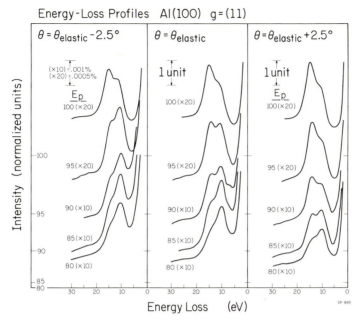

Energy-Loss Profiles   Al(100)   g=(11)

Fig. 1.19. Series of energy-loss profiles in the (11) diffraction beam for different primary energies E_p and collector angles θ. The ordinate marks correspond to the zero levels of each profile [1.66]

The concept [1.70] of volume or bulk plasmons in metals is well established. The plasma mode is a natural mode of oscillation of the electron gas. There are additional plasmon-like modes associated with surfaces and interfaces. This was first recognized by RITCHIE [1.71]. STERN and FERRELL [1.72] named these additional modes surface plasmons, and considered the effect of oxide coatings on them.

To obtain a more quantitative picture of the surface plasmon, one would have to generalize the response function of (1.27) for time dependent effects. This has been done formally by YING [1.73]. There is, in addition, a rather extensive literature on the subject of frequency dependent linear response functions [1.74].

A calculation which is as yet somewhat preliminary but is quite instructive as to the nature of surface plasmons is that of INGLESFELD and WIKBORG (IW) [1.75], who followed much of the earlier work of BECK and CELLI [1.76]. They obtain results for Al, the subject of BURKSTRAND'S experiment. IW dealt with a potential-density response function $P(k_{\parallel}, x, x'; \omega)$

$$n_1(k_{\parallel}, x, \omega) = \int_{-\infty}^{\infty} dx' \, P(k_{\parallel}, x, x'; \omega) \, V_1(k_{\parallel}, x'; \omega), \qquad (1.35)$$

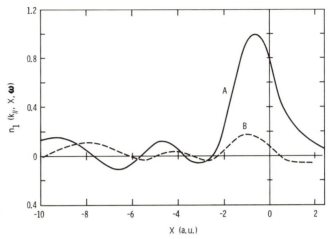

Fig. 1.20. A and B are Re $\{n_1(k_\parallel, x, \omega)\}$ and Im $\{n_1(k_\parallel, x, \omega)\}$ respectively, for Al: $k_\parallel = 0.05$ a.u. (from [1.75])

where n_1, V_1, x, x', and $k_\parallel$ are as defined previously in Section 1.3, and ω is the frequency of the time-varying perturbing potential V_1 (a one dimensional unperturbed system is assumed).

It is desired to compute the fluctuation in the static electron density which accompanies a surface plasmon of frequency ω and wave vector $k_\parallel$

$$n_1(r, t) = n_1(k_\parallel, x, \omega) \exp\left[i(k_\parallel \cdot r - \omega t)\right]. \qquad (1.36)$$

Since the surface plasmon is a normal mode of the electronic plasma, the charge density fluctuation n_1 must produce its own perturbing potential through Poisson's equation

$$V_1(k_\parallel, x; \omega) = \frac{2\pi}{k_\parallel} \int_{-\infty}^{\infty} dx'\, n_1(k_\parallel, x'; \omega) \exp\left(-k_\parallel |x - x'|\right). \qquad (1.37)$$

Thus we encounter our old friend, the self-consistency requirement [c.f. discussion following (1.9)], which in this case is a necessary condition for the occurrence of a plasmon.

IW determined the response function $P(k_\parallel, x, x'; \omega)$ using the random-phase approximation [1.77]. They approximate the surface potential as a step-potential. Thus, while the fluctuations [(1.35) and (1.37)] are determined self-consistently, the response function is not. They chose $E_F = 11.6$ eV and step height $= 15.8$ eV in order to approximate Al. Their procedure is to search for values of ω and

$k_\parallel$ such that (1.35) and (1.37) are solved simultaneously for a fluctuation confined to the surface. Curves A and B in Fig. 1.20 show the real and imaginary parts respectively of the resulting charge fluctuation $n_1(k_\parallel, x, \omega)$ at $k_\parallel = 0.05$ a.u. Presuming that their Friedel-like oscillations eventually damp out (FEIBELMAN [1.78] has argued that the amplitude should fall off as x^{-2}) [1.75], Fig. 1.20 shows that the surface plasmon charge oscillation can be largely confined to within one atomic radius or so.

A bulk plasmon, however, is not confined to the surface region. Thus we see a parallel between the relation between surface and bulk plasmons and that between surface states and continuum states discussed in Section 1.1 and Subsection 1.4.1.

The resultant values of ω and $k_\parallel$ specify the dispersion relation which as FEIBELMAN [1.78] has shown, is unfortunately quite sensitive to the surface potential barrier shape and hence self-consistency. This dispersion relation can be obtained from analysis of LEED data, however. DUKE et al. [1.79] find that for Al(111),

$$\hbar\omega_s = 10.5\,(\pm 0.1) + 2\,(\pm 1)\,k_\parallel + 0\,(+2)\,k_\parallel^2$$

$$\Gamma_s = 1.85\,(\pm 0.5) + 3\,(\pm 2)\,k_\parallel,$$

(1.38)

for energies measured in eV and momenta in Å^{-1}, where $\hbar\omega_s$ is the real part of the energy of the surface plasmon and Γ_s is the imaginary part. The latter provides a measure of the lifetime of the surface plasmon. The $k_\parallel = 0$ limit of $10.5\,(\pm 0.1)$ eV also agrees well with the high energy transmission experiments and with the values obtained by BURKSTRAND for $k_\parallel = 0$ (corresponding to the $\theta = \theta_{\text{elastic}}$ profiles in Fig. 1.17).

FEIBELMAN [1.80a] as well as HARRIS and GRIFFIN [1.80b] have shown that, for a jellium solid and within the RPA (see also [1.81]),

$$\hbar\omega\,(k_\parallel = 0) = (1/\sqrt{2})\,\omega_p,$$

(1.39)

independent of the shape of the barrier, where ω_p is the bulk plasma frequency $(4\pi e^2 n_+/m)^{1/2}$. For Al, (1.39) gives $\hbar\omega\,(k_\parallel = 0) = 11.2$ eV and $\omega_p = 15.8$ eV. Equation (1.39) is approximately consistent with (1.38) for $k_\parallel = 0$, except that the latter shows a nonzero imaginary part to the energy.

Finally we mention that surface plasmon dispersion and damping have been shown to be sensitive to adsorption. We refer the interested reader to [1.82].

1.5. Local Density of States

The density of states weighted by the amplitude squared of the wave function is denoted as the local density of states (LDS)

$$n(E, r) = \sum_i |\psi_i(r)|^2 \delta(E - E_i),$$ (1.40)

where the density of states is given by

$$n(E) = \int n(E, r) \, dr .$$ (1.41)

As we saw in Section 1.1, ψ_i decays into the vacuum at a solid surface. Surface states (see also Subsection 1.4.1) appear as well. Also resonance levels can be associated with chemisorbed particles, as described in Section 1.3. This means that $n(E, r)$ will have a positional dependence at the surface which is interestingly different from bulk behavior. These effects are being seen experimentally, and they are discussed at some length in Chapter 5.

Surface states in band gaps will tend to broaden the local density of states at a surface. There is also a narrowing effect [1.83] which is suggested by the following development. The second moment of the density of states is defined as (see Cyrot-Lackmann et al. [1.84, 85]):

$$\mu_2 = \int (E - E_0)^2 \, n(E) \, dE ,$$ (1.42)

where E_0 is a suitably chosen reference energy. The quantity μ_2 is then a measure of the width of $n(E)$ about E_0. It may be expressed alternatively in terms of the wave functions $\psi_i(r)$ or in terms of local functions such as the generalized Wannier functions (GWF) discussed in Section 1.1 [1.9]

$$\mu_2 = N^{-1} \operatorname{Tr}(\mathcal{H} - E_0)^2 = N^{-1} \sum_j \langle \psi_i | (\mathcal{H} - E_0)^2 | \psi_i \rangle$$

$$= N^{-1} \sum_n \langle a_n | (\mathcal{H} - E_0)^2 | a_n \rangle ,$$ (1.43)

where an example of the Hamiltonian is given in (1.12), a_n is the GWF associated with the lattice site located by the lattice vector n, and the possibility of overlapping bands [1.7] has been ignored. Now let

$$E_0 = E_s \equiv \langle a_{n_s} | \mathcal{H} | a_{n_s} \rangle = \mathcal{H}_{n_s, n_s}$$ (1.44)

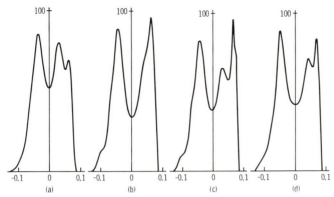

Fig. 1.21a-d. The local density of states of an atom in a) the (111) surface plane b) the first plane and c) the second plane below the surface, and d) in the bulk for a *fcc* d-band [1.88]

where a_{n_s} refers to one of the GWF in the surface plane. Then the contribution to the second moment from a_{n_s} is given by

$$|\mu_2|_s = \sum_{n \neq n_s} |\mathscr{H}_{n,n_s}|^2 . \tag{1.45}$$

Since the number of near neighbors is reduced at a surface, (1.45) suggests that $(\mu_2)_s < \mu_2$ and hence that the surface density of states is narrower than $n(E)$. This is only suggestive, because the surface orbitals are different from the bulk orbitals (see Fig. 1.3). Thus not only the number but the size of the matrix elements changes in going from the bulk to the surface. It has been shown by DAVENPORT et al. (DES) [1.83] that these self-consistency effects can be very important. Self-consistency has not been included in any "first principles" LDS calculations to date. There is a very interesting semi-empirical tight-binding treatment [1.62–64] by PANDEY and PHILLIPS in which the effects of relaxation of the surface plane are included parametrically (see Section 1.4.1).

If one rewrites (1.40) and (1.41) in terms of GWF, it is easily shown [1.7] that $n(E)$ can be written as a sum over lattice sites of terms of the form:

$$n_n(E) = -\pi^{-1} \sum_{\alpha=1}^{p} \lim_{\varepsilon \to 0} \operatorname{Im} \{G_{\alpha,n}(E + i\varepsilon)\}, \tag{1.46}$$

where

$$G_{\alpha,n}(E) = \langle a_{\alpha,n} | (E - \mathscr{H})^{-1} | a_{\alpha,n} \rangle , \tag{1.47}$$

ε is a positive parameter, and there are p overlapping bands. HAYDOCK et al. [1.86–88] have recently provided a new continued fraction method for evaluating a term of the form given in (1.47). The d-band density of states in the surface layers was calculated using the Slater-Koster overlap parameters, as determined by Pettifor [1.89] for (bulk) Ni. Their resultant densities of states for the (111) surface, two sublayers, and the bulk of a *fcc* d-band are shown in Fig. 1.21. The narrowing effects mentioned earlier are readily apparent. Note also that by two layers in from the surface layer, the density of states is quite similar to that of the bulk (cf. Section 1.1).

For a somewhat different approach to the calculation of surface densities of states, the reader is referred to the Green's function theory of Kalkstein and Soven [1.90]. A quite complete solution for the case of a single s-band in a simple cubic lattice is presented.

1.6. Status — Current Challenges

The fundamental or *a priori* theory of those electronic properties of surfaces which we have considered in the preceding sections has often progressed in the following characteristic stages. The first stage is a noncrystalline (one dimensional) nonself-consistent treatment. Next, self-consistency [cf. discussion following (1.9)], is introduced into the noncrystalline calculation. Then the effects of crystallinity are taken into account approximately for nearly free electron metals via perturbation theory. Following that, crystallinity is treated beyond the perturbation approximation, but with a plane wave basis, allowing a wider range of materials to be considered. In the next stage, the array of ions in the surface region are to be allowed to relax from their bulk-like positions to new equilibrium positions. Finally, complex materials such as transition metals and their alloys are dealt with. Of course in all these stages many-electron effects are included in various approximations, and their relative importance depends on the observable being considered.

The aforementioned progression seems to be the most commonly followed, but there has been a most useful companion mode. A semi-empirical tight-binding approach (see, e.g. Section 1.5) allows the inclusion of full crystallinity in a simpler fashion, although full self-consistency is not attempted as yet.

In the following we will attempt to pinpoint the stage at which each of the subject areas alluded to in the preceding section lies. Lang [1] has pointed out that surface energy calculations are presently self-consistent and they include crystallinity in a perturbation approximation (this applies also to the theory of adhesion [1.4]).

Electron work function calculations are self-consistent and now include crystallinity beyond the perturbation approximation in a plane wave basis so that not only good metals [1.24, 25] but also small band gap semiconductors [1.58] are considered. Initial explorations of the effect of ionic relaxation are also available [1.25, 58].

Impurity screening in the surface region is self-consistent but such calculations do not as yet take into account crystallinity [1.23]. In that self-consistent category there is a single, rather crude but *a priori* calculation of the local density of states associated with an adsorbate [1.23].

Surface state theory and, in fact, surface band structure calculations [1.25] are at the same stage as electron work function calculations [1.25, 58].

The theory of surface plasmons as yet includes no crystallinity and self-consistent response functions are not used, although a self-consistent formalism has been completed [1.73]. The sensitivity of the surface plasmon dispersion relation to self-consistency has been revealed [1.77]. This area of surface physics is behind the other fields. That is to be expected, however, since electronic excitations are often inherently more difficult to deal with than ground state properties.

Surface density of states theories are not as yet self-consistent, although full crystallinity is taken into account [1.63, 64, 83–90]. There have also been efforts to include relaxation of the surface lattice (see, e.g., [1.62, 88]).

Of the ground state theories, there are none as yet which treat crystalline transition metals self-consistently [1.91]. This is particularly unfortunate because most of the surface experimental data is for refractory transition metals. There is good reason for this discrepancy in our knowledge, however. For transition metals, one must deal with a mixture of contracted and diffuse orbitals immersed in the inhomogeneous medium of the surface. This makes plane wave bases impractical in general. Perhaps the generalized Wannier function method [1.7, 9], which represents surface observables precisely in terms of local functions, or another local orbital method (see, e.g., [1.83]) will lead to advancement in this area.

There remains a long way to go in surface theory, but the enormous progress of the last three to four years indicates a productive future for the field.

Acknowledgements

The author is indebted to D. HAMANN, J. A. APPELBAUM, K. C. PANDEY, and J. C. PHILLIPS for sending unpublished data and to

L. KLEINMANN and G. ALLDREDGE for preprints of their work. It is a pleasure to acknowledge conversations with P. FEIBELMAN, S. C. YING, E. W. PLUMMER, J. C. TRACY, J. M. BURKSTRAND, and J. G. GAY.

References

1.1. N. D. LANG: Solid State Physics **28**, 225 (1973).
  N. D. LANG, W. KOHN: Phys. Rev. B **1**, 4555 (1970).
1.2. Surface energy considerations pertinent to surface composition of binary alloys have been implemented recently by F. L. WILLIAMS, D. NASON: Surface Sci. **45**, 377 (1974); A recent investigation of correlation energy contributions to metal surface energies has been presented by J. HARRIS, R. O. JONES: Phys. Letters **46** A, 407 (1974).
1.3. H. KRUPP: Advan. Colloid Interface Sci. **1**, 111 (1967).
1.4. J. FERRANTE, J. R. SMITH: Surface Sci. **38**, 77 (1973).
1.5. See, e.g., K. H. JOHNSON, R. P. MESSMER: J. Vac. Sci. Technol. **9**, 561 (1974). See also J. R. SMITH and J. G. GAY (to be published).
1.6. R. F. WALLIS: Progress in Surface Sci. **4**, 233 (1973).
1.7. J. R. SMITH, J. G. GAY: Phys. Rev. Letters **32**, 774 (1974); Phys. Rev. B **9**, 4151 (1974); Phys. Rev. B **11**, 4906 (1975). See also J. J. REHR, W. KOHN: Phys. Rev. B **10**, 448 (1974), for an illuminating investigation of GWF asymptotic behavior.
1.8. H. D. HAGSTRUM, G. E. BECKER: Phys. Rev. B **8**, 1580 (1973).
1.9. W. KOHN, J. ONFFROY: Phys. Rev. B **8**, 2485 (1973).
1.10. N. D. LANG, W. KOHN: Phys. Rev. B **3**, 1215 (1971); 6010 (1973).
1.11. W. JONES, N. H. MARCH: *Theoretical Solid State Physics*, Vol. 2 (Wiley-Interscience, New York, 1973), pp. 814, 1060—1064.
1.12. J. R. SMITH: Phys. Rev. **181**, 522 (1969).
1.13. S. G. DAVISON, J. D. LEVINE: Solid State Phys. **25**, 92 (1970).
1.14. F. G. ALLEN, G. W. GOBELI: Phys. Rev. **127**, 141, 150 (1962).
1.15. J. C. RIVIÈRE: *Solid State Surface Science*, Vol. 1, ed. by M. GREEN (Dekker, New York, 1969), p. 179.
1.16. P. HOHENBERG, W. KOHN: Phys. Rev. **136**, B 864 (1964).
1.17. V. S. FOMENKO: *Handbook of Thermionic Properties* (Plenum Press, Inc., New York, 1966).
1.18. N. D. LANG: Solid State Commun. **7**, 1047 (1969).
1.19. W. KOHN, L. J. SHAM: Phys. Rev. **140**, A 1133 (1965).
1.20. The first treatment of the work function of a single-crystal plane was due to J. R. SMITH: Phys. Rev. Letters **25**, 1023 (1970). SMITH used what should now be considered a crude model, consisting of WIGNER-SEITZ polyhedra protruding into the vacuum.
1.21. N. W. ASHCROFT, D. C. LANGRETH: Phys. Rev. **155**, 682 (1967); **159**, 500 (1967).
  N. W. ASHCROFT: J. Phys. C **1**, 232 (1968).
1.22. N. D. LANG, W. KOHN: Phys. Rev. B **7**, 3541 (1973).
1.23. S. C. YING, J. R. SMITH, W. KOHN: Phys. Rev. B. Feb. 15, 1974. – L. KAHN, S. C. YING: Solid State Commun. (to be published).
1.24. J. A. APPELBAUM, D. R. HAMANN: Phys. Rev. B **6**, 2166 (1972).
1.25. G. P. ALLDREDGE, L. KLEINMAN: Phys. Rev. B **10**, 559 (1974).
1.26. E. W. PLUMMER, A. E. BELL: J. Vac. Sci. Technol. **9**, 583 (1972).
1.27. H. E. IVES: Astrophys. J. **60**, 209 (1924);
  I. LANGMUIR, K. H. KINGDON: Proc. Roy. Soc. (London) A **107**, 61 (1925).

1.28. V. M. GAVRILYUK, A. G. NAUMOVETS, A. G. FEDORUS: Soviet Phys. JETP **24**, 899 (1967);
L. W. SWANSON, R. W. STRAYER: J. Chem. Phys. **48**, 2421 (1968).

1.29. Recently rather a large decrease in the work function (1.5 – 3 eV) has been found for hydrocarbon adsorption on Pt. See J. L. GLAND, G. A. SOMOJAI: Surface Sci. **38**, 157 (1973).

1.30. J. R. SMITH, S. C. YING, W. KOHN: Phys. Rev. Letters **30**, 610 (1973).

1.31. N. D. LANG: Phys. Rev. B **4**, 4234 (1971).

1.32. R. W. GURNEY: Phys. Rev. **47**, 479 (1934).

1.33. J. RUDNICK: Phys. Rev. B **5**, 2863 (1972);
D. M. NEWNS: Phys. Rev. B **1**, 3304 (1970);
D. E. BECK, V. CELLI: Phys. Rev. B **2**, 2955 (1970);
J. W. GADZUK: J. Phys. Chem. Solids **30**, 2307 (1969).

1.34. S. C. YING, J. R. SMITH, W. KOHN: J. Vac. Sci. Techn. **9**, 575 (1972).

1.35. J. R. SMITH, S. C. YING, W. KOHN: Solid State Commun. **15**, 1491 (1974).

1.36. The experimental E_I is obtained from the atomic desorption energy E_a the hydrogen ionization potential I the electron work function ϕ_e, and the BORN-HABER cycle: $E_I = E_a + I - \phi_e$. E_a appears not to be very sensitive to the surface plane, and we used a representative value of 70 kcal/mole (see [1.37]). As mentioned earlier, the model is most appropriate to a close packed plane, and therefore we took $\phi_e = 5.3$ eV.

1.37. See, e.g.: T. E. MADEY, J. T. YATES, JR.: *Structure et Properties des Surface des Solides* (Editions du Centre National de la Recherche Scientifique, Paris, 1970), No. 187, p. 155;
T. W. HICKMOTT: J. Chem. Phys. **32**, 810 (1960).

1.38. E. W. PLUMMER, A. E. BELL: J. Vac. Sci. Technol. **9**, 583 (1972).

1.39. F. M. PROPST, T. C. PIPER: J. Vac. Sci. Technol. **4**, 53 (1967).

1.40. The energy of vibration of molecular hydrogen is 550 MeV, according to G. HERZBERG: *Molecular Spectra and Molecular Structure. I. Spectra of Diatomic Molecules*, 2nd ed. (D. Van Nostrand, New York, 1963).

1.41. T. E. MADEY: Surface Sci. **36**, 281 (1973).

1.42. K. YONEHARA, L. D. SCHMIDT: Surface Sci. **25**, 238 (1971);
P. J. ESTRUP, J. ANDERSON: J. Chem. Phys. **45**, 2254 (1966).

1.43. M. FINK, A. C. YATES: Atomic Data (to be published).

1.44. L. H. GERMER: Surface Sci. **5**, 147 (1966).

1.45. E. BAUER: Surface Sci. **5**, 152 (1966);
J. C. TRACY, J. M. BLAKELY: Surface Sci. **15**, 257 (1969).

1.46. P. J. JENNINGS, E. G. McRAE: Surface Sci. **23**, 363 (1970).

1.47. J. C. TRACY, J. E. ROWE: In *Electron Spectroscopy*, ed. by D. A. SHIRLEY (North-Holland Publishing Co., Amsterdam), p. 587;
H. D. HAGSTRUM, G. E. BECKER: J. Chem. Phys. **54**, 1015 (1971).

1.48. E. W. PLUMMER, B. J. WACLWASKI: Proc. Phys. Elec. Conf. (1973);
E. W. PLUMMER: (to be published);
B. FEUERBACHER, B. FITTON: Phys. Rev. B **8**, 4890 (1973).

1.49. L. ANDERS, R. HANSEN, L. BARTELL: J. Chem. Phys. **59**, 5277 (1973). See also J. W. GADZUK: In *Surface Physics of Crystalline Solids*, ed. by J. M. BLAKELY (Academic Press, New York, 1974).

1.50. I. TAMM: Z. Physik **76**, 849 (1932).

1.51. B. J. WACLAWSKI, E. W. PLUMMER: Phys. Rev. Letters **29**, 783 (1972);
B. FEUERBACHER, B. FITTON: Phys. Rev. Letters **29**, 786 (1972);
E. W. PLUMMER, J. W. GADZUK: Phys. Rev. Letters **25**, 1493 (1970);
N. R. AVERY: Phys. Rev. Letters **32**, 1248 (1974).

1.52. S. G. Davison, J. D. Levine: Solid State Phys. **25**, 1 (1970).
1.53. M. Henzler: Surface Sci. **25**, 650 (1971).
1.54. V. Heine: Proc. Phys. Soc. **81**, 300 (1963).
1.55. E. Carruthers, L. Kleinman, G. Alldredge: Phys. Rev. B **8**, 4570 (1973); **9**, 3325 (1974); **9**, 3330 (1974).
1.56. G. P. Alldredge, L. Kleinman: Phys. Rev. Letters **28**, 1264 (1972); Phys. Rev. B **10**, 1252 (1974).
1.57. J. A. Appelbaum, D. R. Hamann: Phys. Rev. Letters **31**, 106 (1973).
1.58. J. A. Appelbaum, D. R. Hamann: Phys. Rev. Letters **32**, 225 (1974).
1.59. R. O. Jones: J. Phys. C (Solid State Phys.) **5**, 1615 (1972).
1.60. J. A. Appelbaum, D. R. Hamann: Phys. Rev. B **8**, 1777 (1973).
1.61. A. Baldereschi: Phys. Rev. B **7**, 5212 (1973).
1.62. D. R. Hamann, J. A. Appelbaum: Private communication.
1.63. K. C. Pandey, J. C. Phillips: Phys. Rev. Letters **32**, 1433 (1974); Solid State Commun. **14**, 439 (1974).
1.64. K. C. Pandey, J. C. Phillips: To be published.
1.65. L. Kleinman: Phys. Rev. B **11**, 858 (1975).
1.66. J. M. Burkstrand: Phys. Rev. B **7**, 3443 (1973).
1.67. K. D. Sevier: *Low Energy Electron Spectrometer* (Interscience, New York, 1972), Chapter 8.
1.68. A. S. Barker, Jr.: Phys. Rev. B **8**, 5418 (1973).
   J. G. Endriz, W. E. Spicer: Phys. Rev. B **4**, 4144 (1971).
1.69. E. N. Economou, K. L. Ngai: To be published;
   R. H. Ritchie: Surface Sci. **34**, 1 (1973);
   H. Raether: Surface Sci. **8**, 233 (1967).
1.70. D. Pines, D. Bohn: Phys. Rev. **85**, 874 (1952), **92**, 609, 626 (1953).
1.71. R. H. Ritchie: Phys. Rev. **106**, 874 (1957).
1.72. E. A. Stern, R. A. Ferrell: Phys. Rev. **120**, 130 (1960).
1.73. S. C. Ying: Proceedings of the Taormina Conference on Prospectives of Many-Electron Calculations on Solids; Nuovo Cimento (to be published.
   See also S. C. Ying, J. J. Quinn, A. Eguiluz: To be published.
1.74. D. M. Newns: Phys. Rev. B **1**, 3304 (1970);
   V. Peuckert: Z. Physik **241**, 191 (1971);
   J. Harris, A. Griffin: Can. J. Phys. **48**, 2592 (1970);
   D. E. Beck: Phys. Rev. B **4**, 1555 (1971);
   P. A. Fedders: Phys. Rev. **153**, 438 (1967);
   P. J. Feibelman, C. B. Duke, A. Bagchi: Phys. Rev. B **5**, 2436 (1972).
1.75. J. E. Inglesfield, E. Wikborg: Solid State Commun. **14**, 661 (1974); J. Phys. C (Solid State Phys.) **6**, 158 (1973). These authors feel that the increase of the Friedel oscillations into the bulk is due to a numerical approximation — the finite range over which the integral equation is evaluated (private communication).
1.76. D. E. Beck, V. Celli: Phys. Rev. Letters **28**, 1124 (1972).
1.77. L. Hedin, S. Lundqvist: *Solid State Physics*, Vol. 24 (Academic Press, New York, 1969).
1.78. P. J. Feibelman: Phys. Rev. Letters **30**, 975 (1973); Phys. Rev. B **9**, 5077 (1974).
1.79. C. B. Duke, U. Landman: Phys. Rev. B **8**, 505 (1973);
   C. B. Duke et al.: J. Vac. Sci. Technol. **10**, 183 (1973);
   See also Bagchi and Duke: Phys. Rev. B **5**, 2784 (1972).
1.80. P. J. Feibelman: Phys. Rev. B **3**, 220 (1971);
   J. Harris, A. Griffin: Phys. Letters **34**, 51 (1971).
1.81. Hydrodynamic theories have yielded bands of surfaces plasmons in addition to the "usual" band whose frequency is given by (1.39) in the infinite-wavelength limit.

See A.J.BENNETT: Phys. Rev. B **1**, 203 (1970) and L.KLEINMAN: Phys. Rev. B **7**, 2288 (1973).

1.82. P.J.FEIBELMAN: Surf. Sci. **40**, 102 (1973); Phys. Rev. B **9**, 5077 (1974); D.M.NEWNS: Phys. Letters **38**A, 341 (1972).

1.83. J.W.DAVENPORT, T.L.EINSTEIN, J.R.SCHRIEFFER: Japanese J. Appl. Phys., Suppl. 2, Part 2, 691 (1974).

1.84. F.CYROT-LACKMANN, M.C.DESJONQUERES: Surface Sci. **40**, 423 (1973).

1.85. J.P.GASPARD, F.CYROT-LACKMANN: J. Phys. C (Solid State Phys.) **6**, 3077 (1973); **7**, 1829 (1974).

1.86. R.HAYDOCK, V.HEINE, M.J.KELLY: J. Phys. C (Solid State Phys.) **5**, 2845 (1972).

1.87. R.HAYDOCK, V.HEINE, M.J.KELLY, J.B.PENDRY: Phys. Rev. Letters **29**, 868 (1972).

1.88. R.HAYDOCK, M.J.KELLY: Surface Sci. **38**, 139 (1973).

1.89. D.G.PETTIFOR: J. Phys. C; Proc. Phys. Soc. London **2**, 1051 (1969); **3**, 367 (1970).

1.90. D.KALKSTEIN, P.SOVEN: Surface Sci. **26**, 85 (1971).

1.91. There is an interesting recent calculation which sizes some of the phenomena of interest at transition metal surfaces; P. FULDE, A. LUTHER, R. WATSON: Phys. Rev. B **8**, 440 (1973). Transition metal perovskite crystals have been treated by T. WOLFRAM, E. A. KRAUT, F. J. MORIN: Phys. Rev. B **7**, 1677 (1973).

2. Theory of Chemisorption

S. K. Lyo and R. Gomer

With 7 Figures

Chemisorption is defined, somewhat loosely, as the adsorption of atoms or molecules on surfaces with a binding energy in excess of 1 eV. In many cases energies as high as 3 or 4 eV are observed, so that the process clearly corresponds to electron sharing, i.e., chemical bonding. This bonding can be understood at least qualitatively in terms of the usual concepts of chemical bonding. It is not surprising that the principal lines of attack have been extensions of the LCAO-MO (Linear Combination of Atomic Orbitals—Molecular Orbitals) and valence bond methods, respectively. The former is considerably easier to handle at least in the Hartree-Fock approximation; the limits of validity of this approximation are also most easily understood in terms of LCAO-MO arguments. In its simplest form this approach consists of considering the formation of eigenstates of the system from a basis set consisting of eigenstates of the relevant band of the metal plus the relevant adsorbate orbital. Although this approach ignores the fact that this set is incomplete and usually the overlap between the adsorbate and metal states as well, it contains all the qualitative features of more refined theories and is very illuminating. We shall therefore devote considerable attention to it.

2.1. Qualitative Discussion

We start with a very pictorial preview of what we shall find. Consider an adsorbate atom with a filled level of energy E_a as it approaches a metal surface. As the atom comes near the metal the originally sharp level at E_a may broaden by interaction with the metal, i.e. by the fact that tunneling into or from the metal gives it a finite lifetime and hence a half-width

$$\Delta \cong h/2\tau . \tag{2.1}$$

This situation is usually encountered if E_a is relatively close to the Fermi energy E_F, i.e. if the tunneling barrier is not too high. It may also happen, however, that interaction of the adsorbate state leads to splitting off of a relatively sharp localized bonding state near the bottom of the band, and formation of an antibonding state above the Fermi level. In the simplest model which considers the metal band states this level falls outside the band and is also sharp. More realistic theories show that it can in fact be very broad. In either case bonding occurs because there is a net lowering in the energy of all the filled states, i.e. those below E_F.

As in all bonding an essential feature is that two electrons can simultaneously be on the adsorbate; the intra-atomic Coulomb repulsion U of these electrons presents one of the principal difficulties of any calculation. In the Hartree Fock scheme the interaction of an electron of given spin with the average population of electrons of opposite spin is computed. It turns out that this approximation is valid [2.1] when $\pi\Delta/U > 1$ or if the separation of bonding and anti-bonding orbitals exceeds U. If these inequalities are reversed correlation becomes very important; for instance, a generalized valence bond approach must be used. Fortunately the value of U which would apply to the free atom is considerably reduced near a metal surface by screening effects which can be understood in terms of an image interaction. Disregarding any other effects, the effective ionization energy $-E_a$ is decreased at a distance x from the surface by an amount V_{im}, classically given by $e^2/4x$, since the resulting ion interacts attractively with the metal through its image charge; thus the level E_a is pushed up by V_{im}. On the other hand, the electron affinity is increased by V_{im} since an ion A^- would also interact attractively with the metal. Consequently the effective Coulomb repulsion becomes

$$U_{\text{eff}} = U - 2 V_{im}. \tag{2.2}$$

We should note however that recent quantum treatments [2.2, 3] of image interaction give results which deviate significantly from the classical value at small metal-ion separations.

For a quantitative discussion of the problem we introduce a total density of states,

$$\varrho(E) = \sum_m \delta(E - E_m) \tag{2.3}$$

and a local density of states at the adsorbate

$$\varrho_a(E) = \sum_m |\langle a|m\rangle|^2 \delta(E - E_m), \tag{2.4}$$

where $|\varphi_a\rangle \equiv |a\rangle$ and E_m is the eigenvalue corresponding to the eigenvector of the system with the Hamiltonian $\mathcal{H}$ (i.e. $\mathcal{H}|m\rangle = E_m|m\rangle$).

$\varrho_a(E)$ is the weighted sum of the density of states and measures a local property at the adsorbate.

ϱ, ϱ_a can be expressed very conveniently in terms of the Green's function of the metal-adsorbate system defined by

$$G(E - \mathcal{H} - i\alpha) = 1 \tag{2.5}$$

or equivalently by

$$G = \frac{1}{E - \mathcal{H} - i\alpha} \tag{2.6}$$

where α is an infinitesimally small positive quantity. Then

$$G_{mm} = \frac{1}{E - E_m - i\alpha} = \frac{(E - E_m) + i\alpha}{(E - E_m)^2 + \alpha^2} = P\frac{1}{E - E_m} \tag{2.7}$$
$$+ i\pi\delta(E - E_m),$$

where P indicates the Cauchy's principal part. It then follows from (2.3), (2.4), and (2.7) that

$$\varrho(E) = \frac{1}{\pi}\,\mathrm{Im}\{\mathrm{Tr}\,G\} \tag{2.8}$$

and

$$\varrho_a(E) = \sum_m \langle a|m\rangle\langle m|a\rangle\frac{1}{\pi}\,\mathrm{Im}\{G_{mm}\} = \frac{1}{\pi}\,\mathrm{Im}\{G_{aa}\}, \tag{2.9}$$

where Tr and Im mean trace and imaginary part of what follows. This is a central result, since the experimental information obtainable from field emission [2.4] and photoemission [2.5] is known to yield $\mathrm{Im}\{G_{aa}\}$ rather directly.

2.2. Newns-Anderson Model

We treat now the simplest LCAO-MO model in the Hartree-Fock approximation. As already pointed out, the basis consists of the relevant band states of the metal $|k\rangle$ and a single adsorbate wave function φ_a. The approach we shall follow here is largely that of NEWNS [2.6], in turn based on a formalism used by ANDERSON [2.7] to treat impurities *in* rather than *on* a metal. Except for the inclusion of self-consistency the results are entirely equivalent to those obtained earlier by more "chemical", i.e. wave function rather than Green's function methods, for instance by Grimley [2.8].

In the following we consider the chemisorption of hydrogen-like atoms on transition metals surfaces. The relevant wave functions are d-band wave functions of the metal and singly occupied, non-degenerate orbitals of the adsorbate.

The Hamiltonian for electrons of spin σ of the metal-adsorbate system is given in the Hartree-Fock approximation by

$$\mathscr{H}^\sigma = \mathscr{H}_m + V^\sigma , \tag{2.10}$$

where $\mathscr{H}_m$ is the unperturbed metal Hamiltonian, and V^σ is the perturbation introduced by the adatom. Following Newns and Anderson we assume for simplicity that $\{|a\rangle, |k\rangle\}$ $(\mathscr{H}_m|k\rangle = E_k|k\rangle)$ form an orthornormal complete set (i.e. $\langle k|a\rangle = 0$, $\langle k|k'\rangle = \delta_{k,k'}$). The Hamiltonian (2.10) can then be expressed in terms of this basis set: We assume that

$$\mathscr{H}_{kk'} = E_k\delta_{kk'}, \ \mathscr{H}_{ak} \equiv V_{ak}, \ \mathscr{H}_{ka} \equiv V_{ka},$$
$$\mathscr{H}_{aa}^\sigma = E_a + V_{im} + \langle n_{-\sigma}\rangle U_{\text{eff}} \equiv E_{a\sigma}, \tag{2.11}$$

where $\langle n_\sigma\rangle$ is the ground state expectation value of the population of σ-spin electrons on the adatom. V_{ak} describes the hopping of the electron between the adsorbate and the metal and is taken to be independent of spin. The first term of $\mathscr{H}_{aa}^\sigma$ represents the unperturbed adatom level, the second term the upward shift of the level due to the image charge, and the third term the "Coulomb raising" of the σ-spin level due to the presence of-σ-spin electrons.

We can now obtain the Green's functions by taking matrix elements of both sides of (2.5) with respect to the basis set $\{h\} \equiv \{k, a\}$:

$$\sum_{h''} G_{hh''}^\sigma (E - \mathscr{H}^\sigma - i\alpha)_{h''h'} = \delta_{hh'} \tag{2.12}$$

which can be solved straightforwardly [2.7] and yields

$$G_{kk'}^\sigma = g_k\delta_{kk'} + g_k V_{ka} G_{aa}^\sigma V_{ak'} g_{k'} \tag{2.13}$$

and

$$G_{aa}^\sigma = \cfrac{1}{E - E_{a\sigma} - \sum_k \cfrac{|V_{ak}|^2}{E - E_k - i\alpha}} . \tag{2.14}$$

In (2.13) g_k is the Green's function of the metal $\left(\text{i.e. } g_k = \dfrac{1}{E - E_k - i\alpha}\right)$.
The last term in the denominator of G_{aa}^σ can be separated into real and imaginary parts using an identity similar to the third equality in (2.7), yielding

$$G_{aa}^\sigma = \frac{1}{E - E_{a\sigma} - \Lambda - i\Delta},\qquad (2.15)$$

where

$$\Delta(E) = \pi \sum_k |V_{ak}|^2 \delta(E - E_k) \qquad (2.16)$$

and

$$\Lambda(E) = P \sum_k \frac{|V_{ak}|^2}{E - E_k} = \frac{1}{\pi} P \int_{-\infty}^{\infty} \frac{\Delta(E')dE'}{E - E'}. \qquad (2.17)$$

Equation (2.14) enables us to find ϱ_a^σ as

$$\varrho_a^\sigma = \frac{1}{\pi} \operatorname{Im}\{G_{aa}^\sigma\} = \frac{1}{\pi} \frac{\Delta}{(E - E_{a\sigma} - \Lambda)^2 + \Delta^2}. \qquad (2.18)$$

If the energy dependence of $\Lambda(E)$ and $\Delta(E)$ could be neglected, (2.18) would have a simple Lorentzian line shape centered on $E = E_{a\sigma} + \Lambda$, the shifted adsorbate level, with a halfwidth at half maximum of Δ, which would be related to the average, i.e., energy independent tunneling time by the "golden rule" expression

$$1/\tau = \frac{2\Delta}{\hbar} = \frac{2\pi}{\hbar} \sum_k |V_{ak}|^2 \delta(E - E_k) \qquad (2.19)$$

as indicated in (2.1).

In general, the energy dependence of Δ and Λ cannot be neglected, and ϱ_a will be more complicated, even in the simple model depicted here. This fact is responsible for the variety of behavior which may occur. Equations (2.6) and (2.9) show that the energy eigenvalues E_m correspond to poles of G_{aa} on the real axis (i.e. without the imaginary part $i\alpha$ in (2.14)). Poles can also occur for (2.15) (i.e. keeping the imaginary part $i\alpha$) outside the band where $\Delta = 0$ if, from (2.15)

$$E - E_{a\sigma} - \Lambda(E) = 0 \qquad (2.20)$$

has real roots. This situation corresponds to the intersection of the line $E - E_{a\sigma}$ vs. E with $\Lambda(E)$. Possible situations are shown in Fig. 2.1.

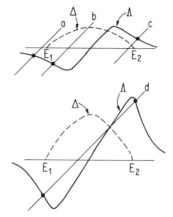

Fig. 2.1. $\Delta(E)$ and its Hilbert transform $\Lambda(E)$ are shown schematically. The roots of $E - E_{a\sigma} = \Lambda(E)$ are indicated by dots. A weak metal-adatom interaction gives rise to a sharp localized state either below (a) or above (c) the band or a virtual level in the band (b). A strong metal-adatom interaction causes a bonding anti-bonding splitting (d). E_1 indicates the band bottom and E_2 band top

It is seen that one (Fig. 2.1a and c), two (Fig. 2.1d), or zero (Fig. 2.1b) states may detach themselves from the band. It is not difficult to show that only one state below (above) the band generally corresponds to a localized state at the adatom formed through a very weak interaction, when the original unperturbed adatom level lies below (above) the band, while a state below (filled) and above (empty) the band corresponds to very strong chemisorption, i.e., the formation of a surface molecule between the adsorbate and its neighboring substrate atoms (Fig. 2.1d).

It is worthwhile to show this more explicitly. If the localized states are far above and below the band we may approximate $\Lambda(E)$ in their vicinity by

$$\Lambda(E) \cong (E - E_c)^{-1} \pi^{-1} \int \Delta(E') \, dE', \tag{2.21}$$

where E_c is the energy of the band center, and the integral runs only over the band. Then we have from (2.20)

$$E - E_{a\sigma} - (E - E_c)^{-1} \pi^{-1} \int \Delta(E') \, dE' = 0 \tag{2.22}$$

or, from the definition of Δ, (2.16)

$$(E - E_{a\sigma})(E - E_c) = \sum_k |V_{ak}|^2. \tag{2.23}$$

We next represent the states $|k\rangle$ in terms of a set formed by taking the most relevant atomic orbitals, say $5d$ orbitals in the case of tungsten, from each substrate atom in the metal. We shall pretend that these form a complete orthornormal set, within the manifold of the relevant substrate band (e.g. $5d$-band), which is of course only an approximation. It is possible to construct orthonormal sets along such lines, for instance Wannier orbitals (which are not localized enough for our purposes) but we shall ignore such refinements. With this approximation we have

$$V_{ak} \cong \sum_j \beta'_j \langle j|k\rangle, \qquad (2.24)$$

where

$$\beta'_j = V_{aj}. \qquad (2.25)$$

Then (2.20) becomes, since the $|k\rangle$ form a complete set (e.g. within the $5d$-band)

$$(E - E_{a\sigma})(E - E_c) = \sum_j |\beta'_j|^2 \qquad (2.26)$$

or

$$E_l = \frac{1}{2}\left[E_c + E_{a\sigma} \pm \sqrt{(E_{a\sigma} - E_c)^2 + 4\sum_j |\beta'_j|^2}\right]. \qquad (2.27)$$

These are just the bonding and antibonding levels of a surface molecule formed between the adsorbate and those substrate atoms for which $\beta'_j \neq 0$. Equation (2.20) may also have a root within the band where $\Delta \neq 0$, as shown by b of Fig. (2.1). In this case the level has a finite width and corresponds to a virtual state.

It is interesting to consider the location of $E_{a\sigma}$ in more detail. We have already seen that it is given by

$$\begin{aligned} E_{a\sigma} &= E_a + V_{im} + U_{\text{eff}}\langle n_{-\sigma}\rangle \\ &= E_a + V_{im} + (U - 2V_{im})\langle n_{-\sigma}\rangle. \end{aligned} \qquad (2.28)$$

Thus, if the total electronic charge at the adsorbate is $1e$ and nonmagnetic (i.e. if $\langle n_\sigma\rangle = \langle n_{-\sigma}\rangle = 1/2$), then

$$E_{a\sigma} = E_a + U/2 \qquad (2.29)$$

which is independent of the image energy V_{im}.

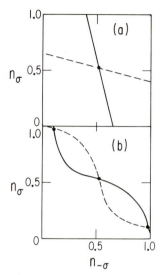

Fig. 2.2a and b. Illustration of occurrence of non-magnetic (a) and magnetic (b) solutions. The solid lines represent (2.30a) and the dashed lines (2.30b). The dots correspond to the self-consistent solutions

We must next evaluate $\langle n_\sigma \rangle$ and $\langle n_{-\sigma} \rangle$. In principle this can be done by noting that

$$\langle n_\sigma \rangle = \int_{-\infty}^{E_F} \varrho_a^\sigma \, dE,$$

(2.30a)

$$\langle n_{-\sigma} \rangle = \int_{-\infty}^{E_F} \varrho_a^{-\sigma} \, dE$$

(2.30b)

Since ϱ_a^σ contains $\langle n_{-\sigma} \rangle$ and vice versa the two equations (2.30) could be solved self-consistently for $\langle n_\sigma \rangle$ and $\langle n_{-\sigma} \rangle$. There will always be a root for which $\langle n_\sigma \rangle = \langle n_{-\sigma} \rangle$, the so called nonmagnetic solution. It may also happen that there are two symmetric magnetic roots $\langle n_\sigma \rangle = a$, $\langle n_{-\sigma} \rangle = b$, and $\langle n_\sigma \rangle = b$, $\langle n_{-\sigma} \rangle = a$, $a \neq b$. Figure 2.2 shows a typical nonmagnetic solution (a), and magnetic solutions (b). The solid lines represent (2.30a), and the dashed lines (2.30b). As is well known, the Hartree-Fock solution has an extremum property. Therefore if there is only one nonmagnetic solution, this should give an energy minimum. If there are two magnetic solutions and one nonmagnetic solution, then the former correspond to minima, and the latter to a maximum, because the end points (cf. Fig. 2.2b) cannot give minima. It is generally known that the Hartree-Fock approximation breaks down entirely when the solutions have magnetic roots, since this case corresponds to so much repulsion that correlation effects are too important to be treated adequately in the Hartree-Fock approximation. We will confine ourselves therefore, at least implicitly, to cases where only nonmagnetic solutions occur, but will continue to apply the validity criterion already discussed.

The density of states for the system is given by (2.8), (2.13), and (2.14)

$$
\begin{aligned}
\varrho^\sigma &= \frac{1}{\pi} \operatorname{Im} \left\{ \sum_k G_{kk} + G_{aa} \right\} \\
&= \varrho_m^0(E) + \frac{1}{\pi} \frac{\partial}{\partial E} \operatorname{Im} \left\{ \ln \left[E - E_{a\sigma} - \sum_k \frac{|V_{ak}|^2}{E - E_k - i\alpha} \right] \right\}
\end{aligned}
$$
(2.31)

with $\varrho_m^0(E) = \sum_k \delta(E - E_k)$, a density of states for the metal. The change of the density of states due to the adsorption of the adatom is thus given by

$$
\Delta\varrho^\sigma \equiv \varrho^\sigma - \varrho_m^0(E) = \frac{1}{\pi} \frac{\partial}{\partial E} \operatorname{Im} \{ \ln [E - E_{a\sigma} - \Lambda(E) - i\Delta(E)] \}. \quad (2.32)
$$

Therefore $\Delta\varrho^\sigma$ is proportional to the derivative of the phase of the argument of the natural logarithm in (2.32). There are two different kinds of roots of $E - E_{a\sigma} - \Lambda(E) = 0$ in Fig. 2.1. One corresponds to negative slopes of $\Lambda(E)$, the other to positive slopes. The phase of the argument of the logarithm increases rapidly at the former and decreases at the latter roots contributing large positive and negative values to $\Delta\varrho^\sigma$, respectively (see, e.g., Fig. 2.7). Therefore the former give rise to resonances and the latter to antiresonances. The local density of states ϱ_a^σ has peaks at the resonances and dips at the anti-resonances as will be shown later (see Fig. 2.6).

We are now ready to evaluate the chemisorption energy as the difference between the system energy when the adsorbate is not interacting and when the interaction is turned on. This is given by

$$
\delta E = \left\{ \sum_\sigma \int_{-\infty}^{E_F} E\varrho^\sigma \, dE - V_{im} \right\} - \left\{ \sum_\sigma \int_{-\infty}^{E_F^0} E\varrho_m^0(E) \, dE + E_a \right\}
$$
$$
- U \langle n_\sigma \rangle \langle n_{-\sigma} \rangle.
$$
(2.33)

The first curly bracket represents the total system energy after chemisorption and the second before chemisorption. V_{im} must be subtracted as the interaction of the ion core with the metal; it takes care of the fact that we have added it to E_a. The U term appears with a negative sign since it has been counted twice in the sum over system states; the factors Σ_σ stands for the summation over spin. It is necessary to distinguish between the Fermi energy of the interacting and non-interacting systems although the difference is infinitesimally small. Equation (2.33) can be rewritten as

$$\delta E = \sum_\sigma \int_{-\infty}^{E_F^0} E(\varrho^\sigma - \varrho_m^0(E))\, dE$$
$$+ \sum_\sigma (E_F - E_F^0)\, \varrho^\sigma(E_F)\, E_F - E_a - U\langle n_\sigma\rangle\,\langle n_{-\sigma}\rangle - V_{im}. \tag{2.34}$$

By making use of charge conservation,

$$\sum_\sigma \int_{-\infty}^{E_F} \varrho^\sigma\, dE = \sum_\sigma \int_{-\infty}^{E_F^0} \varrho_m^0(E)\, dE + 1 \tag{2.35}$$

and multiplying expression (2.35) by E_F and substituting the resulting expression for $(E_F - E_F^0)\,\varrho(E_F)$ in (2.34) we see that

$$\delta E = \sum_\sigma \int_{-\infty}^{E_F} (E - E_F)\,\Delta\varrho^\sigma\, dE + E_F - E_a - U\langle n_\sigma\rangle\langle n_{-\sigma}\rangle - V_{im}. \tag{2.36}$$

If energy is counted from the reference zero of E_F and if (2.32) is used in (2.36), expression (2.33) is equivalent to an expression derived by Newns directly from G_{aa} by means of Levinson's theorem on the poles and zeros of a function, and the fact that the poles of G_{aa}^{-1} correspond to the E_k and its zeros to the E_m.

The quantity $\Delta(E) = \pi \Sigma_k |V_{ak}|^2\, \delta(E - E_k)$ plays an important role in the Newns-Anderson model: It enters into Λ, $\Delta\varrho$, ΔE etc. Unfortunately $\Delta(E)$ cannot be evaluated exactly at present. Nevertheless we can proceed further by introducing the concept of a group orbital (φ_g) [2.9, 10] which simplifies the problem. We assume that the adatom interacts with the metal through a group orbital φ_g (i.e. $V_{ak} \cong V_{ag}\langle g|k\rangle$), which is taken as a linear combination of some substrate atomic orbitals having large overlap with the adatom orbital. We therefore approximate Δ by

$$\Delta(E) \simeq \pi |V_{ag}|^2\, \varrho_g(E), \tag{2.37}$$

where ϱ_g, the surface density of states at φ_g is given by

$$\varrho_g(E) = \sum_k |\langle g|k\rangle|^2\, \delta(E - E_k). \tag{2.38}$$

We have thus couched the problem in terms of overlap integrals between φ_a and φ_g, and the projection of the total density of states of the metal on φ_g. The choice of φ_g depends on the bonding geometry of the adatom. The surface density of states ϱ_g is a very important quantity in the theory of chemisorption. Recently there have been a number of calculations [2.11, 12] of this quantity for transition metals and simple cubic metals.

2.3. Reformulation of the Theory Using a Complete Basis Set

The model we have just sketched has the advantage of great simplicity and shows the qualitative features to be expected from any LCAO-MO theory in a very transparent way. However, it suffers from the fact that it neglects overlap between the metal and adsorbate states, and that it uses a very incomplete set of states. Outside the metal, where the adsorbate is located, the bound states of the metal decay rapidly, but the continuum states (i.e. unbound states) have large amplitude, and should therefore be much more important than in the case of an inpurity *in* the metal. It therefore seems a logical extension of the model to include continuum states of the metal to treat chemisorption. However, we now run into a conceptual difficulty. If the set of metal states is complete, it must contain the adsorbate orbital, i.e. the set of metal states plus the adsorbate orbital is overcomplete.

Since the totality of eigenfunctions of the metal $\{k\}$ form a complete set, we can always expand $\mathcal{H}$ and G in it even if the resultant matrices are not diagonal. The density of states, for instance, would still be given by Tr G since the trace is invariant. The problem then is to bring $|a\rangle$ into the picture somehow. There are various methods of doing so, which turn out to be if not equivalent at least closely related. Perhaps the simplest to understand, if not to justify is an approximation due to PENN [2.13].

The approximation consists of assuming for V^σ in (2.10) that

$$V^\sigma_{kk'} = \sum_b \langle k|V^\sigma|b\rangle \langle b|k'\rangle \simeq \langle k|V^\sigma|a\rangle \langle a|k'\rangle, \qquad (2.39)$$

where $\{|b\rangle\}$ are eigenstates of the free adsorbate of which $|a\rangle$ is the most relevant member. Essentially we are treating $|a\rangle$ as a complete set. This can be justified in terms of a single resonance orbital approximation [2.14]. The equation of motion of the Green's function is still given by (2.12) except that the set $\{h\}$ now comprises $\{k\}$, the totality of the bound and unbound eigenstates of the metal. Inserting (2.39) in (2.12), one obtains [2.13]

$$G^\sigma_{kk'} = g_k\delta_{kk'} + \frac{g_k V^\sigma_{ka}\langle a|k'\rangle g_{k'}}{1 - \sum_k \dfrac{\langle a|k\rangle V^\sigma_{ka}}{E - E_k - i\alpha}}. \qquad (2.40)$$

The local density of states and the change of the total density of states are found from (2.40) using (2.8) and (2.9), respectively

$$\Delta\varrho^{\sigma}(E) = \frac{1}{\pi} \frac{\partial}{\partial E} \operatorname{Im}\left\{\ln\left[1 - \sum_{k} \frac{\langle a|k\rangle V_{ka}^{\sigma}}{E - E_{k} - i\alpha}\right]\right\} \tag{2.41}$$

$$\varrho_{a}^{\sigma}(E) = \frac{1}{\pi} \operatorname{Im} \sum_{kk'} \langle a|k\rangle G_{kk'}\langle k'|a\rangle = \frac{1}{\pi} \operatorname{Im}\left\{\frac{\sum_{k'}|\langle a|k'\rangle|^{2} g_{k'}}{1 - \sum_{k} \frac{\langle a|k\rangle V_{ka}^{\sigma}}{E - E_{k} - i\alpha}}\right\}. \tag{2.42}$$

We can get a more symmetric result by using a different approximation for $V_{kk'}^{\sigma}$. For this purpose we multiply (2.39) by $\langle a|k\rangle$ and sum on k, obtaining $V_{ak'}^{\sigma} \simeq \langle a|V^{\sigma}|a\rangle \langle a|k'\rangle$. Using this in (2.39), we have

$$V_{kk'}^{\sigma} \simeq \frac{\langle k|V^{\sigma}|a\rangle \langle a|V^{\sigma}|k'\rangle}{\langle a|V^{\sigma}|a\rangle}. \tag{2.43}$$

It is to be noted that (2.39) and (2.43) are not equivalent, because they are approximate results. Using (2.43) in the equation of motion of the Green's function, one obtains [2.13]

$$G_{kk'}^{\sigma} = g_{k}\delta_{kk'} + \frac{g_{k}V_{ka}^{\sigma}V_{ak'}^{\sigma}g_{k'}}{V_{aa}^{\sigma} - \sum_{k}|V_{ak}^{\sigma}|^{2} g_{k}}. \tag{2.44}$$

It also follows from (2.8) and (2.44) that

$$\Delta\varrho^{\sigma}(E) = \frac{1}{\pi} \frac{\partial}{\partial E} \operatorname{Im}\left\{\ln\left[V_{aa}^{\sigma} - \sum_{k}|V_{ak}^{\sigma}|^{2} g_{k}\right]\right\}. \tag{2.45}$$

Although the denominator of the second term in (2.44) appears to be entirely different from that of the Newns-Anderson result [cf. Eqs. (2.13) and (2.14)] one can put the former, after some algebra [2.13], into

$$G_{kk'}^{\sigma} = g_{k}\delta_{kk'} + \frac{g_{k}V_{ka}^{\sigma}V_{ak'}^{\sigma}g_{k'}}{E - E_{a\sigma} - \sum_{k}|V_{ak}'^{\sigma}|^{2} g_{k}}, \tag{2.46}$$

where

$$V_{ak}'^{\sigma} = \langle a|\mathcal{H}^{\sigma} - E|k\rangle = V_{ak}^{\sigma} + (E_{k} - E) \langle a|k\rangle. \tag{2.47}$$

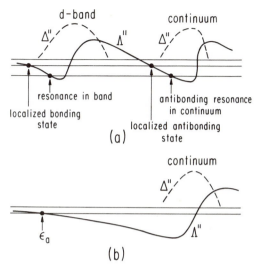

Fig. 2.3a and b. $\Delta''(E)$ and its Hilbert transform $\Lambda''(E)$ are shown when the adatom is near the surface (a) and at infinity (b). The roots of $(\bar{V}^\sigma)^{-1} = \Lambda''(E)$ are illustrated by circles

Equations (2.40) and (2.46) are equivalent to the results of KANAMORI et al. [2.15] and ANDERSON and McMILLAN [2.16] respectively.

The forms (2.40) and (2.44) are in fact rather similar to the Newns-Anderson result, except for the quantititatively significant difference that they include important contributions from continuum states with large amplitudes at the absorbate. In particular, (2.40) and (2.44) can give rise to resonances, antiresonances and localized states and so on. This can be seen qualitatively by approximating V_{ka}^σ and V_{aa}^σ by $\langle k|a \rangle\, \bar{V}^\sigma$ and $\bar{V}^\sigma$, respectively. With these approximations (2.40) and (2.44) become identical

$$G_{kk'}^\sigma = g_k \delta_{kk'} + \frac{g_k \langle k|a \rangle \langle a|k' \rangle g_{k'}}{\dfrac{1}{\bar{V}^\sigma} - \Lambda''(E) - i\Delta''(E)}, \tag{2.48}$$

where

$$\Delta''(E) = \pi \sum_k |\langle a|k \rangle|^2\, \delta(E - E_k) \tag{2.49}$$

and

$$\Lambda''(E) = \frac{1}{\pi} P \int_{-\infty}^{\infty} \frac{\Delta''(E')}{E - E'}\, dE'. \tag{2.50}$$

The general form of Δ'' and Λ'' will be similar to that of Δ and Λ, so that the existence of a localized state below the band of interest, for instance, corresponds to the intersection of Λ'' with the line $1/\bar{V}^\sigma$. Thus the stronger $\bar{V}^\sigma$ the lower in energy the bound state. It is interesting that the analogue of the empty antibonding orbital (the empty upper state in the Newns model) cannot be produced at all now, without invoking the existence of the continuum states, which continue Λ (or Λ'') in such a way as to make an upper intersection possible (Fig. 2.3). Thus overlap has pushed the antibonding orbital up in energy as expected.

If the potential is finite but the overlap with the d-band states is allowed to approach zero, i.e. if the atom is moved far from the surface, the intersection of $1/\bar{V}$ with Λ'' comes about entirely through the contribution of the continuum states. (For the latter the density of states increases beyond bound, but the overlap integral $\langle k|a \rangle \to 0$ as the de Broglie wavelength of the continuum states becomes smaller than the atomic dimensions of the adsorbate, because the positive and negative contributions from φ_k will cancel. This Δ and Δ'' for the continuum are bounded.) This illustrates again the point that the latter were necessary to form $|a\rangle$ in the first place.

For computational purposes it is convenient to use (2.40)–(2.42), and (2.36). The scattering potential V^σ is assumed to be

$$V^\sigma|a\rangle = (V_0 + V_{im} + U_{eff}\langle n_{-\sigma}\rangle)|a\rangle,\qquad(2.51)$$

where V_0 is the ionic potential. The second term V_{im} describes the interaction of the valence electron with the metal electrons (i.e. exchange and correlation energy), and the third term is the Hartree-Fock intra-atomic repulsion at the adatom.

The wave functions corresponding to the continuum states of the unperturbed metal can be approximated by assuming a step-like model potential $W(z)$ given by

$$\begin{aligned}W(z) &= 0 &\quad z > 0 \\ &= -V_c &\quad z < 0,\end{aligned}\qquad(2.52)$$

where $z > 0$ corresponds to the vacuum and $z < 0$ to the region inside the metal. $-V_c$ is the bottom of the conduction band measured from the vacuum level. With these approximations it is possible to carry out fairly realistic calculations. The main parameters entering the result are 1) the metal-adatom separation z_0, 2) the surface density of states ϱ_g which is introduced as before through a group orbital (φ_g) approximation, 3) the adatom-group orbital overlap integral $s = \langle a|g \rangle$, 4) image energy V_{im}, and finally a "Coulomb" parameter defined as

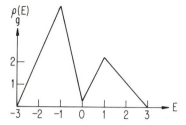

Fig. 2.4. Model surface density of states used for the numerical calculation. The total *d*-band width of tungsten is taken as 6 units, and the origin is at the band center. The Fermi level is approximately at 0.5

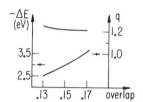

Fig. 2.5. The binding energy (lower curve) and the total electronic charge (in units of *e*) on the adatom (upper curve) as a function of overlap

$\eta = s^{-1} \int \varphi_g(\mathbf{r}) \left[a_0 / |\mathbf{r} - \mathbf{r}_a| \right] \varphi_a(\mathbf{r} - \mathbf{r}_a) d^3r$ ($a_0 \doteq$ first Bohr radius, $\mathbf{r}_a \doteq$ adatom location).

A numerical computation has been [2.14] carried out for hydrogen adsorption on the (100) surface of tungsten, which has a body centered cubic structure. For this system the experimental binding energy [2.17] is 3.0 eV and the total electronic charge in the adatoms is $q = 1.0$ (a.u.). Field [2.18] and photoemission [2.19] measurements show resonance peaks at $0.9 \sim 1.1$ eV and 5.4 eV below the Fermi level E_F with approximate full widths at half maximum of 0.6 eV and 0.7 eV, respectively. The Fermi level [2.18] is at -4.64 eV below the vacuum on (100) surface.

In order to explain these data a model surface density of states, as shown in Fig. 2.4, was introduced. The full band width of tungsten ($\simeq 10$ eV) is taken as 6 units. The origin is at the band center and E_F is at 0.5. This corresponds approximately to the bonding of a hydrogen adatom above the middle of two nearest neighbor tungsten atoms on the 100 surface [2.11].

Figure 2.5 shows the self-consistently determined total charge at the adatom and the binding energy for three different values of the overlap integral $s = 0.13$, $s = 0.15$, and $s = 0.17$ for $V_c \simeq 12.2$ eV, $z = 1.5$ a.u., V_{im}

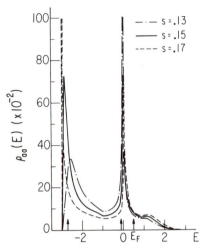

Fig. 2.6. The local density of states for three different overlaps. The energy scale is the same as in Fig. 2.4. The Fermi level, and the experimental values of resonances are indicated by arrows

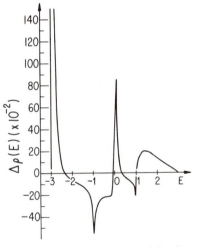

Fig. 2.7. The change of the total density of states for an overlap $s = 0.15$

$= 5.5 \text{ eV}$ and $\eta = 1.0$ [2.14]. It should be mentioned that s, z_0, and V_{im} cannot be uniquely determined at present. The solutions are non-magnetic. Figure 2.6 shows the local density of states for the same values of the parameters. It is seen that the overlap tends to split two resonance levels (i.e. bonding, antibonding levels) apart. The occurrence of the resonance near $E = 0$ is due to a minimum in the surface density of states there. Figure 2.7 shows the change of the total density of states $\Delta\varrho$ for $s = 0.15$ with other parameters unchanged. One observes the anti-resonances as well as the resonances. The results corresponding to $s = 0.15$ with the other parameters taken as above give reasonable agreement with the experimental data. As can be seen from (2.2), (2.51), and (2.36), the main effect of the image energy is to increase the binding energy approximately by $1/2\ V_{im}$ for a non-magnetic neutral binding (i.e. $\langle n_\sigma \rangle = \langle n_{-\sigma} \rangle = 1/2$), as in the present case. The calculation just presented suggests that a generalized LCAO-MO treatment in the Hartree-Fock approximation may be adequate for handling many cases of chemisorption. It should be pointed out, however, that the occurrence of a subsidiary resonance near E_F could only be explained by postulating a dip in the surface density of states. At the moment the existence of this dip is not firmly established, either experimentally or theoretically, and resolution of this question must await further work. It has recently been pointed out by HERTZ [2.20] that structure in ϱ_a including subsidiary peaks of the kind just discussed can also arise by treating spin fluctuation on the adsorbate and the metal in higher order than in Hartree-Fock. It is also conceivable that the subsidiary resonance near E_F arises from interaction of the metal with the hydrogen $2p$ state.

2.4. Adsorbate-Adsorbate Interaction

The interaction of adsorbates with each other through the mediation of the substrate is of considerable interest in connection with the coverage dependence of binding energies, and also the formation of periodic adsorbate arrays. We will not discuss here direct electrostatic inter-actions, i.e. dipole-dipole effects but restrict ourselves to the more subtle level splittings mediated by the substrate. This subject has been investigated by GRIMLEY [2.21] and more recently by EINSTEIN and SCHRIEFFER [2.10]. We give only the briefest sketch of the effect, following an unpublished treatment by LYO. We have already seen that the crucial quantity in calculating chemisorption energies is the quantity L defined by

$$L = V_{aa} - \sum_k |V_{ak}|^2\, g_k = V_{aa} - \langle a| Vg\, V|a\rangle \qquad (2.53)$$

which enters (2.45).

If, say, two adsorbate atoms are being considered, so that we must define state vectors $|a_1\rangle$ and $|a_2\rangle$ corresponding to electrons on A_1

and A_2, respectively, it can be shown that L goes over into the determinantal form

$$L = \begin{vmatrix} V_{aa} - \langle a_1 | Vg\, V | a_1 \rangle & \langle a_1 | Vg\, V | a_2 \rangle \\ \langle a_2 | Vg\, V | a_1 \rangle & V_{aa} - \langle a_2 | Vg\, V | a_2 \rangle \end{vmatrix}, \qquad (2.54)$$

where $V = V_1 + V_2$. If the adsorbate atoms are far apart the coupling between them will be negligible and the off-diagonal elements will vanish. In that case $\ln L_{12}$ for the combined system becomes simply $2 \ln L_1$ as it should and the energy is linear in the number of adsorbate particles. Adsorbate-adsorbate interaction is thus contained in the off-diagonal matrix elements of L and can lead to increases or decreases in E, i.e. to attractive or repulsive interactions.

2.5. Valence-Bond (Schrieffer-Paulson-Gomer) Approach
[2.22, 23]

We have seen from the foregoing that the validity of the LCAO-MO approach in the Hartree-Fock approximation is limited to broad resonances, small U, or localized states straddling the substrate band. The basic problem is to take proper account of the kind of correlation which results from electrons hopping off the adsorbate into the metal. In principle this can be handled in LCAO-MO by including configuration interaction or by more sophisticated definitions of $|a\rangle$. A different approach is to exaggerate correlation from the beginning by setting up the analogue of a valence-bond wave function. It is well known that the LCAO-MO method exaggerates ionic contributions, while the Heitler-London function omits ionic terms altogether. Thus the latter approach has (excessive) correlation built into it. In the valence bond approximation it is customary to consider only electron pair bonds, the spin singlet leading to bonding because of the symmetric space part of the wave function. This is not an iron-clad rule but arises in most cases from quantitative considerations, i.e., the actual magnitudes of the Coulomb and exchange integrals. While HeH is not stable, either in the MO or valence bond schemes, He_2^+ is bonding in both. If the requirement for the electron pair bond is waived, the VB approximation becomes largely equivalent to the LCAO-MO scheme with postulated infinite U, which can be treated more or less along the lines outlined in the last section. If we insist, however, on the importance of spin pairing, the substrate metal as it stands is not a suitable partner since, at ordinary temperatures there are effectively no unpaired spins available. Consequently it is necessary to create electron-hole pairs by promoting electrons above the Fermi energy in order to create free spins which can then pair with the adsorbate spin to form a valence bond. One may think of the adsorbate spin as inducing spin in the substrate. This process would cost energy of course, were it not that the attendant bond formation leads to a net lowering.

It is not difficult to proceed slightly beyond this statement. The energy required to create a spin S on a metal surface atom is

$$\Delta E_{\text{spin}} = \frac{1}{2} \chi H^2 = \frac{(\mu_B S)^2}{2\chi}, \tag{2.55}$$

where μ_B is the Bohr magneton and χ a local spin susceptibility, defined by $\mu_B S = \chi H$, H being the (fictitious) magnetic field which induces S. If a full spin $S = 1/2$ is induced on a metal surface atom, a bond with the adsorbate can be formed, which lowers the energy by an amount W_m. If no spin were present, on the other hand, the adsorbate would interact repulsively with the surface, the energy being increased by W_r. If we interpolate between these limits we can write for the net energy change, regarded as a function of spin S

$$\Delta E(S) = (\mu_B S)^2/2\chi - 2(W_m + W_r) S + W_r \tag{2.56}$$

which reduces to W_r for $S = 0$ and $(\mu_B S)^2/2\chi - W_m$ for $S = 1/2$. By minimizing with respect to S we find the maximum decrease in energy as

$$\Delta E = -(2\chi/\mu_B^2)(W_m + W_r) + W_r. \tag{2.57}$$

It can be shown [1] that

$$2\chi/\mu_B^2 = (2W_b)^{-1}, \tag{2.58}$$

where W_b is the width of the relevant metal band (for approximately flat bands) so that finally

$$\Delta E = -\frac{(W_m + W_r)^2}{2W_b} + W_r. \tag{2.59}$$

---

[1] The total magnetic moment $\chi_{\text{tot}} H$ induced by a field H in a free-electron-like metal by Pauli paramagnetism is $2\mu_B S \varrho(E_F) \Delta E$, where $\Delta E = (1/2)\mu_B H$ is the change in energy and $\varrho(E_F)$ is the density of states at the Fermi level not counting spin. Thus the total susceptibility is $\chi_{\text{tot}} = \mu_B^2 \varrho(E_F)/2$. If the density of states is roughly equated to $N/2W_b$ where N is the number of atoms in the metal the susceptibility per atom is $\chi = \mu_B^2/4W_b$.

This indicates that binding increases as the band gets narrower, in agreement with the fact that binding is strongest on transition metals.

A more quantitative formulation of this theory [2.22] is a rather difficult many-body problem, and goes considerably beyond the scope of this article. Since the basic approach abandons the concept of one-electron energy levels, the theory is also difficult to couch in the language of local densities of state. Very qualitatively, a level spectroscopy should indicate some disturbance in the substrate densities near E_F and should show an electron on the adsorbate near E_a. In the tight binding case, where the VB method also predicts a local state below the band, this quasi one-electron level could be shifted below E_a of the free atom.

2.6. Linear Response (Kohn-Smith-Ying) Method

An entirely different approach to chemisorption applied to date only to hydrogen has been taken by KOHN and his coworkers [2.24], discussed also in Chapter 1. In this method a bare proton is allowed to imbed itself in the electron gas at a metal surface, and the linear response of the resultant electron charge density is found self-consistently by going beyond the Fermi-Thomas approximation. The total energy is expressed in terms of the charge density and its gradient, and then minimized variationally with respect to the charge density. The metal is treated as a jellium. The only free parameter is the Wigner-Seitz radius. Thus the model ignores the band structure of the metal. For transition metals the validity of this approximation is doubtful. Although the calculated binding energy (relative to H^+ and M^-) is not very good, the method deals rather effectively with the charge density at and near the adsorbate and thus explains observed dipole moments rather well. In principle, the self-consistent potential which results can be used to calculate quasi-one-electron energy levels, and thus a local density of states can be extracted. In principle, the method is extendable to other cases, although actual calculations will undoubtedly be very difficult.

2.7. Concluding Remarks

This chapter has attempted to depict the current status of the theory of chemisorption. It seems appropriate to conclude with a short discussion of unsolved problems and possible future developments.

We have indicated that reasonably quantitative calculations of binding energy and local density of states at the equilibrium separation seem within our grasp. In the writers' opinion it is likely that the majority of cases can be handled by LCAO-MO schemes, probably in the Hartree-Fock approximation, because screening of the Coulomb repulsion U at the equilibrium distance reduces it so substantially. This is not to say that many important problems do not remain. Foremost among these are the calculation of self-consistent surface densities of state and dielectric response, i.e. image energy calculations for real transition metals. The first of these problems probably offers no major obstacles, and it is probable that the latter will also be solved before too long. Thus the problem of chemisorption at the equilibrium configuration seems, if not solved, at least soluble.

At large surface-adsorbate separations the problem appears equally soluble, if only because interaction energies are small and perturbative treatments are thus almost guaranteed to work. The situation seems quite different at intermediate separations. Here interaction is reasonably strong, but for cases of large U screening is almost certainly insufficient to justify the Hartree-Fock approximation. In these situations it seems very probable that the valence bond or possibly the linear-response methods developed by SCHRIEFFER and by KOHN, respectively, will turn out to be far more appropriate than the LCAO-method. It seems probable that much future work will concern itself with this region.

References

2.1. J. R. SCHRIEFFER, D. C. MATTIS: Phys. Rev. **140**, 1412 (1965).
2.2. D. M. NEWNS: Phys. Rev. B **1**, 3304 (1970);
      D. E. BECK, V. CELLI: Phys. Rev. B **2**, 2955 (1971).
2.3. J. A. APPELBAUM, D. R. HAMANN: Phys. Rev. B **6**, 1122 (1972).
2.4. D. R. PENN, R. GOMER, M. H. COHEN: Phys. Rev. B **5**, 768 (1972).
2.5. D. R. PENN: Phys. Rev. Letters **28**, 1041 (1972).
2.6. D. M. NEWNS: Phys. Rev. **178**, 1123 (1969).
2.7. P. W. ANDERSON: Phys. Rev. **124**, 41 (1961).
2.8. T. B. GRIMLEY: Proc. Phys. Soc. (London) **90**, 751 (1967) and previous papers.
2.9. T. B. GRIMLEY: J. Vac. Sci. Technol. **8**, 31 (1971).
2.10. T. L. EINSTEIN, J. R. SCHRIEFFER: Phys. Rev. B**7**, 3629 (1973).
2.11. D. R. PENN: Surface Sci. **39**, 333 (1973).
2.12. D. KALKSTEIN, P. SOVEN: Surface Sci. **26**, 85 (1971);
      F. CYROT-LACKMANN, M. C. DESJONQUERES: Surface Sci. **40**, 423 (1973);
      R. HAYDOCK, M. J. KELLY: Surface Sci. **38**, 139 (1973).
2.13. D. R. PENN: Phys. Rev. B **9**, 839 (1974).
2.14. S. K. LYO, R. GOMER: Phys. Rev. B **10**, 4161 (1974).
2.15. J. KANAMORI, K. TERAKURA, K. YAMADA: Progr. Theor. Phys. **41**, 1426 (1969).
2.16. P. W. ANDERSON, W. L. MCMILLAN: In *Scuola internazionale di fisica, Varenna, Italy*, ed. by W. MARSHALL (New York, Academic Press, 1967).
2.17. P. W. TAMM, L. D. SCHMIDT: J. Chem. Phys. **51**, 5352 (1969); **55**, 4253 (1971).

2.18. E. W. PLUMMER, A. E. BELL: J. Vac. Sci. Technol. **9**, 583 (1972).
2.19. B. FEUERBACHER, B. FITTON: Phys. Rev. B **8**, 4890 (1973).
2.20. J. A. HERTZ: To be published.
2.21. T. B. GRIMLEY, S. M. WALKER: Surface Sci. **14**, 395 (1969).
2.22. J. R. SCHRIEFFER, R. GOMER: Surface Sci. **25**, 315 (1971).
2.23. R. H. PAULSON, J. R. SCHRIEFFER: Surface Sci. **48**, 329 (1975).
2.24. J. R. SMITH, S. C. YING, W. KOHN: Phys. Rev. Letters **30**, 610 (1973).

3. Chemisorption: Aspects of the Experimental Situation

L. D. SCHMIDT

With 13 Figures

Because of its obvious relevance to catalysis and corrosion, the characterization of chemisorption has been the major objective of most studies of solid surfaces. It is the intent of this chapter to try to present a brief overall picture of the current situation regarding the interpretations of experiments on chemisorption. This is a rapidly developing and changing subject. Many of the concepts which appear in textbooks as recently as ten years ago have now been shown to be incomplete or wrong, and even monographs tend to become outdated within a few years. In a single chapter it will be impossible to cover chemisorption completely or even to list more than a small fraction of the significant recent developments.

This chapter will therefore be restricted to a consideration of some important recent experimental results regarding adsorbate structures in chemisorption. At the beginning, we note those topics not covered. First, we shall restrict our discussion to the interpretations directly required by experiments rather than those involving theoretical analysis of such data because chemisorption theory has been covered in Chapter 2. Second, we shall consider mainly atomic structures rather than kinetics or electronic structures because these are also covered in other chapters. Third, we shall be concerned only with chemisorption rather than physical adsorption or metal adsorption even though there have been important recent discoveries regarding these adsorbates also. Fourth, we shall consider only chemisorption on metals because, while our knowledge of adsorption on insulators and semiconductors has advanced considerably, the techniques used and the apparent nature of the structures are quite different than on metals. Finally we shall present experimental results with little consideration of the experiments themselves except where experimental uncertainties make interpretations ambiguous. Most of the new experimental methods are covered in other chapters, and earlier ones (methods of work function measurement, field emission microscopy, etc.) have been reviewed extensively in previous monographs.

It is hoped that the discussion will be comprehensible to the reader who is not working in surface physics as well as informative to those who are familiar with the subject. The pertinent quantities used in describing experimental results are adsorbate density n, fractional saturation coverage θ, work function change $\Delta\phi$, activation energy of desorption E_d, sticking coefficient or probability of condensation s, and symmetry of the surface structure, designated $(j \times k)$, where j and k are integers denoting the sepeating distance on the surface in multiples of the solid lattice constant (see Section 6.5 for further discussion of nomenclature). These quantities are readily interpreted without a detailed understanding of the apparatus or experiments from which the quantities are obtained. Interpretation of such data is at times less than obvious, however, and a section is devoted to this.

By adsorbate structures we mean simply the locations of the adsorbate atoms on a surface. This may appear at first to be a very easy task requiring only diffraction measurements. This may be nearly so if LEED theory advances to the stage where adsorbate structure can be obtained from LEED experiments (which are well developed). However even when the structures of perfectly ordered configurations are known, other measurements will be required to interpret the complex structures which exist in many chemisorption systems and the incompletely ordered structures at less than saturation densities and at low or high temperatures.

This chapter is divided into sections covering some of the subjects on which recent advances have been most significant: crystallographic anisotropies, adsorption binding states, adsorbate-adsorbate interactions, and variations between similar substrates. The discussion could also be divided into a few prototype chemisorption systems (H_2, N_2, and CO on body centered cubic metals and CO on face centered cubic metals) because there are only a few of such systems for which data are extensive enough to permit generalizations.

3.1. Structures of Clean Surfaces

Any attempts at locating adsorbate atoms on a surface presuppose a knowledge of the positions of the substrate atoms. This in fact has been, and in some cases still is, a major hindrance to determination of adsorbate structures. Until the 1950's surfaces were generally considered to be structureless (completely disordered or else possessing only the minimum free energy plane) with concepts such as Langmuir's "isolated active areas" invoked to explain any obvious deviations from this assumption. In the 1950's the field emission and field ion microscopes, LEED, and widespread use of macroscopic single crystals and ultrahigh vacuum techniques revealed clearly that polyfacetted surfaces can in no sense be considered uniform. Chemisorption structures and kinetics are now recognized to vary strongly with surface orientation, and as a consequence the proportion of chemisorption papers concerned with polycrystalline and polyfacetted surfaces is rapidly diminishing to situations where primarily engineering information is desired or where single crystal preparation techniques are difficult.

Therefore we must first enquire as to the structure of clean solid surfaces. This involves both the symmetry of the surface atoms and thermal disorder. Symmetry and long range order are studied by LEED, while thermal disorder and the positions of individual atoms are investigated mainly by field ion microscopy. Long range order varies between different metals and between metals, semiconductors and insulators. The trend regarding long range order, at least of metals, appears well established however: field ion microscopy [3.1] clearly indicates that the high symmetry, low free energy planes of metals are *well ordered* with *very low defect densities*, while other planes of a given metal exhibit considerable disorder. Incidentally, most published field ion micrographs are irrelevant to this question because they are obtained after field evaporation, i.e. after removing the top few layers of disordered atoms. Observing a perfect plane in such a micrograph implies nothing about the macroscopic plane. Only after first cleaning a surface by heating in the absence of a field can one use field ion microscopy to infer atom positions on a macroscopic thermally annealed surface.

3.1.1. Body Centered Cubic Transition Metals

These metals — especially W, Mo, Ta, and Nb — are easily studied because they can be cleaned by heating alone or by heating in O_2 at low pressures. Their clean surfaces give only (1×1) LEED patterns, implying that the symmetry is identical to that of the ideal crystal plane obtained by cleaving a perfect crystal (Fig. 3.1). This does not give the possible vertical displacements of the surface atoms or the extent of thermal disorder. From field ion microscopy [3.1] it appears that (110), (100), and (211) planes are perfect, the stepped surfaces consisting of (110) planes, and other planes such as (111) are rather disordered. However, chemisorption variations between these apparently disordered planes imply that specific adsorption sites exist, and that even these surfaces are not without order. For adsorbate structure determination on these metals it is therefore reasonable to assume that the structures are nearly those of the ideal perfect crystal planes, some of which are shown in Fig. 3.1.

Those of us studying chemisorption have been rather defensive of our apparent assumption that tungsten is the only metal in the Periodic

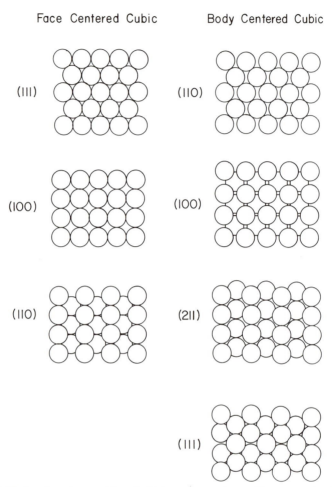

Fig. 3.1. Ideal surface atom positions for high symmetry planes of face centered cubic (fcc) and body centered cubic (bcc) metals. For most transition metals LEED and field ion microscopy indicate that clean surfaces exposing the planes have these structures and are nearly perfect with little disorder

Table. The major reason has admittedly been the ease of preparing clean surfaces of W, but the extensive measurements on this solid have in fact been quite useful because this is almost the only metal on which enough duplication of data exists to give confidence in the validity of results (but, as we shall see, a number of controversies still exist). Further, adsorption on W may prove to be a standard with which to calibrate instruments and to compare adsorption properties (relative densities and sticking coefficients, for example) on other surfaces. Also fortuitous for those studying tungsten is that it is the only metal which was reliably cleaned before 1970, except for vacuum deposited thin films. Auger electron spectroscopy (AES) has shown that many (perhaps most) earlier studies on metals such as Ni and Pt may, in fact, have been on surfaces which contained significant contamination with carbon, sulfur, or oxygen.

3.1.2. Face Centered Cubic Metals

These metals include many of the best catalysts (Pt, Ni, Pd, and Rh) and the noble metals (Cu, Ag, and Au). LEED indicates that (111) planes have (1×1) symmetry for all fcc metals. On Ni, Pd, and Cu the (100) planes also have (1×1) symmetry [3.2–4]. However, from there the situation becomes complex. The clean (100) planes of Pt, Au, and Ir exhibit a (5×1) symmetry [3.5]. It now appears from LEED intensity analysis that this arises from a nearly hexagonal overlayer of metal atoms on the ideal (100) plane. This layer is slightly compressed from the ideal (111) plane, and all atoms are not coplanar. Registry with the underlying (100) plane occurs at five lattice spacings in one direction and one in the other to yield a (5×1) LEED pattern. The (110) plane is the plane of next close packing, and, while on some metals it may have (1×1) symmetry, $(1\bar{1}0)$ Pt exhibits a (2×1) LEED pattern [3.6]. Probably alternate atoms along the rows are displaced or missing, but no clear picture of atom positions has emerged. The stepped planes of Pt, which consist of (111) planes and (100) steps, exhibit (1×1) LEED patterns with regularly spaced steps one atom in height [3.7].

3.1.3. Semiconductors

Silicon and germanium surfaces have been fairly well characterized because of their applications in solid state electronics. While vacuum cleaving may produce (111) planes with (1×1) periodicity, heating this or any other plane usually produces larger unit cell structures. The close packed (111) planes of Si and Ge exhibit (7×7) and (8×8) perodicities while the (100) planes both have (2×1) periodicities [3.8, 9]. Reasonable structures have been proposed to explain these observations [3.1]. The cause of the rearrangement of these surfaces from their bulk structures is the covalent bonding between atoms; the dangling bonds at the surface cannot be satisfied without large changes in the positions of the atoms in at least the first layer. Any detailed attempts at chemisorption structure determination on these surfaces requires a knowledge of the positions of the surface atoms and possible changes in these positions after adsorption. Additional experimental difficulties arise from the strong influences of trace impurities which alter electronic properties of these surfaces and from the fact that most gases have very low sticking coefficients on semiconductors.

3.1.4. Insulators

The structures of very few crystal planes of insulators are known with the exceptions of those prepared by low temperature vacuum cleaving, which are (1×1). A fundamental problem with these surfaces is that upon heating the atomic composition of the surface layer is not known. For oxides there is evidence that the metal oxygen ratio is not always that of the bulk and that it may be varied by heating or exposure to O_2 [3.10]. Oxide catalysts invariably have H_2O or OH^- groups on their surfaces.

3.2. Methods of Adsorbate Characterization

It is appropriate to comment briefly on some of the experimental techniques used to characterize adsorption because, while some are mentioned in other chapters, others are not. Also most of our present knowledge of adsorbate structures comes from techniques which have been widely used for ten years or more and now are rather "classical". The other chapters deal more with newer ones and those aspects of older ones which have not been widely exploited. Here our interest is in the utility and limitations of various techniques and the ways in which they complement each other for adsorbate structure determination.

The basic data one needs to characterize an adsorbate are 1) the number of binding states, 2) their saturation densities, both relative to each other and relative to the surface atom density, and 3) the periodicity of the adsorbate. For a simple system one might be able to construct a model for the adsorbate from such data. However almost without exception such a structure would be either nonunique or there would be gaps or contradictions in data. Therefore one would need additional information such a whether states are atomic or molecular, binding energies, sticking coefficients, and signs and magnitudes of dipole moments. These data, all readily obtained in most modern surface chemistry laboratories, are still insufficient in many cases, and one needs finally either a complete diffraction analysis or spectroscopic information on bonding and electronic structures.

3.2.1. Diffraction

LEED in principle is the most direct means of determining adsorbate structure. As discussed in Chapter 6, the positions of diffraction spots immediately give the size and orientation of the unit cell, and analysis of spot intensity versus electron energy gives in principle the positions of atoms in the unit cell and the distances between adsorbate and substrate atoms. Unfortunately LEED has only been used extensively to determine perodicities of adsorbates and atom positions on clean surfaces, but LEED theory now appears to be capable of yielding information on positions of adsorbate atoms as well.

In addition to perfectly ordered adsorbates, one must also describe the imperfectly ordered configurations obtained at various temperatures and at coverages other than saturation. The applicability of LEED theory for this purpose is uncertain, but measurements of diffraction spot size and intensity can still yield considerable information about the degree of order. The variation in the intensity and width of fractional order adsorbate beams with coverage in a particular state yields information concerning adsorbate-adsorbate interactions [3.11–13]. If intensity $I \sim \theta$, the adsorbate probably exists as islands or domains, while if I increases at greater than the first power of coverage, random occupation is inferred. The width of adsorbate beams $\Delta w_{\frac{1}{2}}$ gives the approximate degree of order, $\Delta w_{\frac{1}{2}} \simeq 2/l + w_0$, where w_0 is the instrumental resolution and l is the distance over which order persists. Typical instrument resolutions are 0.01 Å^{-1}, so that one can determine the degree of order for $l \leq 100 \text{ Å}$.

The variations of adsorbate beam intensities and widths with substrate temperature also gives information on the order of an adsorbate. At sufficiently low deposition temperature the adsorbate should be immobile and thus incapable of ordering, and at high temperature thermal disorder should produce a decrease in spot intensities [3.13]. We shall see that all of these phenomena have been observed.

All of this analysis presupposes that there are nonintegral diffraction beams. In their absence any analysis by LEED appears questionable. It should also be emphasized that perfectly ordered structures (states saturated and annealed) are probably the exception rather than the rule. One must use considerable caution in interpreting LEED data for other than the simplest systems because it is at present impossible to determine from intensity measurements the fraction of an adsorbate which is in a given configuration. Sharp and intense diffraction beams may be observed when only a small fraction of the adsorbate occupies sites with the corresponding configurations with the rest disordered or in binding states with (1×1) periodicity. Care should also be exercised in specifying adsorbate temperatures because many adsorbates which exhibit multiple lattice spacing periodicities may disorder at higher temperatures. Since most LEED experiments have been carried out at 300 K or above, many ordered structures may have been missed entirely. Examples of low temperature ordered configurations are alkali metals [3.14, 15] and CO on fcc metals [3.2–4]; many structures are observed below room temperature but few or none above.

3.2.2. Kinetics

Kinetics are probably the most used and most productive methods for characterizing adsorbate structures. Thermal desorption and especially flash desorption directly yield binding states, relative saturation densities, and desorption rate parameters [3.16, 17]. Desorption kinetics is covered thoroughly in Chapter 4. Analysis of desorption data is generally straightforward, but problems such as induced heterogeneity, bulk solution, and desorption of nonvolatile species must be considered [3.17].

Condensation kinetics provides an indirect means of characterizing adsorption because sticking coefficients depend on the state being populated, and the coverage dependence in a state is controlled by the mechanism of condensation — direct condensation or condensation through a precursor intermediate [3.17]. The magnitude of the sticking coefficient is an important experimental parameter in all measurements because, if too small, it may be difficult to populate a state by gas condensation at low pressures.

Surface diffusion yields information on the potential experienced by an adsorbate as it moves laterally along a surface. Surface diffusion processes govern annealing and order-disorder transformations and may be rate limiting steps in desorption of a dissociated species, in bimolecular reactions, and in bifunctional catalysis. Measurement of surface diffusion rates on single crystal planes are exceedingly difficult, and most data has been obtained using field emission microscopy. Early results have been summarized [3.19–21] and there have been few recent studies. Most information is obtained only as average diffusion coefficients over a field emitter at nominal coverages with qualitative comments on temperatures required for equilibration on particular planes. Almost completely lacking are precise measurements of surface diffusion coefficients on single crystal planes as a function of densities in individual binding states. The major exception is the elegant work of Ehrlich and coworkers on surface self-diffusion using field ion microscopy [3.20, 21]. Field desorption limitations have thus far prevented comparable studies for other than metallic adsorbates. Another study which illustrates qualitatively the crystallographic variations in diffusion coefficients is the work of ENGEL and GOMER who measured temperatures for diffusion of different binding states of O and of CO on most planes of a W field emitter [3.23].

Activation energies vary from 10–20% of binding energies, for many atomic adsorbates; the low values are encountered on atomically, smooth the high values on atomically rough planes, as far as is known. For CO on W the ratio can approach 100% on loosely packed planes.

3.2.3. Auger Electron Spectroscopy (AES)

In the few years since the utility of AES for surface study was demonstrated [3.25], it has rapidly become an essential instrument in surface physics laboratories. With AES and a mass spectrometer to monitor partial pressures in a vacuum system the experimenter can make a complete chemical analysis of an adsorption system — both gases impinging on a surface and the chemical composition of the surface itself. The characteristics of AES which make it so useful are that all elements except hydrogen can be detected with roughly comparable sensitivities, and the height of an AES peak for a surface species is apparently proportional to its density for monolayer or submonolayer densities. The latter assumes that peak shape changes due to chemical shifts can be accounted for and that the adsorbate is confined to the surface layer. Both of these characteristics are predicted theoretically and verified experimentally in all systems so far examined.

Since all of the adsorption systems to be discussed in this chapter have been shown by AES to contain less than a few percent of a monolayer of contaminants (except for possible chance overlap with substrate peaks), it is virtually certain that all of these studies were on clean surfaces. Such a statement could not be made unequivocally for any surface as recently as five years ago.

3.2.4. Miscellaneous Techniques

While LEED and desorption measurements provide the most used and most versatile means for characterizing adsorbate structures, other techniques are useful and sometimes necessary. For adsorbates which do not give stable gas molecules upon desorption, work function changes, condensation rates, AES, and electron stimulated desorption (ESD), [see Chapter 4], are the only methods for determining binding states and densities. Notable use of these techniques has been in O_2 on W which desorbs largely as O atoms and oxides; work function changes and ESD have yielded a fairly detailed picture of this adsorption system [3.24].

Spectroscopic measurements are now recognized as among the most powerful for characterizing adsorbates because they are sensitive to electronic structures, charge distributions, and types and symmetries of bonds. Infrared spectroscopy has been used for many years to examine high area surfaces and more recently for adsorption of CO on well characterized single crystal planes [3.26, 27]. New techniques such as ion neutralization spectroscopy (INS), X-ray photoelectron spectroscopy (XPS), ultraviolet photoelectron spectroscopy (UPS), and field emission energy distributions promise to yield considerable information on electronic structures and symmetries of adsorbates. These are still being developed as surface analytical techniques and are discussed in Chapter 5. It should be noted that spectroscopies are most useful when detailed information on states, densities, and periodicities are available. We shall concentrate on the latter because other chapters deal with the applications of spectroscopy to particular surface and adsorption systems.

3.3. Crystallographic Anisotropies

This section is concerned with the variations in adsorption properties — binding states, condensation and desorption kinetics, and saturation densities — with the crystallographic orientation of the substrate. In the last decade it had become abundantly clear to experimentalists that these variations are in many cases even more significant between crystal planes of a given substrate than between the same planes of different metals. However, models of chemisorption are still proposed in which the substrate is structureless, and elaborate attempts at interpretation are still proposed for data obtained on polycrystalline surfaces.

The adsorption system we shall choose to illustrate crystallographic anisotropies is N_2 on W. The first systematic attempt at observing variations between planes was made on this system by Delchar and Ehrlich [3.28], and there have since been a number of studies which are all in fairly good agreement. Recent references to work on the various planes are summarized in Table 3.1; additional references can be found from these.

On all planes listed in Table 3.1 there appears to be one major tightly bound state which obeys second order desorption kinetics and is atomic. On most planes additional tightly bound states are observed which have much lower sticking coefficients than those indicated, and there are a number of weakly bound or γ states which are molecular. We shall

Table 3.1. Nitrogen on tungsten

Plane	E_{d_0} [kcal/mole]	S_0	N_0 [a] [atoms/cm^2]	Ref.
(110)	79	0.004	1.8×10^{14}	[3.29]
(100)	79	0.4	5×10^{14}	[3.28,30–32]
(211)		<0.01	—	[3.28]
(111)	75	≤ 0.04	—	[3.28]
(210)	~75	0.25	2.2×10^{14}	[3.33]
(310)	~75	0.28	3.2×10^{14}	[3.33]

[a] Saturation density of tightly bound atomic states.

consider mainly the most tightly bound states as they best illustrate crystallographic anisotropies.

First we note that the activation energies of desorption are experimentally almost indistinguishable on all planes, 80 ± 5 kcal/mole. The binding energies of the atoms, E_A, related to the desorption activation energies of the molecule by the relation

$$E_A = \tfrac{1}{2}(E_{dA_2} + D),$$

are higher than this, ~ 150 kcal/mole, are even closer to each other because of the dominance of D, the dissociation energy of N_2, in the above expression.

Table 3.1 and Fig. 3.2 show that the saturation densities (in the tightly bound states) differ by a factor of at least 3 for the different planes and that initial sticking coefficients differ by a factor of ~ 100. There are distinct differences in the shapes of the $s(\theta)$ curves. On (110), $s \sim (1 - \theta)^2$ as predicted by a site occupation mechanism requiring two vacant adjacent sites for condensation, while on (100), (210), and (310) s is initially constant as predicted by condensation through a precursor intermediate

$$N_2(\text{gas}) \rightleftarrows N_2^*(s) \rightarrow 2N(s), \tag{3.1}$$

where $N_2^*(s)$ is a weakly adsorbed species on the surface. Various precursor models similar to that implied by (3.1) have been developed [3.31], and, for N_2 on (100) W, $s(\theta)$ and its dependence on surface temperature can be fitted quantitatively by such expressions.

Nitrogen on the (100) plane has been studied by LEED [3.30, 31] and shown to produce a $c(2 \times 2)$ pattern as expected if N atoms occupy every other site on the surface, Fig. 3.3. The adsorbate beam intensities

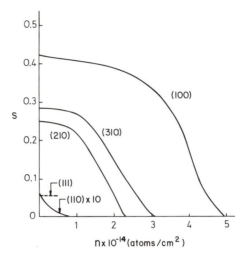

Fig. 3.2. Sticking coefficient versus adsorbate density for N_2 on several crystal planes of W. These results show that there are large variations in both saturation densities and sticking coefficients between different crystal planes

increase at least linearly with coverage, indicating *attractive* adsorbate-adsorbate interactions and island formation [3.32, 13]. The adsorbate-caused beams increase in intensity and sharpen when the surface is heated above 300 K after deposition, suggesting that ordering is a thermally activated process. This will be discussed in more detail later under adsorbate-adsorbate interactions.

The integral diffraction beams appear to remain sharp at coverages and temperatures where the adsorbate beams are broadened by disorder [3.30, 32]. This indicates that adsorption sites probably have four-fold symmetry, as shown in Fig. 3.3 rather than the two-fold symmetry of bridge bonded sites. Nitrogen atoms could, of course, be either on top of the surface W atoms rather than in the sites indicated, but the higher coordination in the latter suggests this location.

3.3.1. Stepped Surfaces

The (210) and (310) planes expose flat planes with four-fold sites identical to those on the (100) plane with steps consisting of substrate atom configurations identical to those on the (110) plane. ADAMS and GERMER [3.33] showed that the LEED pattern from the (210) plane after cleaning was as indicated in Fig. 3.3 with regularly spaced steps.

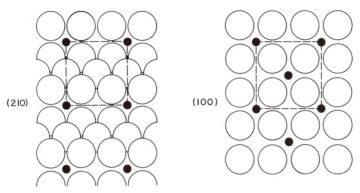

Fig. 3.3. Proposed adsorbate structures for N_2 on the (100) and (210) planes of W. Nitrogen atoms occupy alternate sites of four-fold coordination on both planes, and on the (210) plane atom positions are correlated between rows

ADAMS and GERMER used LEED, work function change, and flash desorption to study nitrogen on the stepped (210) and (310) planes to compare with the (100) plane. Their results are summarized in Figs. 3.2 and 3.4 and Table 3.1. Deposition of N_2 on (310) at 300 K produced weak and broad $p(2 \times 1)$ adsorbate beams. Heating to 900 K increased the order in the [100] direction along the steps (resulting in streaks), and heating to 1200 K produced sharp and intense adsorbate beams with the $p(2 \times 1)$ structure. The structure implied by these results are shown in Fig. 3.3. When completely ordered, N atoms occupy alternate four-fold sites just as they do on the (100) plane. However, there is also a correlation of sites *between rows*. Above 900 K the adsorbate orders both along and between rows, but below 900 K ordering occurs only along rows. Similar behavior is noted on the (310) plane although the unit cell is not rectangular. A most remarkable feature of these results is the long range correlation between rows, a distance of over 10 Å on the (210) plane.

Stepped surfaces of clean platinum also exhibit regularly spaced monatomic steps [3.7]. Ordering of adsorbates is observed on these planes although the adsorbates examined are more complex, and the interpretation of these processes is less clear than for nitrogen on W.

In Fig. 3.4 are shown work function changes versus fractional coverage in the tightly bound states. It is evident that the sign of the dipole moment on the (100) plane is opposite that on the (210) and (301) planes. A simple explanation [3.28, 33] for these variations is that the varying positions of the image planes can produce a reversal in $\Delta\phi$ if the N atom on the stepped planes is below the image plane. This points up the difficulty of interpreting work function changes in terms of adsorbate charges. The magnitude and even the sign of the change depends on the positions

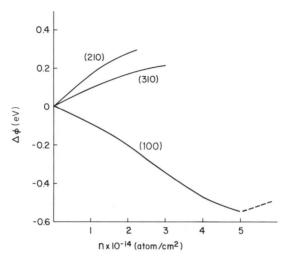

Fig. 3.4. Work function change versus adsorbate density for
N_2 on W

of the atomic and the electronic configurations, neither of which is as
yet established for any adsorption system.

Little mention has been made of weaker binding states for N_2 on W
[3.28, 31]. These have lower sticking coefficients than the most tightly
bound states, and experimental data are consequently much more subject
to artifacts from contamination and electron impact effects. One much
studied binding state is the β_1 state on (100) W. This is almost as strongly
bound as the β_2 state but desorbs with first-order kinetics and has a
dipole moment opposite that of the β_2 [3.34]. It apparently may be
populated readily either by electron impact, by adsorption of NH_3, or
in the presence of contaminants, but has a very low sticking coefficient
otherwise [3.31]. This state has been the subject of much speculation,
but determination of its structure awaits additional, perhaps spectroscopic, examination. For all but the tightly bound states there are possible
discrepancies in saturation densities because of the experimental problem
of saturating a low s binding state. ADAMS and GERMER [3.33], while
noting the problem, assumed that only (100) type sites were populated
on (210) and (310) planes. Higher densities would, of course, be obtained
if (110) sites and weak binding γ sites are populated.

Crystallographic anistropies in both s and saturation density are
probably greater for N_2 on W than for any other well characterized
chemisorption system. This is perhaps because of the large dissociation

energy of N_2 and the availability of three valence electrons in the nitrogen atom. However, as we shall see in the following sections, even H_2 exhibits anisotropies which can in no sense be neglected.

3.4. Binding States

While there have been many careful and comprehensive studies of particular gases on single crystal planes of metals using a variety of techniques, only for a few systems have corresponding data been obtained on several crystal planes of a given metal. Thus comparison of binding states, saturation densities and binding energies is possible in only a few systems. As just discused, nitrogen on W is one such system, but here there is only one binding state and binding energies are approximately identical on all planes examined. The two examples we shall consider here are H_2 on W and CO on W. For these gases there are between two and five states on each plane so far examined, and, although each system has been the subject of over twenty papers, both exhibit sufficient complexity to require many more for understanding. Other particularly well documented systems are CO on Ni, Pd, and Cu. These will be considered in later sections.

3.4.1. Hydrogen on Tungsten

In Table 3.2 and Figs. 3.5 through 3.7 we indicate a summary of data on the (110), (100), (211), and (111) planes [3.35–46]. Flash desorption reveals two major states on the fairly close packed (110), (100), and (211) planes, and at least four states on the (111) plane. All states appear to be "simple" in that they exhibit nearly constant desorption pre-exponential factors and activation energies. Values of pre-exponential factors are approximately those predicted theoretically [3.31, 35], $\sim 10^{-2}$ cm^2 molecule^{-1} sec^{-1} for second-order desorption and 10^{13} sec^{-1} for first-order desorption. Relative densities in the different states are also known fairly accurately from the areas under the flash desorption peaks [3.35], and these are indicated in Table 3.2. The desorption spectra, binding energies, orders of desorption, and relative densities have for all planes been reproduced in two or more laboratories [at least five for (100)W] and there is little question of their validity.

Work function changes with coverage have also been measured by many investigators [3.40], and these are summarized in Fig. 3.6. Again there is quantitative reproducibility except for some early work in which CO contamination was possible or where perhaps some states were not

Table 3.2. H_2 on W

Plane	State	E_{d_0} [kcal/mole]	Relative[a] saturation density	LEED structure	Ref.
(100)	β_2	32	1.0	$c(2 \times 2)$	[3.35, 40]
	β_1	26	$2.0 \pm .2$	(1×1)	
(110)	β_2	33	1.0	$p(2 \times 1)$	[3.35, 40–42]
	β_1	27	$1.0 \pm .1$	$p(2 \times 1)?$	
(211)	β_2	38	1.0	(1×1)	[3.35, 40, 43]
	β_1	20	$1.0 \pm .3$	(1×1)	
(111)	β_4	37	1.0		[3.35, 40]
	β_3	30	$1.5 \pm .2$		
	β_2	22	$1.5 \pm .2$		
	β_1	14	$1.0 \pm .2$		

[a] Density relative to that of state designated as 1.

saturated. There are fairly distinct breaks in these curves which in most cases coincide with coverages where flash desorption shows that one state saturates and another is being populated.

Relative sticking coefficients versus relative coverages [3.44, 40] also are fairly well established, as shown in Fig. 3.7. Each plane has a characteristic $s(\theta)$ curves breaks sometimes observed at coverages where the state saturates and another is being populated.

LEED patterns have also been observed for many of these planes, although some studies have employed substrate temperatures above 300 K and may therefore have missed ordered structures which could exist at lower temperatures. On (100)W Estrup and Anderson [3.36] showed several years ago that H_2 exposure produces a $c(2 \times 2)$ structure which attains maximum intensity at $\sim \frac{1}{4}$ monolayer. At this coverage the adsorbate beams split and their intensity diminishes until at saturation a (1×1) periodicity is again observed. On (110)W early LEED investigations concluded that only (1×1) periodicity occured, but recently Maticek using high energy electron diffraction (RHEED) [3.41] found a (2×1) structure with maximum intensity at $\sim \frac{1}{2}$ monolayer. Only (1×1) periodicities are reported on (211)W, and no recent observations appear to exist for (111)W.

One might conclude from this apparent agreement that the experimental situation for H_2 on W is settled of and that structure determination only awaits model building and testing. However, we shall see that this is by no means the case. A major problem is stoichiometry. While

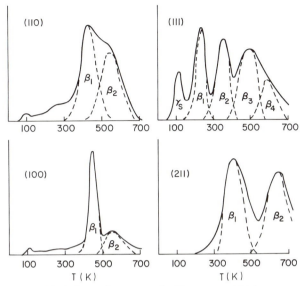

Fig. 3.5. Flash desorption spectra for H_2 on several high symmetry planes of W

relative densities on a given plane are readily obtained (Fig. 3.5), comparisons of densities on different planes are more difficult, and absolute densities are in most experimental systems almost impossible to measure. This is because absolute density determination requires measurement of system pressures, volume, and pumping speeds. While it is easy to estimate these quantities, all three are susceptible to systematic errors.

On (100)W ESTRUP and ANDERSON [3.36] estimated a saturation density of 2.0×10^{14} atoms/cm^2 by noting that a $c(2 \times 2)$ pattern, requiring at least one H atom for two surface W atoms (1.0×10^{15} atoms/cm^2), occurred at approximately one-fourth of the saturation coverage. TAMM and SCHMIDT [3.35] estimated a density by assuming that the β_2 state produced the $c(2 \times 2)$ LEED structure (5×10^{14} atoms/cm^2); the β_1 state has twice this density to give a total of 1.5×10^{15} atoms/cm^2. Note that both of these estimates are *indirect*, one from an assumed density for a given LEED pattern and the other for a density to fit the stoichiometry of flash desorption spectra. The only direct measurement of density is that of MADEY [3.45] who, using a calibrated flux molecular beam method, reported a saturation density of $2.0 \pm 0.3 \times 10^{15}$ atoms/cm^2. This apparently fits the ESTRUP and ANDERSON density although a recalibration of this flux gives a slightly lower value [3.45]. Also a recent measurement of the H/O ratio from H_2O in the

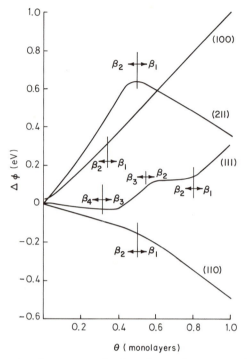

Fig. 3.6. Work function change versus fraction of saturation coverage θ of H_2 on several high symmetry planes of W. Approximate coverages where one state saturates and population of another begins are indicated on the figure. These in most cases correlate fairly well with breaks in the work functions

author's laboratory [3.45] yielded a value of $1.4 \pm 0.3 \times 10^{15}$ atoms/cm^2 for the saturation density of H_2 on (100)W. The unfortunate conclusion of these measurements appears to be that the saturation density of H_2 on (100)W is between 1.5×10^{15} and 2.0×10^{15} atoms/cm^2. This makes it impossible to distinguish between the two proposed structures from present data.

For (110)W the model [3.35] which appears to explain the two atomic states of equal density, the existence of a (2×1) periodicity for one state and a (1×1) peridicity for both, and a saturation density of approximately one H atom per surface W atom is shown in Fig. 3.8. The β_2 state occupies every other site and the β_1 state occupies the remaining sites.

It is not yet established whether there are two distinct states on the (110) plane at saturation. There is a distinct increase in the ESD [3.42] yield of H$^+$ and a decrease in $\Delta\phi$ [3.40] at the coverage where the β_1

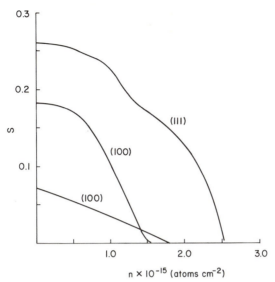

Fig. 3.7. Sticking coefficient s versus density of H_2 on several crystal planes of W

state begins to populate. However, the sticking coefficient exhibits at most a small break at this coverage [3.44]. All of these results are probably compatible with either one distinct state or two if the properties of one single state vary with coverage. The strongest evidence appears to be the RHEED observation [3.41] of a $p(2 \times 1)$ structure at saturation. This can only be explained with distinct β_1 and β_2 states, although it has been suggested [3.42] that the β_1 state may not have been saturated in these experiments.

On (100)W two distinct structure models have been proposed. That of ESTRUP and ANDERSON [3.36] assumes H atoms occupy bridge bond positions, as shown in Fig. 3.8. This obviously leads to a $c(2 \times 2)$ periodicity at one-fourth of saturation and (1×1) periodicity at saturation. However, it does not explain the existence of the two binding states with a 2:1 ratio observed in flash desorption. To do this, TAMM and SCHMIDT [3.35] proposed the model shown in Fig. 3.8. Here at one-third of saturation (assumed sites of four-fold symmetry) a $c(2 \times 2)$ periodicity is predicted. Then if the β_1 state consists of H_2 in the remaining sites with four-fold symmetry, one obtains the 2:1 ratio as observed. This model was proposed merely as the simplest one which gives a 2:1 ratio, occupies only one type of adsorption site, and leaves none of these sites vacant at saturation. One problem is that it does not predict a

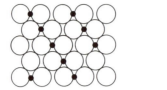

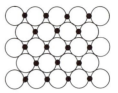

β_2 State, n= 7.0 x 10^{14} atoms/cm^2 Saturation, n= 1.4 x 10^{15} atoms/cm^2

Model Structure for H$_2$ on (110) W

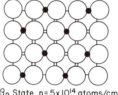

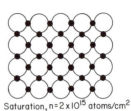

β_2 State, n= 5 x 10^{14} atoms/cm^2 Saturation, n= 2 x 10^{15} atoms/cm^2

Estrup & Anderson Model for H$_2$ on (100) W

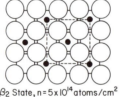

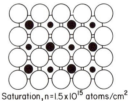

β_2 State, n= 5 x 10^{14} atoms/cm^2 Saturation, n=1.5 x 10^{15} atoms/cm^2

Tamm & Schmidt Model for H$_2$ on (100) W

Fig. 3.8. Proposed adsorbate structures for H$_2$ on the (110) and (100) planes of W. On (110) there are two states of equal density which fill sequentially. On (100) two models have been proposed but neither simultaneously satisfies LEED and flash desorption observations

(1 × 1) periodicity at saturation unless the adsorbate in the two sites were equivalent or disordered.

LEED should in principle be capable of distinguishing between models. If sites had four-fold coordination the substrate beams should not broaden at low coverage where the adsorbate beams are broad, while with two-fold sites some of the substrate beams should broaden also. No broadening of substrate beams has been noted [3.36, 37, 43], but experimental accuracy may not be sufficient to conclusively eliminate two-fold sites. Also the Estrup and Anderson model predicts a maximum

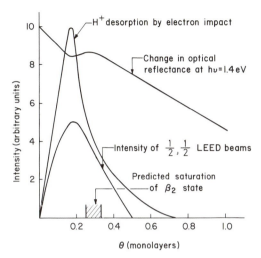

Fig. 3.9. Coverage variation of several properties of H_2 on (100)W. A distinct change at $\theta = 0.16$ is noted in the electron impact desorption cross section, in the intensity of adsorbate beams in LEED, and in the optical reflectivity. This coverage is smaller than those predicted by either structure model for this system, Fig. 3.8

ordering of the $c(2 \times 2)$ structure at 0.25 monolayers while that of TAMM and SCHMIDT determines a maximum at 0.33 monolayers. Results [3.37] indicate that the maximum is attained at 0.16 monolayers (Fig. 3.9) and that the spots begin to split *before* either model predicts a saturated state.

Confirmation that a change is occurring at low coverage comes from electron stimulated desorption [3.45] of H^+. As shown in Fig. 3.9, the H^+ current reaches a maximum at $\theta \simeq 0.16$, a coverage at which the β_2 state is only about one-half populated. Additional evidence for distinct but complex changes in the adsorbate in this coverage interval comes from field emission energy spectra [3.49], photoemission spectra, [3.50, 51] and optical reflectivity [3.52] (Fig. 3.9). These are discussed in Chapter 5.

There appears to be no model which simultaneously gives the 2:1 ratio of state densities and the $c(2 \times 2) \rightarrow (1 \times 1)$ symmetry. This is so even if one uses any combination of sites and any density desired. Therefore it appears that one of the above assumptions must be wrong or the experiments have been improperly interpreted. First it is possible that the 2:1 ratio of states is accidental and not related to specific sites on the surface. ADAMS [3.47] has examined the influence of various neighbor interactions and, while he could predict two peaks in flash desorption on this basis, these peaks do not, with reasonable assumptions, correspond to either a 2:1 ratio nor first-order desorption kinetics from the low temperature peak. First-order desorption from the β_1 state would be observed if the adsorbate were molecular or if desorption occurred only from adjacent pairs of atoms. The latter is certainly more likely, and the H_2 sketched in Fig. 3.8 is merely meant to be a representation of this.

The second possibility is that the LEED data have been misinterpreted. It is entirely possible that at saturation the hydrogen is sufficiently disordered to give a (1×1) periodicity (meaning no long-range order) without requiring one H atom per W atom. The surface diffusion coefficient of hydrogen is fairly high even at zero coverage (mobile at ~ 200 K) [3.21], and at saturation hydrogen could be mobile enough to disorder even at 78 K, the lowest temperature so far examined. A related possibility is that the periodicities observed in LEED are not associated simply with adsorbate atom periodicity but rather with electronic periodicities not correlated with atomic positions. The interpretation of diffraction from a low mass species is especially difficult because it originates almost entirely from multiple scattering.

A final possibility is bulk solution of hydrogen [3.37]. Hydrogen is only slightly soluble in W, but, since it dissolves endothermically, the solubility increases as the temperature increases. This could conceivably cause the apparent contradiction in LEED and desorption data, but no detailed explanations along these lines have as yet been proposed.

The differences in work function changes between the (110), (100), (111), and (211) planes, Fig. 3.6, are striking. They imply significant differences in atomic charges and/or dipole moments of the adsorbates. The decrease in ϕ with hydrogen coverage on the close packed (110) plane, where the H atom is most likely to be outside of the image plane, has the obvious interpretation that the H atom is *positively charged*. The other planes are atomically more open, and the adsorbate could be below the image plane to produced the increase observed on most planes. The Helmholtz equation is of course wholly inadequate to discuss this problem. The point we wish to emphasize is that neither the magnitude nor the sign of the charge on the H atom are experimentally established. Experiments which measure atomic charges (XPS) or adsorbate local densities of state (UPS) and calculations on charge distributions at surfaces appear to be the only way to conclusively answer these questions for this or any other adsorption systems.

3.4.2. Carbon Monoxide on Tungsten

A review of chemisorption experiments would be incomplete if it did not include CO on W [3.53, 54]. This system may exceed H_2 on W as the most often examined adsorption system, but the most significant discovery from all of these studies is probably an appreciation of the complexities which may exist in chemisorption. CO on W differs from H_2 and N_2 on b.c.c. metals and CO on fcc metals in that it is not reversible: properties are not a function of temperature and coverage alone but depend also on the temperature-time history of the adsorbate. This is not unique to CO on W, and a similar situation is observed for O_2 on all metals, for systems which exhibit bulk solution, and probably most of the complex coadsorption systems found in catalysis. The feature that separates CO on W from these is that experimentors have been determined to understand this supposedly straightforward system which has been thought to exhibit neither compound formation, bulk solutions, or surface reactions between species.

We shall not attempt a historical review [3.53, 54] but merely note that studies by REDHEAD [3.55] showed that there were more than 3 high-temperature or β states and several low-temperature or α states on polycrystalline W. Some time previous to this, field emission experiments had indicated that no carbon or oxygen residues remained after repeated adsorption and desorption cycles of CO [3.56], and this was interpreted (perhaps wrongly) as proof that CO on W does not dissociate. GOMER and his coworkers used field emission microscopy [3.57, 59] and more recently macroscopic surfaces [3.60] in an extensive investigation of this system. They have clearly demonstrated that if a surface saturated with CO at low temperature is heated to ~ 400 K, $\sim 50\%$ of the CO desorbs. If then CO is readsorbed, approximately the same coverage is obtained but the work function changes sign. They termed the original configuration the virgin state which, at least, partially distinct from the α and β states obtained upon readsorption. From considerable evidence from field desorption, dipole moment, and electron impact desorption GOMER and coworkers have confirmed earlier speculations that these states of CO must exist in several forms: linear with C bonded to the surface, bridge bonded either through the C atom or through both C and O, and perhaps dissociated. This latter was not a popular position until a few years ago, but now considerable evidence points to at least partial dissociation. Typical flash desorption spectra from (110) and (100) surfaces [3.60–62] saturated at room temperature or below are shown in Fig. 3.10. We shall confine our discussion to the (110) and (100) planes as these have been studied more extensively. It will also be convenient to consider first the β states and then the α and virgin states because, while the former are nearly reversible, the latter certainly are not.

β *States.* These are the states which desorb above 900 K. All are probably electronegative, and have very low electron impact desorption cross sections. As shown in Fig. 3.10 and Table 3.3, about two thirds of

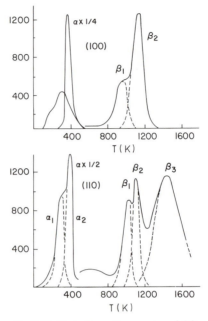

Fig. 3.10. Flash desorption spectra of CO
on the (110) and (100) planes of W

Table 3.3. CO on W

Plane	States	E_{d_0} [kcal/mole]	Fraction of total density	Saturation density [molecules/cm^2]	Surface atom density [atoms/cm^2]	Ref.
(100)	β_3	75	0.43 ⎫			
	β_2	64	0.10 ⎪	$6 \pm 1 \times 10^{14}$	1.0×10^{15}	[3.61]
	β_1	57	0.09 ⎬			
	α's	25–30	0.37 ⎭	$3.8 \pm 1 \times 10^{14}$		
(110)	β_2	66	0.3 ⎫	$\sim 7 \times 10^{14}$	1.42×10^{15}	[3.60, 62]
	β_1	50	0.1 ⎭			
	α's	15–20	0.6	$\sim 8 \times 10^{14}$		

this adsorbate appears as a single state in flash desorption with the rest
appearing as one or two smaller lower temperature states. The desorption
temperature is significantly higher on (100).

Absorbate densities have been measured using effusion methods for
(110)W and a calibration against O_2 saturation using AES for (100)W.
As shown in Table 3.3, these indicate saturation densities in the β states

of approximately one CO molecule for every two surface W atoms on both planes.

There are no (or perhaps very weak) LEED patterns observed upon adsorption at room temperature [3.63–65], but heating to ~900 K produces a $c(2 \times 2)$ structure on (100)W and a complex sequence of structures on (110)W. ESTRUP and ANDERSON [3.65] postulated that the $c(2 \times 2)$ structure was obtained from a state they termed β_H after the other, termed β_L, was desorbed. More recent flash desorption studies show that these states are not as simple as first assumed [3.61, 67]. In both cases the results suggest that reconstruction (motion of the W atoms and possibly incorporation of CO into the top layer of the surface) occurs upon heating to near the desorption temperature.

Next we consider the question of whether CO is dissociated in the β states. KING and coworkers [3.66] showed that the breaking of the CO bond and its reforming in desorption is thermodynamically feasible in spite of the high bond energies of C–O, C–W, and O–W. Also CLAVENNA and SCHMIDT [3.61] showed that the β_3 state on (100)W desorbed with second-order kinetics. This was explainable as dissociative adsorption or as desorption of pairs of molecules, an earlier interpretation used to explain the isotope exchange of isotopically labelled atoms in the β states [3.67]. Finally UPS experiments by BAKER and EASTMAN [3.68] and by PLUMMER [3.69] (see Chapter 5) showed that the spectrum from the β states was almost identical to that of C and O adsorbed separately while that of α and virgin was similar to that of gaseous CO. It appears from this work that some dissociation occurs upon adsorption even at room temperature. Recent work on the recombination of CO from C and O coadsorbed on (100)W show that this is an efficient process [3.70] and that no C or O residues are found on W because neither can dissolve appreciably in the bulk below the desorption temperature. Residues are observed on Ta because bulk solution of C occurs below the desorption temperature.

The simplest interpretation consistent with the data on the β states of CO on the planes (several states in non-integral ratios to substrate densities, complex LEED structures upon heating, and low desorption cross sections) is that considerable dissociation occurs to yield C–W and O–W bonds; these species must then recombine to desorb as CO. Since C and O should have low surface diffusion coefficients (CO is known to be almost immobile up to the desorption temperature) [3.21], the states observed depend on the probabilities of having neighboring pairs of atoms or requiring surface diffusion. The ESCA spectra of the β states on (100)W reveal distinct core electron energies of C and O which seem to correlate with the β_1, β_2, and β_3 states observed in flash desorption [3.71].

α *States.* On both the (100) and (110) planes the saturation density of CO which desorbs below 800 K is approximately one CO molecule for two surface W atoms (Table 3.3). This density is approximately the same for adsorption at 100 or 200, and at 300 K these states can be almost saturated by exposures to high CO pressures [3.60, 62, 72, 73]. Slightly different desorption spectra and perhaps slightly higher amounts are obtained upon readsorption after heating a saturated surface, but this has not been quantified, and we shall term all states in this temperature regime α states. Extensive and fairly reproducible work function data for CO may be found in the references cited. However, work function changes can not be simply considered because values depend on the surface temperatures before, during, and after deposition. Dipole moments in some cases appear to actually change sign upon heating with no accompanying desorption.

The most thorough investigations of the α states of CO are those of KOHRT and GOMER [3.60] for (110)W and YATES and KING [3.72, 73] for (100)W. These are in qualitative agreement with earlier conclusions from measurements on polycrystaline W by EHRLICH [3.74], GOMER and coworkers [3.57–59], and MENZEL [3.75].

On (100)W a state shown in Fig. 3.10 has been observed to consist of two states with almost identical desorption temperatures and roughly equal saturation densities [3.72, 73]. The major experimental distinction between the states is that electron stimulated desorption of the higher binding energy α_2 state produces desorption of primarily O^+ ions while CO^+ ions are produced upon electron bombardment of the α_1 state.

The flash desorption spectra of the α states from both (100) and (110) planes exhibit high temperature "tails" which can be fitted by simple desorption kinetics from one or several binding states and which are not caused by slow pumpout of the desorbed gas. These apparently result from partial conversion into the β states while the surface is being heated. KOHRT and GOMER [3.60] showed that isothermal desorption rates from the β_1 and β_2 states on (110) yielded the same desorption parameters as did flash desorption experiments, while the α and virgin states yielded very low pre-exponential factors and activation energies. Activation energies in Table 3.3 are obtained assuming a pre-exponential factor of 10^{13} sec^{-1} for those states obeying first-order kinetics.

There is as yet no clear consensus as to the structures of these adsorbates. The CO and O^+ yields from the α_1 and α_2 states on (100) could indicate that the α_1 state is bonded to one W atom while the α_2 state is bridge bonded. KOHRT and GOMER [3.60] have discussed possible bonding configurations and electronic structures. It has recently been shown [3.71] that adsorption at 100 K produces ESCA spectra which are distinct from those of either the α or β states. This supports the earlier hypothesis from work function measurements that there exists at low temperature "virgin" states which convert into α or β states upon heating [3.57–59].

3.5. Adsorbate-Adsorbate Interactions

In this section we consider the repulsive and attractive interactions between adsorbate molecules (see also Section 2.4), the exclusion of sites, and phase changes in adsorbed layers. Before 1960 the prevalent picture was that repulsive interactions generally accounted for the observed reduction in heats of adsorption with coverage and the deviations from linearity of work function changes with coverage. Use of single crystals to avoid crystallographic averaging and LEED to directly measure adsorbate periodicities and the degree of order has revealed considerable complexity which was quite unanticipated.

3.5.1. Repulsive Interactions

Experiments on single crystal planes have shown that repulsive adsorbate-adsorbate interactions on metal surfaces are generally very weak and that the variation of adsorption energy with coverage observed on polyfacetted surfaces is primarily due to the existence of multiple binding states on different planes and multiple states on a given plane. To the author's knowledge there are no examples where the binding energy in a single state on a metal surface varies by more than 5 kcal/mole between zero coverage and saturation, and in most cases the variation is immeasurably small. As examples the atomic β_1 and β_2 states of H_2 on (110)W exhibit variations of 2.0 and 3.3 kcal/mole, respectively, between zero and saturation densities, and the first order β_1 state of H_2 on (100)W exhibits a variation of no more than 0.3 kcal/mole, or less than 1% of the desorption activation energy [3.35]. Data for H_2 on W are in fact upper bounds obtained from analysis of shapes of flash desorption spectra; the apparent variations in E_d could be entirely due to variations in pre-exponential factors with coverage or the presence of other binding states on the edges of the crystals.

Heats of adsorption of CO on various planes of Ni and Pd have been measured accurately using adsorption isotherm methods [3.2, 3, 76–78]. The most tightly bound states on (100)Ni, (111)Ni, and (111)Pd (E_{d_0} between 30 and 40 kcal/mole) decrease by no more than 1 kcal/mole at saturation. On (100)Pd, however, E_d, decreases by 2 kcal/mole at saturation of the most tightly bound state. Variations at higher coverages are

Table 3.4. Examples of adsorbate-adsorbate interactions

Effect	State	E_{d_o} [kcal/mole]	ΔE_{sat} [kcal/mole]	LEED pattern	Ref.
Repulsion	β_1 H on (100)W	25	<0.3	(1 × 1)	[3.44]
	β_2 N on (100)W	78	<5	c(2 × 2)	[3.30, 31]
	β_1 and β_2 H on (110)W	33, 26	<3.0	(2 × 1)	[3.41, 44]
	CO on (100)Pd	38	3		[3.3]
	CO on (100)Ni	30	<0.4		[3.2]
	CO on (100)Cu	14	<0.4		[3.4]
Island formation	H$_2$, N$_2$ and Th on (100)W			c(2 × 2)	[3.13, 30, 36]
Order-disorder transition	H$_2$, N$_2$ and Th on (100)W			c(2 × 2)↔(1 × 1)	
	CO on (100)Wi and (100)Cu			c(2 × 2)↔(1 × 1)	[3.2, 4]
One-dimensional order	N$_2$ on (210) and (310)W			streaks	
Short-range order	CO on (100)Pd			rings	[3.3]
Out-of-registry transition	CO on (110)Ni			c(2 × 2)↔hexagonal	
	CO on (100)Cu and (100)Pd			c(2 × 2)↔complex	[3.3, 4]
Structure change	H$_2$ on (100)Mo			c(2 × 2)↔(4 × 2)	[3.82]

larger for these systems due to phase transitions to other configurations as will be discussed later.

The general trend appears to be that for adsorbate-adsorbate distances of two and, in some cases, one lattice spacing, repulsive interactions are at most a few kcal/mole. This is so even when work functions vary by typically 0.2–0.5 eV upon saturation of the state. It appears that electron screening efficiently reduces electrostatic interactions to a small fraction of those predicted assuming no screening. Also the major consequence of adsorbate-adsorbate repulsion may not be a variation in heat of adsorption with coverage but rather the exclusion of bonding sites and induced heterogeneities observed as multiple binding states.

3.5.2. Attractive Interactions and Ordered Structures

Many systems exhibit LEED periodicities greater than those of the substrates. For the tightly bound state of CO on Ni, Pd, and Cu it appears that there is essentially random occupation of sites until the adsorbate density is large enough for core repulsions to become important. For example, as shown in Fig. 3.11, CO on (100)Ni and (100)Cu orders into a $c(2 \times 2)$ structure because the close packed density of CO molecules does not allow every site to be occupied to produce a (1×1) structure. The maximum temperature at which this ordered configuration exists, indicated in Fig. 3.12, increases from 80 K at low coverage to 400 K as the CO density approaches saturation. The existence of a $c(2 \times 2)$ structure at very low coverages on (100)Ni suggests that there may be weak attractive interactions between CO molecules. On (100)Cu ordering occurs only near saturation of the $c(2 \times 2)$ structure and this is preceeded by a ring pattern showing a liquid-like adsorbate configuration.

There are several examples where attractive interactions lead to island formation. Both H_2 and N_2 on (100)W produce $c(2 \times 2)$ structures and the intensities of the half-order adsorbate beams increase approximately linearly with coverage [3.30, 36, 37]. Random occupation of sites predicts [3.12, 13] that these intensities should increase as $\sim \theta^2$; with island formation the intensity should be proportional to θ. The adsorbate beams for both gases also appear to be fairly sharp even at low coverages, indicating that islands are quite large, > 20 Å for H_2 on (100)W at 0.1 of saturation of the β_2 state. It appears that the adsorbate at less than saturation density exists as rather large patches in which every other site is occupied (Fig. 3.8) with essentially bare regions between them. There are two equivalent positions for H atoms in the $c(2 \times 2)$ structure, (by either model) and this results in antiphase domains which presumably prevents the islands from becoming even larger. As

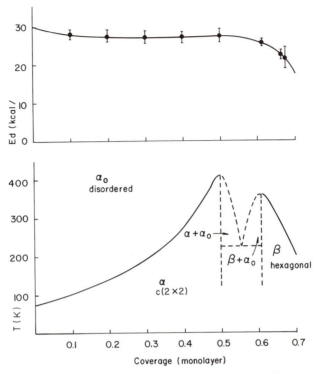

Fig. 3.11. Heat of adsorption versus coverage and proposed phase diagram for CO on (100)Ni. A sequence of ordered structures is observed by LEED at different coverage and temperature

the coverage of H_2 approaches saturation of the β_2 state, these beams split continuously and diminish in intensity. This is interpreted as ordered additional atoms in the $c(2 \times 2)$ structure [3.36].

For CO on (100)Ni and on (100)Cu the $c(2 \times 2)$ structure apparently results from the fact that the adsorbate is too large for closer packing. For H_2 and N_2 on (100)W the atomic diameters are probably small enough that this is not the cause of the $c(2 \times 2)$ being the maximum density, (However, it should be noted that effective adsorbate sizes depend on the charges on the atoms, and these are not well established.) The $c(2 \times 2)$ structures for H and N have been interpreted as resulting from bonding with W atoms in the plane of the surface. Saturation of these bonds limits the adsorbate density, and $s - d$ hybridization offers a possible mechanism for island formation [3.31, 35]. Analogous theories of indirect interactions also predict island formation.

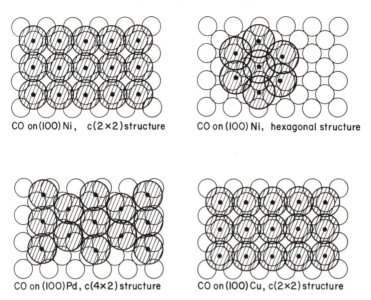

CO on (100) Ni, c(2×2) structure

CO on (100) Ni, hexagonal structure

CO on (100) Pd, c(4×2) structure

CO on (100) Cu, c(2×2) structure

Fig. 3.12. Proposed structures for CO on (100) planes of Ni, Pd, and Cu. On Ni and Cu adsorbates give $c(2 \times 2)$ structures and presumably occupy sites of four-fold coordination while on Pd a $c(4 \times 2)$ structure exists which probably occupies sites of two-fold symmetry. Distinct sequences of higher coverage structures exist on each metal as discussed in the text

3.5.3. Two-Dimensional Phase Transitions

There are now a number of fairly well documented examples of structure transitions of adsorbates. These frequently appear to occur over fairly small ranges in temperature or density, and in some cases heats of transition have been measured. However none appears to be clearly a first-order phase transition. Experiments rely mainly on LEED with desorption kinetics or isotherms to determine coverages and heats of adsorption. Interpretation of LEED is made difficult by experimental problems with instrument resolution (seldom greater than 0.01 Å^{-1}), temperature variations over a crystal (temperatures are only with difficulty measured to better than $\pm 20°$, and $\pm 50°$ is probably typical), and surface imperfections due to disorder, trace impurities, and orientation inaccuracies.

Transitions are mostly of the order vs. disorder or registry vs. out-of-registry type as observed by following LEED patterns as either the temperature is varied at constant coverage or as the coverage is varied at constant temperature. In only one case has an investigator attempted to construct a phase diagram by systematically varying both temperature and coverage [3.2].

Order-disorder transitions are observed when an ordered adsorbate is heated. Most adsorbates which exhibit periodicities greater than that of the substrate are found to disorder before desorption temperatures are reached. The important parameter in ordering and disordering is the surface diffusion coefficient, and this appears to be large enough for most systems (except perhaps CO on W where dissociation is probable for the tightly bound states), to allow rapid equilibrium on the surface. The variation of adsorbate beam intensities with temperature has been measured for H_2, N_2, CO, O_2, and Th on $(100)W$ [3.12, 13, 37]. For many systems one can reversibly follow adsorbate beam intensity versus temperature up to temperature where no adsorbate beams are observed, but in others some desorption occurs. Estrup [3.13] was able to fit the temperature dependence for H_2 on $(100)W$ with an Ising model, but in general one must know interaction energies to predict these transitions. Another complication is that the substrate itself disorders at high temperatures, as shown by the temperature dependence of substrate beam intensities.

As discussed previously, N_2 on the stepped (210) and (310) planes of W exhibits two dimensional ordering at low temperatures, one dimensional ordering along rows at higher temperatures, and probably no ordering at very high temperatures [3.33]. Similar behavior has been noted for alkali metals on $(211)W$ which has a rowed structure (Fig. 3.1).

Carbon monoxide on fcc metals exhibits a number of complex transitions which have been examined in detail by Tracy [3.2, 4], by Ertl and coworkers [3.76, 77], and by Taylor and Estrup [3.78]. CO exhibits registry with substrate lattice sites at low coverages, but it can be forced out of registry at higher coverages into roughly hexagonal adsorbate layers. For CO on $(100)Ni$ Tracy showed that a $c(2 \times 2)$ structure exists at low coverage. This saturates at one CO molecule for every two surface Ni atoms, and at higher coverages the half-order beams split as the adsorbate is forced into a hexagonal structure. This can be further compressed until the heat of adsorption falls to such a low value that no more adsorbate can be added. These data are summarized in Fig. 3.11, while Fig. 3.12 shows the adsorbate structures proposed by Tracy. The phase diagram in Fig. 3.11 has only qualitative significance in many regions, but shows the general behavior to be expected from such systems. There is a definite reduction in the heat of adsorption as the hexagonal layer is compressed but at most a small one for the $c(2 \times 2)$-hexagonal transition. Tracy also speculates that there is a eutectic point where $c(2 \times 2)$, hexagonal, and disordered phases coexist. This elegant experiment clearly shows the desirability of making measurements below room temperature because the LEED pattern observed for $T \geqq 300$ K would probably be (1×1) throughout, and it would not be possible to even form the hexagonal structure because its heat of adsorption is too small for typical pressures used in ultrahigh vacuum systems. A apparently simple and uninteresting system becomes remarkably complex when all states and all possible ordered structures are examined.

It should be noted that these are not actually infinite two-dimensional systems because they always contain high concentrations of imperfections which make the applicability of theories of infinite two-dimensional phase transitions questionable. For finite systems the transition temperature may be strongly affected by these defects. In three-dimensional systems one routinely has impurity concentrations much less than 1%; on surfaces this is probably seldom attained with present standards of cleanliness. It is found that a few percent of CO on (100)W completely destroys the $c(2 \times 2)$ LEED structure of H_2; evidently each CO molecule nucleates a domain of H_2 around it and suppresses long range ordering [3.37].

3.6. Adsorption on Similar Metals

One of the ways of deciding the types of bonds formed in chemisorption is to examine their sensitivity to small changes in the electronic or lattice properties of the solid. Adjacent transition metals in the periodic table frequently possess the same crystal structures so that differences in adsorption should be attributable to differences in lattice constant, number of valence electrons, spatial variations of electron densities, etc. Ideal candidates for this purpose are the bcc metals — W, Mo, Ta, and Nb — and fcc metals — Ni, Cu, Pd. [Most other metals either cannot be cleaned readily or do not have (1×1) surface periodicities.] In this section we shall summarize some comparative studies of these metals for chemisorption of H_2, N_2, and CO. Extensive comparisons of adsorption and catalysis on various metals have been carried out for many years but here we consider only adsorption on single crystal planes. Variation between planes may in fact be as great as that between metals, and therefore comparisons on polycrystalline wires or thin films appear to have only qualitative significance.

3.6.1. H_2, N_2, and CO on W, Mo, and Ta

In Fig. 3.13 are shown saturation flash desorption spectra for these gases on the (100) and (110) planes of W, Mo, and Ta. The original references [3.35, 79–82] give quantitative behavior, but the figure immediately

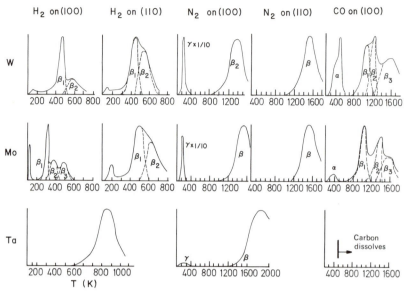

Fig. 3.13. Flash desorption spectra of H_2, N_2, and CO on (100) and (110) planes of W, Mo, and Ta. Close similarities are observed between W and Mo in most cases while on Ta heats of adsorption are higher and bulk solution occurs

indicates the numbers of states (number of peaks), their densities on a plane (relative areas), and desorption activation energies (roughly proportional to desorption temperature). Those peaks which are approximately symmetric about the maximum obey second-order desorption kinetics and those with larger slopes on the high temperature side obey first-order kinetics.

Bulk Solution. Tantalum shows poor correspondence with W and Mo because H, N, and C all dissolve – H even below 80 K and N and C at ~ 500 K. Desorption of H_2 and N_2 exhibits peaks if the heating rates are properly chosen, and these indicate much higher heats of adsorption on Ta than on W or Mo. Carbon from CO dissolves below the desorption temperature on (100)Ta, and therefore no desorption of CO occurs [3.82].

Number of Binding States. Here there is correspondence between planes of W and Mo for H_2 on (110) and N_2 on (110) and (100), but there is an additional state [3.80] of H_2 on (100)Mo which is not found [3.35] on (100)W. The β_1 states of H_2 on (100) planes both obey first-order desorption kinetics and have a saturation density ratio of 2:1 for $\beta_1:\beta_2$. To return briefly to the question regarding the structure of H_2 on (100)W, we note that there appears to be 25 % more H_2 on Mo than on W. This suggests adsorption in the sites of two-fold coordination (Fig. 3.8) with 25% of these unoccupied on W (the TAMM and SCHMIDT density with the ESTRUP and ANDERSON configuration). Bulk solution of this H_2 in W could be the cause of this difference. Also the LEED patterns are different with a $c(4 \times 2)$ observed on (100)Mo rather than the $c(2 \times 2)$ on (100)W. HUANG and ESTRUP have recently observed complex changes in the LEED patterns at low temperatures which have thus far not been explained.

There is little correspondence between the states of CO on (100)W [3.61] and (100)Mo [3.70]. There are three β states, and the β_3 states both obey second-order desorption kinetics. However, the density ratios bear no simple relationship to each other. The absence of stoichiometric ratios fits the suggestion made earlier that the desorption states observed on W may not be completely distinct states on the surface but rather occur because of surface diffusion limited recombination of C and O. Different surface diffusion coefficients (probably higher on Mo than on W) could produce different apparent amounts in the various peaks.

Relative Binding Energies. There are definite differences in binding energies on comparable planes of W, Mo, and Ta. Both H_2 and N_2 are more strongly bound on Ta than on W or Mo. Hydrogen is more strongly bound on the (100) plane of W than of Mo, but on the (110) plane bonding is stronger on Mo. Bonding of N_2 is slightly stronger on both planes of Mo than on W.

These differences have not been explained theoretically. Tantalum metal with approximately $4d$ electrons in its valence shell appears to adsorb all three gases more strongly than does W or Mo which have approximately $5d$ electrons. However, the larger lattice constant of Ta may allow the adsorbates to form stronger bonds (as well as dissolve). The differences between H_2 on W and Mo are more subtle as perhaps expected by virtue of their essentially identical lattice constants and similar electronic structures. Bonding is strongest on the close packed plane of Mo, and equal binding energies are observed on the (100) and (110) planes of W. This does not appear to be explainable with any simple pictures of surface energies or the spatial extensions of valence wave functions.

3.6.2. CO on Ni, Pd, and Cu

TRACY's comparative study [3.2–4] of CO adsorption on the (100) planes of these metals has been considered in the previous section in relation to phase changes at high coverages. The heats of adsorption are much higher on the transition metals Ni and Pd than on the noble metal Cu, although chemical bonds are definitely formed on all three surfaces. On (100) planes of Ni and Cu $c(2 \times 2)$ structures are observed while on (100)Pd a $c(4 \times 2)$ structure occurs. Tracy interprets this as sites of four-fold coordination on Ni and Cu but two-fold sites on Pd. The CO–CO interaction is repulsive on Pd, attractive on Ni, perhaps slightly attractive on Cu. Similar studies have been reported on other planes of fcc metals [3.76–78] but not with sufficient detail to permit close comparison.

As with adsorption on bcc metals, no theories as yet appear close to being able to interpret this behavior.

3.6.3. Comparison between fcc and bcc Substrates

This section would not be complete without mention of the fact that adsorption in general appears to be stronger, as well as more complicated on bcc substrates than on fcc metals. The reasons for this are probably related to the fact that fcc structures are more closepacked. This means first, that surface densities of state are broader than on bcc metals which in turn will tend to reduce adsorption energies, and second that the geometric possibilities, for different binding states are more restricted.

3.7. Summary

We have attempted to be rather conservative with respect to interpretations of chemisorption experiments, first, to be able to cover a number of topics in chemisorption and, second, because adsorbate structures are still somewhat speculative even for the simplest and most studied systems. For example, in spite of the extensive measurements on CO on the (100) planes of Ni, Pd, and Cu, the positions of adsorbate atoms with respect to the substrate atoms and the types of bonds can only be inferred indirectly. These appear to be among the simplest chemisorption systems in that they involve weak bonds, one state, and no dissociation, bulk solution, or motion of substrate atoms.

From the many new experimental techniques and extensive experiments on chemisorption there has evolved a confidence that quantitative and reproducible experiments are possible in spite of the unexpected complexities which have been observed. It also appears that in order to completely specify chemisorption structures it will be essential to employ spectroscopic techniques and all of the capabilities of diffraction as well as all of the now established tools for surface study. The assistance of theoreticians is also sorely needed; experiments appear to be far ahead of theory, with few solid interpretations existing for the numbers of states, binding energies, types of bonds, surface phase transitions, etc.

The ultimate goals of understanding adsorption and reactions of complex molecules such as hydrocarbons appear to the author to be approximately as far away as was the understanding of H_2 on W thirty years ago. Published studies of H_2 adsorption existed at that time just as do those of hydrocarbon adsorption and reactions today; but interpretations of both seem to be so speculative as to be completely untestable. All of the modern experimental techniques and a number of new ones will undoubtedly be required before it will be possible even in principle to specify all adsorption structures.

References

3.1. E. W. Müller: Advan. Electron. Phys. **13**, 83 (1960).
3.2. J. C. Tracy: J. Chem. Phys. **56**, 2736 (1972).
3.3. J. C. Tracy, P. W. Palmberg: J. Chem. Phys. **51**, 4852 (1969).
3.4. J. C. Tracy: J. Chem. Phys. **56**, 2748 (1972).
3.5. Recent summaries may be found in T. A. Clarke, R. Mason, M. Tesari: Surface Sci. **40**, 1 (1973); and J. T. Grant: Surface Sci. **18**, 228 (1969).
3.6. H. P. Bonzel, R. Ku: J. Chem. Phys. **58**, 4617 (1973).
3.7. G. A. Somorjai: Catalysis Rev. **7**, 87 (1972).
3.8. F. Jona: IBM J. Res. Dev. **9**, 375 (1965).
3.9. J. J. Lander, J. Morrison: J. Appl. Phys. **34**, 1403, 2298, 3317 (1963).
3.10. T. M. French, G. A. Somorjai: J. Phys. Chem. **74**, 2489 (1970).
3.11. J. E. Houston, R. L. Park: Surface Sci. **26**, 286 (1971).
3.12. P. J. Estrup, E. G. McRae: Surface Sci. **25**, 1 (1971).
3.13. P. J. Estrup: In *The Structure and Chemistry of Solid Surfaces* (Wiley, New York, 1969), p. 19-I.
3.14. A. G. Naumovets, A. G. Fedorus: Sov. Phys.-JETP Letters **10**, 6 (1969); Surface Sci. **21**, 426 (1970).
3.15. J. M. Chen, C. A. Papageorgopoulos: Surface Sci. **21**, 377 (1970).
3.16. P. A. Redhead: Vacuum **12**, 203 (1962).
3.17. L. D. Schmidt: Catalysis Rev. **9**, 115 (1974).
3.18. J. M. Blakely: Progr. Mat. Sci. **10**, 1 (1963).
3.19. H. P. Bonzel: In *Structure and Properties of Metal Surfaces* (Maruzen, Tokyo, 1973), p. 248
3.20. G. Ehrlich, F. G. Hudda: J. Chem. Phys. **44**, 1039 (1966).
3.21. R. Gomer: Disc. Farad. Soc. **28**, 23 (1959)
3.22. G. Ayrault, G. Ehrlich: J. Chem. Phys. **57**, 1788 (1972).
3.23. T. Engel, R. Gomer: J. Chem. Phys. **50**, 2428 (1969).
3.24. T. E. Madey: Surface Sci. **33**, 355 (1972).
3.25. L. A. Harris: J. Appl. Phys. **39**, 1419 (1968).
3.26. J. Pritchard, M. L. Sims: J. Catalysis **19**, 427 (1970).
3.27. J. T. Yates, Jr., D. A. King: Surface Sci. **30**, 60 (1972).
3.28. T. A. Delchar, G. Ehrlich: J. Chem. Phys. **42**, 2686 (1965).
3.29. P. W. Tamm, L. D. Schmidt: Surface Sci. **26**, 286 (1971).
3.30. P. J. Estrup, J. Anderson: J. Chem. Phys. **46**, 567 (1967).
3.31. L. R. Clavenna, L. D. Schmidt: Surface Sci. **22**, 365 (1970).
3.32. D. L. Adams, L. H. Germer: Surface Sci. **26**, 109 (1971).
3.33. D. L. Adams, L. H. Germer: Surface Sci. **27**, 21 (1971).
3.34. H. F. Winters, D. E. Horne: Surface Sci. **24**, 587 (1971).
3.35. P. W. Tamm, L. D. Schmidt: J. Chem. Phys. **51**, 5352 (1969); and **54**, 4775 (1971).

3.36. P. J. ESTRUP, J. ANDERSON: J. Chem. Phys. **45**, 2254 (1966).
3.37. K. YONEHARA, L. D. SCHMIDT: Surface Sci. **25**, 238 (1971).
3.38. J. T. YATES, JR., T. E. MADEY: J. Chem. Phys. **54**, 4969 (1971).
3.39. M. R. LEGGETT, R. A. ARMSTRONG: Surface Sci. **24**, 404 (1971).
3.40. B. D. BARFORD, R. R. RYE: J. Chem. Phys. **60**, 1046 (1974), see references cited for earlier work function measurements.
3.41. K. J. MATYSIK: Surface Sci. **29**, 324 (1972).
3.42. D. A. KING, D. MENZEL: Surface Sci. **40**, 399 (1973).
3.43. D. L. ADAMS, L. H. GERMER, J. W. MAY: Surface Sci. **22**, 45 (1970).
3.44. P. W. TAMM, L. D. SCMIDT: J. Chem. Phys. **52**, 1150 (1970); and **55**, 4253 (1971).
3.45. T. E. MADEY: Surface Sci. **33**, 355 (1972); **36**, 281 (1973), and private communication.
3.46. G. SANDERS, L. D. SCHMIDT: Unpublished results.
3.47. D. L. ADAMS: Surface Sci. **42**, 12 (1974).
3.48. T. E. MADEY: Surface Sci. **36**, 281 (1973).
3.49. E. W. PLUMMER, A. E. BELL: J. Vac. Sci. Technol. **2**, 583 (1972).
3.50. B. FEUERBACHER, B. FITTON: Phys. Rev. Letters **29**, 786 (1972).
3.51. E. W. PLUMMER: To be published.
3.52. G. W. RUBLOFF, J. ANDERSON, M. A. PASSLER, P. J. STILES: Phys. Rev. Letters **32**, 667 (1974).
3.53. R. R. FORD: Advan. Catalysis **21**, 51 (1970).
3.54. R. GOMER: Jap. J. Appl. Phys. Suppl. 2, Pt. 2, 213 (1974).
3.55. P. A. REDHEAD: Trans. Faraday Soc. **57**, 641 (1961);
    G. EHRLICH, T. W. HICKMOTT, F. G. HUDDA: J. Chem. Phys. **28**, 506 (1958).
3.56. R. KLEIN: J. Chem. Phys. **31**, 1306 (1958).
3.57. L. W. SWANSON, R. GOMER: J. Chem. Phys. **39**, 2813 (1963).
3.58. A. E. BELL, R. GOMER: J. Chem. Phys. **44**, 1065 (1966).
3.59. T. ENGEL, R. GOMER: J. Chem. Phys. **52**, 1832 (1970).
3.60. C. KOHRT, R. GOMER: Surface Sci. **24**, 77 (1971); and **40**, 71 (1973).
3.61. L. R. CLAVENNA, L. D. SCHMIDT: Surface Sci. **33**, 11 (1972).
3.62. C. S. STEINBRUCHEL: Ph. D. Thesis, University of Minnesota (1974).
3.63. J. W. MAY, L. H. GERMER: J. Chem. Phys. **44**, 2895 (1966).
3.64. E. BAUER: Colloq. Intern. CNRS (1969) **187**, 111 (1970).
3.65. J. ANDERSON, P. J. ESTRUP: J. Chem. Phys. **46**, 563 (1967).
3.66. C. G. GOYMOUR, D. A. KING: J. Chem. Soc. Faraday Trans. **169**, 736, 749 (1973); Surface Sci. **35**, 246 (1973).
3.67. T. E. MADEY, J. T. YATES, JR., R. C. STERN: J. Chem. Phys. **42**, 1372 (1965).
3.68. J. M. BAKER, D. E. EASTMAN: J. Vac. Sci. Technol. **10**, 223 (1973).
3.69. E. W. PLUMMER: To be published.
3.70. Y. VISWANATH, L. D. SCHMIDT: J. Chem. Phys. **59**, 4184 (1973).
3.71. J. T. YATES, JR.: To be published.
3.72. J. T. YATES, D. A. KING: Surface Sci. **36**, 739 (1973).
3.73. J. T. YATES, D. A. KING: Surface Sci. **32**, 479 (1972); and **38**, 114 (1973).
3.74. G. EHERLICH: J. Chem. Phys. **34**, 39 (1961).
3.75. D. MENZEL: Ber. Bunsenges. Phys. Chem. **72**, 591 (1968).
3.76. G. ERTL, J. KOCH: *Adsorption Desorption Phenomena* (Academic Presss, New York, 1972), p. 345; Z. Naturforsch. **25**, 1906 (1970).
3.77. H. CONRAD, G. ERTL, J. KOCH, E. E. LATTA: Surface Sci. **43**, 462 (1974).
3.78. T. N. TAYLOR, P. J. ESTRUP: J. Vac. Sci. Technol. **10**, 26 (1973).
3.79. H. R. HAN, L. D. SCHMIDT: J. Phys. Chem. **75**, 227 (1971).
3.80. M. MAHNIG, L. D. SCHMIDT: Z. Phys. Chem. **80**, 71 (1972).
3.81. S. M. KO, L. D. SCGMIDT: Surface Sci. **42**, 508 (1972).
3.82. C. HUANG, P. J. ESTRUP: To be published.

4. Desorption Phenomena

Dietrich Menzel

With 12 Figures

The term "desorption" signifies the rupture of the adsorption bond and the resulting removal of adsorbed particles from the surface. This can be accomplished in different ways. If the temperature of the system is high enough that a sizeable fraction of the adsorbate complexes has energies above the desorption energy in the Maxwellian distribution and can therefore leave the surface, we speak of thermal desorption (TD). Electron impact can lead to transitions to excited or ionized states of the adsorbate whose potential energy at the equilibrium distance of the ground state is higher than that of the respective free particle, so that ions or neutrals can be desorbed; this process is called electron impact desorption (EID) or electron-stimulated desorption (ESD). Similar processes can be brought about by excitation by light; we then speak of photodesorption (PD). The impact of ions or fast neutrals can cause the removal of adsorbates in different ways; these processes could be called ion impact desorption (IID). Finally, a very high electric field (of the order of one $V/\text{Å}$) can bend down the ionic curve of the adsorbate so far, that rapid tunneling occurs from the ground state to the ionic state, and the resulting adsorbate ion is carried away from the surface immediately; these processes are termed field desorption (FD).

Measurements of desorption processes, especially those of thermal and electron impact desorption, have widely been used to define adsorbate states and to measure their populations. As to the kinetic features, both experimental accuracy and theoretical understanding are more difficult to obtain, as is always the case for a time-dependent process. The efforts undertaken to overcome these difficulties are very worthwhile, however, as increased information can help in the understanding of properties of the adsorbate like the binding energy and the energetic coupling to the substrate (TD, EID, and IID), the existence of and transitions to and from excited adsorbate states (EID and PD), and the shape of the ground state potential curves (FD). Furthermore, the practical importance of desorption processes is large: TD is an important step in heterogeneous catalysis; TD as well as EID, PD, and IID are significant processes in vacuum production and measurement, and in accelerators, plasma machines and fusion reactors; EID is a frequent disturbing effect in surface investigations because of the preference for slow electrons as a surface probe; TD and IID can be used to clean samples.

In the following the different processes will be considered with the main emphasis on TD and—to a lesser degree—EID. Because of the limited space and the smaller amount of information available, the other processes will only be briefly discussed. Experimental methods, typical results, and the prevalent theoretical explanations will be covered by examples rather than comprehensively. Emphasis will be placed on modern investigations of well-defined surfaces and adsorbate layers, which have mostly been done on metal surfaces. An attempt will be made to discuss open questions and current trends of experimental as well as theoretical work, as far as space permits.

4.1. Thermal Desorption

Thermal desorption constitutes a normal chemical reaction, in which one of the reaction partners is a solid surface. In the simplest case of independent desorption of single particles, it is similar to unimolecular decomposition, but more complicated mechanisms (association, diffusion, cooperative effects) have to be expected. Analysis can therefore be similar to that of chemical kinetics in general [4.1].

In the following, a discussion of the usual approach used to analyse data is given first; then a description of the most important techniques used and subsequently a survey of typical rate data follow; and finally the current status of the theories of TD is sketched.

4.1.1. Desorption Mechanisms and Rate Parameters

As usual in chemical kinetics, the general dependence of the rates R_d (desorbing particles per unit time and surface area) on the concentration of adsorbed particles per unit surface area, N, and the temperature T,

$$R_d = -dN/dt = f(T, N) \tag{4.1}$$

is analysed in terms of an Arrhenius equation

$$R_d = k_m \cdot N^m = N^m \cdot k_m^0 \cdot \exp(-E_m/RT), \tag{4.2}$$

where k_m is the rate constant, m is the formal order, E_m the activation energy and k_m^0 the pre-exponential factor, frequency factor or simply prefactor. The coverage-dependence is usually assumed to be contained totally in the N^m-term, and the temperature dependence in the exponential term, at least as a first approximation. The rationale for the assumption of such a simple Arrhenius or Polanyi-Wigner equation is the basic concept that the coverage term is produced by the number of particles taking part in the critical step, the pre-exponential is equal to the frequency of attempts of the system to move in the direction of reaction (assumed independent of T to first approximation), and the exponential term represents the relative number of these attempts having the necessary minimum energy. The general case of (4.1) can then be recovered by making E and k^0 functions of N and T, if necessary. As these equations represent macroscopic descriptions of a complicated sequence of microscopic processes, there need not be any simple correspondence between mechanism and order, as known from chemical kinetics. An attempt is usually made, however, to interpret a measured order as indicative of the mechanism of the rate-determining elementary step. This will usually be only the case for very simple sequences, or if that step is clearly much slower than all the others. For instance, if desorption of independent single particles occurs throughout the coverage range,

$$A(ad) \to A(gas) \tag{4.3}$$

the reaction rate at constant temperature will be given by

$$dN/dt = k_1 \cdot N \tag{4.4}$$

and the reaction will be first order. In this very simple concept the prefactor would be given by the number of attempts to leave the surface, i.e. the frequency of vibration v of the adatom; the activation energy would equal the sum of adsorption energy and activation energy of adsorption, which for nonactivated adsorption is equal to the adsorption energy (see, however, Subsection 4.1.4). If two like atoms recombine to desorb as a diatomic molecule,

$$2A(ad) \to A_2(ad) \to A_2(gas) \tag{4.5}$$

the reaction can be first order [if the desorption of $A_2(ad)$ is the rate-determining step or if $A_2(gas)$ is formed directly from 2 neighboring immobile atoms], at least for a certain coverage range, or it can be second order (if the adatoms can diffuse over the surface, and their recombination is rate-determining). In the latter case, the values of E and k^0 can be expected to depend on the degree of mobility. If the adsorbate layer can be regarded as a two-dimensional gas, k^0 can be given by the collision frequency in this gas, and E_d by the desorption energy, so that

$$k_2 = d_A \cdot (\pi kT/M)^{1/2} \exp(-E_d/RT), \tag{4.6}$$

where d_A is the collision diameter, and M the mass of A. If the diffusion is much slower, but still occurs, then for small N

$$k_2 = (v/N_s) \exp[-(E_{diff} + E_d)/RT], \tag{4.7}$$

where N_s is the number of sites on the surface, and E_{diff} the activation energy of surface diffusion [4.2].

In the case of dissociative adsorption, both desorption of atoms and molecules can, in principle, be expected. A simple energy consideration can show which one will take place at not too small coverages [4.3]. If Q is the bond energy per adatom and D the dissociation energy per mole of the gaseous molecule, then the desorption energy of atoms will be Q and that of molecules $2Q - D$ (assuming nonactivated adsorption). Desorption of atoms will then dominate, if $2Q - D > Q$, or $Q > D$. This condition is fulfilled, e.g. for oxygen on W, but not for hydrogen on W. At high temperatures, when the coverage is very small, the argument is not valid, of course, as not enough collisions between atoms occur; H_2 can therefore be atomized on hot filaments [4.4].

Many more complicated situations can be imagined, leading to integral or fractional orders of desorption. The latter are difficult to analyse since the data can always be interpreted in terms of a dependence of E and/or k^0 on N. Even for integral experimental orders, the mechanism can be ambiguous. For instance, if a layer of adsorbed atoms A consists of two different adsorbate states, one of which is mobile and the other immobile, and desorption occurs by recombination of one of each species, so that each desorption step is followed by conversion of another mobile to an immobile species, desorption will be first order until all mobile species are used up, and will then stop. After a temperature increase to make the second species mobile, desorption will resume according to second order [4.2].

This shows that no simple unequivocal conclusions about mechanisms can be made from reaction orders. As always in chemical kinetics, the logic points in the opposite direction: A mechanism can only be shown to be compatible with, but not proven by the kinetics. Nevertheless, the reaction order is one of the principal kinetic parameters, and the determination of m, E, and k^0 are the main objective of kinetic measurements. Apart from their bearing on the kinetics itself, they are also of interest for the understanding of the stationary properties of the adsorbate. From the integral

$$\int_0^\infty R_d \, dt = N \tag{4.8}$$

the number of adsorbed particles present can be obtained; E yields the adsorption energy in simple cases, and N and k^0 are important for the questions of dissociation and mobility. The methods for the determination of these parameters will be considered in the next subsection.

4.1.2. Experimental Methods of Thermal Desorption

The classical method in chemical kinetics is the isothermal measurement of the change of concentrations of reactants and/or products with time, after a sudden disturbance which makes the starting condition unstable. The reaction order can be derived from the rate-law obtained; measurements at different temperatures yield the activation energy and (with smaller accuracy because of the large extrapolation involved) the prefactor. Such isothermal measurements have also been performed for desorption, although not very often, compared to temperature-programmed methods. This is probably due to the fact that step functions in temperature or coverage to cause the initial unstable situation are not easy to accomplish in adsorption systems, so that the starting-point is not well-defined (this is not really necessary, though, as procedures exist for the analysis of rate data without clear start [4.5]). On the other hand, the temperature-programmed method to be described below is quite easy to use and at the same time gives direct information on adsorbate states and coverages, at least in principle.

The usual procedure is to follow the change with time elapsed after the step change, of any quantity x which is connected to the coverage in a known way [$x = f(N)$, for $T =$ const], so that

$$dx/dt = (df/dN) \cdot (dN/dt) \qquad (4.9)$$

can be used to evaluate directly (4.2). Using temperature steps, KOHRT and GOMER [4.6] measured the rate of desorption from a single crystal by placing it in front of a field emission tip and recording the coverage accumulated on this tip (from the change of the field emission current) under conditions where every molecule arriving at the tip would stick to it; their evaluation used the procedure of [4.5] (see Fig. 4.1). PETERMANN [4.7], and JELEND and MENZEL [4.8] used the EID ion current which under certain conditions is proportional to the coverage (see Section 4.2 below), to follow the change of coverage of a certain adsorbate state after step heating. ENGELHARDT and MENZEL [4.9] used the work function change due to adsorption which is also proportional to coverage in certain cases. The amount left on the surface after a certain

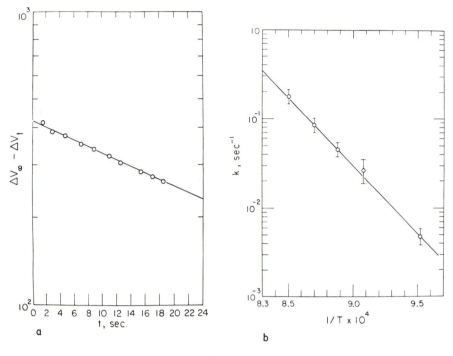

Fig. 4.1. (a) Isothermal desorption kinetics of β_2-CO from W (110), measured by recording the CO molecules condensed on a field emission tip in front of the crystal, by the change of voltage necessary for a certain emission current. (b) Arrhenius plot of data obtained in this way. (After [4.27])

isothermal heating time, measured by integral flash desorption, was used by Tamm and Schmidt [4.10] and others to construct isothermal kinetics.

An isothermal desorption method using pressure steps is the measurement of mean dwell times of the adsorbate on the surface at high temperatures, using modulated molecular or ionic beams. For a first-order desorption reaction, the inverse of the rate constant k_1 is equal to the mean dwell time τ, so that

$$\tau = \tau_0 \exp(E/RT). \tag{4.10}$$

With the assumption of constant τ_0 ($=1/k_1^0$), this equation goes back to Frenkel [4.11]. If a chopped or modulated molecular or ionic beam is directed onto a surface under conditions of reversible adsorption, so that desorption can occur, and the re-emitted particles are detected in a

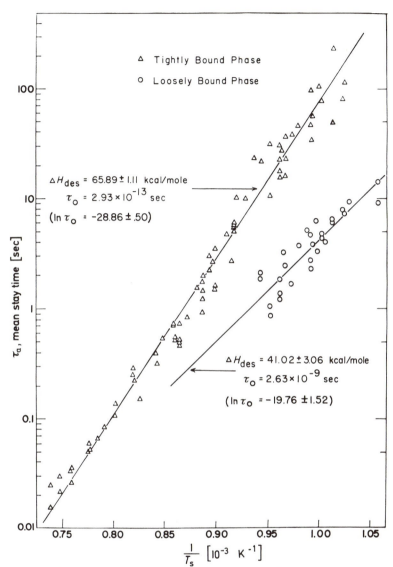

Fig. 4.2. Arrhenius plots for the mean dwell times of Ag on W (110), obtained with the molecular beam decay method. Two states in different coverage regimes are shown. (After [4.19])

mass spectrometer, the desorption kinetics can be either deduced from the decay time of the desorption signal after the beam has been shut off [4.12, 13], or from the phase shift of the output pulses against the input pulses [4.14]. By varying the temperature of the sample, the data for an evaluation according to (4.10) can be obtained. Because of the ease of detection in this case the method has so far been only used for ionic desorption [4.12, 14–17] and for desorption of species which are easily condensed on cooled walls (metals like Cd [4.13] and Ag [4.18, 19], oxides and halides [4.20]). In the first case, direct passage of the desorbing flux into a mass spectrometer is possible; in the second, detection by ionization in a single pass through an electron impact ionizer is possible with good s/n, since no scattering from the cooled walls occurs. Figure 4.2 shows an example. The method allows a less ambiguous determination of the k_1^0 and E values than the flash method (see below), provided only one or two adsorption states are present with first-order behavior throughout (for a discussion of the relative merits of the two methods, see [4.19]).

The method most frequently used to date is temperature-programmed desorption, mostly called flash filament desorption (as it was first performed by rapidly heating a filament or "flashing" it) or simply flash desorption (EHRLICH [4.21], REDHEAD [4.22]), although often rather slow heating rates are used nowadays. The basic idea of this method which goes back to the "glow-curve" method in thermo-luminescence [4.23], is to continuously heat the substrate and follow the rate of desorption as a function of temperature. The rate at any time will be determined by the temperature and the amount of gas left on the surface after the previous desorption; it will then show a maximum at the point, where the increase due to the temperature rise is equal to the decrease from the diminished coverage. Most investigations use the amount of gas evolved to measure the rate (see below), although other parameters coupled to the surface coverage and therefore to the desorption rate (work function change, Auger peak height, EID current) can be used. Essentially the same method has been utilized by CVETANOVIC and AMENOMIYA [4.24] for the investigation of catalysts. The main reasons for the popularity of the the pressure-rise method seem to be that a) a picture of the different adsorption states on the surface can be obtained very rapidly, by correlating every maximum of the desorption rate with a distinct adsorption state; b) an integration of the rates to yield the total coverage, (although mostly in relative units only) can very easily be done [Eq. (4.8)]; c) approximate values of m, E, and (within limits) k^0 can be obtained in a few measurements. The main disadvantages are the often resulting ambiguity of the kinetic parameters, and the fact that distinct desorption peaks need not correspond to distinct states, and vice versa; this will be discussed below.

The basis of the method has been discussed by a number of authors [4.21–26]; the subsequent formulation follows that given by REDHEAD [4.22].

Inserting a linear temperature rise with time

$$T = T_0 + \beta \cdot t, \tag{4.11}$$

as used by most authors, into (4.2) leads to

$$-dN/dt = R_d(t) = N^m(t) k_m^0 \exp[-E_m/R(T_0 + \beta t)] \tag{4.12}$$

which is equivalent to

$$-dN/dT = (N^m \cdot k_m^0/\beta) \exp(-E_m/RT). \tag{4.13}$$

If E and k^0 are assumed to be independent of coverage N, then the temperature T_p at which the rate curve shows a peak, can be obtained from (4.13). It is found that

$$E_1/RT_p^2 = (k_1^0/\beta) \exp(-E_1/RT_p) \quad \text{for} \quad m=1 \tag{4.14}$$

and

$$E_2/RT_p^2 = (2N_p \cdot k_2^0/\beta) \exp(-E_2/RT_p) \quad \text{for} \quad m=2. \tag{4.15}$$

These equations are equivalent to

$$\ln(T_p^2/\beta) = E_1/RT_p + \ln(E_1/k_1^0 \cdot R) \tag{4.16}$$

and

$$\ln(T_p^2 \cdot N_p/\beta) = E_2/RT_p + \ln(E_2/2k_2^0 \cdot R), \tag{4.17}$$

where N_p is the coverage at the rate maximum and $2N_p \approx N_0$ for $m=2$. Formulae for the peak shapes can be obtained from these equations with some approximations [4.21–26].

A similar, and in formal respects simpler, treatment is possible for the case of a reciprocal temperature rise

$$1/T = 1/T_0 - \alpha \cdot t. \tag{4.18}$$

The reader is referred to REDHEAD [4.22] or CARTER [4.25] for the formulation. Instead of a continuous temperature rise, stepwise heating can also been used. For the equivalence of this procedures to flash desorption, see [4.6].

Again, any variable connected to the coverage [Eq. (4.9)] can be used to measure the $R_d(t)$-curves. For instance, the change of work function has been used in this way [4.9]. Condensation of the desorbing particles on a cryogenically cooled field emission tip, as described above, has also been used [4.6, 27], as well as radioactive tracer methods [4.28]. The advantage of these techniques is the absence of disturbing wall effects.

The most frequently used variable connected to R_d, however, is the pressure rise in the surrounding vacuum system resulting from desorption. The pumping equation of a vacuum system is given by

$$dP/dt = (kT/V) \cdot (dN_g/dt) = Q/V - S \cdot P/V, \qquad (4.19)$$

where P is the pressure in the system, V its volume, N_g the number of gas particles contained in it, k the Boltzmann constant, Q the influx of gas (e.g. in Torr $\cdot$ l/sec), and S the effective pumping speed. Before the start of the desorption run, the base pressure is constant, so that

$$Q_0 = S P_0 . \qquad (4.20)$$

If we assume that no change of pumping speed (e.g. by adsorption on the walls or readsorption on the sample) or of influx (e.g. by displacement from the walls or pump) occurs during desorption, simple balancing requires that the rate of desorption be equal to the rate of removal of gas from the system by the pumps plus the rate of increase of gas content of the system:

$$A \cdot R_d(t) = S \cdot \Delta P/kT + (V/kT)(dP/dt), \qquad (4.21)$$

where A is the surface area of the substrate, and $\Delta P = P - P_0$ the pressure increase in the system over the background pressure. This can also be written as

$$dP/dt + \Delta P/\tau_p = a R_d(t), \qquad (4.22)$$

where $\tau_p = V/S$ is the characteristic pumping time of the system and $a = AkT/V$. Two limiting cases are of interest:

1) For small pumping speeds, i.e. if τ_p is large compared to the heating time, the second term can be neglected and $R_d(t) \propto dP/dt$.

2) For large pumping speeds, i.e. if $\tau_p \to 0$, the second term overpowers the first, and $R_d(t) \propto \Delta P$.

Corrections for situations close to, but not exactly equal to one of these cases have been given by REDHEAD [4.22]. Situations between the extremes can best be analyzed using a network of operational amplifiers, simulating (4.22), so that $R_d(t)$ can be directly obtained. In modern uhv systems with large pumping speeds, Case 2 is usually realized for not too large heating rates; the pressure-time curves can then be used directly for the evaluation of R_d. The total amount of liberated gas in relative units is obtained directly from an integration of the $P(t)$-curves; for absolute determinations, an accurate knowledge of S would be required, which is very difficult to obtain, especially for the high S case. In earlier work total pressure measurements were used for the recording of flash filament spectra; in recent years most authors use small mass spectrometers to record only the masses wanted, which eliminates the possibility of disturbances by gases displaced from the walls and makes visible possible disturbing coadsorbates (e.g. CO in hydrogen). Even then, there remain a number of experimental problems, since interactions of the gas with the measuring device as well as with pumps and walls can still occur (when the pressure drops again, re-evolution from the walls is possible; scattering of gas from the walls can make the gas density anisotropic, so that it cannot be analysed in terms of a pressure change). Careful lay-out of the experiments and analysis of the results is necessary to exclude such disturbances (see the discussions given by McCARROLL [4.29], HOBSON and EARNSHAW [4.30], PETERMANN [4.31]). For metallic adsorption which leads to desorption of ions, many of these difficulties can be circumvented by drawing these directly into a mass spectrometer for detection, without the build-up of a partial pressure [4.32]. For the application to fine-grained catalysts [4.24], the desorbed gas is carried away by a flow of inert gas. Temperature-inhomogeneity across the sample can also lead to difficulties, especially for direct Ohmic heating (see EHRLICH [4.21]).

While earlier work mostly used polycrystalline samples (filaments, ribbons), well-defined single crystal faces are being used increasingly in the recent years. Care has to be taken in that case to keep the percentage of surface area with other orientations than the main face as small as possible; in order to assure uniform heating, crystal discs are often suspended on thin wires and heated by light irradiation or electron impact [4.10, 33]. Figure 4.3 shows a famous example of a ·flash spectrum from a polycrystalline filament; in Fig. 4.4 some examples of flash spectra from single crystal faces are given.

The resulting $R_d(t)$-curves obtained by any of these methods can be analysed according to (4.14)–(4.17) or the peak shape formulae obtained from them. Equations (4.14) and (4.16) show that for first-order desorption with constant E and k_1^0, T_p is independent of the initial coverage for linear temperature-programming; the peak is asymmetric about T_p. The relation between E and T_p is then almost linear and for $10^{13} < k_1^0/\beta < 10^8 (K^{-1})$ is given to $\pm 1.5\%$ by

$$E_1/R T_p = \ln(k_1^0 \cdot T_p/\beta) - 3.64 . \tag{4.23}$$

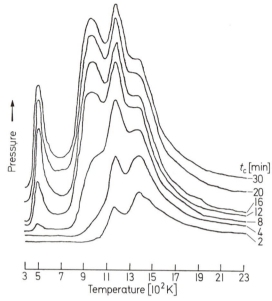

Fig. 4.3. Flash desorption spectrum of CO from a polycrystalline filament, recorded by the total pressure change. 4 states can be recognized. (After [4.34])

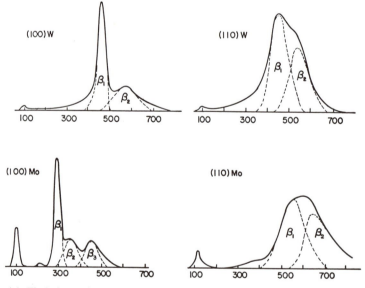

Fig. 4.4. Flash desorption spectra for hydrogen on some W and Mo faces, recorded mass spectrometrically. Resolution into partial peaks is indicated. (After [4.35])

For an evaluation of E from one T_p-value only, a value of k_1^0 must be assumed. This has been done quite often, assuming $k_1^0 \approx 10^{13}$ sec^{-1}. A real determination of E and k^0 is possible from measurements of desorption spectra at different heating rates and evaluation according to (4.16). In order to obtain an acceptable accuracy, β must be varied by two powers of ten or more, which is rarely possible (if β is very small, the accuracy is limited and wall or re-adsorption effects can be very strong; if β is too large, multiple peaks are not resolved any more [4.36]). Variation of β is also important in order to make sure that no redistribution between states occurs during heating, which could falsify the kinetics. If only one peak is present, then a reasonably accurate value of k_1^0 can be deduced from its half-width, which increases with decreasing k_1^0, see e.g. [4.37].

Irrespective of m, flash spectra can be evaluated by Arrhenius plots of the measured rates directly, for constant coverage; these are found by back-integrating the flash-spectra to the desired N-value [4.32].

For second-order desorption T_p is seen to decrease with increasing coverage [Eqs. (4.15) and (4.17)]. However, such behavior can also occur for $m = 1$, but E decreasing with increasing N. The peak should be symmetric about T_p for $m = 2$, but this can usually be checked only for single peaks.

A test for m is obvious from (4.16) and (4.17), if E is constant: a plot of $\log(N_0 \cdot T_p^2 / \beta)$ versus $1/T_p$ must yield a line parallel to the ordinate for $m = 1$ and a straight line (with slope E_2/R) for $m = 2$ (see Fig. 4.5). Plots according to (4.14) and (4.15) can also be used for the determination of m and E. If none of these plots yields a straight line, either E or k^0 or both vary with N, and m cannot be unequivocally determined; wall effects can also be responsible. In such cases and especially for multiple, not totally resolved peak structures, computer analyses can be performed [4.35–39], which can attempt to take account of the experimental disturbances at the same time [4.29]. These are usually done under the assumption that the total spectrum is a sum of independent contributions of different binding states; nonadherence to simple assumptions (values of m, constancy of E_m and k_m^0 values) is then analyzed in terms of coverage-dependent E and/or k^0 values. Because of the large number of parameters involved, such resolutions into partial peaks (e.g. 6 peaks in the case of CO on polycrystalline W [4.38]) and coverage-dependent rate parameters [4.39] can become quite ambiguous. PISANI et al. [4.36] have recently given an illuminating example. For the desorption spectra of nitrogen on polycrystalline W, which consist of two overlapping peaks, they were able to fit a large number of data (120 desorption spectra) equally well assuming first- or second-order desorption for one of the peaks, which of course leads to quite different E and k^0 values also. In the same system,

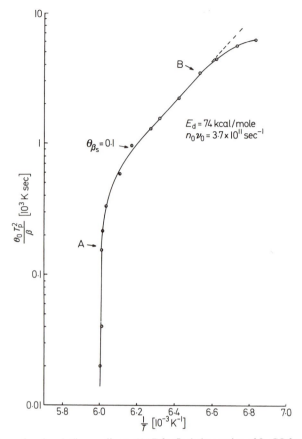

Fig. 4.5. "Second-order plot" according to (4.17) for flash desorption of β_3-CO from W (100). Ranges of first (A) and second order (B) behavior are obvious; deviations occur at higher coverages. (After [4.39])

Madey and Yates [4.40] had earlier encountered complex desorption kinetics, which they analyzed in terms of a variation of m with N (from 4 to 1). Clavenna and Schmidt [4.41] explained similar behavior they found on W (100) by a variation of k_2^0 with N and gave a model for it. Dawson and Peng [4.42] could not distinguish between 6 different models (with $m = 1$ or 2, E between 20 and 80 kcal/mol and a corresponding spread of k^0) for a certain state in this system.

The possibility of conversion between states during heating-up must also be considered carefully, see e.g. [4.43, 44]. Furthermore, the assumption of independent states has to be considered critically as well. For polycrystalline samples, it is sensible to expect surface sites with different binding energies, so that an interpretation of multipeak spectra assuming independent contributions from different binding states is in principle acceptable. However, more than one peak is usually found in desorption from low-index single crystal faces, too. (For instance, the desorption spectra of CO on W (100) [4.39] and other W faces are very similar to those on polycrystalline W [4.34, 45].) If these peaks are clearly separated, then the assumption of distinct binding states is usually warranted here, too; these can also be due to the presence of adsorbed species rather than to a-priori different sites (e.g. α- and β-CO on W). Then two or more binding states coexist simultaneously, as distinct entities in the composite layer. However, the composite layer can also consist of only one binding state only, if there is a variation of desorption energy with coverage strong enough to cause multiple peaks. For a long time the first explanation was assumed to be correct in all cases, and multipeak spectra have therefore been interpreted as representing the equivalent number of distinct binding states. Detailed analyses in recent years (TOYA [4.46], GOYMOUR and KING [4.47], ADAMS [4.48]), have shown, however, that the variation of E with N need not be very strong to lead to distinct peaks, so that a repulsive interaction between adsorbed particles can easily lead to such an effect. For instance, the two β-peaks of hydrogen on W (100) are now thought by some authors to be due to interaction in the adsorbed layer consisting of one distinct species only and not to two distinct binding modes side by side (but see Chapter 3 for alternative views). Such interactions can also lead to unexpected desorption orders (see Subsection 4.1.1).

This discussion had the purpose to show that the flash desorption method, while being a very valuable means for the investigation of desorption kinetics, is also fraught with experimental and interpretational difficulties. While in principle all information on m, E, and k^0 are contained in the desorption peak positions and shapes, provided enough spectra with varied β and N_0 values have been obtained, in practice it is often difficult if not impossible to unfold this information unambiguously. The safest information is usually that on E (however, see [4.36]), and on m for clear first order. The ambiguities are especially large for overlapping peaks. This should be borne in mind when using kinetic data obtained by flash desorption.

4.1.3. Some Results of Thermal Desorption Measurements

In the following some results of desorption parameters, mostly for well-defined polycrystalline or single crystal metal surfaces, will be given and discussed.

Table 4.1. Some rate parameters for the desorption of metallic adsorbates from metals ($m = 1$ in all cases)

Substrate	Adsorbate	Desorbed species	Method	State	k_1^0 [sec^{-1}]	E_1 (kcal/mol)	Ref.
W (poly)	Cs	Cs$^+$	CB	clean	$1 \cdot 10^{12}$	47	[4.15]
W (poly)	Cs	Cs$^+$	CB	contam.	$1.7 \cdot 10^{10}$	36	[4.15]
Re (poly)	Cs	Cs$^+$	CB	clean	$5 \cdot 10^{12}$	44	[4.15]
Re (poly)	Ba	Ba^{2+}	CB	clean	$1.7 \cdot 10^{13}$	109	[4.15]
W (poly)	K	K$^+$	CB	clean	$4.2 \cdot 10^{12}$	54.4	[4.17]
W (poly)	K	K$^+$	CB	C-contam.	$1.7 \cdot 10^{13}$	54.4	[4.17]
W (poly)	Cd	Cd	CB	1	$1.1 \cdot 10^{10}$	41	[4.13]
				2	$7.1 \cdot 10^9$	21	[4.13]
W (110)	Ag	Ag	CB	1	$3.5 \cdot 10^{12}$	66	[4.19]
				2	$3.8 \cdot 10^8$	41	[4.19]
W (poly)	Ag	Ag	CB	clean	$3.6 \cdot 10^{12}$	67	[4.18]
W (poly)	Ag	Ag	CB	C-contam.	$8.2 \cdot 10^{12}$	73	[4.18]
W (poly)	Ag	Ag	CB	O-contam.	$1.4 \cdot 10^{12}$	47	[4.18]
W (poly)	Au	Au	CB	clean	$8.2 \cdot 10^{13}$	105	[4.18]
W (poly)	Au	Au	CB	C-contam.	$1.7 \cdot 10^{14}$	109	[4.18]
W (poly)	Au	Au	CB	O-contam.	$4.7 \cdot 10^{11}$	46	[4.18]
Ni (111)	Na	Na$^+$	TP	$\theta = 0$–0.5	10^{13}	$58 \to 32$	[4.32]
Ni (110)	Na	Na$^+$	TP	$\theta = 0$–0.3	10^{13}–10^{10}	$50 - 32$	[4.32]

CB Chopped beam.
TP Temperature programmed.

For desorption of metallic adsorbates from metal surfaces, both as ions and neutrals, the kinetics seem to follow first order in all cases. Since the corresponding adsorption is always nonactivated, the activation energies of desorption correspond to the binding energies of the species concerned. "Normal" prefactors of $\approx 10^{13}$ sec^{-1} are often found, although lower and higher values have also been reported. Some selected values are given in Table 4.1. An interesting effect is the strong change observed by contamination of the surface, which in part only affects the pre-exponential factor. More complicated results were found for flash desorption of Cu and Au from the basal plane of graphite [4.49]. The behavior of peak temperatures indicated $m < 1$, and the peaks could be fitted well assuming constant E up to a certain coverage and $m = 0.5$; E increased at higher coverages. This behavior seems to be caused by the much stronger interaction between the metal atoms than between metal atoms and C surface, which leads to island formation and to the E increase with coverage. The rate-determining step for desorption is then probably the dissociation of a metal atom from the border of an island, which explains the observed fractional order. This mechanism is also supported by the results of condensation measurements. A somewhat

Table 4.2. Some rate parameters for the desorption of weakly bound adsorbates ($m = 1$ in all cases)

Substrate	Adsorbate	Method	k_1^0 [sec^{-1}]	E [kcal/mol]	Ref.
W (111)	Xe	TP	10^{15}	9.3	[4.51]
W (100)	CH$_4$	TP	$3 \cdot 10^{12}$	7	[4.37]
CO/W (poly)	H$_2$	Iso	10^3	7.5	[4.8]
He (Constantan)	He	RF	$2 \cdot 10^7$	$6 \cdot 10^{-2}$	[4.52]
SiO$_2$ (untreated)	Ar	TP	10^2	$0.9 - 1$	[4.53]
SiO$_2$ (freshly abraded)	Ar	TP	1	$0.9 - 1$	
W (110)	v-CO	Iso	$10^4 - 5 \cdot 10^5$	10	[4.27]

TP Temperature-programmed desorption.
Iso Isothermal desorption.
RF Rapid flash.

similar case has been found for oxygen on Ag (110), where the measured zeroth-order desorption has been explained by desorption from the end of O-atom chains [4.9]. Zeroth order is also found for desorption from oxide layers [4.50].

Complicated desorption spectra for Na on different single crystal faces of Ni have been obtained by GERLACH and RHODIN [4.32]; only the low coverage peaks were therefore analysed. These seemed to obey first order kinetics; the observed shifts of T_p with coverage were attributed to changes of E and/or k^0 with coverage. For Na on Ni (111), Arrhenius plots gave constant k^0 values, while E decreased continuously by about 40 % over the coverage range examined. On the (110) face there was an abrupt change of E by about the same amount at a coverage, where a change of superstructure was observed in LEED, but here k^0 also changed in the same range. The data could also be analysed to yield constant k^0 values, however.

First-order desorption is usually also found for physisorbed or weakly chemisorbed gases. Some results are shown in Table 4.2. The variation of prefactors is seen to be considerable here, which might partly be due to spurious effects. The case of the weakly bound coadsorbed hydrogen on W, however, seems to be reinforced by the fact that the isosteric adsorption energy measured independently agrees very well with the activation energy E [4.8]. The possible reasons for the variation of k^0 values will be discussed in Subsection 4.1.4.

Complicated results are often found for electronegative gases on polycrystalline substrates. The complicated spectrum of CO on W [4.38] and the difficulties and ambiguities for nitrogen on W [4.36, 40–42] have been mentioned above. Interesting kinetic parameters can be derived from the work of SCHMIDT et al. for the simple gases H$_2$, N$_2$, and

Table 4.3. Some rate parameters for the desorption of electronegative adsorbates from metal surfaces

Substrate	Adsorbate	Method	State	Order m	k_1^0 [sec^{-1}]	k_2^0 [cm^2/sec]	E [kcal/mol]	Ref.
W (100)	H_2	TP	β_1	1	$10^{13\pm1}$		26	[4.1?]
			β_2	2		$4\cdot10^{-2}$ a	32	
	N_2	TP	β_2	2		0.23 a	74	[4.4?]
			γ	1	(10^{13})		9–10	
	CO	TP	$\beta_3(\theta<0.2)$	1	(10^{13})		93 ± 5	[4.3?]
			$\beta_3(\theta>0.2)$	2		$\approx10^{-3}$	74 ± 5	
			β_2	1	(10^{13})		62 ± 4	
			β_1	1	(10^{13})		57 ± 4	
			α	1	(10^{13})		21 ± 4	
W (110)	H_2	TP	β_1	2		10^{-2}	27	[4.54]
			β_2	2		$1.4\cdot10^{-2}$ a	33	
W (111)	H_2	TP	β_1	2			14	[4.5?]
			β_2	2			22	
			β_3	2		(0.01)	30	
			β_4	2			37	
			γ	1	(10^{13})		6–11	
W (poly)	H_2	TP		2		$2\cdot10^{-3}$ a	35	
Ir (poly)	H_2	TP		2		$2\cdot10^{-2}$ a	24	[4.5?]
Rh (poly)	H_2			2		$1\cdot10^{-3}$ a	18	
Re (poly)	H_2	TP	β_2	2		$(7\pm3)\cdot10^{-4}$	30	[4.5?]
Mo (100)	H_2	TP	β_1	1	(10^{13})		16	[4.5?]
			β_2	2		(0.05)	20	
			β_3	2		$5\cdot10^{-2}$	27	
Ni (111)	H_2	TP		2		0.2–0.3 a	23	[4.5?]
W (110)	CO	Step	β_2	1	$5\cdot10^{11}$		66	[4.2]
		Iso			$1.2\cdot10^{12}$		69	
		Step	β_1	1	$3\cdot10^9$		40	
		Iso			$3\cdot10^{12}$		55	
		Step	v	1	10^4		9.5	
		Iso			$5\cdot10^5$		10	
W (poly)	CO	TP	1	1	$1\cdot10^{12}$		49	[4.3?]
			2	1	$1\cdot10^{12}$		53	
			3	1	$2\cdot10^{12}$		60	
			4	1	$7\cdot10^{12}$		67	
			5	1	$1\cdot10^{13}$		75	
			6	2		0.01	78	
W (110)	O_2	Step	>1900 K	1	$2\cdot10^8$		92	[4.6?]
		Iso	>1900 K		$3\cdot10^9$		92	
		Iso	<1900 K	1	$2\cdot10^7$		69	[4.6?]
W (poly)	O_2		1900–2400 K	1	$3\cdot10^{13\pm1}$		129 ± 8	[4.5?]
		Step	1600–1800 K	1	$3\cdot10^{16\pm1}$		120 ± 5	
			1300–1600 K	1	$3\cdot10^{16\pm1}$		109 ± 5	

Table 4.3 (continued)

ubstrate	Ad-sorbate	Me-thod	State	Order m	k_1^0 [sec^{-1}]	k_2^0 [cm^2/sec]	E [kcal/mol]	Ref.
(poly)	O_2	TP	Oxide layer 1600–1800 K	0 1	$k_0^0 = 10^{34}$ molec/cm^2 sec $10^{14 \pm 2}$		100 ± 10 110 ± 10	[4.50]
(poly)	O_2	TP		2		6	58	[4.60]

TP   Temperature-programmed desorption.
Step Step desorption.
Iso   Isothermal desorption.

k^0-values in brackets: assumed.
Most other k^0-values from curve-fitting.

[a] Values for low coverages, from plots according to (4.18).

CO on single crystal faces of W and Mo (see Table 4.3). Most strongly
bound states of hydrogen on all faces of both metals showed second-
order kinetics, as would be expected for associative desorption from an
atomic layer. On the (100) faces a strongly bound state exhibiting first-
order behavior was also found, which was originally assumed to be due
to adsorbed molecules. Other work suggests, however, that this state
is also atomic and in fact that the full layer consists of one species only,
the two peaks arising from interactions between the adsorbed atoms,
as discussed above. The spectra could be fitted very well by assuming
constant E and k^0 values for all first-order states (with $k_1^0 = 10^{13}$ sec^{-1})
and for the second-order states at low coverage (with k_2^0 around
10^{-2} cm^2/sec). For the fitting of the higher coverages of the latter either
a linear decrease of E or an increase of k^0 with increasing coverage had
to be assumed. The same behavior has been found for hydrogen on Ir,
Rh [4.55], Re [4.56], and Ni [4.58]. The change of k^0 with coverage
has been explained [4.41] in terms of a random-walk surface diffusion
process as the rate-determining step. This yields the expression

$$k_2^0 = (l^2 \cdot v_0)/[1 - (l_c/l) \cdot \theta^{1/2}]^2 , \tag{4.24}$$

where l is the diffusion jump length, v_0 the vibrational frequency of the
adsorbed atoms, and l_c the critical separation for recombination. Good
fits could be obtained with this equation also, again showing the ambiguity
of fitting. For low coverages $k_2^0 = l^2 \cdot v$, which is ≈ 0.01 cm^2/sec · atom,
as found. This makes it understandable that about the same E-values are
often obtained from the same R_d-values, assuming first- or second-order
desorption: as N_0 is of the order 10^{15} atoms/cm^2, $N_0 \cdot k_2^0 \approx k_1^0$ for normal

k^0-values. The values from the work of KOHRT and GOMER [4.6, 27] for
the desorption of different binding states of oxygen and CO on W (110)
faces, which are listed in Table 4.3, have been obtained both by isothermal
and step desorption with a method described in Subsection 4.1.2. Isothermal measurements gave the clearer picture. Their results for oxygen
desorption disagree strongly with the more recent work of KING et al.
[4.59], which is also listed in Table 4.3. These authors argue that the
very low k^0-values of KOHRT and GOMER are due to a mixture of different
states contributing to their Arrhenius plots.

The data of Tables 4.1–3 show a tendency towards a coupling of E
and k^0 in the sense of a "compensation effect" [4.61]: large values of E
are accompanied by large k^0-values, and vice versa. This relation has
been shown to be linear ($\log k^0 \propto E$) in several cases, for instance, for
multiple binding states [4.62] and continuously varied contamination
[4.63]. The explanation of this effect is not clear at present (for one
interpretation, see DEGRAS [4.64], who also lists more desorption
parameters); in some cases it might even be an artifact.

Finally, results of another kind will be mentioned. Several authors
[4.65–69] measured the angular distribution of hydrogen molecules
desorbing from metal surfaces, both after diffusion through the metal and
after deposition from a molecular beam. Strongly anisotropic distributions were observed, which were peaked in the surface normal up to the
9th power of the cosine of the angle to the surface normal. Recently,
BRADLEY et al. [4.67] showed conclusively that this behavior only
occurs with surfaces containing strongly bound impurity atoms; from
clean surfaces of Ni, Fe, Pt, and Nb, they obtained the expected cosine
distribution. The reason for the different behavior of contaminated
surfaces is not understood. One explanation for peaked distributions
could be that the two hydrogen atoms forming the desorbing molecule
have to move exactly in phase when leaving the surface, in order to be
successful; why such an effect should be enhanced by contamination,
is not clear. Another possibility is an activation barrier for adsorption
[4.67]. These investigations constitute the first step towards a differential
understanding of desorption. Extension to other systems and to energy
resolution besides angular resolution would be the desirable next step.
First experiments of this kind have been reported [4.52, 66]; non-
Maxwellian velocity distributions have been found.

4.1.4. Theories of Thermal Desorption

Some interpretational approaches to desorption kinetics have already
been mentioned above. Virtually all treatments try to retain essentially
the form of (4.2) as a starting point; in most cases m is set equal to 1 or 2,

corresponding to the true molecularity, and additional coverage-dependences are expressed in terms of changes of E and/or k^0. In most cases, E can be assumed to correspond to the adsorption energy plus the activation energy of adsorption for activated adsorption [see, however, the case of (4.7)]. The value of E is therefore essentially a static property, which has to be obtained from a quantum-mechanical theory of the ground state (see Chapter 2). The basic problem of kinetics concerns then the value of k^0.

The simplest approach already mentioned in the beginning and in the discussion of (4.10) assumes k^0 to be independent of N and T and, for unimolecular desorption, to be equal to the frequency of vibration of the adsorbed atoms perpendicular to the surface. While this treatment seems to meet with success for a considerable number of cases for which k_1^0 is between 10^{12} and 10^{13} sec^{-1}, this is a coincidence, as will become obvious from the following.

Most detailed analyses use the transition state theory developed mainly by EYRING [4.70]. This theory is widely applied in chemical kinetics and other transport theories; for its application to desorption, see (Ref. [4.2, p. 141]) and (Ref. [4.70, p. 347]). In this approach, one assumes the existence of a state of the system, called the activated complex, which corresponds to the critical configuration for reaction. Apart from a certain probability of reflection (described by the transmission factor κ), the transition state corresponds to the point of no return in the movement of the system towards reaction in configuration space. For activated reactions it corresponds to the saddle point on the energy hypersurface, but it can be shown that the existence of such a point is not necessary to make the treatment valid. The desorption rate is then given by

$$R_\mathrm{d} = \kappa \cdot N^{\pm} \cdot v^{\pm}, \tag{4.25}$$

where $N^{\pm}$ is the surface concentration of activated complexes and $v^{\pm}$ the frequency of their disintegration, which at least for unimolecular desorption can again be set equal to the frequency of vibration normal to the surface. The crucial assumption is that the transition state is in thermodynamic equilibrium with the reactants (apart from the degree of freedom corresponding to the reaction coordinate), so that the dimensionless equilibrium constant for its formation can be written for desorption as

$$K^{\pm} = (N^{\pm}/N_\mathrm{s})/(N^m/N_\mathrm{s}^m) = N^{\pm} \cdot N_\mathrm{s}^{m-1}/N^m$$
$$= (f^{\pm}/f^m) \exp(-E_0/RT), \tag{4.26}$$

where N_s is the number of sites per unit area.

The f's are the complete partition functions of transition state and adsorbate, respectively, after extraction of the zero-point energy difference E_0. If one extracts the critical degree of freedom from f^{+}, which leaves f_{+}, and replaces it by either a translation along the reaction coordinate or a fully excited vibration [4.70], comparison with (4.2) leads to

$$k_m^0 = \kappa \cdot (kT/h)(f_{+}/f^m) \cdot N_s^{1-m} . \tag{4.27}$$

As

$$K^{+} = \exp(-\Delta G_0^{+}/RT) = \exp[-(\Delta H_0^{+} - T\Delta S_0^{+})/RT], \tag{4.28}$$

where ΔH_0^{+}, ΔS_0^{+}, and ΔG_0^{+} are the changes of standard enthalpy, entropy and free enthalpy, respectively, of formation of the transition state, (4.27) is equivalent to

$$k_m^0 = \kappa(kT/h)N_s^{1-m} \exp(\Delta S_0^{+}/R) . \tag{4.29}$$

The meaning of "normal" k^0-values becomes obvious from this equation. Since $kT/h \simeq 2 \cdot 10^{12}$ to $2 \cdot 10^{13}$ sec^{-1} for the range 100–1000 K, $k_1^0 \approx kT/h \simeq 10^{13}$ sec^{-1} and $k_2^0 \simeq kT/h \cdot N_s \simeq 10^{-2}$ cm^2 sec^{-1} will be found, if $\kappa \approx 1$ and $f_{+}/f^m \approx 1$ (or $\Delta S^{+} \approx 0$). The latter implies identical localization or configurational complexity for reactants and transition state. If the transition state is much more mobile than the reactants, k^0 will be larger than normal; a factor of up to 10^4 can be understood in this way. This explanation has been invoked for the large k_1^0-value of Xe on W (111) (Table 4.2) [4.51]. The large k_1^0-values for desorption of O atoms and of tungsten oxides from W (Table 4.3) have been explained by the assumption of complicated reactant complexes, but simple activated complexes; this will also lead to $\Delta S^{+} \gg 0$ [4.59]. k^0-values below the normal ones must have the opposite meaning, i.e. a transition state which is less mobile or more complex than the reactants. Examples of calculations for different models are found, for instance, in [4.3, 59, 62, 71]; values up to 130 cal/K · mol have been obtained. Another possible explanation for very small k^0-values is a very small transmission factor [4.7, 8]. ARMAND et al. [4.72] have discussed the entropy changes in terms of the phonon properties of the surface. The coverage dependence of k^0 for detailed mechanisms can be evaluated statistically using the proper partition functions [4.3]; an interesting application has recently been given by GOYMOUR and KING [4.47].

For independent particle (first-order) desorption several other treatments have been developed. GOODMAN [4.73] has given a one-dimensional classical theory starting from Slater's theory of unimolecular decomposition [4.74]. He obtained k_1^0-values of the order of 10^{13} sec^{-1}

for several systems, in agreement with experimental results. In essence, this theory assumes an equilibrium distribution also.

This assumption is avoided in the "diffusion model" of chemical kinetics of KRAMERS [4.75] who used a classical Fokker-Planck equation for the movement of the representative point in phase-space for an analysis more general than that of EYRING. An important feature of this model is the coupling between the reactants and the heat bath (which in the case of desorption is the solid), which is represented by a friction coefficient η, equal to the inverse time constant for energy flow between heat bath and reactants. For intermediate η-values, the Eyring result is retained; for very high as well as very low η-values, compared to the characteristic frequencies, the pre-exponentials become much smaller than in the Eyring case, however. The physical meaning is that for low η, the coupling becomes so small that the rate-determining step becomes the energy transfer. In the usual treatment this could be accounted for by treating the energy transfer step as a separate step in the reaction sequence; the Boltzmann-distribution will then be essentially cut off at E_0. If η is large, even near the point of no return, the motion along the reaction coordinate is impeded, and low prefactors result, too.

SUHL and coworkers [4.76] have applied this treatment to surface reactions. They show that the coupling can contain contributions not only from phonons, but also from electrons; the latter will be strongest for metals. An estimate [4.77] suggests that under normal conditions both terms can be of comparable magnitude, but special conditions could lead to a predominance of one term, and also to an overall small coupling. Possibly some of the very low k_1^0 values in Table 4.2, which apply to weakly bound species, are due to very small η-values. SUHL [4.78] has also suggested that a strong change of k^0 could be expected under conditions of increased fluctuation amplitudes in the solid; this could, for instance, be the case near second-order phase transitions; he has cited some experimental evidence. Such effects could also be accounted for within transition state theory, but with a very small κ-value [4.7].

With a different diffusion approach, PAGNI and KECK [4.79] analyzed the time evolution of a non-equilibrium ensemble of adsorbed particles to obtain desorption kinetics. In that treatment, the two time constants of equilibration (energy transfer) and of relaxation of the surface population appear separately. They essentially find an Arrhenius equation with a slightly temperature-dependent prefactor, which leads to a compensation effect [4.61]. Their equations can fit a number of experimental results, but give an incorrect prediction for the case of Xe/W [4.51], for example.

The theoretical approaches discussed so far have all been basically classical treatments. Quantum mechanical approaches considering desorption due to phonon transfer from the solid to the bound adparticle have been given by Lennard-Jones and coworkers [4.80] and recently by Bendow and Ying [4.81]. The Lennard-Jones theory was limited to one dimension and to one-phonon processes, which leads to unrealistic results (Goodman [4.82]). Bendow and Ying give a three-dimensional theory including multi-phonon processes; their treatment can be used to extract energy and angular distributions of desorbing particles. It is only applicable to situations, however, where the desorbing particle leaves the surface in one jump, i.e. where there are no bound vibrational levels of the adsorbate. For Ne desorbing from a layer of Xe on graphite at low temperatures, they deduce a temperature-dependence of the rate according to an Arrhenius law; at higher temperatures deviations occur because of the Bose distribution of phonons. Strongly peaked energy distributions (around E_0) and angular distributions (around the surface normal) are found. The prefactor is calculated to be $\approx 10^5 \sec^{-1}$, which is of the order measured for some low temperature states (Table 4.2). Recently published results [4.52] for the desorption of He seem to agree with these predictions.

4.2. Electron Impact Desorption

Early reports about effects in ion gauges and mass spectrometer ion sources, which could only be explained by assuming that ions are emitted from surfaces under electron bombardment, were the first indication of this effect (for references see the reviews [4.83–86]). Closer investigation started in the early 60's: Moore [4.87] showed mass spectrometrically that O^+ ions are emitted from oxygen layers on Mo surfaces under electron impact and found a direct proportionality between electron and ion current over 7 orders of magnitudes; Redhead [4.88] investigated the energy distribution of the O^+ emission from oxygen and CO on Mo by total current measurements and derived total cross sections; Menzel and Gomer [4.89, 90] measured desorption cross sections for H, O, CO on W field emitters and used the effect for the differentiation between adsorption states. On the basis of these results, Redhead [4.88] and Menzel and Gomer [4.89] independently proposed a mechanism which was able to explain qualitatively and, in part, quantitatively all observations, and which seems to be generally accepted today. Since then, a large number of investigations has appeared on this effect [4.85, 91]. In the following we shall describe first the main experimental methods and procedures, then summarize the general experimental results and give some examples, and then discuss their theoretical explanation. It will become obvious that EID has a threefold importance: as a basic physical process, as a probe for the investigation of adsorbates and as a disturbing feature in other surface work and in vacuum technology.

4.2.1. Experimental Methods of EID and Evaluation of Data

Basically, two different approaches exist to the investigation of EID. The particles liberated from a surface by electron impact are either detected directly (without or with mass separation and energy and angular resolution), or some parameter connected with the surface coverage is monitored and the change induced by electron impact is deduced from its time dependence. Thus the total ion current liberated has been measured with a simple collector assembly and its energy distribution determined by retarding grids, e.g. [4.88, 92, 93]; mass analysis of the ion current with small magnetic or quadrupole spectrometers has been used by many authors ([4.87, 94–97] and others). By combining retarding potential analysis and mass spectrometry [4.98, 99], or by using more sophisticated analysers [4.100], mass and energy analyses of ions have been combined. Neutral desorption caused by electron impact has been detected from the pressure rise, monitored mass spectrometrically [4.95, 101]. The velocity of desorbed particles was measured recently by time of flight methods [4.102, 103]. The indirect methods have mostly used the work-function change coupled with adsorbate coverage, measured by field emission [4.90, 91, 104, 105] or other methods [4.106]. The change of Auger intensity [4.107], of the electron reflection coefficient [4.108], of LEED structures and intensities [4.109, 110], and the gas left on the surface, as detected by flash desorption [4.111], have also been utilized in this way.

All these investigations have shown that the data can be analysed in terms of isolated desorption processes, i.e. the rate of desorption is proportional to the number of impinging electrons per unit area and time, $\dot{n}_e$, and to the number of adsorbed particles per unit area, N_i, of the species concerned

$$-dN_i/dt = q_i \dot{n}_e N_i,$$ (4.30)

where the proportionality constant q_i is the total cross section of removal of species i (see Fig. 4.6). Equation (4.30) can be split up into contributions of the different desorbing species (various ions and neutrals) and other processes like conversion to another adsorbed state or decomposition, so that

$$-dN_i/dt = -\sum_k (dN_i/dt)_k = \dot{n}_e N_i \sum_k q_{ik},$$ (4.31)

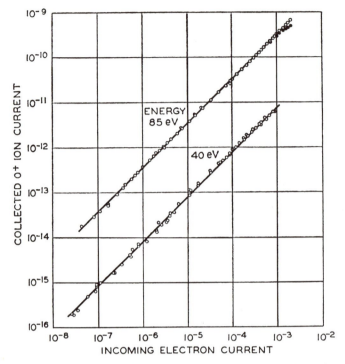

Fig. 4.6. Proportionality between electron current and EID ion signal for CO on Mo. (After [4.87])

where the q_{ik} are the partial cross sections for process k from state i. Equations (4.30) and (4.31) immediately suggest two basic uses:

a) If $\dot{n}_e$ is made large enough to change N_i measurably by EID ("high current mode"), then the time constant of this change can be used to measure the total cross section q_i. Because of the nature of (4.31), any quantity X related linearly to N_i can be used directly, for instance, the EID ion current or the work function:

$$N_i(t)/N_i(0) = X(t)/X(0) = \exp(-\dot{n}_e q t) = \exp(-i_e q t/\varepsilon),\qquad(4.32)$$

where ε is the electronic charge. The q_i-values given below have all been measured in this way (see Fig. 4.7).

b) If $\dot{n}_e$ is so small that N_i is essentially unchanged by EID ("low current mode"), the EID signal can be used to monitor the surface coverage during other processes (adsorption, thermal desorption etc.). This use of EID as a probe depends on the constancy of the q_{ik} within

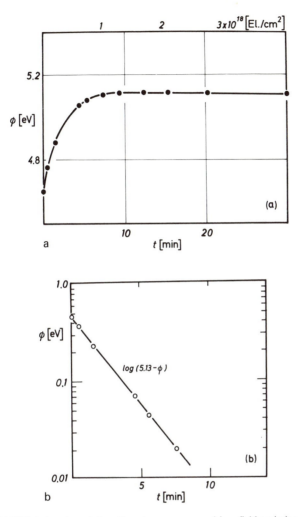

Fig. 4.7. (a) EID-induced work function change, measured in a field emission microscope, for removal of α-CO from W, and (b) plot according to (4.32). (After [4.90])

a given adsorbate state. q_{ik}-values cannot be measured as directly as q_i-values. The directly measured quantity is the desorption probability p_{ik} (number of particles per impinging electron), which is connected to q_{ik} via the coverage:

$$p_{ik} = \dot{n}_{ik}/\dot{n}_e = q_{ik} N_i .$$ (4.33)

Table 4.4. Some examples for EID products and cross sections

System	State	Product	Ionic cross section [cm^2]	Total cross section [cm^2]	Ref.
			(for 100 eV electrons)		
CO/W (poly)	virgin			$2\text{–}5\cdot10^{-19}$	[4.90]
	β			$5\text{–}8\cdot10^{-21}$	
	α			$3\cdot10^{-18}$	
CO/W (poly)	α_1/virgin	CO, CO$^+$	$4\text{–}8\cdot10^{-20}$	$4\text{–}8\cdot10^{-18}$	[4.95]
[mostly (100)]	α_2/β-prec.	CO, O$^+$	$5\cdot10^{-20}$	$1\cdot10^{-18}$	
	β	O$^+$		$<10^{-21}$	
CO/W (110)	physisorbed			10^{-16}	[4.114]
	virgin			$7\cdot10^{-17}$	
	α			10^{-16}	
	β-prec.			$2\cdot10^{-17}$ $-2\cdot10^{-18}$	
	β			$<10^{-21}$	
H$_2$/W (poly)	1			$4\cdot10^{-20}$	[4.89]
	2			$5\cdot10^{-21}$	
H$_2$/W (poly)	β_2	H$^+$	$2\text{–}6\cdot10^{-23}$	$5\cdot10^{-19}$	[4.115, 116]
	β_1	H$^+$	$<10^{-25}$		[4.116]
	κ (on CO)	H$^+$, H$_2$	$8\cdot10^{-20}$	$1.2\cdot10^{-16}$	[4.8]
H$_2$/W (110)	β_2	H$^+$	$5\cdot10^{-22}$	$<1.4\cdot10^{-18}$	[4.117]
O$_2$/W (poly)	1			$4.5\cdot10^{-19}$	[4.89]
	2			$<2\cdot10^{-21}$	
O$_2$/W (110)	1	O$^+$	$3\cdot10^{-20}$	$3\cdot10^{-18}$ $-7\cdot10^{-19}$	[4.97]
O$_2$/W (100)		O$^+$		$2\cdot10^{-18}$ $-4\cdot10^{-19}$	[4.118]

4.2.2. Experimental Results

Most work to date has been concerned with adsorption layers on metals, although some papers on other solids have also been published (see the compilation in [4.85]). The main findings which have been obtained using the methods described are:

1) Impact of electrons with energy above about 10 eV often liberates ions and neutrals from adsorbed layers. The ionic contribution is only a few percent or less. Emission of excited neutrals has also been observed [4.92, 103].

2) The total and partial cross sections are usually much smaller than those of similar processes in molecules (excitation, ionization, dissociation). While the latter are typically between 10^{-16} and 10^{-15} cm^2 for 100 eV electrons [4.112], EID cross sections mostly lie between 10^{-17} and 10^{-22} cm^2. Exceptions to both limits are known.

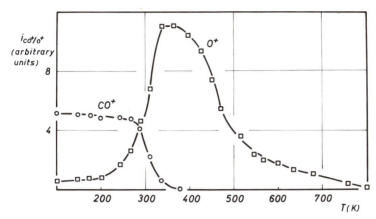

Fig. 4.8. EID of CO^+ and O^+ from CO on W as a function of temperature (low current mode). The two ionic species have been ascribed to emission from two substates of α-CO, whose populations can thus be probed. (After [4.95])

3) For different binding states of the same particle on the same surface, the q_i can be very different (e.g. for different states of CO on W, values between 10^{-17} and 10^{-21} cm^2, and for hydrogen on W, values between 10^{-23} and 10^{-16} cm^2 have been measured; see Table 4.4). In general they tend to be large for weakly adsorbed states and smaller for more strongly bound ones, although there are exceptions. For metallic adlayers, the q_i are immeasurably small ($< 10^{-23}$ cm^2). Co-adsorption also has a strong influence [4.8, 105, 119–121].

The different binding states can also be characterized by EID of different particles. For instance, the weakly bound α-state of CO on W (see Chapter 3 and Section 4.1) was demonstrated by EID to consist of two substates, one of which emits CO^+ ions and the other O^+ ions ([4.95]; for a different interpretation see [4.114]), which can be inter-converted by heating, as shown by EID in the low current mode (Fig. 4.8). This behavior was originally found on polycrystalline ribbons and has recently been reproduced on W (100) [4.122] and also (110) [4.114]; weakly adsorbed CO on other metals shows similar behavior [4.123, 124].

4) Besides desorption, electron impact can also cause a break-up of molecular adsorbates and conversions from one adsorbate state to another. For instance, EID of adsorbed CO leads to carbon or oxygen deposition, as has been shown by field emission microscopy [4.90], LEED [4.125] and Auger spectroscopy [4.126]. The two α-substates of CO on W can be interconverted by electron impact [4.95, 114, 122] (see Fig. 4.9); the minimum energy required for this conversion seems to be equal to that for neutral desorption [4.95].

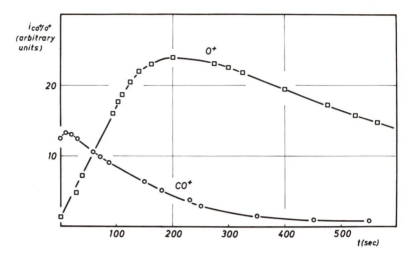

Fig. 4.9. EID of CO$^+$ and O$^+$ from CO on W at 100 K as a function of bombardment time (high current mode). The conversion is seen to be induced by electron impact also. (After 4.95])

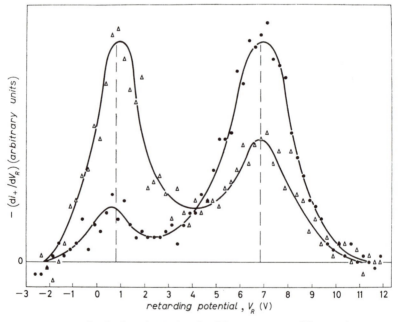

Fig. 4.10. Energy distribution of EID ions for CO on W at two different substrate temperatures (● 300 K; △ 195 K). (After [4.93])

5) EID ions have energies between 0 and ~10 eV. The energy distribution can usually be represented approximately by Gaussian peaks with half widths between 2 and 4 eV. Multiple peak structures have been observed, which were explained by contributions from different coexisting adsorption states [4.92, 93]. For instance, the energy distributions shown in Fig. 4.10 have been found for CO on W for different conditions, which can be correlated to the substates mentioned in 3) and 4) and have been shown to correspond to CO^+ (low kinetic energy peak) and O^+ (high kinetic energy peak) emission [4.93].

6) There are strong isotope effects in the q-values in the sense that higher mass isotopes have smaller q; the effect increases with decreasing q [4.97, 127]. Temperature effects have also been reported [4.128–130].

7) The threshold energies, i.e. the minimum electron energies required for EID, seem to be lower for neutral than for ionic desorption [4.131], although some disagreement exists here [4.132]. For a discussion of the values of ionic thresholds, see e.g. [4.132]. The cross sections have no maxima around 100 eV as for isolated molecules, but keep rising slowly even above a few hundred eV [4.132]; this is probably due to the contribution of secondary electrons to EID [4.133].

These results can be understood in terms of the mechanism developed by REDHEAD [4.88] and MENZEL and GOMER [4.89], which will be discussed next.

4.2.3. Theory of EID

It is easy to show that elastic energy transfer by collisions between electrons and nuclei cannot be responsible for EID [4.89], so that electronic excitations must be the cause. Starting from the normal concepts of electron impact excitation of molecules and of essentially localized adsorbate bonds, the following two-step mechanism has been developed:

1) The adsorbate complex can be characterized by potential curves, as shown in Fig. 4.11. Electron impact causes a Franck-Condon transition from the ground state G to an excited state (repulsive or excited neutral, or ionic state). The cross section for this primary excitation is about that of comparable transitions in molecules. After this transition, the particle (ion or neutral) starts to move away from the surface.

2) During this movement, a recapture process can occur, which transfers the excitation energy into the solid and brings the particle back into this or another ground state (if multiple binding states exist). In the case of ionic desorption this recapturing transition can be approximated by a simple tunneling process (resonance or Auger, depending on the relative situation of the energy levels) of an electron from the

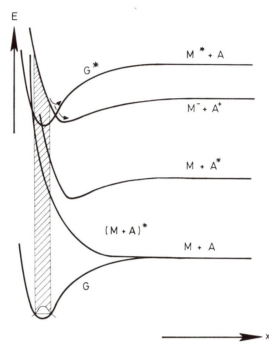

Fig. 4.11. Potential energy diagrams for an adsorbate system. [G: adsorbed ground state. $M^- + A^+$: ionic state. $(M + A)^*$: antibonding state. $M + A^*$: excited state of the adsorbate. $M^* + A$: Adsorbate ground state with excitation energy in the metal (vertically shifted replica of G).] The vibrational distribution in G and resulting ESD ion energy distribution is indicated.

solid into the hole created in the adsorbate complex. If this retunneling occurs after the moving ion has acquired a higher kinetic energy than necessary to surmount the ground state binding energy, neutralization without recapture will occur, so that a neutral particle desorbs. For neutral excitation the process is somewhat more complicated.

Qualitatively this model explains all the results mentioned above. The energy distribution of desorbing ions can be understood as a reflection of the vibrational distribution of the ground state at the ionic curve, skewed by the recapture process; different ground state curves will then lead to different peak energies. The small cross sections point to a high efficiency of the recapture processes, which can be understood in terms of the high density of states in the solid, and of a high transparency of the surface barrier. The unmeasurably small q_i of metallic adsorbates are understandable from the nature of the bond which is assumed to be due to essentially delocalized electrons, i.e. a strongly decreased surface barrier between solid and adparticle, so that tunneling is especially fast. Desorbing neutrals can be created both by direct excitation to an antibonding curve and by neutralization without recapture. Since the treatment below shows that the latter alone leads to more neutral than ionic desorption, the preponderance of neutrals is explained. The first mechanism must also exist, as shown by the existence of neutral EID below the ionic threshold.

The differences of the q_{ik}-values for different adsorbate states are then due to the strong (to first-order exponential) dependence of the recapture rate on the height and width of the barrier between solid and adsorbate. In a one-dimensional model, this should lead to increasing q_{ik} for decreasing bond strength, as the bond length should increase in the same direction, and a variation of the barrier height in the opposite direction is improbable. The true process will be three-dimensional, however; a different variation of total tunneling rate and adsorption energy is then easily envisaged. Such an effect has been invoked for the reverse order of q_i for β_1 and β_2 hydrogen on tungsten [4.116]; it is one of the possible reasons for the very interesting recent finding of strongly peaked angular distributions of EID ions (CZYZEWSKI et al. [4.134]). Since the total tunneling probability depends on the time the particle spends close to the surface after excitation, i.e. on its velocity and therefore its mass, a strong isotope effect is also expected. An increase of q_i with temperature can be understood in terms of population of other vibrational levels leading to an increase of the tunneling distance [4.128].

The quantitative one-dimensional formulation of these ideas [4.88, 89] leads to the following formulae. From a consideration of the ion flux *not* recaptured between excitation and total removal from the surface, the probability of desorption of an ion after excitation is given by

$$P_I(x) = \exp\left\{-\int_{x_0}^{\infty} R(x)\,dx/v(x)\right\}$$

$$= \exp\left\{-m^{1/2}\int_{x_0}^{\infty} R(x)\,dx/[2U(x_0)-2U(x)]^{1/2}\right\},$$

(4.34)

where x is the distance from the surface and x_0 the equilibrium distance in the ground state, $R(x)$ is the tunneling probability as a function of distance x, and $v(x)$ the particle velocity, and $U(x)$ the repulsive potential. Similarly the total probability of desorption after ionic excitation is found by integrating the same formula between x_0 and a critical distance x_c which corresponds to the point at which the kinetic energy of the moving ion $(= U(x_0) - U(x_c))$ is equal to the adsorption energy.

Evaluation of the equations using

$$R(x) = A\exp(-ax)$$

(4.35)

and

$$U(x) = B \exp(-bx), \tag{4.36}$$

i.e. a normal exponential tunneling law and a Born-Mayer repulsive potential, showed semi-quantitatively the correct order of magnitude of the important effects (influence of change of x_0, preponderance of neutrals) [4.89].

The best test of this mechanism is the isotope effect, which should be governed by the appearance of $m^{1/2}$ in the exponential (4.34). Indeed, the experimental values obtained for $^{16}O/^{18}O$ ($q_{16}/q_{18} = 1.5$ [4.97]) and for different states of hydrogen on W (q_1/q_2 between 5 and 150 [4.115, 117, 127]) agree very well with this prediction.

This last finding is the strongest argument against another mechanism proposed by ZINGERMAN and ISHCHUK [4.106] who found periodic maxima and minima in the dependence of q on electron energy on single crystal faces and explained this by the assumption that the primary excitation occurs inside the metal and Bragg reflection decreases the number of these inelastic events. This mechanism cannot explain most of the other points listed above and is therefore probably not applicable.

Very recently, a quantum-mechanical treatment of ionic EID has been developed by BRENIG [4.135]. The process is not taken apart into two steps, but treated as a whole, and the quantum effects in the motion of the escaping particle are considered. This is accomplished by the use of a complex potential, whose imaginary, absorptive part takes care of recapture; the distorted-wave Born approximation is used. The treatment contains the classical two-step mechanism outlined above as the limiting case for large masses, as quantum effects then disappear. For smaller masses, it leads to a decreased overall tunneling rate, as compared to the classical case, as the wave packet representing the particle is distorted by the action of the imaginary potential and has a finite starting velocity in x_0. The isotope effect is unchanged, however.

4.2.4. Practical Importance of EID

This discussion was intended to show the different aspects of EID. EID can provide interesting insights into the nature of electronic levels of adsorbates and excitation and de-excitation processes involving them, because it entails such transitions and the transfer of electrons and energy across the surface barrier. It can therefore be used to test our concepts of these entities. It can further provide a probe for the differentiation and detailed investigation of complex adsorbate systems because of the approximate constancy of cross sections within one state and the large differences between different states. This last property, on the other hand, makes EID quite useless as a general surface analysis method and a tool for cleaning surfaces. It has some other important practical aspects, however. Since low energy electrons constitute *the* favorite probe for surface investigations because of their small mean free path in solids and the consequent high surface specificity (LEED, Auger spectroscopy, electron energy loss spectroscopy), it can cause disturbances in such measurements [4.136] which must be understood in order to be avoided. Since slow electrons are used in many vacuum systems (ion gauges, mass spectrometers) and other apparatus (accelerators, plasma machines), EID can be a disturbing effect in their operation, too [4.83, 137]; this can be very troublesome and is difficult to predict because of the possible large differences of cross sections, depending on circumstances.

4.3. Photodesorption

This short chapter is only concerned with photodesorption resulting from direct excitation of the adsorbate complex by light, i.e. effects which parallel those discussed for electron impact in Section 4.2. The discussion is therefore limited to metals, since the strong effects of illumination on adsorption and desorption from semiconductors and insulators are probably due to absorption of photons by the solid and subsequent transport of the excitation to the surface proper, so that the process is largely not a surface process. For a discussion of these effects, the reader is referred to [4.138].

Photodesorption from metals is a somewhat controversial subject. Some authors have reported clear-cut effects of various magnitude for CO on Ni [4.139–144], W [4.141, 145, 146], and other metals [4.143], while others have ascribed all effects to thermal desorption caused by heating of the metal by the light beam [4.147, 148]. Exclusion of such effects is not as easy as in EID, as in all these cases the photon energy was not sufficient to cause ionic desorption, and neutrals only were desorbed. Arguments were given, however, to support the electronic nature of photodesorption, at least for CO on W [4.146] and on stainless steel [4.149]. Comparison with neutral EID for CO/W [4.131] suggests that basically the same processes take place in the two cases. For the pure metals, the yields are quite small (less than 10^{-7} molecules/photon in the range up to 6 eV); much larger values (above 10^{-3}) were found on stainless steel [4.149]. The measurement of high energy photodesorption, ionic and neutral, by the use of synchrotron radiation [4.150] would be worth-while both in connection with EID and in view of the importance of possible PD-effects in photoelectron spectroscopy of adsorbates, for electron accelerators [4.151], plasma machines and fusion reactor design [4.83].

Another interesting aspect is the possibility that interstellar molecules are produced by photodesorption from interstellar dust grains [4.152].

4.4. Ion Impact Desorption

The impact of ions or fast neutrals (including neutrons) can either knock off adsorbates directly by momentum transfer to them, or can induce collision cascades inside the solid which, after reflection back to the surface, can push off the adsorbate particles as the last member of the collision chain. These processes are essentially the same as sputtering of substrate material and contain large contributions from the bulk properties; the reader is referred to the papers in [4.153]. Besides their use for cleaning surfaces, these processes are important in Secondary Ion Mass Spectrometry [4.154] of adsorbate layers, as a disturbing effect in Ion Surface Scattering [4.155], for ion pumps [4.83], and for the wall problem of plasma machines and fusion reactor design [4.156]. An important question in this connection is the ionisation and excitation of the sputtered particles [4.157]. Conversely, the de-excitation of impinging ions or excited neutrals causes the emission of electrons or can lead to direct excitation of surface species, which in turn can lead to processes similar to those observed in EID. Few investigations of IID as confined to well-defined adsorbate layers and separated from normal sputtering, have become known so far [4.158].

4.5. Field Desorption

Desorption of adsorbed species under the action of very high electrostatic fields (of the order of 10^8 V/cm) was first observed by MÜLLER [4.159] and then by INGHRAM and GOMER [4.160]. As shown by subsequent work, the breaking of the surface bond occurs via a transition from the ground state to the field deformed ionic state. The basic process taking place is similar to field ionization [4.161], and can be understood from Fig. 4.12, which shows schematically the situation for a covalently bound, electronegative adsorbate ($I - \phi$ large). The presence of a strong electric field with positive polarity on the metal bends down the ionic curve so far that it would intersect the ground state curve, which to first approximation (i.e. neglecting polarization effects) is unaffected. Instead of inter-

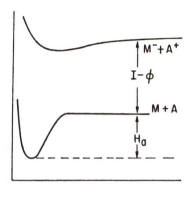
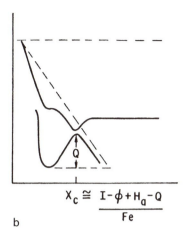

$$X_c \cong \frac{I - \phi + H_a - Q}{Fe}$$

a   b

Fig. 4.12a and b. Potential curves for field ionization of a covalently bound adsorbate.
(a) Field-free case; ground state and ionic state. (b) Under high-field condition. The ionic
curve is bent down; its intersection with the ground state curve produces a Schottky saddle.
(After [4.167])

secting, the two curves separate, of course. An adiabatic transition from
the bound $(M + A)$ state to the free ion is then possible, if the activation
energy Q (which is smaller than the thermal desorption energy) is
available. If the field gets very high, the saddle can disappear altogether;
tunneling through the barrier is also possible in some cases. In the case
of small $I - \phi$, i.e. for ionic or polar bonding of metallic adsorbates, the
applied electric field causes the ionic curve to be the lowest everywhere,
and FD can again occur. In principle the same process, but at higher field
because of the higher energies involved, can occur with the surface atoms
of the substrate proper, and is then called field evaporation [4.161].
Both field desorption and evaporation are extensively used to clean field
emitters [4.161]. Mass analysis of the desorbing species can be carried
out in mass spectrometers [4.162] for the investigation of surface compounds [4.163]; the most sophisticated version is the "atom-probe",
which has atomic spatial resolution by combination with a field ion
microscope [4.164]. As the decisive parameters Q and x_c are clearly
connected to the shape of the potential curves, measurements of FD
can be used to derive the latter, e.g. [4.165]; the ground state desorption
energy can be derived from determination of the conditions for $Q = 0$
[4.166]. One problem in these cases is that the products can be complex
and have high charge states. The analysis then becomes difficult. The
theory of field desorption has largely been developed by GOMER [4.167].

Enhancement effects on FD by the presence of field-ionizing inert gas atoms have been observed and can be explained by EID caused by the electrons liberated in the field ionization [4.168]. Adsorbed particles, on the other hand, can enhance the field evaporation of substrate atoms.

4.6. Conclusion

The field of desorption studies is seen to be interwoven with many aspects of adsorption studies in general, theoretical, experimental, and practical. While the physical mechanisms are not yet clearly understood in all cases and the experimental data still contain many uncertainties, the problems are now reasonably well defined; the experimental methods, though far from flawless, promise significant results, and the theoretical approaches become less dependent on doubtful assumptions. Important developments can, therefore, be expected in the near future, as for the general field of surface physics.

References

4.1.   See, for instance, K. J. Laidler: *Reaction Kinetics,* Vols. 1 + 2 (Pergamon Press, New York, 1963).

4.2.   R. Gomer: *Chemisorption* (to be published in the series *Solid State Physics,* Academic Press).

4.3.   D. O. Hayward, B. M. W. Trapnell: *Chemisorption* (Butterworths, London, 1964).

4.4.   G. E. Moore, F. C. Unterwald: J. Chem. Phys. **40**, 2639 (1964); and references therein.

4.5.   E. A. Guggenheim: Phil. Mag. **2**, 538 (1926);
       W. E. Rosevaere: J. Am. Chem. Soc. **53**, 1651 (1931);
       J. M. Sturtevant: J. Am. Chem. Soc. **59**, 699 (1937).

4.6.   C. Kohrt, R. Gomer: J. Chem. Phys. **52**, 3283 (1970).

4.7.   L. A. Pétermann: In *Adsorption – Desorption Phenomena,* ed. by F. Ricca (Academic Press, London, 1972), p. 227.

4.8.   W. Jelend, D. Menzel: Surface Sci. **42**, 485 (1974).

4.9.   H. A. Engelhardt, D. Menzel (to be published).

4.10. P. W. Tamm, L. D. Schmidt: J. Chem. Phys. **51**, 5352 (1969).

4.11. J. Frenkel: Z. Physik **26**, 117 (1924).

4.12. F. L. Hughes, H. Levinstein: Phys. Rev. **113**, 1029 (1959); and references therein.

4.13. J. B. Hudson, J. S. Sandejas: J. Vac. Sci. Technol. **4**, 230 (1967).

4.14. J. Perel, R. H. Vernon, H. L. Daley: J. Appl. Phys. **36**, 2157 (1965).

4.15. M. D. Scheer, J. Fine: J. Chem. Phys. **37**, 107 (1962); **38**, 307 (1963).

4.16. M. D. Scheer, R. Klein, J. D. McKinley: In *Adsorption – Desorption Phenomena,* ed. by F. Ricca (Academic Press, London, 1972), p. 169.

4.17. J. N. Smith, Jr., J. Wolleswinkel, J. Los: Surface Sci. **22**, 411 (1970).

4.18. A. Y. Cho, C. D. Hendricks: J. Appl. Phys. **40**, 3339 (1969).

4.19. J. B. Hudson, C. M. Lo: Surface Sci. **36**, 141 (1973).

4.20. R. J. Madix, J. M. Schwarz: Surface Sci. **24**, 264 (1971).

4.21. G. Ehrlich: J. Appl. Phys. **32**, 4 (1961).

4.22. P. A. REDHEAD: Vacuum **12**, 203 (1962).
4.23. F. URBACH: Sitzgsber. Akad. Wiss. Wien, Math.-Naturw. Kl., Abt. IIa; **139**, 363 (1930).
4.24. R. J. CVETANOVIC, Y. AMENOMIYA: Advan. Catalysis **17**, 103 (1967).
4.25. G. CARTER: Vacuum **12**, 245 (1962).
4.26. G. EHRLICH: Advan. Catalysis **14**, 256 (1963).
4.27. C. KOHRT, R. GOMER: Surface Sci. **24**, 77 (1971).
4.28. E. LÜSCHER: Annals N.Y. Acad. Sci. **101**, 816 (1963); P. GODWIN, E. LÜSCHER: Surface Sci. **3**, 42 (1965).
4.29. B. MCCARROLL: J. Appl. Phys. **40**, 1 (1969).
4.30. J. P. HOBSON, J. W. EARNSHAW: J. Vac. Sci. Technol. **4**, 257 (1967).
4.31. L. A. PÉTERMANN: In *Progress in Surface Science*, Vol. 3/1 (Pergamon Press, Oxford, 1973), p. 1.
4.32. R. L. GERLACH, T. N. RHODIN: Surface Sci. **19**, 403 (1970).
4.33. T. E. MADEY, J. T. YATES, JR.: *Structure et Propriétes des Surfaces des Solides*, Coll. CNRS No. 187, Paris 1970, p. 155.
4.34. P. A. REDHEAD: Trans. Faraday Soc. **57**, 641 (1961).
4.35. L. D. SCHMIDT: In *Adsorption – Desorption Phenomena*, ed. by F. RICCA (Academic Press, London, 1972), p. 341.
4.36. C. PISANI, G. RABINO, F. RICCA: Surface Sci. **41**, 277 (1974).
4.37. J. T. YATES, JR., T. E. MADEY: Surface Sci. **28**, 437 (1971).
4.38. W. L. WINTERBOTTOM: J. Vac. Sci. Technol. **9**, 936 (1972).
4.39. L. R. CLAVENNA, L. D. SCHMIDT: Surface Sci. **33**, 11 (1972).
4.40. T. E. MADEY, J. T. YATES, JR.: J. Chem. Phys. **44**, 1675 (1966).
4.41. L. R. CLAVENNA, L. D. SCHMIDT: Surface Sci. **22**, 365 (1970).
4.42. P. T. DAWSON, Y. K. PENG: Surface Sci. **33**, 565 (1972).
4.43. L. J. RIGBY: Can. J. Phys. **42**, 1256 (1964).
4.44. C. G. GOYMOUR, D. A. KING: J. Chem. Soc. Faraday I, **69**, 736 (1973).
4.45. M. P. HILL: Trans. Faraday Soc. **66**, 1246 (1970).
4.46. T. TOYA: J. Vac. Sci. Technol. **9**, 890 (1972).
4.47. C. G. GOYMOUR, D. A. KING: J. Chem. Soc. Faraday I, **69**, 749 (1973).
4.48. D. L. ADAMS: Surface Sci. **42**, 12 (1974).
4.49. J. R. ARTHUR, A. Y. CHO: Surface Sci. **36**, 641 (1973).
4.50. D. A. KING, T. E. MADEY, J. T. YATES, JR.: J. Chem. Phys. **55**, 3236 (1971).
4.51. M. J. DRESSER, T. E. MADEY, J. T. YATES, JR.: Surface Sci. **42**, 533 (1974).
4.52. S. A. COHEN, J. G. KING: Phys. Rev. Letters **31**, 703 (1973).
4.53. J. F. ANTONINI: Nuovo Cimento Suppl. **5**, 354 (1967).
4.54. P. W. TAMM, L. D. SCHMIDT: J. Chem. Phys. **54**, 4775 (1971).
4.55. V. J. MIMEAULT, R. S. HANSEN: J. Chem. Phys. **45**, 2240 (1966).
4.56. K. F. POULTER, J. A. PRYDE: J. Phys. D **1**, 169 (1968).
4.57. H. R. HAN, L. D. SCHMIDT: J. Phys. Chem. **75**, 227 (1971).
4.58. J. LAPUJOULADE, K. S. NEIL: J. Chem. Phys. **57**, 3535 (1972).
4.59. C. G. GOYMOUR, D. A. KING: J. Chem. Soc. Faraday I, **68**, 280 (1972).
4.60. B. WEBER, J. FUSY, A. CASSUTO: J. Chim. Phys. **66**, 708 (1969).
4.61. F. H. CONSTABLE: Proc. Roy. Soc. A **108**, 355 (1925); E. CREMER: Advan. Catalysis **7**, 75 (1955).
4.62. J. LAPUJOULADE: Nuovo Cimento Suppl. **5**, 433 (1967); A. K. MAZUMDAR, H. W. WASSMUTH: Surface Sci. **30**, 617 (1972).
4.63. R. MÜLLER, H. W. WASSMUTH: Surface Sci. **34**, 249 (1973).
4.64. D. A. DEGRAS: Nuovo Cimento Suppl. **5**, 420 (1967).
4.65. W. VAN WILLIGEN: Phys. Letters **28** A, 80 (1968).
4.66. A. E. DABIRI, T. J. LEE, R. E. STICKNEY: Surface Sci. **26**, 522 (1971).

4.67. T. L. Bradley, A. E. Dabiri, R. E. Stickney: Surface Sci. **29**, 590 (1972);
       T. L. Bradley, R. E. Stickney: Surface Sci. **38**, 313 (1973).
4.68. R. L. Palmer, J. N. Smith, Jr., H. Saltsburg, D. R. O'Keefe: J. Chem. Phys. **53**, 1666 (1970).
4.69. J. N. Smith, R. L. Palmer: J. Chem. Phys. **56**, 13 (1972).
4.70. S. Glasstone, K. J. Laidler, H. Eyring: *The Theory of Rate Processes* (McGraw-Hill, New York-London, 1941).
4.71. S. Kruyer: Proc. K. Nederl. Akad. Wet. B **58**, 73 (1955).
4.72. G. Armand, P. Masri, L. Dobrzynski: J. Vac. Sci. Technol. **9**, 705 (1972).
4.73. F. O. Goodman: Surface Sci. **5**, 283 (1966).
4.74. N. B. Slater: Proc. Roy. Soc. A **194**, 112 (1948).
4.75. H. A. Kramers: Physica **7**, 284 (1940).
4.76. E. G. d'Agliano, W. L. Schaich, P. Kumar, H. Suhl: In *Collective Properties of Physical Systems,* 24th Nobel Symposium 1973, p. 200 (Academic Press, New York-London, 1974).
4.77. E. G. d'Agliano, P. Kumar, W. Schaich, H. Suhl: To be published.
4.78. H. Suhl, J. H. Smith, P. Kumar: Phys. Rev. Letters **25**, 1442 (1970);
       H. Suhl: To be published.
4.79. P. J. Pagni, J. C. Keck: J. Chem. Phys. **58**, 1162 (1973);
       P. J. Pagni: J. Chem. Phys. **58**, 2940 (1973).
4.80. J. E. Lennard-Jones, C. Strachan: Proc. Roy. Soc. A **150**, 442 (1935);
       J. E. Lennard-Jones, A. F. Devonshire: Proc. Roy. Soc. A **156**, 6, 29 (1936).
4.81. B. Bendow, S. C. Ying: J. Vac. Sci. Technol. **9**, 804 (1972); Phys. Rev. B **7**, 622 (1973);
       S. C. Ying, B. Bendow: Phys. Rev. B **7**, 637 (1973).
4.82. F. O. Goodman: Surface Sci. **24**, 667 (1971).
4.83. P. A. Redhead, J. P. Hobson, E. V. Kornelsen: *The Physical Basis of Ultrahigh Vacuum* (Chapman and Hall, London, 1968).
4.84. D. Menzel: Angew. Chem. Intern. Edit. **9**, 255 (1970).
4.85. T. E. Madey, J. T. Yates, Jr.: J. Vac. Sci. Technol. **8**, 525 (1971).
4.86. J. H. Leck, B. P. Stimpson: J. Vac. Sci. Technol. **9**, 293 (1972).
4.87. G. E. Moore: J. Appl. Phys. **32**, 1241 (1961).
4.88. P. A. Redhead: Canad. J. Phys. **42**, 886 (1964).
4.89. D. Menzel, R. Gomer: J. Chem. Phys. **41**, 3311 (1964).
4.90. D. Menzel, R. Gomer: J. Chem. Phys. **41**, 3329 (1964).
4.91. D. Menzel: Surface Sci. **47**, 384 (1975).
4.92. P. A. Redhead: Nuovo Cimento Suppl. **5**, 586 (1967).
4.93. J. T. Yates, Jr., T. E. Madey, J. K. Payn: Nuovo Cimento Suppl. **5**, 558 (1967).
4.94. D. Lichtman, R. B. McQuistan, T. R. Kirst: Surface Sci. **5**, 120 (1966).
4.95. D. Menzel: Ber. Bunsenges. Phys. Chem. **72**, 591 (1968).
4.96. D. R. Sandstrom, J. H. Leck, E. E. Donaldson: J. Chem. Phys. **48**, 5683 (1968).
4.97. T. E. Madey, J. T. Yates, Jr., D. A. King, C. J. Uhlaner: J. Chem. Phys. **52**, 5215 (1970).
4.98. J. W. Coburn: Surface Sci. **11**, 61 (1968).
4.99. T. E. Madey, J. T. Yates, Jr.: J. Vac. Sci. Technol. **8**, 39 (1971).
4.100. M. Nishijima, F. M. Propst: J. Vac. Sci. Technol. **7**, 420 (1971).
4.101. L. A. Pétermann: Nuovo Cimento Suppl. **1**, 601 (1963).
4.102. R. Clampitt, L. Gowland: Nature **228**, 141 (1970).
4.103. I. G. Newsham, D. R. Sandstrom: J. Vac. Sci. Technol. **10**, 39 (1973).
4.104. W. Ermrich: Nuovo Cimento Suppl. **5**, 582 (1967).
4.105. C. J. Bennette, L. W. Swanson: J. Appl. Phys. **39**, 2749 (1968).

4.106. YA. P. ZINGERMANN, V. A. ISHCHUK: Fiz. tverdogo Tela **7**, 227 (1965); and **9**, 3347 (1967); [Soviet Physics Solid State **7**, 173 (1965); and **9**, 2638 (1968)].

4.107. R. G. MUSKET: Surface Sci. **21**, 440 (1970).

4.108. D. A. Degras, J. LECANTE: Nuovo Cimento Suppl. **5**, 598 (1967).

4.109. J. ANDERSON, P. J. ESTRUP: Surface Sci. **9**, 463 (1968); T. N. TAYLOR, P. J. ESTRUP: J. Vac. Sci. Techn. **10**, 26 (1973).

4.110. T. E. MADEY, D. MENZEL: Jap. J. Appl. Phys. Suppl. 2, pt. 2, 229 (1974).

4.111. J. T. YATES, JR., T. E. MADEY: In *Structure and Chemistry of Solid Surfaces,* ed. by G. A. SOMORJAI (Wiley, New York, 1969), p. 59-1.

4.112. H. S. W. MASSEY, E. H. S. BURHOP: *Electronic and Ionic Impact Phenomena*, Vols. 1 and 2. (Oxford University Press, 1969).

4.113. J. T. YATES, D. A. KING: Surface Sci. **38**, 114 (1973).

4.114. M. VASS, C. LEUNG, R. GOMER: To be published.

4.115. T. E. MADEY: Surface Sci. **36**, 281 (1973).

4.116. W. JELEND, D. MENZEL: Surface Sci. **40**, 295 (1973).

4.117. D. A. KING, D. MENZEL: Surface Sci. **40**, 399 (1973).

4.118. T. E. MADEY: Surface Sci. **33**, 355 (1972).

4.119. G. RETTINGHAUS, W. HUBER: J. Vac. Sci. Technol. **7**, 289 (1970).

4.120. W. P. GILBREATH, D. E. WILSON: J. Vac. Sci. Technol. **8**, 45 (1971).

4.121. D. P. WILLIAMS, R. P. H. GASSER: J. Vac. Sci. Technol. **8**, 49 (1971).

4.122. J. T. YATES, D. A. KING: Surface Sci. **32**, 479 (1972).

4.123. P. R. DAVIS, E. E. DONALDSON, D. R. SANDSTROM: Surface Sci. **34**, 177 (1973).

4.124. R. R. FORD, D. LICHTMAN: Surface Sci. **25**, 537 (1971).

4.125. H. H. MADDEN, J. KÜPPERS, G. ERTL: J. Chem. Phys. **58**, 3401 (1973).

4.126. J. P. COAD, H. E. BISHOP, J. C. RIVIÈRE: Surface Sci. **21**, 253 (1970); J. M. MARTINEZ, J. B. HUDSON: J. Vac. Sci. Technol. **10**, 35 (1973).

4.127. W. JELEND, D. MENZEL: Chem. Phys. Letters **21**, 178 (1973).

4.128. D. MENZEL: Surface Sci. **14**, 340 (1969).

4.129. E. N. KUTSENKO: Zh. Tekhn. Fiz. **39**, 942 (1969). [Sov. Phys.-Techn. Phys. **14**, 706 (1969)].

4.130. T. E. MADEY, J. T. YATES, JR.: J. Chem. Phys. **51**, 1264 (1969).

4.131. D. MENZEL, P. KRONAUER, W. JELEND: Ber. Bunsenges. Phys. Chem. **75**, 1074 (1971); D. MENZEL: J. Vac. Sci. Technol. **4**, 810 (1972).

4.132. M. NISHIJIMA, F. M. PROPST: Phys. Rev. B **2**, 2368 (1970).

4.133. R. M. LAMBERT, C. M. COMRIE: Surface Sci. **38**, 197 (1973).

4.134. J. J. CZYZEWSKI, T. E. MADEY, J. T. YATES, JR.: Phys. Rev. Letters **32**, 777 (1974).

4.135. W. BRENIG: Z. Physik, to be published.

4.136. D. MENZEL: Surface Sci. **3**, 424 (1965).

4.137. P. A. REDHEAD: J. Vac. Sci. Technol. **7**, 182 (1970).

4.138. K. HAUFFE, S. R. MORRISON: *Adsorption* (De Gruyter, Berlin, 1974), p. 88, and references therein.

4.139. A. TERENIN, YU. SOLONITSIN: Disc. Faraday Soc. **28**, 28 (1959).

4.140. W. J. LANGE, H. RIEMERSMA: Trans. Am. Vacuum Soc. (1961), p. 167 (Pergamon, 1962).

4.141. W. J. LANGE: J. Vac. Sci. Technol. **2**, 74 (1965).

4.142. H. MOESTA, H. D. BREUER: Surface Sci. **17**, 439 (1969).

4.143. R. O. ADAMS, E. E. DONALDSON: J. Chem. Phys. **42**, 770 (1965).

4.144. P. GÉNÉQUAND: Surface Sci. **25**, 643 (1971).

4.145. H. MOESTA, N. TRAPPEN: Naturwiss. **57**, 38 (1970).

4.146. P. KRONAUER, D. MENZEL: In *Adsorption – Desorption Phenomena,* ed. by F. RICCA (Academic Press, London, 1972), p. 313.

4.147. J. PAIGNE: J. Chim. Phys. **69**, 1 (1972).

4.148. J. W. MCALLISTER, J. M. WHITE: J. Chem. Phys. **58**, 1496 (1973).

4.149. G. W. FABEL, S. M. COX, D. LICHTMAN: Surface Sci. **40**, 571 (1973).

4.150. J. PEAVEY, D. LICHTMAN: Surface Sci. **27**, 649 (1971).

4.151. G. E. FISCHER, R. A. MACK: J. Vac. Sci. Technol. **2**, 123 (1965);
M. BERNARDINI, L. MALTER: J. Vac. Sci. Technol. **2**, 130 (1965).

4.152. L. T. GREENBERG: In *Interstellar Dust and Related Topics*, ed. by J. M. GREENBERG and H. C. VAN DE HULST (D. Reidel, Dordrecht, 1973), p. 413.

4.153. *Ion-Surface Interactions, Sputtering and Related Phenomena*, ed. by R. BEHRISCH, W. HEILAND, W. POSCHENRIEDER, P. STAIB, H. VERBEEK (Gordon and Breach, London, 1973).

4.154. A. BENNINGHOVEN: Appl. Phys. **1**, 3 (1973).

4.155. D. P. SMITH: Surface Sci. **25**, 171 (1971).

4.156. R. BEHRISCH: Nucl. Fusion **12**, 695 (1972).

4.157. A. BENNINGHOVEN: Z. Physik **220**, 159 (1969);
J. M. SCHROEER, T. N. RHODIN, R. C. BRADLEY: Surface Sci. **34**, 571 (1973).

4.158. A. BENNINGHOVEN, E. LOEBACH, N. TREITZ: J. Vac. Sci. Technol. **9**, 600 (1972);
S. K. ERENTS, G. M. MCCRACKEN: J. Appl. Phys. **44**, 3139 (1973);
H. F. WINTERS, P. SIEGMUND: J. Appl. Phys. **45**, 4760 (1974);
W. HEILAND, E. TAGLAUER: Paper at DECHEMA-Symp. Frankfurt, 1974.

4.159. E. W. MÜLLER: Phys. Rev. **102**, 618 (1956).

4.160. M. G. INGHRAM, R. GOMER: Z. Naturforsch. **10**a, 863 (1955).

4.161. R. GOMER: *Field Emission and Field Ionization* (Harvard University Press, Cambridge, Mass., 1961);
E. W. MÜLLER, T. T. TSONG: *Field Ion-Microscopy* (Elsevier, New York, 1969).

4.162. H. D. BECKEY: *Field Ionization Mass Spectrometry* (Vieweg, Braunschweig, 1969);
H. D. BECKEY: J. Mass Spectrometry Ion Phys. **2**, 500 (1969).

4.163. J. H. BLOCK: Adv. Mass Spectrometry **4**, 791 (1968);
J. H. BLOCK: J. Vac. Sci. Technol. **7**, 63 (1970).

4.164. E. W. MÜLLER, J. A. PANITZ, S. B. MCLANE: Rev. Sci. Instr. **39**, 83 (1968).

4.165. L. W. SWANSON, R. GOMER: J. Chem. Phys. **38**, 2813 (1963).

4.166. G. EHRLICH: Disc. Faraday Soc. **41**, 7 (1968);
E. W. PLUMMER, T. N. RHODIN: J. Chem. Phys. **49**, 3479 (1968).

4.167. R. GOMER: J. Chem. Phys. **31**, 341 (1959);
R. GOMER, L. W. SWANSON: J. Chem. Phys. **38**, 1613 (1963).

4.168. K. D. RENDULIC, Z. KNOR: Surface Sci. **7**, 204 (1967);
D. W. BASSETT: Brit. J. Appl. Phys. **18**, 1753 (1967);
A. E. BELL, L. W. SWANSON, D. REED: Surface Sci. **17**, 418 (1969).

5. Photoemission and Field Emission Spectroscopy

E. W. PLUMMER

With 31 Figures

A surface may be viewed as a distinguishable phase of matter [5.1] with physical and chemical properties which differ from the bulk and from the gas phase molecular properties [5.2]. The termination of the bulk at a surface creates a new boundary condition with a reduced coordination number allowing for both geometrical and electronic rearrangements. To minimize the total energy the surface atoms may rearrange themselves into sites which are not characteristic of the bulk. In the simplest case this may just be a dilation or contraction of the distance between surface plane and the next plane below, while in extreme cases the two dimensional periodicity of the surface may differ from the bulk. The electronic properties of the surface must reflect more localized character than in the bulk, including the possibility of surface states or surface resonances. Clean surfaces may have very localized orbitals equivalent to the "dangling bonds" of molecular chemistry and the bonds formed when a foreign atom or molecule is adsorbed may be localized in a "surface complex". The electron spectroscopy techniques discussed in this paper attempt to characterize the electronic energy level spectrum of a clean surface which has interacted with a foreign atom or molecule. The philosophy is that all interactions of a surface with its surroundings are primarily electronic in nature and must depend upon the distribution of electronic states both in energy and space near the surface.

It should be understood that these techniques are not the whole answer. Even though the geometrical arrangement of the atoms and the electronic energy levels are inescapably intertwined, electron spectroscopies are normally not very useful in determining the geometry. Also, with the exception of X-ray induced photoemission it is very difficult to determine the atomic species present on the surface, since the valence levels depend more upon the bonding configuration than the atomic identity of the constituents. Finally the relation between what is measured and the information desired, namely the ground state configuration of the system depends on the specific spectroscopic technique used, and requires careful analysis. This will be the subject of Section 5.2 which tries to elucidate what we do or do not know about the measurement processes for field emission and photoemission spectroscopy.

There is a pragmatic approach to utilizing electron spectroscopy commonly referred to as the "finger print" technique. It assumes that every bonding configuration will have its own characteristic spectrum so that, when all possible bonding configurations of a given system have been catalogued separately, the state or states can be determined. For example, if one wanted to study the decomposition of a hydrocarbon on a given surface, the spectra of adsorbed H, C, and all decomposition products of the hydrocarbon would be separately catalogued. Then the spectrum of the adsorbed hydrocarbon would be recorded as a function of the parameters of the experiment. The latter spectrum would then be compared to the spectra of the individual components in order to ascertain the nature of the surface molecule at the various stages of the experiment. This is a powerful technique if the spectra of individual species present are additive. It avoids many of the questions of the response of the system to the probe, since one makes no pretense of making absolute measurements. In Subsection 5.5.2 this "finger print" technique will be applied to representative examples of molecular dissociation, decomposition, and multiple surface binding states.

5.1. Preliminary Discussion of Field and Photoemission

Several electron emission processes have been used to study surfaces. In all of these the emitted electrons are energy analyzed so that the energy of the final state is determined, in contrast to an absorption experiment where the energy difference between the initial and final states is measured. The objective then is to infer the initial state from the measured final state energy and the characteristics of the probe. Three of the most widely used techniques are: 1) Ion neutralization spectroscopy, [5.1, 3] where a low energy ion beam is the probe, 2) field emission spectroscopy, where an applied field is the external probe [5.4, 5], and 3) photoelectron spectroscopy, where an incident beam of photons is the probe [5.6, 7]. The energy of the incident photon can range from the ultraviolet [5.6] to the X-ray [5.7]. This article will discuss the capabilities and limitations of the latter two techniques. HAGSTRUM [5.1, 8] has described in detail the comparison of ion neutralization and photoemission. No direct experimental comparisons between ion neutralization and field emission have been made even though these two techniques should be very similar [5.1]. GOMER has also compared photoemission and field emission [5.5] and articles by BRUNDLE [5.9] and MENZEL [5.10] discuss the capabilities of ultraviolet and X-ray induced photoemission.

SCREEN WITH PROBE HOLE

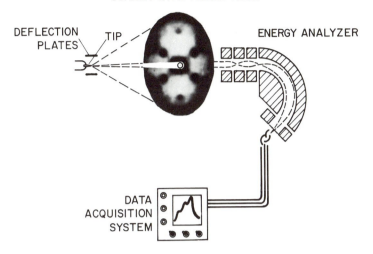

DEFLECTION
PLATES   TIP   ENERGY ANALYZER

DATA
ACQUISITION
SYSTEM

Fig. 5.1. Schematic drawing of a field emission microscope adapted for energy distribution measurement. The (110) plane is positioned over the probe hole

5.1.1. Field Emission

Field emission [5.11, 12] consists of the tunneling of electrons from a solid through the classically forbidden barrier region when the latter is deformed by the application of a strong electrostatic field, $3–6 \times 10^7$ V/cm. In order to achieve these high fields at reasonable voltages the cathode or emitter is usually etched to a sharp point (~ 1000 Å in radius) so that several kilovolts will produce the desired field. MÜLLER [5.11] realized in 1937 that a greatly enlarged ($> 10^6$) image of the spatial distribution of the tunneling electrons could be projected onto a fluorescent screen from the hemispherical emitter. Because of its small size the emitter is part of a single crystal and thus exposes all crystallographic orientations, so that individual crystal planes can be located and identified in the field emission pattern observed on the fluorescent screen. The emission characteristics of any crystal plane may be studied by placing a small "probe hole" in the screen and deflecting the field emission pattern with electrostatic deflection plates [5.13] until the plane of interest is over the probe hole. Figure 5.1 is a schematic drawing of this arrangement, showing the field emitter (tip) on a support loop and the projected field emission pattern of clean tungsten on the screen. In Fig. 5.1 the (110) plane is positioned over the probe hole and the electrons passing through it are being energy analyzed. The field dependence of the total current

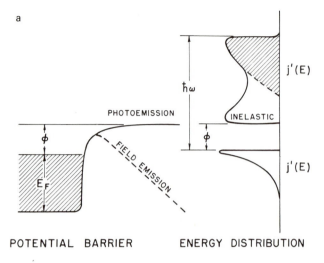

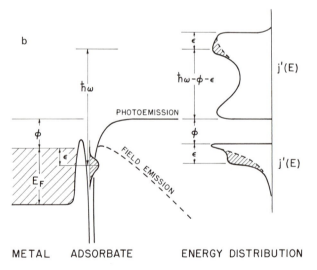

Fig. 5.2. (a) On the left is a schematic representation of the surface potential of a free electron metal, with and without the application of an external field. On the right a typical energy distribution for: 1) electrons which have tunneled elastically from the metal under the application of the applied field, and 2) electrons which have been photoexcited by radiation of energy $\hbar\omega$. (b) Schematic presentation of the surface potential with an idealized adsorbed atom present, both with and without an applied field. On the right are the resultant energy distributions for field emission (bottom) and photoemission (top). The shaded areas of the energy distribution depict the increase in current coming from the "virtual level" of the adsorbate, shown at an energy ε below the Fermi energy on the left

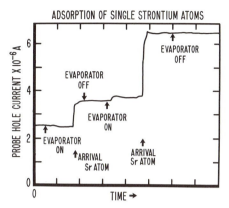

Fig. 5.3. Probe hole current (see Fig. 5.1) vs. time as a strontium source is switched on and off. The step increases in current occur when a single atom arrives on the surface being viewed [5.16]

can also be measured to obtain work function changes. These types of experiments have been reviewed recently by GADZUK and PLUMMER [5.4], SWANSON and BELL [5.14], and GOMER [5.5].

In Fig. 5.2a we show on the left a very schematic drawing of the potential at a metal surface with an electric field applied. On the right is a typical field emission energy distribution, decreasing exponentially as the energy decreases and the barrier becomes wider and higher. The energy distribution is cut off near the Fermi energy by the Fermi-Dirac distribution function. The shape of the field emission energy distribution when viewed on a linear plot, as shown in Fig. 5.2a, is nearly impervious to any changes in the emitter or the external field, and is always exponential in shape. This is a consequence of the tunneling through the field-induced barrier, which may be calculated since the barrier is almost entirely in the vacuum. The measured energy distribution with this exponential tunneling probability removed is extremely sensitive to the electronic properties of the surface [5.4]. Since all electrons which tunnel must originate at the surface, the properly analyzed field emission energy distribution will measure some function of the surface density of states. In Subsection 5.2.1 it will be shown that this function is the one-dimensional density of states evaluated at the classical turning point in Fig. 5.2a.

On the left of Fig. 5.2b we depict adsorption of a foreign atom onto the schematic surface shown in Fig. 5.2a. The bell-shaped curve in the region of the adsorbate centered at an energy ε below the Fermi energy is intended to represent the local density of states or "virtual level" on the adsorbate. This adsorbate level, sharp in the isolated atom, is broadened by interaction with the substrate, i.e., the lifetime of an electron on the adatom is no longer infinite. DUKE and ALFERIEFF [5.15] showed that tunneling through an adsorbate is equivalent to a tunneling resonance: when an electron tunneling from the solid has the same energy as a bound state in the adsorbate, resonance will occur increasing the tunneling probability by 10^2–10^4. This enhancement in tunneling probability as a function of energy can be used to measure the local density of electronic states on the adsorbed atom or molecule [5.4, 5]. Figure 5.3 illustrates quite dramatically the sensitivity of this technique for detecting single adsorbed atoms [5.16].

The limitations of field emission spectroscopy are two-fold: first, the exponential decrease in the current imposes a practical range limitation of 2–3 eV below the Fermi energy, and, secondly, there are a limited number of materials which can be prepared and cleaned for use as emitters.

5.1.2. Photoemission

While field emission is basically an elastic process, photoemission is an excitation process. An incoming photon of energy $\hbar\omega$ raises an electron to an excited state, $\hbar\omega$ eV above the initial state. If the excited electron has sufficient energy, is headed in the right direction and does not lose too much energy, it may escape from the solid to be subsequently energy analyzed. A schematic energy distribution showing both the elastically and inelastically scattered electrons is presented on the top right of Fig. 5.2a. One of the fundamental problems in interpreting photoemission data is our inability to separate the primary unscattered photoelectrons from inelastically scattered ones. The incoming photon beam has an extinction distance in the solid of ~ 100 Å in the ultraviolet region, varying with material and photon energy. The surface sensitivity of photoemission is a consequence of strong inelastic scattering in the excited state. The escape depth for an electron excited to 50 eV above the vacuum level is 2–5 Å. Figure 5.4 shows a plot of the optical absorption depth for normally incident light on tungsten [5.17] and the mean-free path before inelastic scattering of the excited electron as a function of energy. Several authors have compiled lists of the available data on electron escape depths [5.9, 18, 19] which, within experimental error, fall on the general curve shown in Fig. 5.4 for energies $> \sim 20$ eV. At energies < 20 eV the escape depth should increase depending upon the specific material, so that no generalization can be made for this range. Figure 5.4 also shows experimental escape depths for W [5.20], Ni [5.21], and Al [5.19] since these materials will be considered specifically in Section 5.4.

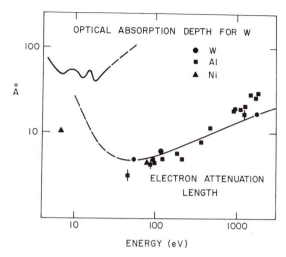

Fig. 5.4. Attenuation lengths for incoming radiation and escaping electrons as a function of energy. The top curve represents the absorption depth for tungsten from the data of JUENKER et al. [5.17]. The bottom curve indicates the excited electron attenuation length. The data for W[1s] is from TARNG and WEHNER [5.20], the Al data is from TRACY [5.19], and the Ni data is from EASTMAN [5.21] and a tabulation by BRUNDLE [5.9]

If the escape depth is 5 Å and the surface has the same optical excitation probability as the bulk, then $\sim 30\%$ of the signal will originate from the surface layer. The strong attenuation of excited electrons which is responsible for the surface sensitivity, also complicates the interpretation of the data. Even in the naive model of photoemission, which assumes that the energy distribution of primary electrons measures the density of initial states, the data can only be interpreted if the bulk and surface densities of states are identical. In the more probable case where the density of states varies layer by layer the signal will be a weighted sum of contributions for the different layers [5.22]. Inclusion of the excitation matrix element complicates matters even more by creating interference effects between the surface and bulk signals (see Subsection 5.4.5), making it nearly impossible to separate the bulk from the surface signal in a measured energy distribution.

When a foreign atom or molecule is adsorbed on the surface, an increase in signal would be expected at a kinetic energy corresponding to a level of the surface molecule, as shown in Fig. 5.2b, for an idealized case. Such bonding also causes a redistribution of energy levels in the substrate, leading to changes in the distribution not shown in the simple picture of Fig. 5.2b. When an energy level of a surface molecule or atom is below the bottom of the bulk band and hence localized the interpretation becomes somewhat easier, since there are then only weak interference effects with the bulk. A convenient way of displaying the changes in the surface properties is to plot the difference between energy distributions taken before and after a change in surface conditions. This will be illustrated in Section 5.3.

All atoms and molecules except hydrogen have core levels not involved in bonding, but the kinetic energy of photoelectrons from these levels may shift in response to the bonding of the valence electrons. The shift in the core levels arises from charge transfer in bonding; energy shifts of the emitted electrons can also be caused by relaxation effects in the surface molecule during the excitation process (see Subsection 5.2.2). When X-rays are used for the excitation, the process is called ESCA (electron spectroscopy for chemical analysis), [5.23] or XPS. By measuring the energies of electrons excited from core levels of adsorbed atoms one should be able to distinguish between different bonding configurations [5.9, 24].

Section 5.2 is aimed at readers interested in details of the measurement processes. For those readers who only want to know what can be done with these techniques, the present section has been written in enough detail to permit omission of Section 5.2.

5.2. The Measurement Process

This section will be devoted to an analysis of the measurement process in field emission and photoemission. What properties of the system are measured by an energy distribution of the emitted electrons? There is no definite answer to this question at the present time, and much of the following discussion will be concerned with what is unknown. In Subsection 5.5.2 the essential ingredients of any microscopic model of surface emission will be discussed: excitation probability, relaxation effects, and interference effects with the bulk.

5.2.1. Field Emission

Field emission was interpreted very early as quantum mechanical tunneling. In 1928 FOWLER and NORDHEIM [5.25] calculated the emitted current from a free electron metal with a work function φ, terminated by a step barrier at the surface and a constant electric field outside. NORDHEIM [5.26] modified this calculation to include the rounding of the triangular barrier by the image potential. Their expression for field emitted current, known as the Fowler-Nordheim equation has the form

$$\ln(i/F^2) = \ln A - 6.83 \times 10^7 \, \varphi^{\frac{3}{2}} \, s(y)/F \,, \tag{5.1}$$

where i is current density, F the applied field in V/cm, φ the work function in eV, $s(y)$ an image correction term close to unity, and $A = 6.2 \, 10^6 \times (E_F/\varphi)^{\frac{1}{2}}(E_F + \varphi)^{-1}$, E_F being the Fermi energy measured from the bottom of the conduction band. There has been considerable effort subsequent to their work to include effects of band structure and of adsorbed atoms or molecules [5.4, 5, 14]. Yet some fifty years after the original paper of FOWLER and NORDHEIM there still exists some controversy over what is being measured, especially for clean surfaces.

5.2.2. Clean Surfaces

The entire field of tunneling has been very carefully reviewed by DUKE [5.27], who pointed out that density of states effects in a normal metal tunnel junction are not readily observable. HARRISON [5.28] calculated the tunneling current in a non-superconducting junction, using an effective mass approximation with WKB tunneling and concluded that the tunneling current does not depend upon the density of states in any direct way. His formulation of tunneling has been adapted to field emission by most theoreticians. The work of STRATTON [5.29] and ITSKOVITCH [5.30] is the most notable using this formulation. GADZUK [5.4] has written a comprehensive review of the efforts in this area. In contrast to HARRISON [5.28], APPELBAUM and BRINKMAN [5.31] concluded from a calculation of interface effects in normal metal tunnel junctions that, "we presently know that tunneling measures the spectral function of the electrode in the vicinity of the metal-barrier interface". PENN [5.32] applied the BARDEEN [5.33] version of the OPPENHEIMER transfer Hamiltonian approximation [5.34] specifically to the case of field emission tunneling. He concluded that the field emission energy distribution can measure the "normal local density of states near the surface". Also, DUKE and FAUCHIER [5.35] calculated the field emission energy distribution for an exactly soluble one-dimensional Kronig-Penny model and found structure which can be related to the surface density of states [5.36].

The available experimental evidence supports the latter point of view. When the exponential nature of the energy distribution is divided out of a measured energy distribution from a single crystal face of the emitter, the resultant curve is usually rich in structure [5.37, 38], and this is very sensitive to the surface conditions [5.4]. In the following paragraphs the conventional application of HARRISON's [5.28] results will be described and an attempt made to show the source of the discrepancy between the two sets of calculations. Finally, the transfer Hamiltonian approach as applied by PENN [5.32, 39] will be described.

The following is based on an excellent paper by POLITZER and CUTLER [5.40] published in 1970, which assumed: 1) a one-dimensional surface potential and 2) the surface to be a perfect crystal plane with two-dimensional periodicity, so that $k_{||}$, the crystal momentum parallel to the surface, is a good quantum number and is conserved upon reflection (and transmission).

The amount of charge crossing a unit area per unit time outside the solid (to the right in Fig. 5.2a) between energy E and $E + dE$ is given by

$$j'(E)\, dE = \frac{2e}{(2\pi)^3}\, f(E) \int \int \int D(E, k_{||})\, V_z d^3 k . \tag{5.2}$$

Spin degeneracy which is assumed accounts for the factor of 2. The question of spin polarization will be addressed later. $f(E)$ is the equilibrium Fermi-Dirac distribution. V_z is the group velocity perpendicular to the surface and $D(E, k_{||})$ is the transmission probability for an electron of energy E and reduced transverse wave vector $k_{||}$. The volume integral in k space is over the region between the constant energy surfaces defined by E and $E + dE$. Equation (5.2) is quite easy to understand; it says: integrate over all states deep in the solid between energy E and $E + dE$ the product of the group velocity (to obtain the supply of electrons) and the transmission probability to obtain the external current.

The transmission probability D is defined as the ratio of the current density of the outgoing wave as $z \to +\infty$ (far to the right in Fig. 5.2a) to the current density of the incoming wave as $z \to -\infty$ (far to the left in Fig. 5.2a), and must be evaluated by solving the wave equation across the barrier. The approximations used for D lead to the apparent discrepancy in the different theories discussed at the beginning of this section.

By using the identity

$$V_z = \frac{1}{\hbar}\, \frac{\partial E(k)}{\partial k_z} \tag{5.3}$$

for the group velocity the integral in (5.2) can be converted to a surface integral over the constant energy surface E, and one obtains for the density in energy

$$j'(E) = \frac{2e f(E)}{h(2\pi)^3} \int \int \frac{D(E_1 k_{||}) \dfrac{\partial E}{\partial k_z}\, dS}{|V_k E|} . \tag{5.4}$$

Let θ be the angle between the surface normal for the incremental surface area dS and the z axis (normal to the interface), and ds its projection on the plane in k space parallel to the interface, $ds = dS \cos\theta$. Since $\hat{z} \cdot \nabla_k E = |\nabla_k E| \cos\theta = \partial E / \partial k_z$ we have

$$j'(E) = \frac{2e f(E)}{h(2\pi)^3} \int \int D(E, k_{||}) \, ds, \tag{5.5}$$

where the integral is over the projection of the constant energy surface E onto the k_x, k_y plane, i.e. the "shadow" on the k_x, k_y plane of the surface of constant energy E.

· Since we have assumed that $k_{||}$ is conserved in crossing the interface the integral in (5.5) can be evaluated using the values of $k_{||}$ outside the barrier where $E_{||} = \hbar^2 k_{||}^2/(2m)$. Converting to polar coordinates we have either

$$j'(E) = \frac{2e f(E)}{h(2\pi)^3} \int_0^{2\pi} d\varphi \int_{k_{||}^{min}(E,\varphi)}^{k_{||}^{max}(E,\varphi)} D(E, k_{||}) \, k_{||} \, dk_{||} \tag{5.6a}$$

or

$$j'(E) = \frac{2em f(E)}{h^3(2\pi)^3} \int_0^{2\pi} d\varphi \int_{E_{||}^{min}}^{E_{||}^{max}} D(E, E_{||}) \, dE_{||}, \tag{5.6b}$$

where the limits on the second integral are the extremes of the projected energy surface on the k_x, k_y plane in k space. The limits on (5.6b) are the extremes in parallel (or tranverse) energy outside the barrier. For elastic tunneling both E and $k_{||}$ are conserved, but $E_{||}$ may be different inside compared to outside.

POLITZER and CUTLER [5.40] pointed out that (5.5) or (5.6) are quite general and valid for any electron dispersion relation $E = E(k)$. The mistake many authors make is approximating $D(E, k_{||})$ by the usual form of the WKB transmission coefficient for an image potential barrier [5.29], based on the assumption that far from the barrier region the WKB asymptotic solutions are the eigenstates of a slowly varying potential; the periodic potential of the solid and solid surface does not satisfy this condition. If a simple WKB exponential tunneling factor is used for D, then all the information concerning the wave function matching at the interface is thrown out and leads immediately to the result that all density of states terms in (5.5) disappear since $\partial E / \partial k_z$ cancels with $|\nabla_k E|$. *The important information about the surface is contained in the transmission factor and much is obviously lost in a calculation which assumes that D does not depend upon the nature of the wave function at the interface.*

There are now several calculations which evaluate D correctly in (5.5). All of them predict structure in $j'(E)$ due to the electronic properties of the emitter. The simplest example is furnished by a model calculation of PLUMMER and YOUNG [5.13] for a free electron emitter with a triangular barrier, and an attractive square-well potential at the surface. Equation (5.5) or (5.6) is very simple for this one-dimensional free electron case,

$$j'(E) = \frac{2em\,f(E)}{\hbar^3(2\pi)^2} \int\limits_0^E D(W)\,dW, \tag{5.7}$$

where W is the normal energy $W = E - \hbar^2 k_\parallel^2/(2m)$.

First let us assume that $D(W)$ for the triangular barrier is given by the WKB form (no wave matching)

$$D_{\mathrm{WKB}}(W) \equiv \exp\left(-2\int\limits_{z_0}^{z_1} \varkappa\,dx\right), \tag{5.8}$$

where

$$\varkappa = \left(\frac{2m}{\hbar^2}\right)^{\frac{1}{2}} \sqrt{V(z) - W}$$

$$= \left(\frac{2m}{\hbar^2}\right)^{\frac{1}{2}} \sqrt{E_F + \varphi - eFz - W}$$

with z_0 and z_1 the classical turning points, and E_F the Fermi energy and φ the work function; $z_0 = 0$ and $z_1 = (E_F + \varphi - W)\,eF$. This gives

$$D_{\mathrm{WKB}}(W) \equiv \exp\left[-\tfrac{4}{3}\left(\frac{2m}{\hbar^2}\right)^{\frac{1}{2}} (E_F + \varphi - W)^{\frac{3}{2}}\right]. \tag{5.8}$$

Since this transmission factor does not account for the properties of the wave functions at the surface, caused by the attractive square well it predicts a free electron energy distribution $j_0'(E)$, obtained by a first-order expansion of W about E

$$(E_F + \varphi - W)^{\frac{3}{2}} \simeq (E_F + \varphi - E)^{\frac{3}{2}}\left(1 - \tfrac{3}{2}\frac{W - E}{E_F + \varphi - E}\right),$$

which gives

$$j_0'(E) \simeq \frac{e\pi\sqrt{2m}\,f(E)}{\hbar^3\,[E_F + \varphi - E]^{\frac{1}{2}}} \exp\left[-\tfrac{4}{3}\left(\frac{2m}{\hbar^2}\right)^{\frac{1}{2}} (E_F + \varphi - E)^{\frac{3}{2}}\right], \tag{5.9}$$

the free electron energy distribution derived by YOUNG [5.41]. On the other hand, if D is calculated correctly by matching across the barrier

[5.27], the energy distribution $j'(E)$ contains structure due to the nature of the wave function near the surface. PLUMMER and YOUNG's [5.13] model calculation showed that

$$\frac{j'(E)}{j_0'(E)} \propto |\psi(z=0)|^2 ,$$

where $z = 0$ is the classical turning point in this model.

POLITZER and CUTLER [5.40, 42] calculated the field emission from ferromagnetic Ni in an attempt to explain spin polarization measurements [5.43]. They showed more rigorously that it is essential to include the matching conditions properly when calculating the transmission factor. The WKB transmission factor given by (5.8) is always multiplied by a pre-exponential term $P(E, k_{||})$ so that

$$D(E, k_{||}) = P(E, k_{||}) \, D_{WKB}(E, k_{||}) . \tag{5.10}$$

$P(E, k_{||})$ must be evaluated from the wave functions at the interface. The ratio of the actual energy distribution to the "free electron WKB" energy distribution, $j_0'(E)$ will be called the enhancement

$$R(E) = \frac{j'(E)}{j_0'(E)} . \tag{5.11}$$

$R(E)$ reflects the properties of the pre-exponential term $P(E, k_{||})$.

POLITZER and CUTLER [5.42] used this approach to calculate $P(E, k_{||})$ for the d-bands in nickel relative to the free electron bands; they found as a consequence of the localization of the d wave functions at the surface, that P is 10^{-1}–10^{-2}. GADZUK [5.44] had previously estimated a decrease of 10^{-3} for d-band tunneling based on a localization argument.

The above should make it clear that the use of WKB tunneling probabilities will, in general, lead to incorrect energy distributions, which can be very misleading. There are exceptions, for example, when there are pronounced extremes in the projected energy surfaces of (5.6), such as gaps or necks [5.45].

Although (5.5) is very useful for treating tunneling from clean metal surfaces its limitations become apparent when attempts are made to apply it to tunneling from adsorbed impurities [5.44, 46]. A more appealing method for handling this case consists of perturbation theory, or more porperly the transfer Hamiltonian method [5.33] whose final result looks exactly like Fermi's golden rule formula for time dependent perturbation theory

$$j'(E) = (2\pi/h) f(E) \sum_k \sum_R |\langle \Phi_k | \tau | \Phi_R \rangle|^2 \, \delta(E - E_R) \, \delta(E - E_k), \qquad (5.12)$$

where

$$\tau = -eFz, \qquad (5.13)$$

and Φ_k and Φ_R refer to wave functions in the metal and beyond the barrier, respectively.

PENN et al. [5.32, 47] have used this approach to evaluate energy distributions from clean as well as adsorbated covered surfaces. They evaluated (5.12) by using Airy functions for Φ_R and insert a normalization factor N_m for the metal wave functions Φ_k at the classical turning point. The final result obtained by PENN [5.32, 48] is the following

$$j'(E) = \frac{2h}{m} f(E) \sum_k D_{WKB}(E, k_{||}) \, N^2(E, k_{||}) \, \delta(E - E_k). \qquad (5.14)$$

If WKB wave functions are used for Φ_k, (5.14) obviously reduces to the WKB result (5.5) and (5.8) with no dependence on the wave function at the surface, i.e. no density of states information. The potential near the classical turning point on the metal side of the barrier changes quite rapidly and the WKB approximation for the wave function is not appropriate.

PENN [5.32] has shown that the normalization constant N_m^2 can be related to the wave function amplitude at the turning point z_0 so that (5.14) can be written as

$$j'(E) \simeq \lambda^{-2}(E) \frac{2h}{m} f(E) \sum_k D(E, k_{||}) |\psi_k(z_0)|^2 \, \delta(E - E_k), \qquad (5.15)$$

where D is now the WKB tunneling probability of (5.8), and $\lambda(E)$ is a slowly varying function of energy. In this form $|\psi_k(z_0)|^2 / \lambda_2(E)$ is equivalent to POLITZER and CUTLER's [5.40] pre-exponential factor $P(E, k_{||})$. Since the tunneling probability $D(E, k_{||})$ falls off exponentially as $k_{||}$ increases from zero, the $|\psi_k(z_0)|^2$ term may be extracted from the sum if it does not change drastically for small changes in $k_{||}$ about $k_{||} = 0$. That is if $\partial |\psi_k|^2 / \partial k_{||}|_{k_{||}=0}$ is small compared to the magnitude of $|\psi_k(k_{||} = 0)|$. This gives

$$R(E) = \frac{j'(E)}{j'_0(E)} \propto \varrho_m^\perp(E)|_{z=z_0}, \qquad (5.16)$$

where $\varrho_m^{\perp}|_{z=z_0}$ is the one-dimensional density of states evaluated at the classical turning point z_0.

Equation (5.16) immediately shows the origin of the reduction in tunneling from localized d states [5.42, 44]. The amplitude of the wave function will be considerably smaller at the turning point for a localized state than for a free electron state.

CAROLI et al. [5.49] have derived the field emission energy distribution applying an out-of-equilibrium formalism using KJELDYSH Green's functions [5.50]. SOVEN [5.51] has shown for the one-dimensional case that this formalism is equivalent to (5.5) and gives $R(E)$ of (5.16) as the one-dimensional density of states at the turning point to order of the tunneling probability.

The electrons which are field emitted may have a spin polarization. PENN [5.52] has shown, using the transfer Hamiltonian approach outlined above, that a spin polarization measurement will measure the one-dimensional "surface" density of states for a given spin band. The problem then reverts back to calculating the one-dimensional density of states for each spin band at the classical turning point. This is in fact what POLITZER and CUTLER calculated for Ni [5.42].

5.3. Adsorbate Covered Surfaces

When an atom or molecule is chemisorbed on a surface the energy levels of both metal and adsorbate will shift, and field emission energy distributions can reveal the characteristics of the local density of states on the adsorbate. Qualitatively, this is obvious from Fig. 5.2b, where electrons with appreciable amplitude on the adsorbate have a considerably smaller barrier to tunnel through than electrons in the metal. It is fairly easy to quantify this statement.

5.3.1. Tunneling Resonance

Without doubt the paper by DUKE and ALFERIEFF [5.15] pioneered in this field. They calculated the transmission through a triangular barrier with an adsorbate potential within the barrier, represented by an attractive square well plus a δ-function repulsive core. The wave functions and the current were calculated exactly for various positions and strengths of the adsorbate potential. For energies corresponding to that of a standing wave in the adsorbate potential well penetration of the barrier is much easier, i.e. tunneling resonance occurs. This approach does not show explicitly how the energy distribution is related to the "local density of states" on the adsorbate. This problem can be overcome by calculating for each energy the amplitude squared $|\psi_a|^2$ of the wave function on the adsorbate.

Subsequent to DUKE and ALFERIEFF's computer calculation several theoretical treatments have appeared which express the energy distribution from the adsorbate, $j_a'(E)$, analytically. All of these calculations [5.47, 49, 53] yield nearly the same result, i.e.

$$\frac{\Delta j'}{j_{cl}'} \equiv \frac{j_a'(E) - j_{cl}'(E)}{j_{cl}'} \equiv U^2(E)\,\varrho_a(E), \qquad (5.17)$$

where ϱ_a is the local density of states on the adsorbate (see Section 2.1), and $U^2(E)$ a term which compensates for the difference in tunneling from the adsorbate relative to tunneling from the metal. The function $j_{cl}'(E)$ denotes the assumed energy distribution from the clean surface which would be obtained if the work function and field were those corresponding to the adsorbate covered surface. This quantity is of course impossible to measure experimentally. Further PENN (Ref. [5.47], Eqs. (14b), and (15a)) has shown that (5.17) is only valid when there is no structure in the clean energy distribution, i.e. when $j_{cl}'(E) = j_0'(E)$. In general, (5.17) should be written as

$$\frac{\Delta j'(E)}{j_{cl}'(E)} = U^2(E)\,\Delta\varrho_a(E). \qquad (5.18)$$

$\Delta\varrho_a$ is the change in the density of states at the adsorbate site caused by the presence of the adsorbate. PLUMMER and YOUNG [5.13] observed an adsorbate induced change in the substrate local density of states for adsorption on (100)W, and DUKE and FAUCHIER [5.35] demonstrated theoretically that $\Delta j'/j_{cl}'$ can display structure which is not present in $\varrho_a(E)$. In practice [5.4, 37] the data are usually plotted in the form of $R(E)$ curves defined by (5.11), with $j_0'(E)$ calculated for the field and work function of the specific adsorption system.

Only a few calculations have considered the effect of structure in clean energy distributions. BAGCHI and YOUNG [5.54] calculated the energy distribution from an adsorbate covered surface, representing the

Fig. 5.5. (a) Field emission energy distribution $j'(\varepsilon)$ [Δ] from clean (112) tungsten at 78 K, $j_0'(\varepsilon)$ [$-$] is the calculated free electron energy distribution for a work function of $\varphi = 4.90\,\mathrm{eV}$ and a field measured from the slope of the Fowler-Nordheim plot [5.4], $R(\varepsilon)$ [$\bigcirc$] on the right hand scale is calculated by dividing j' by j_0' for each energy. R. was arbitrarily normalized to 10 at $\varepsilon = 1.0\,\mathrm{eV}$. (b) Measured energy distribution $j'(\varepsilon)$, calculated free-electron energy distribution j_0' ($\varphi = 6.14\,\mathrm{eV}$) and R factor for $\sim 10^{-6}\,\mathrm{Torr \cdot sec}$ oxygen exposure on (112) tungsten at 78 K

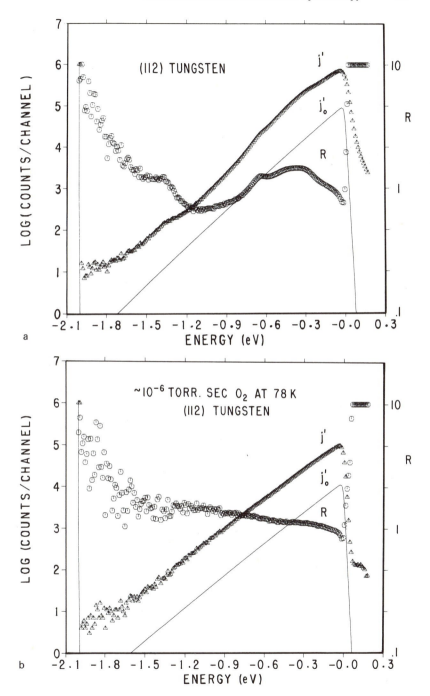

density of states of the metal by two Lorentzian peaks at 2 eV and 3.5 eV below E_F and the adsorbate density by a Lorentzian peak some 6–9 eV below E_F. Since ϱ_a included contributions from the density of states in the substrate, peaks in the latter appeared in ϱ_a and could thus show up in $j'_a(E)$ with enhanced amplitude because of the increased tunneling probability for electrons on the adsorbate. Thus they concluded that the presence of an adsorbate can produce structure in the energy distribution which reflects the density of states of the substrate, at energies far from any resonant levels in the adsorbate.

In concluding this subsection, two examples will be presented to show first that (5.16) is basically correct for clean surfaces and secondly that problems still exist in applying (5.18) for adsorbates. Figure 5.5a is a plot of the measured energy distribution $j'(E)$ for clean (112) tungsten at 78 K. The free electron energy distribution [5.4] $j'_0(E)$ and the $R(E)$ factor are defined by (5.11), and calculated for $\varphi = 4.90$ eV and a field measured from the Fowler-Nordheim plot. Since the pre-exponential terms involving the area sampled were not measured, $j'_0(E)$ is arbitrarily normalized at $\varepsilon = -1.0$ eV where $\varepsilon = E - E_F$. This curve shows the type of structure predicted by (5.16) and in Subsection 5.5.1 it will be compared with actual band structure calculations to show that it is a reasonable surface density of states. The message is that there is structure in the clean energy distribution which is very visible when the exponential tunneling probabilities have been divided out.

In Fig. 5.5b the same (112) plane of tungsten was exposed to $\sim 10^{-6}$ Torr · sec of oxygen at 78 K. The R curve is almost completely flat. Not only have no new levels due to the adsorbate appeared but all the structure due to the substrate has disappeared. When this oxygen layer is heated to 1000 K it orders and a single level appears in the R curve, peaked at $\varepsilon = -1.2$ eV with a half width 0.45 eV [5.4]. At present there is no definite explanation of this penomenon. It could be the result of scattering of tunneling electrons by the adsorbed O atoms, or could result from changes in ϱ_a or the normal surface density of states resulting from surface reconstruction, induced by the presence of O. This suggests that the three-dimensional aspects of tunneling need to be investigated [5.40, 49, 55] in a formulation which does not assume conservation of $k_{\parallel}$. Presumably, the scattering formalism used by Modinos [5.56] and the out-of-equilibrium formulation of Caroli [5.49] could be adapted to study this problem.

5.3.2. Inelastic Tunneling

The importance of impurity assisted inelastic tunneling has been demonstrated by Lambe and Jaklevic [5.57] for tunnel junctions. They

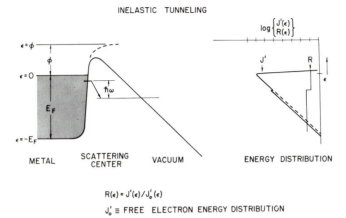

INELASTIC TUNNELING

$R(\epsilon) = J'(\epsilon)/J_0'(\epsilon)$

$J_0' \equiv$ FREE ELECTRON ENERGY DISTRIBUTION

Fig. 5.6. Schematic drawing of the inelastic tunneling process. A tunneling electron loses energy $\hbar\omega$ by inelastically scattering at the scattering center. The sharp Fermi edge produces a cut-off on the energy of the tunneling electrons so that the resultant R curve has a step at an energy $\hbar\omega$ below the Fermi energy

deposited various molecules such as H_2O, CO, and C_2H_2 at one interface of a metal-insulator-metal junction and measured the current voltage characteristics of the junction. The second derivative of the junction current with respect to the bias voltage revealed sharp line structure at voltages near the energies of the infrared active vibrational modes of the molecules or hydroxyl groups. WEINBERG's group [5.58] is now using this technique to identify molecules formed at one of the interfaces after some prescribed chemical reaction has been carried out.

Corresponding processes will occur in field emission, as shown schematically in Fig. 5.6. A tunneling electron may undergo an inelastic collision with an adsorbed molecule or a surface complex.The inelastically scattered electron will appear in the energy distribution with its energy reduced by the energy of the vibrational mode. Since the cross section will usually be small for such a process the change in the signal will be small and appear as a threshold effect (Fig. 5.6), so that the R curve will have a small step at $\varepsilon = -\hbar\omega$. The width of the step will be related to the temperature of the crystal or the sharpness of the Fermi edge, while the height will depend upon the cross section and density of scattering centers. FLOOD [5.59] has presented a theory of this process which assumes equal tunneling probability for inelastically scattered and corresponding elastic electrons. Quantitatively an energy distribution $j_{in}'(E)$ can be written as

$$j_{in}'(E) = j_{el}'(E) + j_{el}'(E + \hbar\omega)\, N\, T(\hbar\omega)\,, \tag{5.19}$$

where N is the density of scattering centers and T the scattering cross section. $T(\hbar\omega)$ contains both the probability that an electron of energy $E + \hbar\omega$ will lose energy $\hbar\omega$ and the ratio of the escape probabilities at energy E and $E + \hbar\omega$. This makes it relatively hard to calculate $T(\hbar\omega)$, since one cannot assume a priori that an electron scatters before or after tunneling.

Experimentally the signals observed both in tunnel junctions [5.57] and in field emission [5.37] for small molecules are much less than the background current. Therefore second derivatives are used to analyze tunnel junctions and computer processing of data is required in field emission. By contrast the inelastic signal from large organic molecules adsorbed on a field emitter may be of the same order of magnitude as the primary signal [5.60].

5.3.3. Many-Body Effects and Photoassisted Field Emission

Neither of these topics will be discussed at any length. Many-body effects have been reviewed by GADZUK [5.4] and photoassisted field emission by BAGCHI [5.61] and LEE [5.62]. Many-body effects will be defined as any electron-electron interaction which modifies the one-electron tunneling picture presented in the previous two sections. Experimentally, these effects give rise to wings on the energy distribution not predicted by the one-electron theory [5.63, 64]. They may be caused by multi-particle tunneling [5.63, 65], by hot-hole electron cascade [5.64], by uncertainty-principle arguments [5.66] or by electron-electron scattering outside the emitter [5.67]. Whatever the mechanism for these tails, there is probably a fundamental limit imposed by the interaction of electrons on the current range over which the one-electron picture is useful. Experimental data [5.63, 64] indicate that this is approximately six orders of magnitude.

Photoassisted field emission [5.61] is an excellent topic to end the discussion of field emission, since it will point out some of the problems we will encounter in the section on photoemission. Photoassisted field emission refers to the process of exciting an electron with an incident photon beam to an energy below the top of the barrier in Fig. 5.2a, so that the electron must still tunnel through the barrier in order to escape. The simplest theories are those of NEUMANN [5.68], and LUNDQUIST et al. [5.69], who view photofield emission as a two-step process in which an electron is first excited by a photon and subsequently tunnels out. This model suggests that the energy of the final state in an optically allowed transition can be mapped as a function of direction in k-space collected by the probe hole. The mean-free path of excited electrons is quite large near the Fermi energy (Fig. 5.4) so that this model should be quite realistic. Unfortunately, experimental observations [5.62, 70] in several directions from a tungsten emitter do not substantiate this theory. All the energy distributions show a peak which is nearly a replica of the initial energy distribution moved up by the photon energy and decreased in amplitude. When the direct transition model of photo-excitation is discussed in the next section it will become obvious that this behavior cannot be reconciled with the band structure of the solid and k conservation in the transition.

BAGCHI [5.61] has developed a theory to explain the data of LEE [5.62], in terms of the surface photoelectric effect. The surface destroys the periodicity in the direction normal to the surface so that the three-dimensional crystal momentum k does not have to be conserved; therefore, the restriction on the allowed transitions in the bulk is removed. This leads to an excited distribution which looks like the ordinary Fermi distribution displaced by the photon energy. If BAGCHI is correct and the surface photoelectric effect is dominant at these low photon energies, where the electron mean-free path must be ~ 100 Å, then it could be even more important at the higher photon energies used in photo-emission where the mean-free path of an electron may be as short as 5 Å.

5.4. Photoemission

A rigorous theoretical treatment of photoemission including surface effects has not been developed [5.71]. In this section the pertinent physical parameters of the measurement process will be discussed.

5.4.1. Photoexcitation; Primarily Atoms and Molecules

Photoionization in gases is much simpler than the analogous process in solids [5.72, 73]. Since gases adsorbed on a surface may retain many of their gas phase properties it is appropriate to begin the discussion of photoemission with a description of gas phase photoionization. The (non-relativistic) Hamiltonian of an electron in a electromagnetic field is [5.74]

$$\mathcal{H} = \frac{1}{2m}(P + eA)^2 - e\Phi + V_0 = P^2/2m + \left(\frac{e}{m}\right)(A \cdot P + P \cdot A)$$

$$+ V_0 - e\Phi + \frac{e^2}{2m}A^2,$$

(5.20)

where A and Φ are the vector and scalar potentials, respectively, and P is the momentum operator. By virtue of gauge invariance, we may demand that either Φ or $\nabla \cdot A$ (but not both) vanish. Here we chose $\Phi = 0$, which means that $\nabla \cdot A$ does not, in general, equal zero [5.74], a point we will use later. Neglecting the last term (quadratic in A) and treating the terms linear in A as a perturbation of the rest of $\mathscr{H}$ leads to a transition rate between states ψ_i and ψ_f of

$$P_{if} = \left(\frac{4\pi^2 e^2}{\hbar^2 m^2}\right)|\langle\psi_f|A(r)\cdot P + P\cdot A(r)|\psi_i\rangle|^2\, \delta(E_f - E_i - \hbar\omega), \quad (5.21)$$

(using lowest-order time-dependent perturbation theory). Here $E_i(E_f)$ is the energy of $\psi_i(\psi_f)$ (an eigenstate of the unperturbed system), and $\hbar\omega$ is the photon energy.

There are several approximations applied to (5.21) to make it easier to handle. In the next few paragraphs each of these steps will be spelled out, indicating why it is usually valid for atomic or molecular calculations and whether it is a valid step when applied to a solid.

In nearly all calculations using (5.21) it is assumed that $\nabla \cdot A = 0$. This is based not on gauge invariance (which was invoked to eliminate the scalar potential) but on the approximation of A by a plane wave

$$A(r, t) = A_0 \exp(-i\omega t + i q \cdot r), \quad (5.22)$$

where $A \cdot q = 0$ so that $\nabla \cdot A = 0$. This reduces (5.21) to

$$P_{if} = (4\pi^2 e^2/\hbar^2 m^2)|\langle\psi_f|A\cdot P|\psi_i\rangle|^2\, \delta(E_f - E_i - \hbar\omega), \quad (5.23)$$

where $A(r)$ in (5.21) is $A(r) = A_0 \exp(i q \cdot r)$. This is the usual form for the matrix element seen in the solid state [5.21] or gas phase literature. In the solid and especially near the surface where the A vector is changing rapidly, $\nabla \cdot A$ does not equal zero and may in fact be very large [5.75]. On physical grounds, it is easy to see why this term is important in UV photoemission. The escape depth of the excited electron is $\sim 5\,\text{Å}$ (Fig. 5.4) and the region where the gradient in the perpendicular component of the field occurs is something like 2–3 Å, so in the region from which emission occurs there may be a large gradient in A_0, i.e., charge imbalance.

In (5.22) or (5.23) the $\exp(i q \cdot r)$ term coming from A, see (5.23), is usually expanded in a power series, with often only the first term, unity, being retained. This approximation is based on the large wavelength of the light compared to atomic dimensions. When this approximation is applied to (5.23), the "electric dipole" approximation is obtained

$$P_{if}(\text{dipole}) = \frac{4\pi^2 e^2}{\hbar^2 m^2} |\langle \psi_f|\boldsymbol{P}|\psi_i\rangle \cdot \boldsymbol{A}_0|^2 \, \delta(E_f - E_i - \hbar\omega). \qquad (5.24)$$

This approximation also ignores any retardation effects across the atom or solid.

In the "electric dipole" approximation the momentum matrix element $\langle \psi_f|\boldsymbol{P}|\psi_i\rangle$ must be evaluated. This can be and is frequently converted to a spatial operator $\boldsymbol{r}$ matrix element or to a gradient in potential ∇V operator by using simple commutation relations [5.76]. If, as we have assumed, ψ_i and ψ_f are eigenstates of H_0 then we can write

$$\langle \psi_f|\boldsymbol{P}|\psi_i\rangle = im\omega \langle \psi_f|\boldsymbol{r}|\psi_i\rangle, \qquad (5.25a)$$

or

$$\langle \psi_f|\boldsymbol{P}|\psi_i\rangle = \frac{-i\hbar}{\omega} \langle \psi_p|\nabla V|\psi_i\rangle. \qquad (5.25b)$$

Using these equalities, (5.24) can be written in the alternate forms

$$P_{if}(\text{dipole}) = \frac{4\pi^2 e^2 \omega^2}{\hbar^2} |\langle \psi_f|\boldsymbol{r}|\psi_i\rangle \cdot \boldsymbol{A}_0|^2 \, \partial(E_f - E_i - \hbar\omega), \qquad (5.26a)$$

or

$$P_{if}(\text{grad } V) = \frac{4\pi^2 e^2}{m^2 \omega^2} |\langle \psi_f|\nabla V|\psi_i\rangle \cdot \boldsymbol{A}_0|^2 \, \partial(E_f - E_i - \hbar\omega). \qquad (5.26b)$$

In calculations (except those for hydrogen) ψ_f and ψ_i are usually approximate wavefunctions which are not true eigenstates of $\mathcal{H}_0$. Thus, (5.25a) and (5.25b), and consequently (5.26a) and (5.26b) are approximations which should be used with some caution. BETHE and SALPETER [5.76] pointed out that (5.26a) with the $\boldsymbol{r}$ matrix elements will accentuate the importance of the wavefunctions at large $\boldsymbol{r}$, while the ∇V matrix element (5.26b) will accentuate the small $\boldsymbol{r}$ terms (for an atom). For the $\boldsymbol{p}$ operator in (5.25), one finds that intermediate values of r are most important. In many atomic calculations of the photo-ionization probabilities, the cross section is calculated using all three methods as a check on the wavefunctions.

Equation (5.26b) is usually applied to calculating the photoemission from the potential step at the surface. It appears that the $1/\omega^2$ term in

(5.25b) has led people to believe that surface photoemission will dominate at low photon energies over bulk emission. SCHAICH and ASHCROFT [5.77] have shown that this is not true.

To this point we have considered transitions of the whole system, but in most cases a one electron approximation is used. Often this helps in visualizing the process, but it should always be remembered that photoemission is not a one-electron process. If the total wave functions ψ_i and ψ_f are written as properly anti-symmetrized determinants of N one-electron wave functions Φ_j, then by virtue of Koopman's theorem [5.78] the matrix elements in (5.24) or (5.26) are just integrals over one-electron wave functions where $N - 1$ of these functions are exactly the same. Note that this approximation assumes an unrelaxed ionic core. This picture is, of course, not exact and the difference between the ionization potential and one-electron orbital energies is called the relaxation energy in this paper. This relaxation energy may be as large as 70 eV for photo-ionization from the $1s$ state of Xe [5.79]. On the other hand, however, COOPER [5.80] has argued that even though the energies of the photo-emitted electrons may be badly estimated in the one-electron approximation, the probability for excitation is fairly accurate.

5.4.2. Cross Section for Photoemission

The relative cross section for photoionizing electrons from different orbits of an atom or molecule has long been known to depend upon photon energy. PRICE [5.81] presented general physical arguments which show the trends in the relative cross sections for photoionization. Everything else being equal, the more localized in space the initial state is, the better it will couple with a higher energy final state, so the maximum in the cross section moves to higher energy as the mean radius becomes smaller.

These same sorts of effects are quite common in spectra from solids [5.82]. A very nice example is shown in Fig. 5.7 for EuS from the work of EASTMAN and KUZNIETZ [5.83]. This figure shows the photoelectron energy distribution from EuS as a function of photon energy from $\hbar\omega = 10.2$ eV up to 40.8 eV. The peak near -2 eV has been identified as the $4f$ level in EuS and the two lower lying peaks as originating from the p bands [5.83]. The insert in the top left of Fig. 5.7 shows the ratio of the photoionization probability of the $4f$ to p-band peak. It increases with the third power of photon energy. The UV data of BRODEN et al. [5.84] on Yb, Ba, and Eu show the same behavior of the $4f$ levels. At photon energies below 12 eV there is little sign of the $4f$ levels in Yb or Eu, and the photoelectron spectra of these metals look much like Ba.

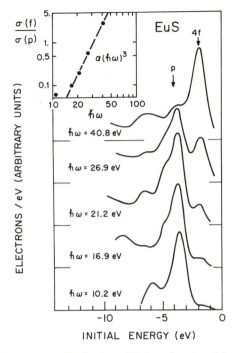

Fig. 5.7. Photoelectron energy distributions of EuS as a function of the energy of the incident photon. The energy scale is the energy of the initial state with zero being the Fermi energy [5.83]

On the other hand, the X-ray photoelectron spectrum [5.82] from Yb and Eu shows only the $4f$ levels with little if any sign of the $6s$ band.

If a photoelectron experiment is to be designed to study the adsorption of molecule X on the surface of metal M the choice of the appropriate photon energy is very important. For example, to study Eu or Ba, one surely would not use a photon energy less than 10 or 15 eV, because the Eu $4f$ levels have a very low photoionization cross section at these low energies [5.84]. These qualitative statements can be made more quantitative by actually calculating the photoionization cross section using one of the forms of (5.24, 26).

The cross sections can be estimated by using a one electron hydrogenic wavefunction for ψ_i and a plane wave approximation for ψ_f, permitting the matrix elements to be calculated in closed form. Then (5.24) becomes

$$P_{if} = \left(\frac{4\pi^2 e^2 B^2}{m^2}\right) |A_0 \cdot k|^2 |\int \exp(ik \cdot r)\, \psi_i d\tau|^2 \, \delta(E_f - E_i - \hbar\omega), \quad (5.27)$$

where k is now the wave vector of the outgoing electron. If ψ_i is a hydrogenic wave function [5.76]

$$\psi_i = R_{nl}(r)\, Y_{lm}(\theta, \varphi) \tag{5.28}$$

then [5.76, 85]

$$\int \exp(i\mathbf{k}\cdot\mathbf{r})\, \psi_f\, d\tau = F_{nl}(\varrho)\, Y_{lm}(\theta, \varphi), \tag{5.29}$$

where θ, φ are the angles of k relative to the orientation of the initial state in momentum space and $F_{nl}(p)$ is the Fourier transform of the radial part of the wave function in (5.28) normalized so that

$$\int_0^\infty dp\, p^2\, |F_{nl}(p)|^2 = 1, \quad \text{with} \quad \hbar k = p.$$

Hence

$$P_{if} \propto p^2\, |F_{nl}(p)|^2 \times \left| \frac{\mathbf{A}_0\cdot\mathbf{k}}{|\mathbf{k}|} \right|^2 Y_{lm}(\theta, \varphi)\, \delta(E_f - E_i - \hbar\omega), \tag{5.30}$$

and if we average over all exit directions k then

$$\langle P_{if} \rangle \propto P^2\, |F_{nl}(p)|^2. \tag{5.31}$$

The $F_{nl}(p)$ functions are given explicitly by [5.76] and [5.85]. The effective radius of the wavefunction in (5.28) can be adjusted to fit experimental values by using an effective nuclear charge Z leaving n and l unchanged. The number of nodes in the wave function is important [5.80] so SLATER type wavefunctions [5.86] cannot be used. Figure 5.8 is a plot of (5.31) for the oxygen 1s and oxygen 2p levels as a function of the energy of the photoemitted electron. For an excitation energy of $\hbar\omega = 1250$ eV the electron from the 2p level would have an energy of ~ 1220 eV and a probability of $\sim 1.6 \times 10^{-3}$, while the electron from the 1s level would have a final energy of ~ 700 eV with a probability of 1.5×10^{-1}. This ratio must be multiplied by the number of electrons in each subshell to give a ratio of 70:1 between emission probabilities for 1s and 2p electrons. This is in good agreement with the ratio of 100:1 obtained by SCOFIELD [5.87]. If the oxygen atom is adsorbed on a transition metal, the excitation probability from a d state will peak at a higher photon energy than the 2p state of oxygen. SCOFIELD's [5.87] calculation indicated the following ratio for the cross section σ

$$\left. \frac{\sigma(O\,2p)}{\sigma(W\,5d)} \right|_{\hbar\omega = 1000\,\text{eV}} \simeq 0.1$$

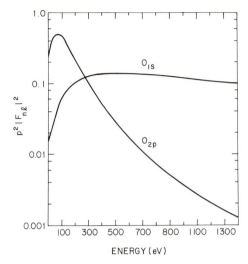

Fig. 5.8. Calculated photoionization probability for the $1s$ and $2p$ levels of oxygen, plotted as a function of the energy of the excited electron

and

$$\frac{\sigma(O2p)}{\sigma(Ni3d)}\bigg|_{\hbar\omega=1000\,eV} \simeq 0.05 .$$

Therefore, one would not expect to see the oxygen $2p$ levels in X-ray induced photoelectron spectra from oxygen on tungsten or nickel, while they should be very pronounced at low photon energies (Fig. 5.8).

Figure 5.9 shows the photoelectron spectra from clean tungsten before and after exposure of $\sim 10^{-5}$ Torr·sec oxygen at room temperature. The top set of curves are for (100) tungsten at a photon energy of 21.2 eV [5.88]. The bottom set of curves are from X-ray [$\hbar\omega = 1254$ eV] photoemission data of MADEY et al. [5.89]. The UV spectrum at the top shows that the levels derived from the oxygen p-levels are very pronounced. The X-ray spectrum show no signs of an oxygen p-band. The dotted line on the bottom is what would have been expected solely from the change in escape depth (Fig. 5.4). [The peak near the Fermi energy in the clean UV data is a surface state (see Subsection 5.5.1.) which probably was not present on the polycrystalline ribbon used for the X-ray experiment. If it had been present, it would not have been seen since WACLAWSKI and PLUMMER [5.90] showed that its photoexcitation probability relative to the d-band peak near -2 eV peaked at very low photon energies.] Figures 5.7–5.9 reveal that it is very important to

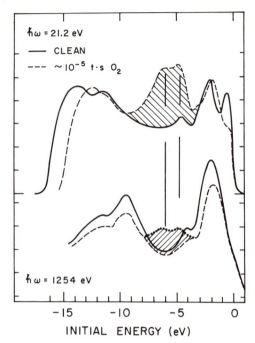

Fig. 5.9. Comparison of the effect of oxygen exposure on the photoelectron spectra from clean tungsten. The top set of curves are for $\hbar\omega = 21.2$ eV [5.88]. The bottom set of curves is for X-rays, $\hbar\omega = 1254$ eV [5.89]. The structure near — 11 eV is due to the W(4d) levels, excited by an impurity X-ray line

choose a photon energy appropriate to the system. The relative changes in the photoexcitation probability as a function of photon energy are usually a much more important consideration in a surface experiment than the electron escape depth as a function of photon energy.

COOPER [5.80] has shown theoretically that if the initial wave-function has nodes, there are nodes in the photoionization cross section. Initial states of the form $1s$, $2p$, $3d$ etc. should not have nodes while all others should. He calculated the photoionization cross section from the $3d$ levels of Cu^+ and $4d$ levels of Ag^+. Ag^+ had a node, and Cu^+ did not. In Figure 5.10 the photoionization probabilities of O ($1p$), S ($2p$), Se ($3p$), and Te ($4p$) are calculated using (5.31). The mean radius shown on the figure was obtained by adjusting the effective Z [5.91]. The nodes move to lower energy as the principal quantum number increases. This figure shows the same trend in excitation probability for O, S, Se, and Te at a given photon energy, as found by HAGSTRUM and BECKER [5.92] for O, S, Se, and Te adsorbed on Ni. It also has the

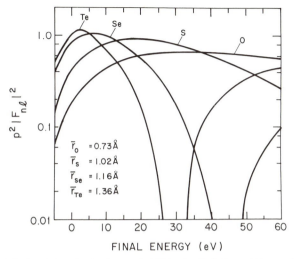

Fig. 5.10. Calculated photoionization probabilities for O, S, Se, and Te as a function of the final energy of the excited electron. Since the ionization potentials are nearly the same the final state energy is just the photon energy minus the ionization potential

same photon energy dependence, with the Te signal dropping faster than that from O as $\hbar\omega$ increased. It would be very interesting to find out whether the Te signal increases for $\hbar\omega > 30$ or 40 eV.

5.4.3. Angular Dependence of Emission

The angular distribution of electrons photoemitted from atoms or molecules in the gas phase has received considerable attention both theoretically [5.93–95] and experimentally [5.96–97]. The objective of these measurements is to determine which molecular orbital is associated with a given photoionization peak in the spectrum of a molecule or, for that matter, an atom. The variation in the angular dependence of one orbital compared to another is never very dramatic because the atoms or molecules in the gas phase have random orientation. On the other hand, a surface can orient all the adsorbed atoms or molecules so that the angular distribution of the emitted electrons has much more structure than the corresponding gas phase spectra [5.98]. A proper analysis of the angular dependence can be used to determine the symmetry of the bonding site [5.98, 99] and potentially the symmetry of each orbital [5.98]. In this section, the theory of the angular distribution from random atoms or molecules will be briefly compared with that from oriented atoms or molecules to illustrate the wealth of new structures produced by orientation. In Subsection 5.46 these angular effects will be discussed within the context of an adsorbed atom or molecule, using the formalism of GADZUK [5.98] and LIEBSCH [5.99].

For simplicity consider an incident beam of polarized photons. If a plane wave were an appropriate description of the final state, then (5.30) would give the probability of observing a photoemitted electron from an oriented atom with an initial state given by the hydrogenic wave function (5.28). θ and φ are the angles between the k vector of the outgoing electron and the orientation of the initial orbital. For a gas phase atom (5.30) must be averaged over all angles θ and φ, i.e., all orientations of the atom. The resulting intensity I as a function of angle is

$$I(\gamma) \propto \cos^2 \gamma,$$

where γ is the angle between the polarization vector A_0 and the direction of emission k. More general calculations for gas phase atoms or molecules [5.94, 95] show that the intensity I can be expressed as

$$I(\gamma) \propto \left[1 + \frac{\beta}{2} (3 \cos^2 \gamma - 1) \right], \tag{5.32}$$

where β is an asymmetry parameter which depends upon the initial and wave final state. The parameter β can range from -1 to $+2$; $\beta = 2$ for a plane.

The form of the continuum function for the final state should be expressed as a sum of spherical harmonics, not a plane wave [5.93, 94]. If the initial state has an angular momentum l_i then the electric dipole selection rules restrict the angular momentum of the out-going photo-electron to $l_f = l_i \pm 1$ [5.82]. Therefore, for an s electron, the ejected electron has $l_f = 1$, leading to $\beta = 2$, but when the initial state is a p state, there are contributions from $l_f = 0$ and $l_f = 2$. The interference of these two out-going waves causes β to be less than 2. For example, $\beta \simeq 1.2$ for photoionization of the $4p$ levels of Kr using He(I) radiation ($\hbar \omega = 21.2$ eV) [5.97].

The effects of orientation can best be illustrated by two simple examples: 1) An atom with a single p orbital, say, boron, and 2) a simple molecule like H_2. For the atomic case assume that the final state is a plane wave. Then in the gas phase the angular intensity $I_g(\gamma)$ is

$$I_g(\gamma) \propto \cos^2 \gamma.$$

But if the atom were oriented on the surface with only a P_z orbital (z is perpendicular to the surface, then the angular intensity of the oriented atom, $I_0(\gamma)$, would be (5.30)

$$I_0(\gamma) \propto \cos^2\gamma \cos^2\theta$$

where θ is the angle between the emission direction and the surface normal. GADZUK [5.98] has illustrated this effect for several different oriented orbitals. In the gas phase the relevant directions are the polarization direction and the emission direction, while for an orientated atom the direction of orientation also becomes important.

The case of an oriented molecule is even more interesting. TULLY et al. [5.96] have calculated β in (5.32) for molecular H_2 in the gas phase. They found $\beta = 1.86$, or an angular dependence of nearly $\cos^2\gamma$ for randomly oriented molecules. Now assume that the H_2 molecule is oriented with its axis along the direction of the photon beam, i.e. A_0 is perpendicular to the axis. KAPLAN and MARKIN [5.100] have calculated the angular dependence of the photoemitted electron from this configuration. They used a wavefunction for the initial state which took into account both the covalent and ionic contributions;

$$\psi_i = N_\perp \{[\varphi_a(1)\,\varphi_b(2) + \varphi_b(1)\,\varphi_a(2)]$$
$$+ \mu[\varphi_a(1)\,\varphi_a(2) + \varphi_b(1)\,\varphi_b(2)]\} \;.$$

When $\mu = 0$, ψ_i is the Heitler-London function and, when $\mu = 1$, it is the molecular orbital type wave function. Their final state is expressible by just a product of a plane wave and an atomic function

$$\psi_f = N_2 \{[\varphi_a(1) + \varphi_b(1)] \exp(i\mathbf{k}\cdot r(2))$$
$$+ [\varphi_a(2) + \varphi_b(2)] \exp(i\mathbf{k}\cdot r(1))\}$$

(N_1 and N_2 are normalization factors). When the matrix element for excitation is calculated using (5.24), the cross section contains an oscillatory factor like

$$1 + \cos(kR_0\cos\gamma),$$

where γ is the angle between the polarization vector and the angle of emission. R_0 is the internuclear spacing. This result can be understand in terms of the interference of two coherent waves emitted from the different centers. If from each center there is emitted a wave $\exp(i\mathbf{k}\cdot r)$, then in a direction θ their phase shift will be determined by the product $k\Delta r = kR_0\cos\theta$. Maxima will be observed for those values of θ at which the path length Δr is an integral number of wave lengths.

The interference pattern from an oriented molecule will therefore give the internuclear spacing R_0 and the orientation with respect to the polarization vector. GADZUK [5.98] has used this fact to show the angular dependence of various surface molecules can be utilized to determine the structure of the molecule.

5.4.4. Relaxation Effects

The energy of a photoemitted electron is always given by

$$E_e = E_0^N - E_\alpha^{N-1} + \hbar\omega, \tag{5.33}$$

where E_0^N and E_α^{N-1} are the total energies of the N electron initial state and the $N-1$, hole final state of the system, respectively. The subscript 0 for the N particle initial state indicates the ground state, which is the only initial state to be considered in this article. The symbol α denotes any one of the possible excited states of the ion. The binding energy E_B of a photoemitted electron is given by

$$E_B = \hbar\omega - E_e \tag{5.34a}$$

or

$$E_B^{(\alpha)} = E_\alpha^{N-1} - E_0^N. \tag{5.34b}$$

In a one electron picture each binding energy $E_B(\alpha)$ can be associated with an ion having a hole in the ith orbital, including the possibility for multiplet splittings.

The term relaxation energy, refers to the change in the energy of the final state E_i^{N-1}, due to the relaxation of the $N-1$ passive electrons towards the ith hole. The relaxation energy cannot be measured, being a theoretical concept, introduced to account for the difference between a binding energy calculated correctly using (5.34b) (including the final state) and a binding energy calculated entirely from the ground state properties of the neutral entity. Since the relaxation energy is a theoretical concept introduced within the one-electron approximation for an N electron system, its meaning may vary from one approximation to another. The following discussion will examine relaxation within the context of a Hartree-Fock (H-F) calculation.

In photoelectron spectroscopy the values of $E_e(i)$ are measured for a number of peaks i at the photon energy $\hbar\omega$. The binding energy of the ith peak is then calculated using (5.34a). Attempts to interpret these binding energies theoretically frequently relate them to the one-electron orbital energies of the initial state, using KOOPMANS' theorem which states that the binding energy of the ith electron in a Hartree-Fock calculation is the orbital energy ε_i of that one electron state, if the $N-1$ orbitals of the ion are taken to be the same as for the neutral atom. This is in fact the meaning of the orbital energy. Therefore, the binding energy using KOOPMANS' theorem with frozen orbitals in the ion, is

$$E_{\mathrm{B}}^{KT}(i) = -\varepsilon_i .$$

In fact the $N-1$ passive orbitals of the ion relax towards the positive hole in the final state, and consequently are not the same as the $N-1$ orbitals of the neutral atom. Within the framework of H-F theory we can define a relaxation energy $E_{\mathrm{R}}(i)$ for the ith orbital as the difference in energy between the binding energy calculated using KOOPMANS' theorem and (5.34b). E_i^{N-1} in (5.34b) is the total energy of the relaxed ion with a hole in the ith orbit,

$$E_{\mathrm{R}} = E_{\mathrm{B}}^{KT}(i) - E_{\mathrm{B}}(i) = -\varepsilon_i - E_{\mathrm{B}}(i) . \tag{5.35a}$$

The binding energy in H-F theory $E_{\mathrm{B}}(i)$ is then given by the orbital energy minus the relaxation energy

$$E_{\mathrm{B}}(i) = -\varepsilon_i - E_{\mathrm{R}} . \tag{5.35b}$$

This subsection will discuss the magnitude of E_{R}(H-F) for different orbitals in a gas phase molecule, [5.101, 102] using calculations for CO as an example. At the end of this subsection the magnitude of the relaxation energy of an atom or molecule (specifically CO) adsorbed on a metal surface will be discussed. When an atom or molcule is adsorbed on the surface of a metal the electrons of the metal atoms will relax towards the positive hole left on the adsorbate so that the relaxation energy will be greater than in the gas phase. This surface induced relaxation will cause a shift in the binding energies of an adsorbate compared to the gas phase binding energies, which can be measured in contrast to E_{R} defined by (5.35b). The important question is how this surface induced relaxation depends upon the properties of the hole state.

The simplest example of relaxation effects in a H-F calculation is the binding energy of the $1s$ electron in He. The H-F orbital energy is -1.79 Ry while the difference between the total energies of He and He$^+$ is -1.70 Ry, so that $E_{\mathrm{R}} = 1.22$ eV. This means that there is a 5% error in using KOOPMANS' theorem to calculate the binding energy of the $1s$ electron in He.

Extensive H-F calculations have been completed for the CO molecule, and for the different related states of CO$^+$ [5.101, 103]. A ground state wavefunction ψ_i is determined in a Hartree-Fock self-consistent field

Table 5.1. Comparison of relaxation energies [eV] in various environments

Configuration	Level	Relaxation energy	Binding energy	Binding energy relative to E_F	Work function φ	Surface shift
Gas phase						
O	O_{1s}	18.0 [a]	544.3[a]			
CO	$O_{1s}(1\sigma)$	20.24[a]	542.6[b]			
	$C_{1s}(2\sigma)$	11.42[a]	296.2[b]			
NO	$O_{1s}(1\sigma)$	20.9 [a]	543.3[b]			
CO	1π	1.90[a]	16.54[c]			
CO	5σ	1.41[a]	14.0 [c]			
Adsorbed CO						
Molecular CO on polycrystalline W						
α_1 state	O_{1s}			534.2[d]		
	C_{1s}			287.2[d]		
α_2 state	O_{1s}			532.8[d]		
Virgin state	O_{1s}			531.5[d]		
	C_{1s}			285.4[d]		
β state	O_{1s}			530.5[d]		
Adsorbed atomic oxygen						
	O_{1s}			530.3[d]	~ 6.0[k]	
	O_{2s}		28	22[k]		
Molecular CO on W(100)						
α_1 state	1π		13.7	8.7[e]	4.98[e]	2.8
	O_{1s}		538.0	533.0[d]	4.98[e]	4.6
	C_{1s}		291.2	286.2[d]	4.98[e]	5.0
α_2 state	1π		13.3	8.3[e]	5.04[e]	3.2
	4σ		16.5	11.4[e]	4.05[e]	3.2
Molecular CO on W(110)						
Virgin state	1π		13.1	7.3[e]	5.75[e]	3.4
	4σ		16.5	10.7[e]	5.75[e]	3.2
α state	1π		13.2	7.8[e]	5.50[e]	3.3

Table 5.1. (continued)

Configuration	Level	Relaxation energy	Binding energy	Binding energy relative to E_F	Work function φ	Surface shift
Molecular CO on Ni(111)	1π		13.6	7.6[f]	6.0 [f]	2.9
	4σ		16.7	10.7[f]	6.0 [f]	3.0
Molecular CO on Ni(100)	1π		13.7	7.8[g]	5.86[g]	2.8
	4σ		17.0	11.1[g]	5.86[g]	2.7
Molecular CO on Fe	1π			7.3[h]		
Organics						
C_2H_4 on Ni(111)	levels		10.9	6.4[f]	4.5	2.1
			12.7	8.2[f]	4.5	2.1
			14.1	9.6[f]	4.5	2.1
C_2H_2 on Ni(111)	3		13.7	9.1[f]	4.6	2.7–3.2[i]
	2		15.8	11.1[f]	4.6	2.7–3.2[i]
C_2H_2 on W(110)	3		13.3	9.1[j]	4.1	3.1
	2		15.2	11.1[j]	4.1	3.2

[a] [5.101].
[b] [5.104].
[c] [5.105].
[d] [5.106].
[e] [5.88].
[f] [5.107].
[g] [5.108].
[h] [5.107].
[i] [5.109] DEMUTH and EASTMAN calculated a relaxation of 3.2 eV. Comparison of their binding energies relative to E_f, including the work function to TURNER [5.105] gives 2.7 eV.
[j] [5.110].
[k] [5.163].

calculation so that the energy is minimized with respect to variations of the orbitals. The ground state wavefunction can be written as [5.101]

$$\psi_0 = [1\sigma_0^2, 2\sigma_0^2, 3\sigma_0^2, 4\sigma_0^2, 5\sigma_0^2, 1\pi_0^4],$$

where the orbitals $1\sigma_0$ and $2\sigma_0$ are essentially the atomic $1s$ orbitals on O and C, respectively. The subscript 0 denotes the orbitals with lowest total energy for the neutral CO molecule. Now we ask what the binding energy of the O_{1s} electron ($1\sigma_0$ level) is. Using Koopmans' theorem, the final state energy is calculated from the frozen orbitals (FO) of neutral CO with an electron missing from the $1\sigma_0$ level

$$E_{1\sigma_0}^{N-1}(FO) = \langle \psi_0^+ |H| \psi_0^+ \rangle$$

where

$$\psi_0^+ = [1\sigma_0^1, 2\sigma_0^2, 3\sigma_0^3, 4\sigma_0^2, 5\sigma_0^2, 1\pi^4]$$

and

$$E_0^N - E_{1\sigma}^{N-1}(FO) = +\varepsilon(1\sigma).$$

On the other hand, Bagus [5.101] calculated the variational "best" orbitals for the O_{1s} hole configuration, i.e., solved the Fock equation for the configuration of an electron missing in the O_{1s} shell. This new relaxed hole-state wavefunction ψ_R^+ was then used to calculate the relaxed final state energy

$$E_{1\sigma}^{N-1}(R) = \langle \psi_R^+ |H| \psi_R^+ \rangle.$$

Using (5.34b) and (5.35b), the relaxation energy is

$$E_R = E_{1\sigma}^{N-1}(FO) - E_{1\sigma}^{N-1}(R). \tag{5.35c}$$

This definition of the relaxation energy is, in principle, more general than the H-F definition of (5.35a). The difference in energy of the ion with frozen and relaxed orbitals can, in principle, be calculated in any one-electron scheme.

The calculated binding energies for CO using (5.34b) with the relaxed final state are in very good agreement with the experimentally measured binding energies [5.103]. The largest error is 4.5% for the 1π level. This means that correlation effects in the CO molecule are not very important or that for some reason they cancel when E_B is calculated. Table 5.1 lists

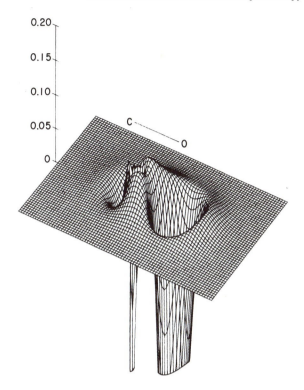

Fig. 5.11. Contour plot of the difference in charge density between frozen orbitals (KOOP-MAN's theorem) and the relaxed ion, for a hole in the $1s$ state of the oxygen. The vertical axis is in units of electrons per a.u. [5.103]

the calculated relaxation energies and the measured binding energies for several levels of CO. The binding energy and relaxation energy for the O_{1s} level in O and NO are also shown for comparison. Notice that a large fraction of the shift in the O_{1s} binding energy between O and CO or NO is a result of the change in the relaxation energy. The relaxation energy of the O_{1s} level in CO is 20.24 eV or 3.7% of the binding energy, while the relaxation energy of the 1π level is 1.90 eV or 11.5% of the binding energy. The relaxation energy or shift of the binding energy with respect to the orbital energy is not a constant or a fixed fraction of the binding energy.

The relaxation of the final state is made much more visible by the electron density difference map [5.103] shown in Fig. 5.11, where the electron density of the relaxed hole state ψ_R^+ is sub-tracted from that given by the "frozen" orbital—KOOPMANS' theorem state ψ_0^+, for an O_{1s} hole. The sigma orbitals (3σ and 4σ) and the 1π

orbital are both contracted. The effect of the π-orbital is discernible in the twin-humped feature between the nuclei.

The orbital energies calculated in H-F cannot be rigidly shifted or uniformly compressed in energy to obtain agreement with the binding energies. Yet the error may only be 10%, so that H-F orbital energies have served a very useful role in identification and ordering of observed binding energies in atoms and molecules. Orbital energies in other one-electron calculational schemes may not have the same significance, since analogues to KOOPMANS' theorem for H-F may not exist. Therefore, all calculations of binding energies should use (5.34b) and not the orbital energies.

When an atom or molecule is adsorbed on or absorbed in a metal surface, a shift in the measured binding energy (relative to the gas phase) of each energy level will result. If we view this "surface shift" in a one-electron picture, then some part of the shift of a specific level is due to bonding shifts (chemical shifts) in the initial state, while the remaining contribution to the shift comes from relaxation effects in the final state. In contrast to the relaxation energies defined by (5.35a) for the energy levels of an isolated atom or molcule, this "surface shift" can be measured. This measurement is analogous to the shift in the binding energy of a core electron in an atom when it is bound in different molecules. For example, Table 5.1 shows a shift of the O_{1s} level of 1.7 eV in CO and 1.0 eV in NO compared to atomic oxygen. If the calculated relaxation energies shown in Table 5.1 are correct then the differential relaxation accounts for 2.2 eV in CO and 2.9 eV in NO. Therefore, the "chemical shift" in the initial state must be -0.5 eV for CO and -1.9 eV for NO. This example illustrates the complexity involved in trying to extract the shift due to the initial state from the measured shift, either in the gas phase or adsorbed on the surface. Obviously, if the binding energy was calculated using (5.34b), both of these effects would automatically be taken into account, but it is not likely that these big systems (bulk plus adsorbate) will be routinely calculated. Therefore, it is useful to discuss the magnitude of the surface shift induced by relaxation in the final state.

The magnitude of this surface induced relaxation effects is important in the following situations: 1) When the photoelectron spectrum of an adsorbed molecule is being compared to gas phase spectra in an attempt to identify the chemical nature of the surface molecule [5.109, 110]; 2) when the shift in a core level of an adsorbed atom or molecule is being used to determine the "chemical shift" due to bonding, and 3) when valence band spectra of an adsorbed atom or molecule are being used to determine the bonding energy shift of a specific energy level [5.107]. The relaxation contribution to the "surface shift" could be formulated in terms of (5.35c), where the relaxation on the surface complex is calculated and the relaxation in the gas phase subtracted. This is a very cumbersome definition, since it relies on the concept of frozen orbitals and necessitates two separate calculations. A much more physical picture of the "surface shift" is obtainable by use of a simple Born-Haber cycle.

If $E_{ion}(i)$ is the bond energy of the ion to the surface, after an electron has been removed from the ith orbital, and $E_{neut.}$ is the bond energy of the atom or molecule to the surface in the ground state, then the binding energy of the ith orbital on the surface $E_B^s(i)$ can be related to the binding energy in the gas phase, $E_B(i)$ by

$$E_B^s(i) = E_B(i) - E_{ion}(i) + E_{neut.} .$$

The "surface shift", which is $E_B(i) - E_B^s(i)$, is given by the difference in the bond strength of the neutral and the ionized molecule. This energy difference will depend upon not only the nature of the ith orbit, but the degree of electronic and spatial relaxation of the ion. This equation illustrates that physically "relaxation shifts" and "bonding shift" are inseparable, unless one or the other can be calculated.

The limiting case of photoionization from a level which is not involved in the bonding or shifted as a consequence of bonding can be discussed within the context of the above equation. This means that we are considering the "surface shift" of an energy level whose H-F orbital energy is the same in the gas phase as it is when bonded to the surface. In addition, we assume that: 1) The relaxation of the outer electrons of the molecule on the surface is the same as in the gas phase and, 2) that the relaxation of the electrons about the hole does not change the bond strength of the neutral molecule. In other words, we will consider only effects due to screening of the hole by the electrons in the metal. This means that the bond energy of the ion is the neutral bond energy plus the change in the energy of the metal due to screening the hole. SMITH et al. [5.111] have calculated the change in energy of a jellium metal [5.112] as a proton is brought up to the surface. The response of the electron gas depends upon the distance of the proton from the jellium surface. This energy is 5.7 eV for a proton 1.5 Å from the surface and reaches a maximum of 8.7 eV at a spacing of 0.5 Å. This calculation is for a high density electron gas so that these values for the "relaxation energy" are probably upper limits. The response of the electron gas will depend upon the density of the gas, the position of the ion relative to the surface and the spatial extent of the hole orbit. The relaxation energy due to the metal electrons screening the ion will decrease as the size of the hole state increases. In a one-electron model like H-F this contribution to the surface shift goes to zero for a completely delocalized hole state. This fact is the basis for assuming KOOPMANS' theorem is correct for excitation from the conduction band of a solid.

Table 5.1 tabulates the "surface shift" for several orbitals of CO adsorbed on different metals, as well as two valence orbitals of C_2H_2 adsorbed on Ni and W. There is always some uncertainty in the binding energies of an adsorbed molecule, since the measurements are made relative to the Fermi energy and it is not clear which value of the work function should be added. The work function used as well as the measured binding energies relative to the Fermi energy are shown in Table 5.1. The work functions used were measured with the adsorbate present.

The measurements for the α_1 state of CO adsorbed on (100) tungsten illustrates the effects of different orbits. The surface shift for the C_{1s} level is 5.0 eV which is larger than the shift of 4.6 eV for the O_{1s}, presumably because the CO is bonded to the surface standing up with the carbon closer to the surface. Both the C_{1s} and O_{1s} have a larger shift than the 1π level, since they are more localized. In a one-electron picture the shift should go to zero for a spatially extended orbital. The surface shift of the 1π and 4σ levels of CO shown for the α_2 state of CO on (100) W and for adsorption of CO on (110) W, Ni (111), and Ni (100), are nearly identical for all cases. The charge distribution in these states is approximately the same with a ratio of 3:1 on the oxygen compared to the carbon. The surface shift for all of the valences orbitals listed in Table 5.1 ranges from 2.7 eV to 3.4 eV, with the exception of C_2H_4 on Ni (111).

Therefore, when a gas phase photoelectron spectrum is being compared to that of an adsorbed molecule, the former should be shifted upward by ~ 3 eV in the energy range of the valence orbitals. If some of the orbitals do not line up properly there is no way at present, without the aid of a calculation, to tell if this is a consequence of a different relation energy or a bonding shift. The experimentalist should operate on the premise that relaxation is not uniform for all levels. There may be situations like the 1π and 4σ levels of CO where the surface shift is constant, presumably as a consequence of both orbits having a similar charge distribution relative to the surface.

5.4.5. Bulk vs. Surface Emission

In this subsection, the concepts of bulk and surface photoemission will be briefly reviewed, always from the point of view of an observer outside trying to see the bulk through the surface. There is an interference between the bulk and surface [5.71, 77] photoemission processes, and at present there is no theoretically justifiable model for extracting either the bulk contribution or the surface contribution from the total distribution. In some cases, there may be so little emission from the surface that the energy distribution is primarily bulk. Likewise, when a state at the surface is spatially localized and split off from the bulk band, it is easy to identify, but in general the surface density of states in the region of the band will be very difficult if not impossible to extract from the energy distribution.

Let us begin with the simplest solid, that is — an infinite free electron gas. The initial and final states are

$$\psi_i \propto \exp(i\mathbf{k}_i \cdot \mathbf{r}); \; \psi_f \propto \exp(i\mathbf{k}_f \cdot \mathbf{r}),$$

where by conservation of energy

$$\hbar^2 k_f^2 / 2m = \hbar^2 k_i^2 / 2m + \hbar\omega.$$

If we apply the momentum matrix element of (5.24), $k_f = k_i$.

This can never be true if energy is conserved and $\hbar\omega \neq 0$. Therefore, there can be no photoexcitation in an infinite free electron gas. The application of the gradient in potential matrix element of (5.25b) to a free electron gas immediately produces the above result since $\nabla V = 0$ for a free electron gas. If this gas is bounded by a surface, then $\nabla V \neq 0$ at this surface and we have what is called the "surface photoelectric effect". This fact led early investigators to conclude that photoemission occurred only at the surface [5.75, 113–116]. The search for this effect has spanned three decades, from the work of MITCHELL in 1934 [5.113] up to the present [5.116]. The theory of the "surface photoelectric effect" has been worked out in detail for a free electron metal by ENDRIZ [5.116]. (A free electron metal allows no bulk excitations so in this case there is no possibility of interference between bulk and "surface emission" [5.77].)

In a real metal, however, the concept of surface emission is not clearly defined. In a non-free electron metal, there are gradients in the potential throughout the bulk caused by the ion cores. "Bulk photoemission" by definition, originates from this three-dimensional, periodic array of the potentials. Near the surface, the magnitude, spacing and periodicity of the potentials may change. The consequence of these changes (see the introduction of this chapter) is that the electronic properties in the vicinity of a surface atom are different from that of an atom in the bulk. The term "surface emission" can be taken to mean either the emission from the potential step at the surface or from the surface layer or layers of atoms. In a real crystal with ion cores, there does not seem to be any theoretical way of defining and separating the "surface" from the "bulk" effect [5.71, 77]. The only cases where a separation can be justified is when either one of the components becomes very small. When one considers a free electron metal, the bulk contribution is zero and the functional form of the surface emission may be predicted. Likewise, when the incident light is normal (so that $A \cdot VV = 0$) and the electron escape depth is much larger than the region of the bulk which has been perturbed by the surface, then the surface contribution should be small and the properties of the emission predicted by the bulk properties. In any intermediate region, the two effects are so mingled that they may be inseparable. For UV photoemission, anything from 10% to 90% of the signal may come from the surface.

In Subsection 5.4.2 where photoexcitation cross sections were introduced it was pointed out that the $P \cdot A$ term in (5.21) was usually dropped assuming that any gradients in A were small. The surface-polarization charge induced by the component of A perpendicular to the surface (A_z) causes a rapid change in A_z over a region of ~ 2 Å. ENDRIZ [5.116] has shown how important this terms is in calculating the "surface photoelectric effect".

Let us now describe a more sophisticated model for bulk photoemission, usually called the "direct transition" model. Here we write the initial and final states as 3-*D* Bloch states.

$$\psi_f \propto \exp(i k_f \cdot r) \, U^n_{k_f}(r) \qquad \psi_i \propto \exp(i k_i \cdot r) \, U^m_{k_i}(r),$$

where n and m are band indices. If we apply the momentum matrix operator of (5.24), we have

$$P_{if} \propto |A_0 \cdot \langle \psi_f | P | \psi_i \rangle|^2$$
$$\propto |A_0 \cdot [\int \exp(i(k_f - k_i)\cdot r) \, U^n_{k_f} V \, U^m_{k_i}$$
$$- i k_i \exp(i(k_f - k_i)\cdot r) \, U^n_{k_f} U^m_{k_i} d\tau]|^2 .$$

The second term is zero unless $n = m$, which cannot be true if the energy of the final state is to be larger by $\hbar\omega$ than the energy of the initial state. The first term gives the criterion that $k_f = k_i$, where k_f and k_i are the crystal momentum in the reduced zone scheme. The K of the final state in the extended zone scheme is $K_f = k_f + G_n$, where n denotes the reciprocal lattice vector associated with the nth band. The energy distribution of excited electrons $P_0(E, \omega)$ is given by summing all bands and integrating over all k in the reduced zone [5.21]

$$P_0(E, \omega) \propto \sum_{n,m} \int d^3 k \, P_{if} \delta[E_n(k) - E_m(k) - \hbar\omega] \, \delta(E - E_n), \qquad (5.37)$$

where

$$P_{if} \propto \int U^n_k \, A_0 \cdot V U^m_k \, d\tau .$$

If we want to calculate the number of electrons excited in a direction K, then the reduced zone scheme of (5.37) is not very useful, since the reduced k_f does not give the direction of propagation of the final state. For a free electron band structure, each band m has a specific G_m which was used to fold the extended zone back to the reduced zone. For example, consider the case of a band structure in the (001) direction of a simple cubic. The first band obviously has $G_1 = 0$. The second band is folded back with $G_2(00\bar{1})$. The next set of bands are composed of reciprocal vectors of the form $G_3(010)$. An excitation from an initial state given by k_i in the first band to a final state k_f (reduced zone) in the second band occurs when

$$\frac{h^2}{2m}\left[k_f + \frac{2\pi}{a}(0,0,\bar{1})\right]^2 = h\omega + \frac{h^2}{2m}k_i^2$$

or since $k_f = k_i$

$$h\omega = -\frac{4\pi}{a}|k_f| + E_G \quad \text{where} \quad E_G = \frac{h^2}{2m}\left(\frac{2\pi}{a}\right)^2.$$

The direction of this excited electron is

$$K = K_f + (2\pi/a)(0,0,1) = \left(0,0,\frac{-2\pi}{a} + k_f\right).$$

If positive k_z is out of the crystal, then this direction is back into the crystal since $k_f < \pi/a$. But the initial state of $-k_i$ excited to $-k_i + (2\pi/a)$ $(0,0,1)$ comes out. In contrast, excitation from $k_i(G=0)$ to k_f in the band associated with $G = (2\pi/a)(0,1,0)$ occurs when

$$h\omega = E_G = (h^2/2m)(4\pi^2/a^2).$$

The direction of the final K is implicitly given by

$$K = (2\pi/a)(0,1,0) + k_i$$

or if θ is the angle from the z axis,

$$\tan\theta = 2\pi/a|k_i| \quad \theta = \tan^{-1}\left(\frac{2\pi}{a|k_i|}\right) \geqq 63°.$$

This excitation would not be seen by a detector normal to the surface. In general, a plot of the bulk energy bands in a reduced zone scheme will indicate which transitions are allowed for a given photon energy, but it will not yield information about the direction of propagation of the excited electron, unless the reciprocal lattice vectors of the initial and final state bands are known. The direction of propagation of the excited electron need not be in the same direction as the k of the initial state.

In a complicated band structure, there are many G's for a given k_f in a band and the weight associated with a given G changes as k_f changes. Therefore, it is not possible to make a unique identification of k_f in the reduced scheme with a single K_f in the extended zone. In the extended zone scheme, the energy distribution of electrons with final energy E and final direction K_f is given by

$$P_0(K, E, \omega) \propto \sum_{i,f,G} P_{if} \delta(E_f - E_i - \hbar\omega) \, \delta(K_f - k_i - G)$$
$$\cdot \delta(K_f - K) \, \delta(E - E_f), \qquad (5.38)$$

where

$$P_{if} \propto |\int U_{K_f,G} A_0 V U_{ki,G} \, d\tau|^2 \, .$$

P_0 in (5.37) or (5.38) is usually multiplied by an escape function, assuming a three step process of light penetration, excitation, and transport and escape [5.117]. This term, even if it is appropriate does not shed much light on the physics of the process; consequently, we will leave it out.

If the matrix element P_{if} of (5.37) is assumed to be a constant for all i or f, then the calculated energy distribution is called the energy distribution of the joint density of states (EDJDOS) [5.118]. If the delta function on crystal momentum is removed from (5.37), the newly allowed transitions are called "non-direct" since momentum is not conserved. If P_{if} is set equal to a constant in this case, the energy distribution is proportional to the product of the initial and final density of states.

Assuming that the excitation process may be separated from the escape function, let us investigate the effect of the short attenuation length on the direct transition model. To begin with, let us ignore the fact that the short mean-free path localizes the excitation near the surface; consider for the moment the excitation process deep in the bulk. The scattering effects can be taken into account in a phenomenological fashion by assigning an uncertainty ΔK to the wave vector of the final state. ΔK can be estimated by using the uncertainty principle in terms of the electron attenuation length λ

$$\Delta K = 1/\lambda \, .$$

The smear in k is over $\sim 20\%$ of a reduced zone for a lattice spacing $a = 3$ Å and an escape depth of 5 Å. This washes out the sharp structure predicted by a "direct transition model" for one electron bands; the energy distribution begins to look like the "non-direct" model.

Now consider the effect of localizing the excitation near the surface. In this region, the component of the K vector perpendicular to the surface (K_z) is strictly speaking not a good quantum number. There will still be conservation of the crystal momentum parallel to the surface

$$k_f^{||} = k_i^{||} + G_{||},$$

where G is a surface reciprocal lattice vector. MAHAN [5.119] has shown that if $a/\lambda \ll 1$ the excitation process is described by conservation of the 3-dimensional k (a is a characteristic spacing in the crystal). In the region of interest to us $\dfrac{a}{\lambda} \sim 1$ so we would expect only a small remnant of k_z conservation. This again will have the effect of washing out both angular dependences and final state structure predicted by a bulk model [5.119]. (A problem which is related to this is the change in the density of both initial and final states near the surface [5.120–123].)

One of the simplest examples in the literature which illustrates the problem of separating bulk and surface effects is the Kronig-Penney model used by SCHAICH and ASHCROFT [5.77]. This is basically the same model used by DUKE and FAUCHIER [5.35] for field emission calculations consisting of two dimensional δ function sheets spaced an equal distance apart and parallel to the surface. The surface is a potential step. SCHAICH and ASHCROFT concluded that, to the extent that the "volume" and "surface" effects may be separated, they *must* interfere since the matrix element given by (5.25b) has a term containing the gradient in potential at the surface and a term containing the periodic bulk potential. The current is given by the square of this probability, and either constructive or destructive interference may occur. In Ref. [5.77], Fig. 1, the effect of this interference on the energy distribution as a function of the electron escape depth is shown. For an escape depth of 5 Å, the energy distribution does not look like what would have been predicted from the bulk, the surface, or any linear combination of the two. Figure 5.12 taken from [5.77] shows the angular dependence of emission for a final energy 1.4 eV above the vacuum level, as a function of the electron escape depth. This illustrates many of the points we want to make. If the escape depth is very large, the curve shown in Fig. 5.12 would be a delta function as MAHAN's theory would have predicted [5.119]. The effect of the inelastic scattering on the final state is to wash out this sharp structure, as can be seen even for an escape depth of 30 Å. The dashed line at the bottom is the surface photoelectric effect from the step potential at the surface [5.113]. As the electron escape depth is decreased, two effects occur — the amplitude decreases with an increased half width and there

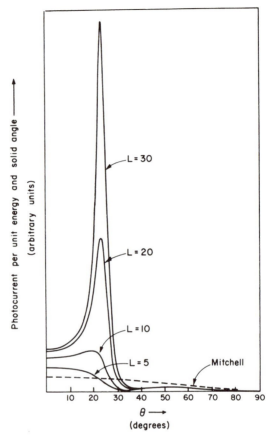

Fig. 5.12. Angular distribution of photoemitted electrons from a modified Kronig-Penney model [5.77]. The emitted electrons have an energy of 1.4 eV above the vacuum. L is the parametrized electron escape depth λ. The dashed curve is the angular dependence of the surface photoelectric effect for the step potential at the surface, first calculated by MITCHELL [5.113]

is both constructive and destructive interference between the bulk and surface effects. The effects seem to be constructive for $\theta < 15°$ and destructive for $\theta > 20°$. This model could be extended by changing the strength and position of the first delta function potential to represent a surface atom, but the effect of the interference is clearly illustrated by Fig. 5.12.

One final observation in this section is that if for any reason the hole state becomes localized, the direct transition model will break down [5.124]. In this case, the final state is not a Bloch state, and there will be

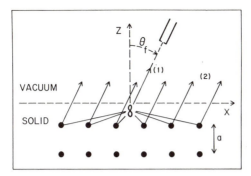

Fig. 5.13. Illustration of two processes contributing to photoemission from an adsorbate p_z orbital 1) direct emission into a plane-wave final state, 2) indirect emission via backscattering from the substrate. Only single scattering from the first layer is indicated [5.99]

no selection rules on crystal momentum. This was suggested by SPICER in 1967 to explain the fact that the energy distributions from many metals appeared as if they were caused by non-direct transitions.

5.4.6. Angular Resolved Surface Emission

The possibility of orienting molecules by adsorbing them on a surface presents great opportunities for angular and energy resolved photoemission. Subsection 5.4.3 already pointed out the expected effects for an oriented gas phase molecule. GADZUK [5.98] calculated the angular dependence for a variety of atomic orbitals and molecular surface complexes, and showed that information about the bond geometry may be obtained from the angular measurements. If one knew the direction of the A vector the symmetry and possibly the direction of the orbital being observed could be measured.

The calculations described in Subsection 5.4.3 and those of GADZUK [5.98] assume a plane wave final state. When the molecule or atom is adsorbed the final state must include the scattering from the crystal. This situation is best described by Fig. 5.13 where a hypothetical adsorbate is pictured above a periodic lattice [5.99]. If the detector is positioned at a polar angle θ_f and an azimuthal angle φ, two coherent waves are detected: 1) The direct excitation into a plane wave (GADZUK's process) and 2) Backscatter waves from the surface. LIEBSCH [5.99] has developed a "one-step" model for photoemission which uses a multiple-scattering theory such as has been applied to LEED to treat the final state. By applying this formalism to the case of localized adsorbate energy levels he could show that the symmetry of the adsorption site was as important

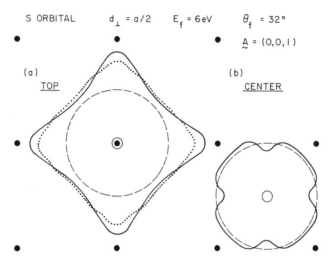

S ORBITAL $d_\perp = a/2$ $E_f = 6\,eV$ $\theta_f = 32°$

$\underset{\sim}{A} = (0,0,1)$

(a)   TOP

(b)   CENTER

Fig. 5.14a and b. Photoemission intensity (arbitrary units) as a function of azimuthal angle for an s orbital adsorbed in top (a) and center (b) positions on the (100) face of a cubic crystal: Single scattering (solid curve), multiple scattering (dotted curve), shown only in panel (a), and no scattering (dashed curves) [5.99]

in determining the angular dependence as the symmetry of the bonding orbital.

Figure 5.14 shows an azimuthal plot of the intensity from an s orbital on a simple cubic substrate. Scattering in the final state produces a significant effect, with the symmetry of the pattern reflecting the symmetry of the bonding site. In these calculations the vector potential is perpendicular to the surface.

At present very little information is available on angular resolved photoemission from adsorbate covered surfaces. Figure 5.15 displays some preliminary work of WACLAWSKI [5.125] for oxygen adsorbed on W(100), at $\hbar\omega = 21.2$ eV. The top set of energy distributions are for clean (100)W and an exposure of 5×10^{-6} Torr sec of O_2 at a crystal temperature of 1500 K. All the emission within a polar angle of 45° was collected. The second set of curves is for the same situation except only those electrons which were emitted at a polar angle of $33° \pm 2.5°$, perpendicular to the plane of incidence of the light were collected. The bottom set of curves are for electrons emitted normal to the surface $+3.8°$. The top set of curves shows a double peak at ~ -5.0 and -6.0 eV derived from the p orbitals of oxygen. The high energy peak is accentuated at normal collection while the low energy peak is more pronounced at 33° collection. The peak at -2.0 eV in the top curves is much more pronounced at 33° than that at 0°, while the peak at -0.4 eV in the clean

ANGULAR DEPENDENCE OF O_2 ON (IOO)W

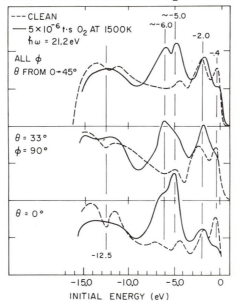

Fig. 5.15. Angular dependence of the photoemission spectra for 5×10^{-6} Torr·sec O_2 at 1500 K on (100)W [5.125]. The top set of curves are for collection of all the photoemitted electron within a polar angle of $\pm 45°$. The middle set of curves is for a collection angle of $33° \pm 2.5°$ normal to the plane of incidence of the light. The final set of curves are for normal emission ($\pm 3.3°$). The incident light was at $45°$ and 21.2 eV

curve which is a surface state (see Subsection 5.5.1) is more pronounced at $0°$ than at $33°$. The dip at -12.5 eV is caused by a band gap in the final state; there are no states in the crystal for the secondary electrons. It is much more pronounced at $\theta = 0°$ than at $\theta = 33°$. If one interpreted these curves in terms of initial state effects then the lower energy oxygen-derived level would be in the plane of the surface and the higher energy level would be more in the perpendicular direction. The -2.0 eV level shown at $\theta = 33°$ could be a d-like level in the substrate mostly in the plane of the surface.

Figure 5.15 indicates a more practical problem: what one sees depends upon where one looks. For example, if the detector was fixed at large θ one would never know that the oxygen derived levels were split. Notice also that the peak position of the high energy peak is shifted by about 0.5 eV between the $\theta = 0°$ curve and the large collection angle at the top. Likewise there is about a 1 eV shift in the "d-band" peak at -2.0 eV in the clean curves. LIEBSCH and PLUMMER [5.126] have applied LIEBSCH's

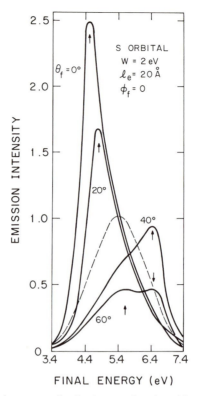

Fig. 5.16. Photoemission energy distribution as a function of final energy for a 2 eV wide p_z orbital adsorbed in the top position on a cubic lattice. The solid curves represent the intensity along four different detector angles. The dashed curve shows the intensity in the absence of scattering. The arrows indicate the effective peak positions caused by final state effects [5.126]

[5.99] "one-step" scattering model to investigate the effects on line shape and peak position in a photoemission spectrum from an adsorbate covered surface as a function of the angle of detection and the photon energy. The initial state of the adsorbate was assumed to be Gaussian in shape centered around a binding energy E_i (relative to the vacuum) with a full width at half maximum given by W. Then for a photon energy $\hbar\omega$ we would expect to see electrons emitted with a final energy in the range

$$-E_i + \hbar\omega - W \leqq E_f \leqq -E_i + \hbar\omega + W$$

peaked at $E_f = -E_i + \hbar\omega$. Because of the coherent scattering in the final state, the photoemission intensities exhibit a considerable amount of structure over the energy range shown above, thus causing the observed peak to deviate in shape and position from the Gaussian distribution centered around $-E_i + \hbar\omega$. This effect is illustrated in Fig. 5.16 where the calculated energy distributions are shown for an adsorbed s orbital sitting in the "top" position of a cubic crystal. The solid curves are for various detector directions θ_f and the dashed curve gives the distribution corresponding to no scattering. Over the 60° range of detector angles the peak is seen to vary considerably in shape and peak position (~ 2 eV). At $\theta_f = 60°$ a weak splitting of the peak takes place. These effects depend upon the final energy E_f (photon energy for a fixed adsorbate level), the electron attenuation length λ and the width W of the adsorbate level.

Averaging over large collection angles has the effect of averaging out the final state scattering effects. Therefore it seems advisable to use as large a collection angle as possible if the objective of the experiment is to look only at the energy level spectra of adsorbates. Photoemission used for the "Fingerprint" technique should certainly use a large collection angle.

5.5. Experimental Results

The last two sections will be devoted to presenting experimental data from photoemission and field emission experiments. In general, the emphasis will be placed on systems where both field emission and photoemission data are available.

5.5.1. Clean Surfaces

It was shown in Subsection 5.2.1 that field emission can measure the "one-dimensional density of states" at the turning point. There are band structure calculations [5.127] and photoemission measurements [5.128], for several directions of tungsten which we will be compared to the field emission measurements. Our objective will be twofold: 1) to determine if the "one-dimensional surface density of states" differs from what a bulk calculation would predict and 2) compare field emission and photoemission to determine the sensitivity of photoemission to the surface density of states. Figure 5.17 shows a comparison of the calculated energy bands in the direction perpendicular to the surface [5.127], the measured field emission R curves (see (5.11)), the smoothed one-dimensional bulk density of states and the photoemission energy distributions of FEUERBACHER [5.128, 129]. The photoemission energy distributions were measured normal to the surface within $\pm 6°$ and the photon energy was chosen to avoid predicted bulk direct excitations [5.127]. CHRISTEN-

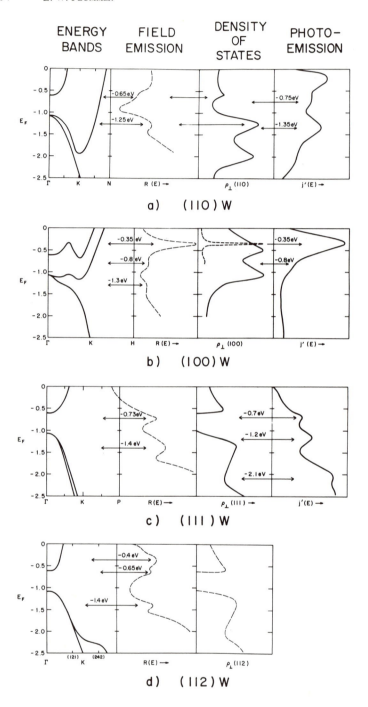

a)   (110) W

b)   (100) W

c)   (111) W

d)   (112) W

SEN has calculated that in the (110) direction there is a gap in the final state extending from approximately 7.8 eV to 9.8 eV above the Fermi energy. The photoemission curve in Fig. 5.17 is for $\hbar\omega = 9.5$ eV, putting the excited state right in this gap.

At first glance the resemblance of the field emission, photoemission and one-dimensional density of states is fairly good, with the exception of the peak at -0.35 eV on (100) W. For all four faces the peak at -1.3 to -1.4 eV seems to line up fairly well with the bulk calculation (third column) while there is a noticeable difference on (111) W between the -1.4 eV level in field emission at the -1.2 eV level in photoemission. The peaks in both the photoemission and field emission distributions at the top of the gap near -0.7 eV seem to be lower than the bulk calculations would predict. Four specific features in the field emission curves cannot be explained by the bulk band structure: 1) the large peak at -0.35 eV on (100) W which is a surface resonance in the spin-orbit split gap in that direction [5.129–131]; 2) a peak and or shoulder on (110) W near -0.4 eV; 3) an additional peak at -0.4 eV in the (112) direction and 4) the current which appears in the total gaps in the (111) and (112) directions.

The first three items are indications of density of states changes near the surface. The most pronounced is the surface resonance on the (100) face. The dashed curve in the third column is the surface density of states calculated by STURM and FEDER [5.133], who used a 3 band tight binding model which takes into account the surface resonance in the spin-orbit induced gap. Their calculation predicts a slightly narrower peak than found in field emission which itself is narrower than the photoemission peak. It has been argued that the photoemission curve is broader because it samples a larger region of k-space. In these measurements FEUERBACHER [5.129] used a 12° collection angle. The 5° collection angle shown in Fig. 5.15 does not produce a peak which is noticeably narrower.

WACLAWSKI and PLUMMER [5.131] examined this surface resonance on (100) W as a function of exposure to hydrogen, in field and photoemission. This comparison is shown in Fig. 5.18. The measured work function changes indicated that < 0.2 of a monolayer of hydrogen was

Fig. 5.17a–d. Comparison of energy bands [5.127], field emission R curves, one-dimensional bulk density of states [5.127] and normal emission photoemission energy distributions [5.128] for four low index faces of tungsten. The energy is $\hbar\omega = 9.5$ eV for (110) W; 10.2 eV for (100)-W and 10.2 eV for (111) W. The density of states shown in Column 3 is the one-dimensional density of states calculated by CHRISTENSEN [5.127] from energy bands (shown in the first column), which have been smoothed by hand to remove the singularities. The dashed curve in the third column for (100) W is from a surface resonance calculation by STURM and FEDER [5.133]

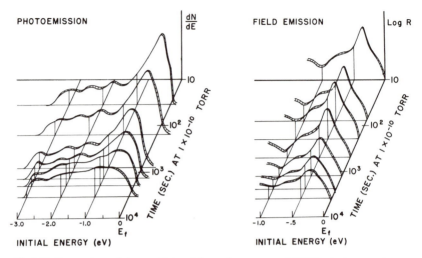

Fig. 5.18. Comparison of the sensitivity of the surface state on (100)W to hydrogen adsorption for photoemission at $\hbar\omega = 7.7$ eV (left) and field emission (right) [5.131]

adsorbed in the final curves. Within the accuracy of two different vacuum gauges these two sets of curves show the surface resonance disappearing in the same manner as hydrogen is adsorbed. Thus photoemission is dominated in this case by the signal from the surface. The latter decreases relative to the bulk signal as the photon energy is increased (see Fig. 5.15) in contradiction to what an escape depth argument would predict. WACLAWSKI and PLUMMER [5.131] measured the optical excitation probability and showed that it peaked at low energies, i.e. the variation in the photoexcitation cross section as a function of energy is more important than the variation of the electron escape depth with energy.

The fourth point of discrepancy between the field emission—photoemission curves and the bulk calculations is the current which is present in the gap regions on (111) and (112) tungsten. It would be fairly easy to attribute this either to electron scattering or to breakdown of conservation of k across the interface. But before jumping to that conclusion one must consider that is measured on these high-index faces. Consider first the case of photoemission, and assume for the moment that the surface is merely a window through which the bulk may be viewed. We now require

$$K_f = k_i + G, \quad K_{f_\parallel} = 0, \quad \text{and} \quad E_f = E_i + \hbar\omega.$$

There are two ways to satisfy the $K_\parallel = 0$ criterion; the first is obvious and corresponds to the slice of k-space shown in Fig. 5.17, that is if z

is the normal direction then

$$k_{ix} = k_{iy} = 0$$

and

$$G_x = G_y = 0 \, .$$

The other solution is more interesting, i.e.

$$\left.\begin{array}{l} k_{ix} = -G_x \\ k_{iy} = -G_y \end{array}\right\} k_{i_\parallel} = -\boldsymbol{G}_i^\parallel$$

so that transitions other than along the cut in k-space shown for each plane in Fig. 5.17 may occur. The criterion for this condition is the existence of a reciprocal lattice vector $\boldsymbol{G}$ such that the vector

$$\boldsymbol{Q} = (\boldsymbol{n} \times \boldsymbol{G}) \times \boldsymbol{n}$$

lies within the first Brillouin zone. The unit vector $\boldsymbol{n}$ lies normal to the surface. For a low-index face this criterion can never be satisfied so that the E vs k curves for (110) and (100) W are the only possibilities for direct transition. For the (111) face there is another slice in k space where $k_{i_\parallel} = -\boldsymbol{G}_\parallel$ besides the $\varGamma$ to P cut shown in Fig. 5.17. This is along the zone face between the points H and P. Comparing the points H and P it is obvious that there will not be a gap in this cut in the energy range -0.6 to -1.1 eV. How much these transitions contribute to the energy distribution is uncertain, but the band structure from $\varGamma$ to P does not tell all the story even if the surface contributions are neglected. All planes of higher index than (111) have other lines of allowed transitions besides the line from $\varGamma$ in k space. Therefore, we can now understand why the intensity in the photoemission spectra should not go to zero in the gaps shown in Fig. 5.17c and d, without involving surface effects.

Even though there are no excitations in field emission the same type of process may occur, if we require that the $\boldsymbol{k}_\parallel$ of the lattice potential be conserved across the barrier then

$$\boldsymbol{k}_\parallel \text{ (outside)} = \boldsymbol{k}_\parallel \text{ (inside)} + \boldsymbol{G}_\parallel \, .$$

If we ignore the slight spread in $\boldsymbol{k}_\parallel$ (outside) then $\boldsymbol{k}_\parallel$ (outside) $= 0$ and

$$\boldsymbol{k}_\parallel \text{ (inside)} = -\boldsymbol{G}_\parallel \, .$$

Thus bulk states with $k_\parallel \neq 0$ can be diffracted by the surface into $k_\parallel = 0$ states. This would allow one to look at the bulk states along the P to H cut in a *bcc* crystal when looking at the (111) surface. Therefore we would not expect to have zero current in the gap in the (111) and (112) directions of tungsten. For (112) W the line in k space where $k_\parallel$ (inside) $= -G_\parallel$, enters the Brillouin zone at N [(110) direction] and leaves the Brillouin zone at a point where another [112] vector intersects. Therefore the peak at -0.4 eV on (112) W and -0.4 eV on (110) W might originate from structure near the K point in the Brillouin zone. For example, the band rising above E_F near N in Fig. 5.17a might intersect the zone face below E_F.

The photoemission energy distributions at low energies, normal to the surface of a single crystal of tungsten seem to reproduce fairly accurately the "one-dimensional surface density of states" at least within 2 eV of E_F. This statement is surely not true at higher photon energies [5.87, 128], as will be seen in the next subsection, so that no general conclusions should be drawn from the work on tungsten. It would be helpul to have field emission distributions for comparison with normal photoemission distributions for several other materials but these data do not exist. How then can one find at least rough guidelines for separation of bulk and surface effects?

In certain cases such as surface states [5.134, 135] or surface resonances [5.131, 132] changes occurring upon adsorption will identify the surface contribution. For tungsten this works only for the surface resonance of the (100) face. CHRISTENSEN [5.127] and FEUERBACHER [5.128] "eliminate" bulk emission by deciding on a model for it, in this case "direct transitions". All the structure in the energy distribution which cannot be identified with the bulk model is then tentatively classified as surface emission. The photon energy dependence of the model is used to decide whether a given peak corresponds to a direction transition. What is left is by definition non-bulk and in some way represents the presence of the surface. It surely cannot be identified with the local density of states of the surface layer, except in rare cases where there is an unusually large surface excitation probability. Even when there is a gap in the final state the excitation goes from initial state to an evanescent wave which penetrates into the bulk. All of the intensity in the photoemission curves shown in Fig. 5.17 comes from non-bulk emission.

ROWE and IBACH [5.136] used a more experimental approach to separate and bulk contributions from the (111) face of Si with different 2-D periodicity, by averaging the energy distributions from 3 different 2-D geometrical arrangements of the Si (111) plane. This averaged distribution was then subtracted from each of the original distributions of obtain the surface contribution. Justification for this procedure comes from the fact

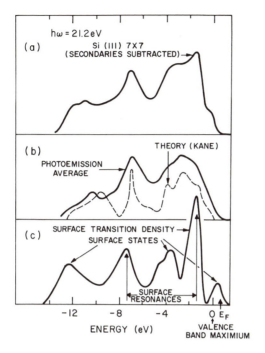

Fig. 5.19. (a) Photoemission energy distribution from Si (111) 7×7 with the estimated contribution from secondary electrons removed. (b) Comparison of "averaged" photoemission curve with the density of states calculated by KANE [5.137]. (c) Surface transition density of states obtained by ROWE and IBACH [5.136] by subtracting the assumed bulk signal [curve b] from the measured energy distribution [curve a]

that the averaged energy distribution looks very similar to the theoretical calculation of KANE [5.137] for bulk Si. There is always an uncertainty in the relative weight to be assigned to the bulk distribution in the subtraction from the measured energy distribution. In Fig. 5.19 we show the assumed bulk distribution for Si and the difference of the Si (111) 7 × 7 surface structure [5.138]. ROWE and IBACH [5.136] identified three states (+0.1, − 3.6, and − 12.3 eV) as surface states and two states as surface resonances (− 1.5 and − 7.5 eV). They maintain that the peak positions of the structure shown in Fig. 5.19 were independent of the scaling factor used in subtracting out the bulk contribution. Yet it is easy to see that if the bulk curve is given more weight the "surface density of states" would become negative around − 6.5 eV, − 3 eV, and 0 eV. These negative regions might arise from interference of bulk and surface emission.

SWANSON and CROUSER [5.139] have measured the field emission energy distribution from (100) Mo and observed a surface state similar to that on W except narrower and shifted up in energy. DIONNE and RHODIN [5.38] have measured field emission energy distributions from the low-index planes of the f.c.c. transition metals (iridium, rhodium, palladium and platinum) and compared them with the band structure calculations of ANDERSON [5.140]. There is systematic agreement if some band edge contraction at the surface is assumed [especially on Ir(111)].

SHEPHERD and PERIA [5.141] have observed a surface state in the energy distribution of field emitted electrons from (100) Ge. The surface state was found to overlap the valence band and, as in the case of tungsten, to be very sensitive to contamination. This surface state which was between 0.6 and 0.7 eV below E_F was found to oscillate quite dramatically in amplitude as the Ge tip was field evaporated. They concluded that this was a result of gradual field stripping plane edge atoms away until the plane edge was being observed by the probe hole. The surface state does not exist near a plane edge so that the observed amplitude decreases. It would be extremely informative to know the minimum number of atoms required for the existence of the surface state. MODINOS [5.46] has calculated the field emission energy distribution from a surface state on Ge (100) and compared his result with SHEPHERD and PERIA's measurements [5.141].

SMITH and PERIA [5.141] have used SHEPHERD's analyzer to look at Ge (111) where they find a surface state overlapping the valence band. EASTMAN and GROBMAN [5.134] found this surface state in their photoemission work on cleaned Ge (111).

5.5.2. Adsorption Studies

Hydrogen Adsorption

The chemisorption of hydrogen on (100) tungsten has been investigated by many experimental and theoretical techniques. The salient experimental facts are reviewed in Chapter 3. Briefly, it is known that the thermal desorption spectrum of a saturated layer has two unequal peaks at ~ 450 K and ~ 550 K, which are referred to as the β_1 and β_2 state, respectively.

PLUMMER and BELL [5.37] studied both the elastic and inelastic tunneling in field emission from hydrogen on (100) W as a function of coverage. Figure 5.20 shows the field emission enhancement factor as a function of the atom density on this face. The surface resonance at $E = -0.35$ eV decreases with increasing hydrogen coverage and a new level associated with β_2 hydrogen builds in at $E = -0.9$ eV with a half width ~ 0.6 eV. In the coverage region $\sim 5 \times 10^{14}$ atoms/cm^2 this level at $E = -0.9$ eV suddenly disappears. This is the same coverage range where the $C(2 \times 2)$ LEED pattern disorders. PLUMMER and BELL con-

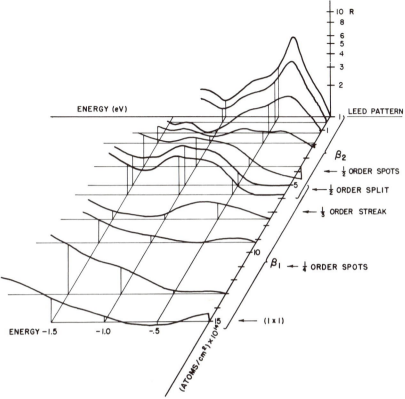

Fig. 5.20. Enhancement factor R for hydrogen and deuterium on (100) W at 300 K as a function of atom density on the surface. The saturated coverage is taken as 1.5×10^{15} atoms $\cdot$ cm^2. LEED data from [5.142]

cluded from these measurements that the β_1 state was not sequentially filling on top of the β_2 state, but that interaction between the chemisorbed hydrogen species caused a density dependent transition in the binding character, accompanied by an order-disorder transition, which is reversible with density.

In Fig. 5.21 the field emission and photoemission energy distribution are compared for clean (100) tungsten, the β_2 state, and the β_1 and β_2 states. All of the photoemission data were taken at $\hbar\omega = 10.2$ eV with collection at normal emission, $\pm 6°$ for the curves of FEUERBACHER [5.143] and ± 15 degrees for those of WACLAWSKI [5.144]. There is an arbitrary scaling factor in the field emission curves so that the amplitudes are not relevant, but the structure is almost identical. Again at these low photon energies the normal photoemission must be sampling the surface region.

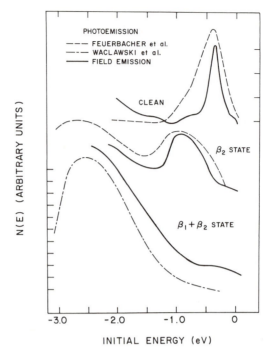

Fig. 5.21. Comparison of field emission and photoemission data for H_2 adsorption on (100) W at 300 K. The top set of curves is for clean (100) W- photoemission data are from [5.143], normal emission ($\pm 6°$). The second set of curves is for the β_2 state $\theta = .2$ and the final set of curves is for saturation coverage. The field emission data are from [5.37], with $R(E)$ curves being plotted with an arbitrary scaling factor. The bottom photoemission curve is from [5.144] for normal collection ($\pm 15°$)

If hydrogen makes localized bonds at the surface forming a "surface complex" (Chapter 2) there should be a corresponding energy level near or below the tungsten band. To observe such a level in photoemission a photon energy > 10.2 eV must be used. The resonance lines of He and Ne at 21.2 and 16.9 eV are intense and narrow enough to be used without a monochromator. The changes in the surface electron density upon adsorption can be enhanced by looking at the difference in the photoemission energy distribution as the surface conditions are changed. Figure 5.22 shows such a difference curve for adsorption of D_2 on (100) W, which should be compared to the clean energy distribution in Fig. 5.15. The scale of the difference curve is related to the clean energy distribution by normalizing the intensity of the -2.0 eV peak to 10.0. The middle set of curves represents the difference with respect to the clean energy

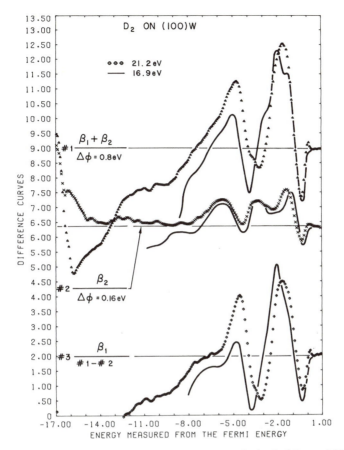

Fig. 5.22. Difference curves for β_1, and β_1 plus β_2 states of adsorbed D_2 on (100) W at 300 K. Curve *1* is saturation coverage of D_2 where both β_1 and β_2 states will desorb. Curve 2 is low coverage ($\theta \simeq 0.2$) where only the β_2 state will desorb. The bottom curves show the difference between Curves *1* and Curve 2 or the β_1 state. The solid curves are for $h\omega = 16.9$ eV and the broken (data) curve is for $h\omega = 21.2$ eV [5.88]

distribution at two photon energies for an exposure of D_2 which maximizes the β_2 state ($\Delta\varphi \simeq 0.16$ eV). The clean energy distribution at $h\omega = 16.9$ eV is very different from that at 21.2 eV, so it is imperative to compare difference curves for more than one photon energy. The dip near -0.3 eV is caused by the disappearance of the surface resonance while the peak near -1.2 eV is a consequence of the -1.0 eV peak shown in Figs. 5.20 and 5.21. There is no observable peak in the actual energy distribution because its intensity is too low and it is riding on the edge of the strong d-band peak at -2.0 eV. There are two additional

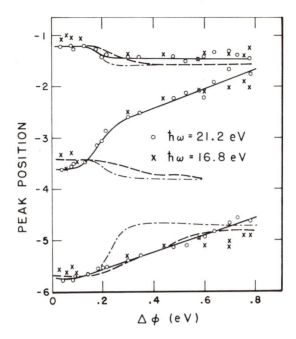

Fig. 5.23. Peak position as a function of work function change for the peaks in the difference curves for D_2 adsorption on (100) W [5.88] [(0) for $\hbar\omega = 21.2$ eV and ($\times$) for $\hbar\omega = 16.8$ eV]. The dashed lines are the peak position variation predicted from a sequentially filling state model, while the dot-dashed lines are predictions of a two state conversion model

peaks in the difference curve, one at -3.6 eV and the other at -5.7 eV. The latter is the bonding orbital mentioned earlier. The top set of curves are difference curves for a saturared adsorption of D_2, or the β_1 and β_2 states. The two peaks visible in the β_2 spectrum are not present in these curves and the lower lying peak has shifted up by nearly 1 eV. The bottom set of curves are for what should have been the β_1 state if the two states were filling sequentially; the β_2 spectrum was subtracted from that labelled $\beta_1 + \beta_2$. The labelling here is meant to correspond to thermal desorption and does not imply that there are distinct β_1 and β_2 states. The large negative regions especially near -3 eV are indicative of conversion, meaning that the adsorbed atoms which were in the β_2 configuration at low coverage changed their electronic configuration, as coverage increased.

This conversion process can be better visualized if the peak positions shown in Fig. 5.22 are plotted as a function of coverage. Figure 5.23 shows such a plot as a function of $\Delta\varphi$ which varies linearly with coverage

[5.145] ($\Delta\varphi = 0.8$ eV at saturation). Below $\Delta\varphi = 0.1$–0.14 eV ($\theta \simeq 0.2$) the peaks are all independent of the coverage; the β_2 state is being filled. For $\Delta\varphi = 0.12$–0.22 eV ($0.16 \leq \theta \leq 0.28$) there is a marked change in the -1.2 eV and -3.6 eV peaks in the difference curves. The low lying level at -5.7 3V does not show any preferential shifting in this coverage range.

Many different experiments have shown this behavior. MADEY [5.146] has measured the cross section for electron impact desorption of hydrogen as a function of coverage. He found that the cross section was 1.8×10^{-23} cm^2 and constant below a coverage of 0.16 ($\Delta\varphi = 0.13$ eV) and fell very rapidly within a coverage range of 0.1 monolayers. The saturation cross section was $< 10^{-25}$ cm^2. The $(1/2, 1/2)$ spot in the Leed diffraction pattern characteristic of the low coverage β_2 state has an amplitude proportional to coverage for $\theta < \sim 0.15$ and then decreases rapidly [5.142]. RUBLOFF et al. [5.147] have measured the change in the reflectance of a (100) W surface as a function of H coverage and wavelength of the incident light. Their data agree exactly with what is shown in Figs. 5.21–23 if the optical transition occurs to the Fermi energy. A plot of the change in the reflectance change $\Delta R(\hbar\omega = 1.4$ eV$)$ with coverage θ is fairly constant for $\theta \leq \sim 0.18$ or $\theta > \sim 0.3$. For $0.18 < \theta < 0.3 - d\Delta R/d\theta$ peaks at $\theta \simeq 0.2$. RUBLOFF et al. conclude that a rapid conversion of β_2 to β_1 is accurring at $0.19 \leq \theta \leq 0.26$. Conversion, even though much slower, continues at $\theta > 0.3$, again in agreement with the results of Fig. 5.23. FEUERBACHER and FITTON [5.143] and EGELHOFF [5.147] have produced photoemission data at different photon energies and collection angles which show the same effects.

PLUMMER and BELL [5.37] used the inelastically tunneling electrons in field emission (Subsection 5.3.2) to measure the vibrational modes for hydrogen and deuterium adsorbed on (100) W at 77 K. In the β_2 region ($\theta < \sim 0.2$ monolayers) they observed two vibrational modes for adsorbed hydrogen, one at 0.140 eV and the other at 0.07 eV, in excellent agreement with the inelastic scattering experiments of PROBST and PIPER [5.149]. For deuterium the inelastic losses are shifted to 0.1 eV and ~ 0.05 eV; which is the shift predicted by the mass ratio. At full coverage PLUMMER and BELL could not see any inelastic losses; even the 0.14 and 0.07 eV losses disappeared at high coverage, indicating that the vibrational structure as well as the electronic properties of the hydrogen-tungsten system had changed.

The cross sections for excitation of the molecular stretching frequencies of H$_2$ (0.55 eV) and D$_2$ (0.4 eV) were measured by looking at the γ state of hydrogen on (111) W at 77 K. This state is believed to be molecular, and produced inelastic losses at the appropriate energies for H$_2$ and D$_2$ stretching. On this basis and from the signal to noise ratio for (100) W it was concluded that $< 10\%$ of the hydrogen could have been molecular on W (100) even allowing for differences in the cross sections on both faces.

We thus require a model for hydrogen adsorption consistent with the following: atomic adsorption at all coverages, into an ordered array at $\theta < \sim 0.2$: a rapid conversion in the range $0.16 < \theta < 0.3$ and a gradual change above this coverage. The LEED pattern must disorder for $\theta > \sim 0.2$, yet $\Delta\varphi$ must increase linearly with θ. We consider briefly two models for chemisorbed hydrogen [5.88]. The first is a sequentially filling state model, where the β_2 state fills for $\theta < 0.2$ ($\Delta\theta \gtrsim 0.16$ eV) and for $\theta > 0.2$ ($\Delta\theta \lesssim 0.16$) the β_1 state fills on top of the β_2 state. This model can be tested by using curve 2 of Fig. 5.22 for the β_2 state and curve 3 for the β_1 state. The dashed curves on Fig. 5.23 are the predictions of this model. The sequential state model reproduces the upper and lower curves shown in Fig. 5.23 but not the middle curve. The second model is a two state conversion model, where for a coverage beyond the saturation of the β_2 state every newly adsorbed hydrogen atom converts one or more adsorbed atoms into a new state. The simplest two state conversion model originated with ESTRUP [5.142] where the β_2 state corresponded to hydrogen atoms adsorbed in every other bridge site. As the coverage increased the lateral interaction of H atoms, which is repulsive at nearest-neighbor distances [5.150] could cause the existing H atoms to be displaced. In ESTRUP's [5.142] model the saturation configuration, which was again ordered, corresponding to hydrogen atoms in every bridge site or two hydrogen atoms per tungsten surface atom. The dot-dashed curves in Fig. 5.25 are for a two state conversion model where every newly adsorbed hydrogen atom for $\theta \gtrsim 0.2$ ($\Delta\theta \gtrsim 0.16$) converts two existing H atoms. The conversion is over at $\theta = 0.3$. This two state conversion model fits only the upper level in Fig. 5.23. Therefore we need a more complicated picture than any two state model [5.147]. At present no obvious resolution of these puzzles is in sight!

CO Adsorption—Multiple Binding States—Dissociation

The adsorption of CO on tungsten is more complicated than the adsorption of hydrogen. This system is of great interest because it was considered as one of the few known cases of non-dissociative molecular adsorption [5.5, 151]. This belief was based on the fact that desorption always occurred as CO without residual C or O on the surface. It is now considered likely that the high temperature β states are dissociated (see Chapter 3). Several general features of CO adsorption seem to be preserved from plane to plane. Low temperature adsorption leads to a rather weakly bound state (binding energy ~ 1 eV) which is called virgin. In the virgin state the ratio of CO to W atoms on the surface is ~ 1.0 upon heating to

300–600 K the virgin state partially desorbs and partially converts to a more tightly bound state (called beta or beta-precursor [5.5]) for which the ratio of CO to W is ~ 0.5. Readsorption on a beta layer results in formation of a new state, alpha, with a ratio of the alpha state to beta state of ~ 1.0. Virgin adsorption results in a work function increase of 0.6–1.6 eV depending upon the plane. In the beta layer the work function change is smaller but usually of the same sign, while alpha adsorption reduces the work function relative to the beta layer [5.151]. The beta layer exhibits from 2 to 3 peaks in thermal desorption depending upon the crystal face while there may be two alpha states and usually only one virgin state.

Photoelectron spectra from CO adsorbed on tungsten can be used to separate and identify these states. We can determine: 1) whether states are being populated sequentially; 2) if they are molecular or correspond to dissociation, and 3) if there is conversion between states.

The virgin state desorbs and converts to beta below 300 K on (100) W so that adsorption at 300 K results in the filling of beta states and after prolonged exposures population of an alpha state or states [5.152]. Figure 5.24 shows the photoelectron spectra for clean (100) W and (100) W with a pressure of 5×10^{-6} Torr of CO in the chamber, recorded at $\hbar\omega = 21.2$ eV; the 16.9 eV spectra show the same features [5.88]. The peak near -8.5 eV is the 1π level of the molecularly adsorbed α state. This can be seen more easily if the difference curves are plotted as a function of heat treatment, as in Fig. 5.25. The top curve is identical to the difference curve in Fig. 5.24. The state called α_1 should desorb at 300 K [5.152], as shown in the second curve recorded after removal of CO and pumping for 15 min. φ has increased by 0.06 eV, i.e. this α state is electropositive. The difference between Curves 1 and 2 shown in Curve 5 is labeled α. It shows that the α state consists of molecular CO. More important is the fact that there is no conversion of the α_1 state to other states. The -8.7 eV peak in the α state spectrum is the 1π CO orbital. The 5σ level which is the lone pair orbital on the carbon atom has disappeared as one would expect from a donor level.

The α_2 state observed by YATES et al. [5.152] can be desorbed by heating to ~ 700 K. The difference curve relative to clean (100) W for the heat treatment is shown in Curve 3 of Fig. 5.25. The peak near -8.5 eV has been completely removed, indicating removal or conversion of all the CO with a 1π type level. Notice that φ decreased in contrast to the assumption that all α states are electropositive. Curve 6 shows the difference between Curves 2 and 3 which should be the α_2 state. It shows the 1π type level at -8.3 eV and a new peak at -11.4 eV (presumably either the 4σ or the bonding orbital from the 5σ bond to the substrate). Notice the negative dip in the region of -4.3 eV, which

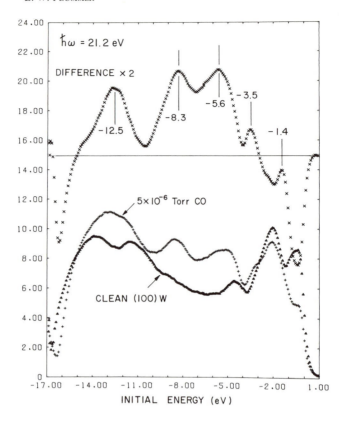

Fig. 5.24. Photoelectron spectra of adsorbed CO on (100) W at 300 K for $h\omega = 21.2$ eV. The two curves at the bottom are clean (100) W and (100) W with a pressure of 5×10^{-6} Torr of CO in the chamber. The top curve is the difference multiplied by 2 [5.88]. $\Delta\varphi = .34$ eV. The peak near -8.5 eV is the level of the molecularly adsorbed 1π state

occurs at the peak in the β state spectrum. PLUMMER et al. [5.88] were able to show that this peak represents conversion of what is called the α_2 state to the β state. If all the β states were saturated by prolonged exposure at a higher temperature the α_2 state did not appear upon readsorption at 300 K. This was interpreted to mean that the α_2 state is in fact a remnant of the virgin state.

Curve 4 of Fig. 5.25 was taken after heating to 1100 K. This results in a reversal in the sign of $\Delta\varphi$ and an ordered $C(2 \times 2)$ LEED pattern [5.153]. Part of the β layer is desorbed by heating to these temperatures [5.154]. The peak near -6.0 eV shows fine structure with the appearance of

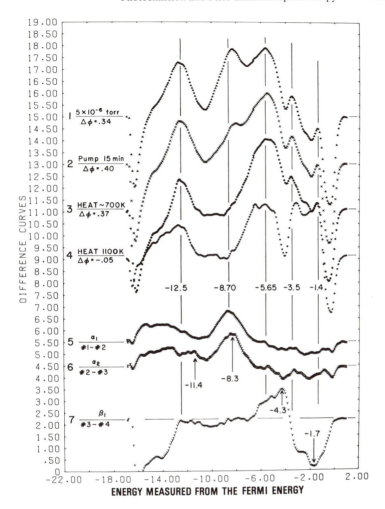

Fig. 5.25. Difference curves for CO adsorption on (100) W for various heating cycles. All of the curves are recorded at 300 K after the indicated heat treatment. The work function changes with respect to clean W are shown on the left [5.88]

three sub-peaks. This peak is very close to that seen for oxygen adsorption giving a $[C(2 \times 2)]$ LEED pattern. This led BAKER and EASTMAN to postulate that CO in this state was dissociated [5.155]. This conclusion cannot be made directly from a curve like 4. What can safely be concluded are the following points: 1) The β states are such that both O

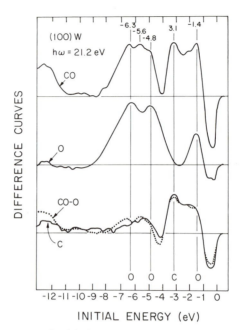

Fig. 5.26. Difference curves for CO, O, and C adsorbed in the C(2 × 2) structure on (100) W. The dashed curve is 0.69 times the CO curve minus 0.35 times the O curve

and C are bound to the substrate, 2) there is no 1π level in the CO molecule and 3) Curve 7 shows that there is conversion within the β layer as the density is changed. We [5.88] were unable to distinguish separate β_1, β_2 or β_3 states, since it appeared that a density dependent conversion process occurred. Recent X-ray data by YATES et al. [5.156] indicate that the broad peak from the O_{1s} level in β–CO can be resolved into three individual peaks. The UV data cannot be decomposed in that fashion.

We now address the question of dissociation. Our definition will be the following: If CO in the high temperature β state (1100 K) is dissociated then the photoelectron spectra should be a linear sum of the spectra from adsorbed oxygen and adsorbed carbon both in a C(2 × 2) surface geometry. This comparison is shown in Fig. 5.26. The top curve is the difference for CO, the middle for oxygen and the bottom for C [5.88]. The dotted curve is the best fit to the C curve obtained by subtracting the oxygen from the CO. The fit is very good especially above −7 eV. The −1.4 and −6.4 eV peaks are primarily O–W while the −3.10 and −5.1 eV peaks are primarily C–W. For our purposes CO in the C(2 × 2) configuration is dissociated.

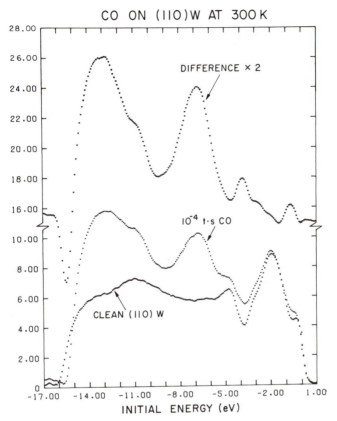

Fig. 5.27. Photoelectron spectra at $h\omega = 21.2$ eV for CO adsorbed on (110) W at 300 K. The two curves at the bottom are for clean (110) W and (110) W after an exposure to 10^{-4} Torr · sec. CO at 300 K. The top curve is the difference multiplied by 2. The peak near -7.0 eV is the 1π level of molecularly adsorbed CO in the virgin state. The shoulder near -10.7 eV is most likely the 4σ level of molecular CO [5.88]

We would now like to compare these results with those YOUNG and GOMER [5.157] for the field emission energy distributions. First observe that the -1.4 eV level which appears in all the CO difference curves of Figs. 5.25 and 5.26 is derived primarily from the O–W bond. O is bonded to W only in the β states so that one would expect an enhancement in the field emission energy distribution near -1.5 eV for 300 K adsorption. This should persist at higher temperatures until desorption begins to occur and it should also be observed with oxygen adsorption [5.88]. This is more or less what was found by YOUNG and GOMER [5.157] so that there seems to be moderately good agreement between field emission and photoemission for the β states of CO on (100) W. YOUNG and GOMER [5.157] pointed out from the temperature behavior of partial layers that there is evidence for strong interaction between C and O to at least 800 K.

Adsorption of CO on (110) W at 300 K results largely in population of the virgin state [5.158]. This is shown in photoelectron spectra of Fig. 5.27 for 10^{-4} Torr · sec exposure of CO on (110) W. The peaks near -7 eV and -11 eV are the 1π and 4σ levels of the molecularly adsorbed virgin state of CO [5.88]. The level at -3.9 eV is indicative of some form of beta CO present at 300 K [5.88]. Figure 5.28 shows the desorption and conversion of the virgin layer. φ increases by 0.5 eV when the virgin state is adsorbed at 300 K. Heating the layer adsorbed at 300 to 400 K (Curve 1, Fig. 5.28) results in desorption of CO without appreciable evidence for conversion from photoemission data, as indicated by the absence of appreciable amplitude in the region 0 to -5 eV. However, there is evidence from electron impact desorption [5.159] that conversion from the low temperature CO^+ yielding state to an O^+ yielding state occurs in this temperature region. The discrepancy may result from the fact that a mixture of virgin, O^+ yielding beta-precursor, and CO^+ yielding alpha-CO can coexist at 300 K. Heating from 390 to 500 K (Curve 2) converts the state remaining after heating to 390 K without appreciable desorption. This is an agreement with the thermal desorption measurements of KOHRT and GOMER [5.158] and the electron impact results, which indicate disappearance of the O^+ yielding state in this temperature range. The 300 K layer is characterized by a 1π type level at -7.0 eV and a 4σ type level at -10.8 eV. There are two unidentified levels at -12.6 eV and -13.0 eV. The work function difference is 0.2 eV. The -10.4 eV and -7.22 eV levels are the 4σ and 1π levels of the state being converted and the -5.3 and -2.2 eV levels are the new levels formed by conversion. Curve 3 shows the conversion between the two β states as the crystal is heated from 500 to 1000 K. The β states are density dependent as on (100) W. The last curve shows the α state which results from readsorption on a layer heated to 700 K. It appears to be slightly electronegative [5.88] again in agreement with the results of LEUNG et al. [5.159] on this plane.

The dissociation of the high temperature states cannot be ascertained as on (100) W because O, C and CO do not form the same Leed patterns. Nonetheless PLUMMER et al. [5.88] performed the same comparison shown in Fig. 5.26 for (100) W. The agreement is not as good, but indicates that β–CO is almost or wholly dissociated.

YOUNG and GOMER [5.5, 155] observed a peak at -2.0 eV in the field emission energy distribution and a shoulder at $E = -0.2$ eV which could be destroyed by heating a layer adsorbed at low temperature to ap-

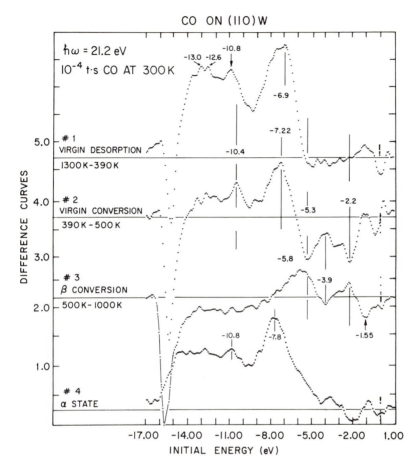

Fig. 5.28. Difference curves for CO adsorbed on (110) W. The top curve shows desorption of the virgin state without conversion. Curve 2 shows the subsequent conversion of the remaining virgin state to the β state of CO. Curve 3 shows the conversion of that occurs in the β states upon heating to 1000 K. Curve 4 shows the alpha state which results from readsorption on a saturated CO layer which had been heated to 700 K [5.88]

proximately 350 K. Readsorption on the heated virgin layer does not change the spectrum. The latter observation agrees with the photoemission observations of the α state in Fig. 5.28. The $E = -2.0\,\text{eV}$ peak which should have disappeared when the virgin layer was heated to 400 K does not appear in Curve 1 of Fig. 5.28. This can easily be explained by the fact that this peak is seen in field emission only at $\theta < 0.75$ [5.157].

In concluding this discussion let us ask what we have learned about the CO on tungsten system that we did not already know. The photoelectron spectra showed that the weakly bound alpha and virgin states consist of molecularly adsorbed CO, but this was known even before the infrared studies of YATES et al. [5.152]. The UV spectra revealed that the multitude of β states observed in a thermal desorption spectrum are not sequentially filling states. Instead, as in the case of hydrogen there is a density dependent transition or conversion. The singly most important observation is the degree of dissociation which exists in the β states, with the high temperature β state on (100)W being completely dissociated as far as photoemission can determine. This type of "finger print" study used to investigate the dissociation of CO is probably the most fruitful experimental application of UV photoemission. Next we shall illustrate this technique for adsorption of C_2H_4 on Ni(111) and W(110).

Hydrocarbon Decomposition

Photoemission energy distribution studies used in the "finger print" mode will become very useful in identifying the chemical nature of adsorbed species or intermediate states. We shall illustrate here the capabilities of this technique by discussing the adsorption of C_2H_4 on Ni(111) and W(110). The photoelectron spectra of these systems have shown that C_2H_4 will adsorb as C_2H_4 at (≤ 250 K) while adsorption at 300 K or subsequent warming of a low-temperature layer results in partial dehydrogenation to a C_2H_4 type adsorbate. Heating a (110)W plane to 500 K results in complete dehydrogenation leaving a C–C bond which is not broken until the crystal is heated to 1100 K. We will now explain how this information can be obtained by comparison of the spectra with gas phase spectra or spectra obtained from adsorption of the intermediate species.

Figure 5.29 shows the difference curves relative to clean (111)Ni obtained by DEMUTH and EASTMAN [5.107, 109] for adsorption of C_2H_2 (Fig. 5.29a) and C_2H_4 (Fig. 5.29b) with $\hbar\omega = 21.2$ eV. The top curve of Fig. 5.29b is for a chemisorbed layer of C_2H_4 on Ni(111) at 100 K. The dashed curves show how the spectra were separated into four peaks. The lower three levels have binding energies of 10.9, 12.7, and 14.1 eV, respectively which, given a 2.1 eV surface induced relaxation shift, agrees with the gas phase spectra from the σ levels of C_2H_4 [5.105]. The binding energy of the peak labelled π does not agree with the gas phase binding energy because it is involved in the bonding to the substrate so that there is a shift [5.109] as well as a different relaxation shift. DEMUTH and EASTMAN confirmed that the asorbed

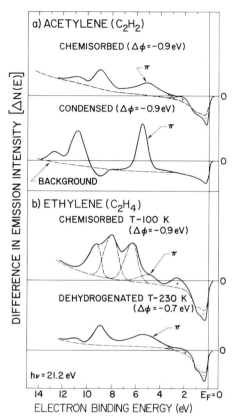

Fig. 5.29. (a) Difference curves for 1.2×10^{-6} Torr · sec exposure of Ni(111) to acetylene at $T \sim 300$ K and for condensed acetylene formed at $T \sim 100$ K with acethylene pressures of 6×10^{-8} Torr. (b) Difference curves for chemisorbed ethylene (exposure of 1.2×10^{-6} Torr · sec at $T \sim 100$ K) and for dehydrogenated ethylene (obtained by warming to $T \sim 230$ K or with initial exposure at $T \sim 300$ K) [5.107, 109]

molecule was C_2H_4 by condensing multilayers of C_2H_4 on the Ni surface. The only observed change in the three σ levels was a reduction in the surface induced relaxation energy by 0.4 eV, as expected for molecules farther from the surface. If the chemisorbed C_2H_4 is warmed to ~ 230 K the photoelectron spectrum changes quite dramatically as in the bottom difference curve of Fig. 5.29b. The adsorbed entity is no longer C_2H_4. A comparison of the two peaks at 9.1 eV and 11.0 eV with gas phase spectra [5.105] suggests that C_2H_4 has been partially dehydrogenated to a C_2H_2 complex. A surface induced relaxation shift of ~ 3.0 eV will align these peaks with the two upper σ levels of the gas phase C_2H_2. DEMUTH and EASTMAN checked this hypothesis by chemisorbing partial

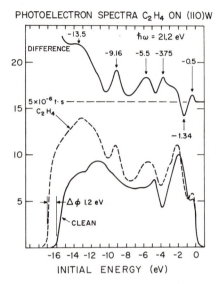

Fig. 5.30. Photoelectron spectra of (110) W at $\hbar\omega = 21.2$ eV. Solid curve (bottom) is clean (110) W, dashed curve is after 5×10^{-6} Torr · sec C_2H_4 exposure at 300 K. At top is shown the difference between the two lower curves. Energy is plotted relative to the Fermi energy [5.110]

layers and condensing multilayers of C_2H_2 on Ni(111). The difference curves for these two cases are shown in Fig. 5.29a; chemisorbed C_2H_2 is nearly identical to dehydrogenated C_2H_4. There may be hydrogen adsorbed on the surface after dehydrogenation since the observed Leed pattern is (2×2) which indicates 0.25–0.5 layers. The condensed C_2H_2 has a reduction in the surface induced relaxation shift of 1.7 eV [5.109]. Room temperature adsorption of C_2H_4 produces adsorbed C_2H_2.

It is interesting to note in passing that SINFELT's [5.160] analysis of the rate law in C_2H_6 hydrogenolysis indicated that ethane was chemisorbed as C_2H_2 on Ni.

The situation for C_2H_4 adsorbed on (110)W seems to be very similar to Ni(111), in that room temperature adsorption of C_2H_4 results in partial dehydrogenation [5.110]. Figure 5.30 shows spectra for clean (110)W and after an exposure of 5×10^{-6} Torr·sec of C_2H_4. The two curves, taken under identical conditions of light intensity and crystal position, were subtracted to obtain the difference curve shown at the top of Fig. 5.30. The original energy distributions were arbitrarily normalized to 10 at the -2.0 eV peak in the clean energy distribution. The -5.7 eV peak is approximately the same position at the "π" peak for the Ni(111) case (Fig. 5.29b) and the -9.16 eV peak and the shoulder

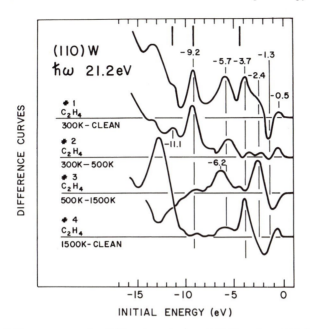

Fig. 5.31. Difference curves for C_2H_4 adsorption on (110)W at $h\omega = 21.2$ eV. Curve *1* is the difference between spectra after 5×10^{-6} Torr · sec exposure to C_2H_4 and clean (110)W. Curve *2* is the difference resulting from heating to 500 K the layer adsorbed at 300 K. Curve *3* is the difference between an adsorbed layer of C_2H_4 heated to 500 K and the 1500 K, and Curve *4* is the difference between the 1500 K heated layer and clean (110)W. The vertical lines at the top are the gas phase photoionization potentials for C_2H_2. They have been shifted up by 3.1 eV using the clean surface work function [5.110]

at -11 eV (which will show up in the subsequent figure) are the same as the two σ peaks. PLUMMER et al. [5.110] concluded that this spectrum corresponded to C_2H_2 adsorption by comparison with the gas phase spectra for C_2H_2 and with the measured photoelectron spectra for adsorbed hydrogen and carbon. The photoelectron spectra in Fig. 5.30 could not be constructed from any linear combination of a hydrogen and a carbon spectrum; therefore, the additional levels must result from C–H and C–C bonds. A 3.1 eV surface induced relaxation shift would bring the σ levels of gas phase C_2H_2 in agreement with the -9.1 eV and -11.1 eV levels.

Room temperature adsorption of C_2H_4 on (110)W results in partial dehydrogenation of C_2H_4 to C_2H_2. The two hydrogen atoms per adsorbed molecule may be adsorbed on the surface or desorbed into the gas phase. The desorption data of BARFORD and RYE [5.161] indicate that the amount of hydrogen desorbed depends on the coverage of

C_2H_2; at the high exposures used for Fig. 5.30 1/3 of the hydrogen is desorbed. Figure 5.31 shows the difference curves as the adsorbed layer is heated. A thermal desorption experiment was simulated by heating the crystal to the indicated temperature, then cooling to room temperature and recording the UV spectrum. The first difference curve is the same as shown in Fig. 5.30; the energy distribution after saturated exposure of C_2H_4 minus the clean energy distribution. The subsequent curves are differences between two different heat treatments.

If the surface molecule does not change upon heating to a prescribed temperature the difference curve comparing spectra before and after heating will be a straight line. If one or more of the energy levels are removed by decomposition or desorption upon heating the difference curve will exhibit a peak where the energy level used to be. If a new energy level is produced by rearrangement upon heating the difference curve will exhibit a negative peak at this energy. Curve 2 shows the difference between the room temperature adsorption and subsequent heating to 500 K. This treatment desorbs all the hydrogen [5.161] and completely dehydrogenates the surface. The -9.2 eV and -11.1 eV levels have been removed as a consequence of breaking the C–H bonds in the C_2H_2 molecule. The only other change in the spectrum is a peak near -5.5 eV, whose origin is not completely understood.

Before discussing Curve 3 of Fig. 5.31 let us examine the fourth curve which is the difference curve relative to clean (110)W after heating the adsorbed layer to ~ 1500 K. This difference curve is characteristic of carbon; it can be obtained by diffusion of small amounts of bulk carbon to the surface, by decomposition of CH_4, or by subtracting the oxygen spectrum from the β spectrum of adsorbed CO [5.88]. The point is that there are peaks at -6.0 eV and -2.4 eV in the original spectrum (Curve 1) which were not removed when the surface was completely dehydrogenated and which are not present in the C–W spectrum shown in Curve 4 of Fig. 5.31. Curve 3 shows that these two peaks are removed by heating above 1100 K. Our contention is that they are energy levels resulting from the C–C bond in the presence of the surface atoms, and that near 1100 K the C–C bond is broken leaving a carbon residue on the surface. The negative dip at ~ -1.0 eV in Curve 3 is a result of charge redistribution into the C–W bond. The decrease in amplitude of these two peaks, associated with the C–C bond, as a function of temperature can be used to measure the activation energy for C–C bond scission energy. This energy is $3.5 - 4.0$ eV, a reduction of > 2 eV from the gas phase.

The observed Leed patterns are consistent with this model. Room temperature adsorption produces no noticeable change in the pattern. Heating to 500 K causing complete dehydrogenation produces a diffuse background with no new spots. Heating above 1100 K breaks the C–C bond and produces an ordered Leed pattern characteristic of a carbon contaminated surface [5.110].

These studies seem to support SINFELT's [5.16] three-step model for hydrogenolysis: 1) dehydrogenative chemisorption, 2) carbon-carbon bond scission, and 3) hydrogenation and desorption. The latter step is currently being checked by performing a dynamic experiment with both C_2H_4 and H_2 beamed onto the surface at high pressure while the energy analyzer is differentially pumped.

Acknowledgements

The author is indebted to T. GUSTAFSSON, C. ALLYN, and T. EINSTEIN for critically reviewing this manuscript and to Professor R. GOMER for a heroic job in editing it. It is a pleasure to acknowledge PAUL SOVEN for the many hours he spent tutoring the author.

References

5.1.   H. D. HAGSTRUM: Science **178**, 275 (1972).
5.2.   C. B. DUKE, R. L. PARK: Physics Today **25**, 23 (1972).
5.3.   H. D. HAGSTRUM, G. E. BECKER: J. Chem. Phys. **54**, 1015 (1971).
5.4.   J. W. GADZUK, E. W. PLUMMER: Rev. Mod. Phys. **45**, 487 (1973).
5.5.   R. GOMER: Advan. Chem. Phys. **27**, 211 (1974).
5.6.   D. E. EASTMAN: *Electron Spectroscopy*, ed. by D. A. SHIRLEY (North-Holland Publishing Co., Amsterdam, 1972), p. 487.
5.7.   C. S. FADLEY: *Theoretical Aspects of X-ray Photoelectron Spectroscopy* (NATO Advanced Study Institute of Electron Emission Spectroscopy, Ghent University, Ghent, Belgium, 1972).
5.8.   H. D. HAGSTRUM, G. E. BECKER: Proc. Roy. Soc. (London) A **331**, 395 (1972).
5.9.   C. R. BRUNDLE: J. Vac. Sci. Technol. **11**, 212 (1974).
5.10.   D. MENZEL: Proc. 2nd Conf. on Solid Surfaces (Madrid, September, 1973).
5.11.   R. H. GOOD, E. W. MÜLLER: In *Encyclopedia of Physics*, ed. by S. FLÜGGE, Vol. 21 (Springer, Berlin-Göttingen-Heidelberg, 1956), p. 176.
5.12.   R. GOMER: *Field Emission and Field Ionization* (Harvard Press, Cambridge, Mass., 1961).
5.13.   E. W. PLUMMER, R. D. YOUNG: Phys. Rev. B **1**, 2088 (1970).
5.14.   L. W. SWANSON, A. E. BELL: Advan. Electron. Electron Phys. **32**, 194 (1973).
5.15.   C. B. DUKE, M. ALFERIEFF: J. Chem. Phys. **46**, 923 (1967).
5.16.   H. E. CLARK, R. D. YOUNG: Surface Sci. **12**, 385 (1968).
5.17.   D. W. JUENKER, L. J. LEBLANC, C. R. MARTIN: J. Opt. Soc. Am. **58**, 164 (1968).
5.18.   C. J. POWELL: Surface Sci. **44**, 29 (1974).
5.19.   J. C. TRACY: J. Vac. Sci. Technol. **11**, 280 (1974), and private communication.
5.20.   M. L. TARNG, G. K. WEHNER: J. Appl. Phys. **44**, 1534 (1973).
5.21.   D. E. EASTMAN: Photoemission Spectroscopy of Metals, Metals **6**, 411 (1972), ed. by BUNSHAH (Wiley, New York).
5.22.   T. L. EINSTEIN: Submitted to Surface Sci.
5.23.   K. SIEGBAHN: *ESCA Applied to Free Molecules* (North-Holland Publishing Co., Amsterdam, 1969).
5.24.   J. T. YATES, JR., T. E. MADEY, N. E. ERICKSON: Surface Sci. **43**, 257 (1974).
5.25.   R. H. FOWLER, L. NORDHEIM: Proc. Roy. Soc. (London) A **119**, 173 (1928).
5.26.   L. NORDHEIM: Proc. Roy. Soc. (London) A **121**, 626 (1928).

5.27. C. B. DUKE: *Tunneling in Solids* (Academic Press, New York, 1969).
5.28. W. A. HARRISON: Phys. Rev. **123**, 85 (1961).
5.29. R. STRATTON: Phys. Rev. **135** A, 794 (1964).
5.30. F. I. ITSKOVITCH: Sov. Phys.-JETP **23**, 945 (1966).
5.31. J. A. APPELBAUM, W. F. BRINKMAN: Phys. Rev. B **2**, 907 (1970); Phys. Rev. **186**, 464 (1969).
5.32. D. R. PENN, E. W. PLUMMER: Phys. Rev. B **9**, 1216 (1974).
5.33. J. BARDEEN: Phys. Rev. Letters **6**, 57 (1961).
5.34. J. R. OPPENHEIMER: Phys. Rev. **31**, 66 (1928).
5.35. E. B. DUKE, J. FAUCHIER: Surface Sci. **32**, 175 (1972).
5.36. Analyzing the ratio of the calculated current per unit energy from a narrow Kronig-Penny band to the free-electron tunneling probability gives an enhancement factor very similar to the surface density of states of a tight binding band.
5.37. E. W. PLUMMER, A. E. BELL: J. Vac. Sci. Technol. **9**, 583 (1972).
5.38. N. J. DIONNE, T. N. RHODIN: Phys. Rev. Letters **32**, 1311 (1974).
5.39. D. PENN, R. GOMER, M. H. COHEN: Phys. Rev. B **3**, 768 (1972); Phys. Rev. Letters **27**, 26 (1971).
5.40. B. POLITZER, P. H. CUTLER: Mat. Res. Bull. **5**, 703 (1970).
5.41. R. D. YOUNG: Phys. Rev. **113**, 110 (1959).
5.42. B. A. POLITZER, P. H. CUTLER: Surface Sci. **22**, 277 (1970).
5.43. W. GLEICH, G. REGENFUS, R. SIZMAN: Phys. Rev. Letters **27**, 1066 (1971).
5.44. J. W. GADZUK: Phys. Rev. **182**, 945 (1969).
5.45. R. D. B. WHITCUTT, B. H. BLOTT: Phys. Rev. Letters **23**, 639 (1969).
5.46. A. MODINOS: Surface Sci. **42**, 205 (1974).
5.47. D. PENN: Phys. Rev. B **9**, 844 (1974).
5.48. In [5.32] PENN used Eq. (5.14), while in the article [Phys. Rev. B **5**, 768 (1972)] his Eqs. (20a) and (20b) have a slightly different form.
5.49. C. CAROLI, D. LEDERER, D. SAINT JAMES: Surface Sci. **33**, 228 (1972).
5.50. L. V. KJELDYSH: Sov. Phys.-JETP **20**, 1018 (1961).
5.51. P. SOVEN: Private communication. Also T. E. FEUCHTWANG, Phys. Rev. B **10**, 4121, 4135 (1974) independently used the Kjeldysch formalism to show that $R(E)$ measures the one dimensional density of states at the surface.
5.52. D. PENN: Private communication.
5.53. J. W. GADZUK: Phys. Rev. **61**, 2110 (1970).
5.54. A. BAGCHI, P. L. YOUNG: Phys. Rev. B **9**, 1194 (1974).
5.55. J. L. POLITZER, T. E. FEUCHTWANG: Phys. Rev. B **3**, 597 (1971).
5.56. A. MODINOS: Surface Sci. **20**, 55 (1970); **22**, 473 (1970);
        A. MODINOS, N. NICOLAUN: Surface Sci. **17**, 359 (1969); J. Phys. C **4**, 2859 and 2875 (1971).
5.57. R. C. JAKLEVIC, J. LAMBE: Phys. Rev. Letters **17**, 1138 (1966);
        J. LAMBE, R. C. JAKLEVIC: Phys. Rev. **165**, 821 (1968).
5.58. B. F. LEWIS, M. MOSEMAN, W. H. WEINBERG: Surface Sci. **41**, 142 (1974).
5.59. D. J. FLOOD: Phys. Rev. Letters A **29**, 100 (1969); J. Chem. Phys. **52**, 1355 (1970).
5.60. L. W. SWANSON, L. C. CROUSER: Surface Sci. **23**, 1 (1970).
5.61. A. BAGCHI: Phys. Rev. B **10**, 542 (1974).
5.62. M. J. G. LEE: Phys. Rev. Letters **30**, 1193 (1973).
5.63. C. LEA, R. GOMER: Phys. Rev. Letters **25**, 804 (1970).
5.64. J. W. GADZUK, E. W. PLUMMER: Phys. Rev. Letters **26**, 92 (1971).
5.65. K. L. NGAI: phys. stat. solidi (b) **53**, 309 (1972).
5.66. J. W. GADZUK, A. A. LUCAS: Phys. Rev. B **7**, 4770 (1973).
5.67. J. A. SIMPSON, C. E. KUYATT: J. Appl. Phys. **37**, 3805 (1966);
        B. ZIMMERMANN: Electron and Ion Beam Tech. Conf. (1969).

5.68. H. NEUMANN: Physica **44**, 587 (1969).
5.69. B. I. LUNDQUIST, K. MOUTFIELD, J. W. WILKINS: Sol. State Commun. **10**, 383 (1972).
5.70. Two other groups have observed basically the same feature seen by LEE [5.66] in different crystal directions: R. POLIZZOTI, R. LIU, G. EHRLICH: 19th Field Emission Symposium (Urbana, Ill., 1972);
T. VORBURGER, B. WACLAWSKI, E. W. PLUMMER: Unpublished. Also see J. WYSOCKI, CH. KLEINT: phys. stat. solidi (9) **20**, K 57 (1973);
H. NEUMANN, CH. KLEINT: Ann. Physik (7) **7**, 237 (1971).
5.71. C. CAROLI, D. LEDERER-ROZENBLATT, B. ROULET, D. SAINT-JAMES: Phys. Rev. B**8**, 4552 (1973), have developed a microscopic model including inelastic scattering which may be quite useful when applied to specific systems.
5.72. U. FANO, J. W. COOPER: Rev. Mod. Phys. **40**, 441 (1968).
5.73. G. V. MARR: *Photoionization Processes in Gases* (Academic Press, Inc., New York, 1967).
5.74. E. MERZBACHER: *Quantum Mechanics* (Wiley, New York, 1962), p. 447.
5.75. R. E. B. MAKINSON: Proc. Roy. Soc. (London) A **162**, 367 (1937).
5.76. H. A. BETHE, E. E. SALPETER: In *Encyclopedia of Physics*, Vol. XXXV (Springer, Berlin-Göttingen-Heidelberg, 1957), p. 88.
5.77. W. L. SCHAICH, N. W. ASHCROFT: Phys. Rev. B **3**, 2452 (1971); Sol. State Commun. **8**, 1959 (1970).
5.78. T. KOOPMANS: Physica **1**, 104 (1933).
5.79. D. A. SHIRLEY: Chem. Phys. Letters **16**, 220 (1972).
5.80. J. W. COOPER: Phys. Rev. **128**, 681 (1962).
5.81. W. C. PRICE, A. W. POTTS, D. G. STREETS: *Electron Spectroscopy*, ed. by D. A. SHIRLEY (North-Holland Publishing Co., New York, 1972), p. 182.
5.82. S. B. M. HAGSTRÜM: *Electron Spectroscopy*, ed. by D. A. SHIRLEY (North-Holland Publishing Co., New York, 1972), p. 515.
5.83. D. E. EASTMAN, M. KUZNIETZ: J. Appl. Phys. **42**, 1396 (1971).
5.84. G. BRODEN: Ph. D. Thesis (Chalmers University of Technology, Göteborg, Sweden, 1972);
G. BRODÉN, S. B. M. HAGSTRÜM, C. NORRIS: Phys. Kondens. Materie **15**, 327 (1973);
G. BRODÉN: Phys. Kondens. Materie **15**, 171 (1972).
5.85. B. PODOLSKY, L. PAULING: Phys. Rev. **34**, 109 (1929).
5.86. J. C. SLATER: Phys. Rev. **36**, 57 (1930).
5.87. J. H. SCOFIELD: *Theoretical Photoionization Cross Sections from 1 to 1500 keV* (Lawrence Livermore Laboratory, TID-4500, UC-34 1973).
5.88. E. W. PLUMMER, B. J. WACLAWSKI, J. VORBURGER: in preparation.
5.89. T. E. MADEY, J. YATES, JR., N. E. ERICKSON: Chem. Phys. Letters **19**, 487 (1973).
5.90. B. J. WACLAWSKI, E. W. PLUMMER: Phys. Rev. Letters **29**, 783 (1972).
5.91. The mean radius was calculated using Eqs. (3.20)–(3.27) of Ref. [5.76].
5.92. H. D. HAGSTRÜM, G. E. BECKER: Private communication.
5.93. S. T. MANSON: Phys. Rev. Letters **26**, 219 (1971).
5.94. For a review see F. A. GRIMM: *Electron Spectroscopy*, ed. by D. A. SHIRLEY (North-Holland Publishing Co., New York, 1972), p. 199.
5.95. J. COOPER, R. N. ZARE: *Lectures in Theoretical Physics XI C* (Gordon & Breach, New York, 1969) also J. Chem. Phys. **48**, 942 (1968).
5.96. J. C. TULLY, R. S. BERRY, B. J. DALTON: Phys. Rev. **176**, 95 (1968).
5.97. T. A. CARLSON, G. E. McGUIRE, A. E. JONES, K. L. CHENG, C. P. ANDERSON, C. C. LU, B. P. PULLEN: *Electron Spectroscopy*, ed. by D. A. SHIRLEY (North-Holland Publishing Co., New York, 1972), p. 207.
5.98. J. W. GADZUK: Phys. Rev. B **15**, 1011 (1974); Jap. J. Appl. Phys. Suppl. 2, Pt. 2, 851 (1974); Sol. State Commun. **15**, 1011 (1974).

5.99.   A. Liebsch: Phys. Rev. **32**, 1103 (1974).

5.100. I. G. Kaplan, A. P. Markin: Sov. Phys.-Doklady **14**, 36 (1969).

5.101. P. S. Bagus: Proc. X-ray Spectra and Electronic Structure Meeting (Munich, 1972).

5.102. D. A. Shirley: Advan. Chem. Phys. **23**, 85 (1973).

5.103. J. Cambray, J. Gasteiger, A. Streitwieser, Jr., P. Bagus: J. Am. Chem. Soc. **96**, 5978 (1974).

5.104. K. Siegbahn, C. Nordling, G. Johannson, J. Hedman, P. F. Heden, K. Hamrin, U. Gelius, T. Bergmark, L. O. Werme, R. Manne, Y. Baer: *ESCA Applied to Free Molecules* (North-Holland Publishing Co., Amsterdam, 1969).

5.105. D. W. Turner, C. Baker, A. D. Baker, C. R. Brunkle: *Molecular Photoelectron Spectroscopy* (Interscience, New York, 1970).

5.106. J. T. Yates, Jr., T. E. Madey, N. E. Erickson: Surface Sci. **43**, 257 (1974). Also see [5.156].

5.107. D. E. Eastman, J. E. Demuth: Japan. J. Appl. Phys. Suppl. 2, Pt. 2, 827 (1974).

5.108. G. E. Becker, H. D. Hagstrüm: J. Vac. Sci. Technol. **10**, 31 (1973).

5.109. J. E. Demuth, D. E. Eastman: Phys. Rev. Letters **32**, 1123 (1974).

5.110. E. W. Plummer, B. J. Waclawski, J. V. Vorburger: Chem. Phys. Letters **28**, 510 (1974).

5.111. J. R. Smith, S. C. Ying, W. Kohn: Phys. Rev. Letters **30**, 610 (1973). In this paper Fig. 3 is a plot of the screening charge density which when the original charge density is subtracted will give the equivalent plot for a proton near a surface as Fig. 11 shows for CO.

5.112. N. D. Lang: Sol. State Phys. **28**, 225 (1973).

5.113. K. Mitchell: Proc. Roy. Soc. (London) A **146**, 442 (1934);
L. I. Schiff, L. H. Thomas: Phys. Rev. B **7**, 3464 (1973);
I. Adawi: Phys. Rev. A **788**, 134 (1964).

5.114. S. A. Flödstrom, J. G. Endriz: Phys. Rev. Letters **31**, 893 (1973).

5.115. P. O. Gartland, S. Berge, B. J. Slassvold: Phys. Rev. Letters **30**, 116 (1973).

5.116. For a recent paper see J. G. Endriz: Phys. Rev. B **7**, 3463 (1973).

5.117. C. N. Berglund, W. E. Spicer: Phys. Rev. **136** A, 1030, 1044 (1964).

5.118. N. V. Smith, M. M. Traum: Phys. Rev. B **9**, 1341, 1353, 1365 (1974).

5.119. G. D. Mahan: Phys. Rev. B **2**, 4334 (1970).

5.120. D. Kalkstein, P. Soven: Surface Sci. **26**, 85 (1971).

5.121. R. Haydock, M. J. Kelley: Surface Sci. **38**, 139 (1973).

5.122. J. A. Appelbaum, R. Hamman: Phys. Rev. B **6**, 2166 (1972).

5.123. J. W. Davenport, T. L. Einstein, J. R. Schrieffer: Japan J. Appl. Phys. Suppl. 2, Pt. 2, 691 (1974).

5.124. W. E. Spicer: Phys. Rev. **154**, 385 (1967).

5.125. B. J. Waclawski, T. V. Vorburger, J. R. Stern: J. Vac. Sci. Technol. **12**, 301 (1975).

5.126. A. Liebsch, E. W. Plummer: Paper presented at Faraday Division of the Chemical Society (Sept. 10–12, 1974).

5.127. N. E. Christensen, B. Feuerbacher: Phys. Rev. B **10**, 2349 (1974).

5.128. B. Feuerbacher, N. E. Christensen: Phys. Rev. B **10**, 2373 (1974).

5.129. B. Feuerbacher, B. Fitton: Phys. Rev. Letters **30**, 923 (1973).

5.130. E. W. Plummer, J. W. Gadzuk: Phys. Rev. Letters **25**, 1493 (1970).

5.131. B. J. Waclawski, E. W. Plummer: Phys. Rev. Letters **29**, 783 (1972).

5.132. B. Feuerbacher, B. Fitton: Phys. Rev. Letters **29**, 786 (1972).

5.133. K. Sturm, R. Feder: Sol. State Commun. **14**, 1317 (1974).

5.134. D. E. Eastman, W. D. Grobmann: Phys. Rev. Letters **28**, 1378 (1972).

5.135. L. F. Wagner, W. E. Spicer: Phys. Rev. Letters **28**, 1381 (1972).

5.136. J. W. Rowe, H. Ibach: Phys. Rev. Letters **32**, 421 (1974).

5.137. E. O. Kane: Phys. Rev. **146**, 558 (1966).

5.138. The 7×7 refers to the LEED pattern observed, 1×1 would be a bulkstructure.

5.139. L. W. SWANSON, L. C. CROUSER: Phys. Rev. Letters **19**, 1179 (1967).

5.140. O. K. ANDERSEN: Phys. Rev. B**2**, 883 (1970).

5.141. W. B. SHEPERD, W. T. PERIA: Surface Sci. **38**, 461 (1973).

5.142. P. J. ESTRUP, J. ANDERSON: J. Chem. Phys. **45**, 2254 (1966).

5.143. B. FEUERBACHER, B. FITTON: Phys. Rev. B**8**, 4890 (1973).

5.144. B. J. WACLAWSKI, E. W. PLUMMER: Unpublished.

5.145. T. E. MADEY, J. T. YATES, JR.: "Structure et Proprietes des Surfaces des Solides" (Editions du Centre National de la Recherche Scientique, Paris) **187**, 155 (1970).

5.146. T. E. MADEY: Surface Sci. **36**, 281 (1973).

5.147. G. W. RUBLOFF, J. ANDERSON, M. A. PRASSLER, P. J. STILES: Phys. Rev. Letters **32**, 667 (1974).

5.148. W. E. EGELHOFF, D. L. PERRY: Phys. Rev. Letters **34**, 93 (1975).

5.149. F. M. PROBST, T. C. PIPER: J. Vac. Sci. Technol. **4**, 53 (1967).

5.150. T. E. EINSTEIN, J. R. SCHRIEFFER: Phys. Rev. B**7**, 3629 (1973); T. B. GRIMLEY, S. M. WALKER: Surface Sci. **14**, 395 (1969).

5.151. R. GOMER: Jap. J. Appl. Phys. (in press).

5.152. J. T. YATES, JR., D. A. KING: Surface Sci. **32**, 479 (1972).

5.153. J. ANDERSON, P. J. ESTRUP: J. Chem. Phys. **46**, 563 (1967).

5.154. L. R. CLAVENNA, L. D. SCHMIDT: Surface Sci. **33**, 11 (1972).

5.155. J. M. BAKER, D. E. EASTMAN: J. Vac. Sci. Technol. **10**, 223 (1973).

5.156. J. T. YATES, JR., N. ERICKSON, S. D. WORLEY, T. E. MADEY: Batelle Colloq. "The Physical Basis for Heterogeneous Catalysis", Gstaad, Switzerland, Sept. 2–6, 1974.

5.157. P. L. YOUNG, R. GOMER: Phys. Rev. Letters **30**, 955 (1973); J. Chem. Phys. **61**, 4955 (1974).

5.158. C. KOHRT, R. GOMER: Surface Sci. **24**, 77 (1971).

5.159. C. LEUNG, M. VASS, R. GOMER: To be published.

5.160. J. H. SINFELT: Advan. Catalysis **23**, 91 (1973).

5.161. B. D. BARFORD, R. R. RYE: J. Vac. Sci. Technol. **9**, 673 (1972).

5.162. P. G. CARTIER, R. R. RYE: J. Chem. Phys. **59**, 4602 (1973).

5.163. T. GUSTAFSSON: Private communication.

6. Low Energy Electron Diffraction (LEED) and Auger Methods

E. BAUER

With 28 Figures

The two phenomena to be discussed in this chapter involve slow electrons: in LEED electrons with energies between approximately 10 eV and 200 eV are used, in Auger electron spectroscopy (AES) the useful energies of the Auger electrons range from 10 eV to 2000 eV. The basis of LEED is the interference between the electron waves scattered from the atoms which comprise the surface region of a crystalline solid, a phenomenon discovered 1927 by DAVISSON and GERMER. The basis of AES is an effect discovered 1932 by AUGER in which electrons are liberated in an atom with energies characteristic for the emitting atom. According to the basic mechanisms, LEED is governed predominantly by the periodocity, in particular by the periodicity parallel to the surface, while AES predominantly responds to the chemical composition of the material studied. The interpretation of LEED data requires the knowledge of the chemical composition of the surface. Therefore AES is complementary to LEED where LEED is applicable. But also when LEED cannot be used, e.g. with polycrystalline and amorphous surfaces, AES is a very important tool for the characterization of surfaces. Although LEED and the Auger effect were discovered more than 40 years ago, they have reached importance in surface studies only during the last ten years. The main reasons for this long delay of their wide-spread application are the past strong interest of science in the bulk of solids and the experimental difficulties of producing well-defined surfaces routinely and keeping them unchanged during observation. The recognition of the importance of surfaces for many solid state properties and many important technical processes as well as the development of ultra high vacuum (UHV) techniques in the early sixties eliminated these reasons and both techniques developed rapidly.

In LEED electrons are produced outside the crystal in form of a nearly parallel electron beam which may be described theoretically as a plane wave. In AES the electrons are produced within the crystal by electrons, X-ray photons, energetic ions or neutrals and are emitted nearly isotropically by the atoms and may be described theoretically by a spherical wave. Whatever their origin, whether incident from the outside or generated within the solid, the electrons have to propagate through the solid and the surface, and in doing so they interact with the solid and its surface. These interactions are decisive for the understanding of both LEED and AES and will therefore be discussed first (Section 6.1). By understanding elastic (Subsection 6.1.1), inelastic (Subsection 6.1.2) and quasielastic (Subsection 6.1.3) scattering processes the limitations of the kinematical and dynamical theory of the elastic LEED method (ELEED) (Subsection 6.2.2) will become evident and the occurrence of inelastic LEED (ILEED) discussed in conjunction with other special topics (Subsection 6.2.4) will become understandable. The reader not interested in the physical basis and the theory of LEED but only in the experimental aspects and results is referred to Subsections 6.2.1 and 6.2.3.

The physical foundations of the Auger methods are discussed next (Subsection 6.3.1), followed by a description of the experimental techniques (Subsection 6.3.2). The applications of AES are illustrated by the results of Subsection 6.3.3 and current basic problems and new developments in Subsection 6.3.4. The article is intended to be an introduction to the physical basis of the technique and as a synopsis of the present state of the art. Because of its brevity it cannot be comprehensive but only illustrative. For more detailed information the reader is referred to the comprehensive reviews (Appendix) which have already appeared on the subject of this article.

Before going into the theoretical discussion of Section 6.1 a few remarks should be made about the experimental limitations common to both methods. Because of the strong interaction between slow electrons and matter the experiments have to be performed in very high vacuum. Hydrocarbons in the system generally lead to strong specimen contamination. This requires special specimen chambers or the whole system must be bakeable unless desorption from the walls is suppressed by cooling. The specimens which can be studied in a meaningful manner should fulfill a number of conditions: 1) they should not be changed by the electron beam (dissociation in ionic crystals, desorption of adsorbed gases, etc.) 2) they should not charge up on electron bombardment, 3) they should have a low vapor pressure or special cooling devices have to be used and 4) they have to have long-range order over a sufficiently large portion of the surface so that diffraction can occur (for LEED only).

The basic properties of the methods outlined and the experimental limitations just mentioned determine the application range of LEED and AES. LEED is only suited for the study of surfaces with sufficient lateral periodicity, i.e., single crystal surfaces, surfaces of specimens with fiber texture (deposited films, rolled sheets, etc.), or surfaces of layered materials with disorder normal to the surface such as pyrolytic graphite. On such surfaces not only the structure but all processes can be studied in which changes in lateral periodicity or order occur such as order-disorder, decomposition, adsorption or condensation processes. In contrast to LEED, AES neither requires a periodic nor a flat surface. Thus it can be applied—and it has with great success—to such unusual samples as fracture surfaces or rocks from the moon. Surface roughness, of course, makes quantitative chemical analysis of the surface layer which is the final goal of AES very difficult, especially if the primary beam is far from normal incidence (shadow effects). But on smooth surfaces after appropriate calibration quantitative surface analysis is already possible with proper care. AES is not limited to chemical analyses, but can also give structural information via the strong attenuation of the Auger electrons on their way to the surface. Furthermore, all processes can be studied which are connected with changes in chemical composition in the surface and which can take place in vacua better than 10^{-4} Torr. The use of sputtering in conjunction with AES not only allows depth analysis but also studies in relatively dirty vacuum because the contamination can be removed continuously. AES is at present by far the most universal surface analysis method with sensitivities down to less than $1/100$ of a monolayer, except for hydrogen and helium which are not detectable.

6.1. Interaction of Slow Electrons with Condensed Matter

6.1.1. Elastic Scattering

Elastic scattering is predominantly due to the ion cores which contain the nucleus and the strongly bound electrons. In order to obtain an understanding of the elastic scattering probability, in particular of the total scattering cross-section of an atom and the angular distribution of the scattered intensity it is useful to neglect initially the phase relations between the waves scattered by the atoms of a solid. This amounts to assuming a random distribution of atoms ("randium") which is approximated to a certain extent in the amorphous state. In such a system the intensities scattered by the individual atoms add up, instead of the amplitudes. Thus the angular distribution, neglecting double scattering, is simply given by that of an individual atom. Figure 6.1 [6.1] shows typical angular distributions for 50 eV electrons scattered by ion cores as used in band structure calculations. Very strong forward and strong backward scattering is evident, as well as the fact that Cu scatters much less than Al, which is quite unexpected from X-ray and high-energy electron diffraction. These deviations from the expectation that the scattering probability increases with nuclear charge Z are even more

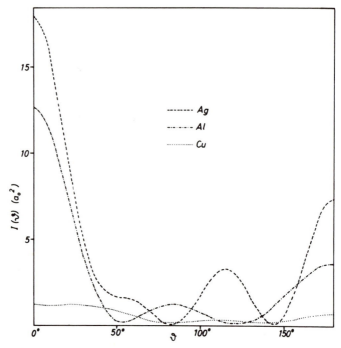

Fig. 6.1. Angular distribution of the intensity scattered by Al, Cu, and Ag ion cores as obtained from band structure calculations in atomic units ($a_0 = 0.529$ Å) [6.17]

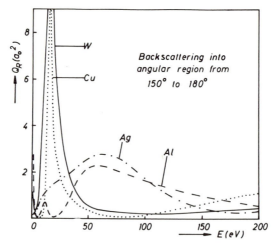

Fig. 6.2. Backscattering into a 30° cone around the backward direction: $Q_b = 2\pi \int_{150}^{180} I(\vartheta)$ · $\sin \vartheta \, d\vartheta$ for Al, Cu, Ag, and W ion cores [6.2]

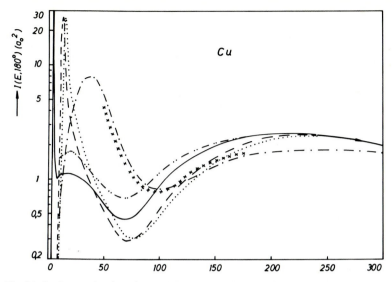

Fig. 6.3. Backscattering into $\vartheta = 180°$ by Cu described by different potentials [6.2]. See text for an explanation

evident in Fig. 6.2 [6.2] which shows the backscattering into a 30° cone around the backward direction: W ($Z = 74$) shows less backward scattering than Al ($Z = 3$) from about 30 eV to 200 eV! It should be noted that such calculated scattering cross-sections become increasingly unreliable with decreasing energy below about 100 eV. This is illustrated in Fig. 6.3 which shows the backscattering ($\vartheta = 180°$) from Cu calculated with six different potentials [6.2]. The results for the two best "solid state potentials" (– – –, …) agree quite well with each other, as do those for free-atom potentials ($\times \times \times$, –·–), but the difference between the two pairs of curves is drastic below 100 eV, indicating that free-atom potentials become rather questionable in the low energy range. But even the results obtained with "solid state potentials" become inaccurate, if correlation (polarization of the electron cloud of the ion core by the incident electron) and exchange ("spin-spin interactions" between incident and ion-core electrons) effects are neglected. Correlation becomes important below about 100 eV, exchange below about 30 eV, but both effects are still noticeable at higher energies [6.3]. It is difficult to take these effects into account quantitatively, which represents one of the major problems of the theory of low energy electron scattering and LEED. These limitations should be kept in mind.

The attenuation $I = I_0 \exp(-\nu x)$ of the incident beam due to the total elastic scattering or the elastic backscattering is determined by the

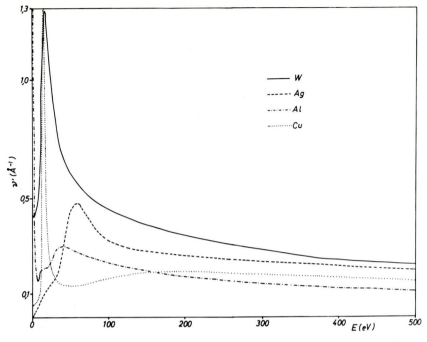

Fig. 6.4. Total attenuation coefficient (neglecting double scattering) for Al, Cu, Ag, W [6.1]

total scattering cross-section $Q_t = 2\pi \int_0^\pi I(\vartheta) \sin\vartheta \, d\vartheta$ or the backscattering

cross-section $Q_b = 2\pi \int_{\pi/2}^\pi I(\vartheta) \sin\vartheta \, d\vartheta$ and the density ϱ of the ion cores:
$v = \varrho Q$. The primary extinction coefficient $v' = \varrho Q_t$ is shown for Al, Cu, Ag, and W in Fig. 6.4 [6.1]. The v' values indicate that the incident intensity has already been reduced by $1/e$ after 1–10 Å which means that double and multiple elastic scattering play an important role. Electrons scattered into the forward half space are not lost from the elastic wave field and thus do not attenuate it. True attenuation due to elastic scattering occurs only by backscattering. Except below 100 eV the calculated v values are below 0.1 A^{-1}, which is a weak attenuation as compared to that caused by inelastic scattering.

6.1.2. Inelastic Scattering

Inelastic scattering can occur by excitation or ionization of valence electrons or inner shell electrons. Inelastic interactions with inner shell electrons are weak compared to those with valence electrons and

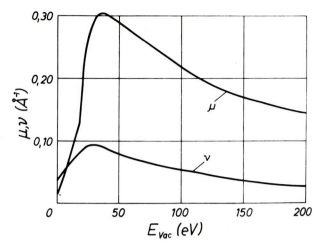

Fig. 6.5. Attenuation coefficients due to inelastic scattering by valence electrons (μ) and due to elastic backscattering (ν) for Al [6.1]

important—in the context of this chapter—only for AES. They will be discussed in Subsection 6.3.1. Inelastic scattering by valence electrons is best discussed in terms of the "jellium" model: the valence electrons are considered as a free electron gas whose charge is compensated by the positive charge of the ion cores which is smeared out to form a homogeneous, isotropic background charge. This model is most applicable to free-electron-like metals such as the alkalis, Al, Be or Mg, but to a certain degree also to other metals, to semiconductors and insulators provided that the group of electrons considered is not bound too tightly ($E_i < 10$–20 eV) and that it is sufficiently separated in energy from the rest of the electrons.

Inelastic scattering in jellium occurs by one-electron excitation and by excitation of plasma oscillations, i.e. by collective excitation of the valence electrons due to the interaction with the incident electron and due to their mutual interaction. This excitation can occur only above a certain threshold, which varies with electron density from $2E_F$ to $1.6E_F$ (E_F: Fermi energy) [6.2]. Below this threshold only one-electron excitations are possible. Figure 6.5 shows the attenuation coefficient μ of slow electrons due to valence (i.e. conduction) electron excitation in Al as calculated in the jellium approximation and for comparison the attenuation coefficient ν due to elastic backscattering. The dominance of inelastic scattering by valence electrons is clearly recognizable. The minimum mean-free path for inelastic scattering in Al is $\lambda_{ee}^{min} = 1/\mu_{max} \approx 3$ Å. The experimental values for Al [6.4] agree well with

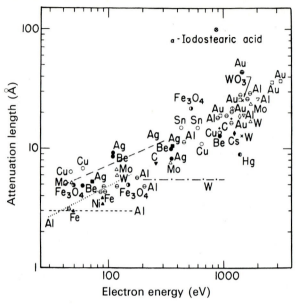

Fig. 6.6. Experimental attenuation length (inelastic mean-free path) values λ_{ee} [6.8]

the jellium predictions. This seems surprising because an important inelastic attenuation mechanism, surface plasmon excitation, has been neglected in the calculation. However, the volume plasmon excitation probability decreases towards the surface in a manner complementary to the increase of the surface plasmon excitation probability [6.5]. Therefore an approximate compensation occurs with the result that inelastic attenuation changes little right up to the surface. Curves similar to that in Fig. 6.5 are obtained for other materials [6.1] and give λ_{ee} values which lie well within the scatter of the experimental values [6.6, 6.7] of mean-free paths for inelastic scattering shown in Fig. 6.6 [6.7]. The weak dependence of λ_{ee} on the kind of material is not surprising because λ_{ee} is basically determined by the valence electron density which does not change strongly from material to material.

For the understanding of ILEED in which inelastically scattered electrons are observed, not only the total scattering cross-section, as expressed by μ, is needed but also the differential scattering cross-section (angular distribution) $I_{ee}(\vartheta)$. There are at present no explicit expressions for $I_{ee}(\vartheta)$ available for slow electrons [6.8] so that to a first approximation the formulas valid for fast electrons ($E \sim 10^4$ eV) [6.9] must be used [6.2]. For volume plasmon excitation the differential attenuation coefficient is $\mu(\vartheta) \sim \varepsilon/(\varepsilon^2 + \vartheta^2)$ which can also be written in the form $\mu(K) \sim \Delta E/K^2$. Here $\varepsilon = \Delta E/2E$ $(\Delta E = \Delta E(K) = $ energy loss $=$ energy of the volume plasmon excited), K is the wave number of the plasmon and E the energy of the incident electron. Thus μ is independent of ϑ for small angles and decreases like ϑ^2 at larger angles. Beyond a critical scattering angle ϑ_c corresponding to a maximal wave number K_c or minimum plasmon wavelength λ_c no plasmon excitation is possible but only one-electron excitation. For example, for 50 eV electrons in Al $\vartheta_c \approx 25°$ [6.2]; similar values are obtained for slow electrons in other materials. Thus electrons which have been inelastically scattered due to excitation of volume plasmons cannot be observed directly in the backward direction but only via *elastic* backscattering. One-electron excitation is not limited by such a critical ϑ_c but drops off so rapidly beyond ϑ_c for volume plasmons ($\sim \vartheta^{-4}$, Rutherford scattering!) that for practical purposes it can also be observed only via elastic backward scattering. Similarly electrons which have lost energy by surface plasmon excitation can generally only be observed by the same mechanism. This coupling between inelastic and elastic scattering necessary for the observation of inelastic scattering is the basis of ILEED.

6.1.3. Quasielastic Scattering

Quasielastic scattering represents the influence of thermal motion of the ion cores on the scattering process. Because of the small energy exchange (10–100 meV) occurring in this process, it cannot be energy-resolved in ordinary LEED instruments but it has a strong effect on the angular distribution of the (quasi)elastically scattered electrons. This effect is most apparent in well-ordered crystals, in which the thermal motion (lattice vibration) reduces the order and thus the intensity of the diffracted beams which depends on the same order. This phenomenon is taken into account in the usual diffraction theory by the Debye-Waller factor $\exp(-2W)$ with $2W = \langle (\boldsymbol{K} \cdot \boldsymbol{u})^2 \rangle \approx 16\pi^2 \langle u^2 \rangle \sin^2(\vartheta/2)/\lambda^2$. Here $\boldsymbol{K} = \boldsymbol{k} - \boldsymbol{k}_0$, $\boldsymbol{k}_0$, $\boldsymbol{k}$ being the wave vectors of the incident and scattered waves, $\boldsymbol{u}$ is the instantaneous displacement of an atom from its equilibrium position, ϑ the scattering angle $\sphericalangle (\boldsymbol{k}, \boldsymbol{k}_0)$ and λ the wavelength of the electron. The mean square displacements of atoms in and near the surface are in general much larger than in the bulk, show strong anisotropy and depend in a complicated manner upon the distance from the surface [6.10]. To a first approximation, however, $\langle u^2 \rangle$ decreases as $\exp(-l)$ with layer number l from the surface to the bulk value $\langle u^2 \rangle_B$. For example, $\langle u^2 \rangle_l / \langle u^2 \rangle_B \approx 3.5$, 1.7, and 1.3 for $l = 1, 2, 3$. Therefore thermal motion reduces the contribution of the first layer to the intensity of diffracted beams much more than the contribution of the second layer. This fact is important for the interpretation of LEED patterns.

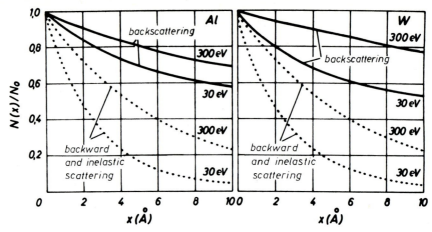

Fig. 6.7. Attenuation of the elastic electron current ($\Delta E = 0$) propagating into the forward half-space due to backscattering only and due to inelastic scattering plus backscattering [6.1]

6.1.4. Consequences of the Scattering Processes

The important features of these scattering processes for ELEED are 1) the strong attenuation due to inelastic scattering by the valence electrons, 2) the large total cross-section for elastic scattering and 3) the strong layer dependence of the quasieleastic scattering. The first feature reduces the thickness of the surface region which contributes effectively to the LEED pattern to about 10–20 Å, depending upon energy. This is illustrated in Fig. 6.7: at a beam energy of 30 eV at which the absorption coefficient is close to its maximum, only 2–4 layers are reached by enough "elastic" electrons to contribute to the LEED pattern. Because of the high elastic scattering probability only a fraction of these elastic electrons propagate in the direction of the incident beam: the electrons form an "elastic" wave field which produces the LEED pattern in contrast to X-ray diffraction where, to a good approximation, the unattenuated incident wave produces the diffraction pattern. The third feature counteracts the first one which suppresses the contributions of deeper layers to the LEED pattern. At high energies, high temperatures or in crystals with low Debye temperatures—that is large $\langle u^2 \rangle$—the second layer may contribute as much as the first layer.

The consequences drawn for ELEED apply also to ILEED, for which still another scattering feature is important: the lack of direct backscattering which requires combination with elastic scattering (diffraction) in order to observe inelastic scattering. The feature most important for

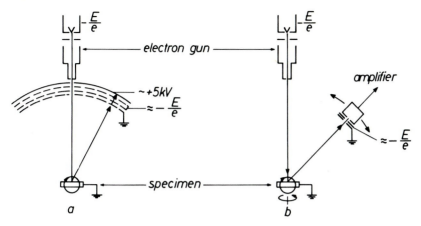

Fig. 6.8. Schematic of the basic types of LEED instruments. See text for an explanation

AES is again the strong inelastic scattering which reduces the escape depth of Auger electrons in the usual energy range to 3–20 Å (see Fig. 6.6) independent of energy, direction and kind of the exciting incident radiation (electrons, X-ray, ions).

6.2. Low Energy Electron Diffraction (LEED)

6.2.1. Experimental Methods

There are essentially two types of LEED instruments: display-type systems and diffractometers. In display-type systems (Fig. 6.8a) the electrons scattered into a large solid angle segment are observed simultaneously on a fluorescent screen. The inelastically scattered electrons and the secondary electrons generated by the incident beam are eliminated by a retarding field between the grids. In a diffractometer (Fig. 6.8b) the electrons scattered into a small solid angle are measured with a Faraday cup or channeltron after passing through a retarding field. Detector and crystal are rotated in a suitable manner so that all desired angles of incidence and diffraction may be covered. The display-type system has the advantage of speedy observation, but for quantitative intensity measurements diffractometers are far superior. There are many versions of both types of instruments, including combinations, e.g. with a channeltron behind a slit in the LEED screen.

The electron gun usually produces a beam on the specimen with $0.1–10 \mu A$ current and a diameter from 10^{-4} to 10^{-3} m depending on electron energy (10–200 eV). The coherence of the beam is determined primarily by the angular divergence and is usually such that specimen regions of the order of several 100 Å diameter scatter coherently. This means that the scattered *amplitudes* have to be added only for atoms within a coherence region and the total scattering is obtained by adding the scattered *intensity* of all coherence regions within the beam cross-section. There are many ways of specimen preparation depending upon its chemical, thermal and mechanical properties: sawing followed by mechanical, chemical or electrochemical polishing and cleaving are the most important ones. If cleaving is not done in the system after establishing UHV then the surface has to be cleaned in situ by ion bombardment or by reaction with gases such as O_2 and H_2. An example is the removal of C or S from metals by O_2, sometimes followed by reduction in H_2. The single-crystalline regions on the specimen obviously should be larger than the beam cross-section if the interpretation should not get to complicated. Utmost surface perfection (e.g. surface orientation within $0.01°$ of the desired plane) is essential for many quantitative studies but LEED patterns can be obtained frequently from microscopically very rough and inhomogeneous surfaces, as long as a sufficiently large fraction of the surface ($> 10\%$) produces the same LEED pattern.

In order to keep the surface clean pressures below 10^{-9} Torr have to be maintained during observation; the best systems work in the 10^{-11} Torr range. In studies of the interaction with gases pressures up to 10^{-4} Torr can be tolerated if proper electron emitters are used. Because of the interpretation difficulties it is useful if not necessary to incorporate other experimental techniques in the LEED system: AES is the most important one, but thermal desorption spectroscopy (TDS), work function measurements and ion scattering spectroscopy (ISS) are also very useful.

6.2.2. Theoretical Methods

Kinematical Theory

This is the simplest theoretical method. In its most elementary form it takes only the diffracted waves produced by the incident wave in the topmost layer into account. More refined versions include also the diffracted waves from "visible" atoms in the second layer without or with inclusion of the attenuation of the incident wave due to inelastic scattering, or the diffracted waves from many layers whose contribution rapidly diminish with increasing distance from the surface due to attenuation by inelastic scattering. All versions of the kinematical theory have in common that only the (unattenuated or attenuated) incident wave is considered to produce diffracted waves while the re-diffraction of diffracted waves (double and multiple scattering) is neglected. Because of the strong elastic scattering (Subsection 6.1.1) this is an extremely serious oversimplification, which considerably limits the application of this theory: it makes it nearly useless for the interpretation of the intensity of the diffracted beams and causes ambiguity even in the interpretation of the geometry of the diffraction pattern from non-ideal surfaces and surfaces covered with adsorbates or thin overlayers. Nevertheless, it is useful in many cases for the interpretation of the position and shape of the diffraction spots, as observed on the fluorescent screen.

A discussion of the simplest version—diffraction only by the topmost layer or in the case of adsorbates by the first two layers—suffices to demonstrate the application of the kinematical theory. The amplitude of the scattered wave is in this approximation obtained by summing over the amplitudes of the waves scattered by all atoms within the coherence region

$$\Psi(r) = \frac{e^{ikr}}{r}\, \psi(K) \quad \text{with}$$

$$\psi(K) = \sum_{l m_1 m_2} f_l(K) \exp[-iK \cdot (r_l + m_1 a_1 + m_2 a_2)]$$

$$= \sum_{l} f_l(K) \exp(-iK \cdot r_l) \cdot \sum_{m_1 m_2} \exp[-iK \cdot (m_1 a_1 + m_2 a_2)]$$

$$= F \cdot G,$$

(6.1)

where F refers to Σ_l and G to $\Sigma_{m_1 m_2}$. Here a_1, a_2 define the periodicity parallel to the surface—the surface unit mesh—r_l is the position of the atoms within the unit mesh, m_1, m_2 are integers, and $K = k - k_0$ as before. The function $f_l(K)$ is the scattering amplitude of atom l and depends only on $K = |K| = 2k \sin(\vartheta)/(2) = \frac{4\pi}{\lambda} \sin(\vartheta)/(2)$ $(\vartheta = \measuredangle(k, k_0))$.

The exponential factor represents the geometrical phase differences between the incident wave $\exp(ik_0 \cdot r_{l m_1 m_2})$ and the waves $\exp(ik \cdot r_{l m_1 m_2})/r$ diffracted by the atom in position $r_{l m_1 m_2}$.

The intensity of the scattered wave is obtained by summing over the intensities $I = |F|^2 |G|^2$ from all coherence regions. The "structure factor" $|F|^2$ varies only slowly with angle and determines mainly the intensity of the diffracted beams. Because of the neglect of the all-important double scattering in the approximation it is not a meaningful quantity and will not be discussed any further. The "lattice factor" or "interference function" $|G|^2$, however, involves only a summation over the unit meshes which are all completely equivalent from the point of view of scattering theory. Thus it is a generally valid expression. Performing the summation in (6.1) for a periodic structure with the dimensions $M_1 \boldsymbol{a}_1 \times M_2 \boldsymbol{a}_2$ (smaller or equal to the coherence region) gives

$$|G|^2 = \frac{\sin^2\left[\tfrac{1}{2}(M_1+1) A_1\right]}{\sin^2\left(\tfrac{1}{2} A_1\right)} \cdot \frac{\sin^2\left[\tfrac{1}{2}(M_2+1) A_2\right]}{\sin^2\left(\tfrac{1}{2} A_2\right)} \tag{6.2}$$

with $A_i = \boldsymbol{K} \cdot \boldsymbol{a}_i = \boldsymbol{K}_\| \cdot \boldsymbol{a}_i$. This function has strong main maxima whenever $A_i = 2\pi h_i$ (h_i integer). If $\boldsymbol{K}_\|$ is expressed in terms of the unit vectors $\boldsymbol{b}_1$, $\boldsymbol{b}_2$ of the reciprocal mesh to $\boldsymbol{a}_1$, $\boldsymbol{a}_2$: $\boldsymbol{K}_\| = 2\pi(n_1 \boldsymbol{b}_1 + n_2 \boldsymbol{b}_2)$, then (6.2) expresses the fact that diffracted waves occur only in certain directions, given by the conditions $\boldsymbol{k}_\| - \boldsymbol{k}_{0\|} = 2\pi(h_1 \boldsymbol{b}_1 + h_2 \boldsymbol{b}_2)$ and $k = k_0$. Thus diffracted beams and diffraction spots (h_1, h_2) are produced on the screen. The size and shape of these spots is determined according to (6.2) by the dimensions M_1, M_2 of the periodic region, the smallest spot size being that determined by the size of the coherence region. If the periodic region is large in the direction $\pm \boldsymbol{a}_1$ then the diffraction spot is small in the direction $\pm \boldsymbol{b}_1$, and vice versa.

Frequently there are within the coherence region several regions with identical periodicity but displaced relative to each other by amounts $\boldsymbol{d} = d_1 \boldsymbol{a}_1 + d_2 \boldsymbol{a}_2$ which do not belong to the periodicity (d_1, d_2: non-integers). The lattice factor of two such "subdomains" is given by

$$|G[1 + \exp(i\boldsymbol{K} \cdot \boldsymbol{d})]|^2 = 2|G|^2(1 + \cos \boldsymbol{K} \cdot \boldsymbol{d}). \tag{6.3}$$

Thus the intensity distribution within a diffraction spot (h_1, h_2) [see Eq. (6.2)] is modulated by $(1 + \cos \boldsymbol{K} \cdot \boldsymbol{d})$. For example the intensity will be zero in the center of the spot when $\boldsymbol{K} \cdot \boldsymbol{d} = (2n + 1)\pi$ or $2\pi(h_1 d_1 + h_2 d_2) = (2n + 1)\pi$; for a $(1, 0)$ spot this condition is fulfilled if $d_1 = (2n+1)/2$, e.g. $d_1 = 1/2$. Such a situation may occur in an adsorption layer which has the same periodicity as the substrate but is displaced relative to it by $\boldsymbol{a}_1/2$. More frequently this spot splitting is seen in adsorption layers which have a larger periodicity than the substrate. A layer with $c(2 \times 2)$ structure on a $\{100\}$ surface of a cubic crystal, i.e. a layer in which the nearest neighbour atoms within the layer are missing, produces, in addition to the integral spots, "extra" half-order spots $[h_i = (2n_i + 1)/2]$. For these spots the condition for splitting is fulfilled also with integral displacements d_1, d_2 of the subdomains. Domain formation is a consequence of the statistical nature of the adsorption process, the limited range of the forces between the atoms and their limited mobility. A detailed analysis therefore requires a statistical treatment.

The location, width and shape of spots can also be analyzed for other forms of surface disorder such as steps, facetting and etch pit formation. The effect of steps is illustrated by a periodic array of steps perpendicular to a unit mesh edge a. If the terraces between the N steps within the coherence diameter are M unit-meshes wide and two steps are separated by the vector s, then

$$G = \sum_{m=0}^{M-1} \exp(im\mathbf{K} \cdot \mathbf{a}) \cdot \sum_{n=0}^{N-1} \exp(in\mathbf{K} \cdot \mathbf{s})$$

so that

$$|G|^2 = \frac{\sin^2 \left[\frac{1}{2}(M-1)A\right]}{\sin^2 \frac{1}{2}A} \cdot \frac{\sin^2 \left[\frac{1}{2}(N-1)S\right]}{\sin^2 \frac{1}{2}S}, \tag{6.4}$$

where $S = \mathbf{K} \cdot \mathbf{s}$. The first term determines the spot position for the ideal surface, the second factor the intensity distribution within the spot. Because $S = \mathbf{K} \cdot \mathbf{s}$, and s has a component normal to the surface, the intensity modulation by the second factor is energy dependent: a spot splitting normal to the steps occurs (see Fig. 6.9) which appears and disappears with electron energy. This effect occurs even when the step periodicity is poor [6.11]. For the determination of the absolute or relative spot intensities as function of energy $|G|^2$, of course, has to be multiplied with the dynamical structure factor [6.13]. In facetting surface elements are formed which are inclined to the original surface. They cause additional diffracted beams with directions determined by the conditions $\mathbf{K}_\parallel \cdot \mathbf{a}_i = 2\pi h_i$, $k = k_0$ applied to the unit mesh vectors of these surface elements. These facet beams can easily be recognized because they move in directions different from those expected for the flat surface when the beam energy is changed.

Thus considerable information can be extracted from LEED patterns with the kinematical theory, even about atomic positions (from domain patterns). But because of the importance of double scattering there are also serious limitations. The problem of interpreting spot intensities has already been mentioned, but even the spot positions cannot be uniquely interpreted if different surface meshes are superimposed. This is illustrated in Fig. 6.10: a) represents a LEED pattern from a {100} surface of a cubic crystal (circles) covered with a layer which produces additional spots (crosses) [(100)–(2 × 1) pattern]. If double scattering would not occur the pattern b) plus the same pattern rotated by 90° would explain the diffraction from the layer. However, each diffraction beam from the substrate (circles) can act as a primary beam for the layer (crosses) (and *vice versa*). Thus patterns c) or d) plus the 90° rotated ones as well as many others can also produce pattern a). Therefore

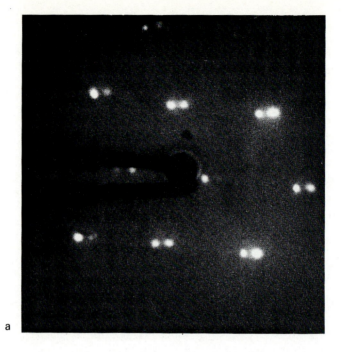

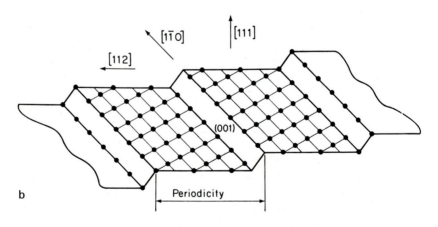

Fig. 6.9a and b. LEED pattern from stepped Pt surface and step structure derived from it [6.12]

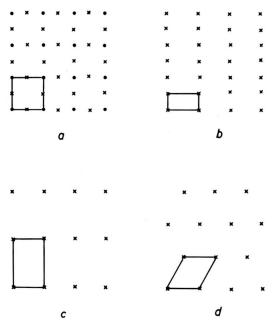

Fig. 6.10a–d. Example for the ambiguity in the determination of the unit cell dimensions due to double scattering. See text for an explanation

additional information is needed for a distinction between these interpretation possibilities which may be obtained with other techniques such as coverage measurements or from an evaluation of the spot intensities.

The evaluation of the spot intensities must take into account all the scattering processes discussed in Section 6.1. There have been attempts to apply standard or modified techniques for the evaluation of X-ray diffraction intensity data to LEED intensity data, such as modifications of the Patterson function method [6.14, 6.15]. An analysis of the Patterson function type assumes implicitly that the wave producing the diffracted wave consists only of the incident plane wave. Applying it to LEED data with the complicated wave field in the specimen should not produce meaningful results unless—as has been suggested to explain the apparent success of the method [6.15]—the transform process used suppresses the contribution of multiple scattering processes and enhances the intensity features produced by the incident wave.

Such suppression and enhancement effects are also used more directly: in LEED data-averaging techniques the observed beam intensities $I_{h_1 h_2}(k, k_0)$ are averaged over a finite energy range [6.16, 6.17]

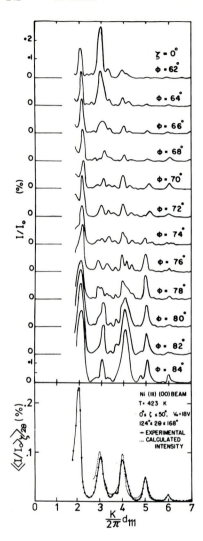

Fig. 6.11. Individual and averaged $I_{00}(V)$ curves of a Ni {111} surface (ξ: azimuth, ϕ: grazing angle of incidence, $2\theta = 9$, $S/S_0 = 2d_{111} \sin\theta/\lambda$) [6.19]

or over many k, k_0 pairs connected by the same $K = k - k_0$ [6.18–6.21] and compared with kinematical model calculations. The rational for the constant K averaging method is the fact that in the kinematical theory $I_{h_1 h_2}$ depends only on K so that an average of sufficient data at constant K should give the kinematical intensity. Figure 6.11 shows that at least a kinematical-like curve is obtained on averaging [6.19]. A comparison of the two averaging methods reveals similar accuracy which is given as ± 0.03 Å for the surface layer spacing [6.22].

Dynamical Theory

The dynamical theory takes the re-diffraction of diffracted waves into account and must in the case of LEED include absorption due to the strong inelastic scattering. Also the reduction of the beam intensities due to quasielastic scattering must be included. There is at present no general theory including all these phenomena accurately. Rather absorption is taken into account by an imaginary, energy-dependent effective potential or by an energy-dependent attenuation length λ_{ee} such as calculated in the jellium approximation (Section 6.1) [6.23, 6.24] or choosen as an adjustable parameter [6.25]. Thermal effects are taken into account by multiplying the atomic scattering amplitudes with Debye-Waller factors which are usually assumed to be layer and direction independent [6.26]. The importance of the various simplifications is still a matter of controversy. Some authors consider the accuracy of the ion-core potential (Subsection 6.1.1) to be most critical, some the shape of the complex energy-dependent surface potential (transition region between crystal and vacuum), and others the deviation of the vibrational behavior near the surface from that in the bulk. Although results obtained with various approximations are accumulating (Subsection 6.2.3) it is still premature to say what simplifications are most serious. Very likely all opinions will prove to be correct depending on specimen, temperature and electron energy.

The basic problem of the dynamical theory can be seen by inspecting the integral equation describing the scattering process

$$\psi(r) = \psi_0(r) + \int G(r, r') V(r') \psi(r') dr'$$
$$\equiv \psi_0(r) + \int G(r, r') T(r') \psi_0(r') dr' ,$$

(6.5)

where $\psi_0(r)$ is the incident wave, $\psi(r)$ the scattered wave, $G(r, r')$ is the Green's function describing the propagation of the wave scattered in the volume element dr' at position r' to the point r, $V(r)$ is the effective scattering potential taking into account correlation, exchange, thermal scattering and the transition region between crystal and vacuum, and $T(r)$ is the "scattering matrix" of the crystal. Thus the determination of the amplitude of the diffracted wave $\psi(r)$ at a large distance from the crystal ($r \gg r'$) requires the evaluation of $\psi(r)$ within the crystal, of $V(r)$ and of $G(r, r')$. For G the function valid for propagation in jellium has been used in general discussions, and V is usually constructed from band structure muffin tin potentials, i.e. core potentials with spherical symmetry. The scattered wave ψ is evaluated by a variety of techniques. The most frequently used techniques are the Darwin or layer method and the Bethe or "wave function matching" method.

In the Bethe method the Schrödinger equation is solved for the three-dimensionally periodic crystal and the wave functions in the crystal are matched at the surface to those in vacuum. This determines the amplitudes of the vacuum waves. Although this method can be generalized by adding a layer with a layer spacing different from that in the bulk, or with different lateral periodicity at the surface to treat lattice expansion or contraction at the surface, the Darwin method is much better adapted to this situation and to adsorbed layers. In it the crystal is divided into layers parallel to the surface. Within each layer multiple scattering between the various atoms is calculated using various methods, while multiple scattering between layers is taken into account by matching the wave functions at the boundaries between planes. Some of the most successful recent calculation procedures, such as the inelastic-collision model [6.25], the layer Kohn-Korringa-Rostocker (KKR) method [6.27], the RFS (renormalized forward scattering) perturbation theory [6.28] or the t-matrix formalism [6.29] belong to this group of methods. All these calculations require large computers. In cases in which calculations have been made for identical models the various methods now give comparable results.

6.2.3. Results

Clean Surfaces

The lateral periodicity of most surfaces is identical to that in the bulk. However there are a number of exceptions such as the {100} surfaces auf Au, Pt, Ir or various surfaces of Si and Ge. These surfaces exhibit superstructures (Fig. 6.12b) which transform reversibly into the normal periodicity at elevated temperatures, e.g. at 1100 K, 1150 K, and 600 K in the case of the Au {100}, Si {111}, and Ge {111} surfaces, respectively. The superstructures can be easily suppressed or modified by impurities (Fig. 6.12a) but there is no doubt now that they are characteristic of the clean surface. On the {100} surfaces they can be attributed to a slightly distorted hexagonal surface layer, while for the superstructures on Si and Ge surfaces many models have been proposed. At present these structures are still subject of speculation [6.30].

The determination of the periodicity normal to the surface requires an analysis of the beam intensities, which can be done in a meaningful manner only with dynamical calculations, i.e. inclusion of multiple scattering in the calculations or with averaging methods, i.e. elimination of multiple scattering in the measurements. Therefore clean surfaces have been and still are the testing ground of the interpretational procedures. Al, Cu, and Ni surfaces have been most thoroughly studied and illustrate

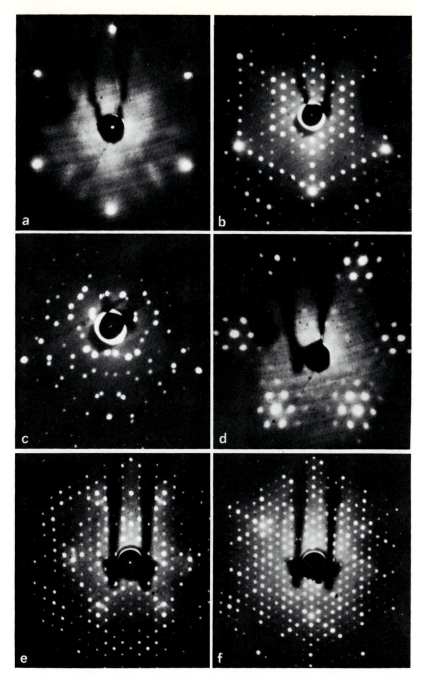

Fig. 6.12a–f. LEED patterns from Si {111} surfaces: (a) impurity stabilized (1 × 1) pattern, (b) (7 × 7) pattern of clean surface, (c) $(\sqrt{19} \times \sqrt{19}) - R(23.5°)$–Ni pattern, (d) (5 × 5)–Cu pattern, (e) (6 × 6)-Au pattern, (f) (7 × 7)-pattern, (a)–(d) 45 eC, (e)–(f) 80 eV

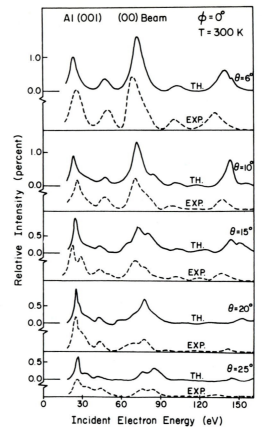

Fig. 6.13. Calculated and measured $I_{00}(V)$ curves from Al {100} surface for various angles of incidence [6.31]

well the present state of the art. The diffraction data most frequently used for comparison are $I_{h_1 h_2}(V)$ curves, i.e. the intensities of diffracted beams $(h_1 h_2)$ as a function of beam energy, obtained at various angles of incidence and temperatures. Criteria for agreement are positions, shapes and widths of the intensity maxima and absolute intensities. The agreement between experiment and recent calculations [6.27, 6.31–6.36] is surprisingly good for {100} and {111} surfaces with bulk lattice spacings normal to the surface (Fig. 6.13), but detailed examination reveals the need for refining the models and calculation procedures. The $I_{h_1 h_2}(V)$ curves for {110} surfaces, as calculated with the same parameters used for {100} and {111} surfaces, differ considerably from the experimental results unless the spacing between the first and second layer is assumed to be 10–15% smaller than that in the bulk [6.31–6.33]. However, even with this surface relaxation agreement is still poor. There are strong indications that steps may, to a large extent, be the cause of the discrepancies [6.12].

Similar results are obtained with data-averaging techniques for Cu, Ni, and Ag [6.18–6.20, 6.22]. The relaxation of the surface interplanar spacing of {100} and {111} surfaces is found to be less than 0.03 Å. The evaluation of the temperature and angle dependence of the intensities indicates that $\langle u^2 \rangle_s \approx 4 \langle u^2 \rangle_B$ in qualitative agreement with theoretical predictions. This suggests again that the layer dependence of the vibrational amplitudes should be included in dynamical calculations. For data-averaging techniques an accuracy of 5% is claimed in the determination of the atomic positions. The results described up to now give some confidence that the evaluation procedures are meaningful and can be applied with caution to more complicated systems.

Adsorption Layers

The most thoroughly studied systems are the $c(2 \times 2)$ structures (Fig. 6.14c) of various adsorbed atoms on the {100} surfaces of Ni and Ag [6.37–6.40]. Models of these adsorption layers are shown in Fig. 6.15. Oxygen on Ni {100} illustrates the results: all authors agree on the fourfold symmetry of the adsorption site so that Model b can be excluded. The normal distances, however, differ considerably: 1.5 ± 0.1 Å (Model a) [6.37], $.9 \pm 0.1$ Å [6.38] and 1.8 ± 0.1 Å (Model c) [6.39], although the same experimental data were used in obtaining the first two values. Figure 6.16 shows how well the calculated curves reproduce the observed $I(V)$ curves [6.39]. Thus there are two problems at present: 1) different methods of analysis lead to different structures for the same experimental data, 2) different authors obtain rather different experimental data. More work, both experimental and theoretical, is therefore necessary before the reliability of the deduced structures can be assessed and before it can be considered as certain that these surfaces are not reconstructed, a question which has been controversial for ten years [6.41]. It is even more premature to judge the reliability of data-averaging and in particular of transform techniques. The energy-averaging technique has been applied to a specific oxygen superstructure on a Rh {100} surface [6.16], the constant momentum transfer(K)-averaging technique to half a monolayer of oxygen on a W {110} surface [6.21] and the Patterson function type analysis to CO on a Pt {100} surface [6.14].

At present the most important application of LEED to adsorption layers is still the determination of the lateral periodicity and of the degree of order (order-disorder transitions, domain size distributions

Fig. 6.14a–c. LEED patterns from a W {100} surface at 60 eV: (a) clean (1×1) pattern, (b) (2×1)-O pattern, (c) $c(2 \times 2)$-Cu pattern

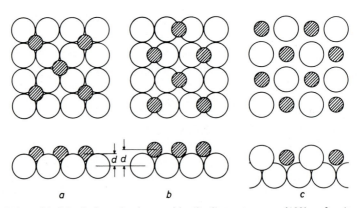

Fig. 6.15a–c. Models of adsorption layers with $c(2 \times 2)$ structure on a {100} surface (top and side views)

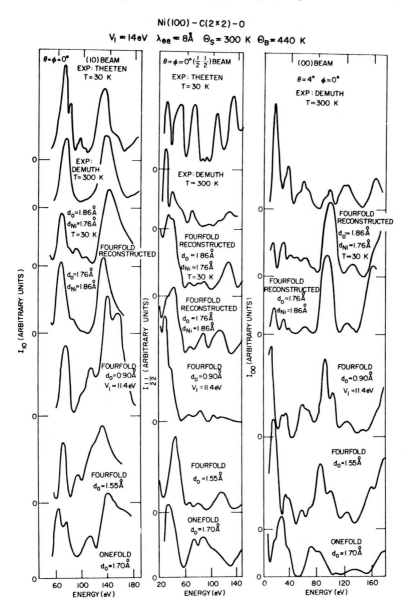

Fig. 6.16. Calculated and measured $I_{h_1 h_2}(V)$ curves for $\mathrm{Ni}\{100\} - c(2 \times 2)$-O structure. From left to right: $(h_1 h_2) = (1, 0)$, $(1/2, 1/2)$ and $(0, 0)$. From top to bottom: Experimental curves (Theeten, Demuth), theoretical curves: Model c (fourfold reconstructed), Model a (fourfold) and onefold cordination [6.39]. (V_i: inner potential, θ_S, θ_B: surface and bulk Debye temperatures)

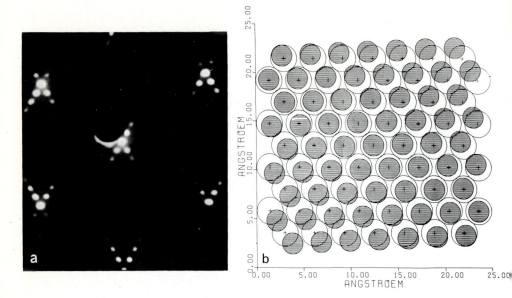

Fig. 6.17a and b. LEED pattern of W{110} – c(14 × 7)O structure and structure model. Open circles: W atoms, full circles O atoms. The relative positions of O and W atoms, and the precise location of the O atoms within the superstructure unit cell cannot be determined at present

etc.). The ambiguity in the determination of the lateral periodicity caused by double scattering with the substrate (Kinematical Theory of Subsection 6.2.2) can be eliminated in general if the coverage is known. If there is one atom per unit mesh, then the coverages producing the $p(2 \times 1)$ pattern of Figs. 6.10a and 6.14b are simply given by the ratio F_A^*/F_0^* of the unit mesh areas of adsorbate and substrate, i.e. by 0.5, 1.5, and 1.0 for the meshes b, c, and d, respectively. Figure 6.17 shows a more complicated example, the W(110)–"$c(14 \times 7)$"–O structure. There are many possible interpretations but the coverage determination and the change of the Auger signal with coverage lead, with reasonable reliability, to the model of Fig. 6.17b.

Order-disorder transitions as function of temperature occur in many adsorption systems and can be studied reliably by measuring the intensity of the extra spots due to the adsorbate, taking into account the Debye-Waller factor. AES is very useful in such studies to assure that the adsorbate does not diffuse into the substrate. Some adsorption layers are thermally so stable that they do not disorder before desorption. High coverage oxygen adsorption layers on a W{110} surface as the one shown in Fig. 6.17 are examples. The comparison of the temperature dependence of extra and normal spot intensities gives information to what extent the substrate is involved in the order-disorder process, which gives indirect evidence for the atomic positions (reconstructed versus unreconstructed surface). Similar indirect information on atomic positions (e.g. twofold versus fourfold symmetry of the adsorption site) has been obtained from the spot splitting caused by domain formation. A detailed kinematical analysis of such domain patterns allows conclusions as to the magnitude and range of the lateral interaction forces between adatoms which cause the ordering [6.42, 6.43]. Another type of order-disorder transition is that occurring on compound and alloy surfaces without and with change in composition during the process. An example is the order-disorder process on a Cu_3Au {100} surface in which it was ascertained by AES that no composition change occurred [6.44]. Studies of this type will remain the major application of LEED until the intensity analysis procedures have become more reliable and convenient to use.

6.2.4. Special Topics

Inelastic Low Energy Electron Diffraction (ILEED)

Inelastically scattered electrons can, in general, be observed only in connection with elastic scattering (Subsection 6.1.2) or—in a crystal—with diffraction. Depending upon the sequence of back-diffraction and energy loss one speaks of two processes: diffraction before loss (DL) and loss before diffraction (LD). In view of the magnitude of the elastic back-scattering and inelastic scattering cross-sections (Section 6.1) the LD process is in general more likely. The significance of ILEED lies in the fact that it allows the study of excitation phenomena in the crystal and on its surface which can be studied only or best with slow electrons [6.45]. Such phenomena are, for example, the excitation functions for volume and surface plasmon creation, the surface plasmon dispersion $E_{SP}(k_{\parallel})$, or eventually the electron band structure $E(k_{\parallel})$ and phonon band structure $\omega(k_{\parallel})$ at the surface. General theoretical treatments exist both for electron and phonon excitation [6.46–6.49], but they are to complicated for the interpretation of the experimental results and have to be simplified considerably [6.50].

   For the study of electronic excitations (energy loss $\Delta E > 0.5\,eV$) diffractometers, as described in Subsection 6.2.1 with variable retarding potential are sufficient but for vibronic excitations ($\Delta E \approx 10$–$100\,meV$) monochromatized primary beams and high-resolution analyzers are necessary. Because of the experimental difficulties of high resolution systems [6.51] most of the ILEED studies have been concerned with electronic excitations, in particular of surface plasmons, and excitations in adsorbed atoms. An example for the first type of study is the determination of the surface plasmon dispersion relation $E_{SP}(k_{\parallel})$ of an Al$\{111\}$ surface [6.50, 6,62], which is important for the understanding of the charge distribution near the surface. Excitations in adsorbed atoms have been studied for CO on a Ni$\{100\}$ surface and have been correlated with other data to determine the energy level diagram of the adsorbed atom [6.53]. In loss measurements, in which no k-dependence of the energy loss is sought, angle-averaging detectors such as display type systems can be used. The interpretation of the observed energy losses is frequently not unique. For example, three losses at about 2, 8, and 15 eV have been observed on Si surfaces [6.46, 6.54], which cannot be assigned to direct interband transitions or plasmon creation. The 15 eV loss is probably due to a surface excitation but the lower two losses can be caused either by non-direct interband transitions [6.46] or by surface excitations [6.54].

Polarized Electrons

In all techniques discussed up to now only the charge and energy of the electron is used to obtain information on the specimen. It has been known for some time that the scattering of slow electrons also depends on its spin [6.55, 6.56]. Therefore it is reasonable to expect that slow electrons can be spin polarized by diffraction and that diffraction of slow polarized electrons is spin dependent. Dynamical theories of the diffraction of slow polarized electrons have been developed [6.57, 6.58]. Recent detailed calculations [6.59] for a W$\{100\}$ surface predict strong polarization effects in the case of the first surface resonance i.e. when the first diffracted beam [the (10) beam] is parallel to the surface. Experiments are in progress or in preparation in some laboratories. Diffraction of slow polarized electrons can be used to obtain information on the electron spin distribution at the surface, e.g. in magnetic superstructures, due to the spin dependence of the scattering amplitudes. They should also allow a distinction between scattering from heavy and light atoms because the scattering by light atoms with paired electrons spins is spin-independent.

Low Energy Electron Diffraction Microscopy

Back scattered or diffracted slow electrons can be used for imaging the surface in a similar manner as emitted or reflected electrons are used in emission and mirror microscopy. To achieve this the specimen has to be made the cathode in an electrical immersion lens. Calculations for a typical electrostatic immersion lens give an optimum resolution of about 20 Å for 50 eV electrons [6.60]. This resolution is better than that of any other imaging method suitable for flat surfaces. Furthermore, imaging and diffraction can be combined in the same system by imaging the primary image plane of the immersion lens with an intermediate lens as it is done in conventional transmission electron microscopy. Thus the lateral distribution of surface features with different structures can be studied. Several systems of this type have been described [6.41, 6.61–6.64], but considerable technological development work still has to be done before the theoretical resolution will be approached.

6.3. Auger Electron Methods

6.3.1. Physical Principles

Free Atoms

Impact of energetic radiation on atoms produces inner shell vacancies (i) which are filled within 10^{-17} to 10^{-12} sec by electrons from outer shells (j). The energy liberated in this process is radiated as characteristic X-ray radiation or it is transferred to another outer shell (k) electron which is then emitted as an "Auger electron". This Auger electron has a kinetic energy characteristic of the atom, which is given by

$$E_{ijk} = E_i(Z) - E_j(Z) - E_k(Z + \Delta Z), \qquad (6.6)$$

where E_i, E_j, and E_k are the binding energies of the electrons in the shells ($K, L, M, ...$) involved. The Auger electron is ejected from a singly charged ion. Therefore its binding energy is somewhat larger than that of the same electron in the neutral atom and can be approximated by that of an atom with somewhat larger nuclear charge $Z (0.5 \lesssim \Delta Z \lesssim 1)$. Auger electron energies calculated with (6.5) from the known atomic energy levels have been tabulated [6.65]. The number of possible Auger transitions increases rapidly with the number of electrons i.e. with Z. The type of coupling between angular momentum and spin of the electrons (LS-, jj- or intermediate coupling) determines the number of Auger lines possible for a given combination of shells. For example, the KLL spectra of very light atoms (LS-coupling) consist of 5 lines, those of very heavy atoms (jj-coupling) of 6 lines while those of intermediate atoms should have 10 lines. Experiment, however, reveals many more lines, as shown in Fig. 6.18 for Ne which has LS-coupling [6.66].

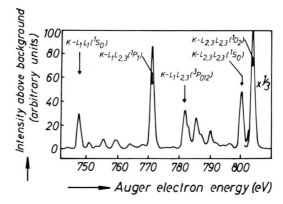

Fig. 6.18. *K LL* Auger spectrum of gaseous Ne excited by 3.2 keV electrons [6.66]

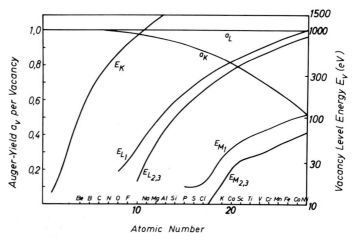

Fig. 6.19. Inner shell ionization energies E_i and transition probabilities a_i for light atoms

The terms between brackets describe the final state configurations of the doubly ionized atom. The weaker additional transitions are due to Auger emission from doubly ionized atoms which produces triply ionized atoms. Such transitions involving initial double ionization are quite common at high primary energies. In Auger-electron excitation by ions even higher degrees of ionization occur giving rise to very complicated Auger spectra. This is well illustrated by comparing Ne *K LL* spectra excited by H^+, He^+, or O^{+5} beams with Fig. 6.18 [6.68, 6.69].

Transitions in which an initial vacancy is filled by an electron from the same shell, e.g. a L_1 vacancy by an electron from the L_2 shell are called Coster-Kronig transitions. These transitions contribute considerably to the production of Auger electrons and thus to the complexity of their spectrum. A rough picture of the dependence of the Auger energies upon the atomic number can be obtained by plotting the energies of the initial vacancy versus Z (Fig. 6.19). This is possible because the levels j and k have frequently binding energies which are small compared to E_i and may be neglected to a first approximation. Figure 6.19 shows what inner shells can be used if the energy analyzer has an upper energy limit of 1500 eV: the K shell up to Al or the L shell up to beyond Ni. Higher Auger-electron energies are frequently impractical for intensity reasons.

The intensity of an Auger line is determined by the probability for creation of an inner shell vacancy, i.e. the ionization cross-section Q_i and the probability a_{ijk} that the filling of this vacancy is accompanied by an Auger or Coster-Kronig transition

$$I(E_{ijk}) \sim Q_i \cdot a_{ijk}. \qquad (6.7)$$

In the case of ionization by electrons Q_i increases rapidly from threshold – which is determined by the ionization energy E_i – to a maximum at about $3E_i$, and decreases afterwards again. Figure 6.20 shows an example for the agreement between experiment $(+,\bigcirc)$ and various theoretical approximations (curves) [6.70]. The dotted curve represents the simple function

$$Q_i = \frac{a}{E_i^2} \frac{\ln U}{U} \ [\text{Å}^2] \qquad (6.8)$$

(E_i in eV, $U = E/E_i$, $a = 960$ in Fig. 6.20) which gives a fair approximation for many ionization processes with a range from 600 to 1100 [6.2]. The function has a maximum

$$Q_i^{\text{max}} \approx 0.38\, a/E_i^2 \ [\text{Å}^2] \qquad (6.9)$$

at $E_{\text{max}} \approx 2.72\, E_i$, somewhat lower than observed. This leads to maximum attenuation coefficients $\mu_i^{\text{max}} = Q_i^{\text{max}} \lesssim 1 \cdot 10^{-2}\,\text{Å}^{-1}$ for all materials and ionization energies $E_i \gtrsim 50$ eV, confirming the statement made in Subsection 6.1.2 that attenuation due to inner shell ionization is small compared to attenuation by valence electrons. Equations (6.8) and (6.9) lead to the following rules for AES with electrons:

1) the energy of the incident beam should be at least 2.5 E_i for efficient ionization,

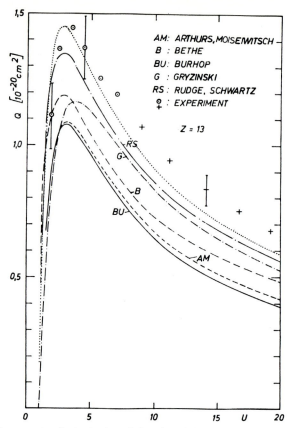

Fig. 6.20. Cross-section for ionization of the Al K shell by electrons according to theory and experiment [6.70]

2) E_i should be smaller than about 1500 eV if an ionization cross-section exceeding 10^{-20} cm^2 is to be obtained.

The second factor in (6.7), the Auger or Coster-Kronig yield a_{ijk} is the probability that a vacancy i is filled by an Auger transition involving levels j and k. It can be obtained reliably only by detailed numerical calculations which have been reviewed recently [6.71]. The results for transitions involving K and L shells are plotted in Fig. 6.19. It is evident that nearly all vacancies are filled by Auger transitions ($a_i = \Sigma\, a_{ijk} \approx 1$) as long as $E_i > 1500$ eV. At higher E_i values X-ray emission becomes increasingly stronger. This fact is a further reason for limiting AES to energies below about 1500 eV.

The Auger-electron line width of free atoms is determined by the lifetime of the vacancy i which ranges from fractions of an eV for small

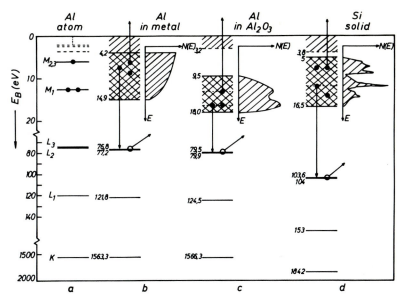

Fig. 6.21a–d. Energy-level schemes and densities of states of Al, in various environments, and of Si

E_i to about 10 eV for high E_i values (≈ 1500 eV), another reason for the use of shells with low ionization energies. The angular distribution of Auger electrons is in general isotropic or nearly isotropic (see *Details of the Auger Emission Process* in Subsection 6.3.4).

Condensed Matter

Figure 6.21 illustrates some of the differences between free atoms and atoms in condensed matter. The major effect of the atomic environment is the broadening of the valence levels into bands with considerable width and variations of the electronic density of state $N(E)$. A second effect is the shift of the energy levels which is, however, similar for all levels and thus has little influence on the energy $E_i - E_j$ available for the Auger electrons. The broadening of the valence levels causes a corresponding broadening of the Auger lines involving these levels. If both states j, k are located in the valence band the Auger line width is in principle twice the valence band width. Because of the variations of $N(E)$ the Auger line is more or less structured. By deconvolution of the Auger line [6.72, 6.73] it is therefore possible in principle to obtain $N(E)$. However, the complications due to the details of the Auger process in solids (*Details of the Auger Emission Process* in Subsection

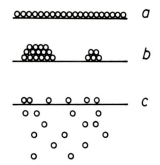

Fig. 6.22a–c. Atomic distributions in the surface region giving rise to different Auger signals in spite of same concentration

6.3.4) and due to inelastic scattering make a reliable analysis rather difficult. The same is true for the derivation of the orbital angular momentum (l) characteristic of electrons in various parts of the band [6.74], [6.75]. A comparison of the valence bands in Fig. 6.21 a and b clearly shows that the chemical environment (metal or oxide) can cause considerable "chemical" shifts of the Auger lines; they may be as large as 15 eV in strongly bound oxides.

The most important effect which the environment exerts on the Auger process in condensed matter is the attenuation of the Auger electrons created at a distance x from the surface on their way because of inelastic scattering (Subsection 6.1.2). Inelastic scattering not only reduces the intensity of the main features of an Auger line, but also redistributes the intensity on the low energy side of the strong features in a manner determined by the energy loss distribution which can be rather complicated. Well defined energy losses such as the volume and surface plasmon losses in Al cause clearly recognizable loss peaks. Energy loss spectra with little structure cause mainly smearing out of features on the low energy side of the main peak.

In principle the attenuation effects can be taken into account rigorously in the evaluations, but the mathematical expressions contain so many poorly known quantities that for practical purposes only highly simplified formulas can be used [6.45]. The consequence is that Auger electron intensities are a good measure for the number of the emitting atoms only if these are distributed in a two-dimensional manner, as indicated in Fig. 6.22a. Other distributions give quite different intensities for low-energy Auger electrons ($\lambda_{ee} \approx 3\text{–}5\,\text{Å}$). If Auger electrons with widely varying energies are emitted (e.g. 50 eV and 1000 eV), the differences in mean-free path cause different effective sampling depths and thus give information on the distribution. Without knowledge of this distribution quantitative AES is not possible. For two-dimensional distributions quantitative measurements can be made easily after calibration with other techniques such as quartz oscillator measurements (mass), radio tracer studies (nucleus) or ion beam deposition (charge). Use of such calibrations for surfaces with different roughness, temperature or surface composition requires considerable caution because the calibrated atoms may be distributed in a different way or the backscattering from the substrate may differ.

6.3.2. Experimental Methods

AES requires energy analysis of the electrons emitted from the surface to be tested with proper subtraction or suppression of the background on which the weak Auger lines are superimposed. The background is small in X-ray and ion bombardment excitation, but large in electron excitation. It is usually suppressed by differentiating—this emphasizes features which vary rapidly with energy—or by pulse counting techniques. There are many types of electron spectrometers suitable for AES, but only the most frequently used ones will be briefly discussed: the retarding field, the cylindrical mirror and the hemi-spherical type. Figure 6.8a suggests immediately the use of the display type LEED system for electron spectroscopy in the retarding field mode: in principle only the retarding potential has to be changed so that the "pass" energy E_a of the electrons varies. In such a "high-pass filter" electrons with energies $E > E_a$ are detected on the collector (fluorescent screen): $I_{a0} = \int_{E_a}^{E_0} I(E)\, dE.$

In order to obtain the energy distribution $I(E)$ the signal has to be differentiated which is done by superimposing an ac voltage with frequency $v\,(10^2–10^5\ \text{Hz})$ on the retarding voltage and by detecting only the ac signal on the detector with lock-in techniques. The resulting ac signal is only due to the electrons in the "energy window" determined by the amplitude of the modulation voltage. By tuning the lock-in detector to frequency v the first derivative of I_{a0}, i.e. $I(E)$, is obtained. In general, however, the signal with frequency $2v$ which is proportional to $dI(E)/dE$ is measured in order to suppress the background. Thus not Auger lines but their derivatives are observed. The amplitudes of the derivatives ("Auger amplitudes") are frequently a good measure for the intensity of the Auger line provided the modulation amplitude is small enough so that no averaging occurs. The maximum modulation amplitude permissible obviously depends on the shape and width of the Auger line and can vary from 1 to 10 V peak to peak. The advantage of this type of energy analyzer is its simplicity, its combination with LEED and its insensitivity to primary beam size and location on the

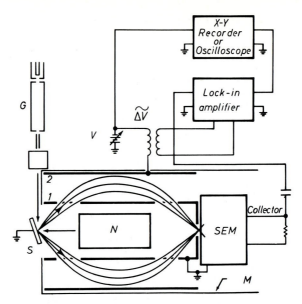

Fig. 6.23. Schematic of cylindrical mirror analyzer. Explanation see text

specimen. It is also very useful if the energy distribution is to be averaged over a large solid angle. Its disadvantage is the high noise $N \sim \sqrt{I_{a0}}$ produced by the electrons with $E_a < E < E_0$. However, by proper averaging and curvefitting techniques this disadvantage can be considerably reduced [6.76].

The high noise of the retarding field analyzers can be avoided if a band-pass analyzer is used which transmits only electrons with the energy of interest so that $N \sim \sqrt{I(E)}$ instead of $N \sim \sqrt{I_{a0}}$. Both the cylindrical mirror analyzer (CMA) shown schematically in Fig. 6.23 and the hemi-spherical analyzer belong to this class of instruments. Energy analysis in a CMA occurs in the radial electrostatic field between the coaxial cylinders 1, 2 in Fig. 6.23, in a hemi-spherical analyzer in the radial field between two concentric hemispheres. The primary electron beam is produced by a normal (N) or grazing (G) incidence electron gun. The Auger signal is very sensitive to beam size and location on the specimen. It is usual to differentiate also in this analyzer by superimposing a modulation voltage $\tilde{\Delta V}$ on the analyzer voltage V and to use lock-in detection. Figure 6.24 shows an example of $N(E)$ and of $dN(E)/dE$ obtained from the same sample with a CMA. For comparable investment in electronics the S/N ratio of a CMA is higher by a factor of 10^3 than that of a retarding field analyzer. Typical analyzer characteristics are:

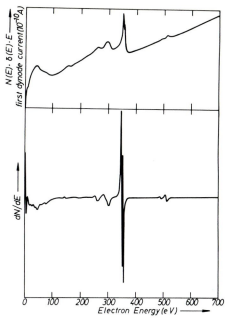

Fig. 6.24. Energy distribution $N(E)$ and its derivative $dN(E)/dE$ of Ag excited by 3 keV electrons as obtained with a CMA. $\delta(E)$ secondary emission coefficient of first dynode (Courtesy of P.E.I.)

energy resolution: 1 %, transmission: 10 % for standard diameter (≈ 10 cm) systems. By scaling up the diameter (≈ 1 m) [6.77] or operating two analyzers in series much higher resolution (<0.1 %) has been obtained.

Major experimental problems are electron beam induced specimen changes such as dissociation, carbon contamination buildup, electron stimulated desorption (ESD) or electron stimulated adsorption (ESA). Therefore, low beam currents e.g. $< 10^{-6}$ Å must frequently be used, increasing the demands on the detection and data processing system, if high resolution is required. Several procedures for optimization of detection and data processing have been discussed [6.76, 6.78, 6.79]. If higher beam currents can be tolerated the large S/N ratio allows very short time constants in the detection system and thus rapid scan times so that rapidly changing surface processes can be studied.

6.3.3. Results

The determination of surface composition, including trace element analysis by AES, has contributed greatly to the understanding of surfaces. For example, the Si $\{111\}$-surface with (7×7) structure (Fig. 6.12b)

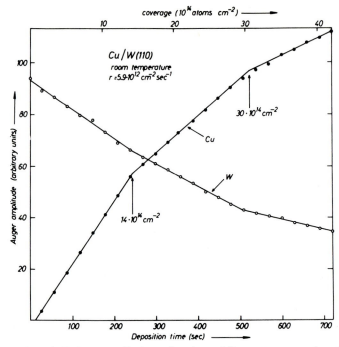

Fig. 6.25. Cu and W Auger amplitudes as functions of Cu coverage on a clean W {110} surface [6.82]

was shown to be clean, while the same surface with $(\sqrt{19} \times \sqrt{19})$ $- R(23.5°)$, (5×5) and (6×6) structures (Fig. 6.12c–e) was found to contain Ni, Cu, and Au, respectively. Similarly, the {100} surfaces of Au, Pt, and Ir with "(5×1)" or "(5×20)" structures are clean by present AES standards. On the other hand, many impurities were revealed by AES on surfaces previously considered to be clean on the basis of their good (1×1) LEED patterns. Some atoms, when located on top of the surface, can be detected if present in less than 1% of a monolayer; in general several percent are sufficient. The surface composition of alloys after or during heating, ion bombardment or chemical reaction has been studied considerably with AES. Information on the distribution of the components normal to the surface could be obtained by using emitted electrons with different characteristic energies from the same specimen. In alloys consisting of a component with low and a component with high specific surface energy, such as Pt–Sn [6.80] or Au–Sn [6.81] alloys, the surface is enriched with the low surface-energy component after equilibration, as expected from thermodynamics. Ion bombardment or chemical reaction can lead to quite different surface compositions depending upon relative sputtering yields and chemical reactivities. The observation of impurity segregation on free surfaces and internal surfaces, as revealed by fracturing, is another important result of AES studies. However, it must be kept in mind that quantitative analysis is difficult when the concentration varies with depth.

The situation is much simpler when the atoms to be studied are distributed only two-dimensionally as is the case in many adsorption systems. An example is shown in Fig. 6.25. Auger amplitudes of Cu and W from a W{110} surface are plotted as a function of the amount of Cu adsorbed on the crystal. Calibration was done with a quartz oscillator microbalance and by mass spectrometry. The Cu Auger signal shows two breaks as does the W signal, caused by the layerwise adsorption of Cu and the short mean-free path of the 60 eV Cu and 170 eV W Auger electrons. The slope ratio allows an accurate determination of the mean-free paths in this system. Of more interest is the fact that the second break does not occur at twice the coverage N_1 of the first break but at $(2.15 \pm 0.03) N_1$ in agreement with the LEED patterns corresponding to the two coverages [6.82]. Another example is the determination of the oxygen coverage producing the LEED pattern of Fig. 6.17 which made an important contribution to the interpretation of this pattern. The fact the AES can be done also at high temperature and gas pressures up to 10^{-5} Torr allows the study of adsorption under quasi-equilibrium conditions [6.83, 6.84]. Caution is necessary in such work because of the temperature dependence of the Auger signal.

Usually undesirable, but potentially useful electron beam effects are the dissociation of oxides (electron beam masking), desorption and adsorption of gases, as well as carbon build-up in the presence of a carbon-containing gaseous environment. Examples are the beam reduction of SiO_2 which leads to Si enrichment in the beam area [6.85], the electron stimulated desorption of C from Be0 in the presence of oxygen gas [6.86] or the electron beam induced adsorption of 0_2 on Si [6.87]. In spite of these beam effects oxidation studies can be done – and many have been done – by intermittent AES with low beam currents. The highest ESD cross-sections of oxygen are of the order 10^{-18} cm^2 [6.88]. At low current density $i = 1 \cdot 10^{-2}$ A cm$^{-2} = 1.6 \cdot 10^{17}$ El./cm^2 sec so that the need for careful experimentation is evident.

6.3.4. Special Topics

Details of the Auger Emission Process

In Subsection 6.3.1 and 6.3.2 a highly simplified picture of the Auger emission process was presented. The Auger emitter was essentially considered to be undisturbed in the emission process except for allowing a somewhat different force acting on the Auger electron, as expressed by the ΔZ term in $E_k(Z + \Delta Z)$. For Auger processes in solids it was assumed that the valence electrons could be described by the three-dimensional band structure $E(\mathbf{k})$ and density of states $N(E)$, which are meaningful only for nonlocalized processes. With increasing number of precise high resolution measurements it has become evident that the Auger process causes a strong localized disturbance of the emitter, so that $\mathbf{k}$ is not a good quantum number. This is true both for free-electron like metals and for d-band metals. Thus the density of states of Al obtained by deconvolution of the $L_{2,3}VV$ Auger line clearly disagrees with the theoretical $N(E)$ [6.89]. The same is true for the $M_{4,5}VV$ spectrum of Ag, which can be explained in terms of atomic-like final states with multiplet splitting [6.89]. Another example is the Cu $L_{2,3}MM$ spectrum which shows strong indications of spin splitting and lines much narrower than expected on the basis of the valence band width [6.90]. Thus conclusions concerning the undisturbed specimen are meaningful only if the localization of the Auger process is taken into account. It cannot be expected that the density of states obtained by deconvolution of Auger spectra should agree with that of three-dimensional band structure calculations. Rather it will be a local density of states, modified by selection rules.

The disturbance [6.91–6.93] caused in the atom from which the Auger electron is emitted may be divided into several parts [6.91, 6.92]: "dynamic" relaxation and "static" relaxation which in turn split into atomic and extra-atomic relaxations. In addition, the multiplet coupling in the final state, which causes the splitting mentioned above, has to be taken into account. Dynamic relaxation describes the rearrangement of the atom accompanying ionization. The dynamic relaxation energies of electrons are automatically included in (6.6) for $\Delta Z = 0$ if experimental binding energies are used. Static relaxation describes the rearrangement of the atom connected with the transition of the j electron into the i hole. Static atomic relaxation is the process which occurs in the free atom, static extra-atomic relaxation represents the response of the atomic environment in the solid to the formation of the j hole. In metals the positive charge on the ionized atom is very likely screened completely by conduction electrons, so that a localized picture is also appropriate for extra-atomic relaxation. The contributions of the various processes to the Auger energy have been determined for the Cu $L_{2,3}M_{4,5}M_{4,5}$ Auger spectrum to be ~ 25 eV, 10 eV and 20 eV for the multiplet, the static atomic and the static extra-atomic relaxation contributions, respectively [6.92]. The Auger energies calculated with (6.6) for $\Delta Z = 0$ but with inclusion of these terms agree within 2–3 eV with experiment.

The magnitude of the extra-atomic relaxation energy which obviously should depend considerably on the immediate environment of the emitting atom suggests that "chemical" shifts have to be analyzed in much more detail than has been done in the past. Another effect of the environment is its influence on the lifetime of the core hole states which determines the i state contribution to the linewidth. This lifetime is found to depend on the valence electron density in the emitting atom and its immediate environment, as determined by the interionic distance [6.94].

The strong localization of the Auger process makes it plausible why another much discussed phenomenon, the plasmon gain of Auger electrons, is very unlikely to occur, at least in d-band metals. Plasmon gains were originally invoked to explain the high energy satellites of the main Auger peaks in various metals [6.95–6.98]. Such a process is expected according to theory, provided that extra-atomic relaxation can be treated in a nonlocalized picture and that the core hole life-time is sufficiently short. Then the plasmons created during the core hole production have not already decayed by the time the Auger electron is emitted and the Auger electron can absorb the energy of one of the plasmons destroyed in its emission process [6.99]. At least the second condition is not fulfilled for the example calculated (the Al $L_{2,3}VV$ Auger process), because the lifetime derived from transition rate calculations [6.100] is $2 \cdot 10^{-13}$ sec, two orders of magnitude larger than required. Alternately the "plasmon gain" peaks have been ascribed to double ionization of core states [6.101–6.104], to internal photoemission [6.102] and to the density of states [6.105]. There is strong evidence that in Li [6.106], Na, Mg, Al, and Si [6.107, 6.108], the first explanation is correct and that the second process is negligable as compared to the first one, even at higher Auger energies [6.109]. The last process appears unlikely because of the localization of the Auger process discussed before. The only material in which plasmon gain cannot be excluded at present seems to be Be in which peaks expected for plasmon gain and double ionization are well separated and observed with the expected intensities [6.110].

After the emission process which apparently has to be treated in a localized picture the Auger electron has to propagate through the solid, which modifies the energy and angular distributions. This has not only negative effects. For example, if the energy losses are very distinct such as in free electron-like metals the plasmon satellites on the low-energy side of the main Auger peaks may be used to determine the depth distribution of the emitting atom by measuring the satellite intensity as a function of exit angle [6.111]. In single crystals the (quasi) elastic scattering of the Auger electrons on their way to the surface modifies the

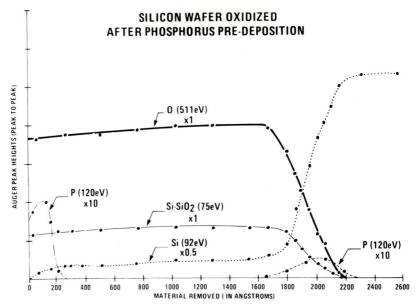

Fig. 6.26. In-depth analysis of an oxydized phosphorus doped silicon surface (Courtesy of P.E.I.)

angular distribution in a manner known from Kikuchi patterns in electron diffraction [6.112–6.114]. This is to be expected because the Auger emission process produces essentially a spherical wave similar to the waves causing Kikuchi patterns. The Auger electrons from atoms located on top of the surface should not show a Kikuchi-like anisotropy, which allows qualitative conclusions on the depth distribution of impurities [6.114]. It should, however, be noted that the angular distribution of Auger electrons from isolated atoms is already somewhat anisotropic if the initial vacancy has a total angular momentum $j > 1/2$ and if the final two vacancy state has a quantum number $J > 1/2$ [6.115].

In-Depth Auger Analysis and Auger Electron Microscopy

The small escape depth of Auger electrons make them an ideal tool for the study of the atomic distribution normal to the surface by successive removal of surface layers. This can be done in several ways but the most convenient method is ion-bombardment sputtering which is possible while the Auger spectrum is being measured [6.116, 6.117]. Typical sputtering conditions are: Ar gas pressure $1–5 \cdot 10^{-5}$ Torr, Ar^+ beam energy 0.5–2 keV, Ar^+ beam current density 0.2–20 $\mu A/cm^2$ and beam diameters on the specimen of several mm to about 1 cm. If the ultimate depth resolution as determined by the escape depth of the Auger electron (≈ 10 Å) is to be achieved, then the ion beam current density must be constant over an area larger than the diameter of the primary electron beam. Otherwise the area from which the Auger electrons are emitted is not flat and the Auger signal represents an average over a range of depths. At sufficiently low sputtering rates (1–10 Å/min depending on concentration gradients) several Auger lines can be monitored sequentially. Figure 6.26 shows an example for such a multiline analysis. Four peaks, the oxygen, phosphorus, silicon 92 eV and the silicon 75 eV line characteristic of Si in SiO_2 are measured while the oxide layer is sputtered away. The availability of convenient commercial data acquisition systems ("multiplexers") has led to a rapid development of in-depth AES.

There are, of course, limitations to this technique: the sputtering cross-sections vary from atom to atom and depend upon its chemical environment. An unusually drastic example is the removal of equal amounts of Mo deposited on various surfaces [6.118]: Mo forms on W a uniform film with a normal sputtering profile while on Cu, Au, and Al it agglomerates and can be observed over a large depth range. Also considerable surface roughening occurs during sputtering, in particular in impure materials. Another disturbing effect is the ion bombardment induced movement of ions in insulating films [6.119] leading to an accumulation of such ions on the boundaries of the film. The problems occurring in ion etching of insulators are also well illustrated by the example of mica [6.120].

The fact that Auger electrons are quite effectively produced by energetic electrons suggests using an Auger analyzer as detector in scanning microscopes in order to produce a high resolusion image of the lateral distribution of the chemical surface composition [6.121–6.123]. Although such an arrangement is, in principle, capable of high resolution due to the small size of the scanning beam on the specimen, the S/N ratio is low. Another approach is to start from a CMA with its high S/N ratio and to incorporate an electron gun which produces a very small spot on the specimen [6.122]. Such a system with a beam diameter of 5–10 μm has recently been developed and some first results are shown in Fig. 6.27, illustrating its capabilities. The specimen is a Si integrated circuit of which an area containing a transistor has been imaged with Si, O, P, and Au Auger electrons, respectively, in the top four panels; the lower half of the picture compares the Au image with the Mo image obtained after removing enough material by ion bombardment so that the Mo interface between the Au leads and the Si substrate becomes visible. Efforts are being made in several laboratories to improve the resolution so that Auger electron microscopy may become an even

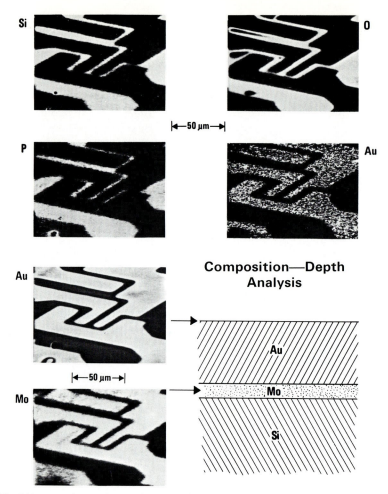

Fig. 6.27. Auger electron images from a transistor on a silicon chip. See text for an explanation (Courtesy of P.E.I.)

more powerful tool in surface and thin film analysis. The significance of these developments for modern technology is well illustrated in a recent review of the industrial applications of AES [6.124].

6.4. LEED Structure Nomenclature and Superstructures

We give here a brief account of commonly used nomenclature. A threefold periodic ideal crystal has a twofold periodic ideal surface lattice. The unit mesh of this two-dimensional lattice is defined by the two unit

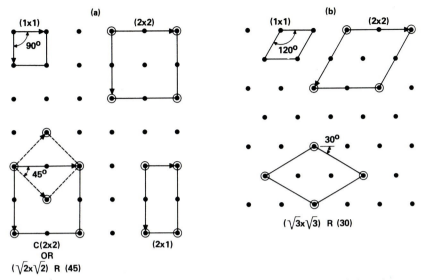

Fig. 6.28a and b. Wood's notation for simple superstructures. Small full circles substrate atoms, large open circles overlayer atoms. (a) Substrate with fourfold symmetry, (b) substrate with sixfold symmetry. The c stands for centered, the (2 × 2) structure is frequently written as p(2 × 2) with p standing for primitive to express the absence of an atom in the center

mesh vectors a_1, a_2. A surface structure with these unit mesh vectors is called a (1 × 1) structure. Frequently the surface periodicity, however, is different from the ideal one due to distortions, reconstruction or adsorbed atoms, for example. For such superstructures two notations are usual, Wood's notation and the matrix notation.

In Wood's notation the length of the unit mesh vectors a_1^s, a_2^s of the superstructures are given as multiples of the lengths of the vectors a_i and their directions are specified by the angle of rotation α^s of the superstructure unit mesh relative to the ideal unit mesh: $\left(\dfrac{a_1^s}{a_1} \times \dfrac{a_2^s}{a_2}\right) R(\alpha^s)$.

Some simple examples for this notation are given in Fig. 6.28. By definition this notation is only applicable if both axes are rotated by the same amount but it can be easily generalized by specifying two angles α_1^s, α_2^s, if this is not the case.

In the matrix notation the vectors a_1^s, a_2^s are expressed by their components a_{11}^s, a_{12}^s, a_{21}^s, a_{22}^s with respect to the ideal unit mesh vectors a_1, a_2

$$\begin{pmatrix} a_1^s \\ a_2^s \end{pmatrix} = \begin{pmatrix} a_{11}^s & a_{12}^s \\ a_{21}^s & a_{22}^s \end{pmatrix} \begin{pmatrix} a_1 \\ a_2 \end{pmatrix} = A^s \begin{pmatrix} a_1 \\ a_2 \end{pmatrix}. \tag{6.10}$$

For example, the matrices of the superstructures shown in Fig. 6.28 are

$$\begin{pmatrix} 1 & 0 \\ 0 & 1 \end{pmatrix}, \quad \begin{pmatrix} 2 & 0 \\ 0 & 2 \end{pmatrix}, \quad \begin{pmatrix} 1 & -1 \\ 1 & 1 \end{pmatrix}, \quad \begin{pmatrix} 2 & 0 \\ 0 & 1 \end{pmatrix}, \quad \begin{pmatrix} 1 & 0 \\ 0 & 1 \end{pmatrix}, \quad \begin{pmatrix} 2 & 0 \\ 0 & 2 \end{pmatrix},$$

and

$$\begin{pmatrix} 1 & -1 \\ 1 & 2 \end{pmatrix}.$$

This nomenclature allows for different angles between ideal and super-structure unit mesh vectors and makes the transition from real to reciprocal lattice – of which LEED provides an image – easy: the corresponding unit mesh vectors in the reciprocal lattice b_i, b_i^s are simply related by the reciprocal transposed matrix $B^s = (\tilde{A}^s)^{-1}$

$$\begin{pmatrix} b_1^s \\ b_2^s \end{pmatrix} = B^s \begin{pmatrix} b_1 \\ b_2 \end{pmatrix} = \frac{1}{|A^s|} \begin{pmatrix} a_{22}^s & -a_{12}^s \\ -a_{21}^s & a_{11}^s \end{pmatrix} \begin{pmatrix} b_1 \\ b_2 \end{pmatrix}. \tag{6.11}$$

Using the matrix notation the interpretation of superstructures can be made purely mathematically without geometrical constructions. It is, however, often convenient to make a graphical analysis based on the physical process which is frequently producing complicated super-structures, i.e., double or multiple scattering: each beam scattered by the surface layer acts as a primary beam for the substrate and *vice versa*. If, therefore, each substrate spot is used as the origin of the spot pattern of the chosen overlayer model the observed LEED pattern should be obtained. The choice of the overlayer model is considerably aided by the knowledge of the absolute coverage associated with the super-structure pattern: the area of the overlayer reciprocal unit mesh in cm^{-2} gives just the coverage in atoms/cm^2 if there is one atom per real space unit mesh. Another criterion is frequently, but not always, the intensity of the superstructure spots: the most intense spots are the most likely candidates for defining the vectors b_i^s. With such aids a relatively reliable interpretation of complex LEED patterns such as that shown in Fig. 6.17 becomes possible in spite of the fundamental ambiguity of the geometry of the LEED pattern.

6.5. Appendix:
Recent Reviews of LEED and Auger Phenomena

1. M. LAZNIČKA: *LEED-Surface Structures of Solids* (Union of Czechoslovak Mathematicians and Physicists, Prague, 1972) (LEED).
2. M. B. WEBB, M. G. LAGALLY: Solid State Phys. **28**, 302 (1973) (LEED).
3. C. B. DUKE: Advan. Chem. Phys. **27**, 1 (1974) (LEED).

4. J.A.Strozier: In *Surface Physics of Crystalline Solids*, ed. by J.M.Blakely (Academic Press, New York 1974) (LEED)).
5. J.B.Pendry: *Low Energy Electron Diffraction* (Academic Press London 1974) (LEED).
6. G.Ertl, J.Küppers: *Low Energy Electrons and Surface Chemistry* (Verlag Chemie, Weinheim 1974) (LEED, AES).
7. C.C.Chang: In *Characterization of Solid Surfaces*, ed. by P.F.Kane, G.B.Larrabe (Plenum Press, New York, 1974) (AES).

References

6.1. E.Bauer: J. Vac. Sci. Technol. **7**, 3 (1970).
6.2. E.Bauer: In 14ème Cours AVCP, Verbier (1972).
6.3. H.N.Browne, E.Bauer: Unpublished Repts. NASA Contr. No. R-05-030-001 (1965–1969).
6.4. J.C.Tracy: J. Vac. Sci. Technol. **11**, 280 (1974); Solid State Commun. (to be published).
6.5. P.J.Feibelman: Surface Sci. **36**, 558 (1973).
6.6. C.R.Brundle: J. Vac. Sci. Technol. **11**, 212 (1974).
6.7. C.J.Powell: To be published.
6.8. P.J.Feibelman, C.B.Duke, A.Bagchi: Phys. Rev. B**5**, 2436 (1972).
6.9. H.Raether: In Springer Tracts Mod. Phys. **38**, 84 (1965).
6.10. R.F.Allen, G.P.Alldredge, F.W.de Wette: Phys. Rev. B**4**, 1661 (1971).
6.11. J.E.Houston, R.L.Park: Surface Sci. **26**, 269 (1971).
6.12. B.Lang, R.W.Joyner, G.A.Somorjai: Surface Sci. **30**, 440 (1972).
6.13. G.E.Laramore, J.E.Houston, R.L.Park: J. Vac. Sci. Technol. **10**, 196 (1973); Surface Sci. **34**, 477 (1973).
6.14. T.A.Clarke, R.Mason, M.Tescari: Surface Sci. **30**, 553 (1972), **40**, 1 (1973); Proc. Roy. Soc. (London) A**331**, 321 (1972).
6.15. U.Landman, D.L.Adams: J. Vac. Sci. Technol. **11**, 195 (1974).
6.16. C.W.Tucker, C.B.Duke: Surface Sci. **23**, 411 (1970); **24**, 31 (1971); **29**, 237 (1972).
6.17. C.B.Duke, D.L.Smith: Phys. Rev. B**5**, 4730 (1972).
6.18. M.G.Lagally, T.C.Ngoc, M.B.Webb: Phys. Rev. Letters **26**, 1557 (1971); J. Vac. Sci. Technol. **9**, 645 (1972).
6.19. T.C.Ngoc, M.G.Lagally, M.B.Webb: Surface Sci. **35**, 117 (1973).
6.20. W.N.Unertl, M.B.Webb: J. Vac. Sci. Technol. **11**, 193 (1974); Surface Sci. (to be published).
6.21. J.C.Buchholz, M.G.Lagally: J. Vac. Sci. Technol. **11**, 194 (1974); Surface Sci. (to be published).
6.22. J.M.Burkstrand, G.G.Kleiman: J. Vac. Sci. Technol. **11**, 192 (1972); Phys. Rev. (to be published).
6.23. E.Bauer, H.N.Browne: 1st LEED Theory Seminar, Brooklyn, 1967 (unpublished).
6.24. J.A.Strozier, Jr., R.O.Jones: Phys. Rev. B**3**, 3228 (1971).
6.25. C.B.Duke, C.W.Tucker, Jr.: Surface Sci. **15**, 231 (1969).
6.26. C.B.Duke, G.E.Laramore: Phys. Rev. B**2**, 4765, 4783 (1970).
6.27. D.W.Jepsen, P.M.Marcus, F.Jona: Phys. Rev. B**5**, 3933 (1972).
6.28. J.B.Pendry: J. Phys. C**4**, 3095 (1971).
6.29. R.H.Tait, S.Y.Tong, T.N.Rhodin: Phys. Rev. Letters **28**, 553 (1972).
6.30. J.C.Phillips: Surface Sci. **40**, 459 (1973).
6.31. S.Y.Tong, T.N.Rhodin, R.H.Tait: Phys. Rev. B**8**, 430 (1973).
6.32. C.B.Duke, N.O.Lipari, U.Landman: Phys. Rev. B**8**, 2454 (1973).
6.33. M.R.Martin, G.A.Somorjai: Phys. Rev. B**7**, 3607 (1973).

272   E. BAUER

6.34. G. E. LARAMORE: Phys. Rev. B. **9**, 1204 (1974).
6.35. S. ANDERSSON, J. B. PENDRY: J. Phys. C**6**, 601 (1973).
6.36. G. E. LARAMORE: Phys. Rev. B**8**, 515 (1973).
6.37. S. ANDERSSON, B. KASEMO, J. B. PENDRY, M. A. VAN HOVE: Phys. Rev. Letters **31**, 595 (1973).
6.38. J. E. DEMUTH, D. W. JEPSEN, P. M. MARCUS: Phys. Rev. Letters **31**, 540 (1973); Solid State Commun. **13**, 1311 (1973); J. Phys. C**6**, 307 (1973).
6.39. C. B. DUKE, N. O. LIPARI, G. E. LARAMORE, J. B. THEETEN: Solid State Commun. **13**, 579 (1973); J. Vac. Sci. Technol. **11**, 180 (1974).
6.40. A. IGNATIEV, F. JONA, D. W. JEPSEN, P. M. MARCUS: Surface Sci. **40**, 439 (1973).
6.41. E. BAUER: In *Adsorption et Croissance Cristalline* (CNRS, Paris 1965), p. 21.
6.42. R. HECKINGBOTTOM: Surface Sci. **27**, 370 (1971).
6.43. C. E. CARROLL: Surface Sci. **32**, 119 (1972).
6.44. V. S. SUNDARAM, B. FARRELL, R. S. ALBEN, W. D. ROBERTSON: Phys. Rev. Letters **31**, 1136 (1973).
6.45. E. BAUER: Vacuum **22**, 539 (1972).
6.46. E. BAUER: Z. Physik **224**, 19 (1969).
6.47. J. I. GERSTEN: Phys. Rev. **188**, 774 (1969; B**2**, 3457 (1970).
6.48. C. B. DUKE, U. LANDMAN: Phys. Rev. B**6**, 2956, 2968 (1972).
6.49. V. ROUNDY, D. W. MILLS: Phys. Rev. B**5**, 1347 (1972); E. EVANS, D. L. MILLS: Phys. Rev. B**5**, 4126 (1972); B**7**, 853 (1973).
6.50. C. B. DUKE, U. LANDMAN: Phys. Rev. B**7**, 1368 (1973); B**8**, 505 (1973).
6.51. H. IBACH: J. Vac. Sci. Technol. **9**, 713 (1972).
6.52. J. O. PORTEUS, W. N. FAITH: J. Vac. Sci. Technol. **9**, 1062 (1972); Phys. Rev. B**8**, 491 (1973).
6.53. J. KÜPPERS: Surface Sci. **36**, 53 (1973).
6.54. J. E. ROWE, H. IBACH: Phys. Rev. Letters **31**, 102 (1973).
6.55. E. BAUER: In *Techniques of Metals Research*, Vol. II, Part 2, ed. by R. F. BUNSHAH (Interscience, New York, 1969), p. 624.
6.56. J. KESSLER: Rev. Mod. Phys. **41**, 3 (1969).
6.57. P. J. JENNINGS: Surface Sci. **20**, 18 (1970); **33**, 1 (1972).
6.58. R. FEDER: phys. stat. solidi (b) **49**, 699 (1972; **56**, K 43 (1973).
6.59. R. FEDER: phys. stat. solidi (b) **62**, 135 (1974).
6.60. D. R. CRUISE, E. BAUER: J. Appl. Phys. **35**, 3080 (1964).
6.61. G. TURNER, E. BAUER: J. Appl. Phys. **35**, 3080 (1964).
6.62. V. DRAHŐS: In *Proc. 5th European Congr. Electron Microscopy* (Institute of Physics, London, 1972), p. 34.
6.63. W. KOCH, B. BISCHOFF, E. BAUER: In *Proc. 5th European Congr. Electron Microscopy* (Institute of Physics, London, 1972), p. 58.
6.64. L. LAYDEVANT, C. GUITTARD, R. BERNARD: In *Proc. 5th European Congr. Electron Microscopy* (Institute of Physics, London, 1972), p. 662.
6.65. W. A. COGHLAN, R. E. CLAUSING: Atomic Data **5**, 318 (1973).
6.66. M. O. KRAUSE, F. A. STEVIE, L. J. LEVIS, T. A. CARLSON, W. E. MODDEMAN: Phys. Letters **31**A, 81 (1970).
6.67. J. D. GARCIA, R. J. FORTNER, R. M. KAVANAGH: Rev. Mod. Phys. **45**, 111 (1973).
6.68. N. STOLTERFOHT, H. GABLER, U. LEITHÄUSER: Phys. Letters **45**A, 351 (1973).
6.69. D. L. MATTHEWS, B. M. JOHNSON, J. J. MACKEY, C. F. MOORE: Phys. Letters **45**A, 447 (1973); Phys. Rev. Letters **31**, 1331 (1973).
6.70. W. HINK, A. ZIEGLER: Z. Physik **226**, 222 (1969).
6.71. W. BAMBYNEK, B. CRASEMANN, R. W. FINK, H.-U. FREUND, H. MARK, C. D. SWIFT, R. E. PRICE, P. VENUGOPALA RAO: Rev. Mod. Phys. **44**, 716 (1972).
6.72. W. M. MULAIRE, W. T. PERIA: Surface Sci. **26**, 125 (1971).

6.73. E. N. Sickafus: Surface Sci. **36**, 472 (1973); Phys. Rev. B**7**, 5100 (1973); J. Vac. Sci. Technol. **12**, 43 (1973).

6.74. R. G. Musket, R. J. Fortner: Phys. Rev. Letters **26**, 80 (1971).

6.75. E. J. LeJeune, Jr., R. D. Dixon: J. Appl. Phys. **43**, 1998 (1972).

6.76. F. Fiermans, J. Vennick: Surface Sci. **38**, 237 (1973).

6.77. P. H. Citrin, R. W. Shaw, Jr., T. D. Thomas: In *Electron Spectroscopy*, ed. by D. A. Shirley (North-Holland Publ. Co., Amsterdam, 1972), p. 105.

6.78. J. E. Houston: Surface Sci. **38**, 283 (1973), Appl. Phys. Letters **24**, 42 (1974); Rev. Sci. Instrum. (to be published).

6.79. J. T. Grant, T. W. Haas, J. E. Houston: Phys. Letters **45**A, 309 (1973); Surface Sci. **42**, 1 (1974).

6.80. R. Bouwman, R. Biloen: Surface Sci. **41**, 348 (1974).

6.81. S. Thomas: Appl. Phys. Letters **24**, 1 (1974).

6.82. E. Bauer, H. Poppa, G. Todd, F. Bonczek: J. Appl. Phys. **45**, 5164 (1974).

6.83. A. E. Dabiri, V. S. Aramati, R. E. Stickney: Surface Sci. **40**, 205 (1973).

6.84. E. B. Bas, U. Bänninger: Surface Sci. **41**, 1 (1974).

6.85. S. Thomas: J. Appl. Phys. **45**, 161 (1974).

6.86. B. Goldstein: Surface Sci. **39**, 261 (1973).

6.87. R. E. Kirby, D. Lichtman, J. W. Dieball: Surface Sci. **41**, 447, 467 (1974).

6.88. T. Madey, J. Yates: J. Vac. Sci. Technol. **8**, 525 (1971).

6.89. J. C. Powell: Phys. Rev. Letters **30**, 1179 (1973).

6.90. G. Schön: J. Electron Spectrosc. **1**, 377 (1972/73); Phys. Letters **42**A, 381 (1973).

6.91. D. A. Shirley: Chem. Phys. Letters **16**, 220 (1972); **17**, 312 (1972); Phys. Rev. A**7**, 1520 (1973).

6.92. S. P. Kowalczyk, R. A. Pollak, F. R. McFeely, L. Ley, D. A. Shirley: Phys. Rev. B**8**, 2387 (1973).

6.93. J. A. D. Matthew: Surface Sci. **40**, 451 (1973).

6.94. P. H. Citrin: Phys. Rev. Letters **31**, 1164 (1973).

6.95. L. H. Jenkins, M. F. Chung: Surface Sci. **26**, 151, 649 (1971); **28**, 409 (1971); **33**, 159 (1972).

6.96. M. Suleman, E. B. Pattinson: J. Phys. F**1**, L21 (1971).

6.97. H. G. Maguire, P. D. Augustus: J. Phys. C**4**, L174 (1971).

6.98. B. D. Powell, D. P. Woodruff: Surface Sci. **33**, 437 (1972).

6.99. C. M. K. Watts: J. Phys. F**2**, 574 (1972).

6.100. D. L. Walters, C. P. Bhalla: Phys. Rev. A**4**, 2164 (1971).

6.101. J. T. Grant, T. W. Haas: Surface Sci. **23**, 347 (1970).

6.102. C. J. Powell: Appl. Phys. Letters **20**, 335 (1972), Solid State Comm. **10**, 1161 (1972).

6.103. J. E. Rowe, S. B. Christman: J. Vac. Sci. Technol. **10**, 276 (1973).

6.104. H. Löfgren, L. Walldén: Solid State Comm. **12**, 19 (1973).

6.105. M. Salmerón: Surface Sci. **41**, 584 (1974).

6.106. D. M. Zehner, R. E. Clausing, G. E. McGuire, L. H. Jenkins: Solid State Comm. **13**, 681 (1973).

6.107. W. F. Hanson, E. T. Arakawa: Z. Physik **251**, 271 (1972).

6.108. M. Salmerón, A. M. Baró, J. M. Rojo: Surface Sci. **41**, 11 (1974).

6.109. J. A. D. Matthew: Solid State Comm. **13**, 1203 (1973).

6.110. L. H. Jenkins, D. M. Zehner, M. F. Chung: Surface Sci. **38**, 327 (1973).

6.111. P. J. Feibelman: Phys. Rev. B**7**, 2305 (1973).

6.112. L. McDonnell, D. P. Woodruff: Vacuum **22**, 477 (1972).

6.113. B. W. Holland, L. McDonnell, D. P. Woodruff: Solid State Comm. **11**, 991 (1972).

6.114. T. W. Rusch, J. P. Bertino, W. P. Ellis: Appl. Phys. Letters **23**, 359 (1973).

6.115. B. Cleff, W. Mehlhorn: Phys. Letters A 37, 3 (1971).
6.116. P. W. Palmberg: J. Vac. Sci. Technol. **9**, 160 (1972); **10**, 274 (1973).
6.117. J. M. Morabito: J. Vac. Sci. Technol. **10**, 278 (1973).
6.118. M. L. Tarng, G. K. Wehner: J. Appl. Phys. **43**, 2268 (1972); **44**, 1534 (1973).
6.119. D. V. McCaughan, R. A. Kushner, V. T. Murphy: Phys. Rev. Letters **30**, 614 (1973).
6.120. P. Staib: Radiation Effects **18**, 217 (1973).
6.121. N. C. MacDonald: Appl. Phys. Letters **16**, 76 (1970); **19**, 315 (1971).
6.122. L. A. Harris: J. Vac. Sci. Technol. **11**, 23 (1974).
6.123. K. Hayakawa, H. Okano, S. Kowase, S. Yamamoto: J. Appl. Phys. **44**, 2575 (1973).
6.124. J. M. Morabito: Thin Solid Films **19**, 21 (1973).

7. Concepts in Heterogeneous Catalysis

M. BOUDART

7.1. Definitions

A single catalytic reaction consists of a closed sequence of elementary processes or steps. Summation of these steps, multiplied each by an appropriate *stoichiometric number* reproduces the stoichiometric equation for the reaction. In the first step, a species called the catalyst enters as a reactant whereas it appears as a product in the last step of the sequence.

The catalyst may be an enzyme, a complex in a liquid solution, a gaseous molecule or a grouping of atoms at the surface of a solid called the *active site* and denoted by an asterisk *. In the latter case, catalysis is called heterogeneous. It is only a special case of a general phenomenon. The great technological advantage of heterogeneous catalysis is the easy separation between the solid catalyst and the fluid reaction medium.

In this chapter, I shall discuss only heterogeneous catalysis, or catalysis for short, remembering that the active site is only a member of a large population of homogeneous chemical analogs. The wealth of chemical catalysis is also illustrated by the number of solids used in catalysis: metals, semiconductors or insulators, X-ray crystalline or amorphous materials, clusters of a few atoms or large crystals.

Table 7.1. Dissociative and associative mechanisms of catalysis: ammonia synthesis: value of stoichiometric number σ

Dissocative	σ	Associative	σ
$2* + N_2 \rightleftarrows 2*N$	1	$* + N_2 \rightleftarrows *N_2$	1
$2* + H_2 \rightleftarrows 2*H$	3	$*N_2 + H_2 \rightleftarrows *N_2H_2$	1
$*N + *H \rightleftarrows *NH + *$	2	$*N_2H_2 + H_2 \rightleftarrows *N_2H_4$	1
$*NH + *H \rightleftarrows *NH_2 + *$	2	$*N_2H_4 + H_2 \rightleftarrows 2NH_3 + *$	1
$*NH_2 + *H \rightleftarrows *NH_3 + *$	2		
$*NH_3 \rightleftarrows NH_3 + *$	2	$N_2 + 3H_2 \rightleftarrows 2NH_3$	
$N_2 + 3H_2 \rightleftarrows 2NH_3$			

The two basic mechanisms of catalysis are *dissociative* and *associative*. As an example, let us postulate two possible sequences of steps in ammonia synthesis (Table 7.1). Qualitative considerations suggest that the steps in a dissociative mechanism will have a higher probability (entropy factor) but also higher energy barrier (energy factor) than their associative counterparts [7.1]. Hence a dissociative mechanism may be favored at high temperatures while at low temperatures associate mechanisms might prevail. For instance, in the case of isotope equilibration reactions involving H_2 or O_2:

$$H_2 + D_2 \rightleftarrows 2HD$$
$$^{32}O_2 + {}^{36}O_2 \rightleftarrows 2{}^{34}O_2$$

it is very remarkable that they proceed at a fast rate on a variety of solids at very low temperatures at which most chemical processes are imperceptibly slow. This suggests associative mechanisms.

Thus, in the case of the H_2–D_2 equilibrium, two possible dissociative and associative mechanisms can be considered. They are normally associated with the names of *Bonhoeffer-Farkas* (or generally *Langmuir-Hinshelwood*) on the one hand and those of *Eley-Rideal* on the other hand [7.2] (Table 7.2). In an Eley-Rideal mechanism, reaction takes place between a chemisorbed species and a non-chemisorbed species. Since the latter may, however, be physisorbed or held molecularly in a precursor state, the distinction between a Langmuir-Hinshelwood and a Eley-Rideal process is unambiguous only if, in the latter case, the non-chemisorbed species strikes the chemisorbed one directly from the fluid phase.

The first quantitative measure of the catalytic act is the rate of the single reaction called the *activity* of the catalyst. The best measure of the rate, which lends itself to comparison of the activity of various catalysts is the *turnover number* defined as the rate per mole of site, that rate itself being defined as the rate of change of the extent of reaction (also in moles) with time. In most cases, only an average or nominal number may be

Table 7.2. Langmuir-Hinshelwood and Eley-Rideal mechanisms [7.2]: H_2–D_2 equilibration: $H_2 + D_2 \rightleftarrows 2HD$

Langmuir-Hinshelwood (or Bonhoeffer-Farkas)	Eley-Rideal
$2* + H_2 \rightleftarrows 2*H$	$*H + D_2 \rightleftarrows *D + HD$
$2* + D_2 \rightleftarrows 2*D$	$*D + H_2 \rightleftarrows *H + HD$
$*H + *D \rightleftarrows HD + 2*$	

obtained, as the number and types of sites may not be known. The method of determination of the number of sites must be specified as well as the conditions under which the rate is measured. Frequently, turnover numbers of heterogeneous catalytic reactions are between 10^{-2} and 10^2 per second [7.3].

The activity of a catalyst is rarely its most important characteristic. *Selectivity*, which is defined as a ratio of rates, that of a desired reaction over the sum of rates of other undesirable side reactions, is often more important to achieve and more subtle to understand. At any rate, no discussion of catalysis is worthwhile without a quantitative assesment of rates.

The habit of catalytic materials is dictated by technological usage and by the frequent need for a very large specific surface area, of the order of 10^2 m^2 g^{-1}. Thus porous materials with average pore dimensions around 10 nm are often used as the catalyst itself or as a *support* or *carrier* for the catalytic material. The use of the word *substrate* to denote the support or the catalytic surface is to be avoided as it has been pre-empted in catalysis to denote the reacting molecules transformes *by* the catalyst. Clearly, the *texture* of a porous catalyst, i.e. the shape of a replica of the material is of great importance in determining activity and selectivity because of the unavoidable gradients of temperature and concentration in the porous medium. The interplay between chemical reactivity and the physical phenomena of heat and mass transfer will not be discussed further in this chapter. It is covered in a number of textbooks [7.4, 5].

Quantitative measures of the texture of catalytic materials, namely the total specific surface area and the pore size distribution, can be obtained from isotherms of physisorbed nitrogen, according to standard methods which have received universal acceptance. The *dispersion* of a supported material, defined as the fraction of atoms of this material which is exposed at the surface, can be determined by selective chemisorption which titrates the surface atoms of interest. Although no general method is available to measure dispersion, reliable methods have been developed in a number of cases [7.6].

7.2. Affinity, Reactivity and Catalytic Activity [7.7]

Consider the reaction $A_1 + A_2 \rightleftarrows B_1 + B_2$ taking place through the simplest two-step catalytic sequence

1) $S_1 + A_1 \rightleftharpoons B_1 + S_2$

2) $S_2 + A_2 \rightleftharpoons B_2 + S_1$

over a constant number of identical sites denoted by S_1 if empty and S_2 if occupied. From the constancy of number of sites and the equality of rates of Steps 1) and 2) at the steady-state, the turnover number is

$$N = \frac{k_1 k_2 (A_1)(A_2) - k_{-1} k_{-2} (B_1)(B_2)}{k_1(A_1) + k_{-2}(B_2) + k_2(A_2) + k_{-1}(B_1)}, \tag{7.1}$$

where the k's denote rate constants with appropriate subscripts for forward and reverse processes, and quantities between parentheses are number densities.

If we now consider different collections of sites, we may ask how N will vary from one collection to the next. We assume that sites differ in their affinity for the reactants and products. Let us call $\underset{\sim}{A}_1$ the standard affinity for adsorption of A_1 divided by RT. Similarly $\underset{\sim}{A}_2$ will be the standard affinity for adsorption of B_2, divided by RT. These affinities are not independent: their differences is equal to the standard affinity for the overall reaction, divided by RT which does not vary with the nature of the sites and therefore may be regarded as a constant

$$\underset{\sim}{A}_1 - \underset{\sim}{A}_2 = \text{const.} \tag{7.2}$$

Now the reactivity of the sites, as expressed by their rate constants must be related to their thermodynamic affinity. A general relationship between rate constants and affinities is that of Brønsted, as found experimentally in acid base catalysis, free radical reactions and chemisorption at solid surfaces [8.8]

$$k = G \exp(\alpha \underset{\sim}{A}), \tag{7.3}$$

where G is a constant, and α is a so-called transfer coefficient

$$0 < \alpha < 1$$

with values frequently in the vicinity of $\frac{1}{2}$. It is easy to use the Brønsted relations (7.3) for the rate constants of our problem, taking into account (7.2) which permits us to retain as sole independent variable the affinity $\underset{\sim}{A}$ without the need for a subscript for adsorption of A_1 divided by RT. We assume that α is the same for both steps and recall that in general the ratio of rate constants for an elementary process is given by $\exp \underset{\sim}{A}$. The resulting relations are

$$k_1 = k_1^0 \exp[\alpha(\underset{\sim}{A} - \underset{\sim}{A}_0)]; \quad k_{-2} = k_{-2}^0 \exp[\alpha(\underset{\sim}{A} - \underset{\sim}{A}_0)]$$
$$k_2 = k_2^0 \exp[(\alpha-1)(\underset{\sim}{A} - \underset{\sim}{A}_0)]; \quad k_{-1} = k_{-1}^0 \exp[(\alpha-1)(\underset{\sim}{A} - \underset{\sim}{A}_0)], \tag{7.4}$$

where rate constants with superscripts ^{0} denote values of the rate constants for the sites with the highest value of A, namely A_0.

For the case $\alpha = 1/2$, it is now easy to answer the question: what are the best sites for the catalytic reaction, i.e. the value of A (namely A_{max}) that maximizes the turnover number. Indeed substitution of (7.4) into (7.2) yields an expression for N with a numerator that does not depend on A. Taking the derivative of the denominator with respect to $A - A_0$ and equating it is zero, gives the required condition for maximizing N:

$$k_1(A_1) + k_{-2}(B_2) = k_2(A_2) + k_{-1}(B_1). \tag{7.5}$$

Comparing this result with the steady state condition expressing the equality of rates of both steps shows at once that (7.5) is satisfied when the concentration of empty sites is equal to that of occupied ones. Thus the optimum sites are those with a value of A corresponding to half coverage. This is an expression of the *principle of Sabatier* according to which the best catalyst is that which has an affinity for reactants which is neither too small nor too large. There are many examples of so-called *volcano-shaped curves* following BALANDIN [7.7] where the rate of a reaction when plotted versus an energy parameter which is a measure of the affinity of the surface for a reactant, first increases, goes through a maximum and then decreases as the energy parameter becomes still higher.

Another consequence of the Brønsted relations (7.4) with $\alpha = 1/2$ is that sites with affinities larger or smaller by the same amount ΔA than those of the optimum sites, have the same turnover number. Moreover, it is easy to show [7.8] that that same turnover number is $\exp(f/4)$ times smaller than that corresponding to the optimum sites, where $f = 2\Delta A$. These are most interesting results. From a *thermodynamic* standpoint alone, sites differing in their adsorption affinity by an amount f would be expected to differ in their occupancy, at least at low coverage, by an amount of $\exp(f)$. From the standpoint of *reactivity*, this amount is reduced to $\exp(f/2)$ by a Brønsted relationship with $\alpha = 2$. But from a *catalytic* standpoint, these sites have the same turnover number, if they have affinities equidistant from the optimum value. This is easy to understand: for adsorption to take place at a certain rate at the steady state of the catalytic reaction, the sites must be reactive but they must also be free. If the affinity is large, the reactivity is high but the number of free sites is low. Conversely, if the affinity is small, the reactivity is low but the number of free sites is high. The optimum catalyst realizes a compromise. But insofar as the fraction of surface cover under optimum conditions may be in the vicinity of 1/2, it appears unlikely that a good catalyst will function under conditions of low surface coverage. Thus, unless active sites are isolated and far removed from each other, a situation which may arise frequently but is inherently far from the optimum, a good catalyst should operate under conditions where interactions between chemisorbed species are likely to be important and cannot be neglected. Besides, active sites may not all be the same. These two situations suggest that a catalytic surface is likely to be *non-ideal*, in the sense that it does not conform to a Langmuir model. In other words, rate constants ought to depend on surface coverage. Two ways to handle this problem will be reviewed briefly in turn.

7.3. Non-Ideal Catalytic Surfaces: the Ammonia Synthesis

If there is any reason to believe that more than one type of site participates in the catalytic reaction, the reasoning that led to the expression for the turnover number (7.1) must be modified, either by a summation or by an integration if the need arises. In particular, the non-uniformity of the surface can be expressed by a distribution function

$$ds = \underline{a} \exp(-\gamma \underset{\sim}{A}) \, d(\underset{\sim}{A}), \tag{7.6}$$

where ds is the number of sites per cm^2 with a value of $\underset{\sim}{A}$ between $\underset{\sim}{A}$ and $d\underset{\sim}{A}$, γ is a parameter characteristic of the distribution, and $\underline{a}$ a constant that can be determined by a normalization condition.

Then, with the same Brønsted conditions (7.4) as before, it can be shown, following Temkin, that for the two step catalytic reaction discussed earlier, the integrated turnover number becomes

$$N = \eta \; \frac{k_1^0 k_2^0 (A_1)(A_2) - k_{-1}^0 k_{-2}^0 (B_1)(B_2)}{[k_1^0(A_1) + k_2^0(B_2)]^m \, [k_2^0(A_2) + k_{-1}^0(B_1)]^{1-m}}, \tag{7.7}$$

where η is a numerical sonstant and $m = \alpha - \gamma$. Details are given in [7.8].

The physical meaning of the distribution function (7.6) lies in the fact that chemisorption isotherms on real surfaces frequently obey the FREUNDLICH form [7.4]

$$\theta \propto p^\gamma \tag{7.8}$$

or the Frumkin-Temkin form [7.4]

$$\theta \propto \ln p, \tag{7.9}$$

where θ is the fraction of surface covered by a gas at pressure p in equilibrium with the surface at temperature T. The isotherms (7.8) and (7.9) can be derived from the distribution function (7.6) for an arbitrary value of γ, $0 < \gamma = 1$, and for $\gamma = 0$, respectively. Besides, the rate of chemisorption of a gas on a non-uniform surface with a distribution function (7.7), in the case $\gamma = 0$, can be shown [7.8] to be

$$r = r_0 \exp(-\beta\theta) \qquad (7.10)$$

which is a very frequently found empirical expression associated with the name of several workers, especially that of ELOVICH [7.9].

Thus, Temkin's phenomenological approach to kinetics on non-ideal surfaces finds its justification in thermodynamics and kinetic studies of surface chemistry. Besides, a simplified form of (7.7) is the famous equation of TEMKIN and PYZHEV [7.10] which has been used successfully since 1939 to represent kinetic data of ammonia synthesis and decomposition at low and high pressures. A slight variation thereof is used today in the design of ammonia catalytic converters. The Temkin-Pyzhev equation is obtained from a simplified mechanism for ammonia synthesis in which it is postulated that nitrogen chemisorption is the rate determining step and that chemisorbed nitrogen is the most abundant surface intermediate [7.4]. These assumptions lead to a two-step mechanism

1) $\qquad * + N_2 \overset{\wedge}{\rightleftarrows} *N_2$

2) $\quad *N_2 + 3H_2 \longleftrightarrow 2NH_3 + *$

in which the symbol $\wedge$ means rate determining and $\leftrightarrow$ stands for equilibrium. Noting that terms in the denominator of (7.7) involving k_1^0 and k_{-1}^0 can be neglected in front of those involving k_2^0 and k_{-2}^0 since the latter parameters refer to a fast equilibrated step, we get for the synthesis reaction sufficiently far from equilibrium [7.11]:

$$N = \eta k_1^0 [K_2^0]^m (N_2) \left[\frac{(H_2)^3}{(NH_3)^2} \right]^m, \qquad (7.11)$$

where $K = k_2^0 / k_{-2}^0$ is the equilibrium constant for the second step. The success of (7.11) in fitting data is not, of course, a sufficient justification of the theory behind it. But there are many other arguments in favor of the latter [7.12]. One of the quantitative ones rests on a comparison of the rates of ammonia synthesis on the same catalyst with H_2 and with D_2. Under identical conditions, it is clear from (7.11) that the ratio of turnover numbers should be

$$N_D/N_H = (K^0_{2,D}/K^0_{2,H})^m \tag{7.12}$$

with subscripts H and D pertaining to the reactions with H_2 and D_2 respectively. However, the right hand side of (7.12) is K^m, where K is the equilibrium constant of the reaction

$$3D_2 + 2NH_3 \longleftrightarrow 3H_2 + 2ND_3$$

which involves only gas phase species and can therefore be obtained from thermodynamic tables. Thus the isotope effect in ammonia synthesis with H_2 and D_2 can be predicted ahead of time of the mechanism behind the equation of TEMKIN and PYZHEV is correct [7.10]. Experiments veryfying these predictions have now been performed over an extended temperature range and the results with $m = 1/2$ are in excellent agreement with expectations [7.13]. It must be stressed that the value of $m = 1/2$ was used in many previous investigations and was therefore not adjusted so as to bring about agreement between theory and experiment in the study of the isotope effect.

In spite of this quantitative success, the nature of the most abundant surface species in ammonia synthesis is not known as yet. Thus an equation identical to that of TEMKIN and PYZHEV is obtained if it is assumed that N_2 dissociates into atoms in the rate determining step and that N atoms are the most abundant surface intermediate. Hence, a choice between associative and dissociative mechanisms of ammonia synthesis (Table 7.1) will have to rely on future direct indentification of the adsorbed intermediates during the reaction by an adequate spectroscopic technique. This need is general in catalysis [7.14]. In particular, even more sophisticated kinetic methods based on the use of tracers are not able to decide between the alternatives presented in Table 7.1. Thus, according to HORIUTI the stoichiometric number of the rate determining process, as determined by rate measurements at equilibrium (by means of tracers) and away from equilibrium, should be unity both for the dissociative and the associative mechanisms if the chemisorption of N_2 is the rate determining process [7.7]. In fact, measurements of the stoichiometric number of the rate determining process in ammonia synthesis do yield a value of unity which confirms the generally accepted view that chemisorption of N_2 is indeed the rate determining process *if* the mechanism is dissociative. But if the mechanism is associative, the obtained value of the stoichiometric number of the rate determining process is clearly ambiguous. A useful concept in catalysis which can be applied quantitatively in the case of ammonia synthesis is that *virtual pressure* of a reactant. Since, on an iron catalyst, adsorbed nitrogen is in equilibrium with gas phase H_2 and NH_3 but not with gas phase N_2, it can be considered to be in virtual equilibrium in the gas phase with H_2 and NH_3 at a virtual pressure defined by the equilibrium constant K of the reaction

$$2\,NH_3 \xrightarrow{\ \ K\ \ } N_2 + 3\,H_2 \,.$$

At 673 K, the value of K is $6 \times 10^3\,atm^2$. Thus, when ammonia decomposes on a catalyst at 673 K in a mixture of NH_3 and H_2 both at 1 atm, the virtual pressure of N_2 over the catalyst surface is 6000 atm. Thus it is possible to control the virtual pressure of a reactant over a catalyst surface over a very wide range of values not readily reached in reality.

In a study of ammonia synthesis, the virtual pressure of N_2 was varied over 4 orders of magnitude while the fraction of the surface of the iron catalyst covered with nitrogen, as determined by microgravimetry, varied only between 0.45 and 0.53 [7.15]. This result is another clear indication of a broadly non-uniform or non-ideal surface with a logarithmic adsorption isotherm of the form (7.9), as determined experimentally in a separate experiment. It also illustrates the quantitative expression of the Sabatier principle according to which the fraction of surface covered is in the vicinity of 1/2 for an optimum catalyst.

7.4. Non-Ideal Catalytic Surfaces: the Water Gas Shift Reaction

There is another way to take non-ideality into account. It rests on the measurement of the *thermodynamic activity* of an element which is transferred from one molecule to the next in the catalytic reaction. This phenomenological approach has been developed by WAGNER [7.16] and his school. A particularly clear example is that of the water gas shift reaction over a foil of wustite FeO

$$CO + H_2O \ \rightleftharpoons\ CO_2 + H_2 \tag{7.13}$$

taking place by oxygen atom transfer between CO and CO_2 on the one hand and H_2 and H_2O on the other hand, in two elementary processes

1) $* + CO_2 \rightleftharpoons CO + *O$

2) $*O + H_2 \rightleftharpoons H_2O + * \,.$

The rate r_1 of the first step is written as usual with the notation $k_1/k_{-1} = K_1$

$$r_1 = k_1(*)(CO_2) - k_{-1}(CO)(O*)$$

$$= k_1(*)(CO_2)\left[1 - \frac{1}{K_1}\frac{(*O)(CO)}{(*)(CO_2)}\right]. \tag{7.14}$$

In these expressions, concentrations have been used instead of thermodynamic activities with the penalty that the rate "constants" may then depend on surface composition. The non-ideality of the surface is handled by defining the *thermodynamic activity* of atomic oxygen at the surface as

$$a_0 = \frac{(*O)}{(*)}. \tag{7.15}$$

But at equilibrium

$$a_0 = \frac{(*O)}{(*)} = K_1 \frac{(CO_2)}{(CO)}. \tag{7.16}$$

The standard state is chosen so that $a_0 = 1$ in an equimolar mixture of (CO_2) and (CO), which is equvalent to writing $K_1 = 1$ in (7.16). Thus finally, the thermodynamic activity of oxygen is

$$a_0 = \frac{(CO_2)}{(CO)}$$

Substitution of (7.15) into (7.14) yields

$$r_1 = k_1'(CO_2)\left[1 - \frac{a_0}{(CO_2)/(CO)}\right], \tag{7.17}$$

where $k_1' = k_1(*)$, clearly not a constant but a function of surface composition. Now, the rate r_1 can be measured by passing a mixture of CO and CO_2 over the surface at a temperature at which a_0 is the same in the bulk and at the surface, so that a bulk physical measurement such as electrical conductivity of the catalyst foil which is determined by the non-stoichiometry of the oxide which in turn depends on a_0, can yield a value of a_0. After equilibrium is reached, the ratio of CO_2 to CO is changed slightly in stepwise manner and the rate r_1 can be determined by following the *relaxation* of the system to a new equilibrium, by means of conductivity measurements [7.16]. By such measurements, STOTZ

[7.17] could not only verify the form of (7.17) but find the dependence of k'_1 on surface composition

$$k'_1 \propto a_0^{-0.6}. \tag{7.18}$$

It can be shown that an expression of this kind is expected also from the treatment of TEMKIN presented in Section 7.3. Thus, both phenomenological approaches, that of WAGNER and that of TEMKIN are two different manners by which the non-ideality of catalytic surfaces can be handled in kinetics. It is somewhat surprising that so much in surface chemistry and catalysis is done routinely without considering explicity the problem of non-ideality of surfaces.

In the case of the water gas shift reaction on FeO, STOTZ [7.17] carried out similar measurements of r_2. He then found that the experimental value of a_0 at which both rates r_1 and r_2 were equal, was the same as that measured during the steady state water gas shift reaction taking place at the same rate $r = r_1 = r_2$. Again, as was the case for ammonia synthesis and the Temkin approach, this result is a remarkable quantitative check of Wagner's approach. But here also other methods are required before more can be said about the nature of the sites or the nature of oxygen bound to these sites.

7.5. Structural or Geometric Factors

The most distinctive feature of a crystalline solid is anisotropy. At the surface, this is manifested by surface atoms with different values of their coordination number C_i, where C_i denotes an atom with i nearest neighbors. Also, especially on metal surfaces, it is easy to recognize groupings of atoms with a symmetry that matches that of a chemisorbed molecule. That grouping is sometimes called a *multiplet* after BALANDIN or an *ensemble* after KOBOZEV [7.5]. A typical multiplet is that found on the (111) faces of a *fcc* metal which matches the hexagonal symmetry of a benzene molecule. I shall refer to these *geometric* factors which depend on atoms with specified values of C_i as *structural* factors. Chemical intuition dictates that the rate of a catalytic reaction should depend on anisotropy or structure. We would normally expect that a catalytic reaction be *structure sensitive* even though the difference in rate between atoms with different C_i may not be as large as anticipated on the basis of differences in affinity alone, for reasons discussed in Section 7.2.

One way to check whether a catalytic reaction is structure sensitive or not, is to measure its rate on different crystallographic plane. Although such experiments have been carried out by various workers in the past, only recent results taking advantage of modern methods of surface analysis can be retained as reliable. One typical result is that of MCALLISTER and HANSEN who showed that the rate of decomposition of ammonia is ca. 10 times larger on the (111) face than on the (100) and (110) faces of *bcc* tungsten [7.18]. A much more surprising result is that of ERTL and KOCH who found no appreciable difference in the rate of oxidation of carbon monoxide on the three low index faces of *fcc* palladium as well as on a polycrystalline palladium wire [7.19]. That the decomposition of ammonia on tungsten is structure sensitive is not surprising. That the oxidation of carbon monoxide on palladium is structure insensitive is an unexpected observation.

But it is not an isolated phenomenon. Several reactions have been found to be structure insensitive over supported Group VIII metals. In the case of supported metals, the experiment consists in preparing a series of catalysts with increasing particle size between 1 and 10 nm. Qualitative and quantitative considerations indicate that the relative fractions of atoms with a given C_i changes appreciably with particle size in that critical range. Thus, as particles of a *bcc* structure grow from 1 to 5 nm, the relative amount of C_7 surface atoms increases by almost an order of magnitude [7.20]. Therefore, if the turnover number for a given reaction does not change over a series of catalysts with metal particles from 1 to 10 nm corresponding to metal dispersion between 1 and 0.1, the evidence is that the reaction is structure insensitive. The reverse is not necessarily true: if the turnover number changes with dispersion, the reaction can be considered to be structure sensitive only after other possible effects such as electronic interaction between metal and support can be ruled out.

An early example of a structure insensitive reaction on supported platinum was the hydrogenation of cyclopropane to propane [7.21]. Striking confirmation of this finding is provided by a recent study of the same reaction on a stepped surface of a platinum single crystal: the turnover number was found to be almost the same as that found in the earlier work on supported platinum particles about 1.5 nm in average size [7.22].

Another example of a structure insensitive reaction is that of the hydrogenation of cyclohexene on supported platinum in the liquid phase [7.23] and in the gas phase [7.24]. Other examples of structure insensitive reactions include hydrogenation of benzene and the H_2-D_2 equilibration [7.25]. By contrast, the hydrogenolysis of ethane [7.26] and of n-hexane [7.27] on rhodium and platinum, respectively, appear to be structure sensitive reactions.

The different behavior of reactions involving C–C bonds on the one hand and C–H or H–H bonds on the other hand is illustrated by a study

Table 7.3. Hydrogenation of cyclohexene on supported platinum at 295 K (g) and 307 K (l): turnover number N on catalysts with degree of Pt dispersion D [7.23]; (g) and (l) stand for gas phase and liquid phase respectively

Support	%-wt. Pt	D	N/s^{-1} (g)	N/s^{-1} (l)
SiO_2	1.5	1.00	2.73	8.90
SiO_2	0.38	1.00	2.64	8.77
γ-Al_2O_3	0.6	0.70	—	8.37
SiO_2	2.3	0.62	2.75	8.43
SiO_2	0.8	0.34	—	8.65
η-Al_2O_3	1.96	0.23	—	7.98
SiO_2	3.7	0.14	2.53	8.37

of the hydrogenolysis (cracking) of cyclopropane running in parallel with its hydrogenation on two forms of chromium oxide: a crystalline form and an X-ray amorphous form [7.28]. The cracking reaction was found to be structure sensitive while the hydrogenation reaction was structure insensitive. Structure here is defined by the difference between short-range and long-range order of the same material. Another example is the reaction between H_2 and O_2 on supported platinum catalysts [7.29]. In excess oxygen, the reaction appears to be structure insensitive while in excess hydrogen, the same reaction is clearly structure sensitive on the same samples under otherwise identical experimental conditions.

The following speculations may explain these latter results. If the interaction between reactants and surface is strong, a reconstruction of the surface with formation of a two-dimensional layer forming a coincidence lattice with the subjacent layer is possible, as indicated by the work of BÉNARD and coworkers [7.30]. If this happens, structure insensitivity becomes understandable [7.31]. On the other hand, if the interaction between reactants and surface is weak, structure sensitivity is expected to be observable. Thus in the case of the reaction between H_2 and O_2 on platinum, the surface may be reconstructed in excess oxygen but not in excess hydrogen because of the strong and weak interactions of these adsorbated with the surface. Thus structure insensitivity may be expected in the first case but not in the other.

To explain the structure sensitivity of hydrogenolysis reactions may require a different concept. Although molecular details are still missing, it is generally agreed that hydrogenolysis of hydrocarbons on metals is accomplished by extensive dissociation of the chemisorbed hydrocarbon [7.11]. This should require a number of sites. i.e. an ensemble of sites, thus a particular surface structure.

These speculations are of great interest in connection with recent results on alloy catalysts. Many studies have been devoted to the activity

Table 7.4. Reaction between H_2 and O_2 on Pt/SiO$_2$ at 273 K: rate constant k on catalysts with degree of Pt dispersion D [7.29]

%-wt Pt	D	$k \times 10^3/\text{cm s}^{-1}$
a) Excess O_2		
3.7	0.14	2.5
2.3	0.62	3.5
0.53	0.625	4.6
0.38	1.00	2.0
b) Excess H_2		
3.7	0.14	3.1
2.3	0.62	10.7
0.53	0.625	10.5
0.38	1.00	20.0

of alloys as catalysts but it is only very recently that *selectivity* has been emphasized. A typical discovery is that of SINFELT et al. [7.32]. When copper is added to nickel the turnover number of the alloy for dehydrogenation of cyclohexane (a structure insensitive reaction) hardly changes until the alloy contains more than 80 mol-% copper. By contrast, the turnover number for hydrogenolysis of ethane (a structure sensitive reaction) goes down by more than three orders of magnitude after addition of less than 10 mol-% copper. Whatever the final interpretation of these results will be, the difference in catalytic behavior from one reaction to the next, i.e. selectivity, is best explained at the present time in terms of geometric or structural or ensemble effects.

7.6. Electronic or Ligand Factors

A recurring theme in surface catalysis has been the vague idea of chemical unsaturation of the sites. With progress in coordination and organometallic chemistry of soluble complexes, the idea has received more attention with the idea that a site exhibits *coordinative unsaturation* by the loss at the surface of one or more ligands [7.33]. Even though this refinement has remained qualitative, for instance in the treatment by BOND of metallic surface orbitals [7.34], it has clarified the old broad concept of *electronic factors* in catalysis. Indeed, with metals and alloys especially, it appears preferable to talk about *ligand effects* rather than electronic factors to designate the influence on a given site of nearest neighbor sites [7.35].

When it comes to compare the activity of different metals for a given reaction from the viewpoint of electronic factors, the only quantitative index that has been used very frequently since first proposed in 1950 [7.36] has been the percentage d bond character from Pauling's theory of metals [7.37]. The relative success of these correlations in bringing some order in *reactivity patterns* especially among Group VIII and Group I b metals [7.38] suggests that even highly approximate theories of the metallic bond are greatly useful in catalysis. This is because of the very large differences in turnover number, differing by as much as ten orders of magnitude, exhibited by different metals.

A much more puzzling problem is that the *specificity* of a given catalyst for a certain reaction can become so important that only one, or perhaps a very few catalysts are capable of carrying out that reaction with a high selectivity. A good example is the specificity of metallic silver in carrying out the oxidation of ethylene to ethylene oxide [7.39]. A reasonable Eley-Rideal mechanism for the reaction postulates that selective oxidation of ethylene takes place when the molecule hits chemisorbed O_2 bound linearly (end-on) to a silver atom. By contrast, if ethylene reacts with O adatoms, complete oxidation of the molecule to carbon dioxide and water place. If this mechanism is correct, the reason for the specificity of silver lies in the unique reactivity of the binding state of O_2 at its surface.

Another example of specificity is the unique ability of supported iridium to catalyze the decomposition of hydrazine in small rocket motors used in space navigation. In spite of intensive research motivated by the scarcity of iridium, no other metal has been found satisfactory. In this case, no mechanism is known.

A third example deals with the reactions of 2,2-dimethylpropane which was found to be readily hydrogenolyzed to smaller fragments on all Group VIII metals as well as on copper and gold but is isomerized to 2 methylbutane *only* on iridium, platinum and gold [7.40]. For the latter reaction, the bond shift mechanism proposed by ANDERSON and AVERY [7.41] may require a shift in *surface valence* so that the specificity of iridium, platinum and gold in this isomerization may well be related to the multiplicity and ready interconversions of multiple valences suggested for these three metals, but not for others, by RHODIN and coworkers [7.42] on the basis of binding energies of foreign metal atoms on a tungsten FIM tip as well as from LEED observations of hexagonal overlayers on cubic faces of Ir, Pt, and Au.

The need for an improved chemical theory of metals is also felt in the interpretation of the many results obtained on alloy catalysts. The challenge for an electronic or ligand interpretation is particularly strong in those cases where large changes in catalytic activity are obtained upon alloying and where also surface composition is relatively well known. The latter is of course not equal in general to bulk composition [7.43].

An alloy which has been studied many times as a catalyst is copper-nickel. In these alloys copper enrichment of the surface takes place as a result of the thermodynamic drive for lowering surface free energy by accumulation at the surface of the component with the lower sublimation energy. There is now general agreement on the fact that Cu addition to Ni yields copper rich surfaces of a composition that changes rapidly as copper is first introduced into nickel and then more slowly after subsequent addition of copper. In a study of nickel-copper alloy catalysts for reactions of n-hexane and hydrogen mixtures, PONEC and SACHTLER reported that with increasing additions of Cu to Ni, up to 23 mol-%, the rate of hydrogenolysis decreases markedly with addition of Cu but the mode of cracking of n-hexane remains that characteristic of pure Ni [7.44]. These observations are explained in terms of structural or geometric or ensemble factors. It must be remembered that, as noted earlier, the hydrogenolysis of n-hexane on platinum has been shown to be a structure sensitive reaction [7,27]. However, as more Cu is alloyed into Ni, the selectivity for the reactions of n-hexane changes markedly although rates are not affected substantially: the selectivity toward isomerization of n-hexane increases sharply while the cracking pattern also changes, both modes of reactivity becoming those observed with platinum rather than with nickel. These observations with copper rich nickel alloys are interpreted in terms of a ligand or electronic effect. A definitive explanation of these phenomena remains to be provided but at a phenomenological level, the contrast between geometric and electronic factors for a given alloy is noteworthy.

Another aspect of the electronic factor in catalysis has been traditionally linked with semiconductors in an *electronic theory of semiconductor catalysis* particularly associated with the name of VOL'KENSHTEIN [7.45]. This is a formal theory which has led over a period of 25 years to an abundant experimental literature. It would be unfair to attempt to review it briefly and equally unfair to ignore it altogether. It will be simply introduced by means of a fairly typical example, the oxidation of carbon monoxide on zinc oxide.

In such a reaction on an oxide surface, it is natural to expect that an oxygen ad-atom will be an intermediate. But what should its charge be? The oxygen anion O^{2-} should be quite unreactive. Thus, naturally, the choice narrows down to O and O^-. The relative population at the surface of these two intermediates must be dictated by an equilibrium

$$O + e \rightleftharpoons O^-, \tag{7.19}$$

the position of which will be determined by the chemical potential of the electrons e or the Fermi level of the semiconductor. The equilibrium can be shifted by doping, by light or by external electric fields. Hence the possibility of controlling catalytic activity by introduction of impurities. Alternatively photocatalytic or electrocatalytic phenomena are conceivable. Indeed they all have been observed on zinc oxide as a catalyst.

For the reaction under discussion, attempts to shift the equilibrium (7.19) by doping zinc oxide with foreign ions (lithium and indium, or gallium) were made by CHON and PRATER on the one hand [7.46] and by AMIGUES and TEICHNER [7.47] on the other hand. The first group of workers found an effect of doping on catalytic activity and a correlation between catalytic rates and the concentration of electronic carriers as measured by the Hall effect. They concluded that the charged surface species O^- was the intermediate in the reaction. By contrast, the second group of workers found no effect of doping on catalytic activity and concluded that the uncharged surface species was the reaction intermediate. But the conditions used by the two groups were different [7.48]. The first group used relatively high temperatures, low pressures and large crystallite sizes. The second group used relatively low temperatures, high pressures and small crystallite sizes. The latter conditions, which are fairly typical of conventional catalysis, may indeed shift the equilibrium (7.19) to the left with the result that the electron concentration is buffered and insensitive to doping. The conditions of the first group of workers are, however, typical of the kind of catalysis practiced by WAGNER and his school [7.16], who pioneered the ideas subsequently developed by VOL'KENSHTEIN and others. Although these conditions are typical of conventional catalysis, they are those encountered in the catalytic treatment of automotive exhaust, a problem of current interest where the electronic theory of semiconductor catalysis may yet find applications.

7.7. Promoters and Poisons

Conceptually, promoters and poisons must be considered together: they consist of additives introduced with the reactants or during the catalyst preparation and they affect catalyst activity or selectivity. Some of the possible mechanisms will be considered in turn.

A first kind of promoter, said to be *textural*, prevents loss of surface area of the catalyst. A typical example is alumina Al_2O_3 introduced in small quantities (ca. 3%) during the preparation of ammonia synthesis iron catalysts. After reduction, the catalyst consists of metallic iron particles with a mean diameter of 35 nm. The alumina Al_2O_3 is unreduced and covers about half of the iron surface, preventing sintering of the metallic particles [7.49]. Another possible mechanism of textural promotion of iron by alumina has been suggested as a result of the examination of Mössbauer spectra[1] of reduced promoted catalysts [7.50]. At least part of the alumina may remain inside the iron crystallites in the form of very small (1.5 nm) inclusions. The latter would contribute to the elastic stress of the slightly strained metallic particles and a stable particle size would result as a balance between elastic stress and surface free energy.

Another kind of promoter is *structural* or *chemical*. An example is chlorine in the selective oxidation of ethylene to ethylene oxide on silver catalysts (see Section 7.6). It appears that chemisorbed chlorine inhibits the activated or non-activated dissociative chemisorption of oxygen on the metal. Since oxygen ad-atoms are responsible for the non-selective oxidation of ethylene, the role of the promoter is to enhance selectivity. Since the promoter occupies part of the surface, its role may also be conceived as that of a *selective poison*.

As an illustration of selective poisoning, and especially of its use in the assignment of sites responsible for one kind of reaction, γ-alumina which has been pretreated in vacuo at 800 K, catalyzes the isomerization of 1-butene to 2-butene at room temperature as well as the H_2–D_2 equilibration [7.51]. The latter reaction is suppressed by the adsorption of 1.2×10^{13} molecules of CO_2 per cm^2 of alumina surface. Under these conditions, the isomerization reaction proceeds at about the same rate as before selective poisoning by CO_2. Clearly, the sites responsible for the two reactions are different. The number density of sites capable of carrying out the isotopic equilibration is less than or equal to 1.2×10^{13} cm^{-2} as CO_2 may have blocked other sites besides the ones responsible for the suppressed reaction. The sites for H_2–D_2 equilibration may be associated with coordinatively unsaturated surface Al^{3+} ions.

There are as many types of poisons as there are types of sites (see Section 7.8). Some are reversibly held, i.e. they can be removed under reaction conditions as is the case for surface oxygen during ammonia synthesis. Some are irreversibly held as are most types of carbonaceous residues accumulating on catalytic surfaces during reactions involving hydrocarbons. These residues must be removed in a special step of catalyst *regeneration*. In fact, catalyst *deactivation* during use is the rule rather than the exception: it is the central problem in the transfer of any catalyst from the laboratory to the plant [7.52].

Reversible poisons are called also *inhibitors* especially when they are participants in the reaction. Thus reaction products are often inhibitors as is the case for ammonia in ammonia synthesis on iron according to (7.11). The reason for this is clear from the postulated equilibrium

$$*N_2 + 3H_2 \longleftrightarrow 2NH_3 + *$$

---

[1] See Topics in Applied Physics, Vol. 5.

which can and has been studied seperately. Similar equilibria involving H_2O and H_2S are

$$*O + H_2 \longleftrightarrow H_2O + *$$

$$*S + H_2 \longleftrightarrow H_2S + *.$$

They explain inhibition of reactions by H_2O or H_2S, respectively. But they also provide a convenient means of covering the surface of a catalyst with small and controlled quantities of oxygen or sulfur adatoms [7.53, 54] by regulating the virtual pressure of oxygen or sulfur (see Section 7.3).

7.8. Active Centers

The fraction of sites which is active in a given reaction depends on the catalyst and on the reaction, as recognized fifty years ago by TAYLOR who called *active centers* the site or group of sites taking part in the reaction [7.55]. The identification of the active centers and the structure of their complexes with the reactive intermediates under reaction conditions is the central goal of research in catalysis. The following examples have been chosen among many to illustrate some possibilities.

As an example of *electronic defects*, paramagnetic V-centers detected and counted by electron spin resonance spectroscopy have been found to be responsible for the H_2–D_2 equilibration at 78 K on magnesium oxide powders [7.56]. The concentration of these centers could be varied over four orders of magnitude by pre-treatment of the samples in vacuo at temperatures between 800 and 1100 K. The catalytic activity could be correlated with the concentration of the V-centers. These are believed to consist of three O^- surface ions in a triangular array corresponding to (111) planes of magnesium oxide. The catalytic site involves two of these O^- defects plus a neighboring OH^- group. A deuterium molecule is pictured as approaching two O^- sites to form a triangular transition state with the neighboring proton. The transition state then dissociates with release of HD. The reaction thus appears to be of the Eley-Rideal type.

Similar electronic defect centers can be produced by X-ray pre-irradiation of silica gel containing aluminum impurities and associated with these impurities, as shown by hyperfine splitting of the electron spin resonance signal [7.57]. These centers were also found to be responsible for the H_2–D_2 equilibration at 78 K [7.58].

The same chemical system, silica-alumina, is an active catalyst for reactions involving carbonium ion intermediates as a result of the *Brønsted acidity* associated with the *protons* required for charge compensation as an Al^{3+} ion is replacing a Si^{4+} ion in the structure [7.59]. These acid sites have been studied in great detail in *zeolites*, especially synthetic faujasite or Y-zeolites which are crystalline porous aluminosilicates, as opposed to silica-alumina which consists of X-ray amorphous gels [7.60]. Many examples of *Lewis acid* sites are also known, for instance, Al^{3+} surface ions with unsaturated coordination on alumina, as already discussed in Section 7.6. Sites consisting of *Lewis bases* are also known, for example, $O^=$ ions which are sufficiently strong electron donors, at corners of magnesium oxide cubic crystallites to catalyze reactions taking place via carbanion intermediates [7.61]. In the latter case, the concentration of the strongly basic sites was determined by electron spin resonance spectroscopy of the radial anion found upon adsorption of tetracyanoethylene on these sites, and the turnover number for the double bond isomerization of 1-butene taking place through carbanion intermediates was found to be almost constant when the turnover number was calculated on the basis of the site concentration measured by electron spin resonance and when the concentration of these sites was varied over a modest range by thermal pretreatment of the samples in vacuo.

In all the examples cited thus far, the concentration of active centers is only a small — sometimes very small — fraction of the total number of sites per unit surface area. Thus in the case of the V-centers at the surface of pure magnesium oxide, the surface density of centers was measured to be only $10^9 \, cm^{-2}$ for the samples with the highest catalytic activity. It follows that the reactions studied on these centers are structure sensitive. For example in the case of magnesium oxide, the sites responsible for the H_2–D_2 equilibration at 78 K are associated with metastable (111) planes of the solid. These are present only when the solid is formed from another phase such as magnesium hydroxide or magnesium hydroxycarbonates. Samples that are recrystallized to form cubic crystals of magnesium oxide which do not expose (111) planes are devoid of any catalytic activity, irreversibly so.

This is just one of the many examples suggesting that electronic or ionic defects associated with small particles of a metastable phase are frequently responsible for catalytic activity. It must be noted that, for the cases discussed thus far, the identification of the active centers as electronic defects or acidic and basic sites is quite conclusive but the mechanism of the reactions on these active centers is not known as yet. For instance, in the case of hydrocarbon cracking reactions proceeding on acid sites through carbonium ion intermediates, inadequate knowledge of the reaction mechanism is illustrated by the lack of explanation for the reported vast difference in catalytic activity for cracking of iso-octane on silica alumina gels and decationated X-zeolites containing only protons as charge compensating cations [7.62]. In both cases, Brønsted acidic sites differ relatively little in their strength or concentration as measured by adsorption of ammonia [7.63], but the catalytic activity of the X-ray amorphous and crystalline materials of similar chemical composition, differs by almost four order of magnitude under comparable conditions.

Another type of active centers consists of coordinatively unsaturated transition metal cations, sometimes in an unusual oxidation state. For example, W^{3+} surface ions found on the edges of WS_2 crystallites and of WS_2 crystallites promoted with Ni^{2+} ions [7.64–66]. The concentration of W^{3+} ions was determined by their electron spin resonance spectra. The role of the Ni^{2+} ions which are inserted between close-packed sulfur ion planes of a layer lattice is to increase the concentration of W^{3+} ions which must be formed from W^{4+} to maintain electrical neutrality. The rate of hydrogenation of benzene was found to correlate with the intensity of the electron spin resonance signal as the concentration of the W^{3+} ions responsible for the signal and the catalytic activity increased by three orders of magnitude. Again, crystalline anisotropy effects are expected to be very important: the hydrogenation of benzene over these WS_2 catalysts cannot take place on the basal planes and is thus structure sensitive since it is energetically prohibitive to remove S^{2-} ions from the basal planes to achieve coordinative unsaturation of the tungsten ions, as calculated by ARLMAN [7.67] for the similar case of layer structures of $TiCl_3$ active in ZIEGLER-NATTA *stereospecific* polymerization of alkenes [7.68]. In the latter case, coordinatively unsaturated Ti^{3+} ions at the edges of the crystallites are part of the active centers responsible for the most selective form of catalysis achieved on an industrial scale by means of solid catalysts in very small particle size.

Ultimately, the identification of the active centers is complete only if the structure of the complexes they form with the reactive intermediates is also determined. This goal has now been achieved in a remarkable series of studies by KOKES and his coworkers [7.69]. The system investigated was the hydrogenation of ethylene in zinc oxide, proceeding through the most durable catalytic mechanism first proposed for this reaction by POLANYI and HORIUTI fourty years ago [7.70].

According to this mechanism, the alkene R is chemisorbed associatively on a catalytic site, H_2 ia chemisorbed dissociatively on two sites, the chemisorbed alkene reacts step-wise with two chemisorbed H atoms to produce first a chemisorbed alkyl radical RH, the so-called halfhydrogenated state, then finally the alkane RH_2

$$* + R \rightleftharpoons *R$$

$$2* + H_2 \rightleftharpoons 2*H$$

$$*R + *H \rightleftharpoons *RH + *$$

$$*RH + *H \longrightarrow RH_2 + 2* \, .$$

Whereas the last step is clearly irreversible at the temperatures at which hydrogenation of alkenes is studied, the first three steps may be reversible. If so, when the alkene is hydrogenated with dideuterium, multiply exchanged alkenes and alkanes can appear. The study of the patterns of exchange for alkane-D_2 and alkene-D_2 over many catalysts has led to a wealth of interesting conclusions and predictions concerning the nature and stereochemistry of chemisorbed intermediates, over metallic [7.71] and non-metallic catalysts [7.72].

In addition, in the case of hydrogenation of ethylene on zinc oxide, possibly because the catalyst has a rather low activity so that the concentration of the active intermediates is relatively large, it has been possible to observe the intermediates directly by infra-red absorption spectrophotometry. In particular, KOKES and coworkers have established that *R is a π-complex between ethylene and Zn^{2+} ions, that *H intermediates are bound to either Zn^{2+} or O^{2-} ions and that the half-hydrogenated state is an ethyl radical bound to the zinc half of the active center. The molecular picture may not be complete but it is much more than a sketch and it rests on direct spectroscopic observations during reaction.

These examples of active centers indicate the progress currently made in the study of heterogeneous catalysis on conventional high surface area catalysts, as well as the great diversity in their chemistry. While catalysis by metals and alloys continues to attract a lot of attention as discussed in Section 7.5 and 7.6, knowledge of catalysis by semiconductors and insulators also progresses rapidly. In fact one of the most interesting forms of industrial catalysis involves both metallic and non-metallic active centers: it is called *bifunctional catalysis* and a good example is the isomerization of n-pentane to i-pentane in the presence of platinum catalysts supported on acidic alumina. The mechanism of the reaction is as follows: n-pentane is first dehydrogenated to n-pentene on platinum, the n-alkene is then isomerized to i-alkene on the acidic sites of the alumina and finally the i-pentene is rehydrogenated on the platinum sites to the final product, i-pentane. The concept of bi- or multifunctional catalysis has many applications in nature and industry [7.74]. Of particular interest is the fact that the two catalytic functions must be sufficiently near to each other to avoid diffusional limitations as intermediates have to be transported from one function to the other. These transport phenomena dictate the size of the particles of both catalytic phases. Thus bifunctional catalysis is another example and for different reason of a catalytic phenomenon which can be observed only with sufficiently small particles and not on large crystals.

Acknowledgement. Partial support of this work by Exxon Research and Engineering Company is gratefully acknowledged.

References

7.1. G. K. BORESKOV: In *The Second Japan-Soviet Catalysis Seminar, New Approach to Catalysis* (Catalysis Society of Japan, Tokyo 1973), p. 114.

7.2. E. K. RIDEAL: *Concepts in Catalysis*, (Academic Press, New York, 1968), p. 113.

7.3. R. L. BURWELL, JR., M. BOUDART: In *Investigation of Rates and Mechanisms of Reactions*, Part I, ed. E. S. LEWIS (John Wiley & Sons, New York, 1974), Chapt. 12.

7.4. J. M. THOMAS, W. J. THOMAS: *Introduction to Principles of Heterogeneous Catalysis* (Academic Press, New York, 1967).

7.5. A. CLARK: *Theory of Adsorption and Catalysis* (Academic Press, New York, 1970).

7.6. S. J. GREGG, K. S. W. SINGH: *Adsorption, Surface Area and Porosity* (Academic Press, New York, 1967).

7.7. M. BOUDART: *Kinetics of Chemical Processes* (Prentice Hall, Engelwood Cliffs, N. Y., 1968), Chapter 9.

7.8. M. BOUDART: *Physical Chemistry*, eds. H. EYRING, D. HENDERSON and W. JOST, Vol. 7, Chapt. 7, *Heterogeneous Catalysis* (Academic Press, New York 1975).

7.9. M. J. D. LOW: Chem. Rev. **60**, 267 (1960).

7.10. A. OZAKI, H. TAYLOR, M. BOUDART: Proc. Roy. Soc. (London) A **258**, 47 (1960).

7.11. M. BOUDART: AIChE Journal **18**, 465 (1972).

7.12. A. OZAKI: In *Fixation of Dinitrogen*, Vol. 1, ed. W. F. HARDY (John Wiley, New York, 1975), Chapt. 4.

7.13. E. I. SHAPATINA, V. L. KUCHAEV, M. I. TEMKIN: Kinet. Katal. **12**, 1476 (1971).

7.14. K. TAMARU: Adv. Catal. Relat. Subj. **15**, 65 (1964).

7.15. J. H. de BOER (ed.): *Mechanism of Heterogeneous Catalysis* (North-Holland Publishing Co., Amsterdam, 1960).

7.16. C. WAGNER: Adv. Catal. Relat. Subj. **21**, 323 (1970).

7.17. S. STOTZ: Ber. Bunsenges. **70**, 37 (1966).

7.18. J. MCALLISTER, R. S. HANSEN: J. Chem. Phys. **59**, 414 (1973).

7.19. G. L. ERTL, J. KOCH: In *Proceedings of Vth Intern. Congress Catalysis*, ed. by J. W. HIGHTOWER (North-Holland Publishing Co., Amsterdam, 1973), p. 969.

7.20. R. VAN HARDEVELD, F. HARTOG: Surface Sci. **15**, 189 (1969).

7.21. M. BOUDART, A. W. ALDAG, J. E. BENSON, N. A. DOUGHARTY, C. G. HARKINS: J. Catal. **6**, 92 (1966).

7.22. D. R. KAHN, E. E. PETERSEN, G. A. SOMORJAI: J. Catal. **34**, 294 (1974).

7.23. M. BOUDART, R. J. MADON: AIChE Journal (to be published), also R. J. MADON, Ph. D. Thesis, Stanford 1974.

7.24. M. BOUDART, E. SEGAL: J. Catal. (to be published), also: R. J. MADON, Ph. D. Thesis, Stanford 1974.

7.25. M. BOUDART: Accounts Chem. Res. (to be published), also: R. J. MADON, Ph. D. Thesis, Stanford 1974.

7.26. D. J. C. YATES, J. H. SINFELT: J. Catal. **8**, 348 (1967).

7.27. J. R. ANDERSON, Y. SHIMOYAMA: In *Proceedings of Vth Int. Congress Catalysis*, ed. by J. W. HIGHTOWER (North-Holland Publishing Co., Amsterdam, 1973), p. 695.

7.28. S. R. DYNE, J. B. BUTT, G. L. HALLER: J. Catal. **25**, 391 (1972).

7.29. F. V. HANSON, M. BOUDART: J. Catal. (to be published); also F. V. HANSON: Ph. D. Thesis, Stanford, 1975.

7.30. J. BÉNARD: Catal. Rev. **3**, 93 (1970).

7.31. M. BOUDART: J. Vac. Sci. Technol. **12**, 329 (1975).

7.32. J. H. SINFELT, J. L. CARTER, D. J. C. YATES: J. Catal. **24**, 283 (1972).

7.33. R. L. BURWELL, JR., G. L. HALLER, K. C. TAYLOR, J. F. READ: Advan. Catal. **20**, 1 (1969).

7.34. G. C. BOND: Disc. Faraday Soc. **41**, 200 (1966).

7.35. Y. SOMA-NOTO, W. M. H. SACHTLER: J. Catal. **32**, 315 (1974).

7.36. M. BOUDART: J. Am. Chem. Soc. **70**, 1040 (1950).

7.37. L. PAULING: Proc. Roy. Soc. (London) A **196**, 343 (1959).

7.38. J. H. SINFELT: Catal. Rev. **9**, 147 (1974).

7.39. P. A. KILTY, W. M. H. SACHTLER: Catal. Rev. **10**, 1 (1974).

7.40. L. D. PTAK, M. BOUDART: J. Catal. **16**, 90 (1970).

7.41. J. R. ANDERSON, N. R. AVERY: J. Catal. **5**, 446 (1966).

7.42. T. N. RHODIN, P. W. PALMBERG, E. W. PLUMMER: In *The Structure and Chemistry of Solid Surfaces*, ed by G. A. SOMORJAI (John Wiley and Sons, Inc., New York, 1969), paper No. 22.

7.43. F. WILLIAMS, M. BOUDART: J. Catal. **30**, 438 (1973).

7.44. V. PONEC, W. M. H. SACHTLER: *Proceedings of Vth Intern. Congress Catalysis* (North-Holland Publishing Co., Amsterdam, 1973), p. 645.

7.45. F. F. VOL'KENSHTEIN: *Fiziko-khimya poverkhnosti poluprovodnikov* (Nauka Publishers, Moscow, 1973), Chapt. 5.

7.46. H. CHON, C. D. PRATER: Disc. Faraday Soc. **41**, 380 (1966).

7.47. P. AMIGUES, S. J. TEICHNER: ibid. p. 362.

7.48. M. BOUDART: Proc. of the Robert A. Welch Foundation Conferences on Chem. Res. XIV: Solid State Chemistry, Houston, Tex. (1970), p. 299.

7.49. P. H. EMMETT: In: *Structure and Properties of Solid Surfaces*, ed. by R. GOMER C. S. SMITH (The University of Chicago Press, Chicago, 1953), p. 414.

7.50. H. TOPSØE, J. A. DUMESIC, M. BOUDART: J. Catal. **28**, 447 (1973).

7.51. J. W. HIGHTOWER: Accounts Chem. Res. 1975 (to be published).

7.52. J. B. BUTT: Advan. Chem. Series **109**, 259 (1972).

7.53. O. D. GONZALES, G. PARRAVANO: J. Am. Chem. Soc. **78**, 4533 (1956).

7.54. J. OUDAR: Compt. Rend. **249**, 91 (1959).

7.55. H. S. TAYLOR: Proc. Roy. Soc. (London) A **108**, 105 (1925).

7.56. M. BOUDART, A. DELBOUILLE, E. G. DEROUANE, V. INDOVINA, A. B. WALTERS: J. Am. Chem. Soc. **94**, 6622 (1972).

7.57. YU. A. MISHCHENKO, B. K. BORESKOV: *Kinet. Katal.* **6**, 842, (1965).

7.58. H. W. KOHN: J. Catal. **2**, 208 (1968).

7.59. K. TANABE: *Solid Acids and Bases* (Academic Press, New York, 1970).

7.60. P. B. WEISZ: Ann. Rev. Phys. Chem. **21**, 175 (1970).

7.61. M. J. BAIRD, J. H. LUNSFORD: J. Catal. **26**, 440 (1972).

7.62. J. N. MIALE, N. Y. CHEN, P. B. WEISZ: J. Catal. **5**, 278 (1966).

7.63. J. E. BENSON, K. UCHIBA, M. BOUDART: J. Catal. **9**, 91 (1967).

7.64. R. J. H. VOORHOEVE, J. C. M. STUIVER: J. Catal. **23**, 228 (1971).

7.65. R. J. H. VOORHOEVE: J. Catal. **23**, 236 (1971).

7.66. R. J. H. VOORHOEVE, J. C. M. STUIVER: J. Catal. **23**, 243 (1971).

7.67. E. J. ARLMAN: Rec. Trav. Chim. Pays-Bas **87**, 1217 (1968).

7.68. T. KEII: "Kinetics of Ziegler-Natta Polymerization", Kodansha, Tokyo 1972.

7.69. R. J. KOKES: Accounts Chem. Res. **6**, 226 (1973).

7.70. M. POLANYI, J. HORIUTI: Trans. Faraday Soc. **30**, 1164 (1934).

7.71. R. L. BURWELL, JR.: Accounts Chem. Res. **2**, 289 (1969).

7.72. C. Kemball: Annals New York Acad. Sci. **213**, 90 (1973).

7.73. P. B. WEISZ: Advan. Catal. **13**, 137 (1967).

Additional References with Titles

Chapter 2

B. BELL, A. MADHUKAR: A Theory of Chemisorption on Metallic Surfaces: The Role of Intra-Adsorbate Coulomb Correlation and Surface Structure (to be published).

W. BRENIG, K. SCHÖNHAMMER: On the theory of chemisorption. Z. Physik **267**, 201 (1974).

T. B. GRIMLEY, C. PISANI: Chemisorption theory in the Hartree-Fock approximation. J. Phys. C **7**, 2831 (1974).

Chapter 4

4.1. Thermal Desorption

M. BALOOCH, M. J. CARDILLO, D. R. MILLER, R. E. STICKNEY: Molecular beam study of the apparent activation barrier associated with adsorption of hydrogen on copper. Surface Sci. **46**, 358 (1974).

R. CHEN: On the analysis of thermal desorption curves. Surface Sci. **43**, 657 (1974).

C. T. FOXON, M. R. BOUDRY, B. A. JOYCE: Evelution of surface kinetic data by the transform analysis of modulated molecular beam measurements. Surface Sci. **44**, 69 (1974).

D. A. KING: Thermal desorption from metal surfaces: A review. Surface Sci. **47**, 384 (1975).

D. A. KING, M. G. WELLS: Reaction mechanisms in chemisorption kinetics: Nitrogen on W(100). Proc. Roy. Soc. **339**, 245 (1974).

E. V. KORNELSEN, D. H. O'HARA: Analysis of thermal desorption spectra using a computer graphics system. J. Vac. Sci. Technol. **11**, 885 (1974).

F. M. LORD, J. S. KITTELBERGER: On the determination of activation energies in thermal desorption experiments. Surface Sci. **43**, 173 (1974).

M. R. SHANABARGER: Clarification of the kinetics observed in isothermal and programmed thermal desorption measurements. Surface Sci. **44**, 297 (1974).

M. SMUTEK: Unified and generalized treatment of thermal desorption data. Vacuum **24**, 173 (1974).

4.2. Electron Impact Desorption and

4.3. Photodesorption

J. L. GERSTEN, R. JANOW, N. TZOAR: Theory of photodesorption. Phys. Rev. B **11**, 1267 (1975).

D. LICHTMAN: Electron- and photon-induced desorption. J. Nucl. Mat. **53**, 285 (1974).

V. K. RYABCHUK, L. L. BASOV, A. A. LISACHENKO, F. I. VILESOV: Time-of-flight determination of the kinetic energy of photodesorption products (the NO/Al_2O_3-system). Sov. Phys. Techn. Phys. **18**, 1349 (1974).

YA. P. ZINGERMAN: Electron-stimulated desorption of oxygen on a single-crystal surface of tungsten. Fiz. Tved. Tela **16**, 1795 (1974) (Sov. Phys. Solid State **16**, 1168 (1974).

4.4. Ion Impact Desorption

S. M. LIU, W. E. RODGERS, E. L. KNUTH: Interaction of hyperthermal atomic beams with solid surfaces. J. Chem. Phys. **61**, 902 (1974).

Z. SROUBEK: Theoretical and experimental study of the ionization processes during the low energy ion sputtering. Surface Sci. **44**, 47 (1974).

4.5. Field Desorption

J. A. PANITZ: The crystallographic distribution of field-desorbed species. J. Vac. Sci. Technol. **11**, 206 (1974).

W. A. SCHMIDT, O. FRANK, J. H. BLOCK: Investigations of field desorption products from silver surfaces by mass spectrometry. Surface Sci. **44**, 185 (1974).

Chapter 6

General

Proc. 2nd Internat. Conf. on Solid Surfaces, 1974, Japan; J. Appl. Phys. Suppl. 2, Pt. 2, 1974; in particular p. 607, p. 795 (LEED, AES).

The Solid-Vacuum Interface (Proc. 3rd Symp. on Surface Physics, 1974); Surface Sci. **47**, Nr. 1 (1975) (AES, LEED).

S. Y. TONG: *Progress in Surface Science* (Pergamon Press, Oxford 1975).

To Section 6.2

Dynamical Calculations

J. E. DEMUTH, D. W. JEPSEN, P. M. MARKUS: Phys. Rev. Letters **32**, 1182 (1974); – Surface Sci. **45**, 733 (1974); – J. Phys. C. (Solid State Phys.) **8**, L25 (1975).

J. E. DEMUTH, P. M. MARKUS, D. W. JEPSEN: Phys. Rev. B **11**, 1460 (1975).

C. B. DUKE, N. O. LIPARI, G. E. LARAMORE: J. Vac. Sci. Technol. **12**, 222 (1975).

M. VAN HOVE, S. Y. TONG: J. Vac. Sci. Technol. **12**, 230 (1975).

S. Y. TONG: Solid State Commun. **16**, 91 (1975).

Averaging and Transform Techniques

D. L. ADAMS, U. LANDMAN: Phys. Rev. Letters **33**, 585 (1974).

J. M. BURKSTRAND, G. G. KLEIMAN, F. ARLINGHAUS: Surface Sci. **46**, 43 (1974).

M. G. LAGALLY, J. C. BUCHHOLZ, G.-C. WANG: J. Vac. Sci. Technol. **12**, 213 (1975).

L. MCDONNELL, D. P. WOODRUFF, K. A. R. MITCHELL: Surface Sci. **45**, 1 (1974).

K. A. R. MITCHELL, D. P. WOODRUFF, G. W. VERNON: Surface Sci. **46**, 418 (1974).

Imperfect Surfaces

C. B. DUKE, A. LIEBSCH: Phys. Rev. B **9**, 1126, 1150 (1974).

W. P. ELLIS: Surface Sci. **45**, 569 (1974).

G. ERTL, M. PLANCHER: Surface Sci. **48**, 364 (1975).

To Section 6.3

S. AKSELA, J. VÄYRYNEN, H. AKSELA: Phys. Rev. Letters **33**, 999 (1974).

G. BETZ, G. K. WEHNER, L. TOTH, A. JOSHI: J. Appl. Phys. **45**, 5312 (1974).

C. R. BRUNDLE: J. Vac. Sci. Technol. **11**, 212 (1974).

M.A.CHESTERS, B.J.HOPKINS, A.R.JONES, R.NATHAN: Surface Sci. **45**, 740 (1974); – J. Phys. C (Solid State Phys.) **7**, 4486 (1974).

J.W.GADZUK: Phys. Rev. B**9**, 1978 (1974).

J.T.GRANT, M.P.HOOKER, R.W.SPRINGER, T.W.HAAS: J. Vac. Sci. Technol. **12**, 481 (1975).

K.O.GROENEVELD, R.SPOHR: Vakuum-Technik **23**, 225 (1974).

T.W.HAAS, D.J.POCKER: J. Vac. Sci. Technol. **11**, 1087 (1974).

L.A.HARRIS: J. Vac. Sci. Technol. **11**, 23 (1974).

L.C.ISETT, J.M.BLAKELY: Rev. Sci. Instr. **45**, 1382 (1974).

A.P.JANSSEN, R.C.SCHOONMAKER, A.CHAMBERS, M.PRUTTON: Surface Sci. **45**, 45 (1974).

S.P.KOWALCZYK, L.LEY, F.R.McFEELY, R.A.POLLAK, D.A.SHIRLEY: Phys. Rev. B **9**, 381 (1974).

T.NARUSAWA, S.KOMIYA: J. Vac. Sci. Technol. **11**, 312 (1974).

D.A.SHIRLEY: Phys. Rev. A **9**, 1549 (1974).

F.J.SZALKOWSKI, G.A.SOMARJAI: J. Chem. Phys. **61**, 2064 (1974).

Author Index

Subject Index

Applied Physics

A monthly journal

Board of Editors	**A. Benninghoven,** Münster · **R. Gomer,** Chicago, Ill. **F. Kneubühl,** Zürich · **H. K. V. Lotsch,** Heidelberg **H. J. Queisser,** Stuttgart · **F. P. Schäfer,** Göttingen **A. Seeger,** Stuttgart · **K. Shimoda,** Tokyo **T. Tamir,** Brooklyn, N.Y. · **H. P. J. Wijn,** Eindhoven **H. Wolter,** Marburg
Coverage	application-oriented experimental and theoretical physics: *Solid-State Physics* *Quantum Electronics* *Surface Physics* *Coherent Optics* *Infrared Physics* *Integrated Optics* *Microwave Acoustics* *Electrophysics*
Special Features	**rapid** publication (3-4 months) **no** page charges for **concise** reports
Languages	Mostly English; with some German
Articles	review and/or tutorial papers original reports, and short communications abstracts of forthcoming papers
Manuscripts	to Springer-Verlag (Attn. H. Lotsch), P.O. Box 105 280 D-69 Heidelberg 1, F.R. Germany Distributor for North-America: Springer-Verlag New York Inc., 175 Fifth Avenue, New York. N.Y. 100 10, USA

Springer-Verlag
Berlin Heidelberg New York

SPRINGER TRACTS IN MODERN PHYSICS

Ergebnisse der exakten Naturwissenschaften

Editor: G. Höhler

Associate Editor:
E. A. Niekisch

Editorial Board:
S. Flügge, J. Hamilton,
F. Hund, H. Lehmann,
G. Leibfried, W. Paul

Volume 66

30 figures. III, 173 pages. 1973
ISBN 3-540-06189-4 Cloth DM 78,–
ISBN 0-387-06189-4
(North America) Cloth $33.60

Quantum Statistics

in Optics and Solid-State Physics

R. Graham: Statistical Theory of Instabilities in Stationary Nonequilibrium Systems with Applications to Lasers and Nonlinear Optics.
F. Haake: Statistical Treatment of Open Systems by Generalized Master Equations.

Volume 67

III, 69 pages. 1973
ISBN 3-540-06216-5 Cloth DM 38,–
ISBN 0-387-06216-5
(North America) Cloth $16.40

S. Ferrara, R. Gatto, A. F. Grillo:

Conformal Algebra in Space-Time

and Operator Product Expansion

Introduction to the Conformal Group in Space-Time. Broken Conformal Symmetry. Restrictions from Conformal Covariance on Equal-Time Commutators. Manifestly Conformal Covariant Structure of Space-Time. Conformal Invariant Vacuum Expectation Values. Operator Products and Conformal Invariance on the Light-Cone. Consequences of Exact Conformal Symmetry on Operator Product Expansions. Conclusions and Outlook.

Volume 68

77 figures. 48 tables. III, 205 pages. 1973
ISBN 3-540-06341-2 Cloth DM 88,–
ISBN 0-387-06341-2
(North America) Cloth $37.90

Solid-State Physics

D. Schmid: Nuclear Magnetic Double Resonance — Principles and Applications in Solid-State Physics.
D. Bäuerle: Vibrational Spectra of Electron and Hydrogen Centers in Ionic Crystals.
J. Behringer: Factor Group Analysis Revisited and Unified.

Volume 69

13 figures. III, 121 pages. 1973
ISBN 3-540-06376-5 Cloth DM 78,–
ISBN 0-387-06376-5
(North America) Cloth $33.60

Astrophysics

G. Börner: On the Properties of Matter in Neutron Stars.
J. Stewart, M. Walker: Black Holes: the Outside Story.

Prices are subject to change without notice
■ Prospectus with Classified Index of Authors and Titles
Volumes 36—74 on request

Volume 70

II, 135 pages. 1974
ISBN 3-540-06630-6 Cloth DM 77,–
ISBN 0-387-06630-6
(North America) Cloth $33.20

Quantum Optics

G. S. Agarwal: Quantum Statistical Theories of Spontaneous Emission and their Relation to Other Approaches.

Volume 71

116 figures. III, 245 pages. 1974
ISBN 3-540-06641-1 Cloth DM 98,–
ISBN 0-387-06641-1
(North America) Cloth $42.20

Nuclear Physics

H. Überall: Study of Nuclear Structure by Muon Capture.
P. Singer: Emission of Particles Following Muon Capture in Intermediate and Heavy Nuclei.
J. S. Levinger: The Two and Three Body Problem.

Volume 72

32 figures. II, 145 pages. 1974
ISBN 3-540-06742-6 Cloth DM 78,–
ISBN 0-387-06742-6
(North America) Cloth $33.60

D. Langbein:

Theory of Van der Waals Attraction

Introduction. Pair Interactions. Multiplet Interactions. Macroscopic Particles. Retardation. Retarded Dispersion Energy. Schrödinger Formalism. Electrons and Photons.

Volume 73

110 figures. VI, 303 pages. 1975
ISBN 3-540-06943-7 Cloth DM 97,–
ISBN 0-387-06943-7
(North America) Cloth $41.80

Excitons at High Density

Editors: H. Haken, S. Nikitine
Biexcitons. Electron-Hole Droplets. Biexcitons and Droplets. Special Optical Properties of Excitons at High Density. Laser Action of Excitons. Excitonic Polaritons at Higher Densities.

Volume 74

75 figures. III, 153 pages. 1974
ISBN 3-540-06946-1 Cloth DM 78,–
ISBN 0-387-06946-1
(North America) Cloth $33.60

Solid-State Physics

G. Bauer: Determination of Electron Temperatures and of Hot Electron Distribution Functions in Semiconductors.
G. Borstel, H. J. Falge, A. Otto: Surface and Bulk Phonon-Polaritons Observed by Attenuated Total Reflection.

Springer-Verlag
Berlin
Heidelberg
New York